Building Teaching Competencies for AI-Driven and Inclusive Learning

Mário Cruz
https://orcid.org/0000-0001-8894-8821
Polytechnic Institute of Porto, Portugal

Ricardo Queirós
https://orcid.org/0000-0002-1985-6285
Polytechnic Institute of Porto, Portugal

Daniela Mascarenhas
Polytechnic Institute of Porto, Portugal

IGI Global
Scientific Publishing
Publishing Tomorrow's Research Today

Vice President of Editorial	Melissa Wagner
Director of Acquisitions	Mikaela Felty
Director of Book Development	Jocelynn Hessler
Production Manager	Mike Brehm
Cover Design	Jose Rosado

Published in the United States of America by
IGI Global Scientific Publishing
701 East Chocolate Avenue
Hershey, PA, 17033, USA
Tel: 717-533-8845 | Fax: 717-533-7115
Website: https://www.igi-global.com E-mail: cust@igi-global.com

Library of Congress Cataloging-in-Publication Data

Names: Queiros, Ricardo, 1975- editor | Mascarenhas, Daniela, 1981- editor | Cruz, Mário, 1979- editor

Title: Building teaching competencies for AI-driven and inclusive learning / [edited by] Mário Cruz, Ricardo Queirós, Daniela Mascarenhas.

Description: Hershey, PA : IGI Global Scientific Publishing, [2026] | Includes bibliographical references and index. | Summary: "This book examines how educators can cultivate the skills needed to teach effectively in AI-enhanced, inclusive environments. Bridging pedagogy, technology, and ethics, it offers global perspectives and practical insights for building human-centered, equitable, and future-ready learning ecosystems in the age of intelligent technologies"-- Provided by publisher.

Identifiers: LCCN 2025052977 (print) | LCCN 2025052978 (ebook) | ISBN 9798337377292 hardcover | ISBN 9798337377308 paperback | ISBN 9798337377315 ebook

Subjects: LCSH: Artificial intelligence--Educational applications | Educational technology | Effective teaching

Classification: LCC LB1028.43 .B85 2026 (print) | LCC LB1028.43 (ebook)

LC record available at https://lccn.loc.gov/2025052977

LC ebook record available at https://lccn.loc.gov/2025052978

British Cataloguing in Publication Data
A Cataloguing in Publication record for this book is available from the British Library.

Table of Contents

Detailed Table of Contents

This chapter provides an overview of seven trends in technology-enhanced teaching and their relationship to cognitive, emotional, and behavioural engagement in learning. In addition to the benefits and challenges, cases are presented that show specific practices in secondary or higher education. Hybrid models extend access and offer students greater control over the place of learning, but they pose challenges for teachers in connecting to all students, both onsite and online. Games and gamification stimulate adaptive learning and motivation for learning through challenge and reward. Data-driven instruction enables educators to make more informed pedagogical decisions, tailoring support to individual needs and preferences. Virtual reality offers immersive experiences that enhance in-situ experiences, while online discussion forums can promote dialogue and collaborative knowledge building. Educational video platforms provide annotated reflections and feedback, and generative AI tools open new possibilities for creativity and personalized support for diverse learners.

Open Educational Resources (OER) are reshaping modern education by enhancing curriculum flexibility and improving access to quality learning. Freely available and openly licensed, OER empowers educators to adapt and customize content, supporting competency-based, interdisciplinary, and inclusive instruction. This adaptability fosters personalized learning and ensures curricula stay relevant to emerging knowledge and industry needs. OER also eliminates financial barriers, promoting equitable access for diverse learners across regions and socioeconomic backgrounds. Challenges such as institutional resistance, sustainability, digital infrastructure, and legal concerns must be addressed. This chapter explores the best practices for adoption of OER, supported by case studies and emerging technologies, and underscores the need for strategic policies and global collaboration to realize the full potential of OER in democratizing education.

This chapter presents a study that aims to investigate how mathematics teachers use ChatGPT in their lessons and to reveal their experience. The research was conducted in accordance with case study design. Within the scope of the research, semi-structured interviews were conducted with mathematics teachers using ChatGPT in their mathematics courses. The results show that mathematics teachers use ChatGPT in problem-solving, problem posing, using different strategies in problem-solving, and to make students discover the basic properties of geometric shapes. The participants of the study also mentioned some of the advantages of using ChatGPT in their lessons, the difficulties, the methods to overcome these difficulties, and made recommendations for other teachers. The results of the study uncover the need for more research and guidelines for the use of ChatGPT and similar artificial intelligence tools in mathematics courses. It is recommended to conduct studies on good examples of using ChatGPT in mathematics courses which overcome possible challenges.

The 21st century education environment necessitates pedagogical changes to develop critical thinking and transversal competencies. Traditional education systems often focus on rote learning, limiting the development of advanced thinking and versatile skills. Artificial Intelligence can be used to promote critical thinking and a broader range of transversal skills, like creativity, collaboration, problem solving, digital literacy, and adaptability. AI tools like intelligent tutoring systems, adaptive learning platforms, and immersive simulations can provide diversified instruction, real time feedback, and procedural learning through experience. Ethically and strategically applied, these tools can lead to the growth of transversal skills needed for lifelong learning. However, ethical issues, algorithm bias, and professional growth for educators are also discussed. The chapter recommends that AI should support human teaching and curriculum, ensuring that education not only provides knowledge but also equips students with the skills needed to adapt to the modern era.

The materials manipulation plays a key role in mathematics education by transforming abstract concepts into concrete experiences. This paper presents an exploratory qualitative study focused on how Pattern Blocks promote computational and geometric thinking in 25 first grade students from a Portuguese private school. Over five formative sessions, children participated in practical activities which echoed the national curriculum such as identifying, composing and decomposing shapes. Observations of classes, video recordings and document analysis were used to collect data. Both physical and digital Pattern Blocks facilitate mathematical learning by promoting spatial awareness, logical reasoning, pattern recognition, and problem-solving skills. The students developed their out-of-the-box and critical thinking, abstraction and collaboration. The study concludes that the integration of structured material promotes meaningful, student centered, active, and collaborative learning, while effectively developing computational and geometric thinking in early mathematics education.

Higher education is rapidly shifting towards distance learning, particularly in health sciences. However, many educators feel unprepared for effective digital tool integration, leading to challenges in teaching quality. The COVID-19 pandemic highlighted this gap, emphasizing the need to equip teachers with both technical and pedagogical digital skills to create engaging learning environments. To address this, the "Technological Modernization in Health: Digital Tools for Distance Learning in Health Education" course was developed. This month-long program covered 5 essential modules and included both formative and summative assessments. Of the 32 participants, 25 successfully completed the course, demonstrating strong interest in utilizing digital resources. This initiative not only helps educators adapt but also drives pedagogical evolution. By enhancing educators' digital fluency, the program aims to democratize access to education, encourage new teaching approaches, and ultimately improve outcomes in health sciences.

Preface

INTRODUCTION

Education today stands at a defining intersection between digital transformation and human-centered inclusivity. The proliferation of Artificial Intelligence (AI) in teaching and learning has redefined how knowledge is created, delivered, and experienced. This paradigm shift presents both unprecedented opportunities and complex challenges, demanding educators who can navigate these evolving landscapes with competence, creativity, and ethical awareness. *Building Teaching Competencies for AI-Driven and Inclusive Learning* emerges as a timely response to these demands, providing a scholarly and practical lens on how teaching can evolve meaningfully in the age of intelligent technologies.

This volume was conceived to explore how educators can develop and refine the competencies necessary to teach effectively in AI-enhanced and inclusive environments. It reflects our shared belief that while technology transforms the mechanics of learning, it is pedagogy—the art and science of teaching—that gives learning its purpose, relevance, and humanity. Each chapter included in this book investigates the interplay between pedagogy, technology, and inclusivity, emphasizing that true educational innovation requires a harmonious balance between human and machine intelligence.

As editors, we have brought together international experts and practitioners whose research, insights, and case studies illuminate the multifaceted nature of this transformation. The contributions represent diverse educational levels, disciplines, and geographic contexts, collectively addressing a central question: *What does it mean to be a competent teacher in an AI-driven world?* The following chapters offer nuanced, evidence-based perspectives that advance this discourse and provide a roadmap for educators, policymakers, and researchers dedicated to building equitable and future-ready learning ecosystems.

CHAPTER OVERVIEW

Chapter 1, *Towards a Pedagogy of Engagement in Technology-Enhanced Teaching*, by Wilfried Admiraal and I Wayan Heka Arcana Putra, explores how emerging technologies—from hybrid models to generative AI—affect student engagement across cognitive, emotional, and behavioral domains. The authors provide practical insights into maintaining meaningful connections in increasingly digital classrooms.

Chapter 2, *Open Educational Resources and Their Impact on Curriculum Flexibility and Accessibility*, by Satya Subrahmanyam, examines how OER empowers curriculum innovation and inclusivity. The chapter highlights OER's transformative potential in removing barriers to access while addressing institutional and legal challenges in its global adoption.

Chapter 3, *Artificial Intelligence in the Classroom: Teachers' Perspectives on the Development of Critical and Creative Thinking*, by Maria Magalhães and colleagues, captures teachers' perceptions of AI as a catalyst for fostering creativity and reflection. It underscores the need for ethical awareness and professional preparation to ensure AI integration enriches, rather than replaces, human pedagogy.

Chapter 4, *Role of AI-Powered Learning Analytics in the Design of Adaptive Curricula within Higher Education*, by Azadeh Eskandarzadeh and Yunona Gogia, focuses on AI's potential to personalize instruction through data-driven insights. The chapter also discusses essential ethical considerations, particularly concerning bias and data privacy, emphasizing the balance between innovation and integrity.

Chapter 5, *Developing Teaching Competencies for AI-Enhanced Learning: Teachers' Evolving Roles in Intelligent Tutoring Systems*, by Seoyeon Park and Wenting Weng, presents a meta-analysis of teachers' shifting roles in AI ecosystems. The authors propose a competency framework that encompasses technical proficiency, pedagogical creativity, and ethical decision-making.

Chapter 6, *Empowering Educators for the AI-Driven Classroom: Strategies for Training and Professional Development*, by Seema Yadav, emphasizes the critical importance of professional training for teachers. The chapter provides strategies to cultivate adaptability, confidence, and ethical literacy, positioning educators as reflective facilitators in AI-integrated classrooms.

Chapter 7, *How Do Mathematics Teachers Use ChatGPT in Their Classes?*, by Zeynep Gül Dertli and Yasemin Saglam Kaya, offers an empirical exploration of ChatGPT's pedagogical use in mathematics education. The authors reveal both the benefits and the challenges of leveraging AI tools for problem-solving, creativity, and student engagement.

Chapter 8, *Pedagogical Shifts in the AI Era Toward Cultivating Critical Thinking and Transversal Skills*, by Sathya Manickam and colleagues, discusses how AI tools can promote transversal competencies such as collaboration, adaptability, and problem-solving. The chapter warns against overreliance on automation, advocating for ethically grounded pedagogical renewal.

Chapter 9, *Enhancing EFL Learning for Neurodiverse Students through Virtual Worlds and the Metaverse*, by Sandra Luna, brings inclusivity to the forefront. It examines how immersive digital environments can support neurodiverse learners and students with disabilities, guided by Universal Design for Learning (UDL) principles.

Chapter 10, *The Power of Games from Traditional to Digital for the 21st Century Survival Skills: A Case Study*, by Emine Sendurur and Neset Mutlu, demonstrates how game-based learning can bridge digital divides and foster essential 21st-century skills. The authors present evidence that playful learning environments can enhance teacher confidence and interdisciplinary collaboration.

Chapter 11, *Piece by Piece – Awakening Computational and Geometric Thinking in the 1st Cycle of Basic Education*, by Joana Martins, Daniela Mascarenhas, and Sara Paredes, highlights the role of hands-on materials in developing computational and spatial reasoning among young learners. It connects tangible learning experiences with abstract mathematical thinking.

Chapter 12, *Distance Learning Tools in Health Sciences: A Training Course for Higher Education Faculty*, by Raquel Simões de Almeida and Maria João Trigueiro, closes the volume with an example of applied innovation. The authors describe a successful professional development initiative that equips health science educators with digital teaching competencies for remote instruction.

CONCLUSION

Collectively, these chapters capture the evolving identity of educators as designers, facilitators, and ethical stewards of learning in the age of AI. The research and reflections presented throughout this book make it clear that the success of AI integration depends less on technology itself and more on the human capacity to wield it with wisdom and inclusivity. By cultivating digital literacy, critical awareness, and emotional intelligence, teachers can ensure that technological transformation remains anchored in the values of equity and accessibility.

This book advocates for a shift from technology adoption to competency development. It calls upon educators and institutions to move beyond surface-level implementation and toward a deeper reimagining of pedagogy—one that embraces adaptability, collaboration, and lifelong learning. Only by empowering teachers with the necessary skills and confidence can we ensure that AI serves as a partner in advancing educational excellence and social justice.

As editors, we extend our gratitude to all the authors and reviewers who contributed to this collaborative endeavor. We hope that *Building Teaching Competencies for AI-Driven and Inclusive Learning* serves as both an inspiration and a practical guide for educators, researchers, and policymakers striving to create inclusive, future-ready educational environments. Together, we can ensure that technology amplifies—not replaces—the human essence of teaching and learning.

Chapter 1
Towards a Pedagogy of Engagement in Technology-Enhanced Teaching

Wilfried Admiraal
https://orcid.org/0000-0002-1627-3420
Oslo Metropolitan University, Norway

I. Wayan Heka Arcana Putra
https://orcid.org/0009-0009-2677-8893
Oslo Metropolitan University, Norway

ABSTRACT

This chapter provides an overview of seven trends in technology-enhanced teaching and their relationship to cognitive, emotional, and behavioural engagement in learning. In addition to the benefits and challenges, cases are presented that show specific practices in secondary or higher education. Hybrid models extend access and offer students greater control over the place of learning, but they pose challenges for teachers in connecting to all students, both onsite and online. Games and gamification stimulate adaptive learning and motivation for learning through challenge and reward. Data-driven instruction enables educators to make more informed pedagogical decisions, tailoring support to individual needs and preferences. Virtual reality offers immersive experiences that enhance in-situ experiences, while online discussion forums can promote dialogue and collaborative knowledge building. Educational video platforms provide annotated reflections and feedback, and generative AI tools open new possibilities for creativity and personalized support for diverse learners.

DOI: 10.4018/979-8-3373-7729-2.ch001

INTRODUCTION

The integration of technology in education has led to the increased use of various tools and methods, such as virtual learning environments, simulation software, educational games, and gamification. Additionally, there are virtual experiments and visualization tools for complex models. These advancements also include communication platforms that allow students and teachers to collaborate via email, electronic forums, and instant messaging systems. At the beginning of this century, technology use mainly aimed at *facilitating* existing teaching approaches such as the use of presentation software, electronic whiteboards, virtual learning environments, and email (Winn, 2002; Wu & Wang, 2016). More recently, technology has been applied to *adapt* teaching approaches, inspired by changing ideas about what effective teaching and learning imply and supported by the increase in smartphones, tablets, social media, smart technologies, and high-speed internet connections (Kimmons et al., 2021). In recent years, the landscape of available technology for education has expanded, with the most influential example being the use of Artificial Intelligence in education (Imran et al., 2024). These tools hold the potential to *transform* education by making learning experiences more interactive, personalized, and responsive to individual student needs. However, despite their growing availability, the pedagogical approaches employed in many educational settings have not evolved at the same pace (Ramdahani, 2025; Sailer et al., 2024). This disconnect presents a critical challenge: how can we redesign pedagogies to make meaningful and effective use of the digital tools now at our disposal?

At the heart of this challenge lies the issue of learner engagement. Decades of educational research underscore that engagement—whether cognitive, emotional, or behavioural—is a vital condition for learning. Yet many learners are not engaged in their education, resulting in high attrition and low interest, motivation, and academic outcomes (Rumberger & Rotermund, 2012). Learner engagement is not a "nice-to-have" addition to learning; it is a prerequisite. Without cognitive, emotional, and behavioural engagement, deep and sustainable learning is unlikely to occur (Ballale, 2024; Perry, 2022). Educators must shift towards pedagogies that put students at the centre of the learning process (Martin & Bolliger, 2018). Technologies can support these pedagogies by offering adaptive learning paths, personalized feedback, and individual learning experiences. This requires not only technical capacity from the teacher but also a renewed commitment to learner engagement as the core principle of effective teaching. Without rethinking pedagogies, technology risks being used in ways that merely replicate teacher-centred practices rather than pedagogies focused on engaging learners in learning. This chapter aims to provide implications of learner engagement at the centre of the learning process for pedagogies using technology in upper-secondary and higher education.

THE LEARNING ENGAGEMENT THEORY

Learner engagement refers to the degree of cognitive and emotional investment a student makes in order to complete a learning task (Schunk & Mullen, 2012). Research has shown that learner engagement is associated with several important educational outcomes, such as academic achievement, persistence, satisfaction, and a sense of community (see, e.g., Filak & Sheldon, 2008; Hughes et al., 2008; Wang & Degol, 2014). Three main types of engagement can be distinguished (Fredricks et al., 2004; 2005): 1) behavioural engagement refers to students' active participation and observable actions in learning, 2) emotional engagement reflects the emotional connections students make with learning activities, and 3) cognitive engagement focuses on the mental effort students invest in learning tasks. Indicators of behavioural engagement are, for example, participation in learning activities and involvement in academic, social, or extracurricular activities. Emotional engagement refers to, for example, affective reactions to teachers and classmates, academics, and school (such as boredom, interest, anxiety, etc.), a sense of belonging, valuing, and being valued. Cognitive engagement has been defined as the amount of mental effort students invest in learning. Two other types of engagement (Van der Rijst et al., 2023), social engagement (the extent to which learners interact with teachers and peers), and agentic engagement (the extent to which students express themselves), can be understood as indicators of behavioural engagement.

The Engagement Theory (Kearsley & Shneiderman, 1998) is a universal learning theory originating from the domain of technology-enhanced teaching and learning. The major premise of the Engagement Theory is that students must be engaged in their coursework and learning tasks for effective learning to occur. Three core learning principles are distinguished: Relate – communication and social skills in a team effort, Create – learning as a creative activity, and Donate – learning in terms of wider community involvement. Other authors took a broader view on teaching and learning with technology. For example, Barak (2006) derived four principles for learning with technology from multiple learning theories. The first principle of learning is that it is contextual. This principle is rooted in theories of situated cognition (Brown et al., 1989), which argue that knowledge is closely tied to the specific contexts and activities in which it is acquired. The second principle emphasizes that learning is an active process. This means that students learn more effectively through their own experiences rather than by passively receiving information from others or through technical means. The third principle states that learning is a social process, drawing on the work of Vygotsky (1978). According to this principle, student learning is enhanced through discourse between the student and various individuals, including teachers, peers, school leaders, parents, and even casual acquaintances. The fourth principle highlights the importance of reflective practice in learning. In a similar vein, Jonassen et al. (1999) proposed learning principles based on a synthesis of several theories of learning in their constructivist approach to technology. They contend that technology fosters meaningful learning only when learners are actively engaged in knowledge construction, conversation, articulation, collaboration, authentic contexts, and reflection.

Based on these learning principles and previous empirical work on technology-enhanced teaching and learning, the Engagement Theory is transformed into The Learning Engagement Theory, which will be used in this chapter to frame research on various types of technology-enhanced teaching and learning (see Figure 1).

Figure 1. The Learning Engagement Theory

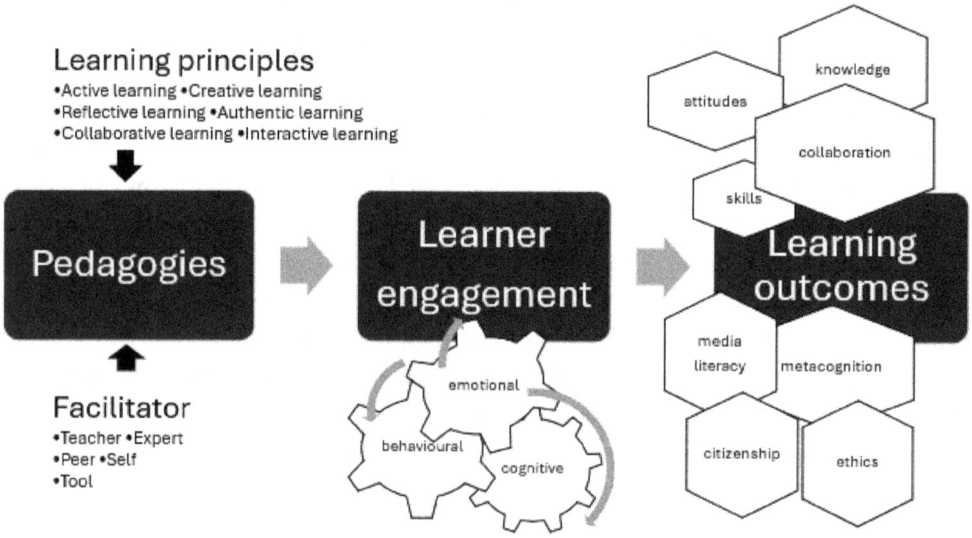

The learning process as presented in Figure 1 resembles the situation of one learner in a specific context, because both *learner characteristics* (e.g., ability, cultural, social and language background, self-efficacy, perseverance, and previous learning experiences) and *learning environment* (e.g., classroom and school characteristics, teacher characteristics, and school subject or discipline) will have a differential effect on the learning process. The pedagogies in The Learning Engagement Theory are not only influenced by the learner characteristics and learning environment; they are also based on the learning principles Active learning, Creative learning, Reflective learning, Authentic learning, Collaborative learning, and Interactive learning (Barak, 2006; Johnson & Aragon, 2003; Jonassen et al., 1999; Salomon,1998). Learners learn better through active engagement with their own experiences rather than passively accepting information or knowledge provided by others or through technical means (*Active learning*). *Creative learning* emphasizes the processing of information and knowledge by the production of artefacts. To facilitate learners in learning from their experiences, it is important to reflect, both individually and in groups, on these learning experiences (*Reflective learning*). *Authentic learning* requires an approach that places learning within the context of real-world situations to create a learning context that is felt as relevant and meaningful by the learner. The principle of *Collaborative learning* views technology as a tool that provides opportunities for shared thinking, joint projects, and peer reviews. It can create an authentic learning environment that replicates collaboration in professional or community settings. An *Interactive learning* environment facilitates active interaction with peers, teachers, parents, and learning materials to apply, evaluate, analyse, and create knowledge.

These learning principles are applied by one or more facilitators, who can be a teacher or an expert (e.g., in workplace-related learning), one or more peers (e.g., in classroom discussion or collaborative work), the learners themselves (as in self-directed and self-regulated learning), a task, or a tool (e.g., in online quizzes or games). In many learning situations, pedagogies will be supported by more than one facilitator and by a variety of learning principles.

As shown in Figure 1, the pedagogies will have an indirect effect on learning outcomes, and their effect is mediated by learner engagement. This means that, without learner engagement, pedagogies will not lead to any learning outcome. In other words, pedagogy should be aimed at supporting learning engagement in the first place. For example, a pedagogical approach that focuses on creating a cognitive conflict in learners, as applied in the use of a mystery in Geography as a task students have to solve (Karkdijk et al., 2013), can trigger higher levels of cognitive reasoning, creativity and divergent thinking in completing a task (*cognitive engagement*), focus student attention on the materials to be learned (*behavioural engagement*), and energize learners to complete an instructional task (*emotional engagement*; Johnson & Johnson, 2009). In many learning situations, pedagogies will be focused on supporting more than one type of learner engagement.

Finally, there are abundant typologies of learning outcomes with a common distinction between outcomes related to the *cognitive domain* (various types of knowledge), the *affective domain* (such as attitudes), and the *psychomotor domain* (such as skills; Guo et al., 2020; Wei et al, 2021). More specific types of learning outcomes are related to collaboration, citizenship, ethics, metacognition, and media literacy, which are all outcomes that go across the cognitive, affective, or psychomotor domains.

The Learning Engagement Theory will be applied and further developed by reviewing empirical work on seven main trends in technology-enhanced teaching and learning:

1. Hybrid Teaching - teaching with some students present on campus and others online at the same time (Van der Rijst et al., 2023).
2. Data-Driven Instruction - the measurement, collection, analysis, and reporting of data about learners and their contexts, for purposes of understanding and optimising learning and the environments in which it occurs (Hershkovitz, 2015).
3. Digital games and Gamification – serious games combine engaging game mechanics (e.g., reward, ranking, competition, collaboration, and challenge) with learning objectives to promote knowledge, skills, or behaviour change, and gamification is the use of game design elements in non-game contexts to create gameful learning environments (Hong et al, 2025).
4. Virtual Reality - technology that creates a fully immersive, computer-generated environment that people can interact with, usually through special equipment like VR headsets and controllers (Atal et al., 2024).
5. Online Discussions - the process by which individuals or groups communicate, exchange information, collaborate, and engage with one another through digital technologies and internet-based platforms (Galikyan et al., 2021).
6. Online video – teacher and peer feedback and self-reflections that are directly linked to the specific parts of an online video clip it refers to (Admiraal, 2014).
7. Generative Artificial Intelligence in Teaching - a type of artificial intelligence that can create new content, such as text, images, music, video, code, or even entire virtual environments based on patterns it has learned from existing data (Belkina et al., 2025).

For each of the seven trends, previous empirical work will be summarized, and benefits and challenges will be presented. For each trend, one case is presented that represents a specific application of the particular trend. The particular tool of each case is explained in a figure. Implications for pedagogies to support student engagement will be integrated in both the text about benefits and challenges and the case description.

HYBRID TEACHING

Hybrid teaching has become increasingly important in both secondary and higher education, particularly in response to evolving technological possibilities after the school closures during the COVID-19 pandemic and the demands for flexible learning environments. Hybrid teaching refers to an instructional modality in which the teacher is physically present in the classroom with a group of on-site students, while simultaneously teaching students who participate remotely via digital platforms.

This approach differs from blended learning, where learners work asynchronously online and on-site with no synchronous engagement across both online and onsite spaces (Raes et al., 2020; Van der Rijst et al., 2023). A successful hybrid teaching setup typically involves the use of videoconferencing platforms (e.g., Zoom, Microsoft Teams), learning management systems (e.g., Moodle, Canvas), and classroom technologies such as microphones, cameras, and smartboards (Fawns, 2022). Hybrid teaching has been widely implemented in both secondary and higher education, often driven by necessity during the COVID-19 pandemic, but it continues to be used due to its flexibility to accommodate diverse learner preferences.

Various setups for hybrid teaching are possible; Bell et al. (2014) identify four configurations, where one teacher and multiple students are connected (see Figure 2). The students in the classroom (blue environment) are virtually connected with the remote students. In the classroom, remote students can be seen and heard through a computer device, and vice versa, remote students can communicate with the students and teacher in the classroom. In most configurations, the teacher is present in the classroom and teaches synchronously to both in-class and remote students.

Figure 2. Various designs of hybrid teaching (Bell et al., 2024)

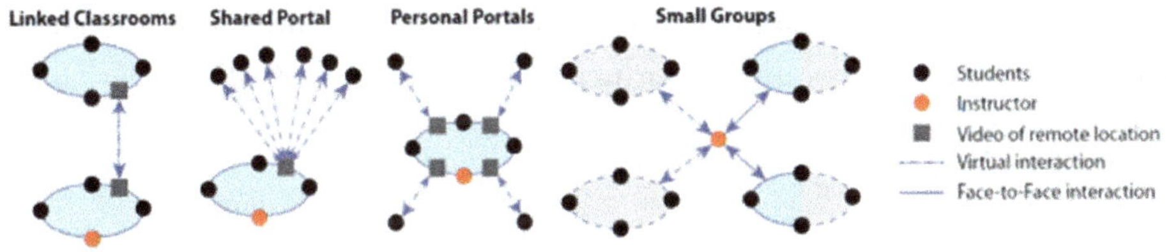

A critical characteristic of effective hybrid teaching is the pedagogical coherence across both offline and online learning environments. Instruction must be designed to ensure that online participants can fully engage with the same learning objectives, content, and activities as their on-site peers (Gudoniene et al., 2025; Raes et al., 2020). This often requires incorporating digital collaboration tools (e.g., shared documents, breakout rooms) and adaptive teaching to address varied learning and access needs.

Moreover, in practice, the context of hybrid teaching can change. The ratio of online to in-person students can vary significantly from session to session because student participation may fluctuate due to interests, illness, geographic constraints, or institutional policies, even during one session. This variability demands a high level of adaptability from educators in terms of pedagogical strategies and student support (Gudoniene et al., 2025).

Benefits of Hybrid Teaching

Hybrid teaching offers a range of benefits for both students and teachers. These benefits reflect the flexibility, inclusivity, and technological affordances of the model.

Benefits for Students

One of the most significant advantages of hybrid teaching for students is increased accessibility of the learning environment. Learners who cannot attend classes in person—due to illness, caregiving responsibilities, employment obligations, or geographical distance—can still participate in real-time teaching experiences (Raes et al., 2020; Van der Rijst et al., 2023).

Hybrid learning environments also support learners as in fully online education, such as students' autonomy and self-regulation, and their digital literacy. Students are often given choices in how they engage with course content, which gives them the chance to tailor their learning experiences according to their needs and preferences (Beatty, 2019). The combination of recorded sessions, asynchronous discussion forums, and synchronous chats, along with online resources, provides a variety of learning opportunities at a personalized pace. Moreover, students enhance their digital literacy by navigating online platforms, using communication tools, managing digital content, and collaborating in virtual spaces (Alsowat, 2022).

Benefits for Teachers

For educators, hybrid teaching can be a start for pedagogical innovation. The necessity of engaging both in-person and online learners prompts teachers to explore new instructional strategies, such as flipped classrooms, interactive multimedia, and collaborative technologies (Van der Rijst et al., 2023). This expansion of the teaching repertoire can result in more varied, inclusive, and student-centred pedagogy that can be used in all learning environments. In addition, hybrid teaching supports ongoing professional development in teachers' digital competences. Teachers who engage with hybrid formats often build stronger digital competencies, including the ability to curate online content, manage online interactions, and assess student performance digitally (Palacios-Hidalgo & Huertas-Abril, 2021). These digital skills also align with broader educational trends toward digital transformation in education.

Challenges of Hybrid Teaching

Hybrid teaching, which combines in-person and online instruction, offers flexibility and broader access to education. However, it also presents several challenges, which means that, overall, hybrid teaching demands a high level of adaptability and support for both educators and learners to be successful. Case studies by Raes et al. (2020), just before the university closed due to the pandemic, and Van der Rijst et al. (2023), just after the university opened again, provide a list of challenges of hybrid teaching reported by both teachers and students of University of Leuven (Belgium) and Leiden (the Netherlands), respectively.

Challenges for Teachers

One major issue is ensuring equal engagement and participation for both online and in-person students. Teachers often struggle to divide their attention effectively, which can lead to uneven engagement (Van der Rijst et al., 2023) and difficulties in maintaining classroom cohesion (Raes et al., 2020). Related to this challenge to engage all students, the pedagogical design for hybrid contexts is also complex. Activities that work well in face-to-face settings may not translate effectively to online formats and vice versa. For example, assessment and feedback become more complex, as teachers must adapt their strategies to suit online and on-site learning environments. Teachers need to develop strategies that ensure equivalent learning experiences for both groups (Bower et al., 2015; Zydney et al., 2019), being intentional in facilitating participation of both online and on-site students.

Moreover, the physical classroom environment may not be adequately equipped for hybrid delivery. Poor audio or video quality, lack of technical support, and insufficient training can hinder effective implementation. These infrastructural issues often require additional preparation time, familiarity with digital tools, and the ability to troubleshoot technical issues, such as unstable internet connections or lack of access to devices, during class (Fawns, 2022).

Challenges for Students

Students also face several challenges in hybrid learning environments. Online students may experience a sense of isolation or exclusion, especially if classroom dynamics favour those who are physically present. Limited access to on-site interaction through a reduced social presence can negatively affect motivation and learning outcomes (Van der Rijst et al., 2023).

In terms of cognitive load, hybrid learning requires students to be self-regulated learners. Online participants must manage their learning environments, stay attentive without direct supervision, and navigate technological tools independently. These demands can be especially challenging for younger students in secondary education or those with limited digital literacy (Kaptanoğlu & Kavanoz, 2024).

Disparities in access to reliable internet, devices, or quiet study spaces can further worsen inequalities. While hybrid teaching aims to enhance accessibility, it can inadvertently widen gaps between students with differing levels of technological and social skills (Beatty, 2019). Some students may struggle to follow group discussions, miss non-verbal cues, or experience delays in receiving feedback. Without careful instructional design, hybrid teaching can result in weakened engagement and learning for both online and on-site participants.

Case 1: Hybrid virtual classrooms with Chronically Ill Children in Secondary Education

Introduction

The case is about a multiple qualitative case study on hybrid teaching chronically ill children in regular secondary school classes in the Netherlands (Klunder et al, 2022, 2023). Mainstream schools in the Netherlands that organize education for their students with a chronic illness (SCIs) at home or in a hospital can apply for assistance from a network of school liaison workers who are experts in the field of education for SCIs. Their guiding principle is that SCIs should stay connected to school and return to school when possible. For SCIs who are absent from school for more than 6 weeks due to their chronic illness, a hybrid virtual classroom is organized using various devices (see Figure 3).

Figure 3. Examples of hybrid virtual classes with one remote student

Hybrid Virtual Classrooms with Chronically Ill Children in Secondary Education

In these hybrid virtual classrooms, the remote SCI at home or in the hospital is connected with the class and attends the on-site lessons simultaneously with their teacher(s) and schoolmates at school. SCIs can remotely control the camera on top of the classroom device and can change the colour of a remote-controlled attention light to attract the teacher's attention without disturbing the class. No video or audio recordings are made to ensure the privacy of the SCIs, teachers, and students in class. Unlike the configurations described above by Bell et al. (2014), this setup includes one remote student connected via a device to an on-site group of students with a teacher.

Data

Each of the seven cases in the study consists of a chronically ill child (the remote student), their caretakers, one or more teachers, some fellow students, two buddies who are responsible for taking the device from class to class, and a school counsellor. The cases were part of different secondary schools in the Netherlands. All participants took part in an individual interview, and two or three classes per case were observed.

Findings

In general, teachers had difficulties engaging with both the remote student and the rest of the class at the same time. All teachers explicitly welcomed the remote student at the start of the class. In many cases, teachers had some additional time after class to respond to questions from the remote student. The buddies not only carried the device from class to class but also supported the remote student with some individual and group work in class, and to get the attention from the teacher. They also had contact after class through social media about the homework to be done. Some of the remote students were assisted by a caretaker (at home or in the hospital) or a nurse (in the hospital) to be sure that all information was received properly.

To ensure the successful integration of a student using a communication or remote presence device in the classroom, Klunder et al. (2023) recommend the following steps: Begin with an introduction where both classmates and the remote student become familiar with the device, Allow time for brief experimentation, and, if the remote student is comfortable, Have them introduce themselves to the class.

It is important to facilitate a class discussion to foster understanding and promote cooperation.

To provide ongoing support, appoint one or more students as buddies responsible for helping with the installation and relocation of the device, as well as maintaining regular contact with the remote student. This arrangement should be reviewed and evaluated regularly to ensure its effectiveness.

In terms of planning, make sure that the remote student receives lesson materials in advance and that there is a clear agreement on when and how they will attend each session. Finally, cultivate empathy by enabling teachers, students, and other stakeholders to experience what it feels like to participate in a lesson remotely, thereby deepening their understanding of the remote student perspective.

To further support the effective participation of a SCI in classroom activities, it is essential to pay attention to several practical and pedagogical aspects. At the start and end of each lesson, ensure that the remote SCI logs in on time, the connection is properly checked, and a brief welcoming chat takes place. Similarly, conclude each session with appropriate attention to the remote student, reinforcing their sense of inclusion.

Careful consideration should also be given to the positioning of the device. Ideally, the remote student should have a clear view of the teacher, the board, and their classmates, while also being visible to the rest of the class. A good audio connection is crucial so that both the teacher and the class can be clearly heard by the remote student.

During the lesson, teachers should actively involve the remote student by encouraging interaction, regularly checking whether they can follow the content, and inviting them to ask questions. It is also important to include the remote student in turn-taking, to check their work, and to provide them with feedback just as one would with physically present students.

Lesson design should include collaborative work formats that allow the remote student to actively participate, as well as opportunities to work together with peers during independent tasks. In exceptional situations, every effort should be made to treat the remote student equally and inclusively as the students who are physically present in the classroom.

Additional attention should be given to the remote student's involvement beyond the core lessons to ensure a holistic and inclusive educational experience. When it comes to homework, it is important to ensure that assignments are communicated and that appropriate schoolwork is provided for times when the remote student is unable to attend lessons.

Social participation is also key. Whenever possible, encourage peers to take the device outside during breaks, allowing the remote student to take part in informal interactions. Portable devices should be used to facilitate contact during external activities, and efforts should be made to include the remote student in school-wide events and celebrations.

Lastly, ongoing support should go beyond academic planning and lesson coordination. Maintaining regular contact with the remote student helps to build a sense of connection, and showing genuine interest in their well-being—such as through brief online chats—reinforces their social inclusion and emotional engagement with the school community.

DATA-DRIVEN INSTRUCTION

Data-driven instruction, referred to in educational discourse as Learning Analytics or Educational Data Mining (cf. Hershkovitz, 2015), represents a pedagogical approach that relies on the systematic collection, analysis, and use of data to inform teaching practices and, consequently, improve student learning outcomes (Siemens & Gasevic, 2012). It involves the use of quantitative and qualitative data from standardized assessments, classroom performance, digital learning environments, and student engagement metrics to guide instructional decisions and provide personalized support for learners (Hershkovitz, 2015; Hamilton et al., 2009; Ifenthaler et al., 2019).

The primary purpose of data-driven instruction is to enhance teaching effectiveness and student learning by identifying gaps in understanding and enabling timely interventions. In blended and online education, the use of digital learning platforms and learning management systems has facilitated the collection of large volumes of learner data such as log data, clickstream analytics, and performance dashboards (Papamitsiou & Economides, 2014), allowing educators to move beyond intuition-based decision-making towards evidence-based instructional planning (Lin et al., 2024; Long & Siemens, 2011).

Key characteristics of data-driven instruction include the continuous cycle of assessment, analysis, and action. Teachers first collect relevant data, such as quiz scores, attendance records, or engagement levels. They then analyse this data to diagnose learning needs and identify patterns or trends at both the individual and group level. Finally, they implement targeted interventions, such as differentiated instruction, peer tutoring, or curriculum adjustments, to address the identified needs (Lee et al., 2024; Mandinach & Gummer, 2016). This data-driven instruction is referred to as *extracted analytics* (Greller & Drachsler, 2012). In contrast, *embedded analytics* refer to data that are used to inform the learner and/or to adapt tasks to the ability levels of students without teacher intervention. An advantage of embedded analytics is that these can be used seamlessly during participation in the learning activity itself; A weakness is that these analytics can be ignored by the learner (see Figure 4).

Figure 4. Embedded and extracted analytics (Admiraal et al., 2020)

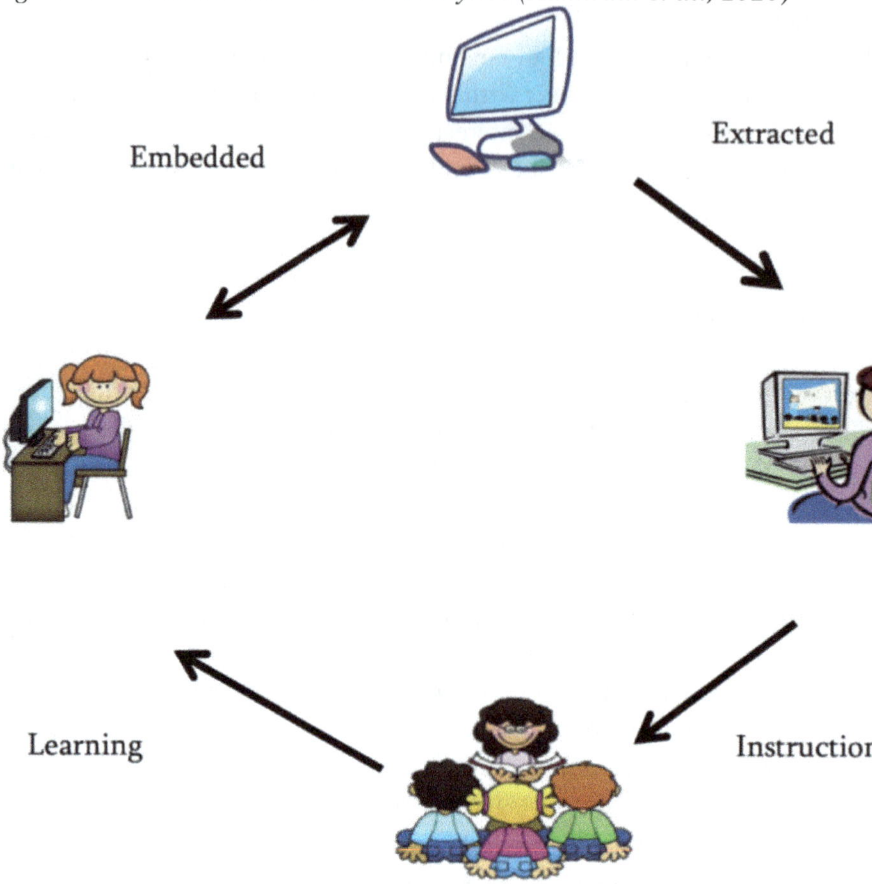

In practice, data-driven instruction manifests in a variety of ways. In secondary education, it may involve teachers using formative assessment results to group students for specific skill development activities. In higher education, instructors might leverage learning analytics dashboards to track students' progress in a course and reach out to those at risk of underperformance with tailored feedback or support (Gašević et al., 2015).

Benefits of Data-Driven Instruction

Data-driven instruction offers several important benefits for both educators and learners. One of the most widely recognized advantages is its potential to enhance teaching effectiveness by providing timely and detailed insights into students' learning progress. Educators are better equipped to identify learning gaps, adjust instruction to meet diverse student needs, and provide targeted interventions (Admiraal et al., 2020; Mandinach & Gummer, 2016).

Another key benefit is the promotion of personalized learning. By analysing individual-level data, teachers can tailor instruction, assignments, and feedback to accommodate varying learning paces and needs. This is particularly suitable in digital learning environments, where adaptive learning technologies use real-time data to adjust content delivery (Ning et al., 2025).

Data-driven instruction can also enhance the collaborative decision-making of teachers. By making student learning data visible and actionable, data-driven instruction can support meaningful dialogue among teachers, administrators, and support staff. This can strengthen professional learning communities and foster a culture of shared responsibility for student success (Schildkamp & Poortman, 2015).

Furthermore, data-driven instruction can improve accountability and transparency in education. When decisions are backed by empirical evidence, stakeholders—including students, parents, and administrators—can better understand how instructional choices are made and how they contribute to learning outcomes (Schildkamp & Poortman, 2015).

Finally, using data as a core instructional tool promotes reflective practice and teacher professional growth. Teachers become more aware of the impact of their strategies, engage in evidence-informed experimentation, and refine their pedagogical approaches over time (Mandinach & Schildkamp, 2021). The process of engaging with data nurtures critical inquiry into what works for whom and under what conditions—essential questions for improving equity and effectiveness in education.

Challenges of Data-Driven Instruction

Despite its promise, the implementation of data-driven instruction in secondary and higher education poses several challenges. One prominent issue concerns educators' data literacy—the ability to accurately interpret, analyse, and act upon data insights. Many teachers and instructors lack sufficient training or confidence in using complex learning analytics tools, which can lead to misinterpretation of data or underutilization of available information (Lee et al., 2024; Schildkamp & Poortman, 2015).

Another major challenge involves data quality and accessibility. Data-driven instruction relies heavily on accurate, timely, and relevant data, yet educational institutions often contend with fragmented, incomplete, or outdated data sets (Ifenthaler et al., 2019). Moreover, the technical infrastructure required to collect and analyse data—such as integrated learning management systems or analytics platforms—might not be available in some schools and universities (Daniel, 2015).

Ethical and privacy concerns can also pose barriers to the adoption of data-driven instruction. The collection and use of student data raises questions about data security, informed consent, and potential misuse. Students and parents may be wary of how their information is collected and stored, and improper handling of sensitive data can erode trust in educational institutions (Slade & Prinsloo, 2013).

Lastly, institutional culture can also limit the effectiveness of data-driven instruction. In some schools and universities, there may be resistance to change or a lack of collaborative practices necessary for meaningful data use. Effective data-driven instruction requires an open culture that values evidence-based decision-making and promotes continuous inquiry and reflection among educators (Schildkamp et al., 2019). Without such a supportive environment, data may be collected but remain unused or underutilized, reducing its impact on teaching and learning.

Case 2: Data-Driven Instruction in Language Teaching in Secondary Education

Introduction

An evaluation of data-driven instruction in a secondary school in the Netherlands has been carried out (Admiraal et al, 2020). In this Dutch secondary school, the software Got it Language (Got it Taal) is commonly used to practice and assess the linguistic components of the Dutch language (e.g., vocabulary, syntax, semantics, and morphology.

Data-Driven Instruction with Got it Language

This online adaptive learning environment includes student tests, each with sub-themes. During one school year in a secondary school, the Dutch language teacher team used Got it Language in 12 cycles of 2 weeks to support their pedagogical choices. The teachers had weekly meetings in the computer room at school, in which students completed online Dutch language tests in Got it Language (guided by the IT support officer). These two weekly meetings were followed by a team meeting with the teachers to prepare one particular lesson for each teacher in the following week. This preparation was based on the learning analytics from Got It Language. After the particular lesson, the teachers participated in an evaluation team meeting, which started a new cycle. When students worked on their tests, they followed this procedure (see also Figure 5):

- Students completed an entry test on a particular subtheme;

- Based on their score on the entry test, students practiced on items that differed in difficulty, starting at the difficulty level set by their entry test score (gridlines in Figure 5);
- If students passed the practice items at a particular difficulty level, they were directed to a final test on that particular subtheme;
- If students passed the final test on a particular subtheme, they were directed to an entry test on a new subtheme, and
- If students failed the final test on a particular subtheme, they returned to the practice items of the same subtheme.

The tests were multiple-choice tests and open-answer tests. With multiple-choice items, students got a second chance if an answer was incorrect. If the second choice was again incorrect, the tool provided students with the correct option. After completing the open-answer items, all correct answers were kept, and incorrect answers were deleted (based on programmed text recognition); in the next step, students only revised the incorrect answers. Students could consult additional written clarifications or explanations presented in a video clip. Students completed the computer-based assessments in weekly sessions in school.

Figure 5. Data-driven instruction with Got.it Language (Admiraal et al., 2020)

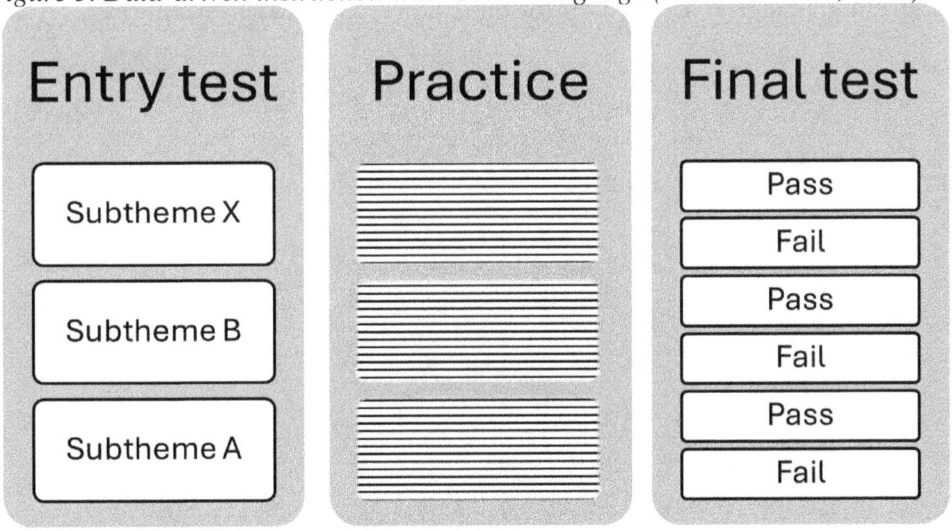

Data

During one school year, five secondary school teachers were observed to address three research questions: (1) What types of student data do teachers utilize in their teaching practice? (2) How do teachers apply student data to inform their instructional methods? and (3) How do students evaluate these classroom instructions?

Findings

Teachers preferred to use data that provided detailed information about each student, their tasks, and their responses in their teaching practice. In the classroom, they focused on giving feedback to low-performing students, either by themselves or through high-performing peers. As a result, low-performing students viewed this formative assessment approach more positively than their high-performing counterparts. They appreciated the opportunity to practice and the additional feedback and instruction they received during class.

Despite the benefits, the teachers mentioned that the data from the tests were too general and difficult to handle, and that qualitative data about the scores were missing. The teachers implemented eight setups in class (see Figure 6). In Figure 6, the black dot is the teacher, and the coloured dots are the students (green = high-performing; orange = medium-performing, and red = low-performing).

Figure 6. Eight class setups of data-driven instruction

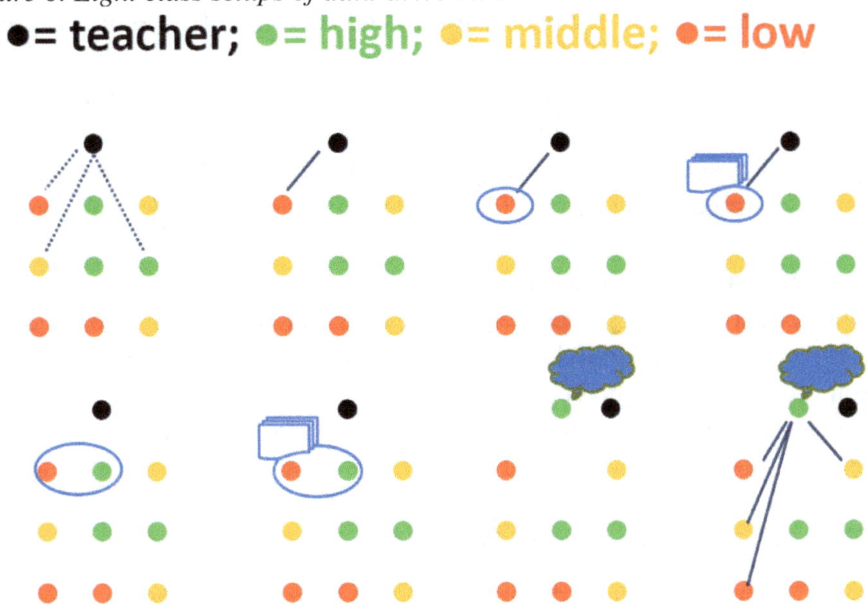

Starting with the first setup (located in the upper-left corner of Figure 6) and moving from left to right, continuing to the second row where the fifth setup is located on the left side, the setups are as follows: 1) a teacher inquires about test scores for a small selection of students; 2) a teacher gives a selected student a turn; 3) a selected individual student completes the same task as their peers, but with teacher support (such as questioning and providing information); 4) a selected individual student completes different tasks from their peers, also with teacher support; 5) pairs of selected students, consisting of one low-performing and one high-performing student, complete the same tasks as their classmates; 6) pairs of selected students, comprising one low-performing and one high-performing student, complete different tasks from their classmates; 7) a teacher invites a student to instruct the class; and 8) a teacher invites a high-performing student to instruct the class and assist other students individually.

Based on these findings, the authors identified two key implications for teachers engaged in data-driven instruction. The first implication concerns the selection of students who receive feedback during class. While data-driven instruction is often seen as most beneficial for low-achieving students, high-achieving students can also benefit. Through peer teaching or feedback activities, these students can build confidence and take pride in helping others, which may boost their motivation to pursue more advanced language learning. Furthermore, as demonstrated in several peer-assessment studies, teaching others is an effective way to learn; providing feedback and instruction requires a strong understanding of assessment criteria and standards.

The second implication highlights the need for additional support for teachers beyond simply providing accurate and relevant assessment data. In this study, teachers expressed a desire for greater pedagogical support in the classroom. Delivering adaptive or individualized instruction is inherently complex. Various forms of professional development could assist teachers in improving their classroom practices to better differentiate instruction based on assessment outcomes. These could include discussion meetings, teacher design teams or data teams, workshops or master classes focused on individualized instruction, collaborative action research, or lesson studies. Such support could empower teachers to make informed decisions about differentiation, ultimately enhancing outcomes for all students.

DIGITAL GAMES AND GAMIFICATION

Digital games and gamification in education share game elements that can support motivation, learning engagement, and cognitive development. An overview of game elements is presented in Table 1.

A central characteristic of both approaches is goal orientation. In digital games, learning is structured around explicit missions, quests, or challenges that players must complete to advance through the game. These goals are often nested within broader narratives that provide purpose and context. For example, in the location-based city game presented as a case (see below), students are told that they can earn citizenship in Amsterdam by collecting as many of the required 366 so-called *Days of Burghership* as possible. These 366 points refer to the medieval year-and-a-day rule, which is how long you had to be living inside the city walls to earn citizenship rights (Huizenga et al., 2009). In gamified environments, goals often take the form of short-term objectives tied to curricular content, such as earning a badge for completing a set of math problems or levelling up after demonstrating mastery of a language skill (Khalil et al., 2018). The presence of clear goals helps learners focus their efforts and track progress over time.

A second key feature is the presence of immediate and informative feedback. In digital games, feedback is intrinsic to the gameplay, enabling learners to understand the consequences of their actions, experiment with different strategies, and adjust their behaviour in real time (Gee, 2003). In gamified systems, feedback typically comes through progress indicators like scores, checklists, or dashboards, which provide learners with an ongoing sense of achievement and status (Hong et al., 2024; Khalil et al., 2018). Feedback, whether embedded in a game narrative or structured through gamified elements, is vital for maintaining learner engagement and scaffolding learning.

Progression and challenge are also defining characteristics. Effective digital games are designed to maintain learners in a state of "flow" (Csikszentmihalyi, 1990), where the challenge level matches the player's current skill, keeping them neither bored nor overwhelmed. Games use levels, increasingly difficult tasks, and adaptive pathways to encourage persistence and a sense of accomplishment (see also Admiraal et al., 2011). Similarly, in gamified education, progression is represented through systems such as ranking levels, unlocking new content, or accumulating experience points (XP). This incremental design motivates learners to continue working toward long-term learning goals by rewarding effort and perseverance.

Another important characteristic is the sense of agency and autonomy that both digital games and gamification can promote. In many digital games, learners are offered choices about how to proceed—what strategy to take, which path to explore, or how to solve a problem. This freedom can increase intrinsic motivation by allowing learners to exercise control and feel responsible for their learning outcomes (Huizenga et al., 2009). While gamification sometimes emphasizes extrinsic rewards, well-designed systems can also incorporate learner choice, such as allowing students to select which challenges to complete or how to earn rewards, thereby supporting self-directed learning and autonomy (Hong et al., 2024).

Furthermore, engagement through narrative and social elements plays a significant role, particularly in digital games. Storytelling is often used to create emotional connections and contextualize learning content, making it more memorable and meaningful (Gee, 2003). Multiplayer or cooperative elements in games can foster communication, collaboration, and shared problem-solving. In gamified educational settings, social presence and motivation are often enhanced by either competition (e.g., leaderboards) or cooperation (e.g., team-based challenges). These social dynamics can support the development of interpersonal competences (Li et al., 2024).

Finally, both digital games and gamification support mastery learning by allowing learners to repeat tasks, experiment with strategies, and receive feedback without fear of failure. This "safe space to fail" or sandbox is particularly needed in education, where mistakes are often stigmatized. In digital games, failure is typically seen as part of the learning journey, encouraging resilience and iterative problem-solving (Gee, 2003).

Table 1. Overview of Game Elements (from Hong et al., 2024)

Cluster game elements	Game element	Description
Performance	Reward	Anything given to the player to praise his/her actions or success in the challenge, which could reinforce students to keep and strengthen their behaviors for achieving more rewards
	Progress	It enables the players to locate themselves and their real-time progress and demonstrates their growth and improvement during the gamified process
	Feedback	It acknowledges the player for his/her inquiry and the correctness or wrongness of his/her learning activities to encourage or discourage a particular behavior
	Punishment	It is imposed when students give an incorrect answer or break the rule of the gamified activity
	Voting	The process of soliciting user feedback to guide the development or progression of the gamified system
Personal	Challenge	A variety of situations or activities that the students need to conquer or make efforts to deal with, in order to achieve the learning goals
	Customization	It provides students with personal experiences by assigning challenges that perfectly fit their skill level, adjusting learning tasks moderated based on player feedback, or allowing students to change the gamified environment by creating their own identities
	Goal	A specific, clear, and defined goal serves as a guideline for student actions, and they can see the direct impact of their efforts
	Free to fail	It creates a low risk of submission for the players
	Novelty	New, updated information presented to the player continuously. Some examples and synonyms are changes, surprises, updates
	Sensation	Use of player senses to create new experiences. Some examples and synonyms are visual stimulation, sound stimulation
Social	Competition	A conflict between players towards a common goal and prompts the players to perform better than others
	Socialization	Social network allows users to create their profiles, add friends and interact with each other in it; Scaffolding allows the users to support others or ask for support from others; Social status is based on the user's social influence, such as the number of followers in the social networks; Social pressure is the pressure through social interactions with other players
	Cooperation	When two or more players collaborate to achieve a common goal
	Reputation	Titles that the player accumulates within the game
Ecological	Access	An exclusive content conditioned to an action of the user to be available
	Choice	It gives the users the possibility to have multiple routes to success, allowing them to decide how to complete the learning tasks
	Time pressure	It requires the players to complete one task in a determined time
	Chance	Any probability to take certain actions or increase outcomes within a gamified activity
	Trading	It represents the transaction in the gamified system
	Rarity	Limited resources and collectables

continued on following page

Table 1. Continued

Cluster game elements	Game element	Description
Fictional	Narrative	Order of events where they happen in a game, which is influenced by the player's actions
	Storytelling	It is the way the story of the game is told (as a script). It is told within the game, through text, voice, or sensorial resources

Benefits of Digital Games and Gamification

The integration of digital games and gamification into educational contexts has been widely studied over the past two decades, with growing evidence pointing to a range of cognitive, motivational, and social benefits.

One of the most consistently cited benefits is the enhancement of learner motivation and engagement. Digital games can be intrinsically motivating due to their interactive nature, immediate feedback, goal-driven tasks, and immersive storytelling (Huizenga et al., 2009; Admiraal et al., 2011). Similarly, gamification leverages game mechanics such as points, badges, and leaderboards to stimulate motivation by tapping into learners' need for achievement, competition, and recognition (Hamari et al., 2014; Khalil et al., 2018). When learners perceive progress and competence, they are more likely to persist in learning tasks.

Beyond motivation, digital games and gamification also support cognitive and active learning strategies. Digital games often require players to engage in problem-solving, critical thinking, and strategic planning—skills that are highly transferable to academic contexts (Squire, 2013). For example, in science and mathematics education, simulations and puzzle-based games encourage learners to test hypotheses, manage variables, and understand cause-effect relationships through experimentation (Ke, 2008). Gamification can also provide learners with monitoring their progress, reflecting on their performance, and setting learning goals based on feedback from the system (Khalil et al., 2018).

Another advantage is the ability of games and gamification to support personalized and adaptive learning. Many digital games adjust difficulty levels, tasks, or content based on individual learner performance. This allows for differentiated instruction, which is particularly beneficial in diverse classrooms with varying levels of ability (Bontchev et al., 2021). Gamified platforms similarly offer opportunities for self-paced learning, where learners can choose the order of tasks or revisit content until mastery is achieved. This flexibility contributes to a more inclusive learning environment in which all students can succeed on their own terms. Four levels of adaptation can be distinguished (Hong et al., 2024): 1) User modelling – no adaptation based on learners' preferences and abilities; 2) Personalization – one-time adjustment based on user profiles with mainly static information; 3) Adaptation – continuous adjustment based on user profiles with dynamic information; and 4) Recommendation - suggesting game elements and activities to the player based on players with user characteristics in the past.

Moreover, digital games and gamification can enhance collaboration and social learning. Multiplayer or cooperative games often require learners to communicate, negotiate roles, and solve problems together, fostering teamwork and peer learning (Voulgari et al., 2014). Gamified classrooms may use team-based challenges or collective goals to build a sense of community and shared responsibility.

From an emotional perspective, both digital games and gamification can promote positive learning experiences by reducing fear of failure and encouraging a growth mindset. In digital games, failure is often reframed as a normal part of the process, providing learners with opportunities to retry, improve, and ultimately succeed. This can support resilience and perseverance (Habgood & Ainsworth, 2011). Gamification can similarly foster a sense of accomplishment by breaking down larger learning goals into smaller, manageable tasks that reward effort, not just outcomes.

Finally, research also suggests that well-designed games and gamified systems can lead to improved learning outcomes. Meta-analyses have demonstrated that digital game-based learning can be as effective or more effective than regular instructional methods, particularly when games are closely aligned with curricular goals and include debriefing or reflection components (Barz et al., 2024). Likewise, gamification has been shown to improve task completion rates, content retention, and classroom participation, especially in digital learning environments (Sailer & Homner, 2020).

Challenges of Digital Games and Gamification

While the integration of digital games and gamification in education offers numerous pedagogical benefits, it also presents a range of challenges that educators should consider. These challenges are related to design, implementation, equity, pedagogical alignment, and long-term effectiveness.

A primary challenge lies in the pedagogical alignment of games and gamified systems with curricular objectives. Not all digital games are designed with educational purposes in mind. In many cases, digital games are used either as a project isolated from the curriculum or as a 'filler' for Friday afternoon (Huizenga et al, 2017). Gamification, too, can risk becoming a superficial layer that prioritizes rewards over learning if not rooted in a sound pedagogical design. When game elements are poorly integrated, learners may focus more on collecting points or badges than on understanding the content. To mitigate this, educators must carefully select or design games and gamified activities that explicitly support learning objectives, promote higher-order thinking, and include reflective elements (Huizenga et al., 2017).

Another, related challenge is the risk of extrinsic motivation overshadowing intrinsic interest in learning. Gamification often relies on external rewards such as badges or leaderboards, which can have short-term motivational benefits but may undermine intrinsic motivation (Przybylski et al., 2013). Learners may become more interested in the rewards than the learning itself, leading to disengagement once the rewards are removed. To counter this, giving students meaningful choices, providing constructive feedback, and fostering collaboration can help maintain intrinsic motivation.

Another concern is the potential for distraction and off-task behaviour. The entertaining nature of games can lead some learners to focus on gameplay mechanics at the expense of educational content (Annetta, 2010). In gamified environments, competition may cause stress or demotivate students who consistently rank lower. To manage this, educators can establish clear guidelines for the use of games, incorporate debriefing sessions to connect gameplay with learning objectives, and design inclusive game elements that emphasize cooperation over competition (Huizenga et al., 2017).

Finally, as with all learning tools and environments, sustainability and long-term engagement are important considerations. The novelty of games and gamified elements can erode over time, potentially reducing their effectiveness. Students may become desensitized to rewards or lose interest if content does not progress (Romero Rodríguez et al., 2025). To ensure sustainability, game-based and gamified systems should offer variety and opportunities for personalization. Regularly updating the content and involving students in the design of activities can help maintain long-term interest and engagement.

Case 3: The Location-Based City Game *Frequency 1550*

Introduction

Admiraal et al. (2011) and Huizenga et al. (2017) examined the impact of a mobile city game called *Frequency 1550* on students' engagement, historical knowledge, and motivation for History in general, with a particular focus on the Middle Ages.

Frequencies 1550

"Frequency 1550" is a game set in medieval Amsterdam, played by student teams over the course of a single school day as part of their History lessons in secondary education. At the beginning of the game day, students are introduced to the game, including its tasks, tools, and objectives. The game is named after the year 1550, during which the medieval city's bailiff reaches out to the present. Students are informed that they can earn citizenship in Amsterdam by collecting a total of 366 points, which correspond to the medieval year-and-a-day rule. This rule established the duration of residence required within the city walls to gain citizenship rights. Participants are randomly assigned the roles of either beggars or merchants, each representing different social statuses typical of the Middle Ages. Along with this distinction, merchants typically have advantages in confrontations throughout the game.

Group and team structure

The activity involved groups of four students, with each group divided into two teams: a city team (CT) consisting of two students who explored the city, and a headquarters team (HQT) made up of the other two students who stayed in the headquarters room using a computer. In the second half of the day, the teams switched roles, allowing each student to participate in both the CT and HQT. The CT was assigned a specific area as their starting point for exploration. Their task was to conduct small, location-based media activities aimed at exploring, mapping, and mastering the area and its theme before moving on to learning tasks in a different location. The HQT, meanwhile, could monitor the CT's real-time movements through the city on a medieval map, illustrated with colored dots, as well as on a current map of Amsterdam. This allowed them to strategize and use their phones to guide the CT to locations where assignments were hidden. Additionally, the HQT collected all the materials produced to complete the tasks. While the CTs had access to a medieval map and a current map of Amsterdam, they could not see their routes on these maps.

Figure 7. The Medieval map of Amsterdam in Frequencies 1550

Assignments

The old city of Amsterdam has been divided into six areas, each representing a different theme from medieval times. The six themes are 'Labour,' 'Trade,' 'Religion,' 'Rules and Government,' 'Knowledge,' and 'Defense.' Students receive an introductory video clip as soon as they enter a specific area, which appears on their phones along with the area's name. These clips provide information that helps the group complete the assignments related to that area, while the audio reflects the sounds characteristic of each theme (e.g., the sound of manual work or sawing).

When a CT reaches a certain location, they automatically receive video assignments. Each area features three types of similar assignments. The orientation assignment aims to enhance environmental awareness by encouraging students to create or select photos or videos, ask questions about the site, and envision the perspectives, work, or actions of historical figures. The imagination assignment focuses on reflecting on historical actions, events, or the roles of historical characters. The symbolic assignment includes texts and tasks that prompt the team to identify details of the site with specific symbolic value.

Each group, consisting of a CT and a HQT, can earn points for completing these assignments, contributing to their success in the game. The groups compete against each other, and each CT must decide whether to avoid other teams or engage in confrontation. Their social status—where merchants rank higher than beggars—determines the outcome of these encounters. The winning team can take points from the losing team. Additionally, the CT has the option to drop virtual medieval rats by pressing a key on their phones, disrupting the communication capabilities of another team with their HQT.

The closing of the game

Each HQT (Headquarters Team) creates a website with all the materials collected throughout the day. At the end of the day, all students gather in the main building where the HQTs are located. Each group is invited to present a selection of their collected media to the other groups. The group that answers the most questions correctly wins the most game points.

Data

Developed by The Waag Society in the Netherlands, the game aimed to help first-year secondary school students learn about medieval Amsterdam in an engaging, playful way. A quasi-experimental study was conducted involving 458 students from 20 classes across five schools. In 10 of the classes, students participated in the mobile history game, while the other 10 classes followed a traditional project-based lesson series.

Findings

The findings indicated that students who played the game were highly engaged and gained significantly more knowledge about medieval Amsterdam compared to their peers who received traditional instruction. Additionally, these students experienced a state of flow during gameplay, although occasional technical and navigational issues caused some distractions. While flow was positively associated with game performance, it did not have a direct impact on learning outcomes. Instead, the level of distraction, the time spent solving problems, and involvement in inter-group competition influenced learning. Specifically, students who experienced fewer distractions and participated more in competitive group dynamics learned more about the medieval history of Amsterdam.

VIRTUAL REALITY

Virtual Reality (VR) is an emerging technology that allows learners to engage with content in new and meaningful ways. VR refers to a computer-generated simulation or recreation of a real or imaginary environment that users can interact with in a seemingly real or physical way. It typically requires the use of specialized hardware, such as head-mounted displays (HMDs), motion sensors, gloves, or hand controllers. VR is distinguished from other related technologies like augmented reality (AR)—which overlays digital content onto the real world—and mixed reality (MR)—which blends real and virtual environments interactively. Unlike AR and MR, VR generally isolates the user from the physical world to deliver a completely virtual experience (Marougkas et al., 2023; Radianti et al., 2020).

In educational settings, VR is used to simulate environments that may be difficult or impossible to access otherwise, such as historical sites, the inside of a human cell, or distant planets. VR can also be used in professional learning, like teachers or nurses, to prevent potential harm to students or patients. Its immersive nature has shown promise for increasing engagement, improving knowledge retention, and supporting experiential learning (AlGerafi et al., 2023; Makransky & Mayer, 2022).

Various levels of immersion of VR can be distinguished based on the technology used. Non-immersive VR includes desktop-based VR experiences where users interact with a virtual environment via a standard computer screen, keyboard, and mouse. Examples include virtual simulations used in educational games or 3D environments navigated with a joystick or touchscreen (Atal et al., 2023). Semi-immersive VR is often used in flight or military simulators and training programs. It combines a projection screen or multiple monitors with spatial audio and some form of user input. While users remain aware of their physical surroundings, they can interact with a partially immersive digital environment (Cross & Hodgson, 2025). Fully immersive VR is the most complete VR experience and typically involves a head-mounted display (HMD), motion tracking sensors, and hand controllers. Fully immersive VR places the user inside a 360-degree environment where they can look around and interact as if they were physically present (Makransky & Mayer, 2025).

Benefits of Virtual Reality

Various benefits of the use of VR in education have been documented (Mazhar & Al Rifaee 2023; Pirker & Dengel, 2021; Radianti et al., 2020). Many studies show the effects of the use of VR on engagement and motivation of the learners. In their scoping review, Jiang and Fryer (2024) concluded that most studies in their literature review reported positive effects of the use of VR on the motivation of students, compared to other pedagogical settings. However, the authors could not rule out novelty effects in VR learning because of the lack of longitudinal research designs. Yet, these effects on motivation and engagement of learners are reported across educational sectors, in primary education (Chen et al., 2025), secondary education (Küçük et al., 2024), and higher education (Yang et al., 2024). VR seems especially useful for students who may struggle with abstract concepts or who require more visual and experiential forms of learning.

A second benefit of VR is that it enables experiential learning by placing students in lifelike scenarios where they can practice skills, conduct experiments, or explore environments. For example, this applies to medical students who develop their surgery skills in an authentic-looking operating room (Radianti et al., 2020). A large body of knowledge about the use of VR as a representation of a realistic professional context in higher education is available in the domains of teacher education (Wang & Li, 2024) and nursing education (Choi et al., 2022).

A third benefit of VR, related to the former one, is that VR provides safe settings for practicing potentially dangerous (e.g., military) or costly (e.g., aviation) procedures as well as accessibility to otherwise inaccessible experiences (such as the bottom of the ocean, outer space, or inside the human brain; Radianti et al., 2020). For instance, chemistry students can perform experiments without the risk of chemical exposure, and engineering students can simulate the operation of heavy machinery without real-world hazards. It also supports inclusive education by providing alternative learning formats for students with disabilities (Carreon et al., 2022).

Challenges of Virtual Reality

Despite its potential, the adoption of VR in education faces several challenges. High-quality VR systems remain expensive, especially when scaled for classroom use. Costs include the hardware (e.g., headsets, sensors, powerful computers), software licenses, maintenance, and potential upgrades. Many schools may not have the budget to support VR implementation.

In addition to the financial challenges, VR systems can be technically complex to set up and operate, often requiring IT support and training. Poor usability, system crashes, or inadequate tracking can lead to frustration among both teachers and students. Additionally, not all students may be comfortable using VR equipment (Araiza-Alba et al., 2022), which might be related to their experiences of motion sickness, eye strain, or disorientation during or after VR sessions. Prolonged use of VR may lead to physical discomfort, and there are also concerns about the potential psychological effects of extended immersion, particularly for younger learners (Cossio et al., 2025).

Finally, while educational VR content is growing, it remains limited in certain subjects and languages. Moreover, integrating VR into existing curricula can be challenging. Educators must align VR experiences with learning outcomes, assessment practices, and pedagogical goals, which requires careful planning and training (Qiao et al., 2021). In their scoping meta-review of how VR can be integrated in medical education, Mergen et al. (2024) particularly emphasized the importance of well-structured curricula grounded in solid learning theories and featuring clearly defined learning objectives.

Case 4: Virtual Reality in Teacher Education

Introduction

Although traditional videos can be seen as a way to 'open the classroom doors', the single focus they provide prevents viewers from noticing other potentially important classroom events. This single restricted view is referred to as the 'keyhole effect' by Sherin and van Es (2009). This 'keyhole effect' is overcome by the much-discussed recent innovation of 360o video technology, which can be viewed on many devices, including PCs, tablets, and phones. Watching 360o videos with a Head-Mounted Display (HMD) is thought to provide a particularly realistic experience.

Virtual Reality in Teacher Education

In a study of Atal et al. (2024) and Theeuwes et al. (2025), virtual reality (VR) with a HMD in teacher education has been examined. Student-teachers had an individual, standardized immersive experience in a near-authentic and realistic multicultural classroom via three Spherical Video-Based Virtual Reality (SV-VR) clips viewed through a Head Mounted Display (HMD, Oculus Go). The use of the HMD and the teaching context were explained at the start of the meeting. Student-teachers were told that they would see three video clips of a 10th-grade class after an assignment on youth drug use had been explained to them. In the first clip, the students were assigned to the table groups by the teacher, while in the second and third clips, the students were allowed to decide for themselves who they wanted to work with. The assignment involved reading, answering questions, and discussing the subject among themselves. The participants would be at the front of the class to observe the students while they were doing their assignment in their table groups (see Figure 8).

Figure 8. Screenshot of participants' view

The three SV-VR clips lasted about 2 minutes each. The scenes in the clips were played by 23 actors, aged about 16 years, working in groups of 4 or 5 on assigned tasks, like in a common Grade 10 classroom. Some actors were given instructions to play a role regarding specific classroom events that can be encountered in all classes. This misbehaviour was reflected in each scenario:

- Scenario 1: Throwing a book, throwing paper, looking out the window, separating desks, changing places, rocking on the chair,
- Scenario 2: Muttering, going to the bathroom without permission, dreamily looking around, sleeping, gossiping, eating cake,
- Scenario 3: Messing around with things, working on something else on the laptop, putting on make-up, verbally abusing a classmate.

Afterwards, the student-teachers discussed their experiences as teachers in the SV-VR classes in groups of 5. They were asked to think about two additional questions: 1) What do you think might be going on in this event? and 2) How would you respond to this event? These questions were intended as stepping stones for a deeper conversation about teaching and classroom management, in particular.

Data

In a study of Atal et al. (2024), the effects of presenting video clips in various ways (as 360 o videos with a HMD, 360o videos on a laptop, or 2D video) on student-teachers' stress levels and self-efficacy in classroom management were studied.

Findings

The VR group with HMD decreased their stress levels and increased their self-efficacy in classroom management, compared to the other conditions. From the interviews, it appeared that student-teachers reported that they felt like a teacher, that the VR setting gave them a very realistic view and a sense of presence, and that they liked to use it as a preparation for their internships. The VR group were significantly more engaged with learning from the experience than the two other groups of students.

ONLINE DISCUSSION FORUMS

Online discussion forums have become an integral component of digital learning environments in education and in higher education, in particular. These forums are typically embedded within Learning Management Systems (LMS), such as Moodle, Canvas, or Blackboard, or integrated into Massive Open Online Courses (MOOCs), where they serve as asynchronous platforms for communication, collaboration, and reflective dialogue among students and instructors. Online discussions allow participants to contribute messages over time, creating a threaded and often thematically organized discourse that supports the social construction of knowledge (Galikyan et al., 2021; Garrison et al., 2001; Hrastinski, 2008).

A key characteristic of online discussion forums is their asynchronous nature, which affords participants the flexibility to engage at their own pace and reflect on the contributions of others before responding (Hrastinski, 2008). This can lead to cognitive engagement, particularly when students are encouraged to justify claims, pose questions, and integrate multiple perspectives (Galikyan et al., 2021). Moreover, online discussions often include prompts or questions from instructors, which serve as scaffolds to guide interaction and encourage critical thinking among learners (Maurino, 2007).

Several types of online discussion structures serve different pedagogical purposes. These include *exploratory discussions*, which focus on open-ended sharing of ideas; *argumentative* or *debate-style discussions*, which require students to take and defend a position; and *collaborative discussions*, in which students co-construct understanding or develop a shared product. Each type elicits different patterns of participation and cognitive presence, and their effectiveness often depends on the instructor facilitation (Darabi et al., 2011).

Online discussions can contribute to multiple dimensions of learning. Cognitively, they can promote critical thinking and articulation of understanding (Garrison et al., 2001; Soylu & Lee, 2024). Socially, they can support a sense of community and peer learning (Rovai, 2002). From a metacognitive perspective, they enable students to monitor their own and others' thinking processes (Soylu & Lee, 2024). However, the success of online discussions is contingent on, amongst others, the discussion prompts, the instructor's role as a facilitator, and the establishment of a safe and respectful communicative climate (Hew & Cheung, 2012).

Benefits of Online Discussion Forums

Online discussions in educational forums offer a range of pedagogical benefits that can support student learning, engagement, and community-building (cf. Almatrafi & Jorhi, 2018). One of the most widely recognized advantages is the promotion of critical thinking and cognitive engagement (Foo & Quek, 2019; Maurino, 2007). The asynchronous nature of most online forums allows learners to reflect on discussion prompts and peer responses before contributing, which can result in more thoughtful, reasoned, and well-supported contributions than those found in real-time classroom discussions.

In addition to cognitive benefits, online discussions facilitate collaborative knowledge construction. Through iterative exchanges, students are able to build on each other's ideas, challenge assumptions, and collectively make meaning of complex topics, when guided effectively by instructors or moderators. The social benefits of engagement in online discussion forums and their effects on collaborative knowledge building is confirmed in recent review studies (Fehrman & Watson, 2021: Moore & Miller, 2022).

Another important benefit lies in the enhancement of student participation and inclusion. Online forums can give all students the chance to contribute, including those who may be less inclined to speak in face-to-face settings due to anxiety or language barriers (Galikyan et al., 2020; Hew & Cheung, 2012).

Related to the potential to enhance student participation, discussion forums can play a significant role in building a sense of community and social presence in online, blended or hybrid courses. Social interaction through consistent and respectful dialogue helps students feel connected to their peers and the learning environment, which in turn positively affects motivation, satisfaction, and persistence (Delahunty et al., 2014; Harvey et al., 2018).

For teachers, online discussions give them opportunities for formative assessment, allowing them to gauge student understanding, identify misconceptions, and adjust instruction accordingly, similar to data-driven instruction. The written nature of forum posts also creates a permanent record of student thinking and dialogue, which can be used for teacher and peer assessment, student reflection, or future learning activities.

Challenges of Online Discussion Forums

Despite their pedagogical potential, as mentioned above, online discussions in educational forums also present several challenges that can undermine their effectiveness if not carefully addressed. One of the most commonly reported issues is superficial participation. While discussion forums are designed to foster critical thinking and collaborative knowledge building, many student contributions tend to be short and unreflective, posted to meet participation requirements rather than to engage in a dialogue (Hew et al., 2010; Hew & Cheung, 2012). This lack of depth often stems from unclear expectations, poorly designed prompts, or a lack of student motivation to engage meaningfully. In addition, online discussions also tend to be off-task, supporting peers emotionally or just short greetings (Lockhorst et al., 2010). One of the most fundamental strategies to fight superficial student participation is the careful design of discussion prompts. Research shows that open-ended, thought-provoking questions that encourage interpretation, debate, and application of concepts are more likely to elicit higher-order thinking than factual or overly general prompts. Prompts that require students to take a position, critique a perspective, or relate content to real-life experiences stimulate richer interaction and more meaningful dialogue (see the recent review of Gehring et al., 2025).

Closely related to this problem of superficial participation is the problem of uneven participation. In many online discussions, a small number of students dominate the conversation, while others remain silent or contribute minimally (Hew et al., 2010). This imbalance can hinder the diversity of perspectives and limit the potential for collaborative learning. Furthermore, some students may feel intimidated by the public and permanent nature of written posts, leading to participation anxiety or reluctance to express views they fear might be incorrect or poorly received (Hew & Cheung, 2012). To address issues of uneven or superficial participation, instructors should establish inclusive discussion norms and actively moderate forums to ensure that all voices are heard and valued. Strategic facilitation—such as prompting quieter students, acknowledging diverse perspectives, and steering discussions back on topic—can enhance the overall quality of interaction (Gehring et al., 2025). At the same time, research suggests that instructors should avoid over-participating, as too much intervention can suppress student agency or shift the focus to instructor-student dialogue rather than peer learning. Equally important is the scaffolding of participation through clear guidelines and expectations. Students often engage more deeply when they know how many posts are expected, what constitutes a quality contribution, and how their participation will be evaluated (Hew & Cheung, 2012). Providing models of effective posts, using rubrics that emphasize critical engagement, and giving early formative feedback can help students develop both confidence and competence in online discussions (Gehring et al., 2025).

Another key challenge is cognitive overload. Online forums often require students to read and respond to numerous posts across multiple threads, which can be time-consuming and overwhelming, particularly when the volume of messages is high or poorly organized (Lockhorst et al., 2010). Without a clear structure or moderation, discussions may drift off-topic or become repetitive, making it difficult for students to follow coherent lines of thought or identify key learning points (Darabi et al., 2011). Breaking a large forum into smaller groups can reduce cognitive overload, create safer spaces for expression, and increase the likelihood of each member contributing meaningfully. Assigning rotating roles, such as summarizer, questioner, or devil's advocate, can further enhance engagement and ensure diverse cognitive tasks are distributed across participants (Hew & Cheung, 2012; Schellens & Valcke, 2006). Regularly summarizing key themes or highlighting particularly insightful contributions can reinforce important ideas and signal that the discussion is a valuable part of the learning process (Fehrman & Watson, 2021; Lockhorst et al., 2010).

As mentioned above, the role of the instructor is crucial but complex. While instructor presence is important for guiding and deepening discussion, excessive intervention can unintentionally limit student agency and turn discussions into question-answer sessions rather than spaces for open exploration. On the other hand, minimal or delayed instructor feedback may cause discussions to stagnate and allow misconceptions to persist unchallenged (Hew et al., 2010; Lockhorst et al., 2010).

Case 5: MOOC Discussion Forums

Introduction

Massive Open Online Course (MOOC) platforms collect digital traces from millions of learners, generating a wealth of data on learner behavior in MOOCs. The study of the case (Galikyan et al., 2021) analysed the content generated by learners in a MOOC discussion forum of *Miracles of Human Language: An Introduction to Linguistics*, which is a MOOC developed by Leiden University in the Netherlands.

Miracles of Human Language: An Introduction to Linguistics

This 6-week course (with each week one module) gives an introduction into the study of languages, the field of linguistics. Together with speakers of many other languages around the world, as well as with famous linguists such as Noam Chomsky and Adele Goldberg, the participants learn to understand and analyse how their native tongue is at the same time similar and different from many other languages. They learn the basic concepts of linguistics, get to know some of the key features of big and small languages, and get insight into what linguists do. The course materials include lecture videos and readings. Assessment consists of six weekly quizzes (10% each) and a final exam (40%). The MOOC provides a discussion board with separate forums for each week for learners to interact and seek help. The course provides a discussion board for learners to interact and seek help; however, participation in the discussion forums is optional.

There are five forum categories: (a) General discussion, (b) Share resources and join study groups, (c) Questions & answers, including feedback, (d) Meet and greet, and (e) Weekly discussions, each corresponding to a particular module (week) of the course. Each weekly forum, in its turn, consists of subforums/threads, through which the instructor assigns discussion tasks on weekly topics (see Figure 9. A sample task reads as follows: "Given the fact that there are different languages and that these languages may contain untranslatable concepts, would you say that people can fundamentally differ in their ways of thinking? Do you think that people agree on the meaning of concepts if they share a native tongue? Try to think of an untranslatable matter in your language and explain its meaning to others, including those who speak your language." Each task asks learners to write a response to the task and respond to at least two other students.

Figure 9. Discussion tasks on weekly topics

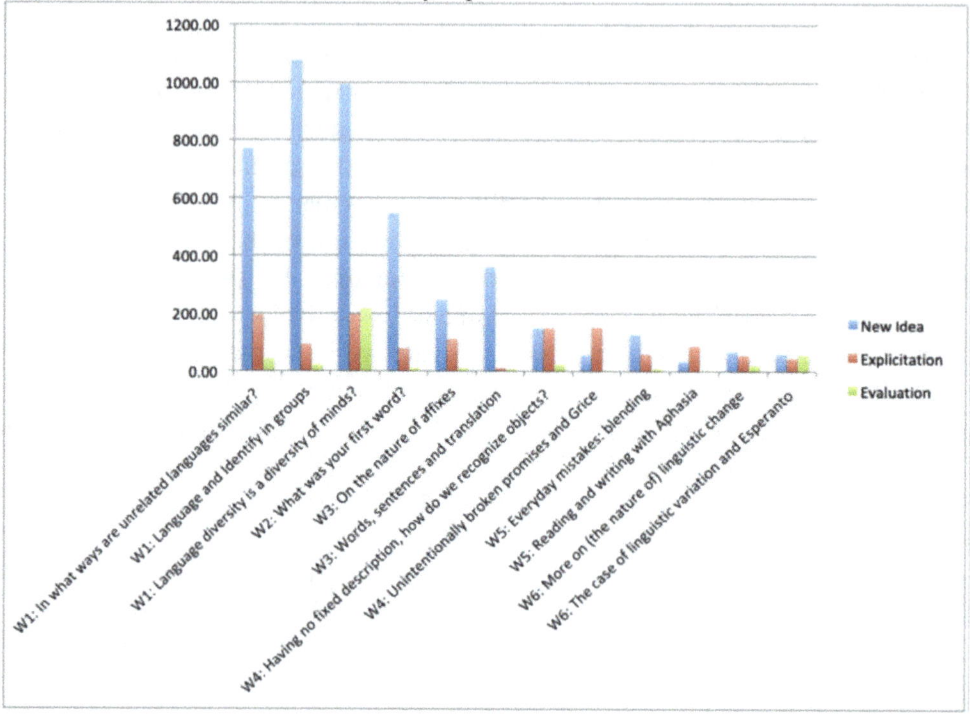

The forum is supervised by volunteer moderators who receive instruction and coaching, in addition to support from Coursera. The moderators are instructed to monitor behaviour, not the content of the course. Students are given community guidelines beforehand, detailing what (positive) behaviour is expected. New threads with the same discussion task on the same topic are started for each course offering by the automated system. Learners, in their turn, can choose to contribute to an existing thread or initiate a new thread. This results in multiple threads on the same topic.

Data

The study by Galikyan et al. (2021) analyzed content generated by learners in a MOOC discussion forum, specifically focusing on the cognitive aspects of learning within MOOCs. It demonstrated how varying levels of cognitive engagement are related to learning outcomes. Additionally, the study explored the relationship between cognitive and social factors, highlighting the moderating role of social elements in connecting the lowest levels of cognitive engagement with learning in a MOOC environment.

Findings

The lowest level of cognitive engagement, which shows the steepest decline over the duration of the course, is negatively linked to learners' MOOC grades. This negative correlation indicates that learners who merely reproduce isolated pieces of information, without understanding the relationships between them, struggle more with grasping the course content. In other words, engagement at this basic cognitive level—such as sharing facts, personal experiences, or opinions, or theoretical ideas without interpretation or connection to previously discussed information—may reflect surface-level processing, which is in turn associated with lower academic achievement. By contrast, engagement at higher cognitive levels, where learners build on each other's ideas through refinement and evaluation, is linked to a deeper understanding of the course material.

The social dimension, measured by the number of different discussion threads a learner contributes to, moderates this relationship. For learners who engage in only a few threads, low-level cognitive engagement has a more detrimental impact, likely because they do not sufficiently participate in the more advanced cognitive levels of discussion. However, learners who contribute to a wide range of discussion threads can compensate for this lack of deep cognitive engagement. Exposure to diverse perspectives and interpretations from others helps mitigate their limited understanding of the course content. In essence, when learners are not cognitively engaged, active social participation can partly offset this deficiency by broadening their exposure to meaningful content.

Understanding how different levels of cognitive engagement influence learning outcomes in MOOCs can assist instructors in designing more effective discussion tasks. To encourage higher-order cognitive engagement, instructors should create tasks that prompt learners to build upon each other's contributions by elaborating on, refining, and critically evaluating shared information. Additionally, fostering learning environments that promote interaction and help learners recognize the knowledge-building potential of discussion forums can enhance their understanding of the link between active participation and meaningful learning in MOOCs.

ONLINE VIDEO

Online video refers to the use of pre-recorded or live-streamed audiovisual content that is delivered via the internet, often through learning management systems (LMS), video-sharing platforms (e.g., YouTube, Vimeo), or institutionally supported tools (e.g., Panopto or Kaltura). Online videos can also be asynchronous, enabling flexible, on-demand access to content, which supports self-paced learning and accommodates diverse learning needs (Noetel et al., 2021; Zhang et al., 2006).

Online video is used in a range of pedagogical formats. It can serve as a substitute for in-person lectures, especially in online and blended learning environments, allowing teachers to allocate classroom time for active learning strategies such as discussions, problem-solving, and peer collaboration. This is the core premise of the flipped classroom model (Baig & Yadegaridehkordi, 2023).

Moreover, online video can enhance student engagement when it incorporates interactive elements, such as embedded quizzes, clickable annotations, and prompts for reflection. Research has shown that interactivity in video increases attention and retention, making learning more effective (Ploetzner, 2024). Effective educational videos are typically short (6–10 minutes), focused on a single topic, and use clear visuals and narration.

Assessment and feedback can also be integrated into online video use. For example, teachers can record personalized feedback via video to support formative assessment or provide scaffolding for assignments (Henderson & Phillips, 2015). Students, in turn, may use video as a medium for creating their content, such as presentations, digital storytelling, or peer instruction videos. The video clips can be assessed and annotated with feedback by peers and teachers (Admiraal et al., 2011).

Benefits of Online Video

The integration of online video in education offers a wide range of pedagogical benefits, from improving comprehension and engagement to supporting differentiated learning and student autonomy (Ploetzner, 2024). One of the primary advantages of online video is its ability to make abstract or complex concepts more accessible through multimodal representation. According to Mayer's (2024) cognitive theory of multimedia learning, learners better understand information when it is presented through both visual and auditory channels. Educational videos capitalize on this principle by combining narration, animation, and real-life demonstrations, thereby reducing cognitive load and supporting learning.

Another well-documented benefit of online video is its potential to increase student engagement. Video content is often perceived as more stimulating and relatable than texts or lectures, especially when it includes storytelling, visual interest, or real-world applications. Engagement is further enhanced when videos are interactive—e.g., including embedded quizzes, reflection prompts, or branching narratives—which can prompt active learning and immediate feedback (see review of Ploetzner, 2024).

In addition, online video supports blended and flipped learning models, in which content is delivered outside of class through video, freeing up in-class time for higher-order learning activities such as discussion, problem-solving, and collaboration. This instructional shift has been associated with improved academic outcomes, greater student satisfaction, and more meaningful classroom interactions (Baig & Yadegaridehkordi, 2023).

Video can also promote accessibility in education. For example, closed captions and transcripts allow students with hearing impairments or language difficulties to access content, while multilingual subtitles can support non-native speakers (Ploetzner, 2024). Moreover, recorded lectures and video explanations can help mitigate educational disruptions, such as illness or school closures, ensuring continuity of learning.

Finally, online video can also be used for annotated feedback and reflection, making comments on assignments more personal, nuanced, annotated, and understandable. In a study on 11 triads of student teachers in Australia (Cavanagh, 2021), a video platform was used for student-teacher self-reflection and for the provision of feedback. Student-teachers made video recordings of one lesson each week during a four-week professional experience placement. They annotated the videos using time-stamped comments and shared them with their supervisors, who added comments to provide feedback. Based on the analyses of the annotations, the authors conclude that the video process only marginally supported the provision of targeted feedback and student-teacher reflection. Stronger effects on feedback and reflection quality of student-teachers of a similar setup are reported by Admiraal & Berry (2016).

Challenges of Online Video

A commonly reported issue is the passive consumption of video content, which may limit learner engagement and retention. Students often watch videos in a distracted or superficial manner, leading to low levels of cognitive processing (Guo et al., 2014). Research suggests that without interactivity, videos may reinforce surface learning rather than deep understanding. To address this, educators are encouraged to incorporate interactive elements into video design, such as embedded quizzes, prompts for reflection, or branching scenarios (Ploetzner, 2024). Tools like Edpuzzle and H5P enable such enhancements, increasing learner activity and attention.

Another challenge is cognitive overload, especially when videos are densely packed with information or include unnecessary visuals or audio. According to Mayer's (2024) cognitive theory of multimedia learning, learners benefit most from concise, well-structured videos that avoid overloading working memory. To manage this, educators should apply multimedia design principles, such as segmenting content into shorter videos (typically under 10 minutes), using signalling to highlight key information, and eliminating irrelevant material (Guo et al., 2014; Mayer, 2024).

Moreover, student self-regulation are key factors in video-based learning success, especially in asynchronous contexts. Without structured guidance, students may delay watching videos or fail to integrate video content into their learning process (Guo et al., 2014). One way to address this is through structured integration of video into course activities, for example, in a flipped-classroom setting. In their study of online video in a flipped-classroom K-12 setting, Lo and Hew (2017) provide 10 guidelines to address challenges with the use of online video. These guidelines include, among other things, starting on-site before using online video in education, retaining the workload, providing an additional communication platform for students, and integrating videos in the rest of the curriculum and materials.

Finally, the widespread availability of online video, including from open platforms like YouTube, raises issues of quality control and alignment with curriculum goals. Videos may be outdated, inaccurate, or inconsistent with instructional aims. Educators need to carefully curate content and evaluate it for pedagogical fit, cultural appropriateness, and academic rigor. When using third-party content, it is also important to consider copyright and licensing terms.

Case 6: Online Video Platform to Assess Student-Teachers' Competences

Introduction

In teacher education programs, written portfolios or self-evaluations are commonly used to document the development of student teachers' competencies (Admiraal & Berry, 2016). However, these methods often fail to capture the complex nature of teaching, as they can lead to evidence that disconnects teacher competencies from actual teaching practice. In one postgraduate teacher education program in the Netherlands, a video platform has been implemented to enhance student-teachers' reflections and assessments.

The Video Platform for Teacher Education

The video portfolios of student teachers were stored in an electronic learning environment that included a fixed set of assignments. These assignments required both written documents (such as lesson plans, personal development plans, and feedback from peers and supervisors) and video documents (including a reflection task, a narrative task, and a review task). Video clips were essential elements in all three tasks.

The first task was a reflection assignment, which required student teachers to collect four video clips from one of their lessons at the beginning of the school year. They needed to store their lesson plans and reflect on the video clips in relation to the lesson plans, teacher competencies, and the perspective of one of the students in the lesson. Additionally, they had to gather feedback on their teaching from peers and teacher educators, followed by a reflection on what they learned from this feedback.

The second task, completed halfway through the program, involved creating several video narratives. A screenshot of the main page for this task is included. The self-portrait assignment required the creation of a 3-minute introductory video clip accompanied by written reflections on the student teacher's teaching qualities, as well as supplementary written documents. The reflection assignment involved analyzing teaching performance using clips of the student teacher's actual lessons. The teaching methodology assignment required a video narrative that included at least four clips showcasing actual classroom performance, connected to the student teacher's written lesson preparation. The subject-related methodology assignment required a video narrative discussing subject-specific methodology. Lastly, the "My Story" assignment required the student teachers to create a narrative linking practice to theory for a particular teaching competence. Feedback is annotated to specific parts of the video clips, which can be accessed by clicking on either the text or the video.

As illustrated in the screenshot for the "My Story" assignment, the assignment details are displayed on the right side of the screen, along with reflection questions. Under the "View Responses" tab, student teachers can read feedback provided by peers and teacher educators. On the lower left side of the screen, under the "My Storyboard" tab, various materials can be collected, such as pictures, video clips, and text. Once activated, these materials appear in the upper left corner of the screen. Under the "My References" tab, student teachers can add additional supportive materials, including lesson plans, evaluations from students and colleagues, and a selection of literature. The "Institute References" tab contains materials published by teacher educators, which may include criteria for assessing the video portfolio and relevant literature on specific topics.

In the third task, which takes place at the end of the teacher training program, student teachers are required to create a video narrative detailing the design, implementation, and evaluation of at least four lessons. This must also include the results of two small-scale studies, video clips of their best practices, and a final self-portrait referencing specific teacher competencies and future plans.

Figure 10. Screenshot of the assignment My Story

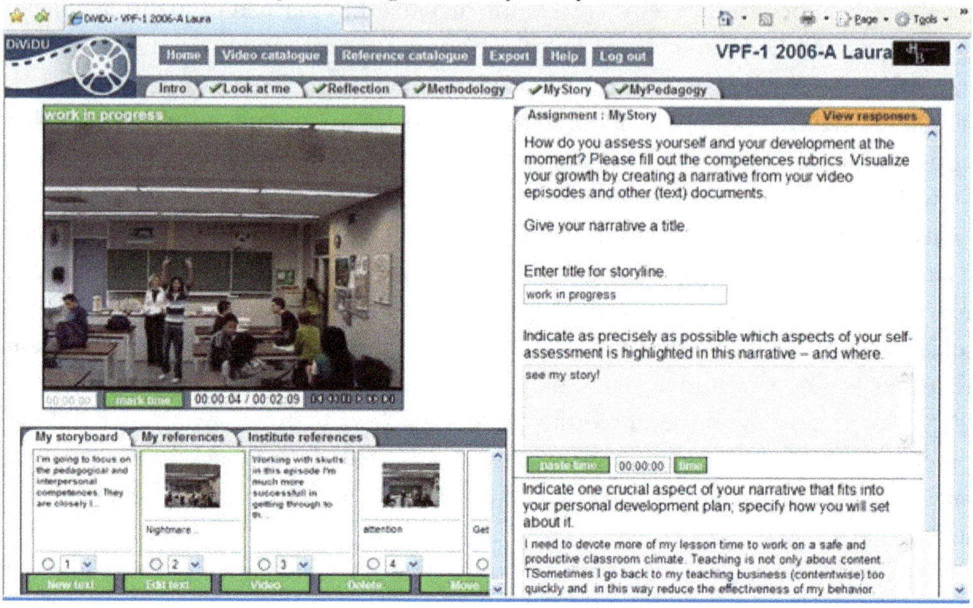

Data

The video narratives from the postgraduate teacher education program in the Netherlands were evaluated by Admiraal and Berry (2016) as an effective method for assessing the teaching competencies of student teachers. This approach fosters connections among various competencies, situates them within practical contexts, and illustrates their development over time.

Findings

Most student teachers were able to meet the established criteria for the video narrative assignment, successfully combining video clips with accompanying text frames. Nevertheless, some student teachers submitted only a limited number of video segments, with loosely connected clips, reflections, and other materials. While most students did engage in explicit reflection on their personal development as future teachers during the programme, few made clear links to their long-term professional growth. The authors conclude that video narratives hold promise as a valid method for assessing teaching competence in student teachers. However, a combination of structured guidance and open-ended assignments is necessary to support effective assessment and student-teachers' cognitive engagement: the former to provide clarity on objectives, format, and evaluation criteria, and the latter to encourage student teachers to reflect in personally meaningful ways.

GENERATIVE ARTIFICIAL INTELLIGENCE

The integration of generative artificial intelligence (GenAI) into secondary and higher education represents a transformative shift in educational practices, offering new ways to support student learning and engagement. GenAI refers to systems capable of producing original content, such as text, code, images, and audio, based on training data, with models like OpenAI's ChatGPT, Google's Gemini, and Anthropic's Claude being widely used in educational contexts (Holmes et al., 2019). There is some evidence that GenAI has potential for automating various learning tasks (Yan et al., 2023), delivering feedback on individual student work (Dai et al., 2023), outperforming average students in reflective writing (Li et al., 2023), and innovating conversational assessments (Yildirim-Erbasli & Bulut, 2023).

A central characteristic of GenAI in education is its capacity to act as an interactive and adaptive tool that facilitates personalized learning. By generating tailored feedback, explanations, and learning materials, AI systems can respond to the specific needs and learning pace of individual students (Yan et al., 2024; Zawacki-Richter et al., 2019). For example, AI-driven writing assistants can help students draft and revise essays, offering grammar corrections, stylistic suggestions, and structural feedback, thereby promoting metacognitive reflection and iterative learning (Kasneci et al., 2023).

Moreover, GenAI supports student engagement by enabling interactive, exploratory learning experiences. Students can use AI tools to simulate problem-solving scenarios, brainstorm ideas, or explore complex concepts through conversational interfaces. Such uses foster active learning, agency, and curiosity, especially when students are encouraged to evaluate AI-generated content critically (Yan et al., 2024)

Another significant use of AI in education is in the automation of formative assessment and feedback. GenAI tools can evaluate short answers, generate quizzes, and provide immediate responses to student input. This feedback loop can improve learning outcomes by supporting timely revision and helping students identify misconceptions early (Chen et al., 2020). Providing detailed feedback regularly is laborious and time-consuming, adding to educators' workload. For example, a recent study found that ChatGPT generates more in-depth and fluent feedback, coherently summarising students' performances compared to human educators (Dai et al., 2023).

However, the use of GenAI in education also raises important pedagogical and ethical considerations. Students must be taught how to engage critically with AI outputs, recognizing the limitations, biases, and potential inaccuracies of generative models. Moreover, the over-reliance on AI-generated content may affect the development of original thinking and academic integrity if not properly guided by educators (Cotton et al., 2024).

Benefits of Generative Artificial Intelligence

The use of GenAI in education offers several pedagogical benefits, particularly in enhancing student learning and engagement (Yan et al., 2023). One of the most significant advantages is the ability of GenAI to provide personalized learning experiences. It can dynamically adapt to students' input and learning pace, offering tailored explanations, examples, and feedback. This personalized support has been shown to increase motivation and academic success (Holmes et al., 2019; Kasneci et al., 2023).

Gen AI also enhances student engagement by promoting active learning. Through conversational interfaces like ChatGPT, students are able to ask questions, receive immediate answers, and explore topics interactively. This dialogic approach can foster curiosity, autonomy, and conceptual understanding—qualities associated with higher-order thinking skills (Kasneci et al., 2023). Additionally, the immediacy of AI-generated feedback enables a more iterative and exploratory learning process, encouraging students to revise their work and reflect on their thinking. Further development of GenAI, like the Khanmigo chatbot (https://www.khanmigo.ai/) shifted from providing direct answers to a guided-learning approach that offers constructive feedback and step-by-step instructions.

Another key benefit lies in supporting the development of academic skills, especially in writing, coding, and problem-solving. For example, GenAI can act as a writing assistant that helps students brainstorm ideas, organize arguments, and revise drafts. This scaffolding can be particularly beneficial for students who struggle with writing, including those for whom the language of instruction is not their first (Kasneci et al., 2023). Some research (Pesovski et al., 2024) suggests that GenAI can only produce a part of relevant learning resources, which makes educators' expertise crucial for ensuring the accuracy, relevance, and pedagogical soundness of the material. This highlights the need for a human-AI collaborative approach to create meaningful learning resources.

GenAI can also increase student confidence and participation, especially among those who may be hesitant to speak up or ask questions in common classroom settings. AI tools offer a low-risk, non-judgmental space for inquiry, helping students to overcome anxiety and take intellectual risks (Smutny & Schreiberova, 2020). This is particularly important in inclusive education, where emotional safety and accessibility are central to engagement and equitable learning.

Finally, when integrated thoughtfully, GenAI can support the development of critical digital literacy. Students learn not only how to use AI tools but also how to question their outputs, check for biases, and evaluate information quality. These are essential skills in today's digital society and align with the broader goals of education to prepare students for informed citizenship and lifelong learning. At the same time, a certain level of critical digital literacy is needed to use GenAI responsibly. Despite the promising design of systems like Khanmigo and students' positive attitudes towards using GenAi for personalised learning support (Chan & Hu, 2023), it is important to acknowledge that currently empirical evidence regarding their short- and long-term impacts on learning outcomes is lacking.

Challenges of Generative Artificial Intelligence

The most often mentioned challenge of GenAI is the challenge of accuracy and reliability. GenAI systems are known to produce content that is plausible-sounding but factually incorrect, a phenomenon often referred to as "hallucination" (Park & Lee, 2024). In the context of AI, hallucinations refer to instances where generative models produce outputs that are incorrect, nonsensical, or fabricated. These errors can occur due to the model's limitations or biases in the training data (Yan et al., 2023). Without appropriate guidance, students may accept AI outputs uncritically, leading to misconceptions or the reinforcement of false information. This challenge highlights the need for students to develop AI literacy—the ability to evaluate the trustworthiness of AI-generated content and understand the limitations of the technology.

One of the primary pedagogical concerns is the risk of undermining critical thinking and academic integrity. When students rely on generative AI tools such as ChatGPT or Gemini to produce essays, solve problems, or answer questions, there is a danger that they may bypass essential cognitive processes such as analysis, synthesis, creating, and evaluation (Kasneci et al., 2023). Furthermore, AI-generated content raises serious questions about plagiarism and authorship. Studies have shown that some students may submit AI-generated work without adequate attribution, creating dilemmas for assessment and academic honesty (Cotton et al., 2023).

Another significant issue is bias and inclusivity. Generative AI models are trained on large datasets that may contain cultural, gender, and racial biases. As a result, the outputs of these systems can spread stereotypes or exclude certain perspectives, potentially leading to discriminatory or non-inclusive learning environments (Sha et al., 2021). Educators must, therefore, be vigilant in monitoring AI tools for bias, and provide students with the skills to recognize and critique biased content.

GenAI poses significant challenges to conventional learning assessment methodologies. Many assessments have focused on evaluating learning products, such as essays, to measure learning outcomes. However, GenAI's ability to produce high-quality, human-like responses calls into question the validity of these approaches (Mao et al., 2023). A central issue is the difficulty in distinguishing between a learner's work and AI-generated output. GenAI, particularly Large Language Models like ChatGPT, can generate responses that closely mimic human reasoning and writing styles, making it difficult to discern the origin of the work.

Lastly, the ethical and privacy concerns surrounding AI use in education cannot be overlooked. GenAI tools often require data input from users, raising questions about data protection, consent, and surveillance. In some cases, student interactions with AI may be logged and used to train future models, leading to concerns about informed consent and ownership of data. A key concern is the transparency of AI-generated solutions, as highlighted in a recent systematic literature review (Yan et al, 2023).

Case 7: ChatGPT as an Addition to Teacher Assessment

Introduction

Lu et al. (2024) conducted a mixed-methods investigation to examine how ChatGPT could be used as an assessment of a writing task, in addition to the teacher assessment. In a short academic writing course at a Chinese university, students were assigned the task of composing a ~300-word abstract in Chinese for a selected empirical article. The article, written in Chinese but lacking an abstract, focused on current challenges in Chinese language teaching classrooms. It contained no complex statistics and was on a topic familiar to all students, who were majoring in education-related fields.

ChatGPT as Assessment in an Academic Writing Course

The course consisted of two sessions held over two weeks. In the first week, the instructor led a 50-minute session on abstract writing and the use of evaluation criteria. This session included presenting a sample abstract and guiding students through a discussion and rating activity to deepen their understanding of abstract writing and assessment standards. Afterwards, students had 80 minutes to read the article, write an abstract, and submit their drafts.

In the second week, students received an assessment form containing feedback from both the teacher and ChatGPT. During a 60-minute session, they were asked to revise their drafts based on the provided feedback and submit the revised version through the online platform.

Abstracts were evaluated across five equally weighted dimensions: (a) research purpose, (b) method, (c) findings, (d) implications, and (e) language conventions. Each dimension was scored on a five-level scale, with scores ranging from 0 to 8, for a total maximum of 40 points. Each level included a brief explanation.

Students received a feedback form featuring two columns—Assessment 1 and Assessment 2—representing the teacher's and ChatGPT's evaluations, though the order was anonymized. Half of the students received the teacher's feedback as Assessment 1 and ChatGPT's as Assessment 2, and vice versa for the other half, to reduce possible bias from preference or column position.

Both assessments included three components:

1. A score for each dimension;
2. A justification for each score (i.e., an evaluation of the student's draft);
3. Suggestions for improving the abstract in each area.

To ensure consistency, three prompts in Chinese were used with ChatGPT version 3.5—identical to those given to teachers on the assessment form:

1. "In your role as a professional Chinese academic writing teacher, you administered a writing task for students. This task required students to read a specific article and then compose an abstract of ~300 words. Your responsibility is to assess the students' abstract writing. Before commencing the actual assessment, you are required to read the article used for the task. Please provide a response indicating your understanding of the article after you have completed your reading." <Insert the article here>.
2. "Recall the article you have just read. Now, review the assessment criteria employed for this task. Provide a response to indicate your comprehension of the criteria following your review." <Insert the criteria here>.
3. "Drawing from the article and criteria you have reviewed, you are now prepared to assess the students' abstract writing. Kindly complete the following three steps in order: (1) assign a score to evaluate the students' writing performance on each dimension as per the criteria, (2) justify each score to elucidate what you think of the students' abstract drafts, and (3) offer suggestions for improvement on each dimension to indicate how the students can revise their compositions for enhanced performance." <Insert the student's abstract here>.

Data

In this study, 46 undergraduate students from a research university in southern China were involved. The students were engaged in a Chinese academic writing task as described above. Both interview data and quantitative data were collected.

Findings

Drawing from both interview data and quantitative findings, the study uncovers three ways in which ChatGPT complements teacher assessment, benefiting students with various writing proficiency levels: (1) fostering deeper comprehension of teacher assessments, (2) encouraging students to make judgments regarding feedback, and (3) promoting independent thinking about revisions.

The authors recommend that teachers utilize ChatGPT's scoring and feedback as a reference for their own assessments, thereby reducing the workload and leveraging the strengths of both approaches. Teachers should provide students with specific guidance on how to effectively utilize ChatGPT and teacher assessment. This guidance can include that students need the skills to conduct comparisons between their text, assessment criteria, and the different feedback sources to evaluate the applicability of diverse feedback and identify potential revision strategies. In addition, low-writing-level students may benefit from instruction on how to respond when ChatGPT provides general, incorrect, or nonsensical feedback. Moreover, medium and high-writing-level students could be encouraged to engage in reflective revision, exploring opportunities for extra revisions and enhancing cognitive engagement.

CONCLUDING REMARKS

The integration of technology in secondary and higher education is rapidly evolving, with seven key trends—hybrid teaching and learning, games and gamification, data-driven instruction, virtual reality, online discussion forums, educational video, and generative artificial intelligence—shaping the future of teaching and learning and rethinking pedagogies. Each of these trends brings distinct opportunities to enhance student cognitive, behavioural and emotional engagement.

Collectively, these innovations support more flexible, interactive, and student-centred learning environments. Hybrid teaching extends access to learning and offers students greater flexibility over the place of learning, but at the same time, it poses challenges for teachers in connecting with all students, both on-site and online. Teachers should think of how to engage both the on-site and online student groups and create in-group feelings, support the interaction between both types of groups, and insert tasks that can easily be done by all students, such as quizzes like Socrative, Mentimeter or Padlet. Games and gamification stimulate, for example, adaptive learning and persistence through challenge and reward, but games are often difficult to integrate into the school curriculum. Gamifying the existing learning environment can have similar positive outcomes compared to digital games if teachers use a variety of game elements in their teaching, align these game elements to students' preferences and needs, integrate the gamified learning environment into their courses instead of using it as an add-on, and regularly provide feedback on students' performance. Data-driven instruction enables educators to make more informed pedagogical decisions, tailoring support to individual needs, but data can also be overwhelming. Online teaching in particular gives teachers the opportunity to collect students' learning data to provide feedback, but also to use for adapting their teaching. Virtual reality (VR)offers students immersive experiences that enhance understanding and empathy, which should be complemented with reflections on these experiences to increase the effects of VR. VR can be used for diagnosis and skills learning, especially as a preparation for real-life or work-related practices. Online discussion forums generally promote reflection, dialogue, and collaborative knowledge building, especially if teachers support student interaction of both the active and not-so-active students, and use a variety of tasks and group settings to support all types of student engagement with learning. Both VR and online discussion forums require time for reflection to be effective for student learning. Educational video platforms provide dynamic, multimodal content that can clarify complex concepts and support skills learning, especially if feedback and assessments are annotated to particular parts of the video clips and the video clips are short. The use of online video also supports the flipped-classroom model in which learning from the video is a preparation on on-site learning activities. Finally, GenAI tools open new possibilities for creativity, personalized feedback, and support for diverse learners, although insights into the effects on engagement and learning are still limited. Instead of trying to exclude GenAI from the classroom, teachers should teach students how to use it wisely.

Effective implementation requires appropriate infrastructure, professional development, and a critical awareness of issues, such as digital equity, data privacy, cognitive overload, and ethical use of AI. Furthermore, the pedagogical value of technology depends not on the tools themselves but on how thoughtfully they are integrated into teaching practices. It is not the technology that matters but the pedagogies that go with it.

Despite these challenges, the strategic and reflective use of these seven trends holds considerable promise for increasing student engagement. The Learning Engagement Theory helps to frame both technology and pedagogies to focus on cognitively, affectively, and behaviourally engaging students in learning. By aligning technological innovation with sound learning principles, educators can create more inclusive, motivating, and meaningful learning experiences that prepare students for the demands of society. The current chapter contributes towards a pedagogy of engagement in technology-enhanced teaching.

ACKNOWLEDGEMENT

This work is partly financed by the project Meta-Scientific Literacies in the (Mis-)Information Age, one of the Teacher Academies funded by the European Commission. Grant Agreement Number 101104523.

REFERENCES

Admiraal, W. (2014). Meaningful learning from practice: Web-based video in professional preparation programs in university. *Technology, Pedagogy and Education, 23*(4), 491–506. DOI: 10.1080/1475939X.2013.813403

Admiraal, W., & Berry, A. (2016). Video narratives to assess student-teachers' competence as new teachers. *Teachers and Teaching, 22*(1), 21–34. DOI: 10.1080/13540602.2015.1023026

Admiraal, W., Hoeksma, M., van de Kamp, M.-T., & van Duin, G. (2011). Assessment of teacher competence using video portfolios: Reliability, construct validity and consequential validity. *Teaching and Teacher Education, 27*(6), 1019–1028. DOI: 10.1016/j.tate.2011.04.002

Admiraal, W., Huizenga, J., Akkerman, S., & ten Dam, G. (2011). The concept of flow in game-based learning. *Computers in Human Behavior, 27*(3), 1185–1194. DOI: 10.1016/j.chb.2010.12.013

Admiraal, W., Vermeulen, J., & Bulterman-Bos, J. (2020). Teaching with learning analytics: How to connect computer-based assessment data with classroom instruction? *Technology, Pedagogy and Education, 29*(5), 577–591. DOI: 10.1080/1475939X.2020.1825992

AlGerafi, M. A. M., Zhou, Y., Oubibi, M., & Wijaya, T. T. (2023). Unlocking the potential: A comprehensive evaluation of augmented reality and virtual reality in education. *Electronics (Basel), 12*(18), 3953. DOI: 10.3390/electronics12183953

Almatrafi, O., & Johri, A. (2018). Systematic review of discussion forums in massive open online courses (MOOCs). *IEEE Transactions on Learning Technologies, 12*(3), 413–428. DOI: 10.1109/TLT.2018.2859304

Alsowat, H. H. (2022). Hybrid learning or virtual learning? Effects on students' essay writing and digital literacy. *Journal of Language Teaching and Research, 13*(4), 872–883. DOI: 10.17507/jltr.1304.20

Annetta, L. A. (2010). The "I's" have it: A framework for serious educational game design. *Review of General Psychology, 14*(2), 105–113. DOI: 10.1037/a0018985

Araiza-Alba, P., Keane, T., & Kaufman, J. (2022). Are we ready for virtual reality in K–12 classrooms? *Technology, Pedagogy and Education, 31*(4), 471–491. DOI: 10.1080/1475939X.2022.2033307

Atal, D., Admiraal, W., & Saab, N. (2024). Effects of 360 video virtual reality-supported reflection on student teachers' classroom management self-efficacy and their stress levels. *Teaching and Teacher Education, 144*(July), 104573. DOI: 10.1016/j.tate.2024.104573

Baig, M. I., & Yadegaridehkordi, E. (2023). Flipped classroom in higher education: A systematic literature review and research challenges. *International Journal of Educational Technology in Higher Education, 20*(1), 61. DOI: 10.1186/s41239-023-00430-5

Barak, M. (2006). Instructional principles for fostering learning with ICT: Teachers' perspectives as learners and instructors. *Education and Information Technologies, 11*(2), 121–138. DOI: 10.1007/s11134-006-7362-9

Barz, N., Benick, M., Dörrenbächer-Ulrich, L., & Perels, F. (2024). The effect of digital game-based learning interventions on cognitive, metacognitive, and affective-motivational learning outcomes in school: A meta-analysis. *Review of Educational Research, 94*(2), 193–227. DOI: 10.3102/00346543231167795

Beatty, B. J. (2019). *Hybrid flexible course design: Implementing student-directed hybrid classes*. EdTech Books. DOI: 10.59668/33

Belkina, M., Daniel, S., Nikolic, S., Haque, R., Lyden, S., Neal, P., Grundy, S., & Hassan, G. M. (2025, April). Implementing Generative AI (GenAI) in higher education: A systematic review of case studies. *Computers and Education: Artificial Intelligence, 8*, 100407. DOI: 10.1016/j.caeai.2025.100407

Bell, J., Sawaya, S., & Cain, W. (2014). Synchromodal classes: Designing for shared learning experiences between face-to-face and online students. *International Journal of Designs for Learning, 5*(1). Advance online publication. DOI: 10.14434/ijdl.v5i1.12657

Bontchev, B. P., Terzieva, V., & Paunova-Hubenova, E. (2021). Personalization of serious games for learning. *Interactive Technology and Smart Education, 18*(1), 50–68. DOI: 10.1108/ITSE-05-2020-0069

Bower, M., Dalgarno, B., Kennedy, G. E., Lee, M. J. W., & Kenney, J. (2015). Design and implementation factors in blended synchronous learning environments: Outcomes from a cross-case analysis. *Computers & Education*, *86*, 1–17. DOI: 10.1016/j.compedu.2015.03.006

Brown, J. L., Collins, A., & Duguid, P. (1989). Situated cognition and the culture of learning. *Educational Researcher*, *18*(1), 32–42. DOI: 10.3102/0013189X018001032

Carreon, A., Smith, S. J., Mosher, M., Rao, K., & Rowland, A. (2022). A review of virtual reality intervention research for students with disabilities in K–12 settings. *Journal of Special Education Technology*, *37*(1), 82–99. DOI: 10.1177/0162643420962011

Cavanagh, M. (2021). Pre-service teacher reflection and feedback using an online video platform during professional experience. *The Australian Journal of Teacher Education*, *46*(2), 72–85. DOI: 10.14221/ajte.2021v46n2.5

Chan, C. K. Y., & Hu, W. (2023). Students' voices on generative AI: Perceptions, benefits, and challenges in higher education. *International Journal of Educational Technology in Higher Education*, *20*(1), 43. DOI: 10.1186/s41239-023-00411-8

Chen, C., Jamiat, N., Rabu, S. N. A., & Du, S. (2025). Effects of augmented reality with pedagogical agent on EFL primary students' vocabulary acquisition, motivation, and technology perceptions. *International Journal of Human-Computer Interaction*, *41*(18), 1–19. DOI: 10.1080/10447318.2024.2443534

Chen, L., Chen, P., & Lin, Z. (2020). Artificial intelligence in education: A review. *IEEE Access : Practical Innovations, Open Solutions*, *8*, 75264–75278. DOI: 10.1109/ACCESS.2020.2988510

Choi, J., Thompson, C. E., Choi, J., Waddill, C. B., & Choi, S. (2022). Effectiveness of immersive virtual reality in nursing education: Systematic review. *Nurse Educator*, *47*(3), 57–61. DOI: 10.1097/NNE.0000000000001117 PMID: 34657101

Cossio, S., Chiappinotto, S., Dentice, S., Moreal, C., Magro, G., Dussi, G., Palese, A., & Galazzi, A. (2025). Cybersickness and discomfort from head-mounted displays delivering fully immersive virtual reality: A systematic review. *Nurse Education in Practice*, *85*, 104376. DOI: 10.1016/j.nepr.2025.104376 PMID: 40267853

Cotton, D. R., Cotton, P. A., & Shipway, J. R. (2024). Chatting and cheating: Ensuring academic integrity in the era of ChatGPT. *Innovations in Education and Teaching International*, *61*(2), 228–239. DOI: 10.1080/14703297.2023.2190148

Cross, J. I., & Boag-Hodgson, C. C. (2025). A collaborative virtual reality flight simulator: Efficacy, challenges, and potential. *IEEE Transactions on Learning Technologies*, *18*, 119–129. DOI: 10.1109/TLT.2025.3526863

Csikszentmihalyi, M. (1990). *Flow: The psychology of optimal experience*. Harper-Perennial.

Dai, W., Lin, J., Jin, H., Li, T., Tsai, Y. S., & Gašević, D.. (2023). Can large language models provide feedback to students? A case study on ChatGPT. In *2023 IEEE International Conference on Advanced Learning Technologies (ICALT)*, (pp. 323–325). DOI: 10.1109/ICALT58122.2023.00100

Daniel, B. (2015). Big Data and analytics in higher education: Opportunities and challenges. *British Journal of Educational Technology*, *46*(5), 904–920. DOI: 10.1111/bjet.12230

Darabi, A., Arrastia, M. C., Nelson, D. W., Cornille, T., & Liang, X. (2011). Cognitive presence in asynchronous online learning: A comparison of four discussion strategies. *Journal of Computer Assisted Learning*, *27*(3), 216–227. DOI: 10.1111/j.1365-2729.2010.00392.x

Delahunty, J., Verenikina, I., & Jones, P. (2014). Socio-emotional connections: Identity, belonging and learning in online interactions. A literature review. *Technology, Pedagogy and Education*, *23*(2), 243–265. DOI: 10.1080/1475939X.2013.813405

Fawns, T. (2022). An entangled pedagogy: Looking beyond the pedagogy—technology dichotomy. *Postdigital Science and Education*, *4*(3), 711–728. DOI: 10.1007/s42438-022-00302-7 PMID: 40477872

Fehrman, S., & Watson, S. L. (2021). A systematic review of asynchronous online discussions in online higher education. *American Journal of Distance Education*, *35*(3), 200–213. DOI: 10.1080/08923647.2020.1858705

Filak, V. F., & Sheldon, K. M. (2008). Teacher support, student motivation, student need satisfaction, and college teacher course evaluations: Testing a sequential path model. *Educational Psychology*, *28*(6), 711–724. DOI: 10.1080/01443410802337794

Foo, S. Y., & Quek, C. L. (2019). Developing students' critical thinking through asynchronous online discussions: A literature review. *Malaysian Online Journal of Educational Technology*, *7*(2), 37–58. DOI: 10.17220/mojet.2019.02.003

Fredricks, J. A., Blumenfeld, P., Friedel, J., & Paris, A. (2005). School engagement. In Moore, K. A., & Lippmann, L. (Eds.), *Conceptualizing and measuring indicators of positive development. What do children need to flourish?* (pp. 419–446). Kluwer. DOI: 10.1007/0-387-23823-9_19

Fredricks, J. A., Blumenfeld, P. C., & Paris, A. H. (2004). School engagement: Potential of the concept, state of the evidence. *Review of Educational Research*, *74*(1), 59–109. DOI: 10.3102/00346543074001059

Galikyan, I., Admiraal, W., & Kester, L. (2021). MOOC discussion forums: The interplay of the cognitive and the social. *Computers & Education, 165*, 104133. DOI: 10.1016/j.compedu.2021.104133

Garrison, D. R., Anderson, T., & Archer, W. (2001). Critical thinking, cognitive presence, and computer conferencing in distance education. *American Journal of Distance Education, 15*(1), 7–23. DOI: 10.1080/08923640109527071

Gašević, D., Dawson, S., & Siemens, G. (2015). Let's not forget: Learning analytics are about learning. *TechTrends, 59*(1), 64–71. DOI: 10.1007/s11528-014-0822-x

Gee, J. P. (2003). What video games have to teach us about learning and literacy. *ACM Computers in Entertainment, 1*(1), 1–4. DOI: 10.1145/950566.950595

Gehring, D. R., Titus, S. K., Bleistein, T. M., & Li, H. (2025). Guidelines of discussion board prompts in higher education: A scoping review protocol. *International Journal of Educational Research Open, 9*, 100470. DOI: 10.1016/j.ijedro.2025.100470

Greller, W., & Drachsler, H. (2012). Translating learning into numbers: A generic framework for learning analytics. *Journal of Educational Technology & Society, 15*(3), 42–57.

Gudoniene, D., Staneviciene, E., Huet, I., Dickel, J., Dieng, D., Degroote, J., Rocio, V., Butkiene, R., & Casanova, D. (2025). Hybrid teaching and learning in higher education: A systematic literature review. *Sustainability (Basel), 17*(2), 756. DOI: 10.3390/su17020756

Guo, P., Saab, N., Post, L. S., & Admiraal, W. (2020). A review of project-based learning in higher education: Student outcomes and measures. *International Journal of Educational Research, 102*, 101586. DOI: 10.1016/j.ijer.2020.101586

Guo, P. J., Kim, J., & Rubin, R. (2014, March). How video production affects student engagement: An empirical study of MOOC videos. In *Proceedings of the first ACM conference on Learning@ scale conference*, (pp. 41-50). DOI: 10.1145/2556325.2566239

Habgood, M. J., & Ainsworth, S. E. (2011). Motivating children to learn effectively: Exploring the value of intrinsic integration in educational games. *Journal of the Learning Sciences, 20*(2), 169–206. DOI: 10.1080/10508406.2010.508029

Hamari, J., Koivisto, J., & Sarsa, H. (2014). Does gamification work?-A literature review of empirical studies on gamification. In *2014 47th Hawaii International Conference on System Sciences* (pp. 3025-3034). Ieee.

Hamilton, L., Halverson, R., Jackson, S., Mandinach, E., Supovitz, J., & Wayman, J. (2009). *Using student achievement data to support instructional decision making* (NCEE 2009-4067). Washington, DC: National Center for Education Evaluation and Regional Assistance, Institute of Education Sciences, U.S. Department of Education. Retrieved from https://ies.ed.gov/ncee/wwc/publications/practiceguides/

Harvey, T., Carlson, J., Struck, M., & Moroz, K. (2018). Feeling real: Social presence within online discussions. *Distance Learning : for Educators, Trainers, and Leaders, 15*(4), 13–27.

Henderson, M., & Phillips, M. (2015). Video-based feedback on student assessment: Scarily personal. *Australasian Journal of Educational Technology, 31*(1). Advance online publication. DOI: 10.14742/ajet.1878

Hershkovitz, A. (2015). Towards data-driven instruction. *Technology, Instruction. Cognition and Learning, 10*, 1–4.

Hew, K. F., & Cheung, W. S. (2012). *Student participation in online discussions: Challenges, solutions, and future research*. Springer Science & Business Media. DOI: 10.1007/978-1-4614-2370-6

Hew, K. F., Cheung, W. S., & Ng, C. S. L. (2010). Student contribution in asynchronous online discussion: A review of the research and empirical exploration. *Instructional Science, 38*(6), 571–606. DOI: 10.1007/s11251-008-9087-0

Holmes, W., Bialik, M., & Fadel, C. (2019). *Artificial intelligence in education promises and implications for teaching and learning*. Center for Curriculum Redesign.

Hong, Y., Saab, N., & Admiraal, W. (2024). Approaches and game elements used to tailor digital gamification for learning: A systematic literature review. *Computers & Education, 212*(April), 105000. DOI: 10.1016/j.compedu.2024.105000

Hong, Y., Saab, N., & Admiraal, W. (2025). EFL university students' game element preferences and learning needs: Implications for the instructional design of digital gamified classes. *System, 131*(July), 103670. DOI: 10.1016/j.system.2025.103670

Hrastinski, S. (2008). Asynchronous and synchronous e-learning. *EDUCAUSE Quarterly, 31*(4), 51–55.

Hughes, J. N., Luo, W., Kwok, O.-M., & Loyd, L. K. (2008). Teacher-student support, effortful engagement, and achievement: A 3-year longitudinal study. *Journal of Educational Psychology, 100*(1), 1–14. DOI: 10.1037/0022-0663.100.1.1 PMID: 19578558

Huizenga, J., Admiraal, W., Akkerman, S., & ten Dam, G. (2009). Mobile game-based learning in secondary education: Engagement, motivation and learning in a mobile city game. *Journal of Computer Assisted Learning*, *25*(4), 332–344. DOI: 10.1111/j.1365-2729.2009.00316.x

Huizenga, J. C., & Dam, G. T. M. (2017). Teachers' practice-based perceptions of the value of game-based learning in secondary education. *Computers & Education*, *110*, 105–115. DOI: 10.1016/j.compedu.2017.03.008

Ifenthaler, D., Mah, D. K., & Yau, J. Y. K. (2019). Utilising Learning Analytics for Study Success: Reflections on Current Empirical Findings. In Ifenthaler, D., Mah, D. K., & Yau, J. Y. K. (Eds.), *Utilizing learning analytics to support study success*. Springer. DOI: 10.1007/978-3-319-64792-0_2

Imran, M., Almusharraf, N., Ahmed, S., & Mansoor, M. I. (2024). Personalization of E-Learning: Future Trends, Opportunities, and Challenges. *International Journal of Interactive Mobile Technologies*, *18*(10), 4–18. DOI: 10.3991/ijim.v18i10.47053

Jiang, J., & Fryer, L. K. (2024). The effect of virtual reality learning on students' motivation: A scoping review. *Journal of Computer Assisted Learning*, *40*(1), 360–373. DOI: 10.1111/jcal.12885

Johnson, D. W., & Johnson, R. T. (2009). Energizing learning: The instructional power of conflict. *Educational Researcher*, *38*(1), 37–51. DOI: 10.3102/0013189X08330540

Johnson, S. D., & Aragon, S. A. (2003). An instructional strategy framework for online learning environments. In Aragon, S. A. (Ed.), *Facilitating learning in online environments. New Directions for Adult and Continuing Education* (Vol. 10, pp. 31–44). Jossey-Bass. DOI: 10.1002/ace.117

Jonassen, D., Peck, K., & Wilson, B. (1999). *Learning with technology: A constructivist approach*. Prentice Hall.

Kaptanoğlu, M. Y., & Kavanoz, S. (2024). Self-regulation and self-efficacy of EFL learners in hybrid educational settings in Türkiye. *Psychology in the Schools*, *61*(12), 4517–4537. DOI: 10.1002/pits.23293

Kasneci, E., Sessler, K., & Küchenhoff, H.. (2023). ChatGPT for good? On opportunities and challenges of large language models for education. *Learning and Individual Differences*, *103*, 102274. DOI: 10.1016/j.lindif.2023.102274

Ke, F. (2008). A case study of computer gaming for math: Engaged learning from gameplay? *Computers & Education*, *51*(4), 1609–1620. DOI: 10.1016/j.compedu.2008.03.003

Kearsley, G., & Shneiderman, B. (1998). Engagement theory. *Educational Technology, 38*(5), 20–23.

Khalil, M., Wong, J., de Koning, B., Ebner, M., & Paas, F. (2018). Gamification in MOOCs: A review of the state of the art. In *2018 IEEE Global Engineering Education Conference (EDUCON)*, (pp. 1629-1638). IEEE. DOI: 10.1109/EDUCON.2018.8363430

Kimmons, R., Rosenberg, J., & Allman, B. (2021). Trends in educational technology: What Facebook, Twitter, and Scopus can tell us about current research and practice. *TechTrends, 65*(2), 125–136. DOI: 10.1007/s11528-021-00589-6 PMID: 33644781

Klunder, S., Saab, N., & Admiraal, W. (2022). A teacher perspective on using a hybrid virtual classroom for students with a chronic illness in mainstream primary and secondary schools. *Technology, Pedagogy and Education, 31*(4), 493–508. DOI: 10.1080/1475939X.2022.2033824

Klunder, S., Smit, B., Slegers, K., Saab, N., Nahon, A., Mainhard, T., & Admiraal, W. (2023). Meedoen op afstand in een hybride klas. Interactie met leerlingen met een chronische aandoening. NWO-NRO 40.5.20500.139. ICLON Universiteit Leiden, the Netherlands.

Küçük, S., Turan, Z., Özkan, Ç. N., Taş, Y. F., & Gürsoy, T. (2024). An innovative approach in middle school science courses: Effects of collaborative augmented reality activities on motivation, cognitive load, and satisfaction. *Interactive Learning Environments, 33*(3), 2355–2373. DOI: 10.1080/10494820.2024.2408582

Lee, J., Alonzo, D., Beswick, K., Abril, J. M. V., Chew, A. W., & Oo, C. Z. (2024). Dimensions of teachers' data literacy: A systematic review of literature from 1990 to 2021. *Educational Assessment, Evaluation and Accountability, 36*(2), 145–200. DOI: 10.1007/s11092-024-09435-8

Li, L., Hew, K. F., & Du, J. (2024). Gamification enhances student intrinsic motivation, perceptions of autonomy and relatedness, but minimal impact on competency: A meta-analysis and systematic review. *Educational Technology Research and Development, 72*(2), 765–796. DOI: 10.1007/s11423-023-10337-7

Li, Y., Sha, L., Yan, L., Lin, J., Rakovič, M., & Galbraith, K.. (2023). Can large language models write reflectively. *Computers and Education: Artificial Intelligence, 4*, 100140.

Lin, L., Zhou, D., Wang, J., & Wang, Y. (2024). A systematic review of big data driven education evaluation. *SAGE Open, 14*(2), 21582440241242180. DOI: 10.1177/21582440241242180

Lo, C. K., & Hew, K. F. (2017). A critical review of flipped classroom challenges in K-12 education: Possible solutions and recommendations for future research. *Research and Practice in Technology Enhanced Learning*, *12*(1), 4. DOI: 10.1186/s41039-016-0044-2 PMID: 30613253

Lockhorst, D., Admiraal, W., & Pilot, A. (2010). CSCL in teacher training: What tasks lead to teacher collaboration? *Technology, Pedagogy and Education*, *19*(1), 63–78. DOI: 10.1080/14759390903579190

Long, P., & Siemens, G. (2011). Penetrating the fog: Analytics in learning and education. *EDUCAUSE Review (Online)*.

Lu, Q., Yao, Y., Xiao, L., Yuan, M., Wang, J., & Zhu, X. (2024). Can ChatGPT effectively complement teacher assessment of undergraduate students' academic writing? *Assessment & Evaluation in Higher Education*, *49*(5), 616–633. DOI: 10.1080/02602938.2024.2301722

Makransky, G., & Mayer, R. E. (2022). Benefits of taking a virtual field trip in immersive virtual reality: Evidence for the immersion principle in multimedia learning. *Educational Psychology Review*, *34*(3), 1771–1798. DOI: 10.1007/s10648-022-09675-4 PMID: 35475019

Mandinach, E. B., & Gummer, E. S. (2016). What does it mean for teachers to be data literate: Laying out the skills, knowledge, and dispositions. *Teaching and Teacher Education*, *60*, 366–376. DOI: 10.1016/j.tate.2016.07.011

Mandinach, E. B., & Schildkamp, K. (2021). Misconceptions about data-based decision making in education: An exploration of the literature. *Studies in Educational Evaluation*, *69*, 100842. DOI: 10.1016/j.stueduc.2020.100842

Mao, J., Chen, B., & Liu, J. C. (2023). Generative artificial intelligence in education and its implications for assessment. *TechTrends*, •••, 1–9.

Marougkas, A., Troussas, C., Krouska, A., & Sgouropoulou, C. (2023). Virtual reality in education: A review of learning theories, approaches and methodologies for the last decade. *Electronics (Basel)*, *12*(13), 2832. DOI: 10.3390/electronics12132832

Martin, F., & Bolliger, D. U. (2018). Engagement matters: Student perceptions on the importance of engagement strategies in the online learning environment. *Online Learning : the Official Journal of the Online Learning Consortium*, *22*(1), 205–222. DOI: 10.24059/olj.v22i1.1092

Maurino, P. S. M. (2007). Looking for critical thinking in online threaded discussions. *Journal of Educational Technology Systems*, *35*(3), 241–260. DOI: 10.2190/P4W3-8117-K32G-R34M

Mayer, R. E. (2024). The past, present, and future of the cognitive theory of multimedia learning. *Educational Psychology Review*, *36*(1), 8. DOI: 10.1007/s10648-023-09842-1

Mazhar, A., & Al Rifaee, M. M. (2023). A systematic review of the use of virtual reality in education. In *2023 International Conference on Information Technology (ICIT), (422-427)*, Amman, Jordan. DOI: 10.1109/ICIT58056.2023.10225794

Mergen, M., Graf, N., & Meyerheim, M. (2024). Reviewing the current state of virtual reality integration in medical education-a scoping review. *BMC Medical Education*, *24*(1), 788. DOI: 10.1186/s12909-024-05777-5 PMID: 39044186

Moore, R. L., & Miller, C. N. (2022). Fostering cognitive presence in online courses: A systematic review (2008-2020). *Online Learning : the Official Journal of the Online Learning Consortium*, *26*(1), 130–149. DOI: 10.24059/olj.v26i1.3071

Ning, J., Ma, Z., Yao, J., Wang, Q., & Zhang, B. (2025). Personalized learning supported by learning analytics: A systematic review of functions, pathways, and educational outcomes. *Interactive Learning Environments*, *33*(8), 1–23. DOI: 10.1080/10494820.2025.2478437

Noetel, M., Griffith, S., Delaney, O., Sanders, T., Parker, P., del Pozo Cruz, B., & Lonsdale, C. (2021). Video improves learning in higher education: A systematic review. *Review of Educational Research*, *91*(2), 204–236. DOI: 10.3102/0034654321990713

Palacios-Hidalgo, F. J., & Huertas-Abril, C. A. (2021). Effects of hybrid education in pre-service EFL and bilingual primary teachers' digital literacy. In *2021 1st Conference on Online Teaching for Mobile Education (OT4ME)*, (pp. 73-77). IEEE.

Papamitsiou, Z., & Economides, A. A. (2014). Learning analytics and educational data mining in practice: A systematic literature review of empirical evidence. *Journal of Educational Technology & Society*, *17*(4), 49–64.

Park, D. M., & Lee, H. J. (2024). Literature review of AI hallucination research since the advent of ChatGPT: Focusing on papers from arXiv. *Informatization Policy*, *31*(2), 3–38.

Perry, A. M. (2022). Student engagement, nol earning without it. *Creative Education*, *13*(04), 1312–1326. DOI: 10.4236/ce.2022.134079

Pesovski, I., Santos, R., Henriques, R., & Trajkovik, V. (2024). Generative AI for customizable learning experiences. *Sustainability (Basel)*, *16*(7), 3034. DOI: 10.3390/su16073034

Pirker, J., & Dengel, A. (2021). The potential of 360° virtual reality videos and real VR for education—A literature review. *IEEE Computer Graphics and Applications*, *41*(4), 76–89. DOI: 10.1109/MCG.2021.3067999 PMID: 33755559

Ploetzner, R. (2024). The effectiveness of enhanced interaction features in educational videos: A meta-analysis. *Interactive Learning Environments*, *32*(5), 1597–1612.

Przybylski, A. K., Murayama, K., DeHaan, C. R., & Gladwell, V. (2013). Motivational, emotional, and behavioral correlates of fear of missing out. *Computers in Human Behavior*, *29*(4), 1841–1848. DOI: 10.1016/j.chb.2013.02.014

Qiao, J., Xu, J., Li, L., & Ouyang, Y. Q. (2021). The integration of immersive virtual reality simulation in interprofessional education: A scoping review. *Nurse Education Today*, *98*, 104773. DOI: 10.1016/j.nedt.2021.104773 PMID: 33497990

Radianti, J., Majchrzak, T. A., Fromm, J., & Wohlgenannt, I. (2020). A systematic review of immersive virtual reality applications for higher education: Design elements, lessons learned, and research agenda. *Computers & Education*, *147*, 103778. DOI: 10.1016/j.compedu.2019.103778

Raes, A., Detienne, L., Windey, I., & Depaepe, F. (2020). A systematic literature review on synchronous hybrid learning: Gaps identified. *Learning Environments Research*, *23*(3), 269–290. DOI: 10.1007/s10984-019-09303-z

Romero Rodríguez, L., Sánchez-Alzola, A., & Salazar, A. (2025). Serious games in engineering education: Assessing novelty effects and the influence of prior gaming experience. *Computer Applications in Engineering Education*, *33*(3), e70021. DOI: 10.1002/cae.70021

Rovai, A. P. (2002). Building sense of community at a distance. *International Review of Research in Open and Distance Learning*, *3*(1), 1–16. DOI: 10.19173/irrodl.v3i1.79

Rumberger, R. W., & Rotermund, S. (2012). The relationship between engagement and high school dropout. In Christenson, S. L., Reschly, A. L., & Wylie, C. (Eds.), *Handbook of research on student engagement* (pp. 491–513). Springer. DOI: 10.1007/978-1-4614-2018-7_24

Sailer, M., & Homner, L. (2020). The gamification of learning: A meta-analysis. *Educational Psychology Review*, *32*(1), 77–112. DOI: 10.1007/s10648-019-09498-w

Sailer, M., Maier, R., Berger, S., Kastorff, T., & Stegmann, K. (2024). Learning activities in technology-enhanced learning: A systematic review of meta-analyses and second-order meta-analysis in higher education. *Learning and Individual Differences*, *112*, 102446. DOI: 10.1016/j.lindif.2024.102446

Salomon, G. (1998). Novel constructivist learning environments and novel technologies: Some issues to be considered. *Learning and Instruction, 1*(1), 3–12. DOI: 10.1016/S0959-4752(98)00007-3

Schellens, T., & Valcke, M. (2006). Fostering knowledge construction in university students through asynchronous discussion groups. *Computers & Education, 46*(4), 349–370. DOI: 10.1016/j.compedu.2004.07.010

Schildkamp, K., Lai, M. K., & Earl, L. (2019). *Data-based decision making in education: Challenges and opportunities*. Springer.

Schildkamp, K., & Poortman, C. (2015). Factors influencing the functioning of data teams. *Teachers College Record, 117*(4), 1–42. DOI: 10.1177/016146811511700403

Schunk, D. H., & Mullen, C. A. (2012). Self-efficacy as an engaged learner. In Christenson, S. L., Reschly, A. L., & Wylie, C. (Eds.), *Handbook of research on student engagement* (pp. 219–235). Springer. DOI: 10.1007/978-1-4614-2018-7_10

Sha, L., Rakovic, M., Whitelock-Wainwright, A., Carroll, D., Yew, V. M., Gasevic, D., ... (2021). *Assessing algorithmic fairness in automatic classifiers of educational forum posts. In Artificial Intelligence in Education: 22nd International Conference, AIED 2021*, (pp. 381-394), Utrecht, The Netherlands. DOI: 10.1007/978-3-030-78292-4_31

Sherin, M. G., & Van Es, E. A. (2009). Effects of video club participation on teachers' professional vision. *Journal of Teacher Education, 60*(1), 20–37. DOI: 10.1177/0022487108328155

Siemens, G., & Gasevic, D. (2012). Guest editorial- learning and knowledge analytics. *Journal of Educational Technology & Society, 15*(3), 1–2.

Slade, S., & Prinsloo, P. (2013). Learning analytics: Ethical issues and dilemmas. *The American Behavioral Scientist, 57*(10), 1510–1529. DOI: 10.1177/0002764213479366

Smutny, P., & Schreiberova, P. (2020). Chatbots for learning: A review of educational chatbots for the Facebook Messenger. *Computers & Education, 151*, 103862. DOI: 10.1016/j.compedu.2020.103862

Soylu, M. Y., & Lee, J. (2024, October). Analyzing interplay of metacognition, cognitive presence, and course performance in MOOCs and Master course forums. In *2024 IEEE Digital Education and MOOCS Conference (DEMOcon)*, (pp. 1-6). IEEE. DOI: 10.1109/DEMOcon63027.2024.10748167

Squire, K. (2013). Video games and learning: Teaching and participatory culture in the digital age. *The Alberta Journal of Educational Research*, *59*(1), 129–132. DOI: 10.55016/ojs/ajer.v59i1.55771

Theeuwes, B., Saab, N., Denessen, E., & Admiraal, W. (2025). Unraveling expert teachers' intercultural competence when facing a simulated multicultural classroom context. *Teaching and Teacher Education*, *162*(August), 105053. DOI: 10.1016/j.tate.2025.105053

van der Rijst, R., Guo, P., & Admiraal, W. (2023). Student engagement in hybrid approaches to teaching in higher education. *Revista de Investigación Educacional*, *41*(2), 315–336. DOI: 10.6018/rie.562521

Voulgari, I., Komis, V., & Sampson, D. G. (2014). Learning outcomes and processes in massively multiplayer online games: Exploring the perceptions of players. *Educational Technology Research and Development*, *62*(2), 245–270. DOI: 10.1007/s11423-013-9312-7

Vygotsky, L. S. (1978). *Mind in society: The development of higher psychological processes* (Cole, M., Vera John-Steiner, S. S., & Souberman, E., Eds. & Trans.). Harvard University Press.

Wang, M. T., & Degol, J. (2014). Staying engaged: Knowledge and research needs in student engagement. *Child Development Perspectives*, *8*(3), 137–143. DOI: 10.1111/cdep.12073 PMID: 27087833

Wang, Q., & Li, Y. (2024). How virtual reality, augmented reality and mixed reality facilitate teacher education: A systematic review. *Journal of Computer Assisted Learning*, *40*(3), 1276–1294. DOI: 10.1111/jcal.12949

Wei, X., Saab, N., & Admiraal, W. (2021). Assessment of cognitive, behavioral, and affective learning outcomes in massive open online courses: A systematic literature review. *Computers & Education*, *163*, 104097. DOI: 10.1016/j.compedu.2020.104097

Winn, W. (2002). Research into practice: Current trends in educational technology research: The study of learning environments. *Educational Psychology Review*, *14*(3), 331–351. DOI: 10.1023/A:1016068530070

Wu, Y. T., & Wang, L. J. (2016). Research trends in technology-enhanced knowledge building pedagogies: A review of selected empirical research from 2006 to 2015. *Journal of Computers in Education*, *3*(3), 353–375. DOI: 10.1007/s40692-016-0065-2

Yan, L., Greiff, S., Teuber, Z., & Gašević, D. (2024). Promises and challenges of generative artificial intelligence for human learning. *Nature Human Behaviour*, *8*(10), 1839–1850. DOI: 10.1038/s41562-024-02004-5 PMID: 39438686

Yan, L., Sha, L., Zhao, L., Li, Y., Martinez-Maldonado, R., & Chen, G.. (2023). Practical and ethical challenges of large language models in education: A systematic scoping review. *British Journal of Educational Technology*, •••, 1–23.

Yang, X., Cheng, P. Y., Liu, X., & Shih, S. P. (2024). The impact of immersive virtual reality on art education: A study of flow state, cognitive load, brain state, and motivation. *Education and Information Technologies*, *29*(5), 6087–6106. DOI: 10.1007/s10639-023-12041-8

Yildirim-Erbasli, S. N., & Bulut, O. (2023). Conversation-based assessment: A novel approach to boosting test-taking effort in digital formative assessment. *Computers and Education: Artificial Intelligence*, *4*, 100135. DOI: 10.1016/j.caeai.2023.100135

Zawacki-Richter, O., Marín, V. I., Bond, M., & Gouverneur, F. (2019). Systematic review of research on artificial intelligence applications in higher education–where are the educators? *International Journal of Educational Technology in Higher Education*, *16*(1), 1–27. DOI: 10.1186/s41239-019-0171-0

Zhang, D., Zhou, L., Briggs, R. O., & Nunamaker, J. F.Jr. (2006). Instructional video in e-learning: Assessing the impact of interactive video on learning effectiveness. *Information & Management*, *43*(1), 15–27. DOI: 10.1016/j.im.2005.01.004

Zydney, J. M., McKimmy, P., Lindberg, R., & Schmidt, M. (2019). Here or there instruction: Lessons learned in implementing innovative approaches to blended synchronous learning. *TechTrends*, *63*(2), 123–132. DOI: 10.1007/s11528-018-0344-z

ADDITIONAL READING

Clark, D. B., Tanner-Smith, E. E., & Killingsworth, S. S. (2016). Digital games, design, and learning: A systematic review and meta-analysis. *Review of Educational Research*, *86*(1), 79–122. DOI: 10.3102/0034654315582065 PMID: 26937054

Gašević, D., Dawson, S., & Siemens, G. (2015). Let's not forget: Learning analytics are about learning. *TechTrends*, *59*(1), 64–71. DOI: 10.1007/s11528-014-0822-x

Hong, Y., Saab, N., & Admiraal, W. (2024). Approaches and game elements used to tailor digital gamification for learning: A systematic literature review. *Computers & Education*, *212*(April), 105000. DOI: 10.1016/j.compedu.2024.105000

Koumpouros, Y. (2024). Revealing the true potential and prospects of augmented reality in education. *Smart Learning Environments*, *11*(1), 2. DOI: 10.1186/s40561-023-00288-0

Mazhar, A. A., & Al Rifaee, M. M. (2023). A Systematic Review of the use of Virtual Reality in Education. In *2023 International Conference on information technology (ICIT)* (pp. 422-427). IEEE. DOI: 10.1109/ICIT58056.2023.10225794

Ploetzner, R. (2024). The effectiveness of enhanced interaction features in educational videos: A meta-analysis. *Interactive Learning Environments*, *32*(5), 1597–1612.

Raes, A., Detienne, L., Windey, I., & Depaepe, F. (2020). A systematic literature review on synchronous hybrid learning: Gaps identified. *Learning Environments Research*, *23*(3), 269–290. DOI: 10.1007/s10984-019-09303-z

Yan, L., Greiff, S., Teuber, Z., & Gašević, D. (2024). Promises and challenges of generative artificial intelligence for human learning. *Nature Human Behaviour*, *8*(10), 1839–1850. DOI: 10.1038/s41562-024-02004-5 PMID: 39438686

KEY TERMS AND DEFINITIONS

Behavioural Engagement: Students' active participation and observable actions in learning.

Cognitive Engagement: The mental effort students invest in learning tasks.

Data-Driven Instruction: The measurement, collection, analysis, and reporting of data about learners and their contexts, for purposes of understanding and optimising learning and the environments in which it occurs.

Emotional Engagement: The emotional connections students make with learning activities, school, and schooling.

Gamification: The use of game design elements in non-game contexts to create gameful learning environments.

Generative Artificial Intelligence: A type of artificial intelligence that can create new content, such as text, images, music, video, code, or even entire virtual environments based on patterns it has learned from existing data.

Hybrid Teaching: Teaching with some students present on campus and others online at the same time.

Online Discussions: The process by which individuals or groups communicate, exchange information, collaborate, and engage with one another through digital technologies and internet-based platforms.

Online video: Teacher and peer feedback and self-reflections that are directly linked to the specific parts of an online video clip it refers to.

Virtual Reality: Technology that creates a fully immersive, computer-generated environment that people can interact with, usually through special equipment like VR headsets and controllers.

Chapter 2
Open Educational Resources and Their Impact on Curriculum Flexibility and Accessibility

Satya Subrahmanyam
https://orcid.org/0000-0003-0441-2742
Holy Spirit University of Kaslik, Lebanon

ABSTRACT

Open Educational Resources (OER) are reshaping modern education by enhancing curriculum flexibility and improving access to quality learning. Freely available and openly licensed, OER empowers educators to adapt and customize content, supporting competency-based, interdisciplinary, and inclusive instruction. This adaptability fosters personalized learning and ensures curricula stay relevant to emerging knowledge and industry needs. OER also eliminates financial barriers, promoting equitable access for diverse learners across regions and socioeconomic backgrounds. Challenges such as institutional resistance, sustainability, digital infrastructure, and legal concerns must be addressed. This chapter explores the best practices for adoption of OER, supported by case studies and emerging technologies, and underscores the need for strategic policies and global collaboration to realize the full potential of OER in democratizing education.

DOI: 10.4018/979-8-3373-7729-2.ch002

1. INTRODUCTION

1.1 Defining Open Educational Resources (OER)

Teaching, learning, and research resources that are either in the public domain or distributed under an open license allow for free access, use, adaption, and redistribution with little or no limitations; these materials are known as Open Educational Resources (OER) (UNESCO, 2019). Some examples of such materials include course materials, software, films, simulations, exams, and textbooks. The ability to modify, remix, and redistribute, as well as the lack of financial expenses, distinguish open educational resources (OER) from proprietary information. This allows for more involvement and customisation in education.

1.2 Evolution Of The OER Movement

Following the official introduction of the phrase "open courseware" at the 2002 UNESCO Forum on Open Courseware, which highlighted the potential of publicly licensed content to increase educational access globally, the OER movement started to gain global momentum in 2003. Important steps forward have been made since then, with the Ljubljana OER Action Plan (2017), the Paris OER Declaration (2012), and the Cape Town Open Education Declaration (2007) all serving as milestones. Policy frameworks and institutional support for open educational resources (OER) have been pushed via these worldwide efforts, which have driven innovation and diversity in education systems (Wiley & Hilton, 2018).

The rapid expansion of internet access, digital technologies, and open-source platforms has further accelerated the spread of OER. Numerous online repositories such as **OER Commons**, **MERLOT**, and **OpenStax** now offer a wide array of high-quality, peer-reviewed resources. The COVID-19 pandemic served as a critical inflection point, highlighting the importance of resilient, flexible, and inclusive educational resources. Many institutions and educators turned to OER as an immediate and sustainable solution to maintain learning continuity during global disruptions (Ribeiro & Subrahmanyam, 2021).

1.3 Relevance Of OER In Modern Pedagogy And Curriculum Development

OER has become central to modern pedagogical approaches that emphasize learner agency, collaboration, and contextual relevance. Their adaptability allows educators to modify content to reflect cultural, linguistic, and cognitive diversity, promoting inclusive education. This flexibility is particularly aligned with constructivist and connectivist learning theories, which support the idea that knowledge is constructed through interaction, experience, and connectivity (Siemens, 2005).

In curriculum development, OER enables dynamic and modular content creation, allowing for continuous updates and integration of interdisciplinary perspectives. They support differentiated instruction by giving educators the ability to tailor resources to different learner profiles and needs, thereby improving engagement and academic outcomes. The openness of these materials encourages academic collaboration and knowledge co-creation, shifting the role of educators from content consumers to active participants in content design and delivery (Ehlers, 2011).

1.4 Purpose And Scope Of The Chapter

This chapter aims to critically examine the impact of Open Educational Resources on curriculum flexibility and accessibility. It explores the theoretical foundations and global trajectory of the OER movement, delves into the ways in which OER empower adaptive and inclusive curriculum models, and assesses how their integration reshapes teaching competencies and pedagogical practices. The chapter addresses institutional and policy considerations, highlights real-world implementations, and discusses the challenges and future directions of OER in education. Through this exploration, the chapter contributes to understanding how OER serve as catalysts for pedagogical and curricular innovation in a rapidly evolving educational landscape.

2. THE CONCEPTUAL FOUNDATIONS OF OER

Open Educational Resources (OER) are teaching, learning, and research materials freely available for use, adaptation, and redistribution under open licenses. Their core characteristics include free access, open licensing, and adaptability. OER encompass diverse formats such as textbooks, multimedia, and assessments. Rooted in principles of openness, collaboration, sharing, and inclusivity, OER aims to democratize education by fostering equitable access, encouraging participatory content development, and enabling personalized learning experiences across educational contexts.

2.1 Definition And Key Characteristics

Materials for instruction, study, and research in any form that are either already in the public domain or made available under an open license that allows others to access, use, modify, and redistribute them without charge are called open educational resources (OER) according to UNESCO (2019). Not only are open educational resources (OER) free to use, but they are also adaptable and may be reused in other settings. Creative Commons and other popular open licenses allow users to do what is often referred to as the "5Rs": retain, reuse, revise, remix, and redistribute (Wiley, 2014). These features encourage creativity and independence in the classroom, setting open educational resources (OER) apart from traditional textbooks.

The key features of OER include open licensing, which defines the legal permissions for using and modifying content; free access, which eliminates financial barriers to learning; and adaptability, which allows educators to tailor content to specific cultural, linguistic, and pedagogical needs. These elements collectively make OER powerful tools for improving curriculum design, increasing educational equity, and encouraging participatory learning environments.

2.2 Categories And Types Of OER

OER encompasses a wide range of educational materials in diverse formats, which allows them to support various learning styles and institutional needs. One prominent category is text-based resources, such as open textbooks, course syllabi, and reading lists. These resources, made available by platforms like OpenStax and BCcampus, provide peer-reviewed content aligned with academic curricula. Another category includes courseware and learning modules, which may consist of complete online courses or modular units that support flexible, self-paced learning, such as those found on MIT OpenCourseWare.

Multimedia OER—videos, podcasts, animations, and simulations—offer engaging, multimodal learning experiences. Resources like Khan Academy and YouTube EDU exemplify the use of multimedia to support conceptual understanding and retention. Open assessment tools, such as quizzes, test banks, and rubrics, support both formative and summative evaluation processes. Open-source software tools and learning management platforms like Moodle and H5P also play a vital role, offering educators the means to design, deliver, and assess learning effectively.

This diversity of resource types not only enriches the teaching and learning process but also enhances curriculum flexibility. Educators can curate and combine different OER formats to create customized learning experiences that align with institutional goals and student needs.

2.3 Principles Underpinning OER

The conceptual framework of OER is grounded in four core principles: openness, collaboration, sharing, and inclusivity. Openness, the foundational principle, is about more than just free access. It reflects a broader ethos of transparency, knowledge sharing, and participatory engagement. By allowing users to adapt and redistribute content, OER promotes a culture of innovation and responsiveness in education (Wiley & Hilton, 2018).

Collaboration is another essential pillar of the OER movement. It encourages educators, students, and institutions to co-create content, peer review materials, and contribute to an evolving ecosystem of shared knowledge. This collective process enhances content quality, contextual relevance, and academic engagement (Ehlers, 2011). Sharing, closely linked to collaboration, facilitates the dissemination of educational resources across boundaries—geographic, institutional, and cultural—thus democratizing access to knowledge.

Inclusivity ensures that OER meets the diverse needs of learners, including those from marginalized or underserved communities. By enabling content to be translated, localized, or adapted for learners with disabilities, OER enhances accessibility and equity in education. Butcher (2015) emphasizes that OER are particularly valuable for tailoring content to suit local contexts, thereby addressing systemic barriers in traditional education systems.

Figure 1. The Conceptual Foundations of OER

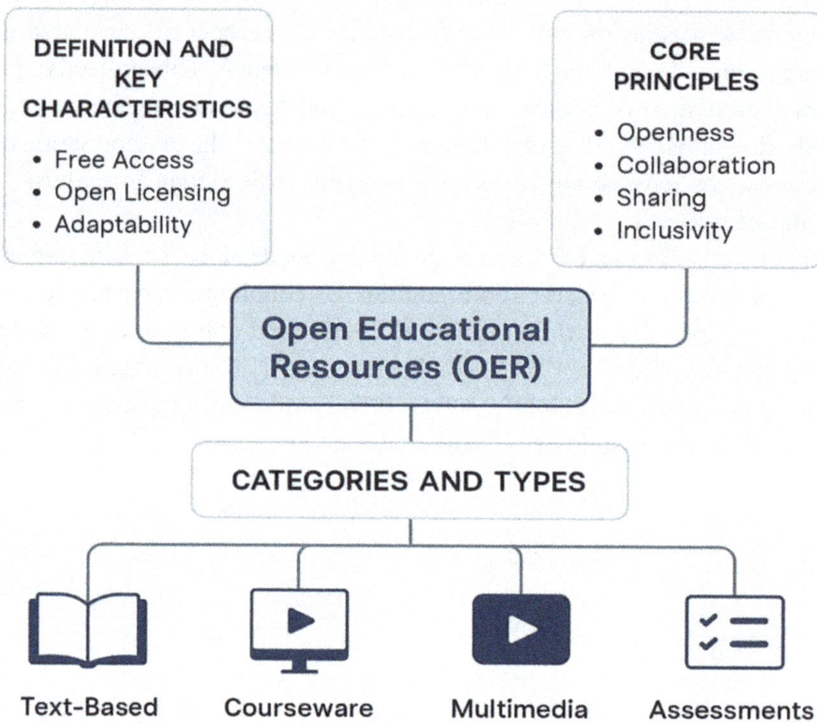

Source: Author (2025)

The conceptual foundations of OER lie in their open, flexible, and inclusive nature. By spanning a broad range of content types and formats, and by adhering to principles of openness, collaboration, sharing, and inclusivity, OER offers transformative potential for curriculum design and educational equity. They empower educators to develop responsive, contextually relevant learning experiences, while also supporting pedagogical innovation and global collaboration.

3. OER AND CURRICULUM FLEXIBILITY

Open Educational Resources (OER) are increasingly recognized as key enablers of flexible and personalized curriculum design. Their open nature allows educators to tailor learning experiences to individual learner needs, promote diversity in content, and respond dynamically to contextual challenges. By removing traditional barriers of access and copyright restrictions, OER empowers teachers to become co-creators of curriculum, rather than passive consumers of standardized textbooks and learning materials. This section explores the various ways in which OER supports curriculum flexibility through personalization, content integration, contextual adaptation, and innovative curricular models.

3.1 Personalized And Learner-Centered Curriculum Design

One of the most transformative impacts of OER lies in their capacity to support personalized and learner-centered curriculum design. Unlike proprietary resources that often follow a rigid instructional design, OER can be adapted to align with diverse learner profiles, learning styles, and competency levels. This personalization is especially important in today's educational landscape, where students come from varied cultural, linguistic, and socio-economic backgrounds.

Personalized learning through OER is facilitated by the 5R framework—retain, reuse, revise, remix, and redistribute (Wiley, 2014). Educators can revise and remix content to meet specific learning objectives or accommodate special education needs. A science module originally designed for high school learners in the United States can be modified to include local examples, cultural references, or additional scaffolding for students in different parts of the world. Such flexibility enhances student engagement, ownership, and motivation (Hilton, 2016).

The learner-centered approach enabled by OER supports constructivist pedagogies where students actively participate in the learning process. Teachers can facilitate collaborative projects using open content, encouraging students to critique, adapt, or create their own educational materials. This participatory model not only deepens conceptual understanding but also cultivates critical thinking and digital literacy skills (Ehlers, 2011).

Table 1. OER Features Supporting Learner-Centered Curriculum

OER Feature	Functionality	Pedagogical Benefit
Open Licensing (5Rs)	Enables reuse, revision, remixing, retention, redistribution	Facilitates customization and localization
Multimedia Formats	Includes videos, simulations, podcasts, interactive modules	Supports varied learning styles and increases engagement
Modular Structure	Allows educators to select and combine learning units	Promotes curricular flexibility and self-paced learning
Language and Cultural Localization	Translating and adapting to specific cultural contexts	Enhances inclusivity and relevance
Community-Sourced Content	Contributions from educators globally	Encourages collaboration, contextual relevance, and innovation

3.2 Integration Of Diverse Content For Varied Learning Needs

The vast and diverse nature of OER allows for the integration of content from multiple disciplines, perspectives, and formats, making the curriculum more inclusive and multidimensional. This diversity is crucial for addressing varied learning needs, including those of students with disabilities, linguistic minorities, or learners in remote and under-resourced settings.

Incorporating multimedia OER—such as videos, simulations, infographics, and podcasts—can cater to different sensory preferences and cognitive styles. A visually impaired student may benefit from audio-based resources, while a kinesthetic learner may engage more deeply with interactive simulations or hands-on open lab activities. Platforms like PhET Interactive Simulations and YouTube EDU offer high-quality multimedia resources that can be seamlessly integrated into classroom instruction or online learning environments.

Open resources can be translated and localized to suit regional languages and cultural contexts, thereby enhancing accessibility and relevance. According to Butcher (2015), the adaptability of OER ensures that learning content can be adjusted to reflect learners lived experiences, identities, and values—elements that are often missing in traditional curriculum materials. This capacity for cultural and linguistic responsiveness supports educational equity and helps bridge the gap between global knowledge and local realities.

Table 2. Comparison of Traditional Curriculum vs. OER-Supported Curriculum

Aspect	Traditional Curriculum	OER-Supported Curriculum
Content Flexibility	Fixed, often proprietary	Editable, remixable, and customizable
Accessibility	Costly, limited by licenses or geographic boundaries	Free, open access from anywhere
Cultural Relevance	Often generalized or disconnected from local context	Can be adapted to specific linguistic and cultural needs
Learner Engagement	Passive consumption of materials	Active participation through adaptation and creation
Curriculum Updates	Slow, dependent on publishers	Real-time updates by educators or institutions

3.3 Flexibility In Content Adaptation And Contextualization

Traditional curricula are often criticized for their inflexibility and lack of responsiveness to evolving learner needs or emerging societal challenges. OER addresses this issue by enabling real-time adaptation and contextualization of content. Educators can update materials to reflect current events, new research findings, or technological developments, ensuring that students receive timely and relevant information.

This capacity for adaptation is especially critical in disciplines that evolve rapidly, such as computer science, health sciences, and environmental studies. During the COVID-19 pandemic, educators used open repositories to quickly disseminate updated health education materials, guidelines, and case studies that reflected the most recent global data (Subrahmanyam, 2021). The open licensing of these materials allowed for immediate contextual adaptation to suit different regions and languages, thereby supporting rapid curriculum responsiveness in crisis situations.

Table 3. Global Examples of Flexible Curriculum Models Using OER

Initiative/Platform	Region	Key Features	Impact
OpenLearn (The Open University)	United Kingdom	Modular free courses, self-paced learning, wide subject range	Enhances lifelong learning and curriculum flexibility
OpenStax	United States	Free, editable textbooks; supports cost savings and curriculum customization	Widely used by community colleges for affordability and flexibility
TESSA (Teacher Education SSA)	Sub-Saharan Africa	Adaptable resources aligned with national curriculum frameworks in multiple African countries	Promotes local ownership of curriculum and teacher professional development
MIT OpenCourseWare	Global	Full university-level courses in open format	Facilitates curriculum enrichment and independent learning

OER allows cross-curricular integration and thematic exploration. A lesson on climate change can include open-access journal articles, statistical datasets, open-source mapping tools, and multimedia content, creating an interdisciplinary learning experience. This not only enriches the curriculum but also promotes higher order thinking skills and real-world problem-solving capabilities.

3.4 Examples Of Flexible Curricular Models Supported By OER

Several educational initiatives across the globe have demonstrated how OER can support flexible curricular models that respond to diverse learner needs and institutional contexts. One such example is the **OpenLearn** platform by The Open University (UK), which offers thousands of free courses designed for flexible, self-paced learning. These courses are structured in modular formats, allowing educators to adopt entire courses or select specific units that align with their curriculum goals.

In the United States, **OpenStax** provides open textbooks that are not only free but also available in editable formats, enabling faculty to tailor chapters, add content, or remove unnecessary material. This has been widely adopted by community colleges and institutions aiming to lower textbook costs while maintaining curricular rigor (Hilton, 2016).

In the Global South, the **TESSA (Teacher Education in Sub-Saharan Africa)** initiative is a prominent example of how OER can support localized curriculum development. TESSA provides adaptable teaching resources aligned with national curriculum frameworks, which have been contextualized for different countries and languages across Africa. The project empowers teachers to modify and integrate materials into their own teaching practices, fostering professional development and learner-centered pedagogy (Wolfenden et al., 2012).

Table 4. Pedagogical and Strategic Benefits of OER in Curriculum Design

Benefit Area	Description	Strategic Outcome
Equity and Access	Removes financial and legal barriers to high-quality educational materials	Promotes social inclusion and democratizes education
Innovation in Teaching	Empowers educators to innovate by remixing and redesigning learning experiences	Encourages experimentation and pedagogical agility
Learner Engagement	Promotes interactive, learner-centered models using collaborative and open content	Improves learning outcomes and motivation
Localization and Inclusion	Enables regional adaptation of global knowledge	Ensures relevance and responsiveness to learner contexts
Professional Development	Engages educators in content creation, peer review, and contextual resource development	Builds faculty capacity and collaboration networks

Open Educational Resources have revolutionized the way curricula can be designed, delivered, and experienced. By enabling personalized, inclusive, and responsive curriculum models, OER supports a dynamic and learner-centered approach to education. Their flexibility in content adaptation, integration, and contextualization allows educators to meet the diverse and evolving needs of learners across the globe. Through practical examples and emerging practices, it is evident that OER are not merely cost-saving tools but vital instruments for educational transformation and curricular innovation.

4. ENHANCING ACCESSIBILITY THROUGH OER

Open Educational Resources (OER) have emerged as powerful instruments in promoting equity and accessibility in education by reducing systemic barriers and expanding opportunities for learning. Their open licensing and digital availability make them particularly valuable in addressing the needs of underserved populations, supporting learners with disabilities, embracing cultural and linguistic diversity, and mitigating the financial burden of educational materials. This section explores how OER enhances educational accessibility across various dimensions and contributes to the global movement for inclusive, equitable, and quality education for all.

4.1 Bridging Educational Gaps In Underserved And Marginalized Communities

OER plays a transformative role in closing educational gaps, particularly in communities with limited access to quality resources, qualified teachers, or physical infrastructure. In many developing regions, educational materials are either outdated or scarce due to high costs or logistical challenges. By contrast, OER offers a scalable and adaptable solution, providing up-to-date, high-quality content that can be freely downloaded, shared, and modified.

A notable example is the **TESSA (Teacher Education in Sub-Saharan Africa)** initiative, which created openly licensed teaching materials contextualized for different African nations. These resources support local educators by aligning with national curricula and being adaptable for classroom use in rural and urban schools alike (Wolfenden et al., 2012). Through such initiatives, OER enables equitable access to instructional content and professional development, thus improving educational outcomes in marginalized areas.

OER allows informal and non-traditional learners—such as refugees, working adults, or those outside formal schooling systems—to access learning opportunities. Platforms like OpenLearn, Khan Academy, and Coursera provide flexible, free courses that empower individuals to pursue lifelong learning regardless of geographic or institutional limitations (Subrahmanyam, 2024).

4.2 Support For Learners With Disabilities

Accessibility in education must extend beyond physical access to include inclusive design practices that accommodate diverse learning needs. OER can be developed or adapted in multiple accessible formats—such as audio descriptions, captions, transcripts, and screen-reader-friendly text—ensuring that students with disabilities can engage with learning materials independently and effectively.

The **Universal Design for Learning (UDL)** framework, which emphasizes providing multiple means of representation, expression, and engagement, aligns closely with the philosophy of OER. Educators can use open resources to design learning experiences that meet varied sensory, cognitive, and emotional needs. An open science lesson could be delivered via text, video, and audio to ensure learners with visual, or hearing impairments can access the content in a format that works best for them.

Some platforms actively promote accessibility in their repositories. For example, **CAST**, a leader in UDL, and **OER Commons** offer resources tagged with accessibility features, helping educators identify materials that can be customized for diverse learners. According to Butcher (2015), OER's adaptability supports inclusive practices by allowing teachers to modify content to suit learners with special educational needs, thus promoting equity in both digital and physical classrooms.

4.3 Role Of OER In Multilingual And Multicultural Education

Linguistic and cultural inclusivity is a significant challenge in conventional curricula, which often reflect dominant cultural narratives and global North-centric knowledge systems. OER offers a solution by enabling content translation, localization, and adaptation to reflect a range of cultural perspectives and languages.

Because OER can be legally modified and redistributed, educators and institutions can translate materials into local languages or incorporate culturally relevant examples to enhance learner engagement and comprehension. This localization not only improves pedagogical relevance but also affirms the cultural identity of learners, thereby enhancing motivation and academic success (Perryman & de los Arcos, 2016).

An example of this is the Open Translation Project by TED, which encourages volunteers to translate educational content into hundreds of languages. The Global OER Graduate Network and initiatives in Latin America and Asia promote multilingual open textbooks and courseware that support indigenous and regional languages. These efforts demonstrate how OER fosters inclusivity and support educational sovereignty by decentralizing knowledge production and dissemination.

OER promotes intercultural dialogue and understanding. Educators can integrate diverse global perspectives into the curriculum by remixing open resources from different cultural contexts. This approach encourages students to critically engage with multiple viewpoints, fostering a more holistic and inclusive educational experience.

4.4 Reduction Of Financial Barriers To Education

One of the most tangible and widely acknowledged benefits of OER is their capacity to eliminate or significantly reduce the cost of educational materials. The high cost of textbooks and proprietary digital content has become a critical barrier, especially for students from low-income backgrounds. In higher education, textbook costs can represent a significant portion of overall student expenses, often forcing learners to forgo required materials or drop out entirely (Hilton, 2016).

By offering free alternatives to costly commercial textbooks, OER help reduce the financial burden on students and institutions alike. In the United States, for example, community colleges adopting OER have reported substantial cost savings for students while maintaining or even improving academic performance (Wiley & Hilton, 2018). Institutions such as the **Z-Degree** programs in Virginia and Texas, which offer zero-cost degree pathways using only OER, highlight how financial accessibility can be institutionalized on a scale.

In addition to cost savings, OER promotes equity by leveling the playing field between students who can afford materials and those who cannot. When all learners have immediate, equal access to course materials from day one, the likelihood of academic success increases, and achievement gaps begin to close (Fischer et al., 2015). In this way, OER contributes not only to affordability but also to student retention and success.

OER holds immense potential in advancing educational accessibility across multiple dimensions. By bridging gaps in underserved communities, accommodating learners with disabilities, embracing multilingual and multicultural inclusivity, and reducing financial barriers, OER provides a holistic approach to equity in education. They are more than digital tools—they are catalysts for structural change, empowering learners and educators to co-create a more inclusive and just educational landscape. As institutions and governments increasingly recognize the value of OER, their role in shaping accessible, equitable, and high-quality education will continue to grow.

5. IMPACT ON TEACHING COMPETENCIES AND PEDAGOGICAL INNOVATION

The integration of Open Educational Resources (OER) into teaching practices has significantly influenced the professional roles, skills, and pedagogical approaches of educators. As the traditional role of teachers evolves in response to open and digital learning environments, OER serves as catalysts for rethinking instructional strategies, fostering professional development, and promoting pedagogical innovation. This section examines the impact of OER on teaching competencies, focusing on the shift in teacher roles, the enhancement of digital and instructional design skills, the promotion of collaborative knowledge creation, and the encouragement of innovation through remixing and localization of content.

5.1 Shifting Teacher Roles: From Content Deliverers To Facilitators And Curators

In conventional educational models, teachers have often been positioned as primary content deliverers, relying on pre-packaged textbooks and standardized materials. The widespread adoption of OER is challenging this model by empowering educators to assume more dynamic roles as facilitators of learning, content curators, and instructional designers. This paradigm shift allows teachers greater autonomy to select, adapt, and organize content in ways that align with learners' needs, institutional goals, and evolving societal contexts (Ehlers, 2011).

With access to a wide array of open resources, teachers are no longer bound to follow a rigid curriculum dictated by proprietary materials. Instead, they can design learning experiences that are contextualized, interactive, and learner-centered. This transition aligns with constructivist pedagogies, where the teacher's role is to guide and support learners in constructing knowledge through inquiry, collaboration, and reflection (Subrahmanyam, 2024). OER requires teachers to engage more actively in pedagogical decision-making, curriculum development, and instructional customization.

5.2 Enhancing Digital Literacy And Instructional Design Skills

One of the most significant impacts of OER adoption is the demand for enhanced digital competencies among educators. The use of OER necessitates a foundational understanding of digital tools, platforms, and licensing mechanisms, particularly Creative Commons licenses, which govern how resources can be used, adapted, and shared legally and ethically (Hilton, 2016).

Digital literacy in the context of OER includes skills such as searching for high-quality resources, evaluating the credibility of content, and editing or remixing materials using various digital formats. Teachers must become proficient in the technical and pedagogical aspects of instructional design—structuring content, sequencing learning activities, integrating multimedia, and ensuring accessibility for all learners.

Instructional design competencies are especially crucial when OER are integrated into blended or online learning environments. Teachers must consider learner engagement, cognitive load, and content interactivity while designing or adapting open content. The ability to scaffold learning experiences using diverse OER formats—such as videos, simulations, open textbooks, and assessment tools—supports inclusive and differentiated instruction (Butcher, 2015). As educators refine these competencies, they become more confident and capable of leveraging technology for deeper learning.

5.3 Promoting Collaborative Teaching And Peer Knowledge Creation

OER also encourages a culture of collaboration among educators, fostering communities of practice where knowledge is shared, refined, and co-created. Teachers can collaborate within and across institutions to create open content, peer review resources, and share best practices. This collaborative spirit shifts educational practice from being isolated and static to collective and dynamic.

Collaborative teaching supported by OER may involve co-authoring open textbooks, develop shared lesson plans, or contribute to repositories like OER Commons or Wikibooks. Such practices not only reduce workload but also improve the quality and relevance of content through diverse perspectives. According to Ehlers (2011), this form of open educational practice leads to professional learning, institutional innovation, and system-level improvements in education.

Peer knowledge creation through OER reflects the principles of open pedagogy, which invites both teachers and learners to become contributors to knowledge rather than passive recipients. This participatory approach enhances academic engagement, critical thinking, and intellectual ownership. Instructors who engage in OER collaboration often report increased professional satisfaction, a sense of community, and empowerment in shaping the curriculum (Kimmons, 2016).

5.4 Encouraging Innovation Through Remixing And Localizing Content

The ability to revise and remix OER allows teachers to innovate by tailoring content to specific learner demographics, local contexts, and emerging educational challenges. This process of localization—modifying resources to include culturally relevant examples, regional data, or vernacular languages—ensures that learning is meaningful and inclusive (Perryman & de los Arcos, 2016). It also allows educators to keep curricula current by incorporating up-to-date information, policy changes, or interdisciplinary perspectives.

Innovation is further fostered by the creative flexibility that OER afford. Teachers can blend open resources with original content, design problem-based learning activities using real-world datasets, or integrate multimedia tools to enhance interactivity. A teacher may remix open videos, datasets, and simulations to create a project-based module on climate change that resonates with the local community. Such practices support the development of higher-order thinking skills and foster real-world application of knowledge.

The iterative nature of remixing OER encourages a mindset of continuous improvement and experimentation in teaching. As educators revise resources based on student feedback and outcomes, they contribute to a living curriculum that evolves in response to learner needs and societal changes. This pedagogical agility is critical in an era marked by rapid technological, economic, and cultural transformations.

Figure 2. OER's Impact

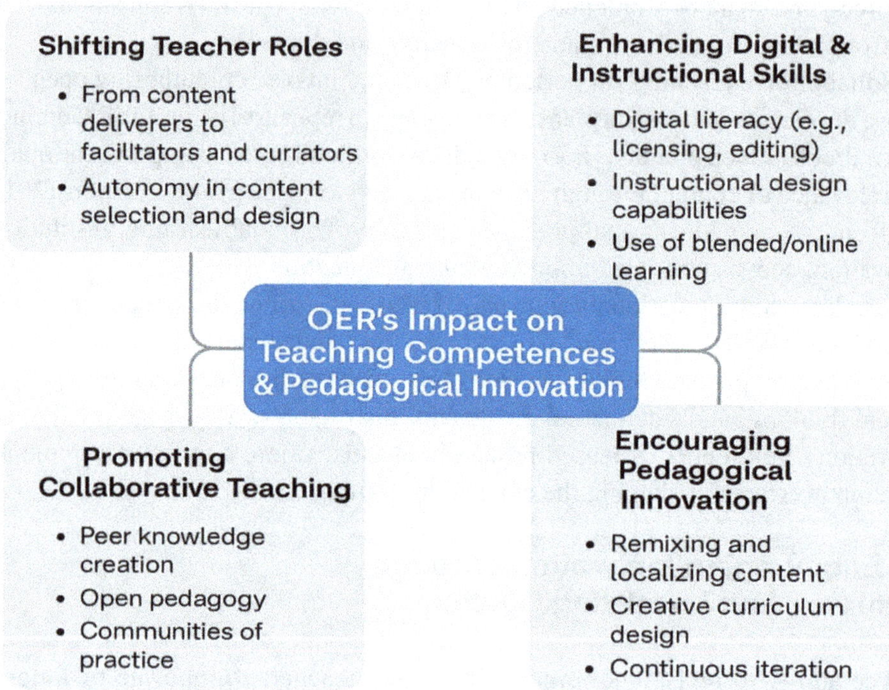

Source: Author (2025)

The integration of OER into educational practice is reshaping the teaching profession by expanding roles, enhancing digital and instructional competencies, and fostering a collaborative and innovative pedagogical culture. Teachers are no longer passive users of static content but are now empowered as facilitators, creators, and collaborators. As they adopt and adapt OER, educators refine their skills in digital literacy, instructional design, and curriculum development, leading to more inclusive, responsive, and engaging learning experiences. Ultimately, the widespread use of OER contributes to a more dynamic, equitable, and future-ready educational system.

6. INSTITUTIONAL AND POLICY FRAMEWORKS SUPPORTING OER ADOPTION

The widespread adoption and sustainability of Open Educational Resources (OER) depend not only on grassroots enthusiasm among educators but also on supportive institutional and policy frameworks. These frameworks are essential for embedding OER into mainstream educational practices and ensuring that their potential for equity, access, and innovation is fully realized. This section explores the global and regional policy landscape surrounding OER, the roles of governments, universities, and consortia in promoting OER, and the institutional strategies necessary for integrating OER into curricula.

6.1 Global And Regional OER Policies And Initiatives

At the global level, the policy push for OER began with UNESCO's pioneering efforts in the early 2000s. The 2002 UNESCO Forum on Open Courseware formally coined the term "Open Educational Resources" and initiated international dialogue around educational openness. Building on this momentum, the **Paris OER Declaration (2012)** called on governments and institutions worldwide to promote open licensing, develop supportive policy environments, and encourage capacity-building for OER adoption (UNESCO, 2012). This was followed by the **Ljubljana OER Action Plan (2017)**, which emphasized strategic areas including capacity building, language and cultural context, and policy development (UNESCO, 2017).

In 2019, UNESCO's Recommendation on OER was formally adopted by 193 member states. This document laid out five strategic objectives: building capacity of stakeholders, developing supportive policies, encouraging inclusive access, fostering sustainability models, and promoting international cooperation (UNESCO, 2019). The recommendation serves as a binding soft law instrument, encouraging countries to align their national educational strategies with open education principles.

Creative Commons, a global nonprofit organization, has also been instrumental in the OER movement by offering standardized open licenses. These licenses (e.g., CC BY, CC BY-SA) enable content creators to specify permissions for reuse, remixing, and distribution. Through Creative Commons licensing, educational institutions can share knowledge freely while maintaining legal clarity and academic integrity (Carson, 2010).

Regionally, several governments have taken proactive measures to integrate OER into their educational frameworks. South Africa's Department of Basic Education has supported OER initiatives for schools and teacher training. Similarly, the European Commission has backed projects such as OpenEdu and OpenLearn to promote open education across EU member states. In Latin America, Brazil's National Institute for Educational Studies (INEP) has encouraged the development of open textbooks and learning materials for basic education (Amiel, 2013).

6.2 Role Of Governments, Universities, And Consortia In OER Promotion

Governments play a critical role in scaling OER adoption by establishing national policies, funding mechanisms, and strategic frameworks that incentivize open educational practices. By allocating public funds for the creation and dissemination of OER, governments ensure that the products of publicly funded education are available to the public. Countries like Poland, the Netherlands, and Canada have launched national OER platforms and repositories supported by public investment (Stacey, 2013).

Universities and higher education institutions are also central to the OER ecosystem. They serve as content creators, distributors, and innovation hubs. Many universities have adopted open education policies, established dedicated OER offices or support units, and incentivized faculty engagement through grants, awards, and tenure considerations. The Massachusetts Institute of Technology (MIT), through its OpenCourseWare initiative, set a precedent for institutional OER leadership, inspiring similar initiatives around the world.

University consortia and inter-institutional collaborations further amplify the impact of OER by pooling resources, sharing best practices, and building collective capacity. The Open Education Consortium (OEC) brings together educational institutions globally to advocate for open education. In the U.S., initiatives like OpenStax (Rice University) and the Community College Consortium for OER (CCCOER) provide infrastructure, content, and support networks for institutions seeking to embed OER into academic programs (Wiley et al., 2014).

Table 5. Roles of Stakeholders in OER Promotion

Stakeholder	Roles and Responsibilities	Examples/Initiatives
Governments	- Create national OER policies - Allocate public funding - Launch national repositories	Poland's OER repository; Canada's open textbook initiative
Universities	- Develop and distribute OER - Create policy and incentives - Train faculty and reward OER engagement	MIT OpenCourseWare; university-based OER grants
University Consortia	- Pool institutional resources - Promote shared content and best practices	Open Education Consortium; CCCOER; OpenStax
Nonprofits and NGOs	- Provide legal tools and infrastructure for open licensing	Creative Commons; SPARC (Scholarly Publishing and Academic Resources Coalition)

6.3 Institutional Policies For Integrating OER Into Curricula

To ensure sustainable OER adoption, educational institutions must develop robust internal policies that support the creation, use, and integration of OER within academic curricula. These policies typically address several key areas: intellectual property and licensing, faculty incentives, professional development, quality assurance, and technological infrastructure.

Intellectual property (IP) policies must align with open licensing norms. Faculty and staff should be educated on Creative Commons licenses, and institutions should establish clear guidelines for open publication of teaching materials. Policies may include mandates or recommendations for using OER in certain courses, particularly those with high enrollment or significant textbook costs.

Faculty engagement and incentives are crucial. Institutions that recognize OER development as scholarly activity—eligible for consideration in promotion and tenure—encourage more educators to participate in open education. Grant programs, release time, and recognition awards also motivate faculty to create and adopt OER (Subrahmanyam, 2025).

Professional development is another essential pillar. Instructors must be trained not only in using digital tools but also in pedagogical strategies for adapting and remixing OER. Workshops, online courses, and peer mentoring programs help build institutional capacity and ensure effective implementation.

Quality assurance mechanisms must be developed to evaluate and maintain the academic rigor of OER materials. Institutions may form review committees, partner with external accrediting bodies, or develop rubrics for assessing the pedagogical and technical quality of OER.

Finally, institutions must invest in **technological infrastructure**—such as learning management systems (LMS), digital repositories, and content authoring tools—that support the discovery, adaptation, and distribution of OER. Libraries often play a central role in curating and managing OER collections, making them accessible to both instructors and students.

Table 6. Key Components of Institutional OER Integration Policies

Component	Policy Focus	Implementation Strategies
Intellectual Property (IP)	Ensure compatibility with open licenses and Creative Commons standards	Guidelines for copyright compliance and open publishing
Faculty Incentives	Motivate participation in OER development and use	Tenure consideration, release time, grant funding, recognition awards
Professional Development	Equip instructors with skills to locate, adapt, remix, and assess OER	Workshops, training modules, online courses, peer mentoring programs
Quality Assurance	Maintain academic rigor and credibility of OER materials	Peer review, rubrics, external partnerships with quality agencies
Technological Infrastructure	Enable creation, access, and sharing of OER	LMS integration, digital repositories, authoring tools; library-based curation and technical support

The effective adoption of Open Educational Resources hinges on the strength and coherence of institutional and policy frameworks. Global initiatives by UNESCO and Creative Commons have provided the vision and tools for OER promotion, while national governments, universities, and consortia have operationalized these frameworks through funding, policy-making, and collaborative action. At the institutional level, supportive policies, infrastructure, and faculty development are essential to integrate OER into academic curricula meaningfully. As more stakeholders align their strategies with the values of openness, equity, and innovation, OER will continue to reshape the educational landscape in transformative ways.

7. CASE STUDIES AND BEST PRACTICES

Open Educational Resources (OER) have been implemented in a variety of educational settings across the globe, demonstrating their capacity to transform learning experiences by promoting accessibility, flexibility, and innovation. From primary and secondary education to higher education and adult learning, numerous case studies showcase successful OER adoption and offer valuable insights into the challenges and strategies that accompany such efforts. This section explores illustrative examples from diverse educational contexts, highlighting best practices in OER implementation and drawing out lessons that inform future policy and pedagogical development.

7.1 OER In K-12 Education: The Utah Open Textbook Project (USA)

One of the most influential K-12 OER initiatives is the Utah Open Textbook Project, launched by the Utah State Office of Education in partnership with Brigham Young University. The initiative replaced traditional commercial textbooks with openly licensed textbooks for core subjects such as math and science in high schools. These OER-based textbooks were created by adapting open content available from platforms such as CK-12 and Saylor Academy, tailored to meet the Utah Core Standards.

The project demonstrated significant cost savings—up to 80% compared to traditional textbooks—and improved student performance and engagement (Wiley et al., 2012). The open format enabled teachers to continuously update and contextualize materials, ensuring that content remained relevant and reflective of student needs. The initiative also encouraged teacher collaboration and professional development as educators worked together to create and revise the textbooks.

This case illustrates the power of OER to make learning more responsive and cost-effective in K-12 contexts. It also underscores the importance of administrative support, professional learning communities, and teacher empowerment in successful OER adoption.

7.2 OER In Higher Education: OPENSTAX At Rice University (USA)

In the higher education sector, **OpenStax**, based at Rice University in the United States, is a leading example of large-scale OER implementation. OpenStax produces peer-reviewed, openly licensed textbooks for high-enrollment university courses, such as physics, biology, economics, and psychology. The initiative has gained widespread adoption across colleges and universities in North America and beyond.

By 2023, OpenStax textbooks had reached over 20 million students, saving learners more than $2 billion collectively (OpenStax, 2023). Empirical studies have shown that student learning outcomes with OpenStax textbooks are comparable to or better than those using commercial alternatives (Hilton, 2016). The textbooks are available in digital and print formats, and instructors are encouraged to adapt the content to fit specific pedagogical goals and institutional requirements.

OpenStax provides an important model for aligning academic rigor with open licensing. Its success has been supported by strong university backing, grant funding from philanthropic organizations, and partnerships with technology providers that integrate OER into digital learning environments. The initiative demonstrates how scalable, high-quality OER can enhance educational equity and curriculum flexibility across diverse academic institutions.

7.3 OER In Adult And Lifelong Learning: Commonwealth Of Learning (COL) And OER For Skills Development

The **Commonwealth of Learning (COL)** has been instrumental in promoting OER for adult and lifelong learning, particularly in low-resource settings across Africa, Asia, and the Caribbean. One such initiative is the Skills for Work program, which offers short, competency-based courses using OER to support employability and entrepreneurship. These courses cover topics such as digital literacy, communication skills, and financial literacy and are hosted on platforms like Moodle and COL's OAsis repository.

A key success story under this initiative is the Partnership with the National Institute of Open Schooling (NIOS) in India, which enabled the translation and localization of OER to serve adult learners in multiple Indian languages. Learners could access the courses freely through mobile devices and low-bandwidth platforms, making education more accessible to rural and marginalized populations.

This case demonstrates how OER can address the specific needs of adult learners, offering flexible, practical, and culturally relevant learning opportunities. It also highlights the importance of localization, language accessibility, and partnerships with national institutions in scaling lifelong learning opportunities.

7.4. Insights Gained And Implications For Future Practice

Across these case studies, several key lessons and best practices emerge:

1. **Contextual Relevance Is Critical**: Successful OER adoption depends on the ability to adapt resources to local curricula, languages, and cultural contexts. Flexibility in content creation and delivery enhances learner engagement and educational relevance.
2. **Institutional Support Drives Sustainability**: Support from educational institutions—through policies, funding, infrastructure, and recognition—plays a vital role in sustaining OER initiatives. Faculty engagement increases when there are incentives, professional development, and clear IP frameworks in place.

3. **Collaboration Enhances Quality and Reach**: Whether in K-12, higher education, or adult learning, collaboration among educators, institutions, and organizations improves the quality of OER and facilitates knowledge sharing. Communities of practice foster innovation and reduce duplication of efforts.
4. **Technology Must Be Inclusive**: Effective OER implementation must consider digital equity. Resources should be accessible across devices and bandwidth levels, and in formats that accommodate learners with disabilities. Offline access and mobile optimization can dramatically expand reach, especially in rural and underserved areas.
5. **Evidence of Impact Strengthens Advocacy**: Demonstrating measurable outcomes—such as cost savings, improved learning outcomes, or increased enrollment—helps build institutional buy-in and attract funding. Rigorous evaluation and research are essential for scaling successful models.

OER has shown transformative potential across educational levels and contexts. From the Utah Open Textbook Project's K-12 innovations to OpenStax's expansive reach in higher education and the Commonwealth of Learning's targeted programs for adult learners, each case provides valuable insights into the power of openness to advance educational accessibility and flexibility. By applying these lessons and best practices, educators, institutions, and policymakers can drive more effective and inclusive OER strategies that address diverse learner needs and promote lifelong learning.

8. CHALLENGES AND CONSIDERATIONS

Despite the transformative potential of Open Educational Resources (OER) in enhancing educational accessibility, affordability, and flexibility, their widespread adoption and integration face several challenges. These include concerns over the quality and credibility of OER, complex intellectual property and licensing issues, persistent digital divides, infrastructural limitations, and resistance to change within traditional educational systems. Understanding these challenges is critical for policymakers, educators, and institutions striving to mainstream OER in a sustainable and effective manner.

8.1 Quality Assurance And Credibility Of OER

A major concern surrounding OER is ensuring their academic rigor and credibility. Unlike commercial textbooks, which typically undergo formal peer review and editorial processes, OER are often developed by individual educators or open communities without centralized quality control mechanisms. This leads to varying standards in content accuracy, instructional design, and pedagogical value.

Quality assurance is especially significant in contexts where educational stakeholders—such as administrators, accreditation bodies, and faculty—are unfamiliar with the open education ecosystem. Perceptions that OER lack credibility or consistency may discourage adoption, particularly in higher education settings where academic standards are closely scrutinized (Wiley et al., 2014).

To address this challenge, several initiatives have developed quality frameworks and reviewed rubrics. Achieve's OER Rubrics provide a structured approach to evaluating OER based on criteria like alignment with learning goals, content accuracy, and usability. Some platforms, like OER Commons, incorporate peer reviews, ratings, and metadata to guide users in selecting high-quality materials (Butcher, 2015). The responsibility for quality assurance ultimately rests with institutions and educators, who must curate and contextualize OER to meet their learners' needs.

8.2 Intellectual Property And Licensing Issues

OER are defined not only by their cost-free nature but also by the legal permissions that allow users to retain, reuse, revise, remix, and redistribute content (Wiley, 2014). Navigating the complexities of open licensing - particularly Creative Commons (CC) licenses - can be daunting for educators unfamiliar with intellectual property law.

Misunderstanding licensing terms can lead to unintentional violations of copyright or the improper attribution of source materials. Combining content licensed under different types of CC licenses may create incompatibility, especially when non-commercial (NC) or share-alike (SA) clauses are involved. In some cases, instructors mistakenly assume all internet content is freely usable, leading to legal and ethical dilemmas.

Institutional policies and training are essential to mitigate these risks. Educators must be equipped with foundational knowledge about copyright, fair use, and open licensing to confidently adopt and create OER. Some universities have developed open licensing toolkits, while others integrate intellectual property guidance into faculty development programs (Amiel, 2013). Legal and technical support from libraries and instructional design teams can empower faculty to navigate licensing issues effectively.

8.3 Digital Divide And Infrastructural Limitations

While OER has the potential to bridge access gaps in education, their digital nature can inadvertently reinforce existing inequalities—particularly in regions with limited internet access, inadequate devices, or unreliable electricity. This digital divide disproportionately affects learners in rural areas, low-income communities, and developing countries, impeding equitable access to digital content and online platforms.

Some OER are created with high-bandwidth requirements, such as video lectures, interactive simulations, or multimedia-rich materials. These formats may be inaccessible to users relying on basic mobile devices or constrained by data costs. Without offline access or low-tech alternatives, the promise of OER for inclusive education may remain unfulfilled for the most marginalized learners.

To overcome infrastructural limitations, OER initiatives must prioritize offline accessibility, mobile optimization, and low-bandwidth content delivery. Projects like the Kolibri platform by Learning Equality offer downloadable OER that can be used without internet connectivity, making them suitable for remote and underserved settings. Text-based OER in PDF or ePub formats can be distributed via USB drives, DVDs, or print-on-demand services.

National governments and development agencies also have a role to play in expanding digital infrastructure—through policies that promote universal broadband, device affordability, and school connectivity. Only by addressing these systemic barriers can the equitable potential of OER be fully realized.

8.4 Resistance To Change In Traditional Curriculum Structures

Educational institutions often operate within deeply embedded traditions and regulatory frameworks that are resistant to rapid change. Curriculum design, textbook selection, and teaching practices are frequently governed by centralized policies, accreditation standards, or bureaucratic procedures that favor established commercial materials over innovative alternatives like OER.

Faculty members may also exhibit skepticism toward OER due to perceived threats to academic autonomy, lack of familiarity, or concerns over the time and effort required to curate and adapt open materials (Belikov & Bodily, 2016). In some cases, educators fear that the push toward OER could devalue their roles as content experts or challenge the authority of conventional instructional resources.

To counteract resistance, institutions must implement change management strategies that promote awareness, capacity-building, and cultural shifts in pedagogical practices. This includes offering professional development workshops, integrating OER into curriculum planning, recognizing OER contributions in faculty promotion, and highlighting successful implementation cases. Leadership support and peer advocacy are also vital in cultivating a positive attitude toward open education.

Policy frameworks must be aligned to incentivize OER adoption. Governments and accrediting bodies can revise curriculum standards to permit the use of openly licensed materials, and universities can include OER metrics in their strategic goals and quality assurance systems.

While OER presents immense opportunities for democratizing education, their adoption is accompanied by significant challenges that must be addressed through thoughtful planning, policy support, and stakeholder engagement. Issues related to quality assurance, intellectual property, digital inequality, and institutional resistance require multi-level interventions and sustained collaboration. By developing comprehensive support systems and fostering a culture of openness, educational institutions and policymakers can unlock the full transformative potential of OER and ensure their benefits are equitably distributed across learning communities.

9. FUTURE PROSPECTS OF OER IN CURRICULUM INNOVATION

Open Educational Resources (OER) continue to evolve as key drivers of educational transformation, enabling curriculum innovation, personalized learning, and broader participation in knowledge creation. With the integration of emerging technologies such as artificial intelligence (AI), adaptive learning systems, and blockchain, OER are poised to offer even more dynamic and responsive learning experiences. Furthermore, the expansion of OER into lifelong and informal learning, and the rise of open pedagogy, signal a shift from consumption to co-creation of educational content. This section explores these future prospects and how they are likely to shape curriculum design, delivery, and participation in the years ahead.

9.1 Emerging Technologies And OER

Emerging technologies, especially AI, adaptive learning systems, and blockchain, are transforming how OER are created, delivered, and used. Artificial Intelligence (AI) has the potential to enhance the personalization of OER by analyzing learner behavior and recommending resources tailored to individual needs. Intelligent tutoring systems and AI-powered search engines can assist educators in curating high-quality OER from vast repositories, reducing the time and effort needed to locate appropriate materials (Zawacki-Richter et al., 2019).

Adaptive learning technologies can integrate with OER to deliver tailored learning pathways, dynamically adjusting content difficulty and pacing based on student performance. By doing so, these systems enhance the flexibility and inclusivity of curricula, especially for learners who require differentiated instruction. Platforms like Smart Sparrow and Knewton exemplify how OER and adaptive technologies can coalesce to improve learning outcomes in real-time.

Blockchain technology also presents novel opportunities for credentialing and content verification in OER ecosystems. Through decentralized and tamper-proof ledgers, blockchain can record learning achievements associated with OER usage, thereby supporting micro-credentialing and lifelong learning portfolios (Grech & Camilleri, 2017). Blockchain can track content usage and authorship, ensure proper attribution and help educators receive recognition for their contributions to open content creation.

As these technologies mature and become more accessible, their integration with OER is likely to enhance curriculum design, ensure data-driven instruction, and promote transparency and trust in educational transactions.

9.2 OER In Lifelong Learning And Informal Education

The role of OER is expanding beyond formal educational settings to support lifelong learning and informal education. In an era marked by rapid technological change and shifting labor market demands, individuals increasingly need to upskill and reskill throughout their lives. OER provides a cost-effective, flexible, and self-directed solution to these needs, enabling learners to access quality content anytime, anywhere.

Major initiatives, such as the Commonwealth of Learning's Skills for Work program and MIT's OpenCourseWare, offer OER-based courses that support vocational training, entrepreneurship, and digital literacy. These platforms often include multimedia materials, assessments, and certificates of completion, making them valuable tools for learners seeking to build competencies outside traditional institutions (COL, 2020).

In addition to upskilling, OER are fostering community-based and social learning environments. Platforms like Peer 2 Peer University (P2PU) encourage learners to form study groups around open resources, enabling peer support and collaborative knowledge building. MOOCs built on OER principles extend access to high-quality learning opportunities for learners in remote or marginalized communities.

The democratisation of education and the realisation of Sustainable Development Goal 4, which is to provide inclusive and equitable quality education and promote lifelong learning for everyone, are both aided by open educational resources (OER) as they encourage informal and lifelong learning (UNESCO, 2019).

9.3 Open Pedagogy And Participatory Curriculum Development

In addition to providing access to material, open educational resources (OER) will continue to thrive if they can facilitate open pedagogy, a style of instruction that places an emphasis on student initiative, group work, and the shared production of new information. By empowering students to actively participate in curriculum creation, open pedagogy transforms them from being just consumers of information to active creators of it.

In practice, open pedagogy involves inviting students to remix, revise, or create OER as part of their coursework. This approach not only deepens subject mastery but also cultivates critical thinking, digital literacy, and civic engagement. Students might collaborate to create an open textbook, develop community-based learning modules, or translate existing OER into local languages (DeRosa & Jhangiani, 2017).

This participatory model aligns with constructivist learning theories, which posit that knowledge is actively constructed through social interaction and reflection. It also enhances curriculum innovation by incorporating diverse perspectives and experiences, thus creating more inclusive and contextually relevant content.

Faculty and institutions that embrace open pedagogy often report increased engagement and motivation among learners. Student-generated OER can be shared with future cohorts, creating a cycle of continual curriculum enhancement and community contribution (Paskevicius & Irvine, 2019).

As open pedagogy gains momentum, it challenges traditional hierarchies in education and fosters a culture of sharing, inclusivity, and innovation. Institutions that support this model are likely to see more agile and responsive curricula that better meet the needs of 21st-century learners.

Figure 3. Emerging Technologies and OER

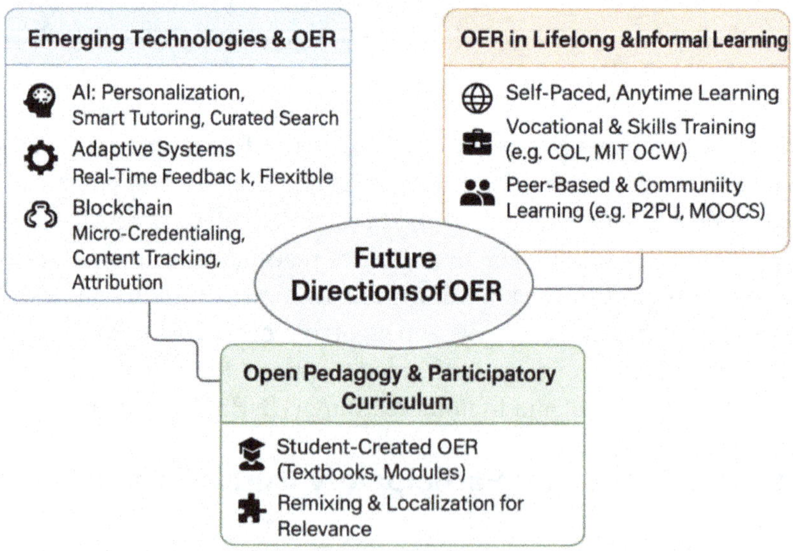

Source: Author (2025)

The future of OER in curriculum innovation is both promising and expansive. Emerging technologies like AI, adaptive learning, and blockchain are enhancing the effectiveness and personalization of OER-based instruction. The growing use of OER in lifelong and informal education underscores its potential to support continuous learning and workforce development. Perhaps most significantly, the rise of open pedagogy is reshaping the educational landscape by fostering participatory, learner-centered curricula. As educational institutions, governments, and communities invest in the infrastructure, policies, and practices that support OER, their role in driving is inclusive, flexible, and innovative education will only grow stronger.

10. CONCLUSION

Open Educational Resources (OER) represent a transformative force in modern education, enabling greater accessibility, flexibility, and equity in curriculum development and delivery. By removing cost barriers, encouraging pedagogical innovation, and fostering participatory learning, OER have redefined how knowledge is created, shared, and consumed across diverse educational contexts. From primary and secondary education to higher education and lifelong learning, OER have demonstrated their ability to personalize learning, engage learners as co-creators, and promote inclusive education for marginalized and underserved communities.

Key insights from this chapter highlight the importance of a supportive ecosystem involving educators, curriculum designers, institutional leaders, and policy-makers. Educators must be empowered with the digital literacy and instructional design skills needed to effectively adopt and adapt OER. Curriculum designers should embrace the open and adaptable nature of OER to create culturally relevant and learner-centered content. Meanwhile, policy-makers and institutional leaders have a vital role in establishing frameworks, funding models, and professional development programs that promote and sustain OER initiatives on scale.

As we look toward the future, it is imperative to act strategically. Stakeholders across education systems are called upon to invest in infrastructure, address challenges such as quality assurance and licensing, and foster a culture of openness and collaboration. Embracing OER not only enhances educational inclusion and innovation but also aligns with broader goals of lifelong learning and global equity. The time is now for institutions and educators to reimagine curriculum development through the lens of open education—one that prioritizes access, flexibility, and empowerment for all learners.

REFERENCES

Amiel, T. (2013). Identifying barriers to the remix of translated open educational resources. *International Review of Research in Open and Distance Learning, 14*(1), 126–144. DOI: 10.19173/irrodl.v14i1.1351

Belikov, O. M., & Bodily, R. (2016). Incentives and barriers to OER adoption: A qualitative analysis of faculty perceptions. *Open Praxis, 8*(3), 235–246. DOI: 10.5944/openpraxis.8.3.308

Butcher, N. (2015). *A basic guide to Open Educational Resources (OER)*. Commonwealth of Learning and UNESCO. https://unesdoc.unesco.org/ark:/48223/pf0000215804

Carson, S. (2010). The unwalled garden: Growth of the OpenCourseWare Consortium, 2001–2008. *Open Learning, 25*(1), 5–10.

Commonwealth of Learning (COL). (2020). *Skills for Work Program*. https://www.col.org/programmes/skills-work

DeRosa, R., & Jhangiani, R. S. (2017). Open pedagogy. In Jhangiani, R. S., & Biswas-Diener, R. (Eds.), *Open: The philosophy and practices that are revolutionizing education and science* (pp. 115–124). Ubiquity Press. DOI: 10.5334/bbc.i

Ehlers, U.-D. (2011). Extending the territory: From open educational resources to open educational practices. *Journal of Open. Flexible and Distance Learning, 15*(2), 1–10.

Ehlers, U.-D. (2011). From open educational resources to open educational practices. *eLearning Papers, 23*, 1–8.

Fischer, L., Hilton, J.III, Robinson, T. J., & Wiley, D. (2015). A multi-institutional study of the impact of open textbook adoption on the learning outcomes of post-secondary students. *Journal of Computing in Higher Education, 27*(3), 159–172. DOI: 10.1007/s12528-015-9101-x PMID: 32269452

Grech, A., & Camilleri, A. F. (2017). *Blockchain in education*. Joint Research Centre, European Commission.

Hilton, J.III. (2016). Open educational resources and college textbook choices: A review of research on efficacy and perceptions. *Educational Technology Research and Development, 64*(4), 573–590. DOI: 10.1007/s11423-016-9434-9

Kimmons, R. (2016). OER adoption and perceptions in American higher education. *Open Praxis, 8*(2), 111–123.

OpenStax. (2023). *About us*. https://openstax.org/about

Paskevicius, M., & Irvine, V. (2019). Open education and learning design: Open pedagogy in practice. *Journal of Interactive Media in Education, 2019*(1), 1–13. DOI: 10.5334/jime.512

Perryman, L. A., & de los Arcos, B. (2016). Women's empowerment through openness: OER, OEP and the Sustainable Development Goals. *Open Praxis, 8*(2), 163–180. DOI: 10.5944/openpraxis.8.2.289

Ribeiro, N., & Subrahmanyam, S. (2021). Emotional challenges of teaching online during pandemic. In Sony, K. K., Verma, N., & Uddin, M. (Eds.), *Psychosocial issues in Covid-19 pandemic* (pp. 244–255). SHINE Publication. RED.

Siemens, G. (2005). Connectivism: A learning theory for the digital age. *International Journal of Instructional Technology and Distance Learning*, 2(1), 3–10.

Stacey, P. (2013). Government support for open educational resources: Policy, funding, and strategies. *International Review of Research in Open and Distance Learning, 14*(2), 67–80. DOI: 10.19173/irrodl.v14i2.1537

Subrahmanyam, S. (2021). Attitudes and beliefs of faculty on teaching online during pandemic. In Sony, K. K., Verma, N., & Uddin, M. (Eds.), *Psychosocial issues in Covid-19 pandemic* (pp. 256–268). SHINE Publication. RED.

Subrahmanyam, S. (2024). Implementing agile talent management practices to adapt to changing higher education landscapes. In Kayyali, M. (Ed.), *Cultivating creativity and navigating talent management in academia* (pp. 187–210). IGI Global Scientific Publishing. DOI: 10.4018/979-8-3693-6880-0.ch009

Subrahmanyam, S. (2024). The role of leadership in nurturing innovation and creativity among faculty and staff. In Kayyali, M. (Ed.), *Cultivating creativity and navigating talent management in academia* (pp. 449–468). IGI Global Scientific Publishing. DOI: 10.4018/979-8-3693-6880-0.ch021

Subrahmanyam, S. (2025). Qualitative Research Designs in Higher Education. In Mdikana, A. (Ed.), *Social Implications of Research in Higher Education* (pp. 263–296). IGI Global Scientific Publishing. DOI: 10.4018/979-8-3373-0654-4.ch010

UNESCO. (2012). *2012 Paris OER Declaration*. https://unesdoc.unesco.org/ark:/48223/pf0000217019

UNESCO. (2017). *Ljubljana OER Action Plan 2017*. https://unesdoc.unesco.org/ark:/48223/pf0000259349

UNESCO. (2019). *Recommendation on Open Educational Resources (OER)*. https://unesdoc.unesco.org/ark:/48223/pf0000370936

Wiley, D. (2014). The access compromise and the 5th R. *Iterating Toward Openness*. https://opencontent.org/blog/archives/3221

Wiley, D., Bliss, T. J., & McEwen, M. (2014). Open educational resources: A review of the literature. In Spector, J. M. (Eds.), *Handbook of research on educational communications and technology* (pp. 781–789). Springer. DOI: 10.1007/978-1-4614-3185-5_63

Wiley, D., & Hilton, J.III. (2018). Defining OER-enabled pedagogy. *International Review of Research in Open and Distance Learning, 19*(4), 133–147. DOI: 10.19173/irrodl.v19i4.3601

Wiley, D., Hilton, J.III, Ellington, S., & Hall, T. (2012). A preliminary examination of the cost savings and learning impacts of using open textbooks in middle and high school science classes. *International Review of Research in Open and Distance Learning, 13*(3), 262–276. DOI: 10.19173/irrodl.v13i3.1153

Wolfenden, F., Buckler, A., & Keraro, F. (2012). OER adaptation and reuse across cultural contexts in Sub-Saharan Africa: Lessons from TESSA (Teacher Education in Sub-Saharan Africa). *Journal of Interactive Media in Education, 2012*(1), 5. DOI: 10.5334/2012-03

Zawacki-Richter, O., Marín, V. I., Bond, M., & Gouverneur, F. (2019). Systematic review of research on artificial intelligence applications in higher education – where are the educators? *International Journal of Educational Technology in Higher Education, 16*(1), 39. DOI: 10.1186/s41239-019-0171-0

KEY TERMS AND DEFINITIONS

Accessible Formats: Materials created or converted into forms usable by learners with disabilities, such as screen reader-compatible texts, captions, or tactile graphics.

Adaptive Learning Technologies: Digital tools that use algorithms to adjust the learning experience in real time based on student performance and needs, often integrated with OER platforms.

Collaborative Teaching: An instructional approach where educators work together to plan, deliver, and assess teaching and learning, often facilitated by sharing and co-creating OER.

Creative Commons (CC): A non-profit organization providing free licenses that allow creators to share their work legally and openly. These licenses are widely used for OER to promote reuse and adaptation.

Digital Divide: The gap between individuals or communities with access to modern information and communication technology and those without, which can hinder the equitable use of OER.

Digital Literacy: The ability to find, evaluate, utilize, share, and create content using information technologies and digital tools—critical for both learners and educators in the OER ecosystem.

Intellectual Property (IP): Legal rights that protect creators' original works; OER challenges traditional IP by promoting open access and reusability under specific licensing conditions.

Open Courseware (OCW): Digitized university-level courses offered freely and openly for anyone to access and use, often as part of institutional OER initiatives.

Open Pedagogy: A set of teaching and learning practices built on the principles of openness, collaboration, and active learner participation in the co-creation of knowledge.

Peer Knowledge Creation: The collaborative process through which learners and educators co-develop content and ideas, a core practice within open pedagogy and OER communities.

Chapter 3
Artificial Intelligence in the Classroom: Teachers' Perspectives on the Development of Critical and Creative Thinking

Maria da Graça Magalhães
https://orcid.org/0009-0009-4689-5464
Centre for Educational Research and Intervention (CIIE), University of Trás-os-Montes and Alto Douro, Portugal

Isabel de Lurdes Pereira do Cabo
https://orcid.org/0000-0002-6482-4653
Lamego School of Technology and Management, IPV, Portugal

Carlos Alberto Lopes
Lamego School of Technology and Management, IPV, Portugal

Romeu Sequeira
Lamego School of Technology and Management, IPV, Portugal

Filipe Ambrósio
https://orcid.org/0000-0001-6048-0542
Lamego School of Technology and Management, IPV, Portugal

Berenice Peñaloza Santos
UNAM, Mexico

ABSTRACT

The digital transformation driven by Artificial Intelligence (AI) is reconfiguring educational contexts, demanding innovative pedagogical practices geared towards the development of critical and creative thinking. This article analyzes the perceptions of 67 primary and secondary school teachers regarding the integration of AI in teaching, as part of the Critical and Creative Thinking Days. The research, of a mixed nature, was based on a questionnaire consisting of fifteen Likert scale items and two open questions. The results show a positive perception of AI's potential to

DOI: 10.4018/979-8-3373-7729-2.ch003

energize teaching, foster creativity and promote reflective skills in students. Teachers recognize AI as an opportunity to transform educational practices, although they warn of significant ethical challenges and urgent training needs. The conclusion is that the critical and responsible adoption of AI can be a catalyst for curriculum renewal and the strengthening of essential skills for the 21st century.

INTRODUCTION

The rapid development and dissemination of Artificial Intelligence (AI) is fundamentally reshaping educational contexts, introducing new pedagogical, ethical, and epistemological challenges. As schools and educators navigate this technological shift, it becomes imperative to reassess the role of AI in promoting essential 21st-century competencies such as critical and creative thinking (Holmes & Miao, 2023). Much like the COVID-19 pandemic exposed systemic weaknesses in teacher digital literacy and the pedagogical integration of educational technologies (Schleicher, 2020), the advent of generative AI models, such as ChatGPT and similar tools, reveals significant gaps in teacher training, policy frameworks, and ethical preparedness (Luckin, 2017; Selwyn, 2019).

In this new landscape of accelerated innovation, educators are increasingly expected to integrate AI-driven tools into their teaching practice, often with limited guidance. They must critically evaluate how these technologies impact learning processes, student agency, classroom dynamics, and the integrity of assessment. Although AI offers the potential to personalize learning, foster creativity, and expand access to knowledge (Holmes et al., 2019), it also raises concerns about algorithmic opacity, bias, surveillance, and dependency (Floridi et al., 2018). Despite this duality, structured professional development programs that equip teachers with the competencies needed to navigate these complexities remain scarce (Zawacki-Richter et al., 2019).

This chapter responds to this urgent context by investigating the perceptions of primary and secondary school teachers regarding the integration of AI in education, specifically its role in supporting students' critical and creative thinking. The study draws on the collaborative experience of the "Critical and Creative Thinking Days", a training initiative that promoted dialogical engagement with AI's pedagogical, curricular, and ethical implications. Such informal communities of practice proved invaluable during the pandemic and continue to be effective spaces for reflective professional learning.

The relevance of this research lies in its empirically grounded contribution to understanding how teachers conceptualize AI, not only as an educational opportunity but also as a professional and ethical challenge. The conscious integration of AI demands more than technical proficiency; it requires critical awareness, ethical sensitivity, and pedagogical intentionality (Popenici & Kerr, 2017). By combining quantitative and qualitative data, this study explores teachers' attitudes, expectations, and concerns about AI, offering insights that can inform more reflective, inclusive, and transformative educational practices.

The structure of this chapter reflects a coherent flow from theory to practice. Section 2 presents the theoretical framework, organized around four analytical axes: AI in education, critical and creative thinking, pedagogical innovation through emerging technologies, and the ethical challenges of AI integration. Section 3 outlines the methodological design, including participant profile, instruments, and analytical procedures. Section 4 presents the results, highlighting teachers' perceptions, the perceived impact of AI on student thinking, and insights drawn from workshop discussions. Section 5 discusses these findings in relation to broader educational challenges and opportunities, while Section 6 concludes the chapter with key takeaways and recommendations for the ethical and formative integration of AI in teaching practice.

Rather than offering definitive conclusions, this chapter seeks to contribute to an open and critical dialogue on the transformative potential of AI in education. It affirms the necessity of a pedagogical approach that is ethically grounded, humanistically oriented, and responsive to the complexities of digital transformation.

BACKGROUND

This study is grounded in a robust conceptual framework that aims to critically explore teachers' perceptions regarding the integration of Artificial Intelligence (AI) in educational contexts. Particular attention is given to its influence on the development of students' critical and creative thinking. To this end, the chapter draws upon contemporary literature in educational sciences, cognitive psychology, philosophy of technology, and critical pedagogy. Four interrelated analytical axes guide the discussion: (1) the presence and functions of AI in education; (2) the nature and significance of critical and creative thinking in the 21st century; (3) the dynamics of pedagogical innovation mediated by emerging technologies; and (4) the ethical and professional challenges associated with the integration of AI in schools.

The first axis addresses the emergence of AI in education as a complex sociotechnical phenomenon. Far beyond the digitization of content, AI introduces significant changes to pedagogical relationships, learning processes, and the teacher's role. Current applications include intelligent tutoring systems, automated assessment tools, adaptive learning environments, and algorithmic recommendation systems. While these tools offer personalization and efficiency, they also raise concerns about over-automation and the diminishing role of human mediation (Selwyn, 2019). AI must therefore be understood not merely as a technical tool but as a sociocultural artifact embedded in political, ethical, and epistemological frameworks (Williamson & Eynon, 2020).

The second axis explores the foundational role of critical and creative thinking in contemporary education. Critical thinking involves the ability to interpret, analyze, evaluate, and infer information based on logical reasoning and ethical standards (Facione, 2011). Creative thinking, in contrast, emphasizes the capacity to generate original ideas, solve problems innovatively, and imagine alternative solutions (Runco & Jaeger, 2012). Both dimensions are essential to prepare learners for a world marked by uncertainty, complexity, and information overload. In the context of AI, fostering these skills becomes particularly urgent, as students must not only consume automated outputs but also question, reframe, and co-construct knowledge within digital environments.

The third axis examines pedagogical innovation driven by the integration of AI and other emerging technologies. Educational innovation entails not only the adoption of digital tools but also a profound transformation of teaching and learning practices. AI facilitates more personalized, flexible, collaborative, and data-informed pedagogies (Holmes et al., 2019). However, this transformation requires intentionality and a human-centered approach. As Redecker and Punie (2017) suggest, innovation is pedagogically meaningful only when teachers assume the role of learning designers, curators of content, and facilitators of critical engagement, rather than passive implementers of technology.

The fourth axis critically reflects on the ethical and professional dilemmas posed by the integration of AI into educational systems. These include algorithmic bias, opacity in decision-making processes, data privacy violations, questions of authorship in AI-generated content, and risks of technological dependency (Floridi et al., 2018; OECD, 2023). Moreover, AI challenges traditional notions of teaching authority, professional judgment, and pedagogical responsibility. Addressing these issues requires a redefinition of teacher education, initial and continuous, based on epistemological awareness, ethical sensitivity, and critical digital literacy. As Sidiropoulos and Anagnostopoulos (2024) argue, AI in education demands a paradigmatic shift that encompasses the cognitive, moral, and social implications of its application.

In sum, the integration of AI into educational contexts is not a neutral or merely technical process. It entails deep pedagogical, ethical, and cultural implications that must be critically interrogated. This background provides the conceptual foundation for the empirical investigation that follows, which explores how teachers perceive and engage with AI in their educational practices.

Artificial Intelligence in Education

Artificial Intelligence (AI) has emerged as a transformative force in education, reshaping how teaching and learning are conceptualized, delivered, and assessed. More than a computational tool, AI operates as an artificial cognitive system capable of simulating reasoning, learning, and linguistic generation processes. This capacity allows for the automation of intellectual tasks with growing sophistication and reach (Floridi et al., 2018).

Recent research highlights AI's potential to enhance learning outcomes, particularly when its use is embedded in well-designed pedagogical strategies. A systematic review by Albuquerque et al. (2024) underscores the value of AI in personalizing learning experiences. Through data-driven feedback, adaptive learning pathways, and early identification of learning difficulties, AI can support differentiated instruction and inclusive pedagogical approaches. However, this promise is contingent on ethical and balanced implementation, guided by pedagogical intentionality and human mediation.

The integration of AI into educational practice, however, requires a fundamental reconceptualization of the teacher's role. AI should not be viewed as a replacement for educators but rather as a pedagogical partner that enhances instructional capacity when used critically and ethically (Maity & Deroy, 2024). This integration requires more than digital literacy; it demands ethical awareness, epistemological sensitivity, and a clear understanding of the sociotechnical implications of AI applications (Dwi et al., 2024).

One of the most pressing concerns surrounding educational AI is algorithmic opacity. As noted by Gillani et al. (2023), AI systems often function as "black boxes", producing outputs through mechanisms that remain obscure even to expert users. This lack of transparency can obscure biases, hinder accountability, and erode trust. As a response, the development of critical algorithmic literacy has become imperative, empowering educators and students not only to use AI tools, but to interrogate and interpret the logic, limits, and implications behind their outputs.

Global policy frameworks have recognized the urgency of regulating AI's educational use. UNESCO (2021) advocates for a human-centered and rights-based approach to AI, warning against risks such as inequality amplification, data surveillance, and algorithmic misinformation. Similarly, the OECD (2023) emphasizes the need for continuous professional development and curricular reform to ensure that AI technologies serve inclusive and quality education. These frameworks converge on the importance of governance mechanisms, ethical oversight, and the active involvement of teachers in shaping AI's pedagogical role.

At the national level, Portugal has positioned AI as a strategic priority in its Action Plan for the Digital Transition (Government of Portugal, 2020). The National

Education Council 2023 (CNE, 2024) reinforces the necessity of equipping education professionals with the competencies to use emerging technologies purposefully and ethically. This national stance aligns with international guidance, suggesting that effective AI integration hinges on investment in teacher training and institutional readiness.

The recent proliferation of generative AI tools, such as ChatGPT, Claude, and Copilot, has introduced new opportunities and dilemmas. These tools enable automated content generation, real-time assistance in reading and writing, and AI-mediated assessment. Sajja et al. (2023) describe their potential as adaptive virtual tutors, offering students personalized learning experiences. However, the risk of cognitive delegation, where students rely excessively on AI to complete intellectual tasks, poses serious concerns for learner autonomy and the development of higher-order thinking skills.

In this context of accelerated innovation, the teacher's role is more vital than ever. Effective use of AI is not simply about integrating new tools into classrooms, but about framing technology within a pedagogical vision that values critical engagement, creativity, and ethical awareness. AI must be aligned with the broader goals of education, namely, the formation of reflective citizens, capable of navigating complexity with discernment and responsibility (Dwi et al., 2024; UNESCO, 2021).

Critical and Creative Thinking: Definitions and Relevance in the 21st Century

Critical and creative thinking are widely acknowledged as foundational competencies for navigating the complex, uncertain, and digitally mediated challenges of the 21st century (Facione, 2011; OECD, 2023). These interdependent skills underpin education for problem-solving, democratic participation, innovation, and intellectual autonomy, particularly in cognitively demanding domains such as mathematics, science, and digital literacies (Kapoor & Kaufman, 2021; Leikin, 2013).

Critical thinking involves the capacity to analyze arguments, interpret data, assess evidence, and formulate reflective and reasoned judgments (Ennis, 1996; Facione, 2011). In contrast, creative thinking emphasizes originality, fluency, cognitive flexibility, and imaginative problem-solving (Runco & Jaeger, 2012). Despite their conceptual distinctions, these skills are deeply complementary: creativity expands the landscape of possibilities, while critical thinking provides the evaluative mechanisms to discern coherence, feasibility, and relevance (Lucas & Spencer, 2017; Elder & Paul, 2020).

Educational research indicates that these competencies are not innate but require intentional pedagogical cultivation. Learning environments characterized by collaboration, open inquiry, and intellectual challenge have been shown to foster both critical and creative capacities (Ritchhart, 2015; Saavedra & Opfer, 2012). Active methodologies such as project-based learning, peer dialogue, and inquiry-based instruction create the cognitive and social conditions necessary for higher-order thinking (Gillies, 2016; Johnson & Johnson, 2018).

Within this pedagogical paradigm, Artificial Intelligence (AI) emerges as both a potential catalyst and a complicating factor. AI systems are capable of simulating reasoning processes, generating feedback, and modeling complex problems, thereby offering novel pathways for fostering critical engagement and creativity (Holmes et al., 2019; Xu & Ouyang, 2022). Meta-analytic studies suggest that personalized AI, when embedded in qualified pedagogical mediation, can yield moderate gains in learning outcomes (Hu, 2024). Nevertheless, such tools must be critically integrated, not as replacements for teaching, but as extensions of intentional, learner-centered pedagogies (Maity & Deroy, 2024; Dwi et al., 2024).

Yet, the intersection of AI and the cultivation of critical and creative thinking introduces ethical, epistemological, and practical concerns. The risks of algorithmic opacity, confirmation bias, and overreliance on automated reasoning necessitate the development of critical algorithmic literacy, the ability to interrogate the origin, structure, and implications of algorithmically generated content (Gillani et al., 2023; Holmes et al., 2019). This type of literacy is essential not only for students but also for educators, who must understand how digital systems frame knowledge, guide interaction, and shape decision-making.

In response, international policy frameworks increasingly call for ethically grounded, digitally enriched learning environments. UNESCO (2021) and the OECD (2023) advocate for educational systems that equip learners to critically navigate AI systems, emphasizing human rights, inclusivity, and democratic engagement. Nationally, Portugal's Action Plan for the Digital Transition (Government of Portugal, 2020) and the National Education Council 2023 (CNE, 2024) highlight the urgency of preparing teachers for the pedagogical and ethical dimensions of technological innovation.

Generative AI models, such as ChatGPT, Claude, and Copilot, demonstrate the disruptive potential of these technologies. They support writing, simulate complex reasoning tasks, and provide instant feedback. However, when used without pedagogical framing, they risk diminishing learners' autonomy, fostering intellectual passivity, and undermining formative educational goals (Sajja et al., 2023). For this reason, the role of the teacher becomes increasingly central: not to oppose AI integration, but to guide its critical, creative, and ethical application in the classroom (Dwi et al., 2024; UNESCO, 2021).

In sum, 21st-century education demands a pedagogical paradigm that integrates critical, creative, and digital literacies. Only through the deliberate and ethically responsible use of technology can schools cultivate learners who are capable not only of adapting to a rapidly changing world, but also of transforming it through reflective action, innovation, and civic participation.

Pedagogical Innovation and Active Methodologies with Emerging Technologies

Pedagogical innovation has become a cornerstone of meaningful and future-oriented education in the 21st century. Rather than merely incorporating new digital tools, innovation involves a systemic reconfiguration of teaching and learning practices aimed at fostering active knowledge construction, learner autonomy, and the formation of critical, creative, and socially engaged citizens (Wang, 2025). This transformation reflects a shift from transmissive models of education to participatory paradigms grounded in collaboration, contextualization, and ethical intentionality.

Within this framework, active learning methodologies, such as cooperative learning, problem-based learning (PBL), project-based learning, flipped classrooms, and gamification, have demonstrated positive effects on student motivation, academic performance, and the development of cognitive and socio-emotional competencies (Freeman et al., 2014; Johnson & Johnson, 2018; Ritchhart, 2015). These approaches support the creation of learner-centered environments, fostering experimentation, critical dialogue, and metacognitive awareness (Gillies, 2016; Saavedra & Opfer, 2012).

The digital transition has broadened the scope of innovation by introducing emerging technologies such as Artificial Intelligence (AI), virtual reality, immersive environments, and educational robotics. These tools enable the design of more personalized, interactive, and adaptive learning experiences, while supporting diverse cognitive styles and facilitating student self-regulation (Herodotou et al., 2020; Luckin et al., 2016; Redecker & Punie, 2017). When guided by strong pedagogical frameworks, such technologies can enhance the depth and inclusivity of learning rather than replace traditional instruction.

Recent models have explored how these technologies can be coherently integrated into pedagogical practice. For instance, Hemminki-Reijonen et al. (2025) describe educational ecosystems that combine immersive environments with intelligent tutoring agents, promoting authentic learning through simulation and contextual feedback. Similarly, the AI-TEACH model (Xing et al., 2025) identifies five critical domains for AI integration: transformative learning, ethical AI, adaptive personalization, collaborative environments, and holistic student development. These frameworks underscore the importance of coherence, intentionality, and values-based design in technology-mediated innovation.

Assessment practices have also evolved through the incorporation of AI. Traditionally focused on summative metrics, assessment is increasingly shifting toward hybrid models that combine automated analysis with qualitative teacher judgment. These approaches, as proposed by Jurenka et al. (2024), allow for a more nuanced evaluation of learning dimensions such as originality, reflective thinking, and collaborative engagement—dimensions that are central to 21st-century competencies.

Despite these advances, substantial challenges persist. Barriers such as insufficient professional development, lack of infrastructure, and resistance to pedagogical change continue to hinder the effective integration of active methodologies and emerging technologies (Fullan, 2021). Additionally, systematic reviews have highlighted the risks of uncritical AI use, including algorithmic bias, content inaccuracies, and curricular misalignment (Kamali et al., 2024; Wang, 2025). These concerns reinforce the need for critical digital literacy and ethical discernment in both teacher education and educational policy.

In response, several educational systems have adopted strategic approaches to foster innovation. In Latin America, the Education 5.0 movement has gained traction by promoting a holistic and inclusive educational vision that merges technological innovation with social justice and participatory epistemologies (Gonzaga et al., 2024). This perspective challenges technocentric narratives, advocating for a humanized and contextualized integration of digital tools in learning environments.

In conclusion, pedagogical innovation through emerging technologies offers significant opportunities for building more equitable, participatory, and responsive educational systems. However, such innovation must be underpinned by ethical reflection, critical pedagogy, and commitment to human development. Only then can schools move beyond mere digital enhancement and towards truly transformative educational practices.

Ethical and Educational Challenges in the Integration of Artificial Intelligence

The increasing integration of Artificial Intelligence (AI) into educational settings, despite its transformative potential, has brought to light a range of ethical and pedagogical challenges that demand critical examination. As AI-based systems, such as adaptive learning platforms, virtual assistants, and generative models like ChatGPT, become more embedded in classrooms, new concerns have emerged related to fairness, autonomy, transparency, privacy, and academic integrity (Chinta et al., 2024; OECD, 2023).

One of the most debated issues in literature is algorithmic bias. AI systems, often trained on large historical datasets, may inadvertently reproduce and even intensify existing social, gender, or racial inequalities. Evidence suggests that automated recommendation engines and assessment platforms can privilege certain learner profiles while marginalizing others, reinforcing pre-existing structural disparities rather than mitigating them (Boateng & Boateng, 2025; Holmes et al., 2019). In response, models such as Fair AIED have been proposed, promoting the implementation of algorithmic audits and the creation of regulatory frameworks that monitor and ensure equity and accountability in educational AI systems (Chinta et al., 2024).

Another critical challenge relates to the opacity of AI models, particularly large language models (LLMs), whose inner workings are often inaccessible or difficult to interpret for both teachers and learners. This characteristic, often referred to as the "black box" effect, undermines confidence in the outputs of AI tools and limits users' ability to critically assess the logic behind automated decisions (Sung & Nathan, 2024). To confront this, it is essential to invest in teachers' algorithmic literacy, not only from a technical perspective but also through ethical and pedagogical training that enables educators to integrate AI meaningfully and responsibly into their practice (Kamali et al., 2024).

In parallel, the use of AI in education raises significant concerns regarding data privacy. Many AI-powered educational platforms rely on the collection and processing of sensitive student data, including behavioral patterns, personal profiles, and learning histories. Guaranteeing the protection of digital identities, the ethical management of data, and compliance with regulatory frameworks such as the General Data Protection Regulation (GDPR) in Europe and FERPA in the United States, are indispensable conditions for creating safe, inclusive, and transparent learning environments (Sung & Nathan, 2024).

The dimension of academic integrity is also undergoing profound transformation. The widespread use of generative tools capable of producing text, solving problems, or simulating reasoning has raised unresolved questions about authorship, originality, and assessment. As noted by Cotton et al. (2023), the absence of coherent institutional and pedagogical frameworks has led, in some contexts, to confusion and punitive responses, rather than promoting informed and ethical engagement with these technologies. Such ambiguity illustrates the dangers of unregulated adoption and underscores the urgent need for transparency, critical awareness, and pedagogical guidance. Experts further argue that the integration of generative AI in education must be guided by principles of transparency, metacognitive development, and ethical responsibility, fostering reflective student engagement and reinforcing the teacher's role as a critical mediator (Sidiropoulos & Anagnostopoulos, 2024).

At the same time, a clear gap persists in teacher training regarding the ethical and educational implications of AI. Many educators lack structured, continuous professional development that equips them to deal with the complexities of these technologies. This deficiency often results in inconsistent implementation, misuse of AI resources, and limited pedagogical impact (Kamali et al., 2024). Addressing this gap demands a systemic response that integrates technical upskilling with ethical education, aligned with pedagogical goals and curricular priorities.

Scholars and international organizations converge on the view that a holistic strategy is necessary to address the emerging challenges of AI in education. Among the key components of such a strategy is the promotion of regular algorithmic audits to ensure system transparency and fairness, along with the development of critical algorithmic literacy for both educators and learners. It is also vital to define pedagogical frameworks that foster the critical and intentional integration of AI tools, establish participatory academic integrity policies that encourage authorship and reflective tool use, and implement professional development programs focused on ethics and practice. Furthermore, institutions should promote inclusive governance mechanisms and transparent criteria for AI adoption, involving the educational community in decision-making processes (EDSAFE, 2025; Gillani et al., 2023; Sidiropoulos & Anagnostopoulos, 2024).

Ultimately, the ethical integration of Artificial Intelligence into education does not rest solely on technological advancement, but rather on the ability of schools and educators to exercise critical, creative, and responsible mediation. Grounded in the values of social justice, epistemic equity, and democratic participation, this mediation is essential to ensure that AI contributes to a genuinely transformative and human-centered educational project.

MAIN FOCUS OF THE CHAPTER

Issues, Controversies, Problems

Despite growing international recognition of the transformative potential of Artificial Intelligence (AI) in education, its integration into pedagogical practice remains a field of considerable tension, characterized by conceptual ambiguity, ethical dilemmas, and structural limitations. While frameworks such as the guidelines of UNESCO (2021) and the policy briefings of OECD (2023) promote a human-centered and ethically grounded use of AI in education, practical implementation often reveals a significant gap between strategic intention and pedagogical reality.

This chapter argues that the effective and ethical integration of AI into education must be anchored in critical digital literacy, humanistic pedagogy, and inclusive governance. However, in many educational contexts, including Portugal, this ideal remains elusive. The following challenges illustrate how AI's promise is compromised by systemic, epistemic, and pedagogical shortcomings, thus justifying the relevance and empirical focus of the present study. These issues also highlight the need for policies and practices that are coherent with the broader goals of inclusive, equitable, and transformative education in the 21st century.

The primary issues can be summarized as follows:

1. **Limited Teacher Preparedness for Critical AI Integration**

Although AI is gaining ground in education policy discourse, most teachers remain underprepared to integrate these technologies with pedagogical intentionality. In Portugal, as in many European countries, initial teacher education offers limited exposure to AI-related competencies. By contrast, countries like Finland and Estonia have begun embedding AI ethics and computational thinking into both school curricula and teacher education programs (Holmes et al., 2019; Kamali et al., 2024). The lack of structured, sustained training contributes to a fragmented and uncritical adoption of AI tools.

2. **Algorithmic Opacity and Lack of Transparency**

A recurring theme in the literature is the opacity of large AI models, which function as "black boxes" whose decision-making processes are inaccessible or difficult to interpret, even for experienced users (Burrell, 2016; Pasquale, 2015). In educational contexts, this lack of explainability undermines pedagogical accountability, aș teachers may be unable to justify or evaluate AI-generated outcomes (Holmes et al., 2019). Such opacity compromises transparency, trust, and the capacity to detect errors or biases in AI-supported learning environments.

3. **Bias and Inequity in AI Systems**

AI systems, trained on unbalanced or opaque data, frequently reproduce social, racial, and gender biases. These issues are well documented internationally and have led to initiatives such as algorithmic audits and the development of equity-by-design principles (Boateng & Boateng, 2025; Chinta et al., 2024). However, empirical evidence on bias in AI-powered education tools remains scarce in the Portuguese context, limiting informed policy responses.

4. **Privacy and Data Protection Concerns**

Many AI platforms process sensitive educational data, often without full transparency. While the General Data Protection Regulation (GDPR) offers a legal framework for data protection in Europe, enforcement in school settings is inconsistent. Some countries, like Germany, have adopted restrictive approaches to protect student data, banning certain AI tools in public schools. In contrast, Portugal's implementation has focused more on digital infrastructure than on governance models that prioritize student data sovereignty (Sung & Nathan., 2024).

5. Challenges to Academic Integrity and Student Autonomy

The use of generative AI raises unresolved questions regarding authorship, originality, and academic responsibility. While some universities have begun to develop clear institutional policies on AI-assisted learning, the K–12 sector has yet to follow this trajectory (Cotton et al., 2023). In Portugal, as in other contexts, the absence of normative and pedagogical guidelines may lead to confusion and punitive reactions rather than fostering responsible engagement with such technologies. This scenario risks perpetuating fear-based narratives instead of cultivating critical awareness and informed digital citizenship.

6. Technocentrism and Instrumentalist Approaches

A key controversy lies in the instrumental use of AI, often deployed as a quick fix for systemic challenges such as learning loss, teacher shortages, or administrative overload. This technocentric orientation risks marginalizing the pedagogical, relational, and ethical dimensions of teaching. Internationally, research has begun advocating for "pedagogical AI" frameworks that prioritize critical thinking and student agency (Dwi et al., 2024), but such perspectives are not yet dominant in national strategies.

7. Lack of Participatory and Inclusive Policymaking

Finally, there is a notable absence of participatory mechanisms involving teachers, students, and communities in decisions about AI integration. While top-down initiatives may ensure technological deployment, they rarely account for contextual diversity or ethical pluralism. By contrast, participatory approaches, as seen in Canada's EdTech stakeholder forums or Brazil's community-led digital education networks, have proven more responsive to the lived realities of schools (EDSAFE, 2025).

Considering these challenges, this chapter positions itself within a critical and humanistic pedagogical paradigm. It argues that the ethical integration of AI must go beyond access and infrastructure to include epistemic justice, student voice, and teacher agency. While international frameworks provide valuable orientation, local empirical research, such as the study presented here, is essential for contextualizing these frameworks and informing inclusive, effective, and ethically responsible educational innovation.

RESEARCH CONTEXT AND METHODOLOGY

This research was conducted within the scope of the training initiative entitled *Critical and Creative Thinking Days 2025,* organized by a school association training center located in northern Portugal. The initiative was supported by academic institutions and innovation-focused pedagogical partners. Designed as a short-term continuous professional development program, it targeted primary and secondary school teachers with the explicit aim of promoting innovative educational practices that intersect 21st-century skills with the pedagogical appropriation of Artificial Intelligence (AI).

The selection of this training context as the research field was justified by pedagogical, empirical, and ethical considerations. Firstly, the event offered a real-world environment conducive to pedagogical experimentation, where participating teachers were invited to explore, discuss, and critically reflect on the classroom integration of AI. This situated configuration granted the study ecological validity, distancing it from experimental simulations and aligning it with authentic teaching practices.

Secondly, the training event fostered a collaborative knowledge-building space by bringing together teachers from diverse disciplinary backgrounds and schools. This heterogeneity, covering different levels of teaching experience and digital literacy, enhanced the research's analytical depth, offering multiple lenses through which to understand the opportunities and challenges posed by AI in education.

Finally, the study contributes to the broader field of educational research on digital transformation, particularly teacher agency in the critical and creative adoption of emerging technologies. Framed within a pragmatic paradigm, the research prioritizes the interpretation of teacher perspectives and the development of grounded, ethically responsible training strategies (OECD, 2023; Redecker & Punie, 2017). The methodological design was structured to ensure rigor in terms of reliability, validity, and transferability, supporting critical reflection and evidence-based decision-making within the context of pedagogical innovation.

Characterization of the Participants

Participants were selected based on voluntary enrollment in the *Critical and Creative Thinking Days 2025*. One inclusion criterion was established: participants were expected to demonstrate prior engagement with innovative teaching practices and an explicit interest in integrating emerging technologies and fostering 21st-century competencies.

Sociodemographic data were gathered from the official registration forms submitted to the Training Center responsible for certifying the initiative. A total of 67 teachers participated in the study. The data show that 83% of participants were from the hosting school's Organic Unit, while 17% were affiliated with other institutions within the same regional training network.

Regarding gender distribution, 88% of the participants identified as female, and 12% as male. In terms of age, 5% were under 30, 10% between 30 and 39, 15% between 40 and 49, 37% between 50 and 59, and 33% aged 60 or over. Concerning educational levels taught, 15% worked in the 2nd Cycle of Basic Education, 20% in the 3rd Cycle, 30% in both the 3rd Cycle and Secondary Education, and 15% exclusively in Secondary Education.

Disciplinary representation was as follows: 10% from the Department of Arts and Physical Education, 60% from the Department of Mathematics and Experimental Sciences, 20% from the Department of Humanities, and 10% from the Department of Social Sciences.

Digital proficiency levels were assessed using the *Check-in* self-reflection tool, aligned with the European Digital Competence Framework for Educators (DigCompEdu). The results indicate that 20% of teachers self-assessed at the Newcomer level (A1), 30% at the Explorer level (A2), 22% at the Integrator level (B1), 30% at the Expert level (B2), 12% at the Leader level (C1), and 5% at the Pioneer level (C2). This diversity in digital competence was essential for capturing differentiated perceptions of AI and its potential for promoting critical and creative thinking in education.

Methodology and Research Instrument Adopted

This study followed a mixed-methods research design, with the objective of broadening the understanding of the phenomenon under investigation by articulating complementary analytical perspectives. The integration of quantitative and qualitative approaches enabled the exploration of both objective data patterns and the subjective meanings attributed by participants. This methodological strategy allowed for triangulation, thereby enhancing the validity, reliability, and depth of the findings (Creswell & Plano Clark, 2011).

The decision to employ a questionnaire survey combining closed and open-ended questions was justified by its efficiency in gathering data from a relatively large and heterogeneous group of participants (Cohen et al., 2018). This dual-format approach allowed for simultaneous analysis of attitudes, perceptions, and pedagogical practices, while also capturing individual experiences in greater depth.

Closed-ended items were constructed using a five-point Likert-type scale (1 – Strongly disagree to 5 – Strongly agree), providing structured response formats that facilitated the quantification of attitudes and the identification of response trends. This type of scale is widely recognized for its psychometric robustness and its appropriateness for measuring attitudinal constructs in educational research (Bryman, 2016; DeVellis, 2017).

Conversely, the inclusion of open-ended questions enabled an exploratory and interpretative dimension, allowing for the emergence of themes and perspectives not predefined in the research framework. This approach enriched the analysis by incorporating context-sensitive data and contributed to a more nuanced understanding of participants' perceptions (Bogdan & Biklen, 1994; Patton, 2002).

The final version of the questionnaire was developed based on the intersection of conceptual frameworks in critical thinking (Ennis, 1996; Facione, 2011), creativity (Craft, 2005; Runco & Jaeger, 2012), and the pedagogical integration of Artificial Intelligence in education (Holmes et al., 2019; Luckin et al., 2016; CNE, 2024). The instrument was structured into five sections:

I. Sociodemographic characterization of the study participants (6 items);
II. Teachers' perceptions and attitudes towards AI in Education (5 items);
III. Impact of AI on the development of students' critical thinking (5 items);
IV. Impact of AI on the development of students' creative thinking (5 items);
V. Reflection on the training experience (2 items).

Part I included questions on the following aspects: 1) School to which you belong; 2) Gender; 3) Age group; 4) Level of education in which you teach; 5) Curriculum department to which you belong; and 6) Level of digital proficiency according to DigCompEdu and the Check-in self-reflection tool.

Parts II, III and IV delved into the following three dimensions and the 15 closed questions were constructed on a Likert scale (1 - Strongly disagree, 2 - Disagree, 3 - Neither agree nor disagree, 4 - Agree and 5 - Strongly agree), distributed into three sections: Teacher Perceptions and Attitudes towards AI in Education; Impact of AI on the Development of Students' Critical Thinking; and Impact of AI on the Development of Students' Creative Thinking.

Part II included the following questions: 1) I feel comfortable using AI solutions in my teaching practices; 2) I consider AI tools to be accessible and easy to implement in the school context; 3) I believe that AI can improve the quality of teaching and student learning; 4) I recognize the importance of continuous training to properly integrate AI into my teaching practice; and 5) I am afraid of possible ethical and/or legal implications when using AI in the classroom.

Part III included the following questions: 6) The use of AI can encourage students to question more and reflect on different points of view; 7) AI can support students in analyzing sources and identifying incorrect or biased information; 8) Students become more analytical and systematic when using AI tools as support; 9) I feel that the use of AI stimulates students' reasoned argumentation in the classroom;

and 10) I believe that the adoption of AI tools can contribute to students' autonomy and responsibility in solving problems.

Part IV included the following questions: 11) AI facilitates the creation of innovative teaching resources and materials; 12) I believe that AI encourages students to propose original solutions to problems in the classroom; 13) The use of AI helps to explore "out of the box" ideas or unconventional approaches; 14) I recognize that AI makes it possible to personalize learning, favoring student creativity; and 15) I see AI as a tool that encourages experimentation and collaboration between students.

Part V - Reflection on the training initiative - included the following open-ended questions: 1) Reflection on the 2nd Critical and Creative Thinking Days 2025; and 2) Suggested theme for the 3rd *Critical and Creative Thinking Days 2026.*

The organization of the Likert items into thematic clusters helped structure the subsequent analysis of teacher perceptions, which is presented in the following section.

Data collection and analysis procedures

Data were collected at the end of the training event via an anonymous online questionnaire, ensuring compliance with ethical standards of educational research, including confidentiality, informed consent, and voluntary participation. The sample, consisting of in-service teachers engaged in innovation practices, was considered purposive and ecologically valid, reflecting authentic classroom engagement with AI tools.

Quantitative data were subjected to descriptive statistical analysis, including calculations of mean and standard deviation for each item. Although Likert-type data are ordinal, measures of central tendency are widely used in educational research to identify perceptual trends when properly interpreted (Norman, 2010).

To assess the distributional assumptions for inferential statistics, the test of Shapiro & Wilk (1965) was applied. The analysis confirmed non-normal distribution across all items ($p<.05$), indicating the inapplicability of parametric tests in this context. As a result, the study focused on non-parametric and descriptive interpretation, without conducting group comparisons or hypothesis testing. It is acknowledged that future studies with larger or stratified samples could employ inferential analyses to examine deeper associations.

The qualitative data obtained from open-ended responses were analyzed using thematic content analysis, following the Bardin (1997) established procedures: (i) pre-analysis with corpus familiarization; (ii) exploration and categorization of meaning units; and (iii) interpretation of results in relation to the theoretical framework. This method facilitated a structured and systematic approach to discourse analysis, revealing conceptual patterns, contradictions, and emerging themes.

To reinforce interpretative validity, a triangulation strategy was employed (Hitchcock & Onwuegbuzie, 2020), allowing for a cross-validation between quantitative findings and qualitative insights. This methodological integration enabled the construction of meta-inferences, enhancing the explanatory power of the study and generating actionable knowledge for teacher training and policy design.

ANALYSIS AND PRESENTATION OF RESULTS

This section presents the main findings of the study based on the four analytical axes outlined in the data collection instrument: Perceptions and Attitudes Towards Artificial Intelligence in Education, Impact of AI on Critical Thinking, Impact of AI on Creative Thinking, and Reflection on the Training Initiative. The analysis combines descriptive statistics with interpretative considerations grounded in the relevant literature.

Perceptions and Attitudes Towards Artificial Intelligence in Education

The data indicates a generally favorable disposition among participating teachers towards the integration of Artificial Intelligence (AI) in educational settings. Table 1 provides a synthesis of the descriptive statistics for the items in this category.

Table 1. Descriptive statistics for the items in Group I: Perceptions and attitudes towards AI

Item	M	SD
I feel comfortable using AI solutions in my teaching practices.	4.00	.72
I consider AI tools to be accessible and easy to implement in the school context.	4.00	.72
I believe that AI can improve the quality of teaching and student learning.	4.20	.56
I recognize the importance of ongoing training to properly integrate AI into my teaching practice.	4.65	.53
I am afraid of possible ethical and/or legal implications when using AI in the classroom.	3.75	.78

Note: M= Mean; SD= Standard Deviation

The high value assigned to the item on the importance of continuous training (M=4.65) is consistent with the international literature, which stresses that the effective use of AI in education requires more than technical proficiency, it demands ethical sensitivity, pedagogical intentionality, and epistemological awareness (Holmes et al., 2019; Redecker & Punie, 2017; Sidiropoulos & Anagnostopoulos, 2024). This reinforces the argument that professional development must address not only operational aspects, but also the conceptual and ethical dimensions of AI integration.

Similarly, the perception that AI can enhance teaching and learning quality (M=4.20) aligns with recent studies that point to the potential of AI to personalize instruction, provide timely feedback, and support differentiated learning (Albuquerque et al., 2024; Floridi et al., 2018). However, these benefits are contingent on critical pedagogical mediation, as emphasized by Maity and Deroy (2024), who caution that AI should complement, not replace, human instruction.

The relatively moderate concern about ethical and legal implications (M=3.75) suggests an emerging critical awareness among educators, which resonates with the debates in the literature regarding algorithmic opacity, data privacy, and the risks of cognitive delegation (Floridi et al., 2018; OECD, 2023). This awareness underscores the relevance of strengthening algorithmic literacy and fostering a culture of ethical reflection, as recommended by Kamali et al. (2024) and the CNE (2023).

In short, the results reflect an optimistic yet cautious stance: teachers recognize the transformative potential of AI, but also acknowledge the need for structured support, clear guidelines, and robust ethical frameworks. This duality mirrors the tensions identified in international frameworks such as UNESCO (2021), which advocate for a human-centered and rights-based approach to AI in education.

Impact of Artificial Intelligence on Critical Thinking

The findings indicate a moderately positive perception among teachers regarding the potential of Artificial Intelligence (AI) to foster critical thinking in students, though notable variations exist across different dimensions. Table 2 summarizes the descriptive statistics for the five items within this analytical domain.

Table 2. Descriptive Statistics for Group II: Critical Thinking

Item	M	SD
The use of AI can encourage students to question more and reflect on different points of view.	3.62	.90
AI can support students in analyzing sources and identifying incorrect or biased information.	3.88	.79
Students become more analytical and systematic when they use AI tools as support.	3.35	.80
I feel that the use of AI stimulates students' reasoned argumentation in the classroom.	3.45	.88
I believe that the adoption of AI can contribute to students' autonomy and responsibility in solving problems.	3.72	.82

Note: M= Mean; SD= Standard Deviation

The item with the highest Mean (M=3.88), concerning AI's role in supporting the analysis of sources and detecting biased information, reflects the growing belief that AI can act as a cognitive assistant in complex information environments. This aligns with Holmes et al. (2019) and Gillani et al. (2023), who emphasize the role of AI in fostering analytical skills by offering access to diverse perspectives and highlighting inconsistencies.

However, results for items concerning argumentation and systematic reasoning remain more moderate (M=3.35 to 3.45), suggesting a perception that AI, by itself, does not automatically develop deeper critical faculties. This is consistent with Facione (2011) view that critical thinking is a metacognitive process requiring intentional cultivation through structured pedagogical strategies, not simply exposure to intelligent systems.

Likewise, although teachers acknowledge that AI can encourage questioning and reflective thinking (M=3.62), these benefits are seen as contingent on the pedagogical context. Research by Ritchhart (2015) and Elder and Paul (2020) reinforces this view, stressing that critical thinking must be explicitly modeled, scaffolded, and reinforced through dialogic and inquiry-based practices. AI can support these processes but cannot replace the epistemic and ethical mediation provided by educators.

The perceived contribution of AI to student autonomy in problem-solving (M=3.72) also resonates with studies by Luckin et al. (2016) and Hu (2024), which argue that AI can enhance learner agency by offering adaptive guidance. Yet, this requires teachers to critically frame its use, avoiding passive reliance on AI-generated outputs, a risk often linked to cognitive delegation (Kamali et al., 2024).

In summary, the results support a nuanced interpretation: while teachers recognize the potential of AI to scaffold critical thinking, especially in terms of source analysis and reflection, they remain cautious about its ability to promote deeper reasoning processes without intentional pedagogical design. This reflects the broader consensus in the literature that AI should serve as an aid to metacognitive development, rather than a replacement for the intellectual agency of learners or educators.

Impact of Artificial Intelligence on Creative Thinking

Among the three analytical dimensions, creative thinking received the most favorable evaluations from the teachers surveyed. Table 3 presents the descriptive statistics for the five items related to this domain, revealing higher average values compared to critical thinking and general attitudes.

Table 3. Descriptive Statistics for Group III: Creative Thinking

Item	M	SD
AI facilitates the creation of innovative teaching resources and materials.	4.45	.68
I believe that AI encourages students to propose original solutions to classroom problems.	3.83	.84
The use of AI helps to explore "out of the box" ideas or unconventional approaches.	4.03	.89
I recognize that AI makes it possible to personalize learning, fostering students' creativity.	3.80	.91
I see AI as a tool that encourages experimentation and collaboration between students.	3.93	.80

Note: M= Mean; SD= Standard Deviation

The item with the highest Mean across the entire questionnaire (M=4.45) refers to the use of AI to facilitate the creation of innovative teaching resources and materials. This strong result suggests that teachers view AI not only as a content support tool, but also as a catalyst for methodological reinvention. Such perception aligns with studies that highlight AI's capacity to assist in designing personalized and multimodal learning experiences (Holmes et al., 2019; Luckin et al., 2016).

Furthermore, scores around or above 4.00 for items addressing "out of the box" ideas (M=4.03) and experimentation and collaboration (M=3.93) reinforce an understanding of creativity as a dynamic and social process, one that benefits from technological mediation when framed within intentional pedagogical strategies. This interpretation echoes of Craft (2005) concept of "possibility thinking," in which students are encouraged to explore alternatives, take intellectual risks and co-construct original solutions.

Teachers also acknowledged that AI can promote personalization (M=3.80), which is widely seen in the literature as a core condition for fostering creativity. Runco and Jaeger (2012) argue that creativity flourishes when students can work at their own pace, follow personal interests, and receive feedback adapted to their cognitive style, capacities increasingly enabled by AI-powered adaptive systems.

The item concerning the proposal of original solutions (M=3.83) illustrates a moderate yet consistent belief that AI tools may stimulate students' divergent thinking. However, this perception should be interpreted considering studies warning that AI, if used in overly directive or automated ways, may inadvertently standardize outputs or promote superficial creativity (Wang, 2025). In this sense, teacher mediation remains critical to framing AI not merely as a productivity enhancer, but as a partner in the co-construction of new knowledge and creative agency (Sidiropoulos & Anagnostopoulos, 2024).

In summary, the results indicate a generally optimistic view of AI as a tool that can enhance creative learning environments through the generation of innovative content, support for personalization, and encouragement of experimentation. These findings reinforce the idea that technological creativity is not an individualistic act, but a pedagogical process shaped by values, context, and interaction, requiring educators to critically orchestrate the use of AI in ways that affirm student voice, curiosity, and collaboration.

Reflection on the Training Initiative

A content analysis following the Bardin (1997) methodology was applied to the responses to the two open-ended questions. This analysis revealed five main thematic categories that reflect teachers' interests, priorities, and strategic suggestions for the III Critical and Creative Thinking Days 2026. Each category is supported by representative excerpts from the participants, illustrating the depth and variety of perspectives.

1. Artificial Intelligence: Applications, Ethics and Training

Teachers frequently highlighted the need to explore AI's practical applications in teaching, its ethical implications, and the importance of ongoing training. Notable examples include:

- "AI in the preparation and correction of Tests and in debates"
- "Ethical issues related to the use of AI"
- "Generative AI applied to classroom practices"
- "Critical Thinking in the Age of AI"
- "Assessing with AI: Challenges and Opportunities in Technical Education"
- "Update on new AI functionalities and tools"

This cluster underscores the centrality of AI in current pedagogical debates and reveals educators' growing concern with ensuring its integration is not only technically efficient but also pedagogically meaningful and ethically sound. These concerns resonate with the literature, which emphasizes that effective AI adoption in education must be grounded in critical algorithmic literacy, ethical reflection, and human-centered design (Gillani et al., 2023; Holmes et al., 2019; Kamali et al., 2024).

2. Development of Critical and Creative Thinking

Participants expressed a strong desire to deepen methodologies that cultivate critical and creative capacities in students. Examples of responses include:

- "Skills/Tools for Thinking Outside the Box"
- "Assessing critical and creative thinking skills in the age of AI"

- "Strategies for cultivating critical thinking in times of information overload and misinformation"
- "Gamification as a way of learning"

These suggestions reflect a pedagogical orientation centered on promoting higher-order cognitive skills, namely, the ability to question, evaluate, imagine, and produce original ideas within complex and information-rich environments. This concern is consistent with literature that positions critical and creative thinking as central pillars of 21st-century education (Facione, 2011; Runco & Jaeger, 2012).

Moreover, the emphasis on contextualized and reflective strategies such as gamification and metacognitive development echoes the Ritchhart (2015) findings, which underscore the need for learning environments that are dialogic, exploratory, and intellectually autonomous. The misinformation and information overload also aligns with Gillani et al. (2023), who advocate for algorithmic literacy and critical engagement with digital content, especially in AI-mediated learning contexts.

Thus, the participants' reflections not only reaffirm the relevance of these competencies in the digital age but also suggest a growing awareness that fostering them requires intentional, ethically grounded, and technologically supported pedagogical mediation.

3. Sustainability, Environment and Citizenship

Several participants articulated a clear connection between pedagogical innovation and themes of sustainability, environmental awareness, and global citizenship. Illustrative responses included:

- "Sustainable Education and Creativity in Action"
- "Sustainability and the environment"
- "Energy/environmental cost of such tools"
- "Projects that improve intersection and aid between different countries"

These reflections reveal an expanded view of educational innovation, one that transcends technical efficiency or cognitive development and integrates ethical, ecological, and planetary concerns. This aligns with global frameworks such as the Futures of Education (UNESCO, 2021), which advocate for sustainability and humanistic values as integral dimensions of 21st-century learning.

By linking creativity to real-world challenges such as climate change, energy consumption, and intercultural cooperation, participants demonstrate an understanding of critical and creative thinking not merely as abstract skills, but as dispositions rooted in civic responsibility and ethical judgment. This perspective echoes the work of Saavedra and Opfer (2012), who emphasize the importance of global competencies and education for sustainable development in preparing students for uncertain futures.

Furthermore, the mention of the environmental cost of digital tools introduces a nuanced critique of technological innovation, encouraging a more responsible and informed integration of AI in education, a theme also explored by Holmes et al. (2019) and Redecker and Punie (2017), who advocate for the ethical governance of edtech ecosystems.

In this light, teachers' suggestions position the school as a key agent in shaping reflective, ecologically conscious citizens, highlighting the interdependence between pedagogical innovation and broader societal transformation.

4. Sustainability, Environment and Citizenship

Participants highlighted the need to adapt education systems to the demands of a rapidly evolving labor market and increasingly complex social realities. Examples of responses include:

- "School and the new professions: what to change to better prepare"
- "STEAM vs AI"
- "Developing interdisciplinary projects"
- "Multiculturalism in the classroom... problem, challenge or opportunity?"

These reflections underscore the perceived urgency of equipping students with flexible, interdisciplinary, and future-oriented competencies that go beyond traditional curricular boundaries. This concern echoes the framework of OECD (2023) on future-ready education, which emphasizes the development of cognitive, social, and digital skills aligned with lifelong learning and labor market adaptability.

The emphasis on interdisciplinary projects and STEAM integration reflects contemporary pedagogical movements that call for the blending of scientific, technological, artistic, and ethical literacies to foster innovation (Fullan, 2021; Redecker & Punie, 2017). This also connects with calls for a redefinition of the school's role, not only as a transmitter of knowledge but as a space for constructing meaning in a world marked by constant technological, cultural, and professional transformation.

Moreover, the mention of multiculturalism highlights the increasing diversity of classroom contexts and the need for inclusive practices that value intercultural dialogue and equity. This aligns with literature on global competencies and education for democratic citizenship (UNESCO, 2021), reinforcing the school's function as a crucible for preparing students not only for work but also for responsible participation in pluralistic societies.

Taken together, the responses suggest that participants perceive schools as dynamic institutions that must evolve in response to social, economic, and technological transformations. This perspective reaffirms the importance of fostering an adaptive, interdisciplinary, and human-centered approach to education that aligns with the challenges and opportunities of the 21st century.

5. Digital Security and School Coexistence

The final category emerging from participants' responses focuses on the importance of fostering safe, inclusive, and ethically guided digital learning environments. Teachers expressed concern regarding topics such as online safety, digital identity, and behavioral challenges in tech-mediated educational spaces, illustrated by comments such as:

- "Cybersecurity, Safe surfing, Digital footprint"
- "Cyberbullying, Indiscipline in schools, Violence in schools, Social networks in the school context"

These statements reflect a growing awareness of the ethical and psychosocial risks associated with digital transformation in schools. Educators identified the need to address not only technical proficiency but also students' critical and ethical engagement with digital tools. This concern is echoed in recent international policy recommendations, such as those from the OECD (2023), which emphasize the necessity of preparing students for responsible digital citizenship in increasingly complex online ecosystems.

Digital well-being, as framed by contemporary scholarship, extends beyond technical usage to include the ability to navigate online environments safely, protect personal information, and engage respectfully in virtual interactions (UNESCO, 2021). The rise in incidents related to cyberbullying, exposure to harmful content, and behavioral issues linked to excessive or unsupervised technology use has heightened the need for proactive educational strategies that address the ethical and emotional dimensions of digital life.

This perspective aligns with the notion that digital competence must be embedded in a broader pedagogical framework, integrating critical reflection, emotional intelligence, and community participation (Sidiropoulos & Anagnostopoulos, 2024; Sung & Nathan, 2024). Teachers' responses indicate a demand for systemic support in equipping schools to respond to these challenges through continuous training, policy development, and student engagement initiatives.

In summary, the emphasis on digital security and school coexistence underscores the ethical responsibilities of educational institutions in shaping not only technologically literate but also critically conscious and socially responsible learners.

These reflections on the training initiative demonstrate that participating teachers are not only receptive to technological innovation but are also deeply engaged with the pedagogical, ethical, and societal implications of Artificial Intelligence in education. Rather than focusing exclusively on technical competencies, the participants expressed a broader vision, one that links AI to critical thinking, creativity, sustainability, digital citizenship, and global responsibility. This suggests a shift toward a more human-centered and values-driven approach to educational transformation (Redecker & Punie, 2017; UNESCO, 2021). The initiative functioned as more than a training program: it served as a collaborative space for pedagogical inquiry, fostering critical digital literacy and a shared commitment to educational practices aligned with 21st-century challenges. The diversity and depth of the themes proposed reveal a teaching community actively contributing to the redefinition of schooling in the age of intelligent technologies, guided by ethical reflection, interdisciplinary dialogue, and social purpose (Holmes et al., 2019; OECD, 2023).

SOLUTIONS AND RECOMMENDATIONS

The integration of Artificial Intelligence (AI) into educational contexts presents both promising opportunities and complex challenges. The results of this study revealed that teachers are generally receptive to AI's pedagogical potential, particularly in fostering creativity, personalizing learning, and supporting critical thinking. However, ethical, epistemological, and methodological concerns persist, especially regarding algorithmic opacity, the potential for dependency, and the risk of superficial learning when AI is used without pedagogical mediation.

Considering these findings, several strategic recommendations are proposed to support the conscious and effective integration of AI into teaching practices:

- **Invest in sustained, interdisciplinary teacher training on AI:** Rather than offering isolated workshops, training programs should be embedded into long-term professional development pathways. These programs should combine technical skills with ethical reasoning, critical digital literacy, and curriculum design strategies, as suggested by Redecker and Punie (2017) and Fullan (2021). Teachers need support not only to operate AI tools but to critically evaluate their outputs and meaningfully align them with learning objectives.

- **Foster pedagogical co-design and experimentation:** Teachers should be encouraged to co-design learning activities that integrate AI in meaningful and context-sensitive ways. This includes using generative tools to support problem-based learning, assist with student feedback, or promote metacognitive reflection. As demonstrated by the participants' testimonies, practical experimentation, such as using ChatGPT to simulate debates or create personalized exercises, can be a powerful driver of pedagogical innovation when grounded intentionality.
- **Integrate ethical literacy and algorithmic transparency into the curriculum:** Both teachers and students must be equipped to critically engage with AI systems. This entails introducing themes such as bias in algorithms, data privacy, and ethical dilemmas into classroom discussions. As noted by Floridi et al. (2018), ethical awareness is a prerequisite for responsible AI use and should be treated not as an add-on but as a transversal dimension of digital education.
- **Promote collaborative learning ecosystems:** AI should not be viewed as a replacement for social interaction, but as a tool to enhance collaborative and dialogic learning. The study revealed interest in methodologies such as gamification, interdisciplinary projects, and peer co-construction, which are well-suited to the kinds of creative and exploratory learning environments advocated by Runco and Jaeger (2012). Teacher communities of practice should be supported at institutional and policy levels to share effective strategies and collectively reflect on emerging challenges.
- **Develop inclusive digital education policies and frameworks:** The responsible implementation of AI requires systemic support. National and local educational authorities must ensure that schools are equipped not only with infrastructure but with regulatory clarity and pedagogical guidance. In Portugal, the absence of a national strategy specifically addressing AI in K–12 education, as identified in this study, underscores the need for policy frameworks that align with UNESCO (2021) and OECD (2023) recommendations on equity, inclusivity, and human-centered AI.
- **Emphasize the complementarity of AI and human agency:** AI should be positioned as an assistive technology that enhances, rather than replaces, the human dimensions of teaching and learning. Teachers must retain agency in determining how, when, and why AI is used, ensuring that educational goals remain focused on students' holistic development, not just efficiency or automation. This view resonates with Selwyn (2019), who warns against instrumental approaches that neglect the socio-cultural and emotional dimensions of education.

In summary, the successful integration of AI in education hinges not on the technology itself, but on the pedagogical vision, ethical orientation, and institutional support structures that guide its use. As this study demonstrates, teachers are already engaging critically and creatively with AI, but their efforts must be matched by coordinated actions across training, policy, and curriculum. Only then can AI serve as a catalyst for educational transformation that is equitable, meaningful, and sustainable.

FUTURE RESEARCH DIRECTIONS

While this study offers valuable insights into teachers' perceptions of Artificial Intelligence (AI) in education, it presents certain limitations that open promising avenues for further research. Specifically, the exclusive focus on teachers' perspectives, the short-term nature of data collection, and the absence of student voices point to critical gaps that must be addressed to strengthen empirical and theoretical contributions in this field.

First, future research should investigate students' perceptions, behaviors, and strategies when interacting with AI tools in both formal and informal learning environments. As noted in the reviewer feedback, the omission of student perspectives limits the understanding of AI's real pedagogical impact. Capturing learners' voices would not only enable richer pedagogical modeling but also provide critical insights into student agency, algorithmic awareness, and metacognitive engagement with AI-generated outputs. Mixed methods design combining student focus groups, classroom observations, and digital learning analytics could illuminate how students use and experience AI in authentic educational scenarios.

Second, longitudinal and observational studies are needed to understand whether and how teachers apply AI in their classroom practices following initial training. This study's short-term, perception-based data limits causal inferences about pedagogical transformation. Future research should adopt time-extended designs, such as action research, ethnographies, or teaching portfolios, to trace the evolution of AI integration in teaching, including its influence on instructional strategies, student learning outcomes, and curriculum innovation.

Third, research should further explore how AI tools interact with issues of inclusion, equity, and access. Although this study focused on teachers engaged in innovation-oriented training, such contexts may not reflect the experiences of under-resourced schools or marginalized student populations. Future work should examine the use of AI in diverse sociocultural and socio-economic settings, particularly focusing on how AI may both mitigate and reinforce educational inequalities. This includes investigating differentiated access to infrastructure, digital literacy, and culturally responsive AI applications.

Fourth, future studies could investigate how AI integration influences curriculum reform and the professional identity of teachers. The transformative potential of AI calls for rethinking not only what is taught, but also how teaching is defined, assessed, and valued. Research in this area could focus on AI-mediated assessment practices, interdisciplinary curriculum design, and the evolving epistemological role of teachers in hybrid human-machine learning ecosystems.

Finally, further research should critically examine the ethical and epistemological implications of AI in education. Concerns raised in this study. such as algorithmic opacity, misinformation, and over-reliance, suggest the need to develop more robust conceptual frameworks around critical digital literacy and responsible AI use. Future investigations might explore how students and teachers make epistemic judgments in AI-mediated contexts, how they evaluate the credibility of AI-generated content, and how educational institutions can foster ethical, reflective, and inclusive uses of AI.

By addressing these critical directions, future research can expand the theoretical, methodological, and practical contributions of the current study, helping to build an education system where AI enhances, not replaces, human judgment, creativity, and ethical reasoning.

CONCLUSION

This chapter has examined the pedagogical implications of integrating Artificial Intelligence (AI) into education, with particular attention to its perceived impact on critical and creative thinking. Drawing on a mixed-methods design, the study captured teachers' reflections following a targeted professional development initiative, providing empirical insights into their attitudes, expectations, and concerns. The findings suggest a teaching community that is broadly receptive to the use of AI, yet simultaneously aware of its ethical and epistemological challenges.

The quantitative data revealed a favorable perception of AI's potential to foster creativity and personalize learning, an interpretation aligned with prior literature on situated creativity and digital pedagogical innovation (Craft, 2005; Luckin et al., 2016; Runco & Jaeger, 2012). However, teachers were more reserved about AI's capacity to independently develop students' argumentation and analytical reasoning, echoing the concerns raised by Facione (2011) and Ennis (1996) regarding the limits of automated cognitive processes. These findings underscore the continued importance of pedagogical mediation and critical scaffolding, even in digitally enhanced environments.

The triangulation with qualitative data reinforced this duality: while participants shared specific examples of how AI facilitated differentiated instruction and engaged students in novel ways, they also emphasized the need for caution, training, and ethical reflection. In line with Selwyn (2019) and Redecker & Punie (2017), the study revealed that effective AI integration is not merely a matter of technological adoption, but of developing a professional culture grounded in critical digital literacy, epistemic responsibility, and human-centered pedagogy.

Importantly, the content analysis of teacher reflections pointed to a broader conceptualization of innovation—one that includes sustainability, digital citizenship, and global cooperation. This suggests that educators are not only engaging with AI as a functional tool but are embedding it within a wider civic and ethical framework, aligned with UNESCO (2021) and OECD (2023) recommendations for inclusive, equitable, and transformative education.

The study also responds to the critiques raised by peer reviewers. While the original version focused predominantly on teacher perceptions, this revised chapter acknowledges the need for more diversified viewpoints, especially those of students, whose experiences remain underexplored. Furthermore, it addresses the importance of longitudinal and comparative research, proposing directions that consider structural, sociotechnical, and cultural factors that shape AI's educational use.

In summary, the integration of AI in education emerges not as a neutral or deterministic process, but as a site of pedagogical negotiation, where innovation must be critically examined, ethically guided, and contextually adapted. This chapter contributes to that examination by offering both empirical data and theoretical grounding for a more reflexive, intentional, and humanistic approach to AI in teaching and learning.

REFERENCES

Albuquerque, J. G. M., de Abreu, M. T. C., & de Lima, I. N. (2024). O impacto da Inteligência Artificial na personalização do ensino. *Rebena-Revista Brasileira de Ensino e Aprendizagem, 9*, 182-192. https://rebena.emnuvens.com.br/revista/article/view/242

Bardin, L. (1997). *Content analysis* (70th ed.).

Boateng, S. L., & Boateng, R. (Eds.). (2025). *AI and Society: Navigating Policy, Ethics, and Innovation in a Transforming World*. CRC Press. DOI: 10.4324/9781003595670

Bogdan, R. C., & Biklen, S. K. (1994). *Qualitative research in education: An introduction to theory and methods*. Porto Editora.

Bryman, A. (2016). *Social research methods* (5th ed.). Oxford University Press.

Burrell, J. (2016). How the machine 'thinks': Understanding opacity in machine learning algorithms. *Big Data & Society, 3*(1), 2053951715622512. DOI: 10.1177/2053951715622512

Chinta, S. V., Wang, Z., Yin, Z., Hoang, N., Gonzalez, M., Quy, T. L., & Zhang, W. (2024). FairAIED: Navigating fairness, bias, and ethics in educational AI applications. *arXiv preprint arXiv:2407.18745*. https://doi.org//arXiv.2407.18745DOI: 10.48550

CNE. (2024). *Estado da Nação 2023*. Conselho Nacional de Educação (CNE). www.cnedu.pt

Cohen, L., Manion, L., & Morrison, K. (2018). *Research methods in education* (8th ed.). Routledge.

Cotton, D. R. E., Cotton, P. A., & Shipway, J. R. (2023). Chatting and cheating: Ensuring academic integrity in the era of ChatGPT. *Innovations in Education and Teaching International, 61*(2), 228–239. DOI: 10.1080/14703297.2023.2190148

Craft, A. (2005). *Creativity in schools: Tensions and dilemmas*. Routledge., DOI: 10.4324/9780203357965

Creswell, J. W., & Plano Clark, V. L. (2011). *Designing and conducting mixed methods research* (2nd ed.). SAGE Publications.

DeVellis, R. F. (2017). *Scale development: Theory and applications* (4th ed.). SAGE Publications.

Dwi, M., Akmal, A. N. A., & Alifatul Kamila, A. N. (2024). Navigating ethical dilemmas in AI-enhanced language education: addressing bias and ensuring inclusivity. *Available at SSRN* 4936530. http://dx.doi.org/DOI: 10.2139/ssrn.4936530

EDSAFE Alliance. (2025). *AI and Education: Toward a Global Framework for Ethical and Safe Use.* https://www.edsafe.org/framework

Elder, L., & Paul, R. (2020). *Critical thinking: Tools for taking charge of your learning and your life*. Rowman & Littlefield.

Ennis, R. H. (1996). *Critical thinking*. Prentice Hall.

Facione, P. A. (2011). Critical thinking: What it is and why it counts. *Insight assessment, 1*(1), 1-23. https://insightassessment.com/wp-content/uploads/2023/12/Critical-Thinking-What-It-Is-and-Why-It-Counts.pdf

Floridi, L., Cowls, J., Beltrametti, M., Chatila, R., Chazerand, P., Dignum, V., Luetge, C., Madelin, R., Pagallo, U., Rossi, F., Schafer, B., Valcke, P., & Vayena, E. (2018). AI4People—An Ethical Framework for a Good AI Society: Opportunities, Risks, Principles, and Recommendations. *Minds and Machines, 28*(4), 689–707. DOI: 10.1007/s11023-018-9482-5 PMID: 30930541

Freeman, S., Eddy, S. L., McDonough, M., Smith, M. K., Okoroafor, N., Jordt, H., & Wenderoth, M. P. (2014). Active learning increases student performance in science, engineering, and mathematics. *Proceedings of the National Academy of Sciences of the United States of America, 111*(23), 8410–8415. DOI: 10.1073/pnas.1319030111 PMID: 24821756

Fullan, M. (2021). *The right drivers for whole system success.* Center for Strategic Education. https://michaelfullan.ca/wp-content/uploads/2021/03/Fullan-CSE-Leading-Education-Series-01-2021R2-compressed.pdf

Gillani, N., Eynon, R., Chiabaut, C., & Finkel, K. (2023). Unpacking the "Black Box" of AI in Education. *Journal of Educational Technology & Society, 26*(1), 99–111. DOI: 10.30191/ETS.202301_26(1).0008

Gillies, R. M. (2016). Cooperative Learning: Review of Research and Practice. *The Australian Journal of Teacher Education, 41*(3), 39–54. Advance online publication. DOI: 10.14221/ajte.2016v41n3.3

Gonzaga, K. V. P., Graça, V. G. D., & Quadros-Flores, P. (2024). A cultura e metodologia maker na formação de professores: Uma proposta criativa, interdisciplinar, inovadora, sustentável e inclusiva. *Dialogia*, (50), e27733–e27733. DOI: 10.5585/50.2024.27733

Government of Portugal. (2020). *Action Plan for Digital Transition*. Council of Ministers Resolution no. 30/2020. https://portugaldigital.gov.pt/wp-content/uploads/2022/01/Plano_Acao_Transicao_Digital.pdf

Hemminki-Reijonen, U., Hassan, N. M., Huotilainen, M., Koivisto, J. M., & Cowley, B. U. (2025). Design of generative AI-powered pedagogy for virtual reality environments in higher education. *npj Science of Learning, 10*(1), 1-15. https://doi.org/DOI: 10.1038/s41539-025-00326-1

Herodotou, C., Naydenova, G., Boroowa, A., Gilmour, A., & Rienties, B. (2020). How can predictive learning analytics and motivational interventions increase student retention and enhance administrative support in distance education? *Journal of Learning Analytics*, *7*(2), 72–83. DOI: 10.18608/jla.2020.72.4

Hitchcock, J. H., & Onwuegbuzie, A. J. (2020). Developing mixed methods crossover analysis approaches. *Journal of Mixed Methods Research*, *14*(1), 63–83. DOI: 10.1177/1558689819841782

Holmes, W., Bialik, M., & Fadel, C. (2019). *Artificial intelligence in education promises and implications for teaching and learning*. Center for Curriculum Redesign. https://discovery.ucl.ac.uk/id/eprint/10139722

Holmes, W., & Miao, F. (2023). *Guidance for generative AI in education and research*. Unesco Publishing.

Hu, S. (2024). The effect of artificial intelligence-assisted personalized learning on student learning outcomes: A meta-analysis based on 31 empirical research papers. *Science Insights Education Frontiers*, *24*(1), 3873–3894. DOI: 10.15354/sief.24.re395

Johnson, D. W., & Johnson, R. T. (2018). Cooperative learning: The foundation for active learning. *Active learning-Beyond the future*, 59-71. https://doi.org/DOI: 10.5772/intechopen.81086

Jurenka, I., Kunesch, M., McKee, K. R., Gillick, D., Zhu, S., Wiltberger, S., . . . Ibrahim, L. (2024). Toward responsible development of generative AI for education: an evaluation-driven approach. *arXiv preprint arXiv:2407.12687.* https://doi.org//arXiv.2407.12687DOI: 10.48550

Kamali, J., Alpat, M. F., & Bozkurt, A. (2024). AI ethics as a complex and multifaceted challenge: Decoding educators' AI ethics alignment through the lens of activity theory. *International Journal of Educational Technology in Higher Education*, *21*(1), 62. DOI: 10.1186/s41239-024-00496-9

Kapoor, H., & Kaufman, J. C. (2021). Basic concepts of creativity. *The Cambridge handbook of lifespan development of creativity*, 5-19.

Leikin, R. (2013). Evaluating mathematical creativity: The interplay between multiplicity and insight1. *Psychological Test and Assessment Modeling*, *55*(4), 385–400.

Lucas, B., & Spencer, E. (2017). *Teaching Creative Thinking: Developing learners who generate ideas and can think critically (Pedagogy for a Changing World series)*. Crown House Publishing Ltd.

Luckin, R. (2017). Towards artificial intelligence-based assessment systems. *Nature Human Behaviour, 1*(3), 0028. https://doi.org/DOI: 10.1038/s41562-016-0028

Luckin, R., Holmes, W., Griffiths, M., & Forcier, L. B. (2016). *Intelligence Unleashed: An Argument for AI in Education*. Pearson Education. https://www.pearson.com/content/dam/corporate/global/pearson-dot-com/files/innovation/Intelligence-Unleashed-Publication.pdf

Maity, S., & Deroy, A. (2024). Human-Centric eXplainable AI in Education. *arXiv preprint arXiv:2410.19822*.https://doi.org//arXiv.2410.19822DOI: 10.35542/osf.io/k5u9b

Norman, G. (2010). Likert scales, levels of measurement, and the "laws" of statistics. *Advances in Health Sciences Education : Theory and Practice*, *15*(5), 625–632. DOI: 10.1007/s10459-010-9222-y PMID: 20146096

OECD. (2023). *Artificial Intelligence and the Future of Skills: Capabilities and Assessments*. OECD Publishing., DOI: 10.1787/5ee71f34-

Pasquale, F. (2015). *The black box society: The secret algorithms that control money and information*. Harvard University Press. DOI: 10.4159/harvard.9780674736061

Patton, M. Q. (2002). *Qualitative research and evaluation methods* (3rd ed.). SAGE Publications.

Popenici, S. A., & Kerr, S. (2017). Exploring the impact of artificial intelligence on teaching and learning in higher education. *Research and Practice in Technology Enhanced Learning*, *12*(1), 22. DOI: 10.1186/s41039-017-0062-8 PMID: 30595727

Redecker, C., & Punie, Y. (2017). *European framework for the digital competence of educators - DigCompEdu*. Publications Office of the European Union. https://data.europa.eu/doi/10.2760/159770

Ritchhart, R. (2015). *Creating cultures of thinking: The 8 forces we must master to truly transform our schools*. John Wiley & Sons.

Runco, M. A., & Jaeger, G. J. (2012). The standard definition of creativity. *Creativity Research Journal*, *24*(1), 92–96. DOI: 10.1080/10400419.2012.650092

Saavedra, A. R., & Opfer, V. D. (2012). Learning 21st-century skills requires 21st-century teaching. *Phi Delta Kappan, 94*(2), 8–13. DOI: 10.1177/003172171209400203

Sajja, R., Sermet, Y., Cwiertny, D., & Demir, I. (2023). Platform-independent and curriculum-oriented intelligent assistant for higher education. *International Journal of Educational Technology in Higher Education, 20*(1), 42. DOI: 10.1186/s41239-023-00412-7

Schleicher, A. (2020). *The Impact of COVID-19 on Education: Insights from" Education at a Glance 2020.* OECD Publishing.

Selwyn, N. (2019). *Should robots replace teachers? AI and the future of education.* John Wiley & Sons.

Shapiro, S. S., & Wilk, M. B. (1965). An analysis of variance test for normality (complete samples). *Biometrika, 52*(3-4), 591–611. DOI: 10.1093/biomet/52.3-4.591

Sidiropoulos, D., & Anagnostopoulos, C. N. (2024). Applications, challenges and ethical issues of AI and ChatGPT in education. *arXiv preprint arXiv:2402.*07907. https://doi.org//arXiv.2402.07907DOI: 10.48550

Sung, H., & Nathan, M. J. (2024). Your body tells how you engage in collaboration: Machine-detected body movements as indicators of engagement in collaborative math knowledge building. *British Journal of Educational Technology, 55*(5), 1950–1973. DOI: 10.1111/bjet.13473

UNESCO. (2021). *Recommendation on the Ethics of Artificial Intelligence.* https://unesdoc.unesco.org/ark:/48223/pf0000380455

Wang, X. (2025). Research and Practice on the Digital Transformation Path of Local Higher Education in the Era of Digital Intelligence. In *Proceedings of the 2nd International Conference on Educational Development and Social Sciences (EDSS 2025)* (Vol. 924, p. 360). Springer Nature. DOI: 10.2991/978-2-38476-400-6_44

Williamson, B., & Eynon, R. (2020). Historical threads, missing links, and future directions. *AI in education. Learning, Media and Technology, 45*(3), 223–235. DOI: 10.1080/17439884.2020.1798995

Xing, W., Song, Y., Li, C., Liu, Z., Zhu, W., & Oh, H. (2025). Development of a generative AI-powered teachable agent for middle school mathematics learning: A design-based research study. *British Journal of Educational Technology, 56*(5), 2043–2077. Advance online publication. DOI: 10.1111/bjet.13586

Xu, W., & Ouyang, F. (2022). A systematic review of AI role in the educational system based on a proposed conceptual framework. *Education and Information Technologies, 27*(3), 4195–4223. DOI: 10.1007/s10639-021-10774-y

Zawacki-Richter, O., Marín, V. I., Bond, M., & Gouverneur, F. (2019). Systematic review of research on artificial intelligence applications in higher education - Where are the educators? *International Journal of Educational Technology in Higher Education, 16*(1), 39. DOI: 10.1186/s41239-019-0171-0

ADDITIONAL READING

Gouseti, A., James, F., Fallin, L., & Burden, K. (2025). The ethics of using AI in K-12 education: A systematic literature review. *Technology, Pedagogy and Education, 34*(2), 161–182. DOI: 10.1080/1475939X.2024.2428601

Mariyono, D., & Nur Alif Hd, A. (2025). AI's role in transforming learning environments: A review of collaborative approaches and innovations. *Quality Education for All, 2*(1), 265–288. DOI: 10.1108/QEA-08-2024-0071

Porayska-Pomsta, K., Holmes, W., & Nemorin, S. (2023). The ethics of AI in education. In *Handbook of artificial intelligence in education* (pp. 571–604). Edward Elgar Publishing., DOI: 10.4337/9781800375413.00038

Roe, J., & Perkins, M. (2024). Generative AI and agency in Education: A critical scoping review and thematic analysis. *arXiv preprint arXiv:2411.00631*. https://doi.org//arXiv.2411.00631DOI: 10.48550

Veldhuis, A., Lo, P. Y., Kenny, S., & Antle, A. N. (2025). Critical Artificial Intelligence literacy: A scoping review and framework synthesis. *International Journal of Child-Computer Interaction, 43*, 100708. DOI: 10.1016/j.ijcci.2024.100708

Walter, Y. (2024). Embracing the future of Artificial Intelligence in the classroom: The relevance of AI literacy, prompt engineering, and critical thinking in modern education. *International Journal of Educational Technology in Higher Education, 21*(1), 15. DOI: 10.1186/s41239-024-00448-3

Williamson, B., & Eynon, R. (2020). Historical threads, missing links, and future directions in AI in education. *Learning, Media and Technology, 45*(3), 223–235. DOI: 10.1080/17439884.2020.1798995

Yang, Y., Zhang, Y., Sun, D., He, W., & Wei, Y. (2025). Navigating the landscape of AI literacy education: Insights from a decade of research (2014–2024). *Humanities & Social Sciences Communications*, *12*(1), 1–12. DOI: 10.1057/s41599-025-04583-8

Yim, I. H. Y., & Su, J. (2025). Artificial intelligence literacy education in primary schools: A review. *International Journal of Technology and Design Education*, •••, 1–30. DOI: 10.1007/s10798-025-09979-w

Zhai, C., Wibowo, S., & Li, L. D. (2024). The effects of over-reliance on AI dialogue systems on students' cognitive abilities: A systematic review. *Smart Learning Environments*, *11*(1), 28. DOI: 10.1186/s40561-024-00316-7

KEY TERMS AND DEFINITIONS

Artificial Intelligence (AI): The simulation of human cognitive processes by machines, particularly computer systems, used in education to support learning, automate tasks, and enhance teaching strategies.

Critical Thinking: A reflective and analytical approach to problem-solving that involves evaluating information and arguments, identifying biases, and drawing reasoned conclusions.

Creative Thinking: The ability to generate new and original ideas, solutions, or approaches, especially in the face of complex or undefined problems.

Pedagogical Innovation: The implementation of new, effective teaching strategies or technologies that improve learning outcomes and adapt to evolving educational needs.

Teacher Perceptions: The views, beliefs, and attitudes of educators towards specific practices, tools, or reforms, which influence their adoption and implementation in the classroom.

Curriculum Renewal: The process of updating and redesigning educational content and methods to reflect contemporary knowledge, skills, and societal needs.

Digital Competence: A set of skills and knowledge that enable individuals to use digital technologies critically, responsibly, and effectively in various contexts.

Ethical Challenges in AI: Dilemmas and concerns related to the use of AI in education, such as data privacy, algorithmic bias, and accountability in automated decision-making.

Professional Development: Ongoing training and education for teachers aimed at improving their knowledge, skills, and practices, particularly in response to technological and pedagogical change.

Educational Transformation: Systemic changes in teaching, learning, and assessment practices driven by technological, social, or policy innovations.

Chapter 4
Transforming Curriculum Design with AI Learning Analytics in the University Context

Azadeh Eskandarzadeh
https://orcid.org/0009-0004-5167-271X
Western Community College, Canada

Yunona Gogia
https://orcid.org/0009-0003-4171-4958
University Canada West, Canada

ABSTRACT

This article examines the potential of AI-based learning analytics to revolutionize adaptive curricula in higher education institutions. Drawing on the synthesis of existing evidence, the study assesses the ability of artificial intelligence to adapt to the individual student through data-driven instructional approaches. It examines key areas of ethics that include data privacy, algorithmic bias, and providing access to the data-driven instructional approaches. It records the preparedness of the institution and teachers. Despite the phenomenal potential of AI integration to enable inclusive and adaptive spaces of learning, the study identifies the need for careful deployment fueled by ethics and instructional fit. The results inspire balanced practice in AI adoption that guarantees that the human aspects of instruction are retained as the data analysis strength of AI comes into play.

DOI: 10.4018/979-8-3373-7729-2.ch004

INTRODUCTION

The integration of digital technology in education signifies a fundamental change in the teaching approach, with the potential to improve accessibility, engagement, and personalization in learning. This review integrates contemporary trends, difficulties, and breakthroughs in digital education, emphasizing the influence of artificial intelligence (AI), and online platforms on student achievement. It emphasizes the necessity of surmounting technological, pedagogical, and social obstacles to guarantee fair access to technology. Successful initiatives such as the Open University exemplify the capacity of digital education to enhance academic results.

The advancement of machine learning and artificial intelligence stands on the cusp of transforming higher education into learning spaces that are personalized and adaptive. Instructors and policymakers can utilize AI-based learning analytics and gain insights into students' real-time performance, hence enabling the creation of responsive learning spaces customized according to individual requirements and areas requiring improvement (Zawacki-Richter et al., 2019). In addition, the system can spot students at risk and implement timely interventions through customized support and resources (Zawacki-Richter et al., 2019). The adaptive learning technology also plays a central role through the ability of the system to adjust the contents, pacing, and difficulties, and adapt them according to the individual educational pathway. These interdisciplinary methods have the potential to transform traditional learning spaces into spaces that are personal, efficient, and adaptable (Rad, 2025). Through the combination of students possessing similar interests or complementary abilities, the incorporation of AI enhances learning spaces into collaborative and creative spaces where students can freely interact and be problem-solvers. These AI-based learning tools will be crucial for developing critical thinking and creativity and enabling students with the ability needed for future problems (Mahmoud & Sørensen, 2024). However, the adoption of the tools necessitates that the educators and policymakers be knowledgeable across the technical and pedagogic sides of AI in order to exploit its potential (Zhang & Miernik, 2025). In addition, the ethics on the issue of data confidentiality and the fairness of the algorithm remain central to the equitable provision and benefit for all students. The incorporation of AI into learning spaces has remarkably changed the face of learning and instruction. The rising acknowledgment of the potential of AI across learning spaces manifests through the rise of publications on the matter.

The transformative potential for AI when it comes to reshaping learning paradigms is a matter for serious review, particularly for learning analytics engines, adaptive learning schemes, and customization technology (Oruganti, 2024). The inclusion of AI within learning has caused real gains for adaptive learning schemes, smart tutoring schemes, and learning analytics, all enabling more customized and streamlined learning. Current trends such as the increase in mobile internet, cloud computing, and big data, and complemented by advancements within artificial intelligence, are causing a transformation throughout learning (Kabudi et al., 2021). The traditional educational atmosphere is evolving, and it holds the potential for opportunities and risks for students and educators (Hakan, 2025). Analyzing learning patterns among students and suggesting knowledge shortcomings, AI-based platforms can customize material and present it based on individual need, generating richer interaction and performance (Zou et al., 2025). As the AI technology continues to advance, the learning realm can anticipate still novel uses, further shaping the future within learning.

The current work realizes a critical examination of the published peer-reviewed materials on the state-of-the-art procedures, benefits, challenges, and ethics for AI-based learning analytics across the landscapes of higher education. The literature review investigates the applications of the technology for the generation of adaptive curricula for the realization of equitable, inclusive, and impactful learning procedures. The future direction for the further advancement of AI towards further automation could lead to the loss of potential for the good kind of AI with higher economic and social returns (Acemoğlu & Restrepo, 2019). The current writing presents the potential for AI-based learning analytics for the redesigning of higher education based on the enabling of individualized and inclusive pathways towards the improvement of students' academic performance and engagement (Adewale et al., 2024). The impact of AI extends across several dimensions within education, such as personalized learning, marking tools based on automation, and the development of smart virtual assistants. The potential for AI in the automation of routine administration, personalization of the learning experience, and the development of evidence-based insights can have the potential for a transformative approach towards the administration and distribution of education. Considering the power, strengths, and shortcomings of AI, the current work strives for the realization of the transformative impact on higher education.

The study also endeavors to build a sound ethical base for the integration of AI into learning, as the research on ethics kept under consideration matters such as data privacy and algorithmic discrimination, but a holistically inclusive and integrated approach for taking these matters does not emerge (Ajani et al., 2024). Perhaps most critically, the study endeavors to empower educators, policymakers, and learning organizations in realizing the full potential for AI and remaining faithful to ideals for ethics while building learning spaces where every student can equally thrive. In the consideration for adoption frameworks for success, countering the risks potential, and non-technical guidelines for practice, the inquiry empowers the stakeholders to oversee the nuances for the integration of AI and build transformative learning opportunities for every learner. The incorporation of artificial intelligence into the learning sector becomes a transformative moment, which can redefine established models for learning and instruction. AI tools are being utilized for automating routine administration, personalization for learning settings, and generation for evidence-based insights and thus increasing the effectiveness and effectiveness for learning organizations (O'Dea & O'Dea, 2023). However, the incorporation of AI into learning settings far from becoming a seamless process since every process for the adoption becomes the cause for concern for the loss of job, ethics implications, and educators' requirements for training and support. AI can bring forth crucial matters such as equitable distribution for quality education and personalization for learning experience. The intent here includes a provision for insights into the ethical considerations, challenges, and opportunities developed when integrating AI into education. The current research emphasizes the integration of AI into education on a prudent footing with a focus on ethics, equitable distribution, and the development for critical thinking capability. AI integration will bring forth the construction for the collaborative and creative learning settings where students sharing the similar interest or complementary for the skill set are congregated for facilitating peer interaction and problem-solving. Ethical implications remain extremely critical for the distribution for equity and the outcome. Ethical issues such as privacy and algorithmic bias should be taken into account so that every student can have equal access and opportunities (Phua et al., 2025). AI-based learning analytics offers educators and policymakers real-time insights into the students' performance, enabling them to develop learning experience sensitive to individual needs and inadequacies. Ethical issues such as privacy, security, and bias should be taken into account nonetheless (Harry & Sayudin, 2023). With the aid facilitated by AI, it's feasible for higher education to augment learning outcomes through more prosperous learning opportunities, higher organizational effectiveness, and gaining real-time, actionable insights into the performance of students (Muhie & Woldie, 2020). AI applications listen for and text chat for keywords and expressions and discern potential customer issues and offer agents real-time pop-up and menu-based fixes. AI can significantly contribute to enhancing higher education, which can be utilized for the construction of individual and adaptive curricula based on individual learning behaviors and needs. Through the application of AI-based learning analytics, educators and policymakers can have real-time knowledge about the performance of students, such as the assessment, patterns of engagement, and monitoring of progress, and based on that knowledge, responsive learning opportunities can be developed based on the needs and inadequacies of every individual. It's still the case that the ethical issues need to be understood and managed, like the issue of data privacy, the problem of algorithmic prejudice, and distributive fairness of learning opportunities for the incorporation of AI into learning spaces (Gkintoni et al., 2025). AI can discern whether a learner gets the correct answer and notify the instructor as to the process followed by the learner for getting the correct answer (Kim & Kim, 2022).

The AI's remodeled potential for higher education is tempered by the realization that it can only be best utilized with a planned strategy and consideration of its capability, limitations, and ethics (Ross & Gillani, 2021). The best possible use of AI for higher education remains a discovery. The integration of AI for higher education necessitates the preparation of educators and policymakers with the relevant competence for the efficient realization of the potential. It could, on the other hand, minimize the enthusiasm and the learning process for students (Akggün & Greenhow, 2021). It necessitates the institution's expenditure on training programmes and professional development programmes that empower educators for the integration of AI tools into their pedagogy. It becomes integral for the consideration of the ethics of AI for education to protect the confidentiality of the students' data and the non-discrimination of the algorithm. Further research and discussion are requisite for the realization of the full potential of AI for the removal of problems for equity, qualification, and ethics (Neji et al., 2023). Predominant writings for AI have been on students or administrators, but the perception, use, and adaptability of AI tools among educators remain understudied, especially since most educators identify the lack of AI literacy.

Key understanding here is the understanding that AI cannot be a silver bullet for the numerous problems that the higher education system faces, but can be seen as one instrument among the numerous that can be deployed for enhancing the process of instruction and learning (Eager & Brunton, 2023). The issue arises in the formulation of policies for enabling humanistic values, fairness, privacy, and openness, and, at the same time, allowing for innovation. Remaining faithful to the understanding that human beings need to find the problems, criticize, identify the risks, and ask big questions which can have a starting point anywhere ranging from the likes of privacy, power relations, and the issue of control to the necessity for developing creativity and keeping the window for the element of surprise and the unintended routes into learning and into instruction (Popenici & Kerr, 2017). AI can potentially set the workers free for more human or high-level work; however, it does require active collaboration with the workers so that the tools for AI can be effectively harnessed. AI also raises questions like the possibilities for automation to displace human workers, exacerbating the existing inequities, and degrading the standard of work.

There's also the use of AI systems within higher education for managerial tasks, which can bring workers into contact with binding decisions that are arbitrary or merciless. As AI reshapes the landscape of higher education, ongoing deliberation among scholars and with AI is called for if the rearranged landscape can be truly inclusive, normatively defensible, and commensurate with scholarly values (Marshall et al., 2024). As AI keeps advancing so rapidly, such deliberation will be iterative and require frequent revisiting, especially as the newest AI tools become available on the commercial market faster and faster still. In response, AI can have the potential for redrawing the landscape of higher education, and its adoption can only be undertaken with caution and intention if scholarly integrity and moral standards are to be maintained (Nguyen, 2025). Toward that end, this research emphasizes the need for education to train folks to be able to think critically, solve problems, and act as humanely as possible within a world where everything's getting automated. AI integration requires a multi-faceted approach, involving infrastructure investment, staff training, and support services. It also requires diligence and forbearance on the issue of the risks for algorithmic discrimination, ethics, and the need for explainable AI. It encompasses active consultation with the on-the-job folks on the front lines, assuring AI tools get deployed effectively and morally. It also emphasizes the need for ongoing review and refinement so AI initiatives align with institutional aspirations and moral ideals. In response, educators and policymakers also need to take into account the broader social implications of AI and what it holds for work, equity, and social justice.

ADVANTAGES OF AI IN EDUCATION

AI can significantly augment student engagement and learning performance with the capacity for individualized curricula and differentiated support .AI adds new ways to improve traditional methods (Dey, 2025) by setting up learning centers that serve a wide range of students and make instruction more effective. AI-based personalized learning adapts the material and pace of learning to each student's needs and fills in specific gaps in their knowledge by giving them a deeper understanding of the subject (AlTwijri & Alghizzi, 2024). AI-based tools like learning platforms that change to fit each student and smart tutoring tools are necessary for helping each student grow and succeed in the changing learning environment (Mello et al., 2023). AI positively contributes towards the higher education sector through the establishment of greater interaction among students and instructors and the capacity for instructors and students alike for refining the learning and instruction process .The use of AI within the educational sector does not attempt the replacement of instructors but the enhancement of their capability through the reduction of non-instructional work, augmented provision for informative information, and the individualization of the learning experience based on individual students' needs (Lampou, 2023). AI frees up teachers' time for more direct contact with students, better learning environments, and personalized help by automating tasks like grades and comments .AI can give teachers useful information about how well their students are doing by looking at their performance data. This can help students who are struggling or need more help, and it can also help teachers create personalized ways to teach and support students.

Some of the benefits of AI that have been mentioned include making learning more personalized, improving the student experience, and cutting down on administrative tasks. AI for Education suggests that students learn in a way that fits their needs by offering a personalized learning experience based on their unique circumstances and past learning (Chaudhry & Kazim, 2021). These observations indicate the central capability played by generative AI for the enhancement based on learning through the capacity for rendering it more individualized, interactive, and immersive (Bura & Myakala, 2024). Besides, AI-based systems have decreased the administrative burden for instructors significantly and granted instructors the capacity for attention towards the creative and interpersonal dimensions for instruction.

AI plays a central role in improving learning and teaching through real-time tracking of performance, facilitating timely support, and the creation of interactive learning spaces (Lin et al., 2023). That holds especially true given that some tasks remain most effectively managed by human beings. In addition, AI can facilitate educational accessibility for disabled students through the adoption of speech recognition, text-to-speech functionality, and real-time language translation. The integration of AI renders educational resources accessible for students regardless of the background and capabilities of the students, hence promoting equity and inclusivity in learning .AI can redesign assessment by gaining a deeper understanding of learners, including their knowledge, learning approach, and learning preferences .Through the monitoring of the patterns of learners using vast quantities of data, AI can evaluate the progress and offer educators knowledge heretofore unavailable. Through automations based on grades and the giving of precise feedback, AI stimulates learner reflexivity and enables students to effect the necessary changes for enhanced learning. Ultimately, AI offers insightful evidence and enables educators to individualize learning experiences for the purpose of responding to the specific needs of every learner and enhancing their potential (Lin et al., 2023).

The use of AI in learning can create group learning spaces where students sharing the same interest or ability work together and develop teamwork and problem-solving (Tan & Maravilla, 2024). These methods help students learn the skills they need for the future and encourage them to be creative and think critically. There are many benefits to using AI in colleges and universities, such as personalized learning, more student involvement, and better learning (Eager & Brunton, 2023). AI gives students feedback that is specific to them, learning plans that can change, and keeps them very interested in school. AI tutors give each student personalized help based on their needs and learning style. This helps them learn better and develop a growth mindset. In order to take full advantage of the power of AI in enhancing learning, it's important to use it ethically, follow moral laws, and build on what human beings can achieve. AI can quickly grade papers, quizzes, and tests and give students quick, useful feedback so they can learn about their strengths and weaknesses right away

(Ha & Painter, 2025). AI can also be used to track how students are engaged in real-time and find students struggling and assist instructors in helping them accordingly. Using the new computer tools mentioned above wisely in lessons can greatly improve learning, make students more interested, and lead to huge gains in school performance (Sharma et al., 2025). But even though AI could make learning better, it also brings up problems and worries that need to be fixed. It is important to deal with problems like keeping the learning data private, making sure the algorithms are fair, and making up for any biases that might come up to ensure fair inclusion and good results for all students in learning (Harry & Sayudin, 2023). AI enhances the accessibility of students with disabilities in learning using the capability of speech recognition, text-to-speech, and real-time translation. The goal is to give teachers the tools they need to learn how to use AI in the classroom in a smart and effective way (Pohn et al., 2025). The main concern about AI has been how it affects the final results and behaviors of students (Ma et al., 2024). While there are known benefits of AI in learning, its use in the real world is still limited. No matter what people say about how well it works, AI definitely makes students more motivated by offering personalized learning paths, more access to learning materials, and more time for teachers to spend on interactive experiences (Roméro et al., 2023).

It is widely used and can be turned into commercial or production technology (Acemoğly & Restrepo, 2019). People are using AI technology more and more to automate jobs, but it can also be used to come up with new ideas and make jobs better.AI technology doesn't have to take away people's freedom or ability to make choices. It is utilized within the place of work, and the employees enjoy the way it has improved their occupations. For example, AI apps can listen for certain words in calls and chats and figure out what problems customers are having and how to fix them. These problems and fixes then show up on agents' desktops in real time. AI can help schools give each student personalized help, keep track of their progress, and build learning spaces that change as needed (Rad, 2025). AI can help make learning more fair and accessible for all students by giving them personalized feedback, customizing their lessons, and stepping in early (Acemoğlu & Restrepo, 2019). Institutions are using evidence-based research to make student support services better, look closely at how they teach, and make sure that resources are used in the best way possible (Long & Magerko, 2020). AI can speed up the discovery process by processing huge amounts of data that people couldn't do on their own. This leads to new ideas and innovations in many fields (Ofosu-Asare, 2024). AI can look at students' data and figure out how well they did, giving teachers information they couldn't get before (Hwang, 2022). Instructors can utilize information to customize learning, which makes students perform and stay engaged, but it poses the issue of ethics and students' privacy. AI programs look for patterns and make decisions by processing a lot of data.

SHIFT TOWARD MODERN DIGITAL EDUCATION

The shift from traditional classrooms to contemporary digital learning settings has been gradual, characterized by the rising use of blended learning models (Regmi and Jones, 2020). Blended learning integrates in-person instruction with digital learning activities, offering students a flexible and individualized educational experience. This method integrates the advantages of both conventional and digital learning, fostering a more dynamic and engaging educational environment (Alam, 2018).

The early 21st century witnessed a notable transition to entirely online learning settings, propelled by technological advancements and an increasing need for flexible educational alternatives. Online learning platforms, notably Massive Open Online Courses (MOOCs), have emerged as a prevalent alternative to traditional education, enabling learners to access high-quality courses from esteemed institutions at little or no cost (Al-Rahmi et al., 2018). This era also witnessed the growth of mobile learning, as smartphones as well as tablets became essential tools for gaining exposure to learning material anywhere and at anytime.

The COVID-19 epidemic of 2020 catalyzed the swift global adoption of online learning. Due to the closure of physical campuses, educators were compelled to swiftly adapt to virtual instruction. This shift emphasized the significance of digital learning technologies and the potential advantages and problems of online education (Zhao and Watterston, 2021). It expedited the advancement and dissemination of new technologies, including virtual learning environments and AI-driven personalized learning platforms, which would ultimately become essential elements of the contemporary educational framework.

ETHICAL CONSIDERATIONS OF AI-DRIVEN LEARNING ANALYTICS

When using AI for learning, it's important to pay close attention to data protection, fairness of algorithms, and responsible implementation (Cordero et al., 2024). It is very important to solve problems with informed consent, data ownership, algorithm responsibility, and possible side effects. It is important to design AI tools that promote fairness, openness, and accountability. This could stop algorithms and data sets from being biased and make sure that all learners get equal benefits.

For fairness in educational outcomes, ethical issues like data privacy and algorithmic fairness must be taken into account. AI adoption requires schools to spend money on infrastructure, training, and professional help for teachers, which can be hard for schools with limited resources. There are moral problems with using AI in education, such as privacy of data, discrimination and bias, and the digital divide

(Chetry, 2024). The main worry is still that AI algorithms could be biased and make the gap even bigger (Delello et al., 2025). For instance, AI algorithms that were made using biased data sets may favor some groups of students and make it harder for others to get a good education. To avoid problems that weren't meant to happen and get the results you want, AI must be monitored and reviewed regularly. To get the most out of AI for learning and lower the risks, we need to make ethical rules and standards for how to use it (Akavova et al., 2023). To get the most out of the benefits and the least number of risks, you need to carefully plan, be ethical, and keep learning professionally. It is still important to train teachers on how to use AI tools correctly in order to avoid the risk of spreading false or biased information and to make sure that the technology is used safely and properly in the classroom. Another important goal is to make AI technology with user-friendly interfaces that make it easy for teachers to use it in the classroom.

Educational AI comes with ethical issues, such as privacy, transparency, and mitigation of bias .AI algorithms used in education can be hard to understand because they are so complex and hidden (Al-Zahrani, 2024). AI-based systems used in schools can unintentionally copy or make worse biases that are already there, which can lead to unfair or discriminatory decisions. Making AI tools transparent and explainable can be crucial for gaining trust among students, educators, and others (Thelma et al., 2024). Addressing the above ethical issues can enable educational establishments to tap into the transformative power of AI for creating personalized, equitable, and efficient learning opportunities for all students (KARAKUŞ et al., 2025).

Concerns about using AI in surveillance, regulation, and evaluation can make people less trusting and free in learning spaces (Vieriu & Petrea, 2025). AI-based learning tools tend to collect a lot of information about students, which raises concerns about privacy and security (Boulay, 2023). To protect student data, use it in a fair way, and not share it without permission, comprehensive data governance models must be put in place. To solve the moral problems, we need to take a multi-faceted approach. This means bringing together teachers, lawmakers, technologists, and ethicists to create clear rules and best practices for using AI in schools.

In addition, frontline workers have witnessed the ability of AI technology to lower the intellectual demand on their jobs, leading to the loss of intellectual stimulation and potentially decreased job satisfaction. The incorporation of AI into the workplace can have a deleterious effect on workers' privacy, dignity, and freedom and can lead to emotional and mental health issues. These can make workers feel less valuable and less able to change things at work. In the development of AI technology for learning that can be trusted and exploited, points of problems relating to prejudice must be corrected, openness be ensured, and user confidentiality protected (Tahir et al., 2024). So, we need a complete and moral approach that makes sure AI helps learning without making things worse. The education sector also needs clear AI governance frameworks in learning spaces to make sure that AI decision-making processes are open and accountable. Holmes et al. (2021) say that the education sector really needs a community-wide system for teaching people how to behave ethically and avoid unintended consequences in order to fully realize AI's potential for learning.

POWERED BY AI PERSONALIZATION IN LEARNING ENVIRONMENTS

Adaptive learning technology uses AI to create personalized content, pacing, and difficulty levels, which means it meets the needs of each learner (Maghsudi et al., 2021). The technology also supports collaborative and creative learning spaces through the connection of the students with shared interests and talents, and for the development of peer collaboration and problem-solving. The AI-based technology will only work if people learn how to use it well (Gligorea et al., 2023). It becomes pertinent for the inspection of the integration and development of traditional talents such as critical thinking, collaboration, and creativity within the AI-based learning. Individualized feedback fine-tunes learning through the provision of personal responses for the students' performance and therefore allows improvement within the development of the talents and the gain in knowledge (Yaseen et al., 2025). AI-based learning analytics support individualized learning through the inspection of the history and the analysis of big data for the discovery of the features and the patterns shared among the learners (Maghsudi et al., 2021). AI applications can process and analyze the information for the educators' benefit and therefore support customized learning .AI transforms the production process and introduces new, high-productivity tasks for the human workforce. AI renders it possible for education to be customized with the recommendation of customized content, the development of extended curricula, the linking of the relevant learners, and the accurate measurement of performance. AI-based technology monitors the students' engagement, measures the gap in the knowledge, and adjusts the scope of the curriculum dynamically for optimizing the learning process (Zou et al., 2025). The system analyzes the students' interaction within the e-learning module and detects the patterns indicating a learning behavior or learning difficulties and therefore supports the generation of the customized instructional contents (Jian, 2023). AI-based platforms can also offer customized support and feedback and guide the learner through problematic concepts and encourage deeper understanding. AI can examine the student performance, strengths, and weaknesses and offer customized learning course (Kamalov & Gurrib, 2023). The real-time adjustment on the learning approach so that it aligns with the students' varying attributes becomes possible with the application of AI.

The platforms offer customized support and resources and informative feedback for instructors for optimizing the approach for learning (Saputra et al., 2023). Personalized learning driven by AI forms the core of meeting the diverse requirements of students and enhancing the efficacy of instruction within the fluctuating learning environment (Akhmadieva et al., 2024). It measures the educational intervention efficacy based on the application of data-based analytics .AI-based learning analytics holds the potential for reshaping higher education based on personalized and equitable learning pathways for improving the students' academic achievements and participation (Zhai et al., 2021). AI can assess the students' attitudes and behaviors based on the identification of facial expressions when students are engaged in learning, and thus extend support on a timely note. The purpose here is moving students towards enhancing their learning process with the customization of learning paths for meeting specific requirements. The concern here includes exploring the potentiality of AI-based personalized learning platforms and testing them on the students' performance and achievement.

TRANSFORMING HIGHER EDUCATION THROUGH REAL-TIME DATA AND ADAPTIVE SUPPORT

AI-based learning analytics gives teachers and policymakers the tools they need to see how well students are doing, how often they are engaged, and how much progress they are making. These kinds of insights help make learning experiences that are tailored to each person's needs and weaknesses. It identifies underperformers and facilitates requisite intervention through targeted support and personalized resources (Joshi, 2023). Adaptive learning technology changes the material, pace, and level of difficulty on the fly to meet the needs of each learner. Integrating AI into the classroom helps create collaborative and creative learning spaces where students with similar interests or strengths can work together, connect, and build peer interaction and problem-solving (Kim & Lee, 2025). AI plays a leading part in the emergence of critical thinking and creativity and gives students the ability to meet future challenges (Zhou & Kevlian, 2025). AI-based personalized learning takes into account each student's performance, preferences, and learning style, and changes the learning path, materials, and speed to fit each student's needs. AI technology could be made customized based on the need for college students (Guo et al., 2025). AI-based m-learning platforms optimize the effectiveness of instruction and convey across the shortcomings of traditional classroom-based methods (Shui & Shui, 2025). AI makes it easier for students with disabilities to get help that is tailored to their needs, like speech recognition and text-to-speech (Asselin & Limbert, 2025). AI finds patterns and insights into how students learn by looking at a lot of data. It then helps train the teacher on how to teach and gives them specific ways to help. These AI-based learning programs also automate the process of grading and administration and let the educator focus on more nuanced instructional tasks (Heckman & Kautz, 2025). AI-based learning programs use AI-based algorithms to look at how well each student is doing and change the difficulty of the material based on what they need to learn. It uses AI for real-time classroom analysis (Ward et al., 2025). AI software construction makes learning styles personal for particular subjects or topics and collects and processes pertinent information.

The continuous integration of machine learning and AI can redefine higher education and support personalized and adaptive curricula. AI-based learning analytics can give teachers, policymakers, and students real-time information about how well students are doing and how engaged they are. This can help create learning experiences that are more responsive to each student's needs and areas for improvement ("Global Educational Studies Review," 2020). The system can find students who are having trouble and help them get help right away by giving them targeted support and personalized resources (Opesemowo & Adewuyi, 2024). Adaptive learning technology changes the content, pace, and level of difficulty on the fly to meet the needs of each learner (Huang et al., 2022). AI tools can help students and teachers learn more relevant information right away and at the right time, which is especially helpful for students and teachers who want to learn more about theory. The tools give quick answers to questions, suggest reading materials, and help students learn more about topics that interest them. The adaptability makes sure that the students get the help and learning they need based on their current level of understanding and ability to learn (Zou et al., 2025). AI-based dashboards that show data in real time and monitor everything from start to finish help teachers make better decisions about how to use resources and how to teach and learn (Egunjobi & Adeyeye, 2024). Using AI helps to evaluate the "effectiveness of curriculum" and measure the "overall happiness" of medical students, which is very important for training the next generation of doctors (Mir et al., 2023). The AI looks at the complicated patterns of emotional states that come from learning data and gives teachers a better idea of what each student needs and what to look for when a student is having an emotional state. AI can also help bring about long-term change in the whole education system and affect how schools and administrators run their schools, just like it can change how students learn and how teachers teach (Rad, 2025). The AI-based system can spot the first signs of disengagement or confusion and help teachers and trainers give students the help, encouragement, and personalized extra help they need. An AI-based system can match students with neighbors who have similar skills and interests. It can also help create collaborative and creative learning spaces that encourage students to work together and solve problems. This kind of plan puts a lot of value on learning from others and working together to develop critical thinking and creativity, which will help students face future challenges with confidence. To get the most out of AI integration, teachers and policymakers need to learn how to use technology and teach it well. At the same time, ethical questions about data privacy and algorithmic fairness need to be given a lot of attention to make sure that everyone has fair access and output. AI can help figure out the best ways to teach people from different educational backgrounds (Qiu et al., 2022). AI can also support the mechanization of repetitive tasks like assessment and grading, enabling instructors to be engaged on more nuanced and individualized facets of instruction. Automation of tasks that are repetitive and can be defined mathematically is a promising part of how AI will change jobs (Acemoğlu & Restrepo, 2019). This frees up human workers to do more creative, compassionate, or intellectually challenging work. AI can also help improve student advising by giving students information about job trends and requirements so they can make better decisions about their academic and professional futures.

TRANSFORMATIVE POTENTIAL OF AI IN HIGHER EDUCATION: PERSONALIZATION, DECISION-MAKING, AND SYSTEMIC INNOVATION

Adding artificial intelligence to higher education is a big change that shows how traditional education models can be changed and how personalized, inclusive, and impactful learning models can be supported can automate everyday administrative tasks and create a personalized support system. This could help educational organizations make the best use of their resources, improve their teaching methods, and make decisions based on evidence at all levels of the organization. (Popenici & Kerr, 2017). Through the automation of day-to-day administration, AI can free the educator for the intent of conceptualizing attractive lessons and providing customized care for the students. Other breakthroughs through AI will lead to transformation on the scale and scope of learning (George & Wooden, 2023). It gives each student a personalized learning support system that helps them learn the most (Akinwalere & Ivanov, 2022). The change affects many parts of the learning ecosystem, from the way the curriculum and learning experience are designed to the student support services and the way the school is run. The adaptive learning system, which uses advanced algorithms to make it work, made it possible to create personalized curricula that fit the needs, choices, and learning styles of each student (Ofosu-Asare, 2024). These adapt and adjust the material, rhythm, and level of intensity on the go and maximize learning achievements. AI gets applied in assessment for the improvement of educational standards (Akinwalere & Ivanov, 2022). It can also perform administrative and managerial duties.

AI-based learning analytics tools grant educators unprecedented insight into real-time information and data on the performance, engagement, and learning behaviors of students. These tools can be utilized for the purpose of identifying students at risk, detecting learning gaps early on, and delivering customized support and interventions. Teachers can use these data-based observations to make better decisions about how to teach, how to design courses, and how to distribute resources, which will lead to better outcomes for students. It empowers higher education providers for the purpose of optimizing resource distribution, improving the process of selection and decision-making, and delivering customized learning experience for the students (Xu, 2025). We can use the constant growth and use of technology to make personalized learning better, improve the learning outcome strategy, and make it easier for more people to access it (Long & Magerko, 2020). AI can help teachers focus on activities that need human interaction, like providing issue-based mentorship and coaching, and helping students develop their critical and higher-order thinking skills. This is possible because it can automate mechanical tasks like grading and giving feedback. Adaptive learning platforms use AI algorithms to constantly check students' interactions and performance data in real time and give them immediate help and feedback. AI can help students even more by giving them personalized advice on their academic and career choices based on job market trends and skill requirements (AlTwijri & Alghizzi, 2024).

AI can be used to automate everyday tasks, make tests, grade them automatically, and give feedback (Chaudhry & Kazim, 2021). AI makes student advising more effective by giving customized advice on coursework and careers using job market trends and skill-based data. It can help students be more honest in school, think critically, and find new connections between subjects. (Rad, 2025). AI integration makes it possible for students with similar interests or complementary skills to find each other, interact, learn from each other, and work together to solve real-world problems in interactive and innovative learning spaces. AI-based programs let students move at their own pace while getting personalized help, which lowers stress and improves both their academic performance and mental health. AI-based platforms can be used for group discussions, giving advice, and encouraging students to work together, which shows their ability to work as a team, communicate, and solve problems (Kaledio et al., 2024). It goes even further by helping with special needs and creating a personalized learning experience so that all students can participate in higher education.

EMOTIONAL INTELLIGENCE AND LEARNING ENVIRONMENTS

AI is also ready to change how tests are given in college with the creation of automated grading programs, plagiarism detectors, and personalized feedback tools. In AI applications in the workplace, foresight for the impact must be a major issue for AI developers and business leaders and managers purchasing and employing workplace AI, or governments implement sufficient safeguards and enforcement so that workers and the general public still suffer injuries for which it was possible to anticipate and prevent. The fact that AI can learn from a lot of different examples of emotional behavior and then analyze them makes it possible for it to understand the personal needs of each student (Vistorte et al., 2024). The impact on higher education instruction and learning created by AI makes it possible to anticipate the future of learning for a world where AI pervades every place ("The Impact of AI on Teaching and Learning in Higher Education Technology," 2022). While AI holds unprecedented promise for enhancing higher education, it also raises numerous challenges and ethical concerns that ought to be handled preventively. These include concerns surrounding the privacy of the data, algorithmic discrimination, intellectual property rights, and academic integrity (Maphalala & Ajani, 2025). It works on letting students master their learning environment based on the experience of their emotions. AI can perceive emotions when interacting with the environment for a deeper understanding of the way they experience it (Vistorte et al., 2024). It necessitates a joint effort on the part of educators, policymakers, technologists, and ethicists for the development of clear guidelines, standards, and best practices for using AI responsibly and ethically within the higher education domain.

Moreover, the development of AI-backed virtual assistants and chatbots provides students with on-demand assistance for questions, advice, and motivation. AI must be deployed within the parameters of values and mission of instructional directions, and students be informed what good use they're getting out of their data (Eager & Brunton, 2023). Colleges must ensure AI complements traditional learning, aids intellectual integrity, and fosters critical thinking (Nguyen, 2025). Moreover, AI can support emotional development and contribute to students' well-being by anticipating warning signs for stress, anxiety, or disengagement and giving individualized tools and interventions .AI can also identify material that aligns with students' passions, interests, and learning objectives and create intrinsic enthusiasm and discovery based on curiosity. Use of AI can construct interactive response material and individual learning experiences for the students (Mallillin, 2024). These intelligent chatbots can also assist educators themselves by addressing frequently recurring questions, providing technical support, and freeing up their time for more intensive endeavors. That way, students can have the privilege of support and direction whenever they need it and experience a high amount of backup and bonding within the learning environment. AI algorithms can also process students' emotional states when they interact within learning spaces and correspondingly gain a greater understanding of the emotional experience (Vistorte et al., 2024). Such systems can monitor tone of voice, loudness, and keywords, and discern emotion, and offer real-time pop-ups and warnings for agents on how they could have managed the emotional dimension of interacting with customers better.

The AI can be capable of supporting the creation of accessible and inclusive learning spaces with the aid of assistive technology, language translator devices, and personalized learning materials. The ethics surrounding the use of AI, such as academic integrity and the potential for AI algorithms to be biased, need to be kept under close watch .AI ought to be deployed for the enhancement and complementation, and not the diminishment of human potential and ability (Lin et al., 2023). Instructors and policymakers need training and education on the best ways of incorporating AI when it comes to learning processes and learning subjects. The impact that AI imposes on learning calls for educators with high AI literacy and professional growth on the best manner it can be utilized ethically (Delello et al., 2025).

INTRINSIC MOTIVATION THROUGH AI-ENHANCED LEARNING PLATFORMS

AI based on natural language processing, sentiment analysis, and recommendation technology that picks the best content for each student's interests, passions, and learning goals can help students develop intrinsic motivation and curiosity-driven learning exploration (Lin & Qiu, 2024). AI-based tutors can provide instant feedback, encourage students, and adjust complexity according to performance. These one-on-one interactions make people feel competent and independent, which are two important things that drive intrinsic motivation and long-term learning (Ma et al., 2024). AI-based learning platforms can also include elements of play, discovery, and learning exploration in interactive simulations and gamification activities to keep students interested. AI helps students move away from the idea of being passive consumers of knowledge and toward the idea of being active agents who are fully involved in the process of building and discovering knowledge.

More and more, teachers and policymakers are seeing how AI-based learning analytics could change the way people learn (Ouyang et al., 2023). For example, AI makes some teaching tasks easier and faster, like grading homework and keeping the classroom in order. AI has a much bigger effect than just making simple robots; it also helps make learning spaces that are more interactive and focused on the students. For example, AI can use information learned during the learning process to figure out complicated emotional behavior patterns and learn more about what a student needs (Vistorte et al., 2024). AI can recommend reading material suitable for the individual, return questions immediately, and invite greater subject explorations. That equally resonates across the administration and running of learning establishments, and the way in which individuals educate and learn. AI can help teachers plan lessons that are specific to each student's learning style and needs. AI-based learning platforms adapt and adjust material, pacing, and difficulty according to students' performance and optimize learning more effectively and efficiently. These tools invite individualized learning and offer insightful information for improving schooling achievements by monitoring where students are running behind and providing specific remedies. AI-based tools are very important for helping people be creative, think critically, and work together on group and activity-based projects. But to stop the replaceable handicapped displacement of human labor, AI implementations need to be watched, and budgets need to be spent on new ideas that help people do their jobs better (Acemoğlu & Restrepo, 2019). So, instead of replacing everything, it's better to use AI to help people learn and create a collaborative learning environment where people and machines can learn at the same time. AI could make interactive response materials and private learning experiences for students, enabling students to learn based on what best meets their requirements and passions and gain desirable learning advantages and engagement (Hwang, 2022).

The AI programs can also tell how students are feeling when they are in learning spaces, which can help them understand their emotional experiences better. These kinds of systems can listen for tone of voice, loudness, and keywords. They can also figure out how the person is feeling and send agents real-time pop-up and alert messages on how to improve the emotional side of dealing with customers. Onesi-Ozigagun et al., (2024) AI can help make learning spaces more accessible and welcoming by using assistive technology, language translation tools, and personalized learning materials.

Augmenting Human Potential: AI's Collaborative Role in Education

The focus on using AI to improve human potential is part of a bigger movement toward cooperative intelligence, where people and machines work together to solve tough problems and achieve common goals. For example, AI-based systems can provide computerized responses on students' writing, so educators can spend more time on high-level instruction and individualized support. AI can free up teachers to focus on high-level instruction, mentoring, and creative experimentation by automating routine tasks and giving each student personalized help (Anghel et al., 2025). It takes a change in the way we think about AI, from seeing it as a replacement for a human teacher to seeing how it could be improved and made more useful. AI lets teachers focus on helping students develop their social, emotional, and creative skills while AI takes care of routine tasks. Besides, employing the collaborative potentiality of AI, learning organizations can design inclusive learning spaces to cater to the diverse requirements of all students. To give teachers the knowledge and skills they need to use AI tools effectively, they need to change the way they think about their roles and responsibilities and make a commitment to professional development and training.

The belief that learning is, above all, a human-centric endeavor and not a technology-centric silver bullet runs through, despite gigantic advancements in machine learning and artificial intelligence (Popenici & Kerr, 2017). AI is great for personalization and efficiency, but it can't match or replace the subtlety, creativity, and moral judgment that human teachers have (Vieriu & Petrea, 2025). So, teachers need to find a balance between using technology and the human element in the classroom. If they don't, they could become too reliant on AI in the learning process (Dey, 2025). It means making sure that AI tools help with, but don't take the place of, important parts of human instruction like coaching, motivating, and teaching critical thinking.

As AI becomes more and more a part of the learning process, we need to think about the moral issues that come with using it in schools. Some of the problems are getting rid of algorithmic biases, protecting students' data privacy, and making sure that everyone has equal access to AI-based tools. AI programs can help students learn life skills, but the observations and personal insights of human teachers are priceless. In a bid to encourage critical thinking and creativity, instructors often utilize questioning methods, group work, and tasks to enable students to evaluate information and develop personal perspectives (Vieriu & Petrea, 2025). AI assists in language learning, providing customized responses and adaptive lessons, enhancing the traditional methods of instruction. When using AI for grading or giving feedback, you need to be extra careful because evaluation is a key part of teaching that has a big impact on learning. Teachers can also use AI-generated feedback to back up their own opinions and keep better track of each student's progress.

When adding AI to learning, you need to take a holistic approach that looks at the technological, human, ethical, and pedagogical aspects all at once. It encompasses ensuring that AI tools are designed and developed in a manner that increases equity, transparency, and accountability and facilitates educators' ability to effectively and ethically exploit the tools (Pohn et al., 2025). Teachers need to be able to use AI in the classroom in a way that is ethical, digital, and technical, as well as be able to read and understand data and be open to changing the way they think about their teacher's role (Kalniņa et al., 2024). By using AI technology to make teaching and learning more interactive, teachers can tailor the learning experience to each student's needs .AI will change the way we learn and teach in the future by automating tasks that are done over and over again and making it easier to learn in a way that is more tailored to each student .For the students and educators, the transition raises the need for the learning of new digital skills and a tendency for accepting technology as a tool for enhancing pedagogy (Kalniņa et al., 2024). This method encourages new ideas, diversity, and success in higher education by making use of AI's capabilities while keeping the focus on the human teacher and the ethical side for educators, it's important to build trust in AI because their lack of trust can make it hard for AI to be used successfully.

ENVISIONING THE EDUCATIONAL PARADIGM SHIFT: AI-POWERED LEARNING ANALYTICS IN THE DESIGN OF ADAPTIVE CURRICULA WITHIN HIGHER EDUCATION

Integrating AI into learning is changing the jobs of teachers. When AI-based apps handle routine and administrative tasks, teachers can spend more time giving students one-on-one attention and helping them think critically. In maximizing AI's impact on educational attainment, it is essential for educators and administrators to build capability in the technical and pedagogical dimensions of AI. Educators need to have a clear understanding of what AI can and can't do to use it effectively to help students learn. AI has also been utilized for improving research, and it is commensurate with the educational industry's perennial need for innovation. It includes helping with data analysis, looking at the literature, and making prediction models to see how learning trends and outcomes will change. Using AI in educational research not only speeds up the research process, but it also gives researchers more information that helps educational organizations make smart decisions and use evidence-based practices (Dey, 2025).

AI not only helps students learn in their way and do their best in school, but it also makes the administration process for educational organizations more effective and efficient. AI platforms can automate tasks like admissions, scheduling classes, and allocating resources. This frees up administrative staff to work on more important projects. The ensuing gains in efficiency can lead to cost-cutting and optimization of resources and have benefits accruing to students and organizations (Acemoğlu & Restrepo, 2019). When bringing AI into the classroom, it is important to think about things like data privacy and algorithm fairness. When it comes to using AI in medical education, we need to pay special attention to things like data security, algorithm transparency, and ethical standards.

AI can help make learning fairer and more inclusive by giving students from historically disadvantaged groups personalized help. This can help fix past differences in learning opportunities. AI-powered tools can figure out how you like to learn and what materials you need, and then suggest resources and ways to learn that are best for you (Oruganti, 2024). By using AI-powered products, schools can create more fair and welcoming learning spaces where every student can reach their full potential (Zaman, 2023). With careful planning, careful execution, and ongoing monitoring and evaluation of the effects on students, teachers, and learning facilities, AI can fully realize its transformative potential for learning. The potential for AI algorithms for the development of bias and issues related to questions of intellectual honesty ought, however, to be approached with diligence and underscore the need for educators to be equipped with technical ability as well as understanding the ethics-based implications of AI. Companies that give AI systems managerial powers can make workers follow decisions that are arbitrary or insensitive.

With the growing integration of AI into all aspects of higher education, it becomes equally crucial for universities to consider the ethical impact of AI on the matters of data privacy, algorithmic fairness, and transparency. Universities require guidelines and policies to be strictly in place so that AI systems can be utilized on the up and up and responsibly and protect the student data and maintain equitable outcomes (Merino-Campos, 2025). AI systems can become biased if they are trained on biased data, so it is important to make sure that AI systems are not biased and do not make existing inequalities worse (Harry & Sayudin, 2023). Important and prospective uses of AI for education include the creation of virtual assistants and chatbots which can be capable of providing students with customized support and counseling. These AI tools can answer students' questions, give them feedback on their assignments, and help them sign up for and choose courses. Students may be more interested and happier with their learning if they have access to virtual assistants and chatbots that can help them right away and tailor their support to their needs. This could lead to higher retention rates and better learning outcomes. AI can also look at how engaged and how well students are doing in school and give teachers ideas about how to improve their teaching and course design.

The capacity for AI to sift through vast collections of information and offer informative insights into the learning behaviors of pupils is one of its major advantages. Instructors can draw on the information so gleaned to differentiate their approach to learning and offer specialized support for pupils falling behind (Eager & Brunton, 2023). The lower intellectual challenge was found unacceptable for some, but the convenience was accepted by others. AI technology is deployed within a variety of workplace contexts for the purpose of mitigating the extent of intellectual challenge on the job. It's also important to remember that the use of AI across the educational sector poses challenges such as cost, trust, issues of privacy, and security concerns. In spite of stringent laws being in place, AI monitoring and surveillance technology dismantles workers' perceptions of a lack of autonomy, dignity, and privacy. Research and development on a continuous cycle are requisite for overcoming the challenges and putting AI effectively and responsibly into the learning environment.

Strategic Foresight: Charting the Trajectory of AI Integration in Educational Frameworks

Adding AI to education is a complex problem that requires both technical and teaching skills (Bancoro, 2024). Teachers need to carefully add AI-powered tools to their existing lesson plans and ways of teaching. Furthermore, educational institutions should invest in professional development initiatives to equip faculty with the knowledge and skills necessary to effectively utilize AI tools in the classroom. For teachers to use AI responsibly and improve student learning outcomes, they need to have a full understanding of its potential, limitations, and moral issues. AI is important for helping students learn on their own and keeping up with the changing needs of education. However, it should not replace the basic rules of good teaching and learning (Bancoro, 2024). When combined with innovative teaching approaches, AI can revolutionize both teaching and learning processes. Educators must be cognizant of the ethical implications of AI in education, particularly concerning data privacy, algorithmic bias, and equity. Education stakeholders need to work together to set rules and best practices for the ethical and responsible use of AI in schools (Baker & Inventado, 2014). For AI tools to be used in schools in a way that is both effective and ethical, academic staff must be involved. To make sure that AI technologies take into account cultural differences, local situations, and the unique needs of different educational systems, countries must work together (Baker & Inventado, 2014). To make sure that AI improves fairness and inclusion in education, everyone needs to work together on this.

IMPLEMENTATION AND SYSTEMIC CHALLENGES

The AI technology is extremely advanced and potentially out of reach for the majority of educators, particularly those without technical experience. To do this, the schools should spend money on professional training so that the teachers can learn how to use AI technology effectively and incorporate it into their teaching. Also, the initial costs of adopting AI technology, such as the cost of the software, hardware, and infrastructure, may be too high for some schools. To make the adoption widespread, governments, learning agencies, and other interested parties need to work together to provide money, resources, and help. To include AI in higher education, major changes need to be made to both the way teachers teach and the places where students learn (Liang et al., 2025). It can be hard to use AI technology in a traditional classroom, which usually prefers traditional methods of teaching.

When businesses start using AI tools, they should think about how they will affect workers' mental and emotional health, as well as the fact that people might misuse their privacy, dignity, and freedom of choice. Researchers found that using AI systems in a variety of jobs made the intellectual challenges less intense, which could make workers prefer a wider range of challenges. Because AI is still used to collect and analyze students' performance data, it was necessary to make it a law that this information be used in the name of ethics and responsibility. AI-based learning tools should also be made available to all students, no matter where they live or what their socioeconomic background is. The issue of surveillance and commodification of personal information is becoming more and more of a concern when it comes to using AI in learning (Roshanaei et al., 2023). Also, problems with emotional intelligence, unfair education, intellectual honesty, and copyright ownership need to be dealt with directly. It is up to the school to make sure that AI is used in addition to traditional learning, to encourage honesty in academics, and to get people to think critically (Nguyen, 2025). The stakeholders can be sure that AI technology will be used in a responsible and good way through the ethics and risks mitigation measures (Al-Zahrani, 2024). The institution should take the initiative and put rules and procedures in place to make sure that AI is used and applied safely and ethically in the learning process. This is because AI has the potential to improve academic performance.

AI-based technologies could cause problems for colleges and universities, but using them also raises moral questions. One of the most important things to pay attention to is data privacy. AI technology analyzes and processes a lot of student data, and there have been big concerns about privacy and security (Pikhart & Klímová, 2025). In return, there are also apprehensions that the students' information is being harvested using the AI technologies without their permission and can result in misuse or exploitation (Swidan et al., 2025). In order to protect the rights of students and gain their trust in AI technology, educational organizations must develop stringent policies for the governance of the data and adhere to ethical procedures for the handling of the data.

The AI can make learning more personal and give you useful information, but the system problems and moral issues that come with using it need to be fixed first. In a bid for responsible and AI-oriented integration, educators, policymakers, and stakeholders must develop regulatory guidelines, best practices, and ethical standards. Including a variety of people on AI development teams can help make AI more inclusive. Without this, there may be blind spots and an unbalanced approach when making AI products. Investing in resources and help for educational organizations and staff can help people learn about AI and use it responsibly (Chetry, 2024). AI-based technology can change colleges and universities, but using it can also raise some moral issues (Delello et al., 2025). Using AI-based tools in schools can bring up some moral issues about the platform for openness, fairness, privacy, ethics, and getting rid of bias (Tahir et al., 2024). Organizations can use AI in schools in a responsible and ethical way by making rules and procedures. This is because AI can give us deeper insights into education.

FUTURE IMPLICATIONS AND CONCLUSION

AI can make learning more interactive and improve how it is taught, but putting AI into the learning system raises serious ethical and practical questions (Ward et al., 2024). The tools can change how schools work and how students learn.AI-based learning analytics give teachers and learning policymakers' real-time information about how well students are doing, how engaged they are, and how well they are being tracked. This information can be used to create learning programs that are tailored to the unique needs and weaknesses of each student. Dynamic learning resources are changing the way people learn by changing the content, speed, and difficulty level of the material to fit the needs of each student. They also make individualized and inclusive pathways that lead to learning success and interaction (Roshanaei et al., 2023). The AI can be the deciding factor in keeping an eye on and helping students who aren't doing well, as well as providing timely support and personalized materials.

AI integration also creates shared and new learning spaces by connecting students who have similar interests or strengths that complement each other, and by making it easier for students to interact with each other and solve problems. By using AI-based tools and good teaching methods, teachers can give students the creativity and critical thinking skills they need to face future problems. However, for AI to have the most positive effect on higher education, educators and policymakers must improve their technical and teaching skills with the technologies. Also, it is important to think about ethical issues related to data protection and algorithmic fairness in order to make sure that access and outcomes are fair. Using AI in schools can change how people learn and teach by using personalized learning, smart tutoring, and automatic testing .AI-based systems can help students stay interested, learn more, and give teachers useful information on how to improve the way they help students learn (Oruganti, 2024). One of the best things about using AI in schools is that it lets students learn at their own pace and in the way that works best for them. This helps improve their learning outcomes.

AI has the power to change things because it can process huge amounts of data and find patterns and insights that can be used to create personalized learning experiences. AI technology is changing the way we evaluate students by using more interactive and informative measures instead of the usual tests and administrative tasks like enrolling students, making schedules, and allocating resources .AI can look at a lot of different things to see how well students are doing, such as how often they are engaged, how quickly they get feedback, and their assignments. This lets teachers tailor their teaching to each student. AI can look at a lot of different things, like how engaged students are, how quickly they get feedback, and what assignments they have, and it lets teachers change how they teach.

Using AI in education opens up a lot of options for students with disabilities. These tools can create personalized learning paths, make learning resources easier to access, and save teachers time that can be used to make the experience more interactive for students with disabilities (Hwang, 2022). Using AI can help teachers save time, make learning resources more accessible, and create personalized learning paths for each student. This can all lead to a more interactive experience for students with disabilities.

AI can automate administrative tasks and give students one-on-one attention, but workers are afraid that AI programs will make the job less intellectually demanding. It can free teachers from boring, repetitive tasks and let them focus on more creative and intellectually challenging parts of teaching, like mentoring and designing courses. But for AI to be fully useful in education, it needs to meet standards for data privacy, algorithmic bias, and equal access. AI-based e-learning platforms also make learning more effective by offering task-specific, real-time learning aids that are in line with the needs of modern educational systems and settings that change all the time (Hazzan-Bishara et al., 2025). When using AI, you should be careful of possible risks, like the automatic creation of invalid or biased content. AI has been used in new ways at work, like having customer service reps monitor calls and chats in real time for coaching, performance ratings, and task optimization. Virtual reality-based technologies that use interactive interfaces to improve people's ability to see, monitor, and manage things could also give workers more power in a machine-assisted workplace and help them make things with high precision and integrated design. AI has come a long way since the 1990s, when computers were first used in schools and smart tutoring and adaptive learning platforms were created. These adapt to each student's learning needs by providing personalized lessons, tracking progress, and giving immediate feedback. As AI continues to improve, teachers will need to learn more about how to use it in the classroom and how it affects students. This could give students new knowledge and chances to learn.

REFERENCES

Acemoğlu, D., & Restrepo, P. (2019). *The wrong kind of AI? Artificial intelligence and the future of labor demand.* DOI: 10.3386/w25682

Adewale, M. D., Azeta, A. A., Abayomi-Alli, A., & Sambo-Magaji, A. (2024). Impact of artificial intelligence adoption on students' academic performance in open and distance learning: A systematic literature review. *Heliyon, 10*(22), e40025. Advance online publication. DOI: 10.1016/j.heliyon.2024.e40025 PMID: 39605813

Ajani, O. A., Gamede, B. T., & Matiyenga, T. C. (2024). *Leveraging artificial intelligence to enhance teaching and learning in higher education: Promoting quality education and critical engagement.* Journal of Pedagogical Sociology and Psychology. DOI: 10.33902/JPSP.202528400

Akavova, A., Temirkhanova, Z., & Lorsanova, Z. M. (2023). *Adaptive learning and artificial intelligence in the educational space.* E3S Web of Conferences, 451, 6011. DOI: 10.1051/e3sconf/202345106011

Akhmadieva, R. Sh., Kalmazova, N., Belova, T. V., Prokopyev, A. I., Molodozhnikova, N. M., & Spichak, V. Y. (2024). Research trends in the use of artificial intelligence in higher education. *Frontiers in Education, 9*, 1438715. Advance online publication. DOI: 10.3389/feduc.2024.1438715

Akinwalere, S. N., & Ivanov, V. (2022). Artificial Intelligence in higher education: Challenges and opportunities. *BORDER CROSSING, 12*(1), 1–15. DOI: 10.33182/bc.v12i1.2015

Al-Rahmi, W., Aldraiweesh, A., Yahaya, N., & Kamin, Y. (2018). Massive open online courses (MOOCS): Systematic literature review in Malaysian higher education. *Int. J. Eng. Technol., 7*(4), 2197–2202. DOI: 10.14419/ijet.v7i4.15156

Al-Zahrani, A. M. (2024). Unveiling the shadows: Beyond the hype of AI in education. *Heliyon, 10*(9), e30696. Advance online publication. DOI: 10.1016/j.heliyon.2024.e30696 PMID: 38737255

Alam, M.Dr. Md. Mahmood Alam. (2018). Digital technologies in teaching and learning. *International Journal of Indian Psychology, 6*(2), 34–39. DOI: 10.25215/0602.045

AlTwijri, L., & Alghizzi, T. M. (2024). *Investigating the integration of artificial intelligence in English as a foreign language classes for enhancing learners' affective factors: A systematic review [Review of Investigating the integration of artificial intelligence in English as a foreign language classes for enhancing learners' affective factors: A systematic review].* Heliyon, 10(10). Elsevier BV. DOI: 10.1016/j.heliyon.2024.e31053

Anghel, G. A., Zanfir, C. M., Matei, F. L., Voicu, C. D., & Neac a, R. A. (2025). The Integration of artificial intelligence in academic learning practices: A Comprehensive approach. *Education Sciences*, *15*(5), 616. DOI: 10.3390/educsci15050616

Baker, R. S., & Inventado, P. S. (2014). Educational data mining and learning analytics. In *Springer eBooks* (p. 61). Springer Nature., DOI: 10.1007/978-1-4614-3305-7_4

Bancoro, J. C.Jaysone Christopher M. Bancoro. (2024). The Relationship between artificial intelligence (AI) usage and academic performance of business administration students. *International Journal of Asian Business and Management*, *3*(1), 27–48. DOI: 10.55927/ijabm.v3i1.7876

Bura, C., & Myakala, P. K. (2024). *Advancing transformative education: Generative AI as a catalyst for equity and innovation.* arXiv (Cornell University). https://doi.org//arxiv.2411.15971DOI: 10.48550

Chaudhry, M. A., & Kazim, E. (2021). Artificial intelligence in education (AIEd): A high-level academic and industry note 2021. *AI and Ethics*, *2*(1), 157–165. DOI: 10.1007/s43681-021-00074-z PMID: 34790953

Chetry, K. K. (2024). Transforming education: How AI is revolutionizing the learning experience. *International Journal of Research Publication and Reviews*, *5*(5), 6352–6356. DOI: 10.55248/gengpi.5.0524.1277

Cordero, J., Torres-Zambrano, J., & Cordero-Castillo, A. (2024). Integration of generative artificial intelligence in higher education: Best practices. *Education Sciences*, *15*(1), 32. DOI: 10.3390/educsci15010032

Delello, J. A., Sung, W., Mokhtari, K., Hebert, J., Bronson, A., & Giuseppe, T. D. (2025). AI in the Classroom: Insights from educators on usage, challenges, and mental health. *Education Sciences*, *15*(2), 113. DOI: 10.3390/educsci15020113

Dey, D. (2025). Enhancing educational tools through artificial intelligence in perspective of need of AI. DOI: 10.2139/ssrn.5031275

du Boulay, B. (2023). Artificial intelligence in education and ethics. In *Handbook of Open* (p. 93). Distance and Digital Education., DOI: 10.1007/978-981-19-2080-6_6

Eager, B., & Brunton, R. (2023). Prompting higher education towards AI-augmented teaching and learning practice. *Journal of University Teaching & Learning Practice, 20*(5). Advance online publication. DOI: 10.53761/1.20.5.02

Egunjobi, D., & Adeyeye, O. (2024). *Revolutionizing learning: The impact of augmented reality (AR) and artificial intelligence.* (AI on Education. *International Journal of Research Publication and Reviews, 5*(10), 1157–1170. DOI: 10.55248/gengpi.5.1024.2734

George, B., & Wooden, O. S. (2023). Managing the strategic transformation of higher education through artificial intelligence. *Administrative Sciences, 13*(9), 196. DOI: 10.3390/admsci13090196

Gkintoni, E., Antonopoulou, H., Sortwell, A., & Halkiopoulos, C. (2025). *Challenging cognitive load theory: The role of educational neuroscience and artificial intelligence in redefining learning efficacy [Review of challenging cognitive load theory: The role of educational neuroscience and artificial intelligence in redefining learning efficacy].* Brain Sciences, 15(2), 203. Multidisciplinary Digital Publishing Institute. DOI: 10.3390/brainsci15020203

Gligorea, I., Cioca, M., Oancea, R., Gorski, A.-T., Gorski, H., & Tudorache, P. (2023). *Adaptive learning using artificial intelligence in e-learning: A literature review [Review of adaptive learning using artificial intelligence in e-learning: A Literature review].* Education Sciences, 13(12), 1216. Multidisciplinary Digital Publishing Institute. DOI: 10.3390/educsci13121216

Global Educational Studies Review. (2020). *In global educational studies review.* https://doi.org/DOI: 10.31703/gesr

Guo, S., Halim, H. B. A., & Saad, M. R. B. M. (2025). Leveraging AI-enabled mobile learning platforms to enhance the effectiveness of English teaching in universities. *Scientific Reports, 15*(1), 15873. Advance online publication. DOI: 10.1038/s41598-025-00801-0 PMID: 40335582

Harry, A., & Sayudin, S. (2023). Role of AI in education. [INJURITY]. *Interdisciplinary Journal and Humanity, 2*(3), 260–268. DOI: 10.58631/injurity.v2i3.52

Hazzan-Bishara, A., Kol, O., & Levy, S. (2025). The factors affecting instructors' adoption of AI technologies: A unified model of external and internal determinants. *Education and Information Technologies, 30*(11), 15043–15069. Advance online publication. DOI: 10.1007/s10639-025-13393-z

Holmes, W., Porayska-Pomsta, K., Holstein, K., Sutherland, E., Baker, T. T., Shum, S. B., Santos, O. C., Rodrigo, M., Cukurova, M., Bittencourt, I. I., & Koedinger, K. R. (2021). Ethics of AI in education: Towards a community-wide framework. *International Journal of Artificial Intelligence in Education, 32*(3), 504–526. DOI: 10.1007/s40593-021-00239-1

Huang, A. Y. Q., Lu, O. H. T., & Yang, S. J. H. (2022). Effects of artificial intelligence-enabled personalized recommendations on learners' learning engagement, motivation, and outcomes in a flipped classroom. *Computers & Education, 194*, 104684. DOI: 10.1016/j.compedu.2022.104684

Hwang, S. (2022). Examining the effects of artificial intelligence on elementary students' mathematics achievement: A meta-analysis. *Sustainability (Basel), 14*(20), 13185. DOI: 10.3390/su142013185

Jiȧn, M. J. K. O. (2023). Personalized learning through AI. *Advances in Engineering Innovation, 5*(1), 16–19. DOI: 10.54254/2977-3903/5/2023039

Joshi, M. (2023). *Adaptive learning through artificial intelligence.* SSRN Electronic Journal. DOI: 10.2139/ssrn.4514887

Kabudi, T., Pappas, I. O., & Olsen, D. H. (2021). AI-enabled adaptive learning systems: A systematic mapping of the literature. *Computers and Education Artificial Intelligence, 2*, 100017. DOI: 10.1016/j.caeai.2021.100017

Kaledio, P., Robert, A., & Frank, L. A. (2024). *The impact of artificial intelligence on students' learning experience.* SSRN Electronic Journal. DOI: 10.2139/ssrn.4716747

Kalniņa, D., Nīmante, D., & Baranova, S. (2024). Artificial intelligence for higher education: Benefits and challenges for pre-service Instructors. *Frontiers in Education, 9*, 1501819. Advance online publication. DOI: 10.3389/feduc.2024.1501819

Kamalov, F., & Gurrib, I. (2023). *New era of artificial intelligence in education: Towards a sustainable multifaceted revolution.* arXiv (Cornell University). https://doi.org//arxiv.2305.18303DOI: 10.48550

Karakuş, N., Gedik, K., & Kazazoğlu, S.KARAKUŞ. (2025). Ethical decision-making in education: A comparative study of instructors and artificial intelligence in ethical dilemmas. *Behavioral Sciences (Basel, Switzerland), 15*(4), 469. DOI: 10.3390/bs15040469 PMID: 40282090

Kim, N. J., & Kim, M. K. (2022). Teacher's perceptions of using an artificial intelligence-based educational tool for scientific writing. *Frontiers in Education, 7*, 755914. Advance online publication. DOI: 10.3389/feduc.2022.755914

Lampou, R. (2023). The Integration of Artificial Intelligence in Education: Opportunities and Challenges. *Review of Artificial Intelligence in Education, 4*(00), e015. Advance online publication. DOI: 10.37497/rev.artif.intell.educ.v4i00.15

Liang, J., Stephens, J. M., & Brown, G. (2025*). A systematic review of the early impact of artificial intelligence on higher education curriculum, instruction, and assessment [Review of A systematic review of the early impact of artificial intelligence on higher education curriculum, instruction, and assessment].* Frontiers in Education, 10. Frontiers Media. DOI: 10.3389/feduc.2025.1522841

Lin, C.-C., Huang, A. Y. Q., & Lu, O. H. T. (2023). *Artificial intelligence in intelligent tutoring systems toward sustainable education: a systematic review [Review of Artificial intelligence in intelligent tutoring systems toward sustainable education: a systematic review].* Smart Learning Environments, 10(1). Springer Nature. DOI: 10.1186/s40561-023-00260-y

Lin, H., & Qiu, C. (2024). Artificial intelligence (AI) -integrated educational applications and college students' creativity and academic emotions: Students' and instructors' perceptions and attitudes. *BMC Psychology, 12*(1), 487. Advance online publication. DOI: 10.1186/s40359-024-01979-0 PMID: 39285268

Long, D., & Magerko, B. (2020). *What is ai literacy? Competencies and design considerations.* 1. DOI: 10.1145/3313831.3376727

Ma, K., Zhang, Y., & Hui, B.-H. (2024). How Does AI Affect College? The Impact of AI Usage in College Teaching on Students' Innovative Behavior and Well-Being. *Behavioral Sciences (Basel, Switzerland), 14*(12), 1223. DOI: 10.3390/bs14121223 PMID: 39767364

Maghsudi, S., Lan, A., Xu, J., & van der Schaar, M. (2021). Personalized Education in the Artificial Intelligence Era: What to Expect Next. *IEEE Signal Processing Magazine, 38*(3), 37–50. DOI: 10.1109/MSP.2021.3055032

Maghsudi, S., Lan, A., Xu, J., & van der Schaar, M. (2021). Personalized Education in the AI Era: What to Expect Next? arXiv. DOI: 10.48550/ARXIV.2101.10074

Mahmoud, C., & Sørensen, J. T. (2024). Artificial Intelligence in Personalized Learning with a Focus on Current Developments and Future Prospects. *Research and Advances in Education, 3*(8), 25–31. DOI: 10.56397/RAE.2024.08.04

Mallillin, L. L. D. (2024). Artificial Intelligence (AI) Towards Students' Academic Performance. *Innovare Journal of Education, 16*, 16–21. Advance online publication. DOI: 10.22159/ijoe.2024v12i4.51665

Maphalala, M. C., & Ajani, O. A. (2025). Leveraging artificial intelligence as a learning tool in higher education. *Interdisciplinary Journal of Education Research, 7*(1), a01. Advance online publication. DOI: 10.38140/ijer-2025.vol7.1.01

Marshall, S., Blaj-Ward, L., Dreamson, N., Nyanjom, J., & Bertuol, M. T. (2024). The reshaping of higher education: Technological impacts, pedagogical change, and future projections. *Higher Education Research & Development, 43*(3), 521–541. DOI: 10.1080/07294360.2024.2329393

Mello, R. F., Freitas, E., Pereira, F. D., Cabral, L., Tedesco, P., & Ramalho, G. (2023). *Education in the age of Generative AI: Context and Recent Developments*. arXiv (Cornell University). https://doi.org//arxiv.2309.12332DOI: 10.48550

Merino-Campos, C. (2025). *The Impact of Artificial Intelligence on Personalized Learning in Higher Education: A Systematic Review [Review of The Impact of Artificial Intelligence on Personalized Learning in Higher Education: A Systematic Review]*. Trends in Higher Education, 4(2), 17. Multidisciplinary Digital Publishing Institute. DOI: 10.3390/higheredu4020017

Mir, R., Mir, G. M., Raina, N. T., Mir, S., Mir, S. M., Miskeen, E., Alharthi, M. H., & Alamri, M. M. S. (2023). *Application of Artificial Intelligence in Medical Education: Current Scenario and Future Perspectives. [Review of Application of Artificial Intelligence in Medical Education: Current Scenario and Future Perspectives.]*. PubMed, 11(3), 133. National Institutes of Health. DOI: 10.30476/jamp.2023.98655.1803

Muhie, Y. A., & Woldie, A. B. (2020). *Integration of Artificial Intelligence Technologies in Teaching and Learning in Higher Education*. Science and Technology, 10(1), 1. http://www.sapub.org/global/showpaperpdf.aspx?doi=10.5923/j.scit.20201001.01

Neji, W., Boughattas, N., & Ziadi, F. (2023). Exploring New AI-Based Technologies to Enhance Students' Motivation. *Issues in Informing Science and Information Technology, 20*, 95. DOI: 10.28945/5149

Nguyen, V. (2025). The Use of Generative AI Tools in Higher Education: Ethical and Pedagogical Principles. *Journal of Academic Ethics, 23*(3), 1435–1455. Advance online publication. DOI: 10.1007/s10805-025-09607-1

O'Dea, X., & O'Dea, M. (2023). Is Artificial Intelligence Really the Next Big Thing in Learning and Teaching in Higher Education? A Conceptual Paper. *Journal of University Teaching & Learning Practice, 20*(5). Advance online publication. DOI: 10.53761/1.20.5.06

Ofosu-Asare, Y. (2024). Cognitive imperialism in artificial intelligence: Counteracting bias with indigenous epistemologies. *AI & Society*. Advance online publication. DOI: 10.1007/s00146-024-02065-0

Onesi-Ozigagun, O., Ololade, Y. J., Eyo-Udo, N. L., & Ogundipe, D. O. (2024). *Revolutionizing education through AI: A comprehensive review of enhancing learning experiences [review of revolutionizing education through AI: A comprehensive review of enhancing learning experiences].* International Journal of Applied Research in Social Sciences, 6(4), 589. Fair East Publishers. DOI: 10.51594/ijarss.v6i4.1011

Opesemowo, O. A. G., & Adewuyi, H. O. (2024). *A systematic review of artificial intelligence in mathematics education: The emergence of 4IR [Review of A systematic review of artificial intelligence in mathematics education: The emergence of 4IR].* Eurasia Journal of Mathematics, Science and Technology Education, 20(7). Modestum Limited. DOI: 10.29333/ejmste/14762

Oruganti, N. R. (2024). The Transformative Impact of AI in Education: A Technical Analysis. *International Journal of Scientific Research in Computer Science Engineering and Information Technology, 10*(6), 1457–1464. DOI: 10.32628/CSEIT241061181

Ouyang, F., Wu, M., Zheng, L., Zhang, L., & Jiao, P. (2023). Integration of artificial intelligence performance prediction and learning analytics to improve student learning in online engineering course. *International Journal of Educational Technology in Higher Education, 20*(1), 4. Advance online publication. DOI: 10.1186/s41239-022-00372-4 PMID: 36683653

Phua, J. T. K., Neo, H. F., & Teo, C.-C. (2025). Evaluating the Impact of Artificial Intelligence Tools on Enhancing Student Academic Performance: Efficacy Amidst Security and Privacy Concerns. *Big Data and Cognitive Computing, 9*(5), 131. DOI: 10.3390/bdcc9050131

Pohn, B., Mehnen, L., Fitzek, S., Choi, K., Braun, R. J., & Hatamikia, S. (2025). Integrating artificial intelligence into pre-clinical medical education: Challenges, opportunities, and recommendations. *Frontiers in Education, 10*, 1570389. Advance online publication. DOI: 10.3389/feduc.2025.1570389

Popenici, Ş., & Kerr, S. (2017). Exploring the impact of artificial intelligence on teaching and learning in higher education. *Research and Practice in Technology Enhanced Learning, 12*(1), 22. Advance online publication. DOI: 10.1186/s41039-017-0062-8 PMID: 30595727

Qiu, Y., Pan, J., & Ishak, N. A. (2022). Effectiveness of Artificial Intelligence (AI) in Improving Pupils' Deep Learning in Primary School Mathematics Teaching in Fujian Province. *Computational Intelligence and Neuroscience*, *1*, 1–10. Advance online publication. DOI: 10.1155/2022/1362996 PMID: 36193186

Rad, H. S. (2025). Reinforcing L2 reading comprehension through artificial intelligence intervention: Refining engagement to foster self-regulated learning. *Smart Learning Environments*, *12*(1), 23. Advance online publication. DOI: 10.1186/s40561-025-00377-2

Regmi, K., & Jones, L. (2020). A systematic review of the factors - enablers and barriers - affecting e-learning in health sciences education. *BMC Medical Education*, *20*(1), 91. DOI: 10.1186/s12909-020-02007-6 PMID: 32228560

Roméro, M., Heiser, L., Lepage, A., Gagnebien, A., Bonjour, A., Lagarrigue, A., Palaude, A., Boulord, C., Gagneur, C.-A., Mercier, C., Caucheteux, C., Guidoni-Stoltz, D., Tressols, F., Henry, J., Alexandre, F., Céci, J.-F., Camponovo, J., Fouché, L., Métral, J.-F., . . . Borgne, Y. L. (2023). *Teaching and learning in the age of artificial intelligence*. arXiv (Cornell University). https://doi.org//arxiv.2303.06956DOI: 10.48550

Roshanaei, M., Olivares, H., & Lopez, R. R. (2023). Harnessing AI to Foster Equity in Education: Opportunities, Challenges, and Emerging Strategies. *Journal of Intelligent Learning Systems and Applications*, *15*(4), 123–143. DOI: 10.4236/jilsa.2023.154009

Saputra, I., Astuti, M., Sayuti, M., & Kusumastuti, D. (2023). Integration of Artificial Intelligence in Education: Opportunities, Challenges, Threats and Obstacles. A Literature Review. *Indonesian Journal of Computer Science*, *12*(4). Advance online publication. DOI: 10.33022/ijcs.v12i4.3266

Sharma, S., Mittal, P., Kumar, M., & Bhardwaj, V. (2025). *The role of large language models in personalized learning: a systematic review of educational impact [Review of the role of large language models in personalized learning: a systematic review of educational impact]*. Discover Sustainability, 6(1). Springer Nature. DOI: 10.1007/s43621-025-01094-z

Swidan, A., Lee, S. Y., & Romdhane, S. B. (2025). College Students' Use and Perceptions of AI Tools in the UAE: Motivations, Ethical Concerns and Institutional Guidelines. *Education Sciences*, *15*(4), 461. DOI: 10.3390/educsci15040461

Tahir, M., Hassan, F. D., & Shagoo, M. R. (2024). *Role of artificial intelligence in education: A conceptual review [Review of Role of artificial intelligence in education: A conceptual review].* World Journal of Advanced Research and Reviews, 22(1), 1469. GSC Online Press. DOI: 10.30574/wjarr.2024.22.1.1217

Tan, M. J. T., & Maravilla, N. M. A. T. (2024). Shaping integrity: Why generative artificial intelligence does not have to undermine education. *Frontiers in Artificial Intelligence*, *7*, 1471224. Advance online publication. DOI: 10.3389/frai.2024.1471224 PMID: 39512399

The Impact of AI on Teaching and Learning in Higher Education Technology. (2022). The Impact of AI on Teaching and Learning in Higher Education Technology. *Journal of Higher Education Theory and Practice*, *22*(13). Advance online publication. DOI: 10.33423/jhetp.v22i13.5514

Thelma, C. C., Sain, Z. H., Shogbesan, Y. O., Phiri, E. V., & Akpan, W. M. (2024). *Ethical* Implications of AI and Machine Learning in Education: A Systematic Analysis. 3(1), 1. DOI: 10.33650/ijit.v3i1.9364

Vieriu, A. M., & Petrea, G. (2025). The Impact of Artificial Intelligence (AI) on Students' Academic Development. *Education Sciences*, *15*(3), 343. DOI: 10.3390/educsci15030343

Vistorte, A. O. R., Deroncele-Acosta, Á., Ayala, J. L. M., Barrasa, Á., López-Granero, C., & Martí-González, M. (2024). Integrating artificial intelligence to assess emotions in learning environments: A systematic literature review. *Frontiers in Psychology*, *15*, 1387089. Advance online publication. DOI: 10.3389/fpsyg.2024.1387089 PMID: 38966729

Ward, B., Bhati, D., Neha, F., & Guercio, A. (2024). *Analyzing the Impact of AI Tools on Student Study Habits and Academic Performance.* arXiv (Cornell University). https://doi.org//arxiv.2412.02166DOI: 10.48550

Ward, B., Bhati, D., Neha, F., & Guercio, A. (2025). *Analyzing the Impact of AI Tools on Student Study Habits and Academic Performance.* 2022 IEEE 12th Annual Computing and Communication Workshop and Conference (CCWC), 434. DOI: 10.1109/CCWC62904.2025.10903692

Xu, X. (2025). *AI optimization algorithms enhance higher education management and personalized teaching through empirical analysis [Review of AI optimization algorithms enhance higher education management and personalized teaching through empirical analysis].* Scientific Reports, 15(1). Nature Portfolio. DOI: 10.1038/s41598-025-94481-5

Yaseen, H., Mohammad, A. S., Ashal, N., Abusaimeh, H., Ali, A. A. A., & Sharabati, A. A. (2025). The Impact of Adaptive Learning Technologies, Personalized Feedback, and Interactive AI Tools on Student Engagement: The Moderating Role of Digital Literacy. *Sustainability (Basel), 17*(3), 1133. DOI: 10.3390/su17031133

Zaman, B. U. (2023). Transforming Education Through AI, Benefits, Risks, and Ethical Considerations. DOI: 10.36227/techrxiv.24231583

Zawacki-Richter, O., Marín, V. I., Bond, M., & Gouverneur, F. (2019). Systematic review of research on artificial intelligence applications in higher education – where are the educators? *International Journal of Educational Technology in Higher Education, 16*(1), 39. Advance online publication. DOI: 10.1186/s41239-019-0171-0

Zhai, X., Chu, X., Chai, C. S., Jong, M. S., Starčič, A. I., Spector, M., Liu, J., Jing, Y., & Li, Y. (2021). *A Review of Artificial Intelligence (AI) in Education from 2010 to 2020 [Review of A Review of Artificial Intelligence (AI) in Education from 2010 to 2020].* Complexity, 2021(1). Hindawi Publishing Corporation. DOI: 10.1155/2021/8812542

Zou, Y. L., Kuek, F., Feng, W. Z., & Cheng, X. (2025). Digital learning in the 21st century: Trends, challenges, and innovations in technology integration. *Frontiers in Education, 10*, 1562391. Advance online publication. DOI: 10.3389/feduc.2025.1562391

Chapter 5

Developing Teaching Competencies for AI-Enhanced Learning: Teachers' Evolving Roles in Intelligent Tutoring Systems

Seoyeon Park
https://orcid.org/0000-0001-5024-9435
University of Nevada, Las Vegas, USA

Wenting Weng
Johns Hopkins University, USA

ABSTRACT

Digital transformation demands new teaching competencies for AI-enhanced learning. This study analyzes teachers' roles in intelligent tutoring systems to inform competency frameworks for pedagogical innovation. Through systematic analysis of 71 studies from the International Journal of Artificial Intelligence in Education (1997-2021), we identified three competency domains: domain expertise (32%), active user capabilities (46%), and developer skills (2%). Teachers function as essential partners in AI-enhanced ecosystems, contributing specialized knowledge and orchestrating technology-integrated experiences. Successful integration requires competencies spanning technical proficiency, pedagogical innovation, data interpretation, and ethical decision-making. Results show AI transforms rather than replaces teaching roles, creating personalized instruction opportunities while challenges persist including technology anxiety and resource constraints. This analysis provides foundation for competency-based professional development programs supporting educational technology integration.

DOI: 10.4018/979-8-3373-7729-2.ch005

INTRODUCTION

Teachers who once worked primarily with textbooks and chalkboards now find themselves collaborating with computer systems that can track how students think through problems, adjust lessons based on each student's learning style, and provide individualized feedback that used to require expensive private tutoring. This isn't just about adding computers to classrooms—it represents a fundamental change in what it means to be an educator.

Intelligent tutoring systems (ITSs) have extensively evolved and contributed to the flourishing of artificial intelligence (AI)-supported education over the last 25 years. ITSs have gained attention for their various learning advantages, such as the ability to capture students' progress in real-time, provide a knowledge example model, and offer timely scaffolding that is not limited to cognitive, metacognitive, or emotional scaffolding (Ma et al., 2014; VanLehn, 2011; Cen et al., 2007). ITSs have been actively applied to K–12 and higher education levels in a variety of areas, such as language, mathematics, sciences, and reading comprehension.

Even though ITSs have been successfully and widely used in diverse subject domains, their effectiveness on students' learning has been a topic of controversy. Many studies strongly contend that ITSs are effective tools for student learning by providing students with highly adaptive and interactive learning environments (Aleven et al., 2009; Koedinger et al., 2004; Blessing et al., 2009; Kodavali et al., 2010; Devasani et al., 2012; Kodaganallur et al., 2005; MacLellan et al., 2014). For example, VanLehn (2011) found that ITSs have a high impact (d = .76) on students' learning in STEM areas, making ITS comparable to human tutoring. Xu et al. (2020) also presented that using ITS can significantly increase students' reading comprehension in K–12 classrooms (d = .60).

However, several rigorous meta-analysis papers have revealed that ITSs have negative or a very small positive effects on students' learning compared to traditional classroom instruction (What Works Clearinghouse, 2010; Steenbergen-Hu & Cooper, 2013) These papers pointed out that the effectiveness of ITS can vary based on many other factors, such as the degree of technology implementation, the context of implementation, or students' prior knowledge levels or metacognitive skills. For example, Belland et al. (2017) contend that low achievers are more likely to struggle with learning content using computer-based learning environments like ITS because they have less prior knowledge, metacognitive skills, or motivation. Ceci and Papiero (2005) also emphasized that using educational technology can result in unwanted learning gaps between different student groups if teachers use these technologies without caution. Steenbergen-Hu and Cooper (2013) found that ITS can have no or very little impact on students' learning when researchers have very limited communication with teachers and cannot ensure that teachers use ITS in their curriculum.

To maximize the advantages and minimize the negative aspects of using ITS in teaching and learning, it is crucial to investigate how teachers have contributed to ITS development and implementation in classrooms and how they can boost meaningful ITS integration into the curriculum. This is because teachers are the ones who can connect students and ITS (and/or ITS researchers) with proper guidance. Teachers have been dominant collaborators of researchers and have shared their knowledge of subject domains and example models of instruction strategies for ITS development. Moreover, they play the main role in using ITS in their teaching and leading AI-based instruction for widespread ITS adoption at the K–12 level. However, most ITS studies have focused more on the effectiveness of ITS interventions on students' attitudes or cognitive outcomes. In the literature related to ITS, how teachers have helped researchers advance ITS and their inputs for the future of ITSs have been somewhat overlooked.

Beyond traditional competencies recommended for teachers such as critical thinking and problem-solving, educators now need to equip new competencies including understanding how AI systems work, interpreting student data meaningfully, and designing lessons that integrate technology in ways that truly support individual learning needs (Reigeluth, 2014). Rather than simply delivering content, teachers are becoming learning facilitators who work alongside intelligent systems to enhance their teaching effectiveness and student learning outcomes. How can we help teachers actually develop these skills? Combining AI technologies and human expertise will be an important task for teachers and teacher educators in the contemporary education era.

The purpose of this study is to provide a comprehensive analysis of the essential teaching competencies required for effective AI-enhanced learning environments by examining teachers' roles in intelligent tutoring system development and implementation. By analyzing 71 empirical studies from the International Journal of Artificial Intelligence in Education (IJAIED), we explore how educators function as domain experts, active users, and developers of intelligent tutoring systems, revealing the specific competency domains and development patterns necessary for successful AI integration.

Through this examination of teachers' roles in ITS ecosystems, we aim to illuminate the competency requirements necessary for successful AI integration in educational settings. The insights gained from this analysis will contribute to more effective teacher preparation strategies, more thoughtful institutional support systems, and more successful implementations of AI-enhanced learning systems that truly serve the needs of both educators and students.

BACKGROUND

Competency-based Frameworks for AI Literacy in Education

Education has changed dramatically in recent decades. Schools have moved away from the old system of "seat time"—where students simply spent a certain number of hours in class—toward focusing on whether students actually master what they're learning. This shift means teachers need new skills to help students apply their knowledge in meaningful ways outside the classroom (Reigeluth, 2014). In the digital age, AI literacy has become essential for teachers, which involves understanding when AI tools can genuinely help students learn (Holmes et al., 2019). Researchers have developed several frameworks to help make sense of what teachers need to know.

Technological Pedagogical Content Knowledge (TPACK) framework remains one of the most traditional and influential frameworks for explaining teachers' competencies in using technology (Mishra & Koehler, 2006). TPACK provides a comprehensive model for understanding how teachers can integrate technology into their instruction effectively. The framework identifies seven interconnected knowledge domains: technological knowledge, pedagogical knowledge, content knowledge, and their intersections. The TPACK framework has been modified to address the unique characteristics of AI use in education, such as understanding AI algorithms and the ability to use AI tools for more adaptive and personalized learning. Teacher attitudes toward AI are also regarded as crucial factors in their competency for using AI within the TPACK framework.

Another popular framework is the European Digital Competence Framework for Educators (DigCompEdu), which identifies six key areas of digital competence: professional engagement, digital resources, teaching and learning, assessment, empowering learners, and facilitating learners' digital competence (Ghomi & Redecker, 2019). This framework describes several different levels of teachers' digital competence. Teachers are regarded as beginners in digital competence if they can use basic technology such as online resources or digital projectors. At the intermediate level, teachers can integrate various digital tools into their lessons and feel more confident using new technology. Teachers with advanced levels of digital competence can share their knowledge with colleagues and act as leaders who inspire other teachers to use innovative teaching techniques.

UNESCO's recent AI Competency Framework for Teachers (2024) suggests an even more detailed framework for AI literacy. Unlike general competency frameworks for digital literacy, UNESCO addresses unique challenges around ethics, fairness, transparency, and specific professional development for using AI in instruction. This framework is unique because it reflects social impacts in explaining and evaluating teachers' competencies around AI use. It is also regarded as a more comprehensive framework due to its emphasis on a human-centered approach and social justice, sustainability, and human dignity when integrating AI into education.

Teacher Roles in integrating ITS into Classrooms

The effectiveness and integration of educational technology into the classroom commonly depend on teachers' approaches to instruction, which can be classified into two categories as either teacher-centered and student-centered (Deng et al., 2014; Ravitz et al., 2000; Tondeur et al., 2017). With a teacher-centered approach, teachers use technology to sustain and reinforce their existing practice, which emphasizes direct guidance, lectures, and demonstrations of the subject matter (Mayer, 2003; Cuban et al., 2001). The teacher can control the process of learning acquisition and provide highly structured content delivery, which makes this approach sometimes more effective than a student-centered approach. However, students may have less motivation and miss learning opportunities, such as participating in authentic disciplinary problems with their peers. In contrast, student-centered approaches allow students to freely interact with technological tools as per their own needs and interests (Kerlinger & Kaya, 1959; Mayer, 2003). With a student-centered approach, students can regulate their learning progress. However, there is a risk that students fail to learn about important content or to receive proper feedback, which can lead to poor performance regarding cognitive tasks.

Even though advanced technologies like virtual reality, mobile apps, or ITSs have been developed and have proven to be significantly effective for students' learning and to have great potential in school settings, much of technology integration in classrooms has occurred as "add-ons" to a teacher-centered curriculum. Examples of "add-ons" include using PowerPoints or e-books (Reighluth & Joseph, 2002; Reigeluth, 2014). To promote students' learning motivation and encourage them to actively participate in authentic problem-solving, it is necessary to embrace a learner-centered approach for integrating technology in the classroom. According to Reigeluth (2014), learner-centered technology integration in education demands several essential characteristics. First, student progress should be based on their learning progress and not an assigned time. Additionally, learner-centered technology integration requires personalization in planning, instruction, recordkeeping, and assessment, which can be achievable by applying technology to help students customize their learning experiences.

Considering that ITS is composed of four modules (expert knowledge, student, tutoring, and user interface), integrating ITS in classrooms can take advantage of both the teacher- and learner-centered approaches. The expert knowledge module includes content that should be taught. This module serves as both the source of knowledge to be presented and the standard for student performance evaluations.

This module is also used to identify any gaps between students' knowledge and that of experts so that the ITS can produce sensible and intermediate steps for students. The tutoring module involves instructional interactions between a tutoring agent and a student in the ITS. This module can be considered parallel to the instruction strategy by embracing creative strategies to present knowledge, learning objectives, and support based on the student model (Self, 1990). Thus, the tutoring module is described as the combination of all kinds of pedagogical interventions. If a student gets stuck or lost, the ITS monitors the students' activity and adapts their tutoring actions to the student's responses based on strategies that are embedded in the systems. These modules allow ITSs to provide students with personalized instruction and planning based on information from the student model module.

The student model module indicates the "dynamic representation of the emerging knowledge and skill of the student" (Nwana, 1990, p.260). This module allows an ITS to offer personalized recordkeeping and assessment by reflecting students' behaviors and how they develop their knowledge through learning tasks. The user interface module controls the interactions between the students and the system itself (Nwana, 1990). Assorted user interfaces, such as text, pictures, graphics, or natural language via computer speech recognition, are employed in ITSs. Given that the effects and power of interactions are influenced by the user interface, it needs to be clear and understandable to students. Students can regulate their learning by using functions, such as hints, discussion, resources, and others, in the user interface of the ITS. Integrating ITS in the classroom in an appropriate manner can be a great way to realize dynamic learning environments for both teachers and students because ITS can provide well-designed practice opportunities, timely feedback, and learner-centered interactions among students, content, and teachers.

The Reality Check: Challenges Teachers Face when integrating ITS in classrooms

ITS have been widely used in diverse areas including mathematics, science, and language learning. For example, Cognitive Tutor by Carnegie Mellon University is one of the most successful ITS for students' learning in mathematics and was used in over 2,600 schools in the United States (Clearinghouse, 2010). Several studies supporting the benefits of using ITS such as Cognitive Tutor have shown that integrating ITS in classroom instruction can help students learn effectively by providing adequate and personalized practice opportunities (Koedinger et al., 1997). In particular, ITS excels at helping students practice fine-grained skills to master required knowledge (VanLehn, 2011). Moreover, ITS also supports teachers' data-driven classroom instruction by identifying students' weaknesses and providing real-time student data (Onyesom, 2024).

However, teachers sometimes face the challenge of addressing unproductive students' learning patterns while integrating ITS into their classroom instruction. Some studies revealed that ITS can waste students' learning time and often threaten their motivation to learn by lacking sufficient support or scaffolding beyond problem-solving steps (Cen et al., 2007; Park, 2023). This phenomenon becomes severe especially when students do not have sufficient prior knowledge or motivation. This requires teachers to make complex decisions about when to intervene while students are working on ITS-directed learning and how to support students' unique challenges. Furthermore, teachers might struggle to identify students who need help if they appear to be working diligently in ITS. Other studies also found that integrating ITS in classroom instruction might challenge teachers to maintain students engaged in classroom activities. Some teachers found that the majority of students did not stay on task consistently while incorporating ITS in their classrooms (Phillips et al., 2020).

Teachers also face additional challenges finding appropriate curriculum and instructional sequences when integrating ITS into their classroom instruction. Considering that the typical class time is relatively short, 40-50 minutes, teachers struggle to have enough time to check on all students and provide remedial instructions for students who might need them, when they also need to give students learning time with ITS. Thus, teachers said it's hard to allocate instruction time effectively when integrating ITS as their main technology (Phillips et al., 2020). They sometimes find it difficult to choose ready-to-learn topics that are already available in ITSs while ensuring alignment with state standards at the same time.

In addition to these pedagogical challenges, teachers also face ongoing concerns about system reliability and ethical issues. Teachers often need to address technical barriers such as updates for optimal effectiveness and software not working properly on either their or students' computers during instruction, which creates severe disruptions (Alsaqqa et al., 2022). Also, they express concerns about privacy and ethics, which are related to student data protection, (Baig et al., 2024). Sometimes teachers find it difficult to trust ITS, which store vast amounts of data collected from students, including their academic performance, access time, location, and other information, and believe these systems have insufficient protection for such data due to lack of encryption or anonymization.

METHOD

Given the theoretical frameworks and competency development models discussed above, empirical analysis is needed to understand how these concepts manifest in practice. The literature reveals significant gaps in understanding the specific competency domains that teachers must develop for AI integration and the developmental pathways through which these competencies emerge. To address these gaps, this study employs systematic content analysis of empirical research on intelligent tutoring systems, which provide a rich context for examining teacher-AI collaboration across development and implementation stages.

Search Database

We focused on The International Journal of Artificial Intelligence in Education (IJAIED) database, considering the profound impact and rigorousness of this journal in publishing research on AI applications in educational contexts. The IJAIED journal has dedicated itself to publishing articles on the frontiers of artificial intelligence in education for decades, providing a comprehensive repository of empirical evidence on technology-enhanced learning systems. This database offers the most extensive collection of peer-reviewed research documenting teacher involvement in AI-enhanced learning environments, making it ideal for identifying competency requirements and development patterns.

The journal covers a broad spectrum of topics relevant to understanding how AI technologies can support and transform educational practice, with particular strength in documenting teacher roles across system development and classroom implementation. According to the IJAIED website, the journal published its first article in 1989. However, the journal's online database provides access to published articles starting from 1997 except 2002. Therefore, our article search included publications from 1997 to 2021 excluding 2002. This 24-year span provides sufficient temporal scope to identify evolution in teacher competency requirements as AI technologies have advanced and become more accessible in educational settings.

Search Criteria and Coding Strategy for Competency Analysis

Understanding how teachers develop competencies for AI-enhanced learning requires comprehensive analysis of their documented involvement across different aspects of intelligent tutoring system implementation. This analysis necessitated examining teachers' contributions from multiple perspectives to identify the knowledge, skills, and abilities required for effective AI integration in educational practice, aligning with the competency-based education frameworks discussed in the literature review.

We adopted a content analysis method (Krippendorff, 2018) to retrieve relevant information from previous studies regarding teacher competency requirements in AI-enhanced learning environments. The procedure of our content analysis included (1) development of a competency-focused data encoding system based on established frameworks for digital competence and AI literacy, (2) implementation of the encoding system to identify competency indicators, (3) organization of retrieved information according to competency domains, and (4) interpretation and reporting of results in terms of competency development patterns and professional development implications.

Two screenings were conducted during the process. The first brief screening was to navigate relevant studies based on our inclusion and exclusion criteria. In the second screening, we used ("teacher" AND "intelligent tutoring systems") as the search string across each article to retrieve information on teachers' contributions and the competencies demonstrated in their involvement. We developed the data encoding system by categorizing information from selected studies based on the competency requirements evidenced in teachers' roles during ITS development and implementation, drawing on the theoretical frameworks for competency-based education and professional development models identified in our literature review.

After completing the coding process, we cross-checked our coding results to ensure consistency and accuracy in identifying competency indicators and requirements across different studies and contexts.

Inclusion criteria

The studies included in this paper had to meet all the specific criteria below:

1. Articles published in IJAIED from 1997 through 2023.
2. Articles pertaining to empirical primary studies investigating the implementation of ITS in educational contexts.
3. Articles providing information about teachers' contributions that demonstrate specific competencies or competency development requirements.

Exclusion criteria

1. Articles that did not report any teacher participation or competency indicators.
2. Articles that merely mentioned teacher participation without providing information about competency requirements or demonstrated capabilities.

3. Articles that focused solely on literature review without empirical evidence of teacher competency requirements.
4. Articles that were not published in IJAIED from 1997 to 2023.

Competency Framework Development

In our coding schema, we established categories that align with competency development frameworks: (1) competency domain indicators, (2) development stage requirements, and (3) demonstrated competency types. The competency domain indicators refer to the specific areas of knowledge, skill, and ability that teachers demonstrate or require for effective AI integration, such as domain expertise for system development, active user capabilities for classroom implementation, or developer competencies for system creation.

The development stage requirements indicate whether teachers' competency development occurs through involvement in AI system development processes or through implementation experiences in educational settings. The demonstrated competency types represent the specific capabilities that teachers exhibit in their documented roles and activities.

During our analysis, we identified an emerging category of teacher competencies related to AI system creation and authoring. While analyzing articles, we found several research studies that document teachers using authoring tools to build and manage intelligent tutoring systems. These tools enable teachers to create problems in tutoring systems, map problems to assessed skills, and manage content over time (Feng et al., 2011). This content authoring capability represents an advanced competency domain that grants teachers roles as educational technology creators rather than merely consumers.

Therefore, we implemented our encoding system to synthesize results in terms of three primary competency domains: (1) domain expertise competencies required for AI system development collaboration, (2) active user competencies for effective classroom implementation of AI-enhanced learning, and (3) emerging developer competencies for creating and customizing AI-enhanced learning tools.

Initially, we identified 445 articles from the IJAIED database across 1997 to 2021 in total. After applying the inclusion and exclusion criteria, 71 articles were selected and prepared for competency analysis.

The analysis revealed that across the selected studies, 38% demonstrated teachers' involvement in competency development related to knowledge domain expertise, 40% involved teachers in developing instructional competencies for AI-enhanced teaching, and 21% documented competencies related to student modeling and learning analytics interpretation. Additionally, 40% of the selected studies documented competency development requirements during AI system development stages, while

58% focused on competencies required for implementation in educational settings. The studies documented teachers demonstrating competencies as active users of AI systems (46%), domain experts contributing specialized knowledge (32%), instructional experts designing AI-enhanced learning experiences (21%), and emerging developers creating educational technology tools (2%).

Research Questions

In this review, we aim to answer the research questions formulated below:

1. What are the essential teaching competency domains that educators must develop for effective AI integration in educational settings, as evidenced by teachers' roles in intelligent tutoring systems?
2. How do teachers progress through different levels of competency development in AI-enhanced learning environments, and what patterns characterize the integration of multiple competency domains?

The first research question examines the specific competency domains that emerge from teachers' documented involvement in intelligent tutoring system development and implementation, identifying the knowledge, skills, and abilities required for effective AI collaboration across domain expertise, active user, and developer roles. The second research question explores the developmental progression pathways that teachers follow as they advance from foundational competency building through practical application to advanced innovation, including how teachers integrate capabilities across multiple competency domains to achieve sophisticated AI integration. Together, these research questions address how empirical evidence from ITS research can inform understanding of the essential competencies and development patterns necessary for preparing educators to effectively leverage AI technologies in 21st-century educational environments.

RESULTS

Our analysis of 71 empirical studies reveals three interconnected competency domains that educators need to develop for effective AI integration in educational settings. These competencies are based on observing what teachers actually do when working with ITS systems, providing evidence-based insights into the knowledge, skills, and abilities required for successful AI-enhanced teaching practice.

Competency Development Progression Patterns

The analysis reveals distinct progression patterns in teacher competency development that mirror established frameworks for AI integration. Teachers demonstrate development across three progressive levels: foundational competency building (acquire), practical application and integration (deepen), and advanced innovation and creation (create). This progression is evidenced by teachers' movement from initial involvement as domain experts contributing basic knowledge (40% of studies documenting development stage activities) to active implementation in classroom settings (58% of studies focusing on implementation stage competencies) to emerging roles as system creators and developers.

The temporal analysis of studies from 1997 to 2021 reveals an evolution in competency expectations and opportunities. Early studies (1997-2010) primarily documented teachers in domain expert roles, contributing subject matter knowledge to system development. The middle period (2011-2015) showed increased emphasis on active user competencies as ITS implementation expanded in educational settings. Recent studies (2016-2021) demonstrate emerging developer competencies, with teachers gaining access to more user-friendly authoring tools and creation platforms.

Educational level analysis indicates differentiated competency development patterns. K-12 implementations (62% of studies) emphasize active user competencies with focus on classroom management and student monitoring, while higher education implementations (38% of studies) show greater emphasis on domain expertise competencies and emerging developer roles. This distribution reflects different institutional contexts and teacher autonomy levels across educational sectors.

Domain Expertise Competencies for AI Collaboration

The analysis reveals that developing domain expertise competencies is fundamental for effective AI integration, with 38% of studies documenting teachers' involvement in knowledge module development and 32% positioning teachers as domain experts during system development stages. These competencies encompass teachers' ability to articulate subject matter knowledge in ways that can inform AI system design and to identify critical learning challenges that students face within their disciplines.

Teachers demonstrating domain expertise competencies contribute specialized pedagogical content knowledge that enables AI systems to provide more effective instruction. The competency development in this domain involves several key elements: knowledge modeling capabilities, where teachers learn to structure and represent their expertise in formats suitable for AI systems; curriculum mapping skills, enabling teachers to align AI capabilities with learning objectives and standards; and learning difficulty identification, where teachers contribute insights about common student misconceptions and challenging concepts.

Subject domain analysis reveals variation in domain expertise competency requirements. Mathematics and science domains (45% of domain expert studies) emphasize procedural knowledge representation and problem-solving strategy modeling. Language arts implementations (28% of domain expert studies) focus on discourse patterns and feedback strategy development. STEM interdisciplinary approaches (27% of domain expert studies) require complex knowledge integration capabilities spanning multiple domains.

The development of domain expertise competencies requires teachers to engage in meta-cognitive reflection about their subject matter knowledge and instructional practices. Teachers must develop the ability to deconstruct their expertise into components that can inform AI system development while maintaining deep understanding of how students learn within their disciplines. This competency domain bridges traditional pedagogical content knowledge with emerging requirements for AI collaboration in educational contexts.

Active User Competencies for Technology-Integrated Teaching

Active user competencies represent the most prevalent competency domain in our analysis, with 46% of studies documenting teachers as primary users of ITS in classroom settings and 58% of studies focusing on implementation stage activities. These competencies encompass teachers' ability to orchestrate AI-enhanced learning experiences, interpret learning analytics, provide adaptive feedback, and customize instruction based on AI-generated insights.

The competency development in this domain demonstrates several key areas of growth. Data interpretation skills enable teachers to understand and act upon AI-generated learning analytics, including student progress tracking, engagement monitoring, and performance prediction. Adaptive instruction capabilities allow teachers to modify their teaching approaches based on real-time AI insights about student needs and learning patterns. Feedback orchestration competencies involve coordinating AI-generated feedback with human judgment to provide comprehensive learning support.

Implementation context analysis reveals differentiated competency requirements across educational settings. Whole-class implementations (52% of active user studies) emphasize classroom management competencies and group dynamics monitoring. Small group settings (31% of active user studies) focus on collaborative learning facilitation and peer interaction support. Individual tutoring contexts (17% of active user studies) emphasize personalized instruction design and one-on-one mentoring skills.

Teachers developing active user competencies demonstrate sophisticated abilities in technology integration that extend beyond basic digital literacy. They develop competencies in learning environment design, creating educational experiences that effectively blend human instruction with AI capabilities. Assessment innovation competencies enable teachers to design and implement continuous assessment approaches that leverage AI monitoring capabilities while maintaining authentic evaluation practices.

Emerging Developer Competencies for Educational Innovation

Although currently observed in only 2% of studies, developer competencies represent an emerging frontier for teaching competency development. These competencies encompass teachers' ability to create, modify, and manage AI-enhanced learning tools using accessible authoring systems and collaborative development approaches. The limited prevalence reflects both the current availability of user-friendly development tools and the specialized skills required for educational technology creation.

The competency development in this domain involves several sophisticated capabilities. Instructional design thinking enables teachers to conceptualize and plan AI-enhanced learning experiences from pedagogical perspectives. User experience awareness allows teachers to consider student interaction patterns and learning preferences in system design. Technical collaboration skills enable teachers to work effectively with software developers and educational technologists in creating and refining AI-enhanced learning tools.

Authoring tool analysis reveals varying levels of technical complexity and competency requirements. Template-based systems (40% of developer studies) enable teachers to create content within predefined structures, requiring primarily content development and pedagogical design competencies. Behavior-based authoring tools (35% of developer studies) allow teachers to model learning interactions and feedback patterns, demanding deeper understanding of learning analytics and student modeling. Advanced programming environments (25% of developer studies) require substantial technical competencies in addition to pedagogical expertise.

Developer competencies mean teachers need to think like instructional designers, understand how users experience technology, and collaborate effectively with technical teams. While these are currently limited in scope, these competencies represent significant potential for expanding teachers' roles as creators of AI-enhanced learning experiences rather than merely consumers of educational technology.

Cross-Domain Competency Integration Patterns

The analysis reveals important patterns in how teachers integrate competencies across the three domains. Teachers demonstrating high-level competencies typically show development across multiple domains rather than specialization in single areas. Domain experts who also develop active user competencies (18% of studies) demonstrate enhanced ability to translate their subject matter expertise into effective classroom implementation. Active users who develop domain expertise competencies (23% of studies) show improved ability to customize AI systems for their specific teaching contexts.

The most sophisticated competency development occurs when teachers integrate capabilities across all three domains. These teachers demonstrate ability to contribute to system development based on their domain expertise, implement AI-enhanced instruction effectively in their classrooms, and adapt or create technological tools to meet specific pedagogical needs. While rare in the current literature, this integrated competency development represents the highest level of AI integration capability.

Sequential competency development patterns suggest that domain expertise often serves as a foundation for developing active user competencies, which in turn can lead to developer competencies. However, alternative pathways exist, with some teachers developing active user competencies first through hands-on implementation experience, later contributing domain expertise insights, and potentially progressing to developer roles.

The analysis of these competency domains reveals that effective AI integration in education requires teachers to develop sophisticated capabilities that extend far beyond basic technology use. These competencies must be systematically developed through comprehensive approaches that address the interconnected nature of domain expertise, active user capabilities, and emerging developer skills in AI-enhanced educational environments.

DISCUSSION AND CONCLUSION

Developing Teaching Competencies Through AI-Enhanced Learning Systems

The findings from this systematic analysis of 71 empirical studies reveal critical insights into how teachers' evolving roles in intelligent tutoring systems can serve as a foundational model for developing teaching competencies in the digital age. Our results demonstrate that effective AI integration in education requires a comprehensive framework of competency development. The framework involves technical proficiency, pedagogical innovation, and leadership capabilities. Our findings also deliver profound implications for professional development programs, policy frameworks, and institutional strategies to help educators in the 21st-century learning environments.

The three primary roles identified in our analysis (i.e., domain expert, active user, and system developer) show the importance for teachers to acquire competency domains for effective AI integration. The empirical evidence supports the development of a comprehensive competency framework for AI-enhanced teaching, which exceeds traditional digital literacy and requires advanced pedagogical and technical capabilities. The comprehensive competency framework aligns with UNESCO's recent AI Competency Framework for Teachers, which emphasizes five key areas: teachers' mindset, AI ethics, AI foundations, AI pedagogy, and AI for professional development (UNESCO, 2024).

Domain expertise competencies emerge from our finding that 32% of studies involved teachers as domain experts contributing to ITS development. This role requires educators to develop competencies in knowledge modeling, curriculum mapping, and pedagogical content representation for AI systems. Teachers functioning as domain experts must possess deep understanding of their subject matter while also developing the ability to articulate this knowledge in ways that can be encoded into intelligent systems. This finding suggests that professional development programs must emphasize not only content knowledge but also meta-cognitive awareness of how knowledge is structured and transmitted, supporting recent research on teacher digital competencies in the post-pandemic context (Ng et al., 2023).

Active user competencies are evidenced by our finding that 46% of studies positioned teachers as primary users of ITS in-classroom settings. Adopting ITS in classrooms requires teachers to comprehend a set of competencies, which include data interpretation, tailored instructional design, and adaptive classroom management. Teachers must also develop the ability to synthesize AI-generated insights by using their professional judgment to make real-time instructional decisions. Our analysis reveals that successful active users possess competencies in analytics interpretation, differentiated instructional strategies, and technology-enhanced assessment design. This result is consistent with findings from systematic reviews on adopting educational technology (Fernández-Sánchez et al., 2022).

Developer competencies represent an emerging frontier, with 2% of studies documenting teachers as ITS creators. While currently limited, this role demonstrates the potential for teachers to become active creators of AI-enhanced learning experiences. This finding suggests the need for professional development programs that build teacher capacity in instructional design thinking, user experience principles, and collaborative development processes with technical teams.

Professional Development Models for Competency Development

Our findings reveal critical insights into the professional development approaches necessary for building these competencies. The evidence suggests that effective professional development for AI-enhanced teaching must be sustained, collaborative, and deeply embedded in authentic teaching practice, aligning with research on technology-mediated teacher professional development in educational contexts (Doherty et al., 2023).

Collaborative professional learning models emerge as essential for competency development across all three domains. Teachers who successfully develop AI integration competencies consistently collaborate with researchers, technical developers, and peer educators. These finding backs professional development models that focus on peer support, communities of practice, and working together to tackle AI integration—echoing what recent reviews say about the value of collaboration in integrating educational technology (Peters et al., 2022).

The progression from domain expertise contribution to active system use to potential developer roles evidences gradual competency advancement that suggests professional development programs should be designed to support teachers through developmental stages, providing appropriate scaffolding and support as competencies advance from foundational to sophisticated levels. Context-embedded learning emerges as critical for effective competency development, requiring professional development to be situated within teachers' actual teaching contexts rather than delivered as decontextualized training programs.

However, significant challenges must be addressed in professional development design. Previous research shows that teachers still face real challenges, such as technology anxiety, lack of time, trouble aligning AI with the curriculum, and institutional roadblocks (Akram et al., 2022). To truly support teachers to successfully adopt AI in classrooms, well-designed AI systems, sufficient technology assistance and training as well as the school administrative support are needed. In addition, AI ethics is another major challenge. A systematic review indicates that teachers often have misconceptions about AI leading to ethical ramifications, jeopardizing the adoption of AI in classrooms (Gouseti et al., 2025). One possible reason is that teachers do not receive proper professional training about AI (Gouseti et al., 2025). To address this challenge, school administrators must prioritize the development and implementation of robust training programs to build teachers' knowledge and competencies in AI use. These programs should include the guideline of using AI ethically to build teachers' awareness of the existence of AI related issues as well as ensure compliance with data protection regulations (e.g., FERPA in the U.S., GDPR in Europe).

Evidence-Based Decision Making

Our analysis reveals the importance of data interpretation and evidence-based decision making when successfully adopting ITS. Data literacy is a key component in digital competence for educators (Durán et al., 2019). Data literacy is a fundamental competency when using AI tools in teaching. Teachers who are equipped with sufficient analytics and information synthesis competences tend to use AI tools effectively. Teachers need to know how to work with different types of data, discover patterns through data, and generate insights to assist their instructions. Studies have shown that teachers with higher data literacy skills could identify student learning needs based on dashboard data, interpret learning trajectories and task difficulty levels, and use this information to adapt instructions (Molenaar & Knoop-van Campen, 2019).

Meanwhile, teachers should know how to use data ethically. Teachers need to understand AI ethical issues, such as student privacy, algorithms bias, and AI's limitations (UNESCO, 2024). Akgun and Greenhow (2022) claims that AI systems, such as facial recognition and predictive analytics, collect detailed data on students' behaviors and preferences. These surveillance mechanisms can threaten student privacy by monitoring actions without transparent consent. For teachers, using social networking sites for pedagogical purposes raises concerns about privacy boundaries and responsibility.

In addition, using multiple sources of information and relying on professional judgment skills are essential for effective data use. Our analysis shows that effective ITS users do not rely solely on AI-generated insights but combine these with factual observational data, formative assessments, professional knowledge, and teaching expertise. This finding supports the research on integrating AI tools into teacher professional learning that emphasizes the need for teachers to maintain agency in AI-integrated environments (Sperling et al., 2024).

International Perspectives and Future Directions

The global nature of AI development in education requires international collaboration and knowledge sharing in developing effective competency frameworks. Our analysis suggests several key policy implications for supporting teacher competency development at national and international levels. In the national level, AI education strategies should specify provisions for teacher competency development to support teachers to build foundational knowledge and skills. These strategies aim to address professional development of implementing AI tools in education, the importance of institutional support, and solutions towards the existing systemic barriers of integrating AI in education (Chen et al., 2024).

International collaboration is a key component in sharing the understanding of effective practices and reducing misconceptions in adopting AI in education. Evidence indicates that countries can yield positive outcomes from successful professional development models, AI competency frameworks, and implementation strategies for both educators and learners (UNESCO, 2024). Furthermore, building ethical frameworks and standards must be a collaborative effort to align AI integration with educational goals and objectives upon protecting student rights and promoting equitable access to learning opportunities.

Several critical areas emerge for future research and development in teacher competency frameworks regarding AI-enhanced learning. Longitudinal studies are needed to understand how teacher competencies develop over time and what factors support their sustained growth in AI integration capabilities to address the identified gaps in teacher digital competence development (Peters et al., 2022). Cross-cultural research is essential for understanding how competency development approaches must be adapted to different educational contexts, cultural values as well as systemic constraints (Doherty et al., 2023). Impact assessment research can also be significant when examining the relationship between teacher competency development and student learning outcomes in AI-enhanced environments (Chen et al., 2024).

Furthermore, some challenges remain when adopting AI in education, especially in diverse contexts, including the access inequality in low-resource areas, rural-urban digital divides, and the lack of cultural relevance in AI. For instance, prior research shows that the generative AI in the Catalonia educational system has great potential but faces complex challenges in rural communities due to unequal resource distributions, teachers shortage and deficits in professional expertise (López Costa, 2025). A mixed-method study conducted in China reveals access inequality of AI tools between urban and rural schools (Li & Mohammad, 2025). Cultural and institutional barriers were found in AI adoption within the Middle East and North Africa higher education settings (Al-Zahrani & Alasmari, 2025). Therefore, future research directions can focus on seeking effective, long-term solutions to increase equitable access, reduce global learning inequalities, and meet different needs in diverse global contexts.

Another significant barrier to effective AI use in K-12 settings is students' and teachers' limited understanding of AI ethics. The lack of knowledge and misconceptions about AI pose risks when using these tools (Gouseti et al., 2025). Generative AI tools can generate biased outputs, which create risks of discriminating against minority groups and negatively impacting student learning fairness (Omughelli et al., 2024). Teachers must decide when and how students can use generative AI and apply ethical frameworks to address student fairness and AI system values.

Implications for Educational Practice

The findings from this analysis have significant implications for multiple stakeholders supporting AI integration in education. For teacher educators, the results suggest improving pre-service teacher preparation programs by including AI literacy and competency development. School administrative leaders are encouraged to support teachers' competency development with a comprehensive strategic plan. Policymakers are suggested to focus on AI ethical concerns and formulate policies to guide schools and individuals. Technology developers should think of AI systems as a supplement rather than replacement to teachers. Successful AI systems must be designed with deep understanding of teacher competency requirements and educational contexts (Sperling et al., 2024). The findings offer valuable insights about teaching practices with AI integration, which requires teachers to equip with sufficient technical skills, pedagogical innovation methods, leadership skills, and AI ethical use. Institutional support and well-design policy frameworks are pivotal to help teachers develop these competences throughout the professional development programs.

We identified three primary roles (i.e., domain expert, active user, and system developer) and provide professional development models for teacher competency development that prepare teachers meeting the demands of AI-enhanced learning environments. As AI technologies continue to evolve and become more prevalent in educational settings, teacher competency development of AI integration in education will become more complex and challenging and require endless efforts. The evidence presented in this analysis provides a foundation and highlights the need for continued research, collaboration, and innovation in supporting teacher competency development in this fast-paced AI age.

REFERENCES

Akgun, S., & Greenhow, C. (2022). Artificial intelligence in education: Addressing ethical challenges in K-12 settings. *AI and Ethics*, *2*(3), 431–440. DOI: 10.1007/s43681-021-00096-7 PMID: 34790956

Akram, H., Abdelrahman, L., & Al Halbusi, H. (2022). Teachers' perceptions of technology integration in teaching-learning practices: A systematic review. *Frontiers in Psychology*, *13*, 920317. DOI: 10.3389/fpsyg.2022.920317 PMID: 35734463

Al-Zahrani, A. M., & Alasmari, T. M. (2025). A comprehensive analysis of AI adoption, implementation strategies, and challenges in higher education across the Middle East and North Africa (MENA) region. *Education and Information Technologies*, *30*(8), 1–51. DOI: 10.1007/s10639-024-13300-y

Alsaqqa, A., Alkahlout, M., & Abu-Naser, S. (2022). Using Deep Learning to Classify Different Types of Vitamin. *International Journal of Academic Engineering Research*, *6*(1), 1–6.

Baig, A., Cressler, J. D., & Minsky, M. (2024). The future of ai in education: Personalized learning and intelligent tutoring systems. AlgoVista. *Journal of AI and Computer Science*, *1*(1), 592648.

Belland, B. R., Walker, A. E., Kim, N. J., & Lefler, M. (2017). Synthesizing results from empirical research on computer-based scaffolding in STEM education: A meta-analysis. *Review of Educational Research*, *87*(2), 309–344. DOI: 10.3102/0034654316670999 PMID: 28344365

Blessing, S. B., Gilbert, S. B., Ourada, S., & Ritter, S. (2009). Authoring model-tracing cognitive tutors. *International Journal of Artificial Intelligence in Education*, *19*(2), 189–210. DOI: 10.3233/IRG-2009-19(2)04

Ceci, S. J., & Papiero, P. B. (2005). The rhetoric and reality of gap closing: When the "have-nots" gain but the "haves" gain even more. *The American Psychologist*, *60*(2), 149–160. DOI: 10.1037/0003-066X.60.2.149 PMID: 15740447

Cen, H., Koedinger, K. R., & Junker, B. (2007). Is Over Practice Necessary?-Improving Learning Efficiency with the Cognitive Tutor through Educational Data Mining. Frontiers in artificial intelligence and applications, 158, 511.

Chen, L., Chen, P., & Lin, Z. (2024). Artificial intelligence in teaching and teacher professional development: A systematic review. Computers and Education: X Reality, 3, 100089. DOI: 10.1016/j.cexr.2024.100089

Cuban, L., Kirkpatrick, H., & Peck, C. (2001). High access and low use of technologies in high school classrooms: Explaining an apparent paradox. *American Educational Research Journal, 38*(4), 813–834. DOI: 10.3102/00028312038004813

Deng, F., Chai, C. S., Tsai, C. C., & Lee, M. H. (2014). The relationships among Chinese practicing teachers' epistemic beliefs, pedagogical beliefs and their beliefs about the use of ICT. *Journal of Educational Technology & Society, 17*(2), 245–256.

Devasani, S., Gilbert, S. B., & Blessing, S. B. (2012). Evaluation of two intelligent tutoring system authoring tool paradigms: Graphical user interface-based and text-based. In *Proceedings of the 21st Conference on Behavior Representation in Modeling and Simulation* (pp. 54-61).

Doherty, I., Sharma, N., & Harbutt, D. (2023). Technology use for teacher professional development in low- and middle-income countries: A systematic review. *Computers and Education Open, 4*, 100088. DOI: 10.1016/j.caeo.2022.100088

Durán, M., Gutiérrez, I., & Prendes, M. P. (2019). Analysis of variables that influence the digital competence of teachers. *Revista Electrónica Interuniversitaria de Formación del Profesorado, 22*(3), 115–132. DOI: 10.6018/reifop.373611

Feng, M., Heffernan, N., & Koedinger, K. (2011). Student modeling in an intelligent tutoring system. In *Intelligent tutoring systems in e-learning environments: Design, implementation and evaluation* (pp. 208–236). IGI Global. DOI: 10.4018/978-1-61692-008-1.ch011

Fernández-Sánchez, M. R., Garrido-Arroyo, M. C., & Porras-Masero, I. (2022). Curricular integration of digital technologies in teaching processes. *Frontiers in Education, 7*, 1005499. DOI: 10.3389/feduc.2022.1005499

Ghomi, M., & Redecker, C. (2019, May). Digital Competence of Educators (DigCompEdu): Development and Evaluation of a Self-assessment Instrument for Teachers' Digital Competence. In CSEDU (1) (pp. 541-548).

Gouseti, A., James, F., Fallin, L., & Burden, K. (2025). The ethics of using AI in K-12 education: A systematic literature review. *Technology, Pedagogy and Education, 34*(2), 161–182. DOI: 10.1080/1475939X.2024.2428601

Holmes, W., Bialik, M., & Fadel, C. (2019). *Artificial intelligence in education promises and implications for teaching and learning*. Center for Curriculum Redesign.

Kerlinger, F. N., & Kaya, E. (1959). The construction and factor analytic validation of scales to measure attitudes toward education1. *Educational and Psychological Measurement, 19*(1), 13–29. DOI: 10.1177/001316445901900102

Kodaganallur, V., Weitz, R. R., & Rosenthal, D. (2005). A comparison of model-tracing and constraint-based intelligent tutoring paradigms. *International Journal of Artificial Intelligence in Education*, *15*(2), 117–144. DOI: 10.3233/IRG-2005-15(2)03

Kodavali, S. K., Gilbert, S., & Blessing, S. B. (2010, June). Expansion of the xPST framework to enable non-programmers to create intelligent tutoring systems in 3D game environments. In *International Conference on Intelligent Tutoring Systems* (pp. 365-367). Springer, Berlin, Heidelberg. DOI: 10.1007/978-3-642-13437-1_72

Koedinger, K. R., Aleven, V., Heffernan, N., McLaren, B., & Hockenberry, M. (2004, August). Opening the door to non-programmers: Authoring intelligent tutor behavior by demonstration. In *International Conference on Intelligent Tutoring Systems* (pp. 162-174). Springer, Berlin, Heidelberg. DOI: 10.1007/978-3-540-30139-4_16

Koedinger, K. R., Anderson, J., Hadley, W., & Mark, M. (1997). Intelligent tutoring goes to school in the big city. *International Journal of Artificial Intelligence in Education*, *8*, 30–43.

Li, F., & Mohammad, M. (2025). Artificial Intelligence and Education in China: Exploring the Future of Personalized Learning and Its Social Implications. *Uniglobal Journal of Social Sciences and Humanities*, *4*(1), 216–222.

López Costa, M. (2025). Artificial Intelligence and Data Literacy in Rural Schools' Teaching Practices: Knowledge, Use, and Challenges. *Education Sciences*, *15*(3), 352. DOI: 10.3390/educsci15030352

Ma, W., Adesope, O. O., Nesbit, J. C., & Liu, Q. (2014). Intelligent tutoring systems and learning outcomes: A meta-analysis. *Journal of Educational Psychology*, *106*(4), 901–918. DOI: 10.1037/a0037123

MacLellan, C. J., Koedinger, K. R., & Matsuda, N. (2014, June). Authoring tutors with SimStudent: An evaluation of efficiency and model quality. In International conference on intelligent tutoring systems (pp. 551-560). Springer, Cham.

Mishra, P., & Koehler, M. J. (2006). Technological pedagogical content knowledge: A framework for teacher knowledge. *Teachers College Record*, *108*(6), 1017–1054. DOI: 10.1111/j.1467-9620.2006.00684.x

Molenaar, I., & Knoop-van Campen, C. A. N. (2019). How teachers make dashboard information actionable. *British Journal of Educational Technology*, *50*(5), 2341–2356. DOI: 10.1111/bjet.12810

Ng, D. T. K., Leung, J. K. L., Su, J., Ng, R. C. W., & Chu, S. K. W. (2023). Teachers' AI digital competencies and twenty-first century skills in the post-pandemic world. *Educational Technology Research and Development*, *71*(1), 137–161. DOI: 10.1007/s11423-023-10203-6 PMID: 36844361

Nwana, H. S. (1990). Intelligent tutoring systems: An overview. *Artificial Intelligence Review*, *4*(4), 251–277. DOI: 10.1007/BF00168958

Omughelli, D., Gordon, N., & Al Jaber, T. (2024). Fairness, bias, and ethics in AI: Exploring the factors affecting student performance. *Journal of International Communication*, *3*(2), 100–110.

Park, S. (2023). Discovering unproductive learning patterns of wheel-spinning students in intelligent tutors using cluster analysis. *TechTrends*, *67*(3), 489–497. DOI: 10.1007/s11528-023-00847-9

Peters, M., Elasri Ejjaberi, A., Martínez, M. J., & Fàbregues, S. (2022). Teacher digital competence development in higher education: Overview of systematic reviews. *Australasian Journal of Educational Technology*, *38*(3), 122–139. DOI: 10.14742/ajet.7543

Phillips, A., Pane, J. F., Reumann-Moore, R., & Shenbanjo, O. (2020). Implementing an adaptive intelligent tutoring system as an instructional supplement. *Educational Technology Research and Development*, *68*(3), 1409–1437. DOI: 10.1007/s11423-020-09745-w

Ravitz, J. L., Becker, H. J., & Wong, Y. (2000). Constructivist-Compatible Beliefs and Practices among US Teachers. Teaching, Learning, and Computing: 1998 National Survey Report# 4.

Reigeluth, C. M. (2014). The learner-centered paradigm of education: Roles for technology. *Educational Technology*, •••, 18–21.

Self, J. (1990). Theoretical foundations for intelligent tutoring systems. *Journal of Artificial Intelligence in Education*, *1*(4), 3–14.

Sperling, K., Stenberg, C. J., McGrath, C., Åkerfeldt, A., Heintz, F., & Stenliden, L. (2024). In search of artificial intelligence (AI) literacy in teacher education: A scoping review. *Computers and Education Open*, *6*, 100169. DOI: 10.1016/j.caeo.2024.100169

Steenbergen-Hu, S., & Cooper, H. (2013). A meta-analysis of the effectiveness of intelligent tutoring systems on K–12 students' mathematical learning. *Journal of Educational Psychology*, *105*(4), 970–987. DOI: 10.1037/a0032447

Tondeur, J., Van Braak, J., Ertmer, P. A., & Ottenbreit-Leftwich, A. (2017). Understanding the relationship between teachers' pedagogical beliefs and technology use in education: A systematic review of qualitative evidence. *Educational Technology Research and Development*, *65*(3), 555–575. DOI: 10.1007/s11423-016-9481-2

UNESCO. (2024). AI competency framework for teachers. UNESCO Publishing. Retrieved from https://unesdoc.unesco.org/ark:/48223/pf0000391104

VanLehn, K. (2011). The relative effectiveness of human tutoring, intelligent tutoring systems, and other tutoring systems. *Educational Psychologist*, *46*(4), 197–221. DOI: 10.1080/00461520.2011.611369

What Works Clearinghouse. (2010, March). WWC intervention report middle school math: Plato Achieve Now. Retrieved from Department of Education, Institute of Education Sciences, website: http://ies.ed.gov/ncee/wwc/interventionreport.aspx?sid378

Chapter 6
Empowering Educators for the AI-Driven Classroom:
Strategies for Training and Professional Development

Seema Yadav
https://orcid.org/0000-0002-8477-5895
Bhopal School of Social Sciences, India

ABSTRACT

Teachers' roles are changing quickly as artificial intelligence continues to change the educational landscape. Teachers must now use AI-powered tools that automate exams, personalise learning, and offer data-driven insights. They are no longer limited to using traditional teaching approaches. Although artificial intelligence (AI) has enormous potential to improve teaching and learning, its successful implementation in classrooms depends on one crucial element: teachers' readiness. The chapter examines the pressing need for professional growth and organised teacher training in order to give teachers the abilities, self-assurance, and ethical awareness needed for teaching with AI. This chapter offers guidance for instructors to become flexible, introspective, and creative facilitators in the era of artificial intelligence by looking at important competencies, professional learning models, and real-world issues.

INTRODUCTION

A revolutionary change in the way teaching and learning processes are planned, carried out, and experienced in the twenty-first century is represented by the incor-

DOI: 10.4018/979-8-3373-7729-2.ch006

poration of artificial intelligence (AI) in education (Kim, 2024). The justification for this integration is AI's capacity to improve administrative effectiveness, broaden access to high-quality learning options, and personalise education. Teachers may customise curriculum, exams, and support systems to match a range of individual needs by using AI-powered tools and platforms that can analyse students' learning habits, preferences, and progress in real-time (Lazarus et al., 2024). This promotes a more welcoming and stimulating learning atmosphere and aids in quickly filling in learning gaps. AI can also automate repetitive administrative duties like resource allocation, attendance tracking, and grading, freeing up teachers' time for engaging and effective teaching methods. AI-driven solutions facilitate sophisticated data analysis, content production, and knowledge management in research and higher education, encouraging creativity and multidisciplinary investigation (Karadag et al., 2023). Additionally, AI can democratise education by providing language translation services, intelligent tutoring systems, and virtual learning environments that transcend socioeconomic, linguistic, and geographic boundaries. The incorporation of AI becomes not only a technological breakthrough but also a strategic necessity to promote quality, equity, and lifelong learning in the current and future educational landscapes, as educational systems around the world work to give students skills they will need in the future and adjust to the quickly shifting demands of a globalised world (Yeadon & Hardy, 2024). In education, artificial intelligence (AI) is revolutionising the field. To fully utilise AI in education, a comprehensive and interdisciplinary framework for AI literacy is needed, one that can guide practice, research, and policy (Allen & Kendeou, 2024).

RATIONALE FOR AI INTEGRATION IN EDUCATION

Artificial Intelligence (AI) in education is not just a fad; rather, it represents a substantial shift in how knowledge is taught, learnt, and handled. Early computer-assisted instruction systems, such as PLATO (Programmed Logic for Automated Teaching Operations), were created in the middle of the 20th century to facilitate learning through preprogrammed instructions. This is when artificial intelligence (AI) first appeared in educational contexts. But as computing power, machine learning algorithms, and data analytics have increased in the twenty-first century, artificial intelligence (AI) has become a potent instrument that can revolutionise traditional teaching methods (Williamson, 2024). The growing need to address enduring issues in educational systems, such as huge class sizes, a variety of learner demands, restricted access to high-quality teaching resources, and administrative inefficiencies, is the justification for incorporating AI into education. AI provides cutting-edge technologies that help automate repetitive administrative and academic processes, personalise learning experiences, and enhance decision-making by using real-time data insights (Yue et al., 2024).

The potential of AI to support adaptive and personalised learning is among the strongest arguments in favour of its inclusion (Abuodha & Kipkebut, 2024). A one-size-fits-all strategy is frequently used in traditional educational systems, which may not adequately accommodate the different learning preferences, styles, and speeds of individual pupils. Customised content and assessments can be delivered thanks to AI-powered platforms that can evaluate enormous volumes of student data to find learning patterns, strengths, and limitations (Dipaola et al., 2023). This fosters inclusion and enhances learning results by guaranteeing that every student receives support catered to their particular educational needs. Additionally, AI-powered virtual teaching assistants and intelligent tutoring programs offer interactive, on-demand learning help, increasing student engagement and encouraging independent, self-paced learning (Habib et al., 2024).

AI greatly simplifies school management in addition to its pedagogical advantages. AI-powered solutions can effectively handle tasks like attendance tracking, grading, arranging timetables, and paperwork that typically take up a significant amount of educators' time. Teachers and academic leaders can devote more time to curriculum creation, student mentoring, and innovative teaching methods as a result of this operational efficiency. AI technologies also make predictive analytics easier, which helps schools spot children who are at danger, track their academic progress, and take prompt action to improve student success and retention (Bobrytska et al., 2024).

AI integration also has the potential to democratise education by providing learners from various socioeconomic backgrounds, languages, and geographical locations with access to top-notch learning materials (Lee et al., 2024). Geographical and linguistic barriers are overcome by AI-enabled applications like virtual classrooms, automatic translation services, and open educational resources, which promote more equal access to education globally. AI tools support multidisciplinary research and innovation in higher education and research by helping with sophisticated simulations, handling large datasets, and producing scholarly content. As the world transitions to Industry 5.0, where digital intelligence and human-machine collaboration influence societal and economic advancement, it is crucial for schools to prepare their pupils with digital competencies and AI literacy (Shal et al., 2024).

Incorporating AI into education not only improves the teaching-learning process but also gets students ready for societies and workplaces powered by AI (Sharples, 2023). AI-integrated education systems help to create knowledgeable, accountable, and future-ready global citizens by promoting abilities like critical thinking, problem-solving, ethical reasoning, and adaptability (Pierres et al., 2024). The case for incorporating AI into education is based on its capacity to solve persistent problems in the field, raise learning standards, boost administrative effectiveness, and encourage fair and inclusive access to information (Lazarus et al., 2024). It is a critical and strategic development for contemporary educational institutions that aim to meet the needs of the 21st-century information economy, technological advancements, and global sustainable development goals.

CHANGING ROLES OF TEACHERS IN AI-ENHANCED ENVIRONMENTS

Teachers' traditional responsibilities are being radically reshaped by the quick adoption of artificial intelligence (AI) in education. In increasingly dynamic and technologically advanced learning environments, they are no longer merely imparting knowledge but also serving as mentors, facilitators, and co-learners. The role of the teacher in AI-enhanced classrooms is changing from giving traditional lectures to planning individualised, student-centered learning experiences, where AI-powered tools help with feedback, evaluation, and content delivery. Teachers are no longer the main information source; instead, they help students navigate enormous digital knowledge networks, evaluate AI-generated content critically, and apply what they have learnt in relevant, real-world situations. In order to create differentiated teaching tactics and prompt interventions, they must also assess data insights from AI systems to determine students' learning patterns, strengths, and limitations (Pierres et al., 2024).

Additionally, educators in AI-integrated environments are vital in developing human qualities that AI cannot duplicate, such as empathy, moral reasoning, creativity, and social collaboration (Sharples, 2023). Teachers can devote more of their time to mentoring, counselling, and fostering the emotional and social growth of their students as AI systems take over repetitive administrative and assessment duties. Furthermore, educators must increasingly take on the role of advocates for digital literacy, making sure that students not only learn the technical skills necessary to use AI tools but also gain an ethical awareness of the societal ramifications of AI, including concerns about bias, privacy, and digital citizenship.

Teachers are encouraged to adapt, innovate, and embrace lifelong learning as a result of the AI-enhanced educational environment, which necessitates ongoing professional development. By investigating novel AI applications, incorporating cutting-edge technologies into teaching, and taking part in cooperative, multidisciplinary learning communities, instructors in this setting become co-learners with students (Sharples, 2023). As a result, teachers' roles in AI-enhanced environments are shifting to represent a move away from traditional, authority-centered instruction and towards dynamic, collaborative, and morally grounded educational leadership that equips students for a world driven by AI that is changing quickly.

CHANGING ROLES OF TEACHERS IN AI-ENHANCED ENVIRONMENTS IN DIFFERENT SECTORS

In addition to changing economies and sectors, the development of Artificial Intelligence (AI) technology in recent decades has had a dramatic effect on education, resulting in a major redefining of the role of the teacher in modern classrooms. As the main keepers and disseminators of knowledge, instructors have historically been seen as being at the centre of the teaching-learning process, in charge of managing the information flow, creating curriculum, and using traditional techniques to assess student performance. This traditional instructional model has been upended by the incorporation of AI-powered systems into educational practices, leading to the development of AI-enhanced learning environments where the teacher's function has expanded beyond information delivery to include collaboration, mentoring, facilitation, and ethical guidance (Yue et al., 2024).

Although they were used in teacher-controlled environments, educational technologies, including computer-assisted instruction, online learning management systems, and overhead projectors, have historically been used to enhance instruction. AI-driven administrative tools, adaptive learning platforms, predictive analytics for student performance, and intelligent tutoring systems are just a few of the previously unheard-of opportunities that have emerged since the advent of AI. Real-time progress assessments, immediate feedback, material customisation according to individual learning preferences, and even intervention recommendations for failing students are all capabilities of these systems. The task of disseminating knowledge can be transferred from teachers to intelligent systems by using AI technologies like Content Technologies and Carnegie Learning in the US or Squirrel AI in China, which can provide individualised educational content and assessments at scale.

The responsibility of the teacher has broadened in this changing environment to include analysing the insights produced by AI to make wise pedagogical choices. Teachers are now expected to examine trends in student performance and engagement metrics, which are supplied by AI technologies, rather than depending only on their instincts and expertise. This will help them identify areas in which students need more help or different teaching strategies. A more individualised, responsive, and student-centered educational experience is fostered by this data-informed teaching, which gives teachers the ability to more precisely meet the varied needs of their students. Furthermore, educators working in AI-enhanced settings are tasked with developing vital human abilities like empathy, emotional intelligence, ethical reasoning, creative problem-solving, and teamwork that AI systems cannot imitate. Teachers have more time to concentrate on their pupils' social, emotional, and moral growth as AI takes care of monotonous duties like grading and attendance management. In an AI-driven world, where the capacity to engage with people and computers in a meaningful, moral, and innovative way is a critical skill, this human-centric component of education becomes even more crucial.

It is also expected of teachers to advocate for digital literacy, equipping pupils to use and assess AI technologies critically. This involves educating students on the ethical ramifications of artificial intelligence, including algorithmic prejudice, data privacy, false information, and the effects of automation on society. Teachers are essential in giving pupils a fair grasp of AI's potential and constraints in nations like Finland, which has implemented a national AI literacy program for its population.

Continuous professional growth is essential in educational settings that are rich in AI. In addition to being acquainted with the features of AI tools, educators need to consider how these tools affect curriculum design, pedagogy, and educational equity. For educators to stay proficient and self-assured in classrooms with AI, professional learning communities, collaborative action research, and interdisciplinary workshops on AI in education are becoming more and more important. Additionally, the use of AI in education is encouraging a change to collaborative teaching methods, in which educators collaborate with digital resources and AI systems to jointly design educational experiences. By experimenting with AI-generated content, investigating novel AI applications alongside their students, and participating in multidisciplinary, project-based learning that tackles real-world issues, educators are becoming co-learners. This change is in line with the global agenda for education, especially Sustainable Development Goal 4 of the UN, which calls for universal access to high-quality, inclusive education and the encouragement of opportunities for lifelong learning.

As a result, the roles that teachers play in AI-enhanced environments are changing dynamically. These changes include a move away from authoritative instruction and towards data-informed facilitation, advocacy for digital literacy, emotional and ethical mentoring, and collaborative learning leadership. In addition to redefining the standards for teachers' careers, this development underscores the timeless importance of human connections, empathy, and wisdom in an increasingly automated and digitalised educational environment. As artificial intelligence develops, the teacher's function as a kind mentor, moral arbiter, and creator of meaningful learning experiences will always be indispensable, guaranteeing that education will continue to promote both social progress and personal growth.

THE NEED FOR TARGETED TEACHER TRAINING AND UPSKILLING

The fast transformation of educational environments across the globe by artificial intelligence (AI) has made the need for focused teacher training and systematic upskilling an urgency. The ability of AI tools to improve assessment, personalise learning, and increase administrative efficiency is enormous, but their successful integration largely depends on how ready and confident educators are to use them responsibly and creatively. Teachers are at the centre of any revolutionary change in education. Yet, many educators today lack the pedagogical techniques, digital literacy, and AI knowledge needed to successfully traverse AI-enhanced learning settings (Imran & Almusharraf, 2023).

Artificial Intelligence (AI) may be adopted superficially without pedagogical purpose or, on the other hand, may be opposed because of technophobia and uncertainty if suitable training is not provided. As a result, focused professional development programs are crucial, providing not only technical expertise but also an emphasis on critical thinking, ethical considerations, data protection, bias awareness, and inclusivity in the application of AI. A one-size-fits-all approach is insufficient in a variety of educational contexts; therefore, training needs to be contextually relevant and customised to various subject areas, educational levels, and institutional capacities. Additionally, upskilling programs ought to prioritise pedagogy-first integration, teaching educators how to create meaningful AI-supported learning experiences that complement a range of learner requirements and curriculum objectives.

To keep teachers up to date with the rapidly changing AI technology and applications in education, it is essential to provide them with chances for continuous learning through workshops, blended courses, experiential learning, and peer mentoring. To guarantee fair, moral, and successful AI deployment, in-service teachers need ongoing, practice-focused capacity-building in addition to pre-service training. In the end, giving teachers AI competencies guarantees that kids reap the full benefits of a technology-enhanced, future-ready education while also enabling them to facilitate classrooms with AI with confidence (Kim, 2024).

UNDERSTANDING AI IN EDUCATION: KEY AI TOOLS AND TECHNOLOGIES USED IN CLASSROOMS

The educational landscape is being rapidly transformed by artificial intelligence (AI), which is providing new tools and technology that improve administrative efficiency, foster individualised learning experiences, and improve the teaching-learning process. Artificial Intelligence (AI) in education refers to the application of intelligent computer systems that are able to analyse data, identify trends, and make judgements or suggestions in order to assist administrators, instructors, and students. Adaptive learning systems, one of the most well-known uses of AI in education, employ algorithms to evaluate students' performance in real time and modify the pace, substance, and degree of difficulty of lessons to meet each student's unique learning requirements. Platforms like as Century Tech for transdisciplinary material and DreamBox Learning for mathematics are prime examples of how adaptive learning customises the learning process and guarantees that every student gets specialised assistance. AI-powered tutoring systems, like Carnegie Learning and Squirrel AI, are another popular AI tool. They give one-on-one virtual teaching and, depending on student performance data, provide instant feedback, extra practice, and clarification of difficult concepts. These tools support classroom instruction by serving as digital learning assistants that are accessible at all times.

Educators and organisations are also increasingly using predictive data analytics technologies to track students' academic progress, uncover learning gaps, and identify at-risk individuals early. By analysing attendance, grades, engagement, and behavioural patterns, AI-based analytics solutions can offer practical insights for prompt interventions that increase academic success rates and student retention. Furthermore, AI-powered automated assessment and grading systems save teachers time by using natural language processing (NLP) to evaluate essays, short answers, and multiple-choice tests. Turnitin's AI writing detection and Gradescope are two examples of tools that provide effective and unbiased grading assistance. AI is also boosting classroom management through chatbots that can respond to students' common academic questions, language translation applications for multilingual learners, and speech-to-text transcription technologies, which improve accessibility and communication. Virtual and augmented reality systems powered by AI, such as ClassVR and Google Expeditions, are also revolutionising experiential learning by using immersive simulations to make abstract ideas relatable and interesting. Together, these AI tools and technologies are making classrooms smarter, more responsive, and inclusive. This ensures that education stays relevant, flexible, and learner-centred in a world that is becoming more and more digital.

PEDAGOGICAL IMPLICATIONS OF AI USE IN EDUCATION

Artificial Intelligence (AI) has profound pedagogical ramifications for educational processes, significantly changing curriculum design, evaluation, teaching, and learning. The transition to learner-centred, individualised education from teacher-centered, one-size-fits-all instruction is among the most significant changes (Frutos et al., 2024). AI-driven adaptive learning platforms support differentiated education in both in-person and virtual settings by customising content, tempo, and feedback according to each student's needs, learning preferences, and development. This allows teachers to concentrate more on higher-order abilities like creativity, critical thinking, teamwork, and problem-solving, while AI handles repetitive duties like attendance, grading, and content delivery. Additionally, by using AI's predictive analytics capabilities, educators may detect at-risk kids early on and implement timely, data-driven interventions that can enhance learning outcomes and lower dropout rates.

AI not only personalises education but also encourages a shift to competency-based and project-based learning paradigms. AI-enhanced simulations, augmented reality apps, and virtual labs provide inquiry-driven, experiential learning that connects theoretical ideas to real-world situations (Frutos et al., 2024). This pedagogical change calls for teachers to assume facilitative roles that include mentoring, guiding, and co-learning with students rather than only teaching knowledge. It also underlines how important it is to include digital literacy, AI ethics, and data privacy awareness in the curriculum in order to enable children to securely navigate a world that is rich in AI.

But there are pedagogical issues with AI's use in education as well, which call for serious consideration. Instructors must assess AI systems closely for appropriateness, biases, and limitations to make sure they don't unintentionally perpetuate inequality or limited educational opportunities. If AI-driven content and evaluation are used excessively, human interaction, empathy, and moral reasoning—all crucial components of holistic education—may be undervalued. Furthermore, for AI to be successfully incorporated into education, teachers must engage in ongoing professional development to give them the technical know-how and pedagogical approaches they need to employ AI tools in an ethical and efficient manner. In summary, whereas AI has revolutionary possibilities to improve efficiency, inclusivity, and personalised learning, its pedagogical implications necessitate a fair, thoughtful, and morally motivated strategy that protects the human values at the core of education.

MYTHS AND REALITIES ABOUT AI IN EDUCATION

There are a number of myths and misconceptions regarding the function and potential of artificial intelligence (AI) as it becomes more prevalent in educational settings. The idea that AI would eventually supplant teachers and make human educators obsolete is a common misconception (Lydia et al., 2023). Actually, AI is meant to support instructors rather than replace them by taking care of repetitive administrative and teaching duties. This frees up teachers to concentrate on creating intricate cognitive and socioemotional learning opportunities. The idea that AI can ensure student achievement or address all educational issues is another widespread misconception. As a tool, AI actually requires human monitoring, high-quality data, and careful pedagogical integration to be effective. The human attributes that instructors supply in a unique way, such as empathy, moral direction, creativity, and ethical reasoning, cannot be replaced by it.

There is also the idea that AI systems are naturally impartial and objective. As it turns out, AI systems frequently carry over the biases of the data sets they are trained on, and if they are not closely watched, they may unwittingly perpetuate prevailing societal injustices or cultural preconceptions (Klimova et al., 2023). The idea that AI-based education is available to everyone and advantageous to all students is another misconception. Digital divides still exist, though, since students in low-resource environments could not have the equipment, infrastructure, or connectivity needed to take advantage of AI-enhanced learning, increasing the likelihood of educational inequalities. Furthermore, despite some people's concerns that AI will make education impersonal and mechanical, research indicates that, when used carefully, AI can enhance individualised, interesting, and differentiated learning experiences by facilitating adaptive learning pathways, modifying content, and offering instant feedback (Klimova et al., 2023).

Lastly, there is a false belief that AI is too complicated for teachers to comprehend or apply successfully. In actuality, a lot of AI-powered teaching resources have intuitive user interfaces, and teachers can successfully incorporate AI to improve teaching methods with the right professional development. To responsibly, ethically, and fairly use AI's transformative potential in education, educators, legislators, and students must acknowledge these beliefs and address them with accurate knowledge.

COMPETENCY FRAMEWORK FOR AI-INTEGRATED TEACHING: BUILDING DIGITAL AND AI LITERACY FOR TEACHERS

Giving teachers a thorough competency framework that guarantees they are ready to successfully navigate, integrate, and critically engage with AI-enhanced learning environments has become crucial in the quickly changing educational landscape shaped by artificial intelligence (AI) and digital technologies. The fundamental knowledge, abilities, attitudes, and values that educators need to use AI technologies in their pedagogical practice in a responsible and secure manner are outlined in a competency framework for AI-integrated education. Digital and AI literacy, which goes beyond fundamental digital skills to encompass a deeper comprehension of AI systems' operation, pedagogical implications, ethical issues, and potential social influence, is at the heart of this approach.

Technical skills like using AI-powered learning platforms, deciphering data analytics, and customising instruction with adaptive learning systems are important parts of this framework. Designing AI-enhanced learning experiences, managing blended and hybrid learning environments, and preserving a learner-centred approach while using AI tools are all examples of pedagogical competencies that are equally crucial. In order to evaluate the fairness, transparency, and biases of AI applications and make sure that AI is applied inclusively and equitably without endangering the rights and welfare of students, educators must also cultivate ethical and critical thinking skills.

The framework highlights the significance of data privacy awareness, wherein instructors receive training on how to responsibly handle student data in AI-supported systems and inform students about their privacy and digital rights. Additionally, it promotes continual professional development because AI technologies are developing quickly, and teachers need to stay current through collaborative learning communities, certificates, and regular workshops. Collaborative skills are also essential because integrating AI frequently calls for interdisciplinary cooperation between educators, technologists, data scientists, and legislators in order to jointly develop significant, contextually relevant educational solutions.

In the end, a well-designed competency framework equips educators to be not only proficient AI tool users but also critical thinkers, moral role models, and teachers of AI literacy, enabling them to create classrooms that are ready for the future and where innovation in technology and human values coexist peacefully. By placing educators at the forefront of responsible AI adoption, the framework guarantees that they will actively contribute to the development of the moral, inclusive, and significant application of AI in education.

COMPETENCY FRAMEWORK FOR AI-INTEGRATED TEACHING: CRITICAL THINKING, ETHICAL AWARENESS, AND DATA PRIVACY

As artificial intelligence (AI) becomes increasingly pervasive in educational environments, it is imperative that teachers develop critical thinking, ethical awareness, and data privacy skills in addition to technical knowledge as part of an AI-integrated teaching framework. This competency framework's core component is the capacity for instructors to use critical thinking when evaluating, choosing, and utilising AI technologies and systems. Teachers need to be able to think critically about how AI systems work, what data they utilise, whose viewpoints they represent, and what educational ideals they uphold. This entails going beyond using AI technologies passively and actively examining their assumptions, design, and effects on student outcomes, teaching, and learning (RASHMI, 2023).

Ethical awareness is a fundamental component of AI-integrated teaching competencies, along with critical thinking. The ethical conundrums raised by AI, such as algorithmic bias, justice, accountability, and transparency in automated decision-making processes, must be recognised by educators. Being ethically aware entails being aware of the possible drawbacks of relying too much on AI, keeping in mind the human values that ought to direct educational procedures, and making sure that AI applications promote rather than jeopardize equity, inclusion, and the holistic development of learners. In order to enable students to develop into knowledgeable, thoughtful digital citizens who can properly navigate an AI-driven society, educators should also encourage class debates on AI ethics.

The competency framework also highlights data privacy and security literacy as a crucial need for teachers working in AI-enhanced settings. Teachers need to be able to protect sensitive data, comprehend data protection concepts, and ensure compliance with privacy laws and institutional rules because AI systems rely largely on student data for personalisation and analytics. Additionally, they must to be able to inform students about their data footprints, digital rights, and privacy options on AI-powered platforms. This entails encouraging ethical data practices within their organisations and fostering openness in the way AI tools use data.

A competency framework that includes ethical awareness, critical thinking, and data privacy essentially prepares teachers to handle the potential and difficulties presented by AI in education with judgment, accountability, and integrity. In the digital age, it equips them not only as proficient AI tool users but also as moral leaders and proponents of secure, equitable, and human-centered teaching methods.

MODELS OF PROFESSIONAL DEVELOPMENT FOR AI INTEGRATION: IN-SERVICE AND PRE-SERVICE TRAINING PROGRAMS

There is a pressing need for carefully considered professional development models that give teachers the skills they need to successfully integrate artificial intelligence (AI) into their lessons as these technologies become more and more integrated into contemporary educational institutions. Both pre-service teacher education, which prepares aspiring educators before they enter the field, and in-service training programs, which help working educators adjust to quickly changing digital settings, must be covered by these models. In order to give prospective educators the chance to investigate AI applications in curriculum design, personalised learning, classroom management, and assessment, AI integration should be incorporated into core courses on educational technology, pedagogy, and ethics in pre-service teacher education (Sanusi et al., 2024). Pre-service programs must promote critical thinking, ethical awareness, and data privacy consciousness in respect to AI systems, going beyond operational abilities. To develop AI literacy among aspiring teachers, teacher education institutions might use experiential learning strategies like case study analysis, collaborative digital projects, and AI tool simulations (Sperling et al., 2024).

In order to close knowledge gaps and support ongoing upskilling, in-service professional development programs are essential for working teachers. Teachers' differing levels of digital competency should be accommodated by these applications' flexibility, modularity, and responsiveness. AI applications in education can be better understood and meaningfully incorporated into teaching practices by teachers with the help of models like webinars, blended learning modules, online certification courses, workshops, and school-based learning communities (Sharrab et al., 2023). Crucial topics like algorithmic bias, student data protection, ethical AI use, and inclusive digital pedagogy should also be given top priority in in-service training. Action research projects, collaborative inquiry projects, and peer mentorship provide educators with excellent chances to experiment, co-learn, and think critically about integrating AI in real-world classroom environments (Sharrab et al., 2023).

Micro-credentialing and competency-based certification are becoming more and more important in innovative professional development models. These enable educators to show that they are proficient in particular AI-related competencies, such as adaptive learning management, AI-assisted formative assessment, or ethical AI literacy. Additionally, the quality, scalability, and relevance of these training programs can be improved by forming alliances between policy agencies, educational technology firms, and teacher education institutions. The human-centered values at the heart of teaching and learning are ultimately protected by a strong professional development framework for AI integration, which guarantees that both new and seasoned educators are prepared to successfully, morally, and confidently traverse AI-enhanced educational environments.

MODELS OF PROFESSIONAL DEVELOPMENT FOR AI INTEGRATION: BLENDED AND EXPERIENTIAL LEARNING APPROACHES

Teachers can gain the flexibility, practical experience, and real-world context they need to successfully traverse AI-enhanced learning settings by integrating blended learning and experiential learning into professional development programs for AI integration. Together with the quickly developing nature of AI in education, these two strategies make sure that teachers not only comprehend abstract ideas but also acquire useful, real-world skills (Kitcharoen et al., 2024).

Blended learning offers a flexible, individualised experience by combining online learning components with in-person education. This method makes it possible to combine synchronous and asynchronous learning activities in the framework of AI professional development. In addition to self-paced online courses, video tutorials, and reading materials (asynchronous), educators can take part in live, interactive webinars, workshops, and virtual conversations (synchronous). Blended learning's adaptability accommodates various learning preferences and enables teachers to manage their demanding teaching schedules with professional development.

Blended learning for pre-service teachers might involve a mix of online assignments, simulations, and access to AI-powered learning platforms with on-campus courses on AI tools and technology. This enables aspiring educators to test out practical AI applications and modify them for use in their future classes. Through live discussions on the newest developments in AI, online certifications in AI integration, and the ability to integrate these tools into their classes, blended learning provides in-service instructors with continuous professional development opportunities. After that, they can discuss their experiences with peers, mentors, and professionals in person or by webinar. Blended learning's main benefit is its flexibility and capacity to establish a self-directed, scalable learning environment where educators can improve their AI skills on their own time and with the help of a learning community (RASHMI, 2023).

EXPERIENTIAL LEARNING APPROACH

When working with AI technologies that demand practical knowledge and abilities, experiential learning is crucial since it places an emphasis on hands-on experience and learning by doing. Teachers actively interact with AI technologies and integrate them into their teaching practices as part of experiential learning in professional development for AI integration. Kolb's Experiential Learning Cycle, which consists of the phases of active experimentation, abstract conceptualisation, reflective observation, and real experience, serves as the foundation for this methodology. Opportunities for pre-service teachers to interact directly with AI tools in a controlled setting, such as developing lesson plans with AI enhancements, simulating classroom activities with AI, and utilizing AI-powered feedback systems to gauge student progress, may be included in experiential learning. This practical method increases proficiency and self-assurance in incorporating AI tools into regular teaching procedures.

Experiential learning for in-service teachers is usually accomplished through AI-driven action research projects, in which educators use AI tools in the classroom, consider their effects, and then adjust their methods in response to data and feedback from the real world. Teachers might, for instance, employ adaptive learning systems to tailor their lessons to each student, evaluate the outcomes, and share these findings in reflection workshops or professional learning communities. This method fosters a deeper comprehension of AI's practical implications by enabling educators to gain knowledge from both achievements and setbacks. As educators learn how to handle the intricacies of AI tools, modify them for a variety of classroom scenarios, and critically evaluate their efficacy, experiential learning fosters the growth of critical thinking, problem-solving, and creative pedagogical approaches.

SYNERGY BETWEEN BLENDED AND EXPERIENTIAL LEARNING APPROACHES

A dynamic and comprehensive approach of professional development for AI integration is offered by the mix of blended and experiential learning. While experiential learning makes sure that these resources are used in real-world, practical contexts, blended learning provides flexibility and scalability, guaranteeing that educators have access to a range of learning resources and may participate in self-paced learning.

When these strategies are combined, professional development initiatives can provide:

- Real-world AI application: Teachers get hands-on experience with AI tools and technologies, which guarantees they can apply theory to real-world situations.
- Collaborative learning: Teachers exchange knowledge by sharing their experiences, perspectives, and difficulties in synchronous and asynchronous modes.
- Continuous reflection: Teachers can evaluate how well AI technologies work in their classrooms, consider their methods, and make adjustments in light of their practical experiences.

In conclusion, a strong framework for ensuring that educators are not only knowledgeable about AI technologies but also capable of incorporating them in ways that improve student learning and encourage moral, responsible use of AI in the classroom is offered by the combination of blended and experiential learning approaches.

DESIGNING EFFECTIVE TRAINING PROGRAMS

In order to create training programs that effectively integrate AI into education, it is imperative to adhere to the philosophy of "pedagogy first, technology second" while developing material. Although artificial intelligence (AI) and digital technologies present significant potential to improve teaching and learning, this philosophy highlights that these tools must be motivated by strong educational goals and pedagogical frameworks rather than the attraction of technology per se. The first step in creating content should be determining the main learning objectives, instructional goals, and pedagogical techniques that teachers want to accomplish in their courses. AI tools should only be chosen and presented as facilitators to support, enhance, or revolutionise these instructional approaches if these goals have been precisely established. For instance, adaptive AI systems can be investigated to differentiate education according to students' needs if the pedagogical objective is to promote personalised learning. Similar to this, AI-driven analytics tools can be incorporated to monitor student development and offer data-driven feedback if the goal is to enhance formative evaluation. This method guarantees that technology does not control the teaching process but rather acts as a deliberate tool to improve student engagement and instructional efficacy. Furthermore, training materials ought to concentrate on assisting teachers in critically assessing when and how to employ AI tools suitably, taking into account variables such as topic matter, context, learner diversity, and ethical considerations. Programs that prioritise pedagogy help instructors develop the skills necessary to create inclusive, relevant, and curriculum-aligned AI-supported learning experiences. By doing this, educators are given the ability to employ technology as they see fit and become intelligent, introspective professionals who can decide how best to incorporate AI tools into their lessons in ways that actually improve student learning results.

NEEDS ASSESSMENT FOR AI-READINESS

A thorough needs assessment for AI-readiness is a crucial and fundamental step in creating training programs that effectively integrate AI into education. As educators are ready to incorporate artificial intelligence into their teaching practices, this approach entails methodically identifying their current capabilities, knowledge gaps, technology resources, and contextual challenges (Labadze et al., 2023). Clarifying the intended scope of AI integration, including whether it involves data analytics platforms, intelligent tutoring systems, adaptive learning systems, or AI-driven assessment tools, and figuring out how these technologies fit with curriculum objectives and teaching strategies, is the first step in the assessment process. The assessment of educators' present knowledge of AI principles, their proficiency with digital technology, and their familiarity with currently available AI-powered teaching resources is then necessary.

Structured surveys, diagnostic tests, focus groups, and interviews can all be used to collect this data. The evaluation must take into account both human competency and infrastructure, including digital equipment, dependable internet connectivity, and helpful school administration. Furthermore, training programs are guaranteed to be realistically applicable and contextually relevant when instructors' distinct pedagogical approaches and the subject-specific requirements of AI integration are understood. To guarantee accessibility and engagement, it is equally crucial to record instructors' preferences for the training delivery method, whether it be in-person workshops, online courses, or blended learning settings.

The information acquired from this requirements assessment helps to create precise, focused training goals and individualised learning paths that cover both basic AI knowledge and sophisticated classroom applications. Finally, a thorough needs analysis for AI-readiness guarantees that professional development programs are intelligently matched with educators' practical requirements, promoting self-assurance, proficiency, and moral consciousness in negotiating AI-enhanced learning environments.

CONTENT DEVELOPMENT: PEDAGOGY FIRST, TECHNOLOGY SECOND

A key tenet for content production in the context of creating training programs that successfully integrate AI into education is "pedagogy first, technology second." This method makes sure that the employment of AI tools and technologies in the classroom is motivated by good teaching methods, well-defined learning goals, and the requirements of students as a whole, not only by the newness or accessibility of technology. The first step in creating effective content is determining the educational objectives, pedagogical intentions, and student-centered results that teachers want to accomplish. Only once these educational priorities have been established can choices about suitable AI technologies and digital resources be made (Alharbi, 2023).

To assist the educational goal of improving collaborative learning, for example, AI-powered discussion platforms or adaptive group work tools might be carefully chosen. AI-driven analytics solutions, on the other hand, can be taken into consideration if the goal is to support formative assessment and prompt feedback in order to collect data on student performance and guide instructional modifications. This guarantees that technology is used to improve learning opportunities rather than to take the place of pedagogical knowledge. Furthermore, by encouraging teachers to critically assess the appropriateness, usability, and moral implications of different AI applications in their classroom, this method promotes technology use that is both responsible and significant.

AI tools should therefore be incorporated into training materials as supplementary resources that complement and enhance those pedagogical frameworks when a solid basis in learner-centred approaches, curricular alignment, and effective teaching techniques has been established. Training programs that put pedagogy at the centre of content development can enable educators to make deliberate, well-informed choices about when, how, and why to implement AI in the classroom, which will eventually result in more impactful, inclusive, and purposeful learning environments.

ADDRESSING CHALLENGES AND BARRIERS

Resolving educators' aversion to change and technophobia is one of the biggest obstacles to incorporating AI into the classroom. Particularly for educators who may be unfamiliar with these developments or who are used to more conventional teaching approaches, the quick development of digital tools and artificial intelligence technology can be both thrilling and daunting. Fear of the unknown, doubts about the usefulness and dependability of AI tools, anxiety about job security, and a fear of losing control over classroom dynamics are all common causes of resistance to change. Teachers' use of AI-enhanced teaching methods may also be hampered by technophobia, which is the fear or hesitancy to interact with technology (Lydia et al., 2023).

The perceived complexity of AI systems, the time commitment needed to acquire new tools, or concerns about their capacity to effectively manage technology can all contribute to this opposition (Abuodha & Kipkebut, 2024). Professional development programs must be created with empathy, expose participants gradually, and provide ongoing assistance in order to overcome these obstacles. Training programs should start by demythologising AI and offering relatable, understandable examples of how technology might complement conventional teaching methods rather than take their place. It's critical to establish secure, accepting learning environments where educators may ask questions, voice concerns, and experiment with new resources at their own pace (Alharbi, 2023).

Teachers' confidence can also be bolstered by presenting success stories, peer-led seminars, and practical experiences that illustrate how AI can be used to improve teaching outcomes. Leadership support is also very important; school administrators need to encourage a culture of innovation, offer ongoing technical help, and acknowledge teachers' efforts to adopt new technologies. By tactfully handling resistance, fostering digital literacy over time, and highlighting AI's role as a helpful collaborator in the teaching-learning process, educators can get over their technophobia and become engaged, self-assured members of AI-integrated learning environments (Kizilcec, 2024).

INFRASTRUCTURE AND ACCESS INEQUALITIES

Disparities in access and infrastructure, which can exacerbate the digital divide and lead to unequal learning opportunities, are a major obstacle to the successful integration of AI in education. Access to dependable internet connectivity, contemporary digital gadgets, and AI-powered learning platforms is still scarce or irregular in many educational settings, especially in rural areas, under-resourced schools, and developing nations. Disparities between government or public schools with antiquated or rudimentary infrastructure and private institutions with sophisticated technical setups can also be found inside metropolitan schools. In addition to impeding the adoption of AI-driven teaching methods, these disparities run the risk of denying educators and students access to the advantages of tailored, data-driven, and adaptable learning environments.

In order to overcome this obstacle, a multifaceted, systemic strategy combining both localised fixes and policy-level initiatives is needed. In order to guarantee that schools have access to fast internet, working devices, and the technical assistance required to maintain them, governments and educational authorities must give priority to investments in digital infrastructure. Training programs should be made to work in a variety of settings at the same time. Where needed, they should provide low-tech or offline alternatives to AI-based learning, like community learning hubs with shared resources or AI-powered educational apps that don't require constant internet access. In order to close these gaps, public-private collaborations can be extremely helpful in giving underserved schools access to resources, infrastructure funding, or subsidised AI products. In order to ensure that no learner is left behind because of technical restrictions, professional development programs should also be designed to overcome these infrastructure limits by giving teachers solutions for fair AI integration. Education systems can transition to more inclusive, egalitarian, and productive AI-enhanced learning environments by recognising and actively attempting to lessen infrastructural and access disparities.

POLICY AND INSTITUTIONAL SUPPORT

Education is one of the many facets of society that artificial intelligence (AI) is quickly changing (Uygun, 2024). Strong institutional and governmental support is crucial for the effective integration of AI in education since it acts as a foundation and a catalyst for long-lasting change. Without explicit, progressive rules and institutional frameworks, the use of AI tools frequently results in disorganised, disjointed initiatives that are inconsistent, ineffectual, or even morally dubious. Despite their lack of institutional support, financial allocation, and official rules, many educators and schools are keen to investigate AI-enhanced teaching practices in a responsible and confident manner. Infrastructure development, teacher training, ethical standards, data privacy safeguards, curricular reforms, and equality measures are just a few of the many aspects that require strong policy backing to ensure that AI integration is inclusive, safe, and purposeful. By encouraging an innovative culture, facilitating ongoing professional growth, and offering incentives for the integration of AI into teaching methods, educational leaders at the institutional level play a critical role in fostering an enabling environment. Institutional frameworks should also provide explicit procedures for assessing how AI tools affect student results and guarantee that educators have access to trustworthy technical support and curriculum-specific AI resources. Additionally, in order to guarantee that AI initiatives are contextually appropriate and in line with the larger objectives of the educational system, policy interventions should actively involve stakeholders at all levels, including educators, administrators, technology suppliers, students, and parents. In order to overcome digital gaps, national and regional education policies should also incorporate AI literacy into teacher preparation programs and offer fair funding mechanisms. In the end, tackling the difficulties and obstacles of integrating AI requires consistent, well-thought-out policy and institutional support, allowing educational systems to utilise AI's potential in a way that is inclusive, ethical, and responsible.

MONITORING AND EVALUATING IMPACT: TOOLS AND INDICATORS TO ASSESS TEACHER GROWTH AND STUDENT OUTCOMES

Establishing a systematic method for tracking and assessing the effects of professional development programs and AI-enhanced teaching techniques is an essential part of any successful AI integration plan in education. This entails determining and putting into practice suitable instruments and metrics to evaluate the development of teachers' AI competencies as well as the ensuing learning outcomes for students (Ray & Ray, 2024). Improvements in AI literacy, self-assurance while utilising AI technologies, incorporating AI-driven teaching techniques into lesson planning, and understanding of ethical and data privacy issues should all be considered important indicators for educators. Self-assessment questionnaires both before and after training, reflective journals, lesson observations, AI competency assessments, and digital portfolios exhibiting AI-supported teaching methods can all be used to gauge these (Ray & Ray, 2024).

Impact assessments for students should look at things like better personalised learning experiences, higher levels of engagement, improved performance in activities supported by AI, and the growth of critical and digital thinking abilities.

Tools that can offer important insights into learning progress and areas in need of intervention include AI analytics dashboards, adaptive learning reports, student feedback forms, and formative assessment data. Furthermore, in order to ensure a comprehensive knowledge of AI's educational influence, qualitative techniques like focus groups, interviews, and case studies can capture complex experiences and perceptions from both teachers and students. Institutions can address issues, improve their AI implementation plans, and make sure that the usage of AI technology is in line with equality considerations and pedagogical objectives by conducting ongoing monitoring. Educational institutions may show the worth of AI integration projects, influence policy choices, and advance evidence-based practices that lead to significant, long-term educational improvement by putting in place a strong assessment system with precise, quantifiable indicators (Sumakul & Hamied, 2023).

FEEDBACK LOOPS AND CONTINUOUS IMPROVEMENT

To keep the use of AI tools dynamic, responsive, and pedagogically useful, a successful plan for integrating AI in education must be supported by strong feedback loops and methods for ongoing improvement. In order to improve both the teaching strategies and the technology being used, feedback loops entail methodically gathering, evaluating, and acting upon inputs from administrators, teachers, students, and AI system analytics. These loops facilitate continuous communication between human stakeholders and AI systems, enabling modifications to training curricula, policy frameworks, and teaching methodologies in response to empirical data and real-world experiences. In order to promote a culture of cooperative growth, teachers can benefit greatly from regular feedback sessions that are conducted through peer observations, reflective conversations, and professional learning communities.

In order to better customise instructional tactics, students' experiences, challenges, and preferences can be recorded through built-in feedback mechanisms in AI-powered adaptive learning systems, as well as through open feedback surveys and periodic self-assessment. Academic leadership at the institutional level should routinely examine AI-generated learning analytics reports along with qualitative input from classrooms to spot patterns, weaknesses, and areas where the program could be improved. This ongoing, iterative process of feedback and improvement builds educator confidence and capacity while ensuring that AI integration stays in line with educational goals, moral principles, and student needs. In the end, well-designed feedback loops foster creativity and resilience in a quickly changing digital learning environment by integrating adaptive, evidence-based decision-making practices into the educational system and assisting in maintaining the relevance and efficacy of AI-driven initiatives.

REFLECTION-BASED PRACTICES FOR ADAPTIVE LEARNING

The use of reflection-based techniques, especially in adaptive learning settings, is a crucial component of tracking and assessing the effects of AI integration in education. AI-powered adaptive learning systems continuously modify feedback, tempo, and material based on performance data and the needs of each individual learner. But in order to fully realise their potential and guarantee significant learning outcomes, these methods must be supplemented by organised chances for both teacher and student reflection. By encouraging teachers to critically assess how AI technologies are affecting their teaching methods, student engagement, and learning results, reflection-based approaches promote a culture of ongoing pedagogical development. Teachers can record their experiences integrating AI by keeping reflective journals, lesson logs, or post-session feedback forms. They can note accomplishments, difficulties, moral dilemmas, and ideas for future work.

Reflective learning diaries, self-assessment checklists, or guided feedback prompts should also be used to help students think back on their experiences learning in AI-supported settings. Through the development of metacognitive awareness, these reflections assist students in identifying areas in which they need more support, defining individualised goals, and recognising how adaptive technologies influence their learning trajectories. In order to meet training needs, improve the use of AI tools, and modify teaching methods, educational institutions can gather and examine reflective narratives, journals, and discussion summaries as qualitative data for monitoring purposes. In addition to increasing learner autonomy and teacher agency, integrating reflection-based practices into adaptive learning ecosystems fosters a feedback-rich environment where human and AI inputs continuously inform one another, guaranteeing that technology continues to be a tool in support of ethical, learner-centred, and thoughtful education.

FUTURE DIRECTIONS: EVOLVING ROLE OF THE TEACHER IN AI-POWERED LEARNING ECOSYSTEMS

The role of the teacher is changing dramatically as artificial intelligence continues to reshape educational environments. It is now going beyond the traditional role of imparting knowledge to become a mentor, learning designer, and ethical steward in AI-powered learning ecosystems (Guha et al., 2024). Teachers will no longer be the only information source in future AI-enhanced classrooms; instead, they will serve as facilitators of individualised, inquiry-based, and competency-driven learning experiences, using AI tools to supplement human education rather than replace it (Sumakul & Hamied, 2023). Routine chores will be automated by AI-driven assessment tools, intelligent tutoring systems, and adaptive learning platforms, freeing up teachers' time for higher-order learning activities like developing students' creativity, critical thinking, teamwork, and emotional intelligence (Sumakul & Hamied, 2023).

By curating and creating hybrid learning pathways that combine AI recommendations with their professional judgement, teachers will increasingly assume the role of learning architects, ensuring that education stays socially and culturally responsive. Teachers will also have to take on the role of ethical guardians, guiding pupils through AI-generated information critically, interpreting algorithmic choices, and comprehending data protection, digital bias, and responsible AI use. The future educator will also be a lifelong student, constantly improving their skills to stay up to date with new educational developments and emerging technologies (Samuel et al., 2023).

Teachers will increasingly take on the role of learning architects by curating and developing hybrid learning pathways that integrate AI recommendations with their professional judgement, guaranteeing that education remains culturally and socially appropriate. Teachers will also need to act as ethical guardians, helping students understand data protection, digital bias, and responsible AI use, as well as critically guiding them through AI-generated content and interpreting algorithmic decisions. In order to stay current with new advancements in education and emerging technology, the future teacher will also be a lifelong learner who continuously enhances their skills.

LIFELONG LEARNING AND TEACHER RESILIENCE IN THE AGE OF AI

Lifelong learning and teacher resilience are more important than ever as artificial intelligence continues to change the educational landscape. In a time where AI technologies are constantly developing, educators need to adopt a mindset of constant improvement and flexibility, understanding that professional development is now a continual, career-long commitment rather than a one-time event (Zhou & Zhang, 2024). In order to effectively traverse hybrid, data-driven, and technology-augmented classrooms, educators will need to continuously refresh their understanding of new AI tools, digital pedagogies, and ethical frameworks (Griffiths et al., 2024). Building resilience is crucial for managing the quick speed of change, the unknowns of new educational paradigms, and the difficulties of striking a balance between machine-assisted systems and human-centered instruction. This goes beyond developing technical skills (Griffiths et al., 2024).

Teachers who are resilient exhibit adaptability, emotional intelligence, and a proactive approach to change, seeing setbacks as chances for creativity rather than dangers. Additionally, they act as role models for pupils, showing them how to use technology critically while upholding fundamental human values like empathy, inclusion, and moral responsibility. Teachers will be empowered to continuously improve their competencies and stay relevant in an educational ecosystem that is prepared for the future, thanks to lifelong learning opportunities, micro-credentialing systems, and collaborative digital learning communities, all of which are supported by AI-enabled personalised professional development platforms. The ability of a teacher to learn, unlearn, and relearn, along with resilience and ethical awareness, will ultimately be crucial in the era of artificial intelligence to guarantee that technology is a useful instrument for enhancing rather than undermining the profoundly human aspect of education.

VISION FOR EQUITY, INCLUSION, AND HUMAN-CENTERED AI

It is imperative to create a future where technology enhances human potential without escalating societal injustices or undermining moral principles as AI becomes more integrated into educational systems around the globe. The fair and responsible design, implementation, and use of AI technologies that respect the rights, dignity, and various needs of every student are given top priority in an educational vision for equity, inclusiveness, and human-centered AI. AI systems must be transparent, explicable, and free from algorithmic biases that can reinforce current inequalities based on socioeconomic class, geography, gender, aptitude, or cultural background, according to this perspective (Ballantine et al., 2024). In order to ensure that vulnerable, under-represented, and marginalised learner groups have fair access to AI-enhanced resources, adaptive learning technologies, and data-informed support systems, future-ready AI in education should be purposefully inclusive.

In order to put human interactions, ethical consciousness, and wellbeing at the centre of AI-enhanced learning settings, educators and educational leaders will be essential in promoting human-centered AI. Institutional frameworks and policies must protect data privacy, require the ethical auditing of AI tools, and support an inclusive curriculum that enables students to interact critically with AI systems as responsible, knowledgeable citizens. Furthermore, a truly human-centered vision for AI in education places a high value on traits that are exclusive to humans and cannot be replaced by machines, such as empathy, creativity, critical thinking, and cultural intelligence. This ensures that technology is a supportive rather than a driving force in the educational process. To co-create AI solutions that promote social justice, provide inclusive learning environments, and honour the diversity and complexity of human learning, educators, technologists, legislators, and communities must work together in this future.

CONCLUSION: CALL TO ACTION FOR STAKEHOLDERS IN EDUCATION POLICY AND TEACHER EDUCATION

All educational stakeholders urgently need to respond in a coordinated, forward-looking manner, given the revolutionary possibilities and intricate obstacles presented by the integration of artificial intelligence in education. Together, policymakers, teacher preparation programs, school administrators, and tech developers must design an inclusive, moral, and pedagogically sound framework for integrating AI that meets the many demands of both educators and students. This necessitates putting educators at the centre of AI-enhanced educational systems and making sure they are empowered by supportive institutional policies that promote innovation while preserving human values, equal access to digital infrastructure, and ongoing professional development. In order to incorporate ethics, equity, data privacy, and the human aspects of learning into AI-related tactics and curricular reforms, education policy must go beyond the surface acceptance of technology. Pre-service and in-service teacher education programs urgently need to update their frameworks to incorporate crucial data skills, AI literacy, and abilities for navigating AI-powered learning environments with empathy, resilience, and ethical discernment. Additionally, human-centered, inclusive AI solutions that take into account the contextual realities of various educational contexts should be designed collaboratively, especially in marginalised and resource-constrained regions. In order to ensure that the principles of inclusivity, critical thinking, and lifelong learning remain firmly anchored in the future of education, this call to action exhorts stakeholders to embrace AI not just as a technological advancement but also as a tool for social good, educational equity, and human development. Acting now will help educators be ready, rethink regulations, and co-create learning ecosystems where AI can be a valuable partner in forming fair, moral, and future-ready education for everyone.

REFERENCES

Abuodha, L., & Kipkebut, A. (2024). Disruptive AI in Education: Transforming Learning in the Digital Age. *International Journal for Research in Applied Science and Engineering Technology*, *12*(2), 195–199. DOI: 10.22214/ijraset.2024.58283

Alharbi, W. (2023). AI in the Foreign Language Classroom: A Pedagogical Overview of Automated Writing Assistance Tools. *Education Research International*, *2023*, 1–15. DOI: 10.1155/2023/4253331

Allen, L. K., & Kendeou, P. (2024). ED-AI Lit: An Interdisciplinary Framework for AI Literacy in Education. *Policy Insights from the Behavioral and Brain Sciences*, *11*(1), 3–10. DOI: 10.1177/23727322231220339

Ballantine, J., Boyce, G., & Stoner, G. (2024). A critical review of AI in accounting education: Threat and opportunity. *Critical Perspectives on Accounting*, *99*, 102711. Advance online publication. DOI: 10.1016/j.cpa.2024.102711

Bobrytska, V. I., Krasylnykova, H. V., Beseda, N., Krasylnykov, S. R., & Skyrda, T. S. (2024). Artificial intelligence (AI) in Ukrainian Higher Education: A Comprehensive Study of Stakeholder Attitudes, Expectations and Concerns. *International Journal of Learning. Teaching and Educational Research*, *23*(1), 400–426. DOI: 10.26803/ijlter.23.1.20

de Frutos, N. D., Carrasco, L. C., de la Maza, M. S., & Etxabe-Urbieta, J. M. (2024). Application of Artificial Intelligence (AI) in Education: Benefits and Limitations of AI as Perceived by Primary, Secondary, and Higher Education Teachers. *Revista Electronica Interuniversitaria de Formacion Del Profesorado*, *27*(1). Advance online publication. DOI: 10.6018/reifop.577211

Dipaola, D., Moore, K. S., Ali, S., Perret, B., Zhou, X., Zhang, H., & Lee, I. (2023). Make-a-Thon for Middle School AI Educators. *SIGCSE 2023 - Proceedings of the 54th ACM Technical Symposium on Computer Science Education, 1*, 305–311. DOI: 10.1145/3545945.3569743

Griffiths, D., Frías-Martínez, E., Tlili, A., & Burgos, D. (2024). A Cybernetic Perspective on Generative AI in Education: From Transmission to Coordination. *International Journal of Interactive Multimedia and Artificial Intelligence*, *8*(5), 15–24. DOI: 10.9781/ijimai.2024.02.008

Guha, A., Grewal, D., & Atlas, S. (2024). Generative AI and Marketing Education: What the Future Holds. *Journal of Marketing Education*, *46*(1), 6–17. DOI: 10.1177/02734753231215436

Habib, S., Vogel, T., Anli, X., & Thorne, E. (2024). How does generative artificial intelligence impact student creativity? *Journal of Creativity*, *34*(1), 1–7. DOI: 10.1016/j.yjoc.2023.100072

Imran, M., & Almusharraf, N. (2023). Analyzing the role of ChatGPT as a writing assistant at higher education level: A systematic review of the literature. In *Contemporary Educational Technology* (Vol. 15, Issue 4, pp. 1–14). DOI: 10.30935/cedtech/13605

Karadag, I., Güzelci, O. Z., & Alaçam, S. (2023). EDU-AI: A twofold machine learning model to support classroom layout generation. *Construction Innovation*, *23*(4), 898–914. DOI: 10.1108/CI-02-2022-0034

Kim, J. (2024). Types of teacher-AI collaboration in K-12 classroom instruction: Chinese teachers' perspective. *Education and Information Technologies*, *29*(13), 17433–17465. DOI: 10.1007/s10639-024-12523-3

Kitcharoen, P., Howimanporn, S., & Chookaew, S. (2024). Enhancing Teachers' AI Competencies through Artificial Intelligence of Things Professional Development Training. *International Journal of Interactive Mobile Technologies*, *18*(2), 4–15. Advance online publication. DOI: 10.3991/ijim.v18i02.46613

Kizilcec, R. F. (2024). To Advance AI Use in Education, Focus on Understanding Educators. In *International Journal of Artificial Intelligence in Education* (Vol. 34, Issue 1). DOI: 10.1007/s40593-023-00351-4

Klimova, B., Pikhart, M., & Kacetl, J. (2023). Ethical issues of the use of AI-driven mobile apps for education. *Frontiers in Public Health*, *10*, 1–8. DOI: 10.3389/fpubh.2022.1118116 PMID: 36711343

Labadze, L., Grigolia, M., & Machaidze, L. (2023). Role of AI chatbots in education: systematic literature review. In *International Journal of Educational Technology in Higher Education* (Vol. 20, Issue 1). DOI: 10.1186/s41239-023-00426-1

Lazarus, M. D., Truong, M., Douglas, P., & Selwyn, N. (2024). Artificial intelligence and clinical anatomical education: Promises and perils. *Anatomical Sciences Education*, *17*(2), 249–262. DOI: 10.1002/ase.2221 PMID: 36030525

Lee, J., Hong, M., & Cho, J. (2024). Development of a Content Framework of Artificial Intelligence Integrated Education Considering Ethical Factors. *International Journal on Advanced Science, Engineering and Information Technology*, *14*(1), 205–213. DOI: 10.18517/ijaseit.14.1.19558

Lydia, E. G., Vidhyavathi, P., & Malathi, P. (2023). A Study On "Ai In Education: Opportunities And Challenges For Personalized Learning. *Industrial Engineering Journal, 52*(05), 750–759. DOI: 10.36893/IEJ.2023.V52I05.750-759

Pierres, O., Christen, M., Schmitt-Koopmann, F. M., & Darvishy, A. (2024). Could the Use of AI in Higher Education Hinder Students With Disabilities? A Scoping Review. *IEEE Access, 12*(December 2023), 27810–27828. DOI: 10.1109/ACCESS.2024.3365368

RASHMI. (2023). Unlocking the Potential of AI in Education: Challenges and Opportunities. *International Journal For Multidisciplinary Research, 5*(4), 1–11. DOI: 10.36948/ijfmr.2023.v05i04.5955

Ray, S., & Ray, D. P. (2024). Artificial Intelligence in Education: Navigating the Nexus of Innovation and Ethics for Future Learning Landscapes. *International Journal of Research -GRANTHAALAYAH, 11*(12), 163–174. DOI: 10.29121/granthaalayah.v11.i12.2023.5464

Samuel, Y., Brennan-Tonetta, M., Samuel, J., Kashyap, R., Kumar, V., Krishna Kaashyap, S., Chidipothu, N., Anand, I., & Jain, P. (2023). Cultivation of human centered artificial intelligence: Culturally adaptive thinking in education (CATE) for AI. *Frontiers in Artificial Intelligence, 6*, 1–13. DOI: 10.3389/frai.2023.1198180 PMID: 38106981

Sanusi, I. T., Ayanwale, M. A., & Tolorunleke, A. E. (2024). Investigating pre-service teachers' artificial intelligence perception from the perspective of planned behavior theory. *Computers and Education: Artificial Intelligence, 6*(100202), 1–15. DOI: 10.1016/j.caeai.2024.100202

Shal, T., Ghamrawi, N., & Naccache, H. (2024). Leadership styles and AI acceptance in academic libraries in higher education. *Journal of Academic Librarianship, 50*(2), 102849. Advance online publication. DOI: 10.1016/j.acalib.2024.102849

Sharples, M. (2023). Towards social generative AI for education: Theory, practices and ethics. *Learning: Research and Practice, 9*(2), 159–167. Advance online publication. DOI: 10.1080/23735082.2023.2261131

Sharrab, Y., Almutiri, N. T., Tarawneh, M., Alzyoud, F., Al-Ghuwairi, A. R. F., & Al-Fraihat, D. (2023). Toward Smart and Immersive Classroom based on AI, VR, and 6G. *International Journal of Emerging Technologies in Learning, 18*(2), 4–16. DOI: 10.3991/ijet.v18i02.35997

Sperling, K., Stenberg, C.-J., McGrath, C., Åkerfeldt, A., Heintz, F., & Stenliden, L. (2024). In search of artificial intelligence (AI) literacy in teacher education: A scoping review. *Computers and Education Open*, *6*(100169), 1–13. DOI: 10.1016/j.caeo.2024.100169

Sumakul, D. T. Y. G., & Hamied, F. A. (2023). Amotivation in AI injected EFL classrooms: Implications for teachers. *Indonesian Journal of Applied Linguistics*, *13*(1), 26–34. DOI: 10.17509/ijal.v13i1.58254

Uygun, D. (2024). Teachers' perspectives on artificial intelligence in education. *Advances in Mobile Learning Educational Research*, *4*(1), 931–939. Advance online publication. DOI: 10.25082/AMLER.2024.01.005

Williamson, B. (2024). The Social life of AI in Education. In *International Journal of Artificial Intelligence in Education* (Vol. 34, Issue 1, pp. 97–104). DOI: 10.1007/s40593-023-00342-5

Yeadon, W., & Hardy, T. (2024). The impact of AI in physics education: A comprehensive review from GCSE to university levels. *Physics Education*, *59*(2), 1–19. DOI: 10.1088/1361-6552/ad1fa2

Yue, M., Jong, M. S.-Y., & Ng, D. T. K. (2024). Understanding K–12 teachers' technological pedagogical content knowledge readiness and attitudes toward artificial intelligence education. *Education and Information Technologies*, *29*(15), 19505–19536. DOI: 10.1007/s10639-024-12621-2

Zhou, C., & Zhang, W. (2024). Computational Thinking (CT) towards Creative Action: Developing a Project-Based Instructional Taxonomy (PBIT) in AI Education. *Education Sciences*, *14*(2), 1–14. DOI: 10.3390/educsci14020134

KEY TERMS AND DEFINITIONS

AI Integration in Education: The strategic use of artificial intelligence technologies to enhance teaching, learning, assessment, and educational management processes. This involves incorporating AI tools such as adaptive learning systems, intelligent tutoring, and predictive analytics into educational practice.

Teacher Professional Development: Ongoing programs, workshops, and training initiatives aimed at improving teachers' pedagogical, technological, and AI-related competencies. It ensures educators are equipped to navigate and lead in AI-powered learning environments.

Human-Centered AI: An approach to designing and implementing AI systems that prioritizes human values, ethical considerations, social well-being, empathy, and inclusivity. It ensures that AI technologies enhance rather than replace the human elements of education.

Educational Equity and Inclusion: The principle of providing fair, unbiased, and meaningful access to quality education for all learners, regardless of socio-economic status, gender, ability, geographic location, or cultural background — particularly important in AI-supported environments.

Ethical AI Use in Education: The responsible and transparent application of AI tools in educational contexts, ensuring the protection of student data, privacy rights, and preventing algorithmic bias. It involves aligning AI practices with ethical standards and legal frameworks.

AI Literacy for Educators: The essential knowledge and skills that teachers need to understand, evaluate, and effectively use AI tools and applications in classrooms, while also fostering AI awareness and critical digital literacy among their students.

Future-Ready Learning Ecosystems: Flexible, technology-enriched educational environments designed to prepare learners and educators for future careers and societal roles in an AI-driven world. These ecosystems prioritize adaptability, innovation, and inclusivity.

Lifelong Learning and Resilience: The commitment to continuous, self-directed learning throughout one's professional career, alongside the ability to cope with, adapt to, and thrive amid technological change and pedagogical transformation.

Adaptive Learning Systems: AI-powered platforms that personalize the learning experience by analyzing students' performance data and automatically adjusting instructional content, feedback, and pacing to meet individual learning needs.

Feedback Loops in AI-Enhanced Education: Dynamic cycles of real-time data collection, reflection, instructional decision-making, and continuous improvement within AI-supported classrooms. They help teachers refine strategies and optimize student outcomes based on ongoing analysis.

Chapter 7
How Do Mathematics Teachers Use ChatGPT in Their Classes?

Zeynep Gül Dertli
https://orcid.org/0000-0002-4750-5343
Istanbul Aydin University, Turkey

Yasemin Sağlam Kaya
https://orcid.org/0000-0002-1615-0041
Hacettepe University, Turkey

ABSTRACT

This chapter presents a study that aims to investigate how mathematics teachers use ChatGPT in their lessons and to reveal their experience. The research was conducted in accordance with case study design. Within the scope of the research, semi-structured interviews were conducted with mathematics teachers using ChatGPT in their mathematics courses. The results show that mathematics teachers use ChatGPT in problem-solving, problem posing, using different strategies in problem-solving, and to make students discover the basic properties of geometric shapes. The participants of the study also mentioned some of the advantages of using ChatGPT in their lessons, the difficulties, the methods to overcome these difficulties, and made recommendations for other teachers. The results of the study uncover the need for more research and guidelines for the use of ChatGPT and similar artificial intelligence tools in mathematics courses. It is recommended to conduct studies on good examples of using ChatGPT in mathematics courses which overcome possible challenges.

DOI: 10.4018/979-8-3373-7729-2.ch007

INTRODUCTION

The rise of artificial intelligence is opening new and unexplored avenues in educational contexts. Artificial intelligence (AI) is the technology that enables a machine to mimic and perform human-like behaviors such as learning, decision making, problem solving and prediction (Kennedy & Wanless, 2022). AI in education provides the opportunity to address gaps in content and teacher competence (Busuttil & Calleja, 2025), support teachers and students by providing purposeful learning experiences and intelligent learning systems (Crompton & Song, 2020), and equip students with new skills for an AI-driven world (Slimi, 2023). One of the main reasons for the recent rise of AI is thought to be the development of large language models and the associated increasing potential of chatbots (Lokman & Ameedeen, 2019). Chatbots, also known as conversational agents, enable humans to interact with computers through natural language by applying natural language processing (NLP) technology (Adamopoulou, & Moussiades, 2020). Natural language processing is a system designed to create a representation of human spoken language to perform tasks such as answering questions and making inferences (Bender et al., 2021). The latest evolution of chatbots is important, because it has enabled people to communicate directly with computer systems without the need for any intermediary (Asha et al., 2023). Today's modern chatbots can understand spoken or written commands, fulfill many of them, and answer questions (Adamopoulou, & Moussiades, 2020).

One of the clearest examples of the rise of modern chat bots is ChatGPT. ChatGPT (Chat Generative Pre-Trained Transformer) is an artificial intelligence language model developed by the research company OpenAI (Cooper, 2023). Due to its design using deep learning, ChatGPT is able to generate the kind of text that humans would write and maintain a conversational style that allows for more realistic natural dialog (Tlili et al., 2023). Deep learning methods make it possible for a machine to be fed with raw data and automatically discover the representations needed for detection or classification (LeCun et al., 2015; Lee & Yeo, 2022). Therefore, ChatGPT is continuously improving itself through user feedback (Floridi, 2023). While ChatGPT's primary function is to mimic human speech, its capabilities extend far beyond this. For example, it can generate text such as a poem, a story or a novel, give feedback on such text, or behave in any other way appropriate to the role assigned to it. (Su et al., 2023; Tlili et al., 2023).

The incorporation of artificial intelligence into educational settings is an emerging field due to its potential benefits (Adamopoulou, & Moussiades, 2020; Farrokhnia et al., 2023). Integrating AI into education makes the learning process personalized, flexible, inclusive and fun (Luckin et al., 2016). In parallel, chatbots are thought to provide opportunities in education by engaging students, personalizing learning activities, supporting educators, and developing deep insights into students' behavior (Kuhail et al., 2023). The use of ChatGPT as an artificial intelligence chatbot in education offers learning opportunities in some subjects such as lesson planning, personalized student support, question answering, assessment and evaluation, writing and supervision, and programming learning (Rahman & Watanobe, 2023). In terms of mathematics education, it is stated that ChatGPT can show success in a mathematics exam, provide students with immediate support and feedback on problem solving, and improve students' learning experiences and mathematical skills (Korkmaz Guler et al., 2024; Li et al., 2023; Wardat et al., 2023). For teachers, it is thought to have benefits such as asking and answering questions in a mathematics lesson and simulating possible interactions with a student with misconceptions (Lee & Yeo, 2023). Although there are studies in the literature investigating teachers' experiences of using ChatGPT through specific scenarios (Seebut et al., 2024; Tlili et al., 2023; Vasconcelos & Santos, 2023), there is a need to investigate applications that integrate ChatGPT as a tool into mathematics classes.

It may not always be easy to use new technologies and technological tools in mathematics lessons and to integrate them with the subjects and outcomes appropriate to the student level. In order for this process to take place and progress smoothly, the technology to be used needs to be adapted to the lesson, integrated in a meaningful way and the curriculum content needs to be reorganized (Oates, 2011). In addition, teachers who want to incorporate a new technology into mathematics education settings need to be able to use this technology and its tools effectively in the classroom for successful integration (Viberg et al., 2020). Professional development and strategic planning are important to identify and overcome potential barriers to the use of technology in the classroom (Wachira & Keengwe, 2011).

In this context, the aim of this study is to investigate how mathematics teachers use ChatGPT, an artificial intelligence chatbot, in their classes and to reveal their views about this experience. The research problem was stated as "How do mathematics teachers use ChatGPT in their lessons and what are their views on using ChatGPT in their lessons?"..

BACKGROUND

Artificial Intelligence in Education

Artificial intelligence refers to machine systems that simulate human-like characteristics such as perception, communication, and cognitive behavior (Coleman, 2021; Zhang, 2023). Although artificial intelligence is a technology that mimics human intelligence, there are some points where it resembles and differs from human intelligence (Zhang, 2023). These similarities and differences make artificial intelligence an effective and noteworthy technology in terms of education. For example, thanks to its human-like intelligence, it enriches the learning experience by offering personalized learning experiences (Kok et al., 2024; Zaharuddin et al., 2024), can demonstrate cognitive thinking skills such as reflective thinking and critical analysis for challenging tasks (Almazrou et al., 2024), can be used as a mentor that understands personal needs, and creates an experience that is indistinguishable from human interaction while doing all of this (Castañeda et al., 2024). Examples of the effects of aspects that differ from human intelligence include the ability to process data impartially, leading to successful predictions and assessments (Liu, 2024). Additionally, there is the capacity to create a learning system that considers the characteristics of both teachers and students (Echeverria et al., 2023). Moreover, there is the capability to transform large amounts of data into a personalized decision-making system (Mohd Amin et al., 2025). There are views that these capabilities of artificial intelligence could serve as a balancing factor in reducing inequality of opportunity in education and making education more accessible. The literature reports that artificial intelligence is supportive because of its potential to compensate for the shortage of qualified teachers for disadvantaged students in rural areas and to respond to students' individual needs (Khazanchi et al., 2025).

Artificial intelligence for education is a technology that requires addressing both opportunities and challenges. Especially with ChatGPT, AI has spread very quickly, catching many educators off guard. Many educators have pointed out that AI harms students' academic integrity in assignments and exams. Additionally, there have been discussions about how misleading and inaccurate information generated by AI is used without critical thinking, and how the lack of transparency in the use of AI systems has led to a trust issue between students and educators (Giannakos et al., 2024). Furthermore, some educational institutions have banned the use of AI by students but have gradually changed their policies and moved towards applications for the controlled integration of tools such as ChatGPT (Huang et al., 2024; McDonald et al., 2025). The current consensus is that rather than ignoring AI, which is already part of the educational context, and avoiding its use, it is better to understand it and adapt it to educational environments (Wang et al., 2024). Eaton (2025) argues that, especially in today's world where the use of generative AI tools such as ChatGPT has become quite widespread in individual production, the definition and approach to plagiarism need to be re-examined. Based on this view, he has proposed a conceptual framework that encompasses new paradigms related to the use of AI in education and ethics. Some of the important points emphasized in this framework are as follows:

- Collaboration between humans and AI in the production process should not be considered plagiarism but rather become the norm. Students and educators can seek ideas from AI and request support for structure and draft formation during the production process. It is believed that this collaboration between AI and humans will not stifle creativity but rather enhance it.
- Support provided by AI, such as translation, correction, and explanation, can eliminate linguistic inequality. Students and educators whose native language is not English will have an assistant in accessing content and expressing their thoughts in a global context.
- Even with AI support, it should not be forgotten that the individual bears full responsibility throughout the production process. Educators and students should be aware that ethical and academic responsibility cannot be delegated.
- The definition of plagiarism should be approached in relation to culture and context and restructured in a way that does not ignore the benefits of new technology (Eaton, 2025).

It is important to clarify the role of educators in the process of leveraging the full potential of human–AI interaction for educational purposes, while doing so within ethical boundaries. In order to ensure effective and transparent AI use among younger students, it is essential that teachers first develop sufficient competence in this area and recognize their responsibilities. ***What is the Role of the Teacher?***

The careful, critical, and utilitarian use of artificial intelligence poses a challenge for teachers as well as students (Kasneci et al., 2023). Hu et al. (2024) define four fundamental challenges facing teachers in the age of artificial intelligence: the application of digital technologies in the teaching process, ethical issues raised by AI, increased teacher training requirements, and the need for teachers to continuously improve themselves and adapt to a changing learning environment that requires new technologies. On the other hand, teachers who do not experience these difficulties or who are able to overcome them successfully are more likely to use AI, a constantly evolving technology, in their educational processes, involving their students (Hu et al., 2024). In other words, the effective use of AI in education requires that teachers are able to make sense of it (Chiu & Chai, 2020). The fact that an AI-supported educational experience can also contribute to the development of AI-literate individuals underscores the critical role of teachers in this process (Velander et al., 2023).

A teacher who wants to integrate artificial intelligence into their lessons must consider issues such as how to strike a balance between artificial intelligence and the learning objectives of the lesson, which teaching strategies to choose, and how to use time and resources efficiently (Park et al., 2023). Although policymakers have made some moves toward integrating artificial intelligence into education, policies and curricula are generally lacking in specific content related to artificial intelligence applications, so teachers need guidance to implement these applications (Velander et al., 2023). The introduction of AI into the educational context requires teachers to transition from their traditional role as knowledge transmitters to a role focused on understanding student thinking and making appropriate pedagogical decisions. It is important for teachers to be equipped with pedagogical content knowledge (PCK), trained in questioning strategies, and to understand the limitations and potential of AI so that they can use it not only as a teaching tool but also as a tool to help design individualized learning experiences (Lee et al., 2025). Research has revealed findings related to teachers' AI competencies (Delcker et al., 2025), perspectives on AI education (Jatileni et al., 2024), perceptions of AI (Chounta et al., 2022), and attitudes (Perla et al., 2025). One study discussed an example of integrating an AI-based prediction application into a middle school science class (Park et al., 2023). In the context of mathematics education, a study discussed the potential use of ChatGPT in tasks such as subject presentation, activity design, creative scenario development, and providing alternative explanations to students through lesson plans prepared by teacher candidates (Yanar & Ergene, 2025).

The National Council of Teachers of Mathematics (NCTM, 2023) has reported that generative artificial intelligence has the potential to shift the focus in mathematics classrooms away from computation and procedural tasks toward more creative problem solving. Accordingly, mathematics teachers are expected to provide both the environment and the competence necessary for students to critically evaluate the outputs generated by such technologies. To this end, mathematics teachers should be able to use AI tools strategically, create classroom environments that encourage students to question the mathematical concepts and content contained in AI-generated responses, and encourage students to think about the accuracy and validity of AI-generated content throughout this process (Dilling, 2025). Aqazade et al. (2025) have stated that teachers who integrate AI tools such as ChatGPT into mathematics lessons can produce more effective outcomes by consciously using types of knowledge such as pedagogical knowledge (PK), subject knowledge (CK), contextual knowledge (CxK), and technological knowledge (TK). Thus, the teacher will no longer be a passive user who merely requests content from AI; instead, they will become an active process designer who guides the process with their knowledge and experience, evaluates mathematical content for accuracy and appropriateness for the student, and adapts it as needed.

Most studies conducted in the literature on the use of AI in mathematics education aim to evaluate the mathematical abilities of AI tools rather than directly involving students or teachers (Dilling, 2025). For example, Wei (2024) tested the success of current versions of ChatGPT in solving math problems at different grade levels. The research results showed that ChatGPT performed excellently in tasks related to algebra, number properties, and computation, but performed poorly in tasks involving geometry, measurement, and spatial reasoning. Etcuban (2025) reported that when ChatGPT was used as a helpful tool by students in learning algebra, it was effective in reducing algebra anxiety and increasing test performance. In a study where students interacted with ChatGPT to solve specific calculus problems, it was concluded that this interaction led to positive development in students' questioning and verification skills, and the importance of tasks such as formative assessment, structuring the process, and early intervention for students with negative attitudes was emphasized for teachers (Zhuang, 2025). Another mathematics education study suggesting that the dialogue-based learning method can be enriched by flipped it with ChatGPT describes a learning process in which students take an active role, search for information by engaging in dialogue with ChatGPT, reformulate their questions, and identify the AI's errors. The study predicts that this process will enhance students' critical thinking skills and question-asking strategies, and that questioning AI errors can be leveraged as an advantage in the learning process education (Pavlova, 2024). These studies are important in helping educators recognize the potential and limitations of artificial intelligence in mathematics. However, more research is needed on concrete examples and outcomes of AI-integrated lesson processes. The research presented in this section shares the experiences of teachers who have used an AI tool like ChatGPT, which provides practical applications, in mathematics lessons with their students.

METHOD

Design of the Study and Participants

This research was conducted in accordance with the case study design, one of the qualitative research methods. Case study design is used to reveal, describe and evaluate the details that make up a current phenomenon, event or situation (Creswell, 2021). In this study, it was investigated how mathematics teachers use ChatGPT, an artificial intelligence tool that can be considered new in the context of education, in their lessons. The participants of the study consisted of four middle school mathematics teachers who used ChatGPT in their lessons. Participants are working in different regions of Türkiye. The participants were determined by criterion sampling method. Accordingly, teachers who had experience in using ChatGPT in mathematics lessons were included in the study. The participants were coded as T1, T2, T3, and T4 to keep their identities confidential. Demographic information of the participants is given in Table 1.

Table 1. Demographic information of the participants

Participants	Gender	Level of Education	Professional Experience	Status of receiving a training on AI
T1	Female	Bachelor's degree	22 years	Received Training
T2	Male	Graduate degree	5 years	No Training
T3	Female	Graduate degree	8 years	Received Training
T4	Female	Graduate degree	6 years	Received Training

As seen in Table 1, a total of four mathematics teachers, three female and one male, participated in the study. The participants' teaching experience ranged from 5 to 22 years. The education level of one of the participants was undergraduate (T1) and three of them were postgraduate. T1 received training on artificial intelligence by attending in-service seminars from the Teacher Information Network (TIN) education platform and free courses through e-government. T3 received artificial intelligence education within the scope of a doctoral course. T4 stated that she participated in certified training courses provided by academics at several universities and attended lectures on AI in education at various conferences and workshops. T2 stated that he did not receive any formal training on artificial intelligence and that he improved himself with the content created on social media platforms.

Data Collection Tools

Semi-structured interviews were conducted within the scope of this research. For this purpose, an interview form consisting of 15 questions was prepared by the researchers. The interview questions were prepared to obtain demographic information about the participants, participants' initial attitudes towards ChatGPT, how they use ChatGPT in their lessons, which methods/techniques they prefer, at which stages of their lessons they use ChatGPT, the difficulties and advantages of using ChatGPT in mathematics lessons, methods of overcoming difficulties, and recommendations for teachers who want to use ChatGPT in mathematics lessons. The participants were asked questions such as "For what purposes and how do you use ChatGPT in your lessons?", "What are the challenges of using ChatGPT in mathematics lessons?", "What advice would you give to mathematics teachers who want to use ChatGPT in their lessons?". The interviews lasted approximately 15-25 minutes.

Analysis of Data

The data obtained from semi-structured interviews were analyzed in accordance with the inductive approach. The inductive approach aims to define the collected data, to reveal the facts that may be hidden in the data and the relationships that can explain the data (Yıldırım & Şimşek, 2021). In this study, themes and codes were obtained based on the answers given to the interview questions. According to the interview questions and the answers given, the themes were determined as "the first encounter with ChatGPT", "first views about ChatGPT", "the use of ChatGPT in lessons", "the things to be considered in interaction with ChatGPT", "advantages and difficulties of using ChatGPT", "methods to overcome the difficulties that may be encountered in the use of ChatGPT" and "recommendations for teachers who will use ChatGPT in their lessons.

FINDINGS

In this section, the codes corresponding to the themes identified through data analysis are presented, along with direct quotations from participant responses

First Meeting with ChatGPT

Within the scope of the research, the participants were asked when and how they met ChatGPT. While Participant T1 stated that her first encountered ChatGPT on the TIN educational platform, Participants T2 and T4 reported hearing about it on social media, and Participant T3 indicated being introduced to it through a doctoral course. The codes related to this theme are presented in Table 2.

Table 2. Codes Related to the Theme of First Meeting With Chatgpt

Codes	Participant
TIN education platform	T1
Social media	T2, T4
Doctoral course	T3

Initial Views Against ChatGPT

The participants were asked what they thought about ChatGPT when they first met it. T2, T3, and T4 stated that they had positive views in general, whereas T1 stated that she had negative views. The codes related to this theme are presented in Table 3.

Table 3. Codes Related to the Theme of Initial Views Against ChatGPT

View Orientation	Codes	Participant
Negative	Concern that it will make teachers passive	T1
	Concern about professional prestige	
	Concern that it could replace teachers	
Positive	Excitement	T2
	Significant development	
	Potential for application in lessons	
Positive	Supportive and complementary role for teachers	T3, T4

T1 stated that when she first met ChatGPT, she thought that it could passivate the teacher, reduce her professional prestige and replace the teacher, but as she gained experience in ChatGPT, she saw its advantages and this negative perception changed. T1's view is as follows:

T1: I thought that artificial intelligence would make a teacher passive, reduce the dignity of the teacher... In short, I thought that it could replace the teacher... As I saw what it did or tried to do, I saw that it could be productive for me and even taught me ways to motivate students in my lessons.

The view of T2, who stated that he was excited when he first met ChatGPT, that it was an important development and that he thought about its potential application in lessons, is as follows:

T2: It excited me a lot. Because I could guess that it was a very important development. Soon after, I started to think about how I could use it in my lessons.

Similarly expressing a positive perspective, Participant T3 stated that although she is aware of the ethical and social concerns in society regarding artificial intelligence, she is not influenced by them. An excerpt from the interview with Participant T3 on this topic is as follows:

T3: Well, ethical concerns about AI and emotional issues—these are already in the literature. People talk about them when it comes to AI, but honestly, I didn't really care much about that side of it. What matters more to me is whether it's useful. And it really guides me well, especially when I'm overwhelmed or stuck... it helps me get out of those situations. That's what I thought even when I first started using it. It shows direction, so I didn't have any negative feelings or thoughts. And right now, I feel quite positive about it.

Interviewer: You mentioned concerns related to emotional states. Could you explain a bit more about what those are exactly?

T3: Sure, like... the idea is that if students start using ChatGPT instead of their teacher, it might have some negative effects because it's a robot, artifi-

cial intelligence—it doesn't have emotions like a human. For example, when a student reacts in a certain way, ChatGPT will respond based on its algorithm. But a student might want to feel understood, or expect an emotionally attuned response, or maybe even some kind of praise like "well done" after giving the correct answer. But ChatGPT would just say something like "this is correct" or "this is incorrect." It wouldn't have the same emotional impact as a human. That's what people are saying. But I don't agree. I think a teacher can train AI to be used in a way that accounts for this..

Using ChatGPT in Classes

In order to determine the use of ChatGPT in mathematics lessons, the participants were asked how and at which stages of their mathematics lessons they used ChatGPT, how they integrated ChatGPT into their lessons, whether they made any preparation for its use, and which teaching method/technique they preferred to use while integrating it into their lessons. Based on the responses received, it was observed that mathematics teachers can use ChatGPT for different purposes in the preparation, implementation, and evaluation stages of their lessons. Teachers use ChatGPT in mathematics lessons for various purposes, such as generating different strategies for problem-solving, providing feedback on incorrect solutions, creating problems, designing activities, finding the basic properties of geometric shapes through estimation, and generating tasks targeting student deficiencies. Participating teachers reported conducting these applications using question-and-answer, discussion, group work, and inquiry-based approaches. Additionally, teachers stated that they made preparations such as determining an appropriate topic for using ChatGPT in mathematics lessons, informing students about AI usage, preparing students for the topic to be integrated with AI, planning the content, and testing, monitoring, and evaluating its use in the classroom. The codes related to this theme are presented in Table 4.

Table 4. Codes Related to the Theme of Using ChatGPT in Classes

Subcategory	Codes	
Practice	Problem solving	T1
	Generating different strategies for problem solving	
	Providing feedback on incorrect solutions	
	Creating problems based on scenarios	T2
	Drawing pictures and creating problems based on them	
	Designing STEM activities	T3
	Discovering the basic properties of geometric shapes through estimation	
	Providing students with compensation tasks	
	Creating scenarios that match the different meanings of fractions	T4
	Creating images that describe the context	
Course stage	Preparation	T2, T3, T4
	Implementation	T2, T3
	Reinforcement	T1
	Evaluation	T1, T2, T3
Preparations	Subject selection	T1
	Content planning	T2, T4
	Literature review	T4
	Preparing students in terms of subject matter	T1,T2
	Preparing students in terms of AI usage	T3
	Testing the accuracy of answers	T3
	Testing the suitability of the content for students	T3
	Testing appropriate questions	T3
Teaching method/ technique	Question and answer	T1
	Discussion	T2, T4
	Collaboration	T3
	Inquiry-based approach	T3

T1, who stated that she used ChatGPT during problem solving activities in her lessons, stated that students were able to gain different perspectives for problem solving. T1's view is as follows:

T1: They have a general prejudice about using problem solving strategies and even solving problems using different strategies. So I make them solve a problem and ask them how they solve it. Then we make them solve the same problem with ChatGPT to see how they solve it. If it does not solve it differently, we tell it what we have and tell it to solve it with a different strategy... Sometimes students can make wrong solutions for different things. Let's ask ChatGPT, let's see what it says about his solution, and I make them get feedback directly from it...When I think about it, they gain a different perspective from both mine and their own.

The practices of T2, who used ChatGPT in problem solving activities like T1 in her lessons, were printing a problem to ChatGPT according to the scenario and having ChatGPT draw a picture and construct a problem accordingly. T2's view explaining these applications is as follows:

T2: For example, I ask the children randomly. Tell a story...write an equation problem about two stubborn goats who meet on a bridge. I ask ChatGPT for this and the children solve the problem that ChatGPT wrote for this. Then we take it one step further. I think of a situation that fits the problem, for example the problem of the age difference between Ali and his mother. Draw a picture suitable for this... I have ChatGPT draw this without showing it to the students. Then I show this picture to the students. I say, "Come on, write a problem suitable for this." I force them. Then we choose among them and solve them together.

The views of T3, who stated that she used ChatGPT in her lessons to find the basic properties of geometric shapes by guessing and to present make-up tasks to the students, are as follows:

T3: Children may have difficulty in learning the properties of geometric shapes... square, rectangle, trapezoid...to learn the basic properties of these...I determine a shape, I ask the ChatGPT with the class if they can find it. ChatGPT asks questions to find the shape... how many sides it has, are the angles equal, are the sides equal. So we are trying to get ChatGPT to find the shape. The students try to guess with it. It attracts the children's attention. Apart from that...for example, there are things that a student or a few students cannot do about probability. We open them and write them on ChatGPT. We ask it to give the students tasks to make up for it. Sometimes it gives homework, sometimes it prepares questions or ... there are things it needs to emphasize. Sometimes I see that children are more motivated when they get the task from the robot and not from me. This is how I use it in general.

T4 shared an example of how he used ChatGPT to help students understand the different meanings of fractions with the following statements:

T4: I use ChatGPT in class when I want to do something myself but don't have the time to design it or can't think creatively at that moment. For example, I'm going to explain fractions, but I want to make a point before I start. I want what I'm going to do to encourage my students to think. I want them to start by understanding fractions and thinking about them from there. Let's say I want to design such an activity. I actually have a general idea in mind. I ask ChatGPT, "What are the meanings of fractions?" ChatGPT lists them: part-whole, ratio, operator, etc. Now I say, create a scenario for each of these. I specify that I want them to be long if I want them to be long, or short if I want them to be short. What I'm aiming for is this... to define the different meanings of fractions in context and have the students extract them from within... I'm actually expecting them to notice them. I am showing from the beginning that the concept of fractions can exist in different contexts, not just in slices of cake, but also, for example, in the number of students going on a trip, the red beads on a necklace, or the sugar ratio in lemonade. If I want to involve my students even more, I want ChatGPT to create visuals that describe the scenarios it creates. I directly show these visuals to the class and have them discuss them. I want them to discuss what might be explained here, how fractions might be used in this context, and what fractions might represent. I explain what's in my mind to it, and I use what it produces based on my ideas in the classroom, in short.

As shown in Table 4, participating teachers stated that they used these sample applications in the Preparation, Implementation, Reinforcement, and Evaluation stages of their lessons. According to this, while T2 and T3 expressed their opinions on the use of ChatGPT in almost every stage of the lesson, T1 expressed her view on its use only in reinforcement and evaluation, and T4 expressed her view on its use in the preparation stage. A section of T1's interview and T4's interview is provided below.

T1: Reinforcement and evaluation. I think we still need to teach the subject using traditional methods.

Interviewer: Why?

T1: ChatGPT can do amazing things, but I don't think it's a tool that can teach students a subject from scratch. It's great for creative tasks, but it's not good at creating content suitable for students. It can also give wrong answers sometimes. There's no need to take that risk when children are just starting to learn a subject.

T4: I prefer to use it in situations that require creativity and attention, so it is the preparation stage of the lesson. I think it is an effective way to engage students in discussion and arouse their curiosity.

Participating teachers stated that they made preparations related to determining subject, planning content, reviewing literature, preparing students in terms of subject, preparing students in terms of AI use, testing the accuracy of answers, testing the suitability of content for students, and trying out appropriate questions in order to use ChatGPT in mathematics lessons. Some views regarding the preparation subcategory are as follows:

T3: After all, even though it generally works well, it is still a robot. If I am going to use it in class, I try it out myself first and check the answers it gives... I look at the assignments it will give beforehand to see what it might suggest. I ask questions based on that. Sometimes we need to explain what we want clearly...

I had explained it to the class beforehand. What ChatGPT is, what it does, how we will use it, and so on.

T4: I usually do a literature review beforehand. The reason for this is to check which concepts are important in relation to the topic I will be teaching, what has been done before, and whether there are any activities that I can adapt to my ChatGPT lesson.

Mathematics teachers have stated that the teaching methods/techniques they prefer to use when integrating ChatGPT into their lessons are question-and-answer, discussion, collaboration, and inquiry-based approaches. Examples of relevant views are provided below.

T1: I would say question and answer. Even in class, they do not interact directly with ChatGPT. We use ChatGPT's output through question and answer sessions with my mediation.

T2: Discussion, I guess. I want the children to explain and evaluate their ideas and discuss them. In other words, I encourage them to do so.

Interaction Considerations with ChatGPT

In order to examine how the participants created their inputs when they used ChatGPT for practice in their lessons, they were asked how they interacted with ChatGPT and what they paid attention to in order to increase the potential of their answers. T1 stated that she used clear and descriptive sentences, rephrased the questions by changing them when necessary and paid attention to ask questions in a descriptive way. T2 stated that he specified the target audience and the subject of the lesson for which he would create content for the ChatGPT, briefly explained what was asked, and did not pay attention to details other than that. T3, on the other hand, stated that she experimented by forming the question in different ways, asked it clearly, defined a role for ChatGPT and specified the format of the answers. The codes related to this theme are presented in Table 5.

Table 5. Codes related to the theme of Interaction Considerations with ChatGPT

Codes	Participants
Use clear and descriptive sentences	T1,T3
Rewrite the prompt	T1,T3
Specify the target audience	T2,T4
Specify the subject of the lesson	T2
Briefly explain what is required	T2

continued on following page

Table 5. Continued

Codes	Participants
Define a role for ChatGPT	T3
Specify the format of the answers	T3
Provide the prompt in stages	
Improve based on feedback on the output	T4

The relevant views of T1, T2, T3, and T4 are as follows:

T1: I use clear and descriptive sentences when I ask questions. I want them to be clear and precise because when I don't ask questions like this, I see that I don't get clear answers...I asked by changing the form of the question. Actually, I am asking the same thing, but I expanded the sentence, I tried to explain exactly what I wanted. I really saw that the answers also changed.

T2: Yes, I try to be more descriptive when I ask my questions. There are very fine details about this, but I cannot say that I pay much attention. I just emphasize that the children should prepare according to their grade level and the topic. I also briefly explain what I want.

T3: The questions we ask are very important to get good answers from the ChatGPT. For example, I ask my questions by constantly trying different ways. It is necessary to ask clearly, without taking too long. For example, it is important to give it a role. You are a 6th grade student, I am a math teacher. If we want the answers as questions, for example, I indicate it and it answers accordingly.

T4: I am careful to explain the student's level, such as "for a middle school student." Rather than long prompts, it is more efficient to divide what I want into stages and proceed as I go along. I also give feedback based on the answers they give, such as "can you write more concisely" or "can you give a more creative answer."

Advantages and Challenges of Using ChatGPT

Participants mentioned the advantages of using ChatGPT in mathematics lessons such as providing practicality for the teacher, developing different solution strategies, giving direct feedback to incorrect answers, facilitating classroom control, reinforcing the topics, providing remarkable content, being motivating for students, and reducing workload, supporting and enriching creative ideas. On the other hand, they stated that the use of ChatGPT in mathematics lessons posed difficulties such as writing long inputs during the lesson, inconsistency, producing irrelevant answers, creating content by associating it with learning outcomes, making it interactive with students, and requiring preparation before class. The codes related to this theme are presented in Table 6.

Table 6. Codes related to the theme of Advantages and Challenges of Using ChatGPT

Subcategory	Codes	Participants
Advantages	Providing practicality to teachers	T1
	Developing different solution strategies	T1
	Providing direct feedback on incorrect answers	T1
	Facilitating classroom control	T2
	Reinforcing the topics	T2
	Providing remarkable content	T2
	Reducing workload	T4
	Supporting and enriching creative ideas	T4
Challenges	Writing long input during the lesson	T1
	Inconsistency	T2
	Producing irrelevant answers	T2
	Creating content by associating it with learning outcomes	T3
	Making it interactive with students	T3
	Requiring preparation before class	T4

Some of the participants' views on the advantages and challenges of using ChatGPT in mathematics lessons are as follows:

T1: When I use it for problem solving, it is difficult to write every problem in class during the lesson. It is the same for any other long text. Students can be distracted while waiting for me to write it.

T3: I mean, I think it is a bit difficult to associate these kinds of things with learning outcomes. Okay, I can use it in geometry and so on, but for example... I have difficulty in creating content by associating it with the learning outcomes related to algebra. I mean it is difficult to use ChatGPT in a way that is always appropriate for the purpose of the lesson.

T4: It is very advantageous when I want to create and use creative ideas. Let's say I have an activity idea in mind that I want to use in class, but it's not clear yet. When I tell ChatGPT that I have such an idea, it gives me ideas that support or enrich it. It also lightens my load because it creates details of the content. This saves me time.

How to Overcome Challenges in Using ChatGPT

In order to overcome the difficulties of using ChatGPT in mathematics lessons, participants made suggestions such as preparing questions in advance, giving feedback to unwanted answers, planning before use, sharing different ideas and experiences, making trainings practical, and bringing experts and teachers together in trainings. The codes related to this theme are presented in Table 7.

Table 7. Codes related to the theme of How to Overcome Challenges in Using ChatGPT

Codes	Participants
Preparing questions in advance	T1
Giving feedback to unwanted answers	T2
Planning before use	T2
Sharing different ideas and experiences	T3
Making trainings practical	T3
Bringing experts and teachers together in trainings	T3
Using adaptable examples	T4

Some of the participants' views on how to overcome the difficulties they encounter when using ChatGPT in their classes are as follows:

T2: ChatGPT continues to improve itself. I definitely give feedback to the answers I don't like. Apart from that, if it is planned in advance and used in the classroom, such situations can be prevented to some extent.

T3: Of course, it is important to receive education and to read, but I think it is very important to experience. The more you try, the more you have the opportunity to think about it. Also, mathematics teachers can share these experiences with each other. I said I cannot integrate it into algebra, but maybe someone else can. It is important to see different ideas. In fact, I think that teachers and experts in this field should come together in the trainings and do it in a practical way, because there are many problems in the field. If experts realize these problems, it may be easier to prepare content for them.

T4: I prepare for class by researching previous examples. I look for things that I can adapt to both ChatGPT and my students' level. This makes my job a little easier.

Recommendations for Teachers to Use ChatGPT in Their Classes

The participants made recommendations for teachers who want to use ChatGPT in their classes; following innovations, attending trainings, researching, following local and foreign content, making efforts to adapt the content to the lesson, eliminating their deficiencies in artificial intelligence, attending practical trainings, receiving training from experts in artificial intelligence and continuous experience. The codes related to this theme are presented in Table 8.

Table 8. Codes related to the Theme of Recommendations for Teachers to Use ChatGPT in Their Classes

Codes	Participant
Following innovations	T1
Attending trainings	T1
Researching	T1
Following local and foreign content	T2
Making efforts to adapt the content to the lesson	T2, T4
Eliminating their deficiencies in artificial intelligence	T3
Attending practical trainings	T3
Receiving training from experts in artificial intelligence	T3
Continuous experience	T3, T4

The views of the participants regarding their recommendations for teachers who will use ChatGPT in their lessons are as follows:

T1: They should definitely continue to research and use new things. There are new things coming out all the time because... I think they should attend seminars and so on if they can find them.

T2: I think they should do some research. Local and foreign content producers produce a lot. ChatGPT is very popular right now. They should look at the work done and think a little bit about how I can adapt it to my lesson.

T3: First of all, as far as I understand artificial intelligence, as far as I can see, we are still very deficient. In order to overcome this, if they have the opportunity to receive training from people who know mathematics education and artificial intelligence well, they can evaluate it. Then, as I said, they can constantly experiment and find out how they can use and apply it in accordance with their own students and needs.

DISCUSSION AND CONCLUSION

In this study, how mathematics teachers use ChatGPT in their lessons and their views about it were investigated. As a result of the research, it was seen that mathematics teachers used ChatGPT in problem solving, problem posing, using different strategies in problem solving, knowing the basic properties of geometric shapes, and understanding the meanings of fractions. It is noteworthy that the topics preferred by mathematics teachers who integrate ChatGPT into their lessons are often those in which students experience difficulties or hold preconceived notions. It is also stated in the literature that ChatGPT is very successful in solving complex mathematical problems and having basic geometric knowledge (Farrokhnia et al., 2023). It was observed that the mathematics teachers participating in this study used ChatGPT to provide immediate, direct feedback for students' incorrect solutions and missing points. It is important for the teacher to immediately review the answers during the lesson and ask for a review of inconsistent answers, but it is very difficult to provide real-time feedback to all students in the class (Urrutia & Araya, 2024). It is thought that AI tools such as ChatGPT can form a powerful combination to support the teacher in such situation (Davenport et al., 2019).

There are also some criticisms and concerns in the literature regarding the use of artificial intelligence by students. Although artificial intelligence provides an advanced learning experience thanks to its ability to produce effective text, it is thought to pose risks in terms of academic integrity and unethical use (Khatri & Karki, 2023). There are also concerns that if students become overly dependent on artificial intelligence, their cognitive skills such as originality, analysis, and critical thinking may be negatively affected (Méndez Alarcón et al., 2025). In a study that approached this issue from a neurological perspective, individuals' brain activities were measured in real-time through a writing task. The results showed that individuals who used ChatGPT during writing tasks exhibited less cognitive effort and brain activity compared to those who did not use it. Accordingly, it is thought that individuals who directly accept and use AI-generated information may experience immediate comfort, but in the long term, they may experience a decline in skills such as critical thinking, evaluation, problem solving, and mental structure development (Kosmyna et al., 2025). The mathematics teachers who participated in this study stated at various stages of the interview that they did not use ChatGPT-generated content directly in their lessons; instead, they evaluated the content from different perspectives, such as its suitability for the students' level, learning objectives, ethical and cultural values, before presenting it to the students. Generative artificial intelligence tools, especially when used to enrich individuals' own ideas, as exemplified and emphasized by T4, will not stifle creativity and mental capacity but rather play a developmental role (Eaton, 2025). It is believed that this understanding, when adopted and disseminated by teachers, will also be imparted to students.

A notable finding of the study is that teachers prefer to integrate ChatGPT into different stages of their mathematics lessons. In this regard, a participating teacher with 22 years of professional experience stated that she uses ChatGPT in the reinforcement and assessment stages of their lessons and that the relevant topic should be taught using traditional methods beforehand. Research indicates that age influences attitudes toward AI, with younger teachers exhibiting higher levels of AI acceptance and finding it easier to adopt (Bakhadirov et al., 2024; Cabero-Almenara et al., 2024). Although the participating teacher who holds this view has integrated ChatGPT into their lessons, they may perceive traditional methods as more effective and acceptable than AI-supported education.

As a result of the study, it was seen that although mathematics teachers who used ChatGPT in their lessons expressed the difficulties of this use, they also offered solutions to overcome them. In the literature, there are concerns that ChatGPT may produce inaccurate, incomplete or inconsistent content (Duan et al., 2019; Dwivedi et al., 2023). However, in order to avoid these concerns and to use ChatGPT to its maximum potential, it is important to know how to interact with it (Lo, 2023). As a result of this study, it was seen that mathematics teachers who had a lot of experience in integrating ChatGPT into their lessons increased their competencies in this regard. Teachers' ability to keep up with the artificial intelligence era and actively use artificial intelligence tools in their lessons will have positive effects on their students. It is believed that when teachers do not actively use new technologies while integrating them into their lessons, collaborative practices and student learning do not take place (Viberg et al., 2020). When students experience artificial intelligence tools with their teachers in their lessons, they can have the skills and equipment required by new technologies. Other challenges mentioned by participating teachers include writing long entries during class, creating content related to learning outcomes, making it interactive with students, and the need for preparation before class. In a study conducted with teacher candidates, the challenges of using ChatGPT in a mathematics teaching method included concerns about the risk of generating incorrect answers and the clarity and simplicity of problem solutions (Kim et al., 2025).

Mathematics teachers who used ChatGPT in their lessons stated that they had different interactions with ChatGPT in order for it to produce appropriate outputs. Since ChatGPT is trained with a very large dataset and generates its answers by selecting from this dataset, it is very important to customize the requests (Grabb, 2023). It is known that an incorrect or incomplete answer produced by ChatGPT is not always due to a technical problem, and better results can be obtained with appropriate questioning styles (Spasić & Janković, 2023). In line with their experiences, the participant teachers of this study used clear and understandable sentences, defined a role for ChatGPT, asked their questions in different formats and rephrased the question differently when necessary. Similarly, a study using the self-study method reported that mathematics teacher educators first assigned ChatGPT a teacher role to create mathematical tasks, provided the basic mathematical concepts to be addressed in the task, and specified the target audience's grade level. In addition, participants selected words in an educational context to produce purposeful output (Aqazade et al., 2025).

In this research, which aims to present effective examples of integrating ChatGPT into mathematics lessons, four teachers were reached in the Turkish context. The reason why the research was limited to four participants is that mathematics teachers do not widely integrate ChatGPT into their lessons; instead, they use it for individual purposes outside of preparation, consultation, and educational contexts, or they do not use it at all. This situation may be influenced by teachers' lack of knowledge about how to integrate ChatGPT into mathematics lessons and learning outcomes, their perception of its effective use in the classroom as a risk, their distrust of artificial intelligence, or their belief that the preparation and planning required for integration would be an additional burden. Generative artificial intelligence tools are used in many fields such as health, finance and education and provide advantages to their users (Luo et al., 2022). Instead of staying away from these developments, individuals should strive to become competent in learning, gaining experience and using them effectively (Wang et al., 2023).

The mathematics teachers who participated in the study advised other teachers who want to use ChatGPT in their lessons to improve themselves by attending related trainings and following innovations. They also suggested that they should create opportunities to integrate ChatGPT and similar tools into their lessons by continuously experiencing them. Similarly, educational researchers should design AI-assisted learning tasks to engage students in solving complex and innovative problems with content aligned with instructional objectives (Zhai, 2022). These recommendations from participating teachers may help promote the adoption and widespread use of AI in the classroom among teachers. The literature indicates that social influence is an important factor in determining teachers' views on the adoption and integration of AI (Khlaif et al., 2024; Velli & Zafiropoulos, 2024). It is believed that those who adopt artificial intelligence early in the classroom will influence their colleagues through their contributions to user experience, trust building, risk awareness, and methods for overcoming challenges, thereby promoting the adoption and widespread use of artificial intelligence. The results of the study show that ChatGPT can be used to explain mathematical concepts to students. With the help of ChatGPT, learning scenarios and activities can be designed in which mathematical concepts, their definitions and properties can be recognized. ChatGPT can be used in and out of the classroom to provide real-time feedback to students' problem solving. It is thought that students who have knowledge about how to use productive artificial intelligence tools such as ChatGPT in the classroom and what they can do can use artificial intelligence support in their educational activities outside of school. Teachers can design a lesson in which they can simultaneously monitor the questions asked by students and the answers produced by ChatGPT, and conduct discussions based on the questions and answers. In this way, teachers can successfully manage a classroom interaction process where discussion and collaboration are experienced and provide more effective support to students.

CONCLUSION AND RECOMMENDATIONS

This chapter presents a snapshot of insights into how mathematics teachers utilize ChatGPT in their classrooms, a tool whose use has become widespread among a significant portion of society in recent years due to its outstanding performance in generating text and visual content, as well as its capacity for continuous self-improvement. Despite providing valuable insights, the results of this study should be interpreted in light of various limitations that also point to directions for further research. One of these limitations is that the participants in the study were mathematics teachers in Türkiye who used ChatGPT in their lessons and were available for interviews. This situation limits the diversity of concrete examples and perspectives related to the application. While the current data provides guidance for educators and researchers, it reflects a specific educational and cultural context. In the future, these findings could be expanded to include participants from countries with different policy frameworks, curriculum standards, or levels of digital readiness.

Another limitation of the study is that the practical applications it presents are based solely on the statements of participating teachers. Due to the fact that the researchers and participants were located in different cities, it was not possible to conduct observations. In the future, the consistency of the results could be improved by supporting the participants' views with observations. The findings of this study highlight the need for future research that not only includes teachers but also incorporates the perspectives of students who have experienced this process in mathematics classrooms, as well as studies that provide an external view of the classroom environments where the process took place. For the integration of new technologies into lessons to be considered successful, it must be evaluated using a holistic approach that includes not only usage behavior but also factors such as pedagogical alignment, participant encouragement, and technological creativity. Considering the results of the research, it is thought that there is a need to increase the number of studies and guidelines for integrating ChatGPT into mathematics courses. It is suggested that studies on good examples should be carried out on the possible difficulties that may arise from using ChatGPT in mathematics lessons and solution suggestions.

REFERENCES

Adamopoulou, E., & Moussiades, L. (2020). Chatbots: History, technology, and applications. *Machine Learning with Applications*, *2*, 100006. DOI: 10.1016/j.mlwa.2020.100006

Almazrou, S., Alanezi, F., Almutairi, S. A., AboAlsamh, H. M., Alsedrah, I. T., Arif, W. M., & Attar, R. W. (2024). Enhancing medical students' critical thinking skills through ChatGPT: An empirical study with medical students. *Nutrition and Health (Berkhamsted, Hertfordshire)*, *02601060241273627*. Advance online publication. DOI: 10.1177/02601060241273627 PMID: 39150341

Aqazade, M., Mauntel, M., & Atabas, S. (2025, January 29). Empowering mathematics teacher educators: Exploring Artificial Intelligence-driven mathematical tasks. *School Science and Mathematics*, ssm.18339. Advance online publication. DOI: 10.1111/ssm.18339

Asha, V., Reddy, G. P., Nithya, B., Tungal, K., Durgaprasad, V., & Kruthik, T. N. (2023). Implication and advantages of machine learning-based chatbots in diverse disciplines. In *2023 International Conference on Sustainable Computing and Data Communication Systems (ICSCDS)* (pp. 22–28). IEEE. DOI: 10.1109/ICSCDS56580.2023.10104649

Bakhadirov, M., Alasgarova, R., & Rzayev, J. (2024). Factors influencing teachers' use of artificial intelligence for instructional purposes. *IAFOR Journal of Education*, *12*(2), 10–32. DOI: 10.22492/ije.12.2.01

Bender, E. M., Gebru, T., McMillan-Major, A., & Shmitchell, S. (2021). On the dangers of stochastic parrots: Can language models be too big? In *Proceedings of the 2021 ACM Conference on Fairness, Accountability, and Transparency* (pp. 610–623). DOI: 10.1145/3442188.3445922

Busuttil, L., & Calleja, J. (2025). Teachers' beliefs and practices about the potential of ChatGPT in teaching mathematics in secondary schools. *Digital Experiences in Mathematics Education*, *11*(1), 140–166. DOI: 10.1007/s40751-024-00168-3

Cabero-Almenara, J., Palacios-Rodríguez, A., Loaiza-Aguirre, M. I., & Rivas-Manzano, M. R. (2024). Acceptance of educational artificial intelligence by teachers and its relationship with some variables and pedagogical beliefs. *Education Sciences*, *14*(7), 740. DOI: 10.3390/educsci14070740

Castañeda, R., Martínez-Gómez-Aldaraví, A., Mercadé, L., Gómez, V. J., Mengual, T., Díaz-Fernández, F. J., Sinusia Lozano, M., Navarro Arenas, J., Barreda, Á., Gómez, M., Pinilla-Cienfuegos, E., & Ortiz de Zárate, D. (2024). Use of ChatGPT as a virtual mentor on K-12 students learning science in the fourth industrial revolution. *Knowledge (Beverly Hills, Calif.)*, *4*(4), 582–614. DOI: 10.3390/knowledge4040031

Chiu, T. K. F., & Chai, C. (2020). Sustainable curriculum planning for artificial intelligence education: A self-determination theory perspective. *Sustainability (Basel)*, *12*(14), 5568. DOI: 10.3390/su12145568

Chounta, I. A., Bardone, E., Raudsep, A., & Pedaste, M. (2022). Exploring teachers' perceptions of artificial intelligence as a tool to support their practice in Estonian K-12 education. *International Journal of Artificial Intelligence in Education*, *32*(3), 725–755. DOI: 10.1007/s40593-021-00243-5

Coleman, J. P. H. (2021). AI and our understanding of intelligence. In Arai, K., Kapoor, S., & Bhatia, R. (Eds.), *Intelligent systems and applications* (pp. 209–223). Springer., DOI: 10.1007/978-3-030-55180-3_15

Cooper, G. (2023). Examining science education in ChatGPT: An exploratory study of generative artificial intelligence. *Journal of Science Education and Technology*, *32*(3), 444–452. DOI: 10.1007/s10956-023-10039-y

Creswell, J. W. (2021). *Qualitative research methods* (Bütün, M., & Demir, S. B., Trans.). Siyasal Kitabevi. (Original work published 2013)

Crompton, H., & Song, D. (2020). El potencial de la inteligencia artificial en la educación superior. *Revista Virtual Universidad Católica Del Norte*, (62), 1–4. DOI: 10.35575/rvucn.n62a1

Davenport, T., Guha, A., Grewal, D., & Breßgott, T. (2019). How artificial intelligence will change the future of marketing. *Journal of the Academy of Marketing Science*, *48*(1), 24–42. DOI: 10.1007/s11747-019-00696-0

Delcker, J., Heil, J., & Ifenthaler, D. (2025). Evidence-based development of an instrument for the assessment of teachers' self-perceptions of their artificial intelligence competence. *Educational Technology Research and Development*, *73*(1), 115–133. DOI: 10.1007/s11423-024-10418-1

Dilling, F. (2025, July). ChatGPT's Perspectives on Real Numbers, Straight Lines and Probability-A Quantitative Study on the Influence of Prompting. In *Frontiers in Education* (Vol. 10, p. 1577322). Frontiers., DOI: 10.3389/feduc.2025.1577322

Duan, Y., Edwards, J. S., & Dwivedi, Y. K. (2019). Artificial intelligence for decision making in the era of Big Data – Evolution, challenges and research agenda. *International Journal of Information Management*, *48*, 63–71. DOI: 10.1016/j.ijinfomgt.2019.01.021

Dwivedi, Y. K., Kshetri, N., Hughes, L., Slade, E. L., Jeyaraj, A., Kar, A. K., Baabdullah, A. M., Koohang, A., Raghavan, V., Ahuja, M., Albanna, H., Albashrawi, M. A., Al-Busaidi, A. S., Balakrishnan, J., Barlette, Y., Basu, S., Bose, I., Brooks, L., Buhalis, D., & Wright, R. (2023). "So what if ChatGPT wrote it?" Multidisciplinary perspectives on opportunities, challenges and implications of generative conversational AI for research, practice and policy. *International Journal of Information Management*, *71*, 102642. DOI: 10.1016/j.ijinfomgt.2023.102642

Eaton, S. E. (2025). Global trends in education: Artificial intelligence, postplagiarism, and future-focused learning for 2025 and beyond–2024–2025 Werklund Distinguished Research Lecture. *International Journal for Educational Integrity*, *21*(1), 12. DOI: 10.1007/s40979-025-00187-6

Echeverria, V., Yang, K., Lawrence, L., Rummel, N., & Aleven, V. (2023). Designing hybrid human–AI orchestration tools for individual and collaborative activities: A technology probe study. *IEEE Transactions on Learning Technologies*, *16*(2), 191–205. DOI: 10.1109/TLT.2023.3248155

Etcuban, J. O. (2025). The use of ChatGPT in addressing Algebra anxiety and promoting confidence. *International Electronic Journal of Mathematics Education*, *20*(2), em0825. Advance online publication. DOI: 10.29333/iejme/16008

Farrokhnia, M., Banihashem, S. K., Noroozi, O., & Wals, A. (2023). A SWOT analysis of ChatGPT: Implications for educational practice and research. *Innovations in Education and Teaching International*, •••, 1–15.

Floridi, L. (2023). AI as agency without intelligence: On ChatGPT, large language models, and other generative models. *Philosophy & Technology*, *36*(1), 15. DOI: 10.1007/s13347-023-00621-y

Giannakos, M., Azevedo, R., Brusilovsky, P., Cukurova, M., Dimitriadis, Y., Hernandez-Leo, D., & Rienties, B. (2024). The promise and challenges of generative AI in education. *Behaviour & Information Technology*, •••, 1–27. DOI: 10.1080/0144929X.2024.2394886

Grabb, D. (2023). The impact of prompt engineering in large language model performance: A psychiatric example. *Journal of Medical Artificial Intelligence*, *6*, 6. DOI: 10.21037/jmai-23-71

Hu, X., Sui, H., Geng, X., & Zhao, L. (2024). Constructing a teacher portrait for the artificial intelligence age based on the micro ecological system theory: A systematic review. *Education and Information Technologies, 29*(13), 16679–16715. DOI: 10.1007/s10639-024-12513-5

Huang, J., Wu, J., Wang, Q., Yuan, K., Li, J., & Lu, D. (2024). From Prohibition to Adoption: How Hong Kong Universities Are Navigating ChatGPT in Academic Workflows. *arXiv preprint arXiv:2410.01695*. https://doi.org//arXiv.2410.01695DOI: 10.48550

Jatileni, C. N., Sanusi, I. T., Olaleye, S. A., Ayanwale, M. A., Agbo, F. J., & Oyelere, P. B. (2024). Artificial intelligence in compulsory level of education: Perspectives from Namibian in-service teachers. *Education and Information Technologies, 29*(10), 12569–12596. DOI: 10.1007/s10639-023-12341-z

Kasneci, E., Seßler, K., Küchemann, S., Bannert, M., Dementieva, D., Fischer, F., Gasser, U., Groh, G., Günnemann, S., Hüllermeier, E., Krusche, S., Kutyniok, G., Michaeli, T., Nerdel, C., Pfeffer, J., Poquet, O., Sailer, M., Schmidt, A., Seidel, T., & Kasneci, G. (2023). ChatGPT for good? On opportunities and challenges of large language models for education. *Learning and Individual Differences, 103*, 102274. DOI: 10.1016/j.lindif.2023.102274

Kennedy, H., & Wanless, L. (2022). Artificial intelligence. In *The Routledge Handbook of Digital Sport Management* (1st ed.). Routledge. DOI: 10.4324/9781003088899-29

Khatri, B. B., & Karki, P. D. (2023). Artificial intelligence (AI) in higher education: Growing academic integrity and ethical concerns. *Nepalese Journal of Development and Rural Studies, 20*(01), 1–7. DOI: 10.3126/njdrs.v20i01.64134

Khazanchi, R., Di Mitri, D., & Drachsler, H. (2025). The effect of AI-based systems on mathematics achievement in rural context: A quantitative study. *Journal of Computer Assisted Learning, 41*(1), e13098. DOI: 10.1111/jcal.13098

Khlaif, Z. N., Ayyoub, A., Hamamra, B., Bensalem, E., Mitwally, M. A. A., Ayyoub, A., Hattab, M. K., & Shadid, F. (2024). University teachers' views on the adoption and integration of generative AI tools for student assessment in higher education. *Education Sciences, 14*(10), 1090. DOI: 10.3390/educsci14101090

Kim, Y. R., Park, M. S., & Joung, E. (2025). Exploring the integration of artificial intelligence in math education: Preservice Teachers' experiences and reflections on problem-posing activities with ChatGPT. *School Science and Mathematics*, ssm.18336. Advance online publication. DOI: 10.1111/ssm.18336

Kok, C. L., Ho, C. K., Koh, Y. Y., & Heng, W., J. B., & Teo, T. H. (2024). Psychological aspects of AI enhanced learning experiences. In *Proceedings of TENCON 2024 – 2024 IEEE Region 10 Conference* (pp. 1302–1305). IEEE. DOI: 10.1109/TENCON61640.2024.10902839

Korkmaz Guler, N., Dertli, Z. G., Boran, E., & Yildiz, B. (2024). An artificial intelligence application in mathematics education: Evaluating ChatGPT's academic achievement in a mathematics exam. *Pedagogical Research*, *9*(2), em0188. Advance online publication. DOI: 10.29333/pr/14145

Kosmyna, N., Hauptmann, E., Yuan, Y. T., Situ, J., Liao, X. H., Beresnitzky, A. V., . . . Maes, P. (2025). Your brain on ChatGPT: Accumulation of cognitive debt when using an AI assistant for essay writing task. *arXiv preprint arXiv:2506.08872*. https://doi.org//arXiv.2506.08872DOI: 10.48550

Kuhail, M. A., Alturki, N., Alramlawi, S., & Alhejori, K. (2023). Interacting with educational chatbots: A systematic review. *Education and Information Technologies*, *28*(1), 973–1018. DOI: 10.1007/s10639-022-11177-3

LeCun, Y., Bengio, Y., & Hinton, G. (2015). Deep learning. *Nature*, *521*(7553), 436–444. DOI: 10.1038/nature14539 PMID: 26017442

Lee, D., Son, T., & Yeo, S. (2025). Impacts of interacting with an AI chatbot on preservice teachers' responsive teaching skills in math education. *Journal of Computer Assisted Learning*, *41*(1), e13091. DOI: 10.1111/jcal.13091

Lee, D., & Yeo, S. (2022). Developing an AI-based chatbot for practicing responsive teaching in mathematics. *Computers & Education*, *191*, 104646. DOI: 10.1016/j.compedu.2022.104646

Li, P. H., Lee, H. Y., Cheng, Y. P., Starčič, A. I., & Huang, Y. M. (2023). Solving the self-regulated learning problem: Exploring the performance of ChatGPT in mathematics. In *International Conference on Innovative Technologies and Learning* (pp. 77–86). Springer. DOI: 10.1007/978-3-031-40113-8_8

Liu, H. H. B. (2024). Learning evaluation method based on artificial intelligence technology and its application in education. *Journal of Electrical Systems, 20*(1833), 1842. DOI: 10.52783/jes.1722

Lo, L. S. (2023). The CLEAR path: A framework for enhancing information literacy through prompt engineering. *Journal of Academic Librarianship*, *49*(4), 102720. DOI: 10.1016/j.acalib.2023.102720

Lokman, A. S., & Ameedeen, M. A. (2019). Modern chatbot systems: A technical review. In *Proceedings of the Future Technologies Conference (FTC) 2018: Volume 2* (pp. 1012–1023). Springer. DOI: 10.1007/978-3-030-02683-7_75

Luckin, R., Holmes, W., Griffiths, M., & Forcier, L. B. (2016). *Intelligence unleashed: An argument for AI in education.* Pearson. https://www.pearson.com/content/dam/one-dot-com/one-dot-com/global/Files/about-pearson/innovation/open-ideas/Intelligence-Unleashed-Publication.pdf

Luo, B., Lau, R. Y., Li, C., & Si, Y. W. (2022). A critical review of state-of-the-art chatbot designs and applications. *Wiley Interdisciplinary Reviews. Data Mining and Knowledge Discovery*, *12*(1), e1434. DOI: 10.1002/widm.1434

McDonald, N., Johri, A., Ali, A., & Collier, A. H. (2025). Generative artificial intelligence in higher education: Evidence from an analysis of institutional policies and guidelines. *Computers in Human Behavior: Artificial Humans*, *3*, 100121. DOI: 10.1016/j.chbah.2025.100121

Méndez Alarcón, C. M., Lasekan, O. A., & Godoy Pena, M. T. (2025). AI concerns among educators: A thematic analysis. [IRJMS]. *International Research Journal of Multidisciplinary Scope*, *6*(1), 1031–1045. DOI: 10.47857/irjms.2025.v06i01.01929

Mohd Amin, M. R., Ismail, I., & Sivakumaran, V. M. (2025). Revolutionizing education with artificial intelligence (AI)? Challenges, and implications for open and distance learning (ODL). *Social Sciences & Humanities Open*, *11*, 101308. Advance online publication. DOI: 10.1016/j.ssaho.2025.101308

National Council of Teachers of Mathematics (NCTM). (2023). Artificial Intelligence in mathematics teaching: A position of the National Council of Teachers of Mathematics. https://www.nctm.org/standards-and-positions/Position Statements/Artificial-Intelligence-and-Mathematics-Teaching/

Oates, G. (2011). Sustaining integrated technology in undergraduate mathematics. *International Journal of Mathematical Education in Science and Technology*, *42*(6), 709–721. DOI: 10.1080/0020739X.2011.575238

Park, J., Teo, T. W., Teo, A., Chang, J., Huang, J. S., & Koo, S. (2023). Integrating artificial intelligence into science lessons: Teachers' experiences and views. *International Journal of STEM Education*, *10*(1), 61. Advance online publication. DOI: 10.1186/s40594-023-00454-3

Pavlova, N. H. (2024). Flipped dialogic learning method with ChatGPT: A case study. *International Electronic Journal of Mathematics Education*, *19*(1), em0764. Advance online publication. DOI: 10.29333/iejme/14025

Perla, L., Agrati, L. S., & Beri, A. (2025). Post-teaching and professional learning: An investigation on teachers attitudes towards AI. *Professional Development in Education, 51*(3), 1–12. DOI: 10.1080/19415257.2025.2465970

Rahman, M. M., & Watanobe, Y. (2023). ChatGPT for education and research: Opportunities, threats, and strategies. *Applied Sciences (Basel, Switzerland), 13*(9), 5783. DOI: 10.3390/app13095783

Seebut, S., Wongsason, P., & Kim, D. (2024). Combining GPT and Colab as learning tools for students to explore the numerical solutions of difference equations. *Eurasia Journal of Mathematics, Science and Technology Education, 20*(1), em2377. DOI: 10.29333/ejmste/13905

Slimi, Z. (2023). The impact of artificial intelligence on higher education: An empirical study. *European Journal of Educational Sciences*. DOI: 10.19044/ejes.v10no1a17

Spasić, A. J., & Janković, D. S. (2023, June). Using ChatGPT standard prompt engineering techniques in lesson preparation: Role, instructions and seed-word prompts. In *2023 58th International Scientific Conference on Information, Communication and Energy Systems and Technologies (ICEST)* (pp. 47–50). IEEE.

Su, Y., Lin, Y., & Lai, C. (2023). Collaborating with ChatGPT in argumentative writing classrooms. *Assessing Writing, 57*, 100752. DOI: 10.1016/j.asw.2023.100752

Tlili, A., Shehata, B., Adarkwah, M. A., Bozkurt, A., Hickey, D. T., Huang, R., & Agyemang, B. (2023). What if the devil is my guardian angel: ChatGPT as a case study of using chatbots in education. *Smart Learning Environments, 10*(1), 15. DOI: 10.1186/s40561-023-00237-x

Urrutia, F., & Araya, R. (2024). Who's the best detective? Large language models vs. traditional machine learning in detecting incoherent fourth grade math answers. *Journal of Educational Computing Research, 61*(8), 187–218. DOI: 10.1177/07356331231191174

Vasconcelos, M. A. R., & Santos, R. P. D. (2023). Enhancing STEM learning with ChatGPT and Bing Chat as objects to think with: A case study. *arXiv preprint arXiv:2305.02202*.

Velander, J., Ahmed Taiye, M., Otero, N., Milrad, M., & Zijlema, A. (2023). Reflections on methods for eliciting teachers' understanding, attitudes and emotions about AI. In M. Milrad et al. (Eds.), *Methodologies and intelligent systems for technology enhanced learning. 13th International Conference, MIS4TEL 2023* (Lecture Notes in Networks and Systems, Vol. 764, pp. 124–135). Springer. https://doi.org/DOI: 10.1007/978-3-031-41226-4_13

Velli, K., & Zafiropoulos, K. (2024). Factors that affect the acceptance of educational AI tools by greek teachers—A structural equation modelling study. *European Journal of Investigation in Health, Psychology and Education, 14*(9), 2560–2579. DOI: 10.3390/ejihpe14090169 PMID: 39329837

Viberg, O., Grönlund, Å., & Andersson, A. (2020). Integrating digital technology in mathematics education: A Swedish case study. *Interactive Learning Environments, 31*(1), 232–243. DOI: 10.1080/10494820.2020.1770801

Wachira, P., & Keengwe, J. (2011). Technology integration barriers: Urban school mathematics teachers perspectives. *Journal of Science Education and Technology, 20*(1), 17–25. DOI: 10.1007/s10956-010-9230-y

Wang, M., Wang, M., Xu, X., Yang, L., Cai, D., & Yin, M. (2023). Unleashing ChatGPT's power: A case study on optimizing information retrieval in flipped classrooms via prompt engineering. *IEEE Transactions on Learning Technologies, 17*, 629–644. DOI: 10.1109/TLT.2023.3324714

Wang, N., Wang, X., & Su, Y. S. (2024). Critical analysis of the technological affordances, challenges and future directions of Generative AI in education: A systematic review. *Asia Pacific Journal of Education, 44*(1), 139–155. DOI: 10.1080/02188791.2024.2305156

Wardat, Y., Tashtoush, M. A., AlAli, R., & Jarrah, A. M. (2023). ChatGPT: A revolutionary tool for teaching and learning mathematics. *Eurasia Journal of Mathematics, Science and Technology Education, 19*(7), em2286. Advance online publication. DOI: 10.29333/ejmste/13272

Wei, X. (2024, September). Evaluating chatGPT-4 and chatGPT-4o: performance insights from NAEP mathematics problem solving. In *Frontiers in education* (Vol. 9, p. 1452570). Frontiers Media SA. DOI: 10.3389/feduc.2024.1452570

Yanar, A. N., & Ergene, Ö. (2025). Integrating artificial intelligence in education: How pre-service mathematics teachers use ChatGPT for 5E lesson plan design. *Journal of Pedagogical Research, 9*(2), 158–176. DOI: 10.33902/JPR.202533163

Yıldırım, A., & Şimşek, H. (2021). *Qualitative research methods in social sciences* (12th ed.). Seçkin Publishing. [in Turkish]

Zaharuddin, C. Y., Chen Yu, , & Yao, G. (2024). Enhancing student engagement with AI-driven personalized learning systems. [ITEE]. *International Transactions on Education Technology, 3*(1), 1–8. DOI: 10.33050/itee.v3i1.662

Zhai, X. (2022, December 27). *ChatGPT user experience: Implications for education. SSRN.* https://doi.org/DOI: 10.2139/ssrn.4312418

Zhang, H. (2023). Similarities, differences, and limitations of humans and AI behavior. *Computer Sciences & Mathematics Forum*, *8*(1), 43. DOI: 10.3390/cmsf2023008043

Zhuang, Y. (2025). Lessons from Using ChatGPT in Calculus: Insights from Two Contrasting Cases. *Journal of Formative Design in Learning*, *9*(1), 25–35. DOI: 10.1007/s41686-025-00098-2

Chapter 8
Pedagogical Shifts in the AI Era Toward Cultivating Critical Thinking and Transversal Skills

Sathya Manickam
https://orcid.org/0009-0009-7539-0318
SASTRA University, India

R. Alamelu
https://orcid.org/0000-0003-0539-2480
SASTRA University, India

J. Leema Christina
https://orcid.org/0009-0004-8855-2965
SASTRA University, India

R. Purushothman
https://orcid.org/0009-0003-0941-8462
SASTRA University, India

ABSTRACT

The 21st century education environment necessitates pedagogical changes to develop critical thinking and transversal competencies. Traditional education systems often focus on rote learning, limiting the development of advanced thinking and versatile skills. Artificial Intelligence can be used to promote critical thinking and a broader range of transversal skills, like creativity, collaboration, problem solving, digital literacy, and adaptability. AI tools like intelligent tutoring systems, adaptive learning platforms, and immersive simulations can provide diversified instruction, real time

DOI: 10.4018/979-8-3373-7729-2.ch008

feedback, and procedural learning through experience. Ethically and strategically applied, these tools can lead to the growth of transversal skills needed for lifelong learning. However, ethical issues, algorithm bias, and professional growth for educators are also discussed. The chapter recommends that AI should support human teaching and curriculum, ensuring that education not only provides knowledge but also equips students with the skills needed to adapt to the modern era.

1. INTRODUCTION

In the dynamically changing environment of the 21st-century education, teaching students to develop critical thinking and transversal competencies has become a teaching necessity. As international needs are becoming knowledge-based economies, the capacity of learners to examine, interpret, and combine data with meaning is crucial to personal, educational, and professional achievement. Specifically, critical thinking is considered one of the most important transversal skills because it empowers learners to address complicated problems, provide knowledge synthesis, and make evidence-based decisions (Saleh, 2019; Rönnlund et al., 2019). Such skills are not optional anymore; they are now necessary skills that students need to function effectively in real-world environments involving problem solving, flexibility, teamwork, and innovativeness.

The traditional education system, however, still focuses on rote learning and passive access to information. Such concentration suppresses higher-order thinking skills, including reasoning, evaluation and metacognition. The principles of Higher Order Thinking Skills (HOTS) that enable more profound knowledge and learning in life have not been fully developed and applied in most teaching activities. The structural constraints of global education systems include training too many students per teacher and using assessment based on rote learning. According to UNESCO (2023), the pupil-teacher ratio in low-income countries averages more than 30:1, and does not allow personal attention and teaching focused on critical thinking. At the same time, the data provided by OECD (2018) identify that a small percentage of students can complete tasks involving higher-order thinking, demonstrating the inefficiency of conventional assessment practices in measuring a range of cognitive abilities. These structural obstacles produce conditions under which students can leave school with factual expertise but not the analytical and reflective abilities to allow academic or professional involvement (Saleh, 2019).

In addition, the subjectivity of critical thinking creates serious challenges for instructors regarding teaching and evaluation. Since metacognition also contributes to the growth of critical thinking, students will be asked to think and reflect on the thinking processes (Saleh, 2019). This dual demand needs pedagogical practices that are reflective, student-centred and supported with continuous feedback. However, in the current teacher shortages, high student classes, and little personalised attention, many educational systems are not becoming effective in addressing those needs.

This chapter considers the possibilities of Artificial Intelligence (AI) to overcome such pedagogical issues. AI has introduced practical tools to transform traditional classrooms into more interactive, student-centred learning environments. Because of real-time analytics, adaptive learning, and personalised feedback systems, AI can be used to address the drawbacks of traditional teaching. Innovative tutor systems, learning analytics tools and immersive simulation systems are the AI tools that can drive the engagement of the students and facilitate their progress to higher levels of inquiry and critical evaluation (Buskist & Irons, 2008; Lai, 2011). The tools provide differentiated instruction and support the needs of diverse learners, which can ensure that students' progress at their own pace and develop critical cognitive and metacognitive knowledge.

Moreover, AI creates experiential learning conditions, involving students' active exploration, questions and problem-solving abilities. Within the said contexts, learning is less internalisation than the discovery process. AI has the potential to analyse massive data that students produce to detect patterns and misconceptions in learning, and educators can then provide interventions with purpose (Saleh, 2019). Such a high degree of individualisation plays a central role in building strong critical thinking abilities because it guarantees that tuition is arranged in a highly time-sensitive manner, as well as highly personal, in terms of individual learning paths.

However, the question of AI in education is not unconcerned with ethics and pedagogy. The question of data privacy, the bias of the algorithms, and the danger of using automated feedback mechanisms too aggressively have to be carefully approached. Although AI can be helpful in education, it should not replace the critical insight, personal sensitivity, and situation sensitivity that educators provide during instruction. There is also the risk that poorly designed AI systems may inadvertently stifle creativity and discourage non-linear thinking, essential components of transversal competencies.

The fact is that educators should be adequately trained not only in terms of technical utilisation of AI tools but also pedagogical application of such tools. The professional development program should empower educators to learn how to analyse the information created by AI, apply it in instructional design, and balance an instructional approach (Sanabria-Z et al., 2023). AI can further permit educators, in particular, to concentrate on stimulating critical inquiry and interaction with students once routine administrative work is processed by AI (Lai, 2011).

Aligning AI with curriculum design and assessment frameworks is also considered a way of effectively utilising technology to develop critical thinking. AI tools should not determine learning outcomes and instructional aims but rather support them. For example, the learning environment in an intelligent tutoring system may contain increasingly complex problems to solve that imply the usage of an analytical approach and decision-making. Meanwhile, this information through AI solutions allows teachers to adjust their teaching methodologies, making the educational environment more responsive to individual needs.

Finally, the vision is to use AI to develop a wide range of transversal skills that would enable lifelong learners to become active citizens. These involve critical thinking, method solving, inventiveness, information and communications technology literacy, and flexibility. An ethical incorporation and steady approach to AI can make education meaningful and empowering under constant global change.

The presented challenges, including crowded classrooms, the absence of individualised instruction, and the use of rote-based examinations, demonstrate the inefficiency of the traditional pedagogical practices in developing critical thinking and transversal abilities. Those systemic barriers require systemic and innovative solutions that are scalable and more than typical reform. Respondently, this chapter examines the possible implementation of artificial intelligence (AI) with a rational approach to improving educational settings through authoritative support of varied instruction, emphasis on student-oriented learning, and the ability to provide data-based teaching approaches. These possibilities are explored with the following objectives.

Objectives of the Chapter:

1. To analyse the limitations of traditional pedagogical approaches in developing students' critical thinking and transversal skills.
2. To examine the potential of AI-driven educational tools in enhancing learner engagement, metacognitive development, and differentiated instruction.
3. To propose ethical and pedagogical considerations for integrating AI into curriculum design and teaching practices to cultivate critical and transversal competencies.

2. BACKGROUND

2.1. Theoretical Framework

The **OECD learning compass 2030** is a comprehensive student learning framework beyond what people consider as academic success, such as social, emotional, and metacognitive aspects. It focuses on the agency of students and their ability to respond effectively to dynamic and multifaceted real-world challenges with the help of a set of core competencies including cognitive, interpersonal, and intrapersonal, that is, includes instrumentality, responsibility, and collaborative problem-solving. The model affirms that the capacity of learners to reflect, to act ethically, and to co-design sustainable futures is important and this borders heavily on the transversal learning outcomes (OECD, 2019).

The **partnership for 21st-century skills**, which designed the P21 framework of 21st-century learning, considers 4cs (critical thinking, communication, collaboration, and creativity) to be the predominant skills necessary in a knowledge-based economy. As transversal skills of the baseline, these competencies should be developed carefully, and that can be done by integration into the curriculum, project-based learning, and technology-enhanced environment (Battelle for kids, 2019). This model helps in promoting instructional innovation to achieve lifelong learning and readiness for the world.

To supplement such areas of cognition and cooperation, the **social and emotional learning (SEL)** framework of CASEL emphasises the relevance of emotional intelligence as a transversal skill to acquire the competencies of self-awareness, relationship skills, and responsible choices. SEL aims to enhance not only academic success but also the wellbeing of students and their ethical participation, which are the key parameters in ai-facilitated human-oriented learning environments (Home - Casel Schoolguide, 2025).

Bloom's Taxonomy of Cognitive Domains, formulated by Benjamin Bloom, classifies cognitive abilities into six tiers: RUAEC Bloom's Revised Taxonomy (Remember, Understand, Apply, Analyse, Evaluate, Create), fostering the critical and inferential thinking skills essential for contemporary learning and professional environments.

The Paul-Elder **critical thinking framework** improves critical thinking by emphasising three pillars: categories of thought, traits of thought, and critical thinking skills, orientation, and dispositions that ensure accuracy, complexity, and inclusiveness.

Piaget's and Perry's **cognitive developmental theory** illustrates the progression of critical thinking from concrete to formal stages and from dualistic to relativistic perspectives.

Metacognition and reflective thinking theories pertain to the regulation of reasoning during critical thinking, wherein an individual engages in self-examination, modification, and judicious actions. Dewey's Reflective Thinking model advocates for reflective belief assessment through reflexive reflection-in-action and reflection-on-action inquiry.

Complexity theories and systems thinking develop critical thinking skills in that they introduce a holistic perspective through which learners can learn how the individual elements of a system relate to each other. The most common components of systems thinking, finding interrelationships, spotting patterns, feedback loops, non-linear causality, are all closely linked to skills of critical thinking, i.e analysis (dividing up a complex into its parts), evaluation (analysing how each part functions and what its effects are) and inference (concluding about the consequences of those interactions). This strategy improves learners' problem-solving, strategic thinking, and critical thinking skills in a dynamic and uncertain world.

Figure 1. Theoretical and Framework Integration

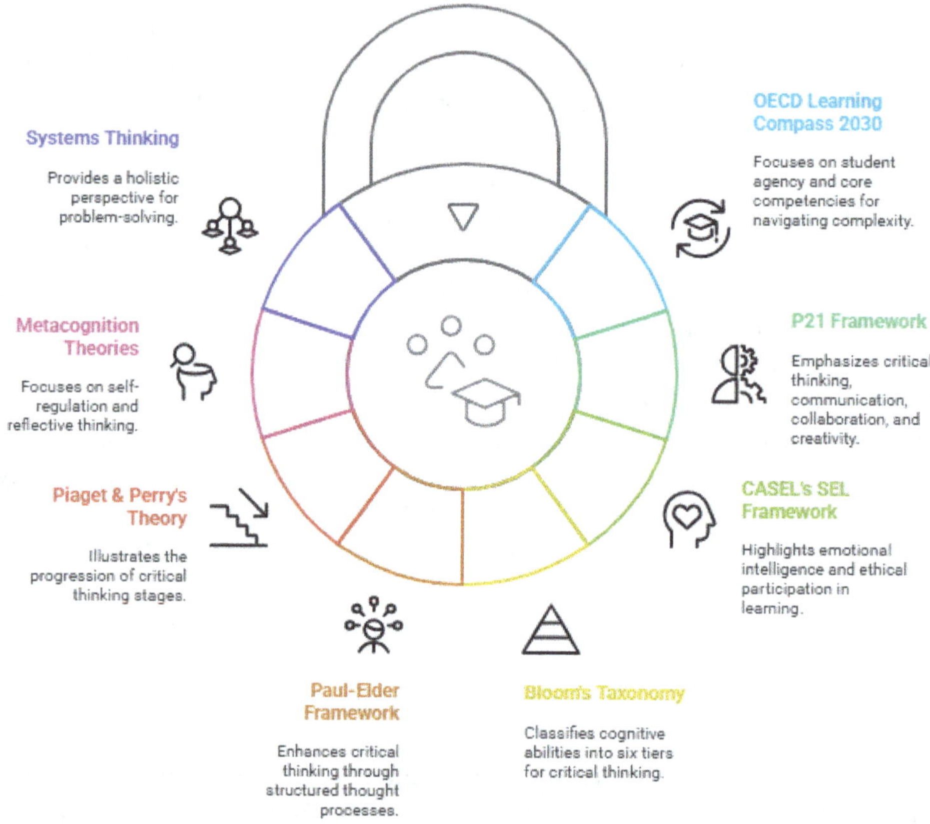

Source: Author(s)

Fig. 1 presents a synthesised model of key cognitive, reflective, and global educational frameworks that collectively support the development of critical thinking and transversal skills. It integrates theories such as Bloom's Taxonomy, Piaget & Perry's developmental stages, and the Paul-Elder framework, alongside modern frameworks like the OECD learning compass 2030, P21, and CASEL SEL, to emphasise cognitive, emotional, and collaborative competencies essential for 21st-century learning.

This chapter has offered theoretical frameworks that enable students to develop critical thinking skills, including Bloom's Taxonomy, the metacognitive theory, systems thinking and the OECD Learning Compass, which are necessary as an essential source of knowledge. However, the connection with the current trends in the context of AI-based pedagogy makes them especially powerful. For example, the adaptive learning systems based on AI adhere to the hierarchical model introduced by Bloom and gradually raise the level of cognitive stimulation of assignments. Likewise, intelligent feedback systems, intelligent tutoring processes, and computer-based pedagogical aids are all forms of metacognitive support equipment considering the theory of self-regulation and reflection that form the basis of metacognition. Systems thinking is comparable to creating AI learning environments, which track feedback pathways and enable adaptable learner accounts. Resting their application of AI on such theories helps educators and developers ensure that using technological tools leads to deep and meaningful learning instead of keeping students superficially interested in the given tasks. Such a combination enhances the pedagogical validity of using AI and contextualises it as part and parcel of broader learning objectives. Table (1) provides a comparative overview of how these frameworks contribute to critical thinking and how their principles align with AI-enhanced educational practices.

Table 1. Integration of Learning Frameworks in AI-Based Pedagogy Source: Author(s)

Framework	Core Educational Focus	Relevance to Critical Thinking and Transversal Skills	Pedagogical Applications in AI Context
OECD Learning Compass 2030	Student agency, global competencies, lifelong learning	Encourages ethical decision-making and future-oriented thinking	Guides AI tools to promote learner autonomy and adaptability
P21 Framework	4Cs: Critical thinking, communication, collaboration, creativity	Frames critical thinking as part of holistic transversal skills	AI supports collaborative tools, simulations, and feedback
CASEL SEL Framework	Emotional intelligence, wellbeing, social skills	Supports ethical reasoning and interpersonal judgment	AI can enhance SEL through emotion-aware learning platforms
Bloom's Taxonomy	Six cognitive domains from remembering to creating	Structures higher-order thinking processes	Adaptive AI can align task complexity to the cognitive level
Paul-Elder Framework	Elements of thought, intellectual standards, and traits	Deepens structured reasoning and reflective thinking	AI systems can model and prompt critical questioning

continued on following page

Table 1. Continued

Framework	Core Educational Focus	Relevance to Critical Thinking and Transversal Skills	Pedagogical Applications in AI Context
Piaget & Perry's Theories	Cognitive development and epistemological positions	Outlines developmental stages of reasoning	AI can scaffold learning based on the learner's developmental stage
Metacognition Theories	Self-regulation, awareness of thinking processes	Enables learners to reflect and adjust their thinking	AI facilitates reflective feedback, goal setting, and self-assessment

2.2. Review of Literature

2.2.1. Critical Thinking Skills

Critical thinking is an essential competency for academic and professional achievement, encompassing the analysis of arguments, assessment of evidence, and resolution of problems (Lai, E. R., 2011; Onions, P. E. W., 2009). It includes cognitive abilities and traits like open-mindedness, curiosity, and adaptability (Lai, E. R., 2011). Although critical thinking originates from multiple fields, such as philosophy and psychology, it is teachable and assessable (Haber, J., 2020). Effective instructional methods encompass actively involving students in project-based activities, emphasising the learning process, and employing rigorous assessment techniques (Snyder, L.G., & Snyder, M., 2008). Nonetheless, obstacles such as insufficient training and time limitations can hinder the instruction of critical thinking (Snyder, L.G., & Snyder, M., 2008). To augment critical thinking abilities, educators ought to deliver explicit instruction, facilitate transfer to novel contexts, and employ collaborative learning methodologies (Lai, E. R., 2011). Ultimately, critical thinking helps move through the complexities of the modern world and maintain a democratic society (The MIT Press, Massachusetts Institute of Technology, 2025). Such essential characteristics of critical thinking as open-mindedness and adaptability translate into the wider transversal skills functional in collaboration, innovation, and lifelong learning across various studies.

2.2.2. Critical Thinking In Education

In education, cognitive abilities are highly valued, and the ability to evaluate reasons, argue on facts and distinguish justifiable and faulty arguments are moulded by reasoning abilities (Fahim & Ghamari, 2011). Physical education is a critical means of developing active citizenship, sustainable development, and individual advancement

(Uribe-Enciso et al., 2017). The educational goal is critical thinking; in this case, the teachers use particular teaching strategies (Fahim & Ghamari, 2011). However, the critique of existing research indicates that not every student is outstanding at critical thinking, and some teachers might not develop the necessary skills in that area (Pithers & Soden, 2000). Teachers are advised to adopt practices promoting critical thinking skills, including Content and Language Integrated Learning (CLIL) in language courses (Uribe-Enciso et al., 2017). To become an educated, complete person who can comprehend complicated matters and come up with a solution, it is necessary to develop critical thinking skills. Furthermore, transversal skills such as communication and collaboration are often cultivated alongside critical thinking when active learning strategies like project-based learning and CLIL are employed. Annual practice and enhancement of these skills are necessary to cultivate them into genuine competencies (Benavides Caruajulca, 2021).

2.2.3. Critical Thinking Vs. Traditional Education

Critical thinking is a crucial skill presumed to be utilised in the teaching-learning process; however, its integration presents distinct challenges. Traditional teaching methods are often criticised for their inability to cultivate critical thinking due to resource deficiencies and the emergence of new demands that burden educators (Ironside, 2000). Cultural barriers are apparent, as exemplified in Singapore, where the socially and culturally anticipated role of teachers as purveyors of knowledge, coupled with the association of critical thinking with adversarial practices, impeded adoption (Tan, 2017). Educators are discovering new approaches to surmount these challenges. Computer-based instruments and micro-level technological requirements can be employed to enhance critical thinking skills as a supplement to traditional classroom learning, as identified (Mandernach, 2006). Proposed methods for addressing cultural differences include cooperative learning strategies that involve grouping students into collaborative teams and fostering a secure learning environment (Tan, 2017). In Nepal, various cognitive skills have been advocated to address the challenges of English Language Teaching (ELT) by fostering relaxed, meaningful engagement through active participation and democratic education (Kandel, 2015). These innovative approaches enhance critical thinking and foster transversal skills such as teamwork, adaptability, and problem-solving through learner-centred and context-sensitive pedagogies. These methods aim to transform conventional teaching practices while also introducing novel techniques.

2.2.4. Artificial Intelligence (AI) And Critical Thinking

AI is increasingly influential in education, particularly in enhancing critical thinking. Beyond cognitive development, AI tools are increasingly used to nurture transversal competencies like self-direction, creativity, and digital literacy, which are interdependent with critical thinking processes. Intelligent tutor systems based on artificial intelligence can enhance self-reflection, responding to integrated questions, and decision-making skills (Malik et al., 2018). All these systems provide comprehensive learning solutions with customised approaches to accommodate various learning needs (Yoshija Walter, 2024). However, the challenges of employing AI in education include a deficiency of sufficiently trained educators and the necessity to adapt the curriculum to facilitate the integration of AI. Students assert that AI positively contributes to various aspects of critical thinking, such as research and theory evaluation; however, they express concerns regarding AI's limited ability for personalisation and nuanced understanding (Darwin et al., 2023). Regarding the augmented generation of content, cognition-enhancing applications for artificial intelligence assist in organising substantial material and aid in developing students' critical thinking skills (Kouzov, 2019). Thus, a balanced use of AI can enhance critical reasoning and broader 21st-century skills essential for collaborative and adaptive learning. Moderation means that students should learn to utilise the benefits of AI and consider the limitations, which is a critical element in developing strong critical thinking skills (Darwin et al., 2023).

An emerging global literature emphasises that AI has the transformative potential in the educational sphere and has shown the potential to lead to better tool results, stimulate critical thinking, and personalise education in various teaching settings. European, East Asian, and North American studies indicate the potential of AI tools, such as intelligent tutoring systems and adaptive learning environments, to boost critical thinking, metacognitive regulation and student engagement. For example, formative assessment and real-time feedback reportedly proved positive outcomes in the ViLLE platform in Finland (ViLLE, n.d.). An inquiry-based Science learning is also supported considerably using AI chatbots in Korean middle school examinations (Davar et al., 2025). AI-supported self-regulated learning received attention in Germany, where researchers focused on its positive impact on reflective practices among students (Holmes et al., 2019). Likewise, in Singapore and Taiwan, AI platforms enhanced students' writing according to reasoning and arguments (Akram et al., 2025). The paper by Zawacki-Richter et al. (2019) also confirms through a worldwide systematic review that educational advantages of AI are not restricted to any given region but are being realised and demonstrated in diverse socio-cultural backgrounds. The international results raise awareness of possible applications of

AI in teaching worldwide and emphasise the necessity of culturally responsible and ethically sound implementation approaches.

2.2.5. AI Tools For Critical Thinking

Educational use of AI tools opens new opportunities and challenges to promoting critical thinking skills. Through AI, students can obtain and use the necessary information in their critical thinking (Kouzov, 2019). The tools like Intelligent Tutoring Systems, data analytics for personalised learning, AR/VR, and adaptive learning platforms are also instrumental in promoting transversal skills like content generation, creativity, collaboration through peer feedback design, and adaptability through customisation of learning in real-time. Although AI tools for content generation can save time and effort, students must comprehend the associated risks and limitations, highlighting the importance of critical thinking skills (Zou et al., 2023). Integrating the 7E learning cycle model with pedagogy and AI applications in the instructional process enhances the critical thinking skills of Generation Z students, particularly when AI is utilised for verifying or validating learning outcomes in the final phase (Baskoro et al., 2023). Nevertheless, technological advancements necessitate implementing novel strategies to cultivate critical thinking within the educational framework, thereby empowering students to analyse information provided by AI (Moustaghfir & Brigui, 2024). The influence of AI on cognitive abilities raises ethical concerns, particularly regarding the interplay between critical thinking and technology within educational frameworks (Moustaghfir & Brigui, 2024).

2.2.6. Challenges In Implementation

Artificial intelligence in education can enhance personalised learning, instructional methods, student engagement, and other aspects (Grace et al., 2023; Chima Abimbola et al., 2024). In the future, AI is expected to increase critical thinking among the students and broaden the educational opportunities to learners with diverse learning disabilities, which will help the latter to undergo the learning process with much ease (Yoshija Walter, 2024; Chima Abimbola et al., 2024). Some challenges also impact the broader growth of the transversal competencies because all learners should have equitable access to the tools of AI that ensure problem-solving, innovations, and teamwork. However, ethical concerns, data privacy rights, and possible biases are among the obstacles to using AI in educational establishments (Grace et al., 2023; Mohammed Rizvi, 2023).

These efforts should consider access difficulties, issues of the digital divide, and the need for responsible evolution as referenced by attaining integration (Chima Abimbola et al., 2024). Trucano (2005) highlights that in many low-income regions, insufficient infrastructure and limited digital readiness impede the effective integration of advanced educational technologies like AI. Teachers may resist AI adoption due to lack professional development, fear of de-skilling, or cultural scepticism toward automation in pedagogical decision-making (Zawacki-Richter et al., 2019). Guan et al., 2024 further observe that many educators feel underprepared to integrate AI meaningfully into their instruction, citing a global lack of training resources and institutional support. Cultural factors, including differing educational values and expectations, also shape how AI tools are perceived and implemented across regions (Luckin et al., 2016).

Moreover, AI presents new possibilities for dynamic and formative assessment redesign, yet raises questions about validity, transparency, and student agency in automated grading systems (Popenici & Kerr, 2017). So that these tools can be appropriately used, educators should be sufficiently competent in AI and gain competencies in timely engineering (Yoshija Walter, 2024). Although the transformative potential of AI in educational technology is notable, it is crucial to anticipate the ethical challenges that may arise from its implementation and to develop well-thought-out strategies to address them. However, as Jobin et al. (2019) argue, existing AI ethics guidelines are fragmented and inconsistent across regions, complicating efforts to implement these technologies equitably in diverse educational settings (Mohammed Rizvi, 2023; Chima Abimbola et al., 2024). Overcoming these shortcomings, educational establishments will have a chance to create an AI-empowered environment where critical thinking will not be the only attribute enhanced by such an approach, but rather the whole set of transversal skills to better prepare individuals to face the modern world.

While AI presents significant opportunities to enhance critical thinking, its implementation must be approached with caution and critical awareness. Algorithmic bias remains a pressing concern, as AI systems trained on non-inclusive or culturally limited datasets may unintentionally reinforce stereotypes or exclude marginalised learner groups (Moustaghfir & Brigui, 2024). Moreover, scholars such as Binns (2018) stress that educational AI systems often reflect data biases, resulting in hidden discrimination in feedback systems. It is imperative to embed fairness-aware algorithms and include diverse datasets to avoid perpetuating social inequities. Similarly, equity of access is a significant challenge—students from rural areas or low-resource contexts often lack consistent internet access, digital tools, or localised content, limiting their ability to benefit from AI-based learning (UNESCO, 2023).

In addition, over-reliance on AI-generated feedback can impede the development of independent judgment and reflective thinking, as students may begin to accept automated responses uncritically (Darwin et al., 2023). AI tools must be used as supplements, not substitutes, for teacher-led instruction, human feedback, and culturally contextualised learning to mitigate these risks. A balanced and inclusive approach—rooted in critical pedagogy and human-centred design—ensures that AI supports, rather than undermines, equitable and meaningful critical thinking development.

2.2.7. Transversal Skills In The AI-Powered Learning Environment

Recent studies describe the key role of Artificial Intelligence (AI) in developing transversal skills in higher education. Using AI-assisted tools, students interact and share more effectively, become more critical-minded and perform more creatively (Sajid Hasan et al., 2025; Ismail Çelik et al., 2024). It is fundamentally important to accomplish academic and professional success in the 21st-century (Kumar, 2023). The use of AI in the educational process provides a customised experience and feedback, which in turn is associated with the development of multiple skills simultaneously (Ismail Çelik et al., 2024). Nevertheless, it is essential to balance technological progress and human-focused education (Chan, 2024). AI can influence creativity levels, which are not definite, although it significantly enhances collaboration, communication, and critical thinking (Sajid Hasan et al., 2025). Responsible AI use should maximise good, combining AI literacy and traditional values, allowing the institution to receive optimal benefits (Chan, 2024). In this way, students will be adequately prepared to operate in the modern technologically changing environment and acquire the most valuable human skills (Kumar, 2023).

2.3 Conceptual Model: AI-Supported Transversal Skill Development

Figure 2. Conceptual Model Source: Author(s)

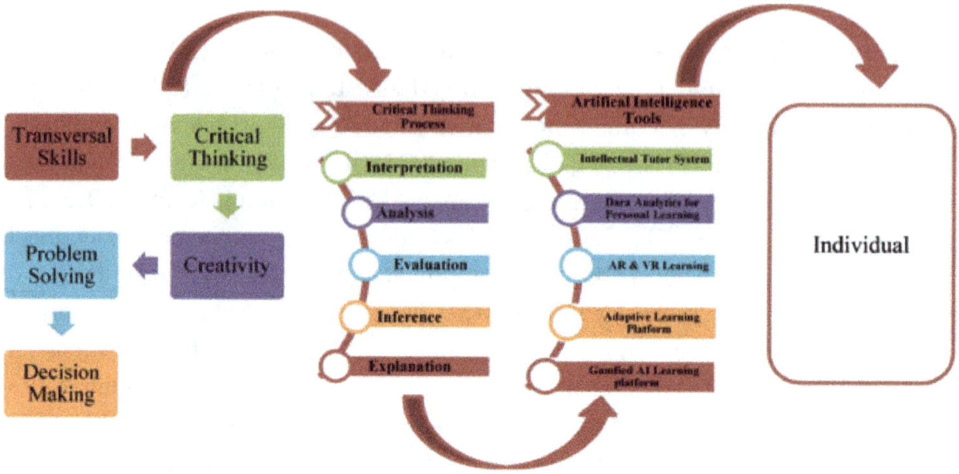

The conceptual model presented in Fig. 2 is a graphical illustration of the functionality of artificial intelligence tools and their interactions with the critical thinking process to foster the emergence of transversal skills among learners. The distinguishing feature of the model is in the acknowledgement that transversal competencies, which include creativity, adaptability, decision-making, and problem-solving, can be developed through intentional involvement with higher-level thinking and AI-assisted learning. The model places the learning result of Transversal Skills in the middle of the model, with structured critical thinking processes on one hand and AI-based instructional platforms on the other. Such synergy results in meaningful and individualised learning experiences that eventually produce individuals prepared to learn a lifetime and adapt to a global environment. The transition from theoretical models to practical implementations can be clarified by connecting key model nodes (e.g., metacognition, reflection) to real AI use cases in the classroom, facilitating a clearer narrative thread.

3. FROM CRITICAL THINKING TO TRANSVERSAL COMPETENCE: PROCESSES AND APPLICATIONS

3.1. Critical Thinking Process

It is essential to integrate critical thinking into our educational systems to enable students to analyse information critically. This is a concise overview of the critical thinking process and its elements within the educational framework:

Interpretation is the ability to clarify or explain the meaning of information, experience or data. Learners judge personal understanding of texts, lectures or experiments. They learn to ask the question. Interpretation is the pillar of more efficient comprehension in different fields.

Analysis involves subdividing materials or content in order to analyse it, separating an argument, or a chain of thoughts and ascertaining possible links to other materials or content. In complex topics, analysis will help the students to break down issues into simpler terms. They interpret such subjects and resources in literature or history to understand the principles or motives behind it. Analysis creates a better and all-inclusive idea of the material.

Evaluation refers to the evaluation of information, argument or evidence according to credibility or relevancy. In the course of evaluation, students can evaluate sources successfully, decide the reliability of a particular material and compare different opinions.

Inference is a deduction made on information available or a process of establishing a systematic solution to a problem or reasoning. When students make inferences, they develop hypotheses, make reading predictions of the outcomes or come up with new learning things by using the information that is already established to make logical conclusions. It is the ability to apply learning to solving problems within unfamiliar situations of their practical lives.

An **explanation** is the principal method of articulating thought processes and offering justification for the conclusions reached. Students obtain it through a PowerPoint presentation, written assignments such as essays, and verbal communication, where they must elucidate their thought processes and the rationale behind their conclusions. Elaboration improves learning by enabling students to articulate their thoughts and organise them into more coherent structures.

The application of the aforementioned critical thinking skills in education enhances academic success and equips learners to make sound decisions in their daily lives.

3.2. Application Of Critical Thinking Through Transversal Competencies

Utilising critical thinking skills in the classroom will improve an individual's workplace performance in problem-solving, decision-making, creativity, and adaptability. All of these skills are essential for addressing issues and fostering development in both academic environments and professional settings. Here is a summary of each application.

Creativity is defined as the ability to generate novel ideas or, typically, a resolution to complex or unfamiliar situations. In professional contexts, creativity is advantageous in various domains that require innovation, such as public relations, advertising, graphic design, and product development. Adversarial thinking aims to fulfill customer needs innovatively, introduce new products or services, and distinguish professional work from competitors. Creativity fosters growth and can initiate differentiation within an industry.

Problem solving encompasses the ability to identify issues and subsequently determine appropriate solutions through logical application. Problem solving in the workplace involves addressing organisational issues, project challenges, or customer complaints. This skill enables professionals to conduct a critical analysis of any environment and identify potential issues that may arise in the future, facilitating the determination of optimal practical solutions. Problem-solving enhances work efficiency and improves the quality of output.

The **decision-making** process entails evaluating multiple options and selecting the most appropriate one. In every professional setting, individuals make decisions that influence projects, teams, or organisational outcomes. In devising or executing a strategy, distribution or employment of resources, choice of strategies or actions, critical thinking enables the formulation of rational decisions. Making informed decisions enhances performance and mitigates potential repercussions in practice.

3.3. Integration Of Transversal Skills In Educational And Professional Contexts

Most efficient in transversal skills development (such as communicative, collaborative, digital, creative, emotional intelligence, and adaptive skills) are when combined with the critical thinking processes in the context of an AI-enhanced learning environment. These competencies can help students operate in a complex environment and resolve problems and operate in different academic/professional settings. Students are enabled to build upon their communication skills and collaborative work with a well-organised dialogue, peer interaction and project-based learning, and develop their digital literacy and creativity through working with adaptive platforms, creation tool set, and problem-based simulations. Self-awareness and empathy as the components of emotional intelligence facilitate ethical judgment and rational decision-making. Artificial intelligence enhances these effects because it provides individual feedback, current information, and an immersive experience. These skills can be combined so that they fulfill a comprehensive model to make the learners active, innovative and responsible individuals characterised by the capabilities of meeting the challenges of the 21st -century.

4. ARTIFICIAL INTELLIGENCE TOOLS FOR ENHANCING CRITICAL THINKING AND TRANSVERSAL SKILLS

Integrating essential AI applications aids students in exercising critical thinking about their attitudes, interests, and the content's complexity. These are the highlights of how specific AI technologies, namely the Intelligent Tutoring Systems (ITS), Data Analytics, AR/VR, Adaptive Learning platforms, and Generative AI learning platforms, contribute to the development of critical thinking abilities in the fields of education.

4.1. Intelligent Tutoring System (ITS)

An intelligent tutoring system is the it system of training, which is designed to simulate human tutoring through advice, suggestions, and encouragement in the necessary form and guided by the needs of students. The learner uses critical thinking to assess and solve problems using practical thinking. To illustrate, it can ask a set of sequential questions that progress to another level depending on how well the learner responds with various concepts and efficiency on problem-solving techniques. The system provides a direct feedback to the learners and, in a way, students will be able to correct their line of thinking and also develop self-assurance in their ability to think abstractly.

4.2. Data Analytics For Personalised Learning

Data analytics in education refers to the process of systematically collecting data from students throughout the learning process to serve the purpose of evaluating both educational experience and improving it. Data analysis gives teachers a chance to address specific student learning problems, which promotes autonomous thinking as the areas of learning weaknesses are addressed, yet making better use of already possessed strengths. In case data analysis shows that a certain student has difficulties solving the inference questions, which can be located in the reading subtest, one can recommend practicing more of this sort. Analysis of educational data is expected to provide educators with the relevant data which can help students get important assistance in thinking, processing information, and logically integrating thoughts.

4.3. Augmented Reality (AR) And Virtual Reality (VR)

Augmented Reality (AR) and Virtual Reality (VR) Learning involve the use of models, educational simulations and environments through which students can interact with the use of objects that are not easy to explain in a regular classroom. Augmented Reality (AR) and Virtual Reality (VR) can foster critical thinking by enabling students to engage in immersive, scenario-based learning, analysing problems, testing hypotheses, and making real-time decisions in safe, simulated environments. These technologies promote higher-order cognitive processes such as analytical reasoning, spatial thinking, and evaluative judgment, as learners interact with complex content rather than passively consume information. For instance, Baskoro et al. (2023) found that integrating AI and AR-based tools using the 7E instructional model enhanced critical thinking among Generation Z students by stimulating inquiry, prediction, and reflection. Similarly, Walter (2024) reported that VR-enabled science simulations improved students' ability to formulate and test hypotheses, supporting evidence-based reasoning and iterative learning. In social studies, as an example, students can learn about the essence of history to understand context, functions, and perspectives. In scientific studies, augmented reality simulations could provide scenarios where students can perform hypothesis-based experiments and process the results, thus helping facilitate experiential learning and inquiry. Such integrated exhibitions actively encourage criticism, analysis and self-reflection during the learning process.

4.4. Adaptive Learning Platform

In adaptive learning platforms, AI modifies the difficulty level, delivery methods, and duration based on the student's classroom behaviour. Initially, these platforms facilitate the cultivation of essential skills by offering problems that are adequately challenging, yet attainable for students. As students' progress, the system escalates the complexity of the problems presented; students are anticipated to analyse information, infer data, and synthesise facts mentally using adaptive platforms. They articulate their reasoning and conduct step-by-step analyses, thereby enhancing their reasoning capabilities.

4.5. Generative Learning Platform

Generative AI environments allow students to produce original works, including essays, computer code, or art, and utilise AI for peer-reviewing the structure, creativity, and reasoning processes involved. The utilisation of AI, specifically generative platforms, facilitates students in contemplating idea generation, intricacy, and stylistic choices. In a language arts class, students can create drafts for a specific course and receive guidance on enhancing their arguments, coherence, and structure within that course. While generative AI and peer-review tools can promote objectivity by offering consistent, criterion-based feedback, they also risk reinforcing biases. To ensure meaningful outcomes, students must be taught to critically evaluate both AI and peer inputs, promoting fairness, reflection, and diverse perspectives (Zou et al., 2023; Darwin et al., 2023).

Figure 3. AI tools for Critical Thinking and Transversal Skills Source: Author(s)

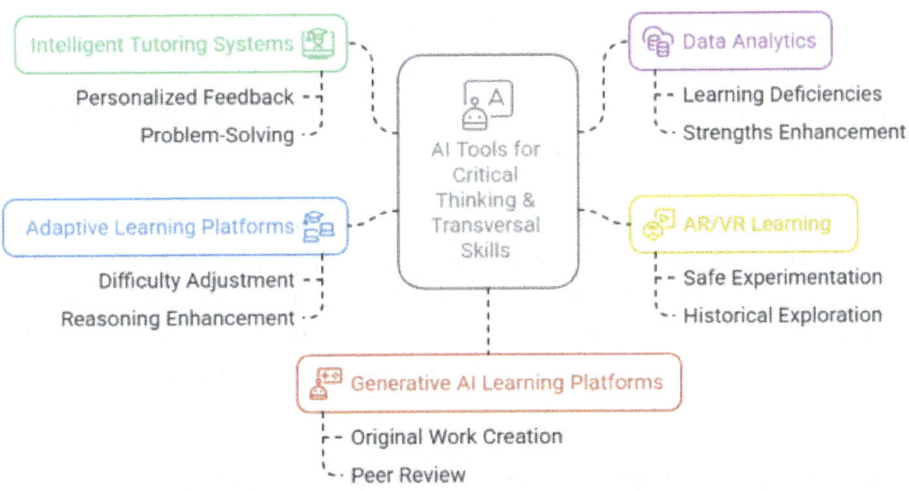

Figure (3) highlights key AI tools used to develop critical thinking and transversal skills in education. It categorises five main platforms—Intelligent Tutoring Systems, Adaptive Learning, Data Analytics, AR/VR, and Generative AI—based on their specific contributions to personalised learning, reasoning, and creative output.

5. BENEFITS OF USING AI IN DEVELOPING STUDENTS' CRITICAL THINKING PROCESS

Artificial intelligence in educational settings is transforming how students learn and interact with course material, particularly in the context of problem-solving. Concerning individual learning requirements, particularly in analysing extensive data sets and realistic modelling, AI is increasingly being utilised to support the development of critical thinking skills, particularly by facilitating personalised learning, immediate feedback, and engagement with complex problem-solving tasks. While promising, its impact is context-dependent and requires careful pedagogical design. The subsequent benefits can be attained by employing AI to design students' critical thinking processes. Although AI's advantages in improving reasoning and self-regulated learning are widely understood, some studies warn that one should not expect uniform effectiveness. For example, Holmes et al. (2021) explain that AI tools can further deepen the disparities or even fixate on the superficial learning process in the absence of deliberate pedagogy.

5.1. Personalisation Learning Models

AI educational tools facilitate the identification of key figures, deficiencies, and learning styles, enabling the customisation of learning experiences for each student. The utilisation of AI personalises information delivery and problem-solving, thereby compelling students to engage more deeply with the content. It is essential for critical thinking that students learn to analyse their thought processes; thus, this personalisation is beneficial in aiding students. As an example, when a student faces difficulties in solving complicated tasks, AI can distribute assignments to work on them step-by-step and provide the chance to work on them with different perspectives (Saleh, 2019).

5.2. Technology Integrated Activities, More Specifically Interactive Problem-Solving And Simulations

AI allows various exercises to be implemented imitating real-life conditions, where the students have to make choices and analyse their consequences with zero consequences in an artificial environment. An AI science laboratory (Malik et al., 2018) placed in the educational system will help student's complete experiments without severe consequences in a realistic environment that helps to see the practical outcome of various actions, thus encouraging the formation of critical thinking. Such situations demand that students apply their minds and develop the hypotheses, which are the elements of critical thinking.

5.3. There Is Always An Option For The Instructor To Provide Feedback Soon After The Interactive Learning Process

The main advantage of employing an AI system lies within its ability to give immediate answers to questions or actions of a student, which play a pivotal role in the understanding of the student on the reasoning and analytical process of whether an action is correct or incorrect. The immediate response that comes also helps the students to be aware of their mistakes, review their ways and use other kinds of tactics; instead of solving problems, they learn to think logically. The model of learning allows the reiterative learning process whereby a learner understands the various solutions without necessarily having the possibility of choosing the wrong solution. Students have support in all the stages of learning, and AI makes students skillful problem solvers (Darwin et al., 2023).

5.4. Analysis And Interpretation Of Data Acquired Skills

Analysis is another ability that most AI tools have and allows students to analyse information in their learning process. It can introduce long sets of data to the students in mathematics and sciences, ask them to speculate about parameters, generate predictions, and draw conclusions (Kouzov, 2019). The exercise enhances identification, collection, and analysis of data, which are crucial in being able to think critically, since information is a major tool in solving problems.

5.5. Increasing Proactivity Of Metacognition

Artificial intelligence will safeguard students' progress and elucidate their learning processes, which is crucial for enhancing metacognition. Certain AI tools may raise inquiries or reflections regarding decision-making processes, potentially necessitating that students evaluate the various steps they undertake (Sanabria-Z et al., 2023). AI-facilitated metacognition enhances student awareness in problem-solving, thereby fostering self-regulation and reflective thinking, which are foundational to critical thinking.

5.6. Questioning Techniques For Diverse Learner Groups

AI can utilise self-adjustive quizzing, which progressively increases the difficulty of both content and form and can raise students' critical-thinking capacities. For example, after a student responds to a problem, the AI tutor can propose a follow-up exercise to focus on more profound reasoning or a correlated sub-skill, which promotes thinking at a higher level, e.g., analysis and evaluation (Zou et al., 2023).

Nevertheless, the task's difficulty level does not necessarily imply learning more profoundly, as when inaccurately controlled, it may result in cognitive overload and/or anxiety or passive engagement, particularly among students with lower background knowledge (Çelik et al., 2024). This can be overcome by introducing well-designed AI systems that work contextually to adjust to the challenges and provide scaffolding, hints and real-time feedback that enables an efficient cognitive load and productive struggle instead of frustration (Walter, 2024).

5.7. Cultivating Cooperation And Discussion Environments Using Artificial Intelligence Systems

AI-based platforms can facilitate collaborative activities when students are tasked, working in teams, engaging in discussions, and debating issues. Consequently, these interactions enhance students' critical thinking as they encounter diverse perspectives and cultivate the skills to substantiate their viewpoints. AI systems can therefore document engagement and provide analytics to the student concerning collective participation, thereby emphasising the importance of incorporating diverse perspectives in the development of critical thinking skills.

Artificial intelligence is transforming education by markedly enhancing students' critical thinking abilities, achievable through technology-driven, engaging, and feedback-oriented instruction. AI tools cultivate essential skills such as problem-solving, data analysis, metacognition, and adaptive reasoning, thereby enabling students to become analytical, reflective, and independent learners, which are crucial in the 21st-century. The future of AI technology will also be based on developing critical thinking skills among students, which will enable them to adapt to the ever-changing world. However, the process of incorporating AI tools into an educational context to enhance critical thinking faces a wide variety of obstacles.

Although AI has many pedagogical applications that can be used in making students learn more, the value it has reached is whether it will be used in creating independent, reflective, and collaborative thinkers who can excel in unpredictable and rapidly changing conditions. These advantages further support the strategic use of AI in training the transversal skills required of the 21st-century learner (Sajid Hasan et al., 2025).

6. CHALLENGES IN IMPLEMENTING AI FOR ENHANCING CRITICAL THINKING AND TRANSVERSAL SKILLS

Even though artificial intelligence has a great promise to improve learners' critical thinking and transversal skills, the use of artificial intelligence tools in education has its complications. Numerous pitfalls, from infrastructure capabilities to ethics, complicate AI's immense potential to transform education. The challenges have been identified as technical shortcomings, financial factors, ethical concerns, and the need to create capacity-building for educators. These are critical parameters that educators need to understand in order to incorporate AI in classrooms. Using AI applications to foster critical understanding among learners brings forward some challenges.

6.1. Costs And Resources

Artificial intelligence may be expensive, especially when a school has a small budget. Administrative investment involves buying new AI resources, upgrading the current ones or switching to better ones (via forking or upgrading), which requires significant money. In addition, most educational institutions lack IT support and the necessary infrastructure to implement AI as a core component. The issue of costs is especially apparent in the case of schools located in rural settings.

6.2. Data Privacy And Security Concerns

The majority of app-based feedbacks and learning activities require large amounts of information in order to deliver intelligent yet personal solutions to each user. There are serious privacy concerns associated with the collection and keeping of such data, and it is necessary to protect the personal and academic data of students. In order to use AI in education, schools have to undertake different legal challenges like GDPR and FERPA to protect information about students. Any violation or mishandling of the information and security may greatly compromise the trust of students, parents and instructors. It will prevent the creation of an environment leading to critical thinking.

6.3. Lack Of Teacher Training And Familiarity With AI

To be efficient in improving critical thinking processes using AI tools, teachers should learn how to implement them in the learning process. However, many instructors do not spend enough time on AI systems to manage the systems within their lifetime experience or have the training to allow them to handle the systems. Without any professional development that would increase the AI literacy of teachers, these educators will not be capable of using AI in order to engage in critical thinking. Without this knowledge, the use of AI tools can become rather ineffective in the dissemination of critical thinking skills.

6.4. Potential Over-Reliance On AI

The AI tools provide students with quick feedback, which, despite being rather helpful, contributes to overdependence on the resources. Students having too much reliance on AI to be able to answer or solve problems might not experience enough challenges and chances to learn and practice free critical thinking of a situation. Overreliance on AI prevents the fostering of persistence as well as the ability to excel at thinking. To avoid such a scenario, a new balance between AI assimilation and conventional learning processes needs to be reached.

6.5. Equity And Accessibility Concern

AI can improve critical thinking among students, but not every student who might need AI would even have access to the best possible instruments and does not belong to economically well-off families or live in cities. The problem is that the imbalanced distribution of AI in training produces digital inequity, which means that some students could enjoy the comforts of better learning with AI compared to their peers who are forced to deal with rote learning. It is necessary to address such paradoxes to create relations that will provide all learners with fair chances to work with AI and implement it in critical thinking.

6.6. Ethical Issues And Bias In Handling Algorithms

Of greater concern is their vulnerability to biases that may have negative impacts on students, learning, and general performance. Since the algorithms used to drive the current application of AI are stereotyped, it can aid the work of stereotyping or prevent the success of some students. For example, gender or ethnicity can either provide or deny the chance to the students in studying humanities, sciences, or any other subject, hence affecting the self-esteem and critical thinking skills. As revealed in this paper, there is a need to design AI models based on transparent and fair algorithms to avoid bias in AI applications in education.

6.7. Difficulty In Measuring Critical Thinking Progress

One of the primary goals of applying AI in education is to enhance students' critical thinking skills. However, unlike memorisation or factual recall, critical thinking is a complex, multidimensional cognitive process that is not easily quantified. While AI can track specific learning indicators—such as problem-solving patterns, reasoning sequences, and response times—it still struggles to capture the depth, context, and reflective aspects of critical thinking. Therefore, AI-generated analytics should complement human-centred methods such as teacher evaluations, reflective journals, and performance-based assessments to validate students' cognitive growth meaningfully. Additionally, educators may find it challenging to assess the effectiveness of AI tools in fostering critical thinking due to the absence of standardised parameters that link tool use to observable, higher-order learning outcomes.

The idea to incorporate AI to improve critical thinking and transversal abilities among students is a well-heeled idea, but not risk-free. The obstacles that affect the implementation of AI in classrooms are economic limitations, privacy concerns, lack of training, and ethics. These problems require differences, which should involve social investment, broad and thorough training of teachers, and ethical use of AI. As a result, these barriers are capable of reduction, hence enabling AI to become an excellent tool in inculcating critical thinking into the future.

7. CASE STUDIES: FOSTERING CRITICAL THINKING AND TRANSVERSAL SKILLS

To illustrate the prospects of AI integration, new curriculum design and experiential learning to facilitate the development of critical thinking and transversal skills, the case study below outlines the most advanced initiatives within the Indian education sector and other countries like Finland, South Korea, Singapore and Taiwan. These examples showcase practical models for enhancing problem-solving, creativity, adaptability, and reflective thinking across diverse learner groups. Presented the concepts and development of the above-mentioned initiatives and platforms to foster transversal skills like critical thinking, creativity, problem-solving, adaptability, and practicality in every student.

7.1. Delhi Government's Happiness Curriculum

In 2018, the Delhi government implemented the 'happiness curriculum' in all government schools to enhance students' wellbeing and development, following the CBSE board exams. This curriculum is founded on the principles of mindfulness, precise emotional identification, and reflection, aiming to enhance students' wellbeing and the efficacy of their learning processes. Consequently, the happiness curriculum facilitates students' understanding of their moral values and the practical application of those values. By integrating the arts and daily mindfulness practices that encompass guided discussions about emotions, students are encouraged to engage in critical thinking regarding their feelings, the feelings of others, and the resolution of conflicts and disagreements. Preliminary research suggests enhanced student empathy, emotional wellbeing, and/or advanced critical thinking abilities when they participate in the program.

7.2. Design Thinking At IIT Gandhinagar

Design thinking has been incorporated into the educational framework of the school of artificial intelligence at the Indian Institute of Technology Gandhinagar (IITGN), enabling students to address real-world problem scenarios systematically. The design thinking workshops are integrated into the program as students refine their idea generation and problem-solving skills. By employing the design thinking pedagogical approach, students can articulate problems, perform user analysis, generate ideas, and create models. This process compels them to think creatively by exploring all potential methods of defining a problem, questioning their existing paradigms, and devising practical and innovative solutions. The development of economic purification systems exemplifies the critical and innovative thinking necessary to tackle real-world issues.

7.3. Ekstep Foundation's Digital Learning Platform

Ekstep is a Bengaluru-based foundation which uses learning to make it available to students who do not have normal access to schools. A non-profit solution provider in education, Ekstep provides its own math and science content and an inquiry-based learning approach. This means that students using the Eksteps platform will not only have to be able to create questions but also test and discover different concepts in different ways and measure the results. The adaptive learning model used on the platform provides conceptualisation, relationships, and personal reflection to the students and allows critical analysis of fundamental material in subjects that are critical to their growth.

7.4. ATAL Tinkering Labs By Niti Aayog

Atal innovation mission was launched in July 2016 by the government and is a part of NITI Aayog, which is a passion-driven movement of students being set up with Atal Tinkering Labs (ATLs) in schools. The tools used in the ATLs (3D printers, robotics kits, etc.) are also produced in these schools so that the students could develop through practice. These are supposed to stimulate creative imaginations and reason. Through robotic, electronic and green solutions, the students will come with the mandate to work on formulating a hypothesis, designing to error, and redesigning an idea. Such an approach to learning makes students develop better problem-solving skills. It demands that they analyse the available information and the consequences of all the prototypes while they improve the design based on systematic suggestions, which is greatly beneficial to them in their future undertaking of stem.

7.5. Mindspark By Educational Initiatives

MindSpark is a learning platform that uses machine learning to educational initiatives created to enable students to grasp their knowledge about complex mathematics and science concepts. It utilises the evaluation of the pupil's performance before the presentation of more demanding questions that need critical thinking, but not memory. MindSpark encourages the students to think and analyse in resolving concepts of interest to understand the core concept of the subject matter. It is based on the potential to meet the individual needs of the students and apart from this feature, students can learn to analyse and reason in a good manner, and this imparts better academic performance with time. Studies have shown that using MindSpark in learning mathematics is also more effective and critical for thinking between students.

These case studies represent strong examples of successful Indian initiatives promoting critical thinking and transversal skills, selected based on their measurable impact (e.g., improved student engagement or academic performance), alignment with national education policy goals (e.g., NEP 2020), scalability across diverse educational settings, and sustained implementation over multiple years. The use of the happiness curriculum, which helps to increase self-reflection, and the practice of MindSpark, which helps to add analytical thinking, proves that introducing critical thinking methodology in curricula helps students academically and in the real world. In this respect, these initiatives equip students with the skills they need to succeed academically and personally.

7.6. Finland – Ville Learning Platform

Finland has implemented the ViLLE platform, developed at the University of Turku, as a national-level formative assessment tool. ViLLE uses AI-driven learning analytics to provide real-time feedback, personalise learning pathways, and track student progress across subjects. Empirical evaluations show that ViLLE students demonstrate improved metacognitive regulation, better engagement with complex problem-solving, and stronger learning outcomes in mathematics and science. Teachers, in turn, can adjust instruction based on the AI-generated insights, reinforcing reflective and critical thinking.

7.7. South Korea – AI Chatbots For Inquiry-Based Science

In South Korea, AI chatbots have been introduced into middle school science classrooms to support inquiry-based learning. These bots guide students through hypothesis generation, experimentation, and analysis by asking critical prompts and offering contextual feedback. This method supports evidence-based reasoning, encourages student curiosity, and helps learners iterate through reflective cycles of questioning and evaluation—key components of transversal skill development.

7.8. Singapore & Taiwan – AI Scaffolding For Argumentative Writing

A cross-national study conducted in Singapore and Taiwan explored using AI-powered writing platforms that provide scaffolded feedback to secondary students. The AI systems support students in organising arguments, evaluating evidence, and refining their reasoning. Results showed significant improvements in argumentative structure, critical literacy, and metacognitive awareness, demonstrating AI's effectiveness in language and humanities education.

Table 2. Case Studies on AI and innovation-based Critical Thinking and Transversal Skills in India

Initiative / Institution	Key Tool / Approach	Targeted Skills	Outcomes / Impact	Analytical Commentary / Alignment with Educational Context
Happiness Curriculum (Delhi Govt.)	Mindfulness, reflection-based curriculum	Emotional intelligence, self-awareness, empathy, and conflict resolution	Improved emotional regulation, enhanced self-reflection, and development of critical social reasoning	Supports NEP 2020's focus on holistic and value-based education; adaptable for SEL integration in AI-driven emotional learning platforms
Design Thinking (IIT Gandhinagar)	Design thinking pedagogy, AI-linked problem solving	Creativity, problem-solving, innovation, and adaptability	Enhanced student capacity to ideate, prototype, and solve real-world problems creatively	Aligns with SDG 4 (Quality Education) and NEP's call for experiential and innovation-based learning; scalable in engineering education
EkStep Foundation	Digital learning platform with an inquiry-based model	Digital literacy, critical inquiry, and self-directed learning	Improved access to conceptual learning, strengthened reasoning and question-generation skills	Nationally scaled open-source platform; policy-backed via DIKSHA; well-positioned for integration into rural and urban AI-mediated learning contexts

continued on following page

Table 2. Continued

Initiative / Institution	Key Tool / Approach	Targeted Skills	Outcomes / Impact	Analytical Commentary / Alignment with Educational Context
Atal Tinkering Labs (NITI Aayog)	Hands-on STEM tools (AI, robotics, 3D printing)	Collaboration, data analysis, critical thinking, and innovation	Boost in practical design thinking, team-based innovation, and iterative problem-solving	Government-supported initiative promoting AI readiness and innovation; scalable across socio-economic contexts; aligns with India's AI for Youth vision
MindSpark (Educational Initiatives)	AI-powered adaptive learning platform	Logical reasoning, math/science comprehension, decision-making	Demonstrated gains in analytical thinking and subject mastery through personalised learning feedback	Strong empirical backing; integrated into low-resource schools; exemplifies AI-aligned pedagogy addressing both personalisation and equity
University of Turku, Finland (ViLLE Platform)	AI-powered formative assessment and analytics	Metacognitive regulation, problem-solving, and reflection	Improved student performance, real-time feedback, enhanced teacher adaptability	Aligns with Finland's strong focus on data-driven formative assessment and student autonomy. ViLLE supports personalised instruction and system-level monitoring.
Korean Middle Schools	AI chatbots in science inquiry-based learning	Hypothesis generation, evidence-based reasoning, evaluation	Greater engagement, improved scientific thinking, and iterative problem-solving	Reflects South Korea's integration of edtech in STEM fields. AI supports constructivist, inquiry-based pedagogy, encouraging self-guided exploration.
Singapore & Taiwan Secondary Schools	AI-based scaffolding for writing and argumentation	Critical writing, analytical reasoning, and metacognitive reflection	Enhanced argumentative structure, stronger critical literacy, and self-assessment	Supports bilingual, high-achievement cultures. AI tools scaffold language learners and promote deep thinking that is aligned with curriculum goals.

Source: Author(s)

Integrating AI and innovative pedagogical approaches across diverse educational contexts demonstrates the global shift toward cultivating transversal competencies. Table (2) summarises select initiatives from India and other countries, highlighting their tools, targeted skills, outcomes, and alignment with broader educational goals.

8. SOLUTIONS AND RECOMMENDATIONS

In this section, the effective implementation of AI tools that will have the practical potential to support the development of students in critical thinking and transversal skills is described. The solutions will be laid out by the three main objectives of the chapter.

8.1. Addressing Limitations Of Traditional Pedagogies

Development of critical thinking is central to the participation of the students, as it enables the analysis of the content and evidence in analysesing the decision-making process. The reason why constructing their knowledge base and understanding how they can apply it to another area is more significant to the students is that they gain more meaning from it when they can undertake critical analysis. However, critical thinking is not an easy task in conventional classes, which are characterised by retaining information rather than using their analytical abilities. The higher class size, the wide range of students, and the nature of critical thinking evaluation that is subjective at the same time, makes the task more difficult.

Artificial intelligence (AI) has to be seen as the best solution, which provides students with tools to improve the learning process, receive feedback, and allow an individual to train their cognitive abilities. AI allows customised learning and allows the student to learn at their own pace and ability. As an example of such, when two students work on the same math problem, AI can identify underlying misconceptions and force the learners to apply different, critical and independent thinking. Such an interactive engagement can be challenging to achieve in the ordinary classroom since instructors do not have ample time and class size.

8.2. Leveraging AI For Engagement, Metacognition, And Differentiated Instruction

It is considered that the effectiveness of AI in education is determined by the fact that it allows for personalising feedback and improving independent thought and analysis. AI has a chance to analyse large amounts of data concerning the performance of students and help them realise the pattern, comprehend the links within sets of information, and employ critical thinking more efficiently. That development of reflective and analytical skills requires personal feedback that accommodates the ideal learning pace of an individual.

AI also saves instructional time in the automation of various administrative activities like grading, attendance and assessments. This will enable teachers to concentrate on theoretical education and use new instructional methods, including the development of substantive activities and class discussions. Teachers can recognise the students that require further assistance and structure the learning path channels differently with the aid of AI, increasing student performance.

Metacognition through AI also improves awareness on the students' part when solving problems through the need for self-regulation and thinking. The students are prompted to assess how the students make decisions and come up with ways of making the process more effective, and this is one of the most essential cornerstones in developing critical thinking.

8.3. Ethical And Pedagogical Considerations For AI Integration

AI applications in the educational environment should be implemented with references to ethical and practical issues. To begin with, privacy and security should be given the first priority in order to protect the students ' personal data. The application of AI tools must be presented under transparency aspects and explainable to all, including the students and the educators, the rationale behind the AI-generated feedback.

Moreover, AI should not substitute human wisdom in the processes of teaching and learning. Teachers can contribute in an invaluable way to assisting students to understand data insights, providing moral support, and developing a classroom atmosphere of empathy, collective thinking, and moral judgment. In order to do so, educators need to be offered constant professional growth, which should be aimed at technical fluency and pedagogical integration of AI applications.

With artificial intelligence (AI), assessments can also be improved, including more consistent, objective, and scalable student learning measurement. AI can deliver objective evaluation without bias and can offer useful feedback to the educators to target development in each learner better. Regular evaluations, as well as the knowledge of educators, provide a healthy mix of technological effectiveness and human supervision.

An efficient combination of conventional and AI-supported techniques promises a positive way ahead. Although AI is effective when it comes to data-based personalisation and real-time feedback, empathy, imagination, and critical thinking are where educators should succeed. Active learning-based classroom establishments with AI will allow students to chance to practice critical thinking collectively and/or on their own.

Institutions are, therefore, expected to develop policies and guidelines regarding ethical AI use that meet the criterion of transparency, fairness, and student wellbeing. The students will need to be informed that AI is an auxiliary tool and not a substitute for deep learning. Through this balance between innovativeness and responsibility, schools would be in a position to make AI implementation fully worthwhile, when it comes to the development of critical and transversal skills.

9. FUTURE RESEARCH DIRECTIONS

The chapter has discussed the pedagogical transition achieved due to the artificial intelligence (AI) powered learning, emphasising the improvement of critical thinking and transversal skills among the learners. Although it has found a variety of AI tools and their educational value, further study is required to explore more evidence and inform the implementation process.

Future research on determining the most effective AI tools in establishing the evolution of different aspects of critical thinking (i.e., inference, evaluation, and reflection) in different subjects should be considered. In addition, it needs an empirical study that can come up with valid and reliable assessment frameworks for the measurement of the progress of the students in critical and transversal competencies in an AI-based learning environment.

The need to investigate longitudinal effects of AI-informed pedagogy on the adaptability, collaboration, and problem-solving skills is evident in the research as well, since it is quite important to understand how these impacts can change in the long run and how those changes can vary across a range of educational settings, e.g., rural vs. urban schools or schools in the private vs. public sectors.

Advanced research combining the application of AI in the field of inclusive education, or education of students with different needs and learning styles, will assist in maximising the equal effects of the practice. Also, studies need to look into the ethical aspects of AI-assessment-based measures, such as the bias in the algorithm, data privacy, and the self-autonomy of students.

Finally, research needs to be done in future about the professional development frameworks of making teachers ready with the competencies required for making a meaningful use of AI in curriculum planning, classroom practice, and reflection teaching.

10. CONCLUSION

Critical thinking of students is important in their development of the ability to tackle the multifaceted problems of the real world. However, traditional educational approaches fail in this respect as they commonly fail to develop any forms of higher order thinking, changeability, and observational learning. This chapter has established that artificial intelligence will facilitate the development of novel ways of closing these gaps, namely, personalised instruction, real-time feedback, performance analytics, and adaptive learning environments.

With the help of the AI tools, educators can design learner-centered experiences to not only foster critical thinking but a wider range of transversal skills such as collaboration, creativity, digital literacy, and problem-solving. They are essential skills that people need to succeed in the 21st-century, which is a fast-moving and unpredictable world.

To make this vision possible, the implementation of AI should be based on a definite pedagogical intent, ethics, and teacher preparedness. This involves evaluating the knowledge of teachers, creating the ideals of accountability with AI, and ensuring data privacy and algorithmic transparency. It is also crucial to provide students with critical awareness regarding the AI mechanics and how to employ them in a responsible manner.

AI, when introduced, implemented responsibly and thoughtfully, proves a potent tool of the educational revolution that helps develop not just cognitive, but emotional, and socially relevant skills, far beyond stepping across the wall of the classroom. With the transformation of the educational system, the development of the integrated process of learning and teaching based on human-scale educational approaches and the application of AI will be crucial to raise educated, ethical, and future-proof learners.

REFERENCES

Aayog, N. I. T. I. (2022). Atal Innovation Mission: Atal Tinkering Labs and STEM Education in India. https://niti.gov.in

Akram, N. A., Kiren, N. A., Sabir, N. S., & Aslam, N. S. (2025). The effect of AI based scaffolding on problem solving and metacognitive awareness in learners. ˜the œCritical Review of Social Sciences Studies, 3(3), 1074–1089. DOI: 10.59075/ja7dvy78

Baskoro, G., Mariza, I., & Sutapa, I. N. (2023). Innovation to Improve Critical Thinking Skills in the Generation Z using Peeragogy as a Learning Approach and Artificial Intelligence (AI) as a Tool. *Deleted Journal*, *25*(2), 121–130. DOI: 10.9744/jti.25.2.121-130

Battelle for Kids. (2019). Framework for 21st Century Learning Definitions. https://www.battelleforkids.org/wp-content/uploads/2023/11/P21_Framework_DefinitionsBFK.pdf

Binns, R. (2018). Fairness in machine learning: Lessons from political philosophy. Journal of Machine Learning Research. https://ora.ox.ac.uk/objects/uuid:2ff2785b-b0d4-447a-8326-a1fcc4c80840

Buskist, W., & Irons, J. G. (2008). Buskist, W., & Irons, J. G. (2008). Simple Strategies for Teaching Your Students to Think Critically. American Psychological Association, 49–57. DOI: 10.1002/9781444305173.ch5

Caruajulca, C. B. (2021). CRITICAL THINKING IN THE EDUCATIONAL IN THE FIELD OF EDUCATION. *ASEAN Journal of Psychiatry*, *22*(10). Advance online publication. DOI: 10.54615/2231-7805.47233

Celik, I., Gedrimiene, E., Siklander, S., & Muukkonen, H. (2024). The affordances of artificial intelligence-based tools for supporting 21st-century skills. *Australasian Journal of Educational Technology*. Advance online publication. DOI: 10.14742/ajet.9069

Chan, C. (2024). Holistic competencies and AI in education: A synergistic pathway. *Australasian Journal of Educational Technology*, *40*(5), 1–12. DOI: 10.14742/ajet.10191

Darwin, N., Rusdin, D., Mukminatien, N., Suryati, N., Laksmi, E. D., & Marzuki, N. (2023). Critical thinking in the AI era: An exploration of EFL students' perceptions, benefits, and limitations. *Cogent Education*, *11*(1), 2290342. Advance online publication. DOI: 10.1080/2331186X.2023.2290342

Davar, N. F., Dewan, M. A., & Zhang, X. (2025). AI chatbots in education: Challenges and opportunities. *Information (Basel)*, *16*(3), 235. DOI: 10.3390/info16030235

Educational Initiatives. (2020). MindSpark Adaptive Learning Platform: Enhancing Student Understanding and Critical Thinking in Mathematics. https://uplink.weforum.org/uplink/s/uplink-contribution/a012o00001pTbgMAAS/personalised-adaptive-learning-with-mindspark

EkStep Foundation. (2021). Digital Learning for All: Case Studies and Impact of EkStep's Personalised Learning Platform. EkStep Foundation (https://ekstep.org). Home - EKStep. (2023, August 12). EkStep. https://ekstep.org/

Fahim, M., & Ghamari, M. R. (2011). Critical thinking in Education: Globally developed and locally applied. *Theory and Practice in Language Studies*, *1*(11). Advance online publication. DOI: 10.4304/tpls.1.11.1632-1638

Grace, E., & Vidhyavathi, P. L., & P. Malathi, L. (2023). A STUDY ON "AI IN EDUCATION: OPPORTUNITIES AND CHALLENGES FOR PERSONALISED LEARNING. Industrial Engineering Journal (Vol. 52, Issue 5, pp. 750–759). http://www.journal-iiie-india.com/1_may_23/82_online.pdf

Guan, L., Zhang, Y., & Gu, M. M. (2024). Pre-service Teachers Preparedness for AI-integrated Education: An Investigation from Perceptions, Capabilities, and Teachers' Identity Changes. *Computers and Education Artificial Intelligence*, *100341*. Advance online publication. DOI: 10.1016/j.caeai.2024.100341

Hasan, S., Nasreen, N. S., & Rasul, N. S. S. U. (2025). Leveraging artificial intelligence (AI) in higher education: fostering soft skills communication, collaboration, creativity and critical thinking among university students. *Insights-Journal of Life and Social Sciences*, *3*(2), 1–7. DOI: 10.71000/c42srm97

Holmes, W., Bialik, M., & Fadel, C. (2019). Artificial intelligence in Education: Promises and implications for teaching and learning. https://oro.open.ac.uk/60255/

Home - Casel schoolguide. (2025, August 12). Casel Schoolguide. https://schoolguide.casel.org/

Indian Institute of Technology Gandhinagar. (2020). Innovative Approaches in Education: Design Thinking at IIT Gandhinagar. https://dic.iitgn.ac.in/wp/

Ironside, P. M. (2000). Thinking in nursing education. Part II. A teacher's experience. PubMed, 20(5), 243–247. https://pubmed.ncbi.nlm.nih.gov/10754846

Jobin, A., Ienca, M., & Vayena, E. (2019). The global landscape of AI ethics guidelines. *Nature Machine Intelligence*, *1*(9), 389–399. DOI: 10.1038/s42256-019-0088-2

Kandel, R. K. (2015). Resolving ELT Challenges Through Critical Thinking Strategies. https://www.researchgate.net/publication/281692231_Resolving_ELT_Challenges_Through_Critical_Thinking_Strategies

Kouzov, O. (2019). The New Paradigms In Education and Support of Critical Thinking with Artificial Intelligence (AI) Tools. *Serdica Journal of Computing*, *13*(1–2), 27–40. DOI: 10.55630/sjc.2019.13.27-40

Kumar, S. (2023). Developing human skills in the era of Artificial intelligence: challenges and opportunities for education and training. Scholedge International Journal of Multidisciplinary & Allied Studies ISSN 2394-336X, 10(2), 11. DOI: 10.19085/sijmas100201

Lai, E. R. (2011). Critical Thinking: a literature review. http://paluchja-zajecia.home.amu.edu.pl/seminarium_fakult/sem_f_krytyczne/Critical%20Thinking%20A%20Literature%20Review.pdf

Luckin, R., Holmes, W., Griffiths, M., & Forcier, L. B. (2016). Intelligence unleashed: An argument for AI in education. Pearson Education. https://www.pearson.com/content/dam/one-dot-com/one-dot-com/global/Files/about-pearson/innovation/open-ideas/Intelligence-Unleashed-Publication.pdf

Malik, G., Tayal, D. K., & Vij, S. (2018). An analysis of the role of artificial intelligence in education and teaching. In Advances in intelligent systems and computing (pp. 407–417). DOI: 10.1007/978-981-10-8639-7_42

Mandernach, B. J. (2006). Thinking Critically about Critical Thinking: Integrating Online Tools to Promote Critical Thinking. *InSight a Journal of Scholarly Teaching*, *1*, 41–50. DOI: 10.46504/01200603ma

Moustaghfir, S., & Brigui, H. (2024). Navigating Critical Thinking in the Digital Era: An informative exploration. *International Journal of Linguistics Literature & Translation*, *7*(1), 137–143. DOI: 10.32996/ijllt.2024.7.1.11x

OECD. (2019). OECD Learning Compass 2030: A series of concept notes. oecd/en/about/projects/edu/education-2040/1-1-learning-compass/OECD_Learning_Compass_2030_Concept_Note_Series.pdf

OECD. (2019). PISA 2018 results (Volume I): What students know and can do. OECD Publishing. https://www.oecd.org/en/publications/2019/12/pisa-2018-results-volume-i_947e3529.html

Onions, P. (2009). Thinking Critically An introduction. https://www.semanticscholar.org/paper/Thinking-Critically-An-introduction-Onions/0409cf62b55da25a6ebbe64a3114c921edb43f5a

Pithers, R., & Soden, R. (2000). Critical thinking in education: A review. *Educational Research, 42*(3), 237–249. DOI: 10.1080/001318800440579

Popenici, S. D., & Kerr, S. (2017). Exploring the impact of artificial intelligence on teaching and learning in higher education. *Research and Practice in Technology Enhanced Learning, 12*(1), 22. Advance online publication. DOI: 10.1186/s41039-017-0062-8 PMID: 30595727

Rizvi, M. (2023). Exploring the landscape of artificial intelligence in education: Challenges and opportunities. (2023, June 8). IEEE Conference Publication | IEEE Xplore. https://ieeexplore.ieee.org/document/10156773

Rönnlund, M., Ledman, K., Nylund, M., & Rosvall, P. (2019). Life skills for 'real life': How critical thinking is contextualised across vocational programmes. *Educational Research, 61*(3), 302–318. DOI: 10.1080/00131881.2019.1633942

Saleh, S. E. (2019). *CRITICAL THINKING AS a 21st CENTURY SKILL: CONCEPTIONS, IMPLEMENTATION AND CHALLENGES IN THE EFL CLASSROOM*. European Journal of Foreign Language Teaching., DOI: 10.46827/ejfl.v0i0.2209

Sanabria-Z, J., Alfaro-Ponce, B., Argüelles-Cruz, A., & Ramírez-Montoya, M. S. (2023). AI-Based Platform Design for Complex Thinking Assessment: A case study of an Ideathon using the Transition Design approach. *Computers in the Schools, 40*(4), 391–411. DOI: 10.1080/07380569.2023.2256711

Snyder, L. G., & Snyder, M. (2008). Teaching critical thinking and problem solving skills. In The Delta Pi Epsilon Journal (Vols. 2–2). https://dme.childrenshospital.org/wp-content/uploads/2019/02/Optional-_Teaching-Critical-Thinking-and-Problem-Solving-Skills.pdf

Tan, C. (2017). Teaching critical thinking: Cultural challenges and strategies in Singapore. *British Educational Research Journal, 43*(5), 988–1002. DOI: 10.1002/berj.3295

The MIT Press, Massachusetts Institute of Technology. (2025, June 23). Book details - MIT Press. MIT Press. https://mitpress.mit.edu/9780262538282/critical-thinking/

Trucano, M. & Information for Development Program. (2005). Knowledge Maps: ICT in Education. infoDev / World Bank. https://documents1.worldbank.org/curated/en/457411468341334749/pdf/319530WP0REVIS0800PUBLIC0Box379827B.pdf

UNESCO & Teacher Task Force. (2023). *Global report on teachers: Addressing teacher shortages*. UNESCO Publishing. https://www.unesco.org/en/articles/global-report-teachers-addressing-teacher-shortages-and-transforming-profession

Uribe-Enciso, O. L., Uribe-Enciso, D. S., & Vargas-Daza, M. D. (2017). Critical thinking and its importance in education: Some reflections. *Rastros Rostros*, *19*, 78–88. DOI: 10.16925/ra.v19i34.2144

Walter, Y. (2024). Embracing the future of Artificial Intelligence in the classroom: The relevance of AI literacy, prompt engineering, and critical thinking in modern education. *International Journal of Educational Technology in Higher Education*, *21*(1), 15. Advance online publication. DOI: 10.1186/s41239-024-00448-3

Zawacki-Richter, O., Marín, V. I., Bond, M., & Gouverneur, F. (2019). Systematic review of research on artificial intelligence applications in higher education – where are the educators? *International Journal of Educational Technology in Higher Education*, *16*(1), 39. Advance online publication. DOI: 10.1186/s41239-019-0171-0

Zou, X., Su, P., Li, L., & Fu, P. (2023). AI-generated content tools and students' critical thinking: Insights from a Chinese university. *IFLA Journal*, *50*(2), 228–241. DOI: 10.1177/03400352231214963

Chapter 9
Enhancing EFL Learning for Neurodiverse Students Through Virtual Worlds and the Metaverse

Sandra Luna
https://orcid.org/0000-0001-9185-0593
Polytechnic Institute of Porto, Portugal

ABSTRACT

This chapter examines the intersection of English language learning, neurodiversity, and the use of virtual worlds and the metaverse. It considers the needs and characteristics of neurodivergent learners and students with cerebral palsy, analysing the affordances and potential drawbacks of immersive environments for English as a Foreign Language (EFL) instruction. The chapter is structured around four strands: an analysis of virtual worlds, the metaverse, and their educational uses; a critical comparison of their affordances and limitations; a discussion of inclusive design practices for neurodivergent and physically disabled students; and practical recommendations for integrating these technologies into EFL instruction in effective and equitable ways. The Universal Design for Learning (UDL) serves as a recurring conceptual and practical anchor, guiding the exploration of accessibility, learner agency, and inclusive instructional design across theoretical, technological, and pedagogical dimensions.

DOI: 10.4018/979-8-3373-7729-2.ch009

1. INTRODUCTION

Digital education has undergone a profound transformation in recent decades, driven by the increasing integration of emerging technologies into teaching and learning processes (Bailenson, 2018). This movement has recently gained momentum, especially following the COVID-19 pandemic, which accelerated the interest in digital solutions across all levels of education and exposed both the potential and the limitations of current educational models (Aragon et al., 2024; Hupont Torres et al., 2023; Mystakidis, 2022). For both educators and policymakers in the field of English as a Foreign language (EFL), these changes raise urgent questions about equitable access, particularly for learners, who may also face additional challenges due to physical or neurological differences.

As Aragon et al. (2024) aptly observed, "during this rush of innovation, there was some attention paid to the way that many on-site experiences are exclusionary to blind/low-vision people, d/Deaf/hard-of-hearing people, and people with invisible disabilities, physical disabilities, or mental health conditions" (p.1). The authors note that, for many in the disability community, the pandemic initially sparked hope for a long-overdue reckoning with accessibility - but that this promise largely went unfulfilled. Since then, virtual learning environments, virtual reality (VR), augmented reality (AR), and more recently the metaverse have gained increased prominence in pedagogical innovation. These technologies are associated with what is often referred to as the fourth wave of computing, with the metaverse in particular holding the potential to transform online education, business, remote work, and entertainment (Mystakidis, 2022). More than a shift in format, they introduce immersive, interactive, and sensory educational approaches that seek to overcome "the fundamental limitations of web-based 2D e-learning tools" (p. 486).

This turn toward immersive, sensory-rich environments is particularly meaningful in foreign language education, where authentic interaction thrives in contexts that closely mirror real-world communication. In such settings, virtual worlds and the metaverse offer three-dimensional environments that mimic real-life experiences, enabling real-time linguistic interaction through visual, auditory, and sometimes tactile stimuli. As W. Chen et al. (2023) point out, the metaverse can enhance educational outcomes by providing immersive and interactive spaces that satisfy learners in both physical and virtual dimensions (p. 36).

In the EFL context, these immersive approaches have shown strong potential for developing communicative skills, while also offering more engaging, motivating, and contextually rich learning settings (W. Chen et al., 2023; Peterson & Jabbari, 2022). Yet, this technological transformation, while promising, is neither pedagogically neutral nor inherently inclusive. For example, Yong et al. (2024) highlight that VR accessibility challenges include a lack of standards, reliance on limited modalities, and physical constraints related to movement. They further note that the underrepresentation of many marginalized groups in design processes has resulted in products that fail to be inclusive. For teachers and instructional designers, these gaps translate into practical challenges when selecting, adapting, or implementing immersive tools in ways that meet a wider range of learners' needs.

A particularly pressing issue is the pedagogical invisibility of neurodivergent learners in most immersive learning environments. Even if research on the educational potential of immersive technologies is expanding, it seldom addresses the needs of neurologically diverse students, in part due to the absence of consistent theoretical and methodological frameworks in VR research (Savickaite, 2023). Savickaite further notes that many VR features, such as visual perception and 3D interaction, are often poorly aligned with neurodivergent learning profiles. This lack of individualization - rooted in a 'one-size-fits-all' design logic (Creed et al., 2024) - means that students with Attention Deficit Hyperactivity Disorder (ADHD), Autism Spectrum Disorder (ASD), or Cerebral Palsy (CP) continue to face substantial cognitive, sensory, or motor barriers in digital environments. For instance, students with ADHD may struggle to maintain focus in overstimulating settings; those with ASD could experience sensory overload or difficulties interpreting social cues; and students with CP may encounter persistent interface or navigation challenges. In practice, these barriers can limit participation, reduce engagement, and require teachers to invest considerable effort in adapting activities, often without sufficient institutional guidance or technical support.

This gap is specifically troubling given that inclusive education is now a policy priority enshrined in international and national frameworks, such as the Salamanca Declaration (UNESCO, 1994), Portuguese legislation (DL-54/2018[1] and DL-55/2018[2]), and curriculum guidelines grounded in epistemological and pedagogical equity (Cosme, 2018). For policymakers, these instruments set clear expectations for equitable participation; for educators, they establish a mandate, and an opportunity, to translate these commitments into classroom practice, including within immersive learning environments.

Hupont Torres et al. (2023) suggest that eXtended reality (XR) technologies can contribute to more effective and inclusive education by offering immersive, engaging, and accessible experiences that promote both technical and interpersonal development. However, a considerable disconnect remains between political aspiration and classroom reality, especially when it comes to ensuring the accessibility and meaningful participation of learners with specific needs (Wehrmann & Zender, 2023). Bridging this gap requires not only technological adaptation, but also targeted teacher training, clear institutional guidelines, and ongoing evaluation of how immersive tools perform in real teaching contexts.

Many immersive environments, including virtual worlds and metaverse platforms, are built around a universalised experience model, which often overlooks the need to adapt stimuli, interfaces, and modes of interaction to diverse users. As a result, neurodivergent learners, particularly those with motor or sensory differences, may face increased barriers when using standard navigation tools. Addressing these barriers from the beginning calls for the integration of Universal Design for Learning (UDL) principles, as advocated by Meyer et al. (2014) and K. Novak & Rose (2016), thus ensuring that technological development reflects user diversity (Casarez et al., 2023). Framing design in this way also lays the groundwork for more equitable pedagogical practices, as we will see throughout this chapter.

Simply making virtual or augmented environments available, without deliberate pedagogical mediation, risks replicating, or even exacerbating, the exclusionary dynamics found in traditional classrooms. Creed et al. (2024) highlight the lack of research into accessibility barriers in immersive learning for neurodivergent and physically diverse learners, while Aragon et al. (2024) warn of "potentially overlooked harms in immersive and embodied virtual spaces" (p. 1). Similarly, Yong et al. (2024) note the scarcity of research on ethical, cultural, and usability protocols in inclusive VR adoption. Taken together, these findings underscore a central point: technical innovation, by itself, does not ensure equity.

This chapter explores the pedagogical potential of virtual worlds and the metaverse for EFL instruction, with a focus on neurodivergent students and those with cerebral palsy.

It critically examines both the possibilities and limitations of immersive technologies and proposes principles for inclusive instructional design grounded in current research, digital accessibility practices, and insights from language education. The underlying premise is that, when designed thoughtfully, immersive environments can enhance learning outcomes while fostering more equitable, learner-centred educational experiences.

The discussion unfolds in four interconnected strands: (i) a theoretical clarification of virtual worlds and the metaverse and their educational uses; (ii) a critical comparison of their pedagogical benefits and limitations; (iii) a discussion of inclusive design practices for neurodivergent and physically disabled students; and (iv) practical recommendations for their equitable integration into EFL instruction. Across these strands UDL serves as a recurring conceptual and practical anchor, guiding the exploration of accessibility, learner agency, and inclusive instructional design.

Section 2 explores the educational foundations of neurodiversity in relation to language learning and digital inclusion. Section 3 presents the theoretical framework, including the Interaction Hypothesis, Socioconstructivism, distributed agency, and UDL. Section 4 examines the pedagogical affordances of immersive technologies, particularly virtual worlds and the metaverse, alongside its main challenges, best practices, and core educator competences. The final section synthetises key insights while proposing future research directions in immersive learning, inclusion and language education.

Ultimately, the chapter argues that achieving true inclusion in immersive environments requires more than technical fixes: it calls for a pedagogical paradigm shift, one that places neurological diversity at the centre of instructional design. Such an approach stands to benefit more learners by making language education more humane, flexible, and effective.

2. INCLUSIVE EDUCATION, NEURODIVERSITY AND LANGUAGES: A JOURNEY IN THE MAKING

Learning a language is more than memorising vocabulary or grammar rules; it involves stepping into a universe of meanings, rhythms, and communicative gestures. In EFL contexts, embracing neurodiversity as part of our human landscape invites us to acknowledge that there is no single right way to communicate, learn, or perceive the world. In fact, as Savickaite (2023) notes, "there is no single way for a brain to be normal, as there are numerous ways for the brain to be wired up and mature" (p. 294). Inclusive language education, therefore, offers a chance to reconceptualise learning spaces as environments where diverse ways of thinking, being, and expressing are not merely accommodated but genuinely valued.

2.1 The Origin and Concept of Neurodiversity

The concept of neurodiversity recognises that neurological variations - such as ASD, ADHD, and dyslexia - are natural expressions of human diversity, rather than pathologies. In education systems worldwide, from Finland to Japan, this view is slowly influencing curriculum design. While clinical frameworks like the DSM-5 (American Psychiatric Association, 2013) categorise these conditions as disorders, the neurodiversity paradigm shifts emphasis from **deficit** to **difference** (T. Armstrong, 2010; Kapp, 2020; Singer, 1999).

This reconceptualization invites educators, including those in EFL settings, to design learning environments that support neurological differences, rather than seeking to normalise or remediate them. For example, by allowing a learner with ADHD to complete a vocabulary matching task in short, time bursts with movement breaks, rather than in one longer, uninterrupted sitting.

Coined by sociologist Judy Singer in the 1990s, the term *neurodiversity* emerged as part of her advocacy for neurological minorities, i.e. individuals whose cognitive profiles diverge from the statistical norm (Singer, 1999). Drawing on sociological analogies like cultural or gender diversity, Singer reframed neurological difference as a matter of human rights and social justice (Jones & Orchard, 2024). Singer's ideas then gained wider visibility through journalist Harvey Blume, whose *Atlantic* article (1998) helped introduce the term to mainstream discourse.

In *The Power of Neurodiversity*, T. Armstrong (2010) reinforces this perspective, suggesting that just as biodiversity and cultural diversity enrich our world, so too does variability among brains. "There is no standard brain," he writes, "just as there is no standard flower" (p. 3) – a view that underpins inclusive approaches to language learning and teaching.

As neurodiversity gained ground in public and institutional discourses, it was increasingly adopted in education, healthcare, and employment contexts (Baumer & Frueh, 2021; Jones & Orchard, 2024). Nonetheless, in educational practice, including EFL, this interest has sometimes diluted its transformative potential. Jones & Orchard (2024), for example, caution that neurodiversity is often invoked as a rhetorical gesture of inclusion, without meaningful structural change to teaching methods or learning environments. One factor sustaining this gap is linguistic framing: terms like "deficit" or "special needs" perpetuate clinical framings that emphasise pathology and limitation (T. Armstrong, 2010; Craine, 2020; Savickaite, 2023). In contrast, expressions such as "neurodivergent" or "neurodivergent profile" reflect a more humanistic orientation that focuses on the person rather than the diagnosis, a shift that can meaningfully shape interaction and identity within the EFL classroom.

Alongside neurodivergent conditions, other neurological and physical conditions, such as cerebral palsy (CP), also require tailored educational responses. While CP is not technically part of the neurodivergent spectrum, the challenges it presents - motor, sensory, cognitive - similarly call for inclusive and differentiated pedagogy (Gronseth & Dalton, 2020; K. Novak & Rose, 2016). This need becomes quite evident in language learning, where oral expression and interaction are central, and in immersive environments where navigation tools may demand fine motor control, making accommodation of motor variability crucial.

2.2 Cerebral Palsy: Cognitive, Motor and Technological Challenges in the Context of Language Learning

Cerebral palsy is a non-progressive neuromotor condition caused by early brain damage, which can impair coordination, posture, and sometimes communication (I. Novak et al., 2013; Pennington et al., 2004). While many students with CP have strong cognitive and communicative potential, their participation depends on accessible, responsive environments (Portugal. Ministério da Educação, 2018a, 2018b; UNESCO, 1994). In an EFL setting, this might mean adapting a VR role-play in a virtual café so that a student with CP can navigate the activity using an on-screen eye-gaze menu instead of gesture-based controls. Through gaze selection, they could choose menu items, request the bill, or respond to the waiter's small talk. This adaptation ensures they can practise the same functional language, such as polite requests and transactional exchanges, as their peers, while removing the barrier posed by interfaces that require fine motor movement.

To support this sort of participation, pedagogical strategies must go beyond technical adaptations and integrate modes of interaction suited to individual needs (T. Armstrong, 2010; K. Novak & Rose, 2016). In digital contexts, conventional tools like keyboards or dropdown menus often pose barriers (Bekteshi et al., 2020; Borgestig et al., 2016; Yong et al., 2024), since these can hinder communication, collaboration, and language development, particularly when interfaces are inflexible or overly reliant on fine motor control (Aragon et al., 2024; Creed et al., 2024). Addressing these challenges requires that educators be familiar with alternative input methods and adaptable technologies to support these students' active participation. In EFL, this might mean that activities relying on rapid text input (e.g. a timed vocabulary quiz), small on-screen icons, or precise cursor movements, become inaccessible unless they are adaptated.

Conversely, Augmentative and Alternative Communication (AAC)[3] systems, including pictorial boards and speech-generating devices, offer important solutions (I. Novak et al., 2013). One of the most promising tools is eye-gaze technology, which allows users to select items or generate speech via gaze fixation (Borgestig et al., 2016; Karlsson et al., 2019), and for some, this is the only viable method of interaction. Such systems can also be adapted for use in virtual worlds to facilitate interaction in immersive language tasks.

Nevertheless, implementing such systems requires careful calibration, customisable visual and auditory interfaces, and contextually relevant vocabulary (CAST, 2018; Savickaite, 2023). Failure to address these design factors could possibly result in frustration or disengagement (Bekteshi et al., 2020; Lui et al., 2021), for example, if an AAC device's vocabulary bank contains general or unrelated terms instead of target EFL vocabulary, such as the words and structures currently being taught, it may limit opportunities for practice and meaningful communication, such as role-plays or group discussions.

To prevent issues such as mismatched AAC vocabulary in EFL contexts, involving students and caregivers in the design process, aligned with the "nothing about us without us" principle. (Raymaker, 2020; Savickaite, 2023). This also requires that teachers be prepared to work collaboratively with families, assistive technology specialists, and other professionals to ensure effective integration into learning contexts. For teachers, this co-design approach also supports the development of specialised competencies, like adapting learning materials, integrating multimodal participation strategies, and collaborating effectively with support staff and special education teachers, when and if needed.

Such considerations reflect the principles of UDL, which advocate for multiple means of representation, action, and engagement (CAST, 2018; Meyer et al., 2014; K. Novak & Rose, 2016). Multimodal content delivery, alternative response formats, and personalised sensory inputs all have the potential to contribute to increased accessibility (Borgestig et al., 2016; Lui et al., 2021). And although CP is not typically classified within neurodivergence (T. Armstrong, 2010; Singer, 1999), the pedagogical strategies that benefit neurodivergent learners, such as personalisation, multimodal expression, and differentiated instruction, also apply to students with CP. These approaches also help affirm learners' identities as active members of the language classroom community, ensuring that their contributions are valued and visible, regardless of their mode of expression. As we will see in the next section, these ideas align closely with sociocultural and interactionist principles in language learning, which emphasise that communication skills develop most effectively through meaningful, supported interaction within a learner's zone of proximal development (ZPD, Vygotsky, 1978).

2.3 Challenges to Digital Inclusion

Though awareness of neurodiversity has grown within educational discourse, translating this recognition into truly accessible digital learning environments remains a significant challenge. For example, an autistic learner may experience both sensory overload and attention fatigue during a metaverse-based group task. In a busy virtual classroom filled with moving avatars, flashing icons, and overlapping conversations, the absence of features to reduce on-screen clutter or mute background noise can quickly make the activity disorienting and exhausting. In such cases, the tools intended to increase engagement can, instead, create barriers to participation, reinforcing the earlier point that technology alone does not guarantee equity (see Introduction).

Authors such as Aragon et al. (2024), Creed et al. (2024), and Hupont Torres et al. (2023) highlight the persistent gap between technological potential and inclusive implementation. Structural barriers, including limited teacher training, insufficient guidelines, and resource constraints, undermine the enactment of inclusive policies like Portugal's Decree-Laws 54/2018 and 55/2018 (Portugal. Ministério da Educação, 2018a, 2018b). In practice, these barriers directly impact both teachers and learners in EFL classrooms with many teachers reporting that available professional development on digital tools is either too basic or narrowly focused on specific platforms, leaving them without strategies to adapt immersive technologies for students with diverse cognitive or motor profiles (Cowie & Alizadeh, 2022; Hupont Torres et al., 2023; Stickler & Emke, 2015).

As a result, a teacher may struggle to facilitate collaborative activities in a metaverse-based environment because the interface presupposes fine motor control, or because their training did not address alternative navigation methods (Cowie & Alizadeh, 2022; Creed et al., 2024; Harrison et al., 2024; Hehir et al., 2016). For a neurodivergent learner with ADHD, for example, excessive visual stimuli or multiple simultaneous interaction cues in a busy metaverse space can lead to cognitive overload, making it hard to follow instructions or engage with peers. In such cases, simplifying the environment by, for example, reducing moving objects, or creating clearer visual focal points, can help sustain attention and make the activity more manageable while including the learner in the activity.

Pedagogical inclusion must then go beyond content digitisation. Effective virtual environments must be adaptable, responsive, and accessible, offering tools like screen readers, voice control, and customisable interfaces (Casarez et al., 2023; CAST, 2018). Yet in practice, many digital platforms unintentionally privilege analytic, text-based processing, disadvantaging students who learn best through multimodal or experiential approaches (Bland, 2023; Hu-Au & Lee, 2017; K. Novak & Rose, 2016; Rose & Meyer, 2002). Unless immersive environments are designed with diverse sensory and cognitive processing styles in mind, they risk replicating the same inequities present in traditional materials, only this time in a digital format. Ensuring that accessible technologies translate into meaningful learning experiences requires more than just the right tools; it demands a supportive institutional culture and inclusive pedagogical vision.

School leadership plays a vital role in this transformation, by fostering inclusive digital cultures and supporting professional development (Hehir et al., 2016; Zhang & Zhao, 2019). Such leadership should promote pedagogical approaches that align with these values; as Chen (2024) and Rose (2014) argue, co-constructive pedagogies that empower student agency and personalisation are essential for meaningful digital inclusion.

2.4 Bridges to Inclusive Practice

As established so far, supporting neurodivergent and physically disabled learners requires more than isolated accommodations; it calls for a systemic redesign of learning environments. In an EFL setting, this might mean rethinking lesson formats to include options for oral, written, or visual expression; adapting participation structures to allow both real-time and asynchronous interaction and modifying assessment methods so that success is not solely measured through timed performance. Returning to the earlier example of an autistic EFL learner who also had ADHD, and who found it difficult to sustain attention in a visually busy metaverse-based group task, such redesign could involve offering the same communicative activity in multiple formats, such as simplified VR space with fewer moving objects, muted background visuals, and clearer focal points, combined with the option to contribute responses in short, timed segments. This would allow participation to be possible without cognitive overload while recognising neurological and physical diversity as integral aspects of the human condition, rather than deviations from a norm (Alvarez et al., 2020).

Building on the principles outlined in Section 2.2, UDL provides a framework for redesigning learning environments to offer flexible pathways for participation and engagement (CAST, 2018; K. Novak & Rose, 2016).

In foreign language education, these principles are especially pertinent, as language learning engages multiple cognitive and sensory modalities. For neurodivergent learners, dominant communicative patterns may not align with their preferred ways of expression (Godwin-Jones, 2024; Savickaite, 2023). For instance, a learner who struggles with rapid spoken interaction may excel when given time to respond in writing or through visual media. UDL strategies, such as offering multiple modes for input and output, providing scaffolds, and creating safe spaces for linguistic experimentation, may help bridge this gap (CAST, 2018; Gronseth, 2020).

Moreover, digital environments can support these practices, if designed thoughtfully. Yet many VR applications still neglect accessibility dimensions like 3D navigation or visual sensitivity (Savickaite, 2023). An example of this would be a metaverse-based language activity relying on head-tracking navigation that is inaccessible to students with limited neck mobility. Also, premature adoption without critical reflection may amplify inequities (Creed et al., 2024).

Godwin-Jones (2024) highlights the promise of AI-powered conversational agents, which serve as non-judgmental partners that foster learner autonomy. In immersive environments, these agents can simulate rich communicative contexts, blending verbal and non-verbal elements (Bailenson, 2018; Hupont Torres et al., 2023; Yong et al., 2024). For example, EFL learners could rehearse job interviews with a responsive AI avatar before engaging in live role-plays with peers.

So, aligning UDL with digital innovation thus presents an opportunity for inclusive, transformative pedagogy (Gronseth & Dalton, 2020; K. Novak & Rose, 2016). In practice, this means leveraging immersive tools not simply for novelty, but to provide multiple, flexible pathways for participation, such as in when pairing spoken interaction in a VR environment with visual prompts, text chat, or haptic feedback[4] so that learners can choose the mode that best suits their strengths. Such integration has the potential to lower barriers, foster learner agency, and ensure that technological advancement serves pedagogical equity rather than undermining it.

The next section builds on this foundation, examining how virtual worlds and the metaverse can serve as ethical, dynamic spaces for inclusive language education.

3. FOSTERING INTERACTION, MEDIATION AND AGENCY IN LANGUAGE LEARNING

Understanding how students interact with content, peers, and learning environments is essential to shaping inclusive pedagogy (Bekteshi et al., 2020). W. Chen et al. (2023) further emphasise that such interaction is central to building inclusive, participatory learning spaces. This section explores key theoretical contributions, from interactional and Socioconstructivism perspectives, examining the role of mediation and distributed agency, and connecting these with pedagogical differentiation and curricular flexibility.

3.1 Interaction and the Social Construction of Language

Language is not merely a system of abstract rules, but a situated social practice deeply embedded in interaction and context (Bakhtin, 1981). This sociocultural perspective has shaped research in Second Language Acquisition (SLA), where language learning, particularly in EFL classrooms, is increasingly understood as a socially mediated, multimodal process (Godwin-Jones, 2024). As learners participate in social contexts, they acquire language through embodied, culturally situated communication, and not just through exposure as Godwin-Jones (n.d.) notes.

This orientation, widely developed by authors such as Bakhtin[5] and Vygotsky (1978), positions linguistic development as inseparable from social activity. Vygotsky's insight - that "every function in the child's cultural development appears twice: first on the social level [...] and then inside the child" (1978, p. 57), remains foundational. Recognising this social dimension has strong implications for inclusive language education, particularly for neurodivergent learners with diverse communicative profiles (CAST, 2018; Savickaite, 2023).

This sociocultural orientation highlights interaction not merely as social context, but as the core mechanism through which language development unfolds. It also lays the conceptual groundwork for interactionist theories like Long's, which emphasise negotiated meaning as central to acquisition. For neurodivergent learners, this reinforces the need to design interactional settings that are flexible, scaffolded, and attuned to diverse cognitive and communicative profiles (Lantolf & Thorne, 2006).

Long's (1996) Interaction Hypothesis underscores the centrality of meaning negotiation in authentic interaction. Through feedback, reformulations, and recasts, learners refine their output and integrate new language forms, especially when scaffolded by more competent interlocutors. For example, in an EFL speaking activity, a student might say *"He go to school yesterday,"* prompting a peer to reformulate with *"Oh, he WENT to school yesterday?"* – drawing attention to the past tense form without interrupting the flow of conversation. This negotiation process, rich in semantically contingent speech, connects input with learners' attentional resources and output (Long, 1996).

At this juncture, Vygotsky's (1978) concept of the Zone of Proximal Development (ZPD), i.e. the distance between what a learner can do independently and what they can achieve with guidance, becomes relevant, framing learning as a mediated process supported by interaction. In EFL contexts this often translates into designing activities that stretch learners' abilities without overwhelming them, such as pairing a less proficient speaker with a supportive peer in a role-play task. Intelligent tutoring systems and virtual reality platforms can play a similar mediational role, offering adaptive support tailored to individual needs (Bailenson, 2018; Bekteshi et al., 2020; CAST, 2018; Godwin-Jones, 2024; K. Novak & Rose, 2016). These tools align with Wood, Bruner, and Ross's (1976) scaffolding model, whereby temporary supports are gradually withdrawn as learners gain autonomy.

For neurodivergent learners, such scaffolding may require personalised, visual, or sensory-based approaches that resonate with their processing styles and learning pace (CAST, 2018; Godwin-Jones, 2024; K. Novak & Rose, 2016). For example, the autistic student with ADHD introduced earlier might benefit from a VR-based role-play where prompts and visual clues are presented sequentially rather than simultaneously, reducing sensory overload and attention fatigue, two challenges that often intersect in ADHD-ASD profiles. Importantly, scaffolding must avoid infantilisation, instead supporting autonomy and agency (Creed et al., 2024; Jones & Orchard, 2024; UNESCO, 1994).

Sociocultural theory (SCT) and the Interaction Hypothesis together reposition language learning as a co-constructed activity embedded in meaningful interaction (Lantolf, 2006). Language is a cultural artefact, "the most pervasive and powerful" for mediating our relationship to the world and others (Lantolf & Thorne, 2006, p.201). For some learners, this means that interaction is not just an opportunity for language practice, but a space where pacing, turn-taking, and feedback can be intentionally shaped to accommodate diverse attentional rhythms, sensory preferences, or motor abilities. This perspective reframes the teacher's role as a designer of experiences that prioritise communication and flexibility over form correction (K. Novak & Rose, 2016; Rose & Meyer, 2002).

To operationalise these principles, UDL offers a practical framework for translating inclusive interactional design into concrete classroom practice. It does so by embedding multiple pathways for accessing content, participating in activities, and demonstrating learning, ensuring that the interactional flexibility described above is built into the learning environment from the outset (CAST, 2018; K. Novak & Rose, 2016). This flexibility can take the form of multisensory instruction (digital texts, podcasts, animated videos, or comics) that supports diverse processing preferences (Savickaite, 2023; Suwannawut, 2019). Virtual reality tools further extend these possibilities by enabling sensory-based and individualised feedback (Godwin-Jones, 2024; Koreeda & Tsuge, 2020).

UDL also supports self-regulation strategies through prompts, reflection spaces, and collaborative help-seeking, thereby promoting autonomy (CAST, 2018). This focus on learner agency can be further extended through immersive environments, including simulations and 3D avatar-mediated interactions, which offer powerful tools for expanding access to language learning (W. Chen et al., 2023; Hupont Torres et al., 2023; Mystakidis, 2022). As Godwin-Jones (n.d.) suggests, these spaces facilitate "incidental language learning through informal chats, simulations, and games" (p. 7) which when grounded in inclusive pedagogy, enhance interaction, reduce anxiety, and promote equity.

Thus, conceptualising language as a social practice calls for inclusive, interactive, and multimodal approaches to teaching, grounded in the realities of diverse learners and supported by thoughtful mediation and flexible design (W. Chen et al., 2023; Lantolf, 2006). In EFL, this means creating environments where interaction is not only encouraged but structured to accommodate varied communication styles, processing speeds, and participation preferences, ensuring that more (and ideally all) learners can engage meaningfully with language and with one another.

3.2 The Role of Mediation and Collaboration in the Learning Process

Building on the interactional foundation discussed in Section 3.1, mediation refers to the process through which humans interact with their environment using tools and signs, particularly language, which shape mental functioning in essential ways (Wertsch, 1991). From a sociocultural standpoint, the mind is mediated through cultural artefacts that evolve over generations (Daniels, 2001; Lantolf, 2000; Vygotsky, 1978), which in educational contexts include: peers, teachers, visual aids, and digital platforms (Lantolf & Poehner, 2024). Therefore, effective mediation must be tailored to learners' cognitive and sensory profiles, especially for neurodivergent students for whom one-size-fits-all approaches may lead to exclusion (K. Novak & Rose, 2016; Savickaite, 2023).

One way to operationalise mediation in language education is through a structured, staged process that supports learners as they move from initial exposure to deeper mastery. SCT-informed instruction supports systematic, explicit teaching of language concepts through four interconnected stages: (i) conceptual introduction, where the target idea or skill is first explained (Koreeda & Tsuge, 2020; Lantolf & Poehner, 2024); (ii) visual materialisation, which anchors understanding through diagrams, images, or physical models (K. Novak & Rose, 2016; Savickaite, 2023); (iii) verbalisation or "languaging," in which learners articulate their understanding and test ideas in interaction (Daniels, 2001; Swain, 2000); and (iv) internalisation, when skills or concepts are consolidated through guided and independent practice (Godwin-Jones, n.d.; Lantolf, 2006). Figure 1 shows these stages as a continuous cycle, emphasising how learners move through them in an ongoing process.

Figure 1. Four interconnected stages of SCT-informed instruction (adapted from Koreeda & Tsuge, 2020; Lantolf & Poehner, 2024; and others), illustrating the cyclical process through which learners move from conceptual introduction to internalisation.

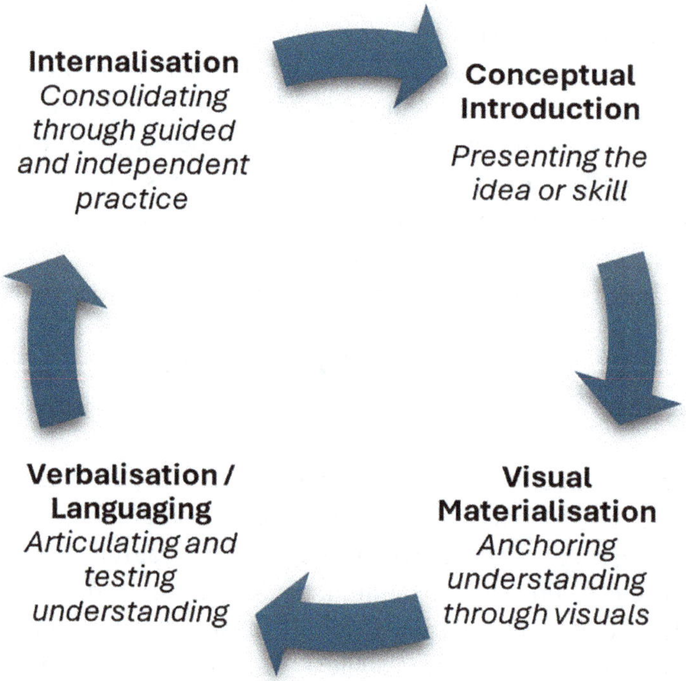

This cycle not only fosters linguistic development but also affirms cognitive diversity by embracing varied mediational modes (CAST, 2018; Rao et al., 2014). This process is further strengthened when embedded in collaborative contexts, where learners build on each other's contributions. Collaboration, more than task division, requires active listening, adaptive communication, and shared meaning-making

(Daniels, 2001; Godwin-Jones, 2024; Long, 1996), stimulating metacognition and linguistic awareness, particularly through feedback and negotiation (Lantolf, 2006; Swain, 2000). Furthermore, Swain's Output Hypothesis (2005) asserts that trying to produce language reveals gaps in knowledge and pushes learners to process language more deeply. This cognitive engagement, often triggered by collaborative work, supports internalisation and accuracy (Long, 1996; Swain, 2000).

For neurodivergent learners, structured group work, with clearly defined roles, predictable routines, and explicit objectives, can support equitable participation and agency (CAST, 2018; Raymaker, 2020). For instance, in an online EFL project, a student who finds spontaneous speaking challenging might summarise discussion points in a shared document, while another contributes through recorded audio comments. Such arrangements ensure that collaboration accommodates diverse strengths and comfort levels. Daniels (2001) describes how mind is co-constructed and distributed within mediated activity, placing responsibility on educators to create interactive, accessible learning conditions.

The concept of distributed agency further illuminates how cognition and participation are shaped by social, material, and institutional factors (Godwin-Jones, 2024; Lock et al., 2020). In EFL, this reminds educators that a learner's ability to engage is shaped by the accessibility of tools, tasks, and social structures, not just individual skills. Mediation and collaboration thus align with UDL principles by promoting environments in which learning is actively co-constructed and supported through multiple means of engagement, representation, and expression.

One such approach is the pedagogy of multiliteracies, which advocates for diverse forms of engagement, including multimodal communication, assistive technology, and digital media (W. Chen et al., 2023; Cope & Kalantzis, 2009; Creed et al., 2024). In practice, this could mean that an EFL learner who struggles with extended writing produces a multimedia project combining short text segments, images, and audio narration. Tasks like visual scripting, collaborative editing, and multimedia presentations offer inclusive entry points and recognise diverse strengths.

Assistive tools, such as alternative keyboards or voice input, can further support learners with motor or speech challenges by enabling them to participate in communicative tasks without being limited by physical constraints. In an EFL class, for example, a student with limited fine motor control might use speech-to-text software to contribute to a group writing project in real time. As Tomlinson (2017) and Hansen (2017) argue, rich, varied, and emotionally meaningful content fosters deeper learning by engaging both analytical and imaginative faculties.

When integrated into digital environments, such assistive tools can further amplify these possibilities by reconfiguring classroom dynamics and expanding opportunities for interaction. Tools such as moderated chats, forums, and virtual spaces allow learners to contribute in formats that suit their processing speed and communication preferences (Germain-Rutherford & Ernest, 2015; Kessler, 2018). As Godwin-Jones (2020) notes, they offer the potential for truly transformative pedagogy.

Finally, inclusive educational research must employ diverse methods - qualitative, multimodal, collaborative - to reflect the complexity of teaching and learning today (Cosme, 2018; Peterson & Jabbari, 2022). Approaches such as learner diaries, multimodal portfolios, and co-designed studies can reflect not only linguistic outcomes but learners' sense of agency and belonging. This ensures that pedagogical design is grounded not only in theory, but in lived, inclusive practice, informing strategies that are responsive to the diversity of EFL classrooms.

3.3 Distributed Agency and the Centrality of the Learner

Language learning involves more than acquiring grammatical structures or memorising vocabulary, as previously mentioned. It is a socially situated process shaped by interaction, mediation, and participation, within cultural, historical, and institutional contexts (Wertsch, 1991). It involves constant choices: what to say, how to say it, when to intervene, through which agency emerges: the learner's ability to influence their own development by acting on goals and using available mediational tools (Swain, 2000).

For neurodivergent learners, who are often subject to normalising approaches that seek to mould them into predetermined patterns (Raymaker, 2020; Savickaite, 2023; Singer, 1999), education should instead provide opportunities to construct lives that reflect their own needs, styles, and assets (T. Armstrong, 2010). This requires a structural transformation of educational environments - one that embeds diversity not as an exception but as an intrinsic value (Suwannawut, 2019). Therefore, this vision demands a rethinking of the learning environment itself, moving from fitting learners to systems toward designing systems around learners.

Central to this paradigm shift is the principle of "*Nothing About Us, Without Us*," which underscores the importance of involving neurodivergent individuals directly in decisions that affect them (Jones & Orchard, 2024; Kapp & Ne'eman, 2020). Here, agency is not simply a matter of choice but of co-creation, with learners shaping their own participation through the tools, contexts, and practices available to them (CAST, 2018; Daniels, 2001; Lantolf & Poehner, 2024; Wertsch, 1991).

Supporting agency, therefore, requires designing environments where options are not tokenistic but meaningful and matched to learners' strengths (CAST, 2018; Ikuta & Hisatsune, 2020). For instance, a learner with ADHD might be offered structured task sequences with embedded breaks, while a student with motor challenges could use speech-to-text or eye-tracking tools, ensuring that mediating resources align with individual needs and foster ownership of the learning process. Tools that match learners' expressive and cognitive needs, such as word-prediction keyboards, visual-assist software, multimodal input systems, or adaptive virtual interfaces, can significantly enhance self-expression and foster a stronger sense of ownership (Creed et al., 2024; Ikuta & Hisatsune, 2020; Yong et al., 2024). In an EFL context, this might mean, for example, allowing a student to use a mind-mapping platform to organise vocabulary visually. These supports, when embedded in lesson design rather than added reactively, normalise diverse ways of communicating and reduce barriers to participation.

Such practices align closely with the broader philosophy of pedagogical differentiation, as articulated by Tomlinson (2014), which is grounded in equity, aiming to provide "access to excellence for every student" (p. 27). Rather than simplifying content, it creates rich, personally relevant experiences that nurture talents and potential (T. Armstrong, 2010; Cope & Kalantzis, 2009; Cosme, 2018; Hehir et al., 2016). Differentiation thus acts as a structural partner to agency, ensuring that learner choice is supported by inclusive design.

Allowing learners to choose topics, formats, or working pace - as proposed by CAST (2018), C. A. Tomlinson (2014), and K. Novak & Rose (2016) - reinforces agency and self-representation which aligns with sociocultural frameworks (Cope & Kalantzis, 2009; Godwin-Jones, 2024; Lantolf & Poehner, 2024) and, for example, is enshrined in Portuguese legislation (DL 54/2018).

These principles strongly align with UDL, which places learner agency at the core of inclusive, accessible education, a connection explored in more detail in Section 3.4.

3.4 Universal Design for Learning: Principles for Building Inclusive Virtual Environments

In a continually evolving educational landscape, marked by increasing diversity and the rapid advancement of emerging technologies, the creation of inclusive learning environments has become a pedagogical imperative. This view is supported by scholars such as T. Armstrong (2010), (CAST, 2018), W. Chen et al. (2023), Creed et al. (2024), and K. Novak & Rose (2016), and is reinforced by key frameworks such as Portugal's Decree-Laws 54/2018 and 55/2018.

This imperative extends beyond accommodating specific challenges, calling for intentional design that is accessible, flexible, and responsive to all learners from the outset (Rao et al., 2014; Rose & Meyer, 2002; Yong et al., 2024).

Originally developed by the Center for Applied Special Technology (CAST), UDL adapts the architectural notions of "design for all from the outset" (Rose & Meyer, 2002) to education, integrating insights from cognitive science and educational neuroscience (CAST, 2018; K. Novak & Rose, 2016). Rather than relying on retrofitted accommodations, it promotes inclusive design from the start, an approach already outlined in section 2.2 and supported by scholars such as Cope & Kalantzis (2009), Hehir et al. (2016), Rao et al. (2014), and C. A. Tomlinson (2014), who argue that learner diversity must be treated as a foundational principle, not an exception.

As outlined earlier, UDL rests on three core principles, or "pillars," that guide pedagogical planning: (i) Multiple Means of Representation, (ii) Multiple Means of Action and Expression, and (iii) Multiple Means of Engagement (CAST, 2018; K. Novak & Rose, 2016; Rose & Meyer, 2002).

These ensure that learners can access content, engage in tasks, and express learning in ways that align with their strengths and needs.

These principles clarify the distinction between **equality** (uniform treatment) and **equity** (different supports for different needs), embedding inclusion through flexible options for accessing content, engaging in tasks, and expressing learning (CAST, 2018; K. Novak & Rose, 2016; Rose & Meyer, 2002). For neurodivergent learners, this flexibility is essential: standard classroom practices, like strictly timed comprehension tests or simultaneous listening and writing tasks, often present significant barriers. By contrast, UDL-aligned environments allow students to choose participation modes, production formats, and working rhythms that match their strengths (Cope & Kalantzis, 2009).

This emphasis on flexibility aligns with cognitive research, particularly Richard Mayer's Multimedia Learning Theory. Mayer (2009) argues that people learn more effectively when words and visuals are presented together rather than separately - this is known as the Multimedia Principle. For example, an EFL learner using a VR scene of a café may understand new vocabulary more easily if they hear the phrases while seeing the related objects, rather than only reading or listening.

However, Mayer also cautions against cognitive overload, which happens when too much information competes for the learner's attention. His Modality Principle suggests that, when showing a visual, spoken explanation is more effective than presenting identical on-screen text, because it spreads processing across sight and hearing (Godwin-Jones, n.d.; Mayer, 2009). The Redundancy Principle further advises avoiding identical text and narration alongside visuals, as it can cause unnecessary mental strain. These guidelines are especially relevant in immersive environments - such as virtual worlds - where learners already process rich visual input and need careful design to focus on the most relevant cues (Aragon et al., 2024; W. Chen et al., 2023; Creed et al., 2024; Mystakidis, 2022; Peterson & Jabbari, 2022).

To address these design challenges, educators and developers must carefully coordinate visual, auditory, and textual elements so they work together rather than compete for attention. This can be done by breaking content into manageable segments and avoiding unnecessary repetition across modes. For example, instead of showing subtitles that exactly match the narration during a VR tour of a historical site, captions could be simplified to key words while the spoken explanation adds details. This reduces mental strain and helps learners focus on meaning rather than juggling identical inputs. Designing for inclusion from the onset means embedding practical tools that reduce barriers and enable authentic self-expression. Avatars, mind maps, audio recordings, and adaptive interfaces, for example, can give neurodivergent students more control over how they participate and communicate (Buckle, 2020; W. Chen et al., 2023; Savickaite, 2023). Such tools are integral to communicative diversity, not optional add-ons (CAST, 2018; K. Novak & Rose, 2016).

It is important to remember that these resources work best when paired with intentional scaffolding and flexible participation options. By allowing learners to select interaction mode, content formats or pacing that align with their strengths, educators move beyond a one-size-fits-all approach and create spaces where participation feels accessible and meaningful from the start (CAST, 2018; Cope & Kalantzis, 2009; K. Novak & Rose, 2016).

This principle is central to the broader philosophy of differentiation, which C. A. Tomlinson (2014) frames not as a set of isolated strategies but as a philosophy rooted in equity. This too aligns with UDL's foundational aim: to reject one-size-fits-all models and embrace learner variability as a starting point (Alvarez et al., 2020). These approaches emphasise that diversity enriches learning, and that flexible, responsive environments enable all students to work toward excellence on their own terms.

UDL's value in immersive environments, then, lies in both removing barriers and embedding equity into the fabric of leaning design from the start. As noted by Menke et al. (2020), W. Chen et al. (2023) and Creed et al. (2024), this requires moving beyond adjustments toward systemic, equity-driven approaches.

The next section builds on this foundation, exploring how immersive technologies, particularly virtual worlds and the metaverse, can enact these principles in practice while addressing the real-world challenges of implementation, equity, and ethics.

4. DESIGNING IMMERSIVE VIRTUAL ENVIRONMENTS TO FOSTER INCLUSIVE LANGUAGE LEARNING

Immersive technologies such as VR and virtual worlds have gained prominence in education, offering the promise of more engaging, personalised, and multisensory learning experiences (Almufarreh & Arshad, 2023; H. J. Chen, 2024). Beyond their novelty, these tools can support neurodivergent learners who face persistent barriers in traditional settings (T. Armstrong, 2010; Ashburner et al., 2008; Dahlstrom-Hakki et al., 2024; Silva et al., 2025).

A wide range of platforms illustrate these possibilities:

- **Browser-based 2D environments** such as *Gather* offer accessible, low-barrier entry points without installation, enabling informal dialogue, small-group interaction, and role-play in low-pressure settings (H. J. Chen, 2024).
- **Social VR platforms** like *Mozilla Hubs*[6], *AltspaceVR*[7], *Engage, Virbela,* and *Second Life* support thematic discussions, scenario-based learning, debates, and guided tours. Their use of avatar, spatialised audio, and customisable settings can enhance pragmatic language skills and provide safe spaces for learners with social anxiety (Altum & Lee, 2020; Cowie & Alizadeh, 2022; Godwin-Jones, 2023; Gomez, 2020; Mystakidis, 2022).
- **Sandbox and game-based worlds such as** *Minecraft: Education Edition* enable project-based tasks, cooperative storytelling, and functional language use embedded in gameplay, particularly effective for younger learners (Bland, 2023; Menke et al., 2020).

These platforms vary in immersion levels - from basic 360° video to fully embodied headset experiences (Mystakidis, 2022), and in their accessibility. While many align with inclusive frameworks such as UDL and differentiated instruction (Harrison et al., 2024; I. Novak et al., 2013; C. A. Tomlinson, 2014), usability limitations, cybersickness risks, and uneven implementation remain (Aragon et al., 2024; CAST, 2018; Harrison et al., 2024; Hehir et al., 2016; Menke et al., 2020).

Augmented Reality (AR) also offers valuable potential. Although not immersive in the same way as VR, AR's ability to augment real-world experiences with digital overlays has been associated with improved learning outcomes across disciplines. In EFL contexts, which rely heavily on sensory, communicative, and social processes, AR serves as a complementary tool. Meta-analyses by Garzón & Acevedo (2019) and Fajari et al. (2023) (though not EFL-specific) support its instructional value, echoing findings from Wu et al. (2024).

Research consistently highlights the motivational and inclusive potential of immersive environments for language learning. Bacca et al. (2014) report increased engagement and motivation, while Melchor-Couto (2016) finds that avatar-mediated communication can lower anxiety in socially anxious learners and promote authentic interaction. Kruk (2022) similarly identifies motivational gains in *Second Life* due to its authentic, interactive features. For students on the spectrum, adjustable VR settings can support sensory regulation and create safe, developmentally appropriate communicative spaces (Silva et al., 2025).

These benefits are maximised when immersive technologies are embedded within inclusive design frameworks, differentiated instruction and when educators have the skill, support, and resources to apply them effectively. The following sections examine these dimensions in turn: pedagogical affordances (4.1), practical design implications (4.2), strategies for supporting neurocognitive diversity (4.3), challenges and ethical considerations (4.4), and the development of educator competencies for inclusive immersive learning (4.5).

4.1 Harnessing the Potential of Immersive Technologies for Language Learning and Teaching

Over the past two decades, immersive technologies, especially VR and AR, have evolved to enable complex, socially meaningful digital spaces such as virtual worlds and the metaverse. Bailenson (2018) describes VR as context where "the user becomes engulfed in a virtual environment that simultaneously engages multiple senses, in ways similar to how we are accustomed to experience things in our daily "real" lives" (p. 38). These affordances allow language learning experiences to be more context-rich, multisensory, and emotionally resonant - conditions often missing from conventional classrooms.

While VR immerses learners in fully digital environments and AR overlays digital content onto the physical world, persistent virtual worlds offer additional affordances such as sustained social interaction, contextualised communication, and continuity of identity (W. Chen et al., 2023; Hupont Torres et al., 2023; Mystakidis, 2022). For example, guided tours of culturally relevant locations and simulated café dialogues in *Second Life* fostered oral communication, with avatar-mediated anonymity reducing anxiety and promoting spontaneity (Bailenson, 2018; Kruk, 2022; Melchor-Couto, 2016). These curriculum-aligned activities reflect content-integrated language learning (Swain, 2000) and demonstrate how immersive tasks can reinforce institutional objectives while embedding inclusivity into classroom practice (Cosme, 2018).

The metaverse, defined as "an interconnected web of social, networked immersive environments in persistent multiuser platforms" (Mystakidis, 2022), extends these possibilities by allowing fluid movement between virtual spaces as noted by H. J. Chen (2024), W. Chen et al. (2023), Godwin-Jones (2024), and Hupont Torres et al. (2023), while retaining avatars and interaction histories, as well as customised identities (Almufarreh & Arshad, 2023; Godwin-Jones, 2024). Such features expand the scope for both human-human and human-AI interaction, fostering sustained presence, co-creation, and collaborative learning (H. J. Chen, 2024; Godwin-Jones, 2024; Hupont Torres et al., 2023; Silva et al., 2025). Table 1 summarises the core distinctions between VR, virtual worlds, and the metaverse in terms of access, experience mode, and interaction modality.

Table 1. Comparative Overview of Virtual Reality, Virtual Worlds, and the Metaverse

Technology	*Interface / Access*	*Experience Mode*	*Interaction Modalities*
Virtual Reality (VR)	VR headsets or compatible mobile/computer setups; enclosed immersive environments	Simulated, immersive, usually individual	Pre-defined, controlled scenarios; guided sensory exploration
Virtual Worlds	Computer, tablet or mobile device; persistent avatar in continuous digital environment	Continuous, social, focused on interacting with other users	Collaborative activities, cultural simulations, communicative tasks
Metaverse	Varied devices (computer, tablet, mobile, VR headsets); interconnected worlds and interoperable platforms	Expansive, multimodal; persistent user identity and a continuous interaction history	Seamless transitions between environments, co-creation, and integrated experiences

While Table 1 outlines structural and technical distinctions between immersive technologies, Table 2 maps these differences against their pedagogical affordances and risks in EFL instruction, with a focus on inclusion and accessibility. The aim is not to prescribe rigid choices but to give educators a practical reference for experimenting with these tools, adapting them to local contexts, and seeking support where needed.

Table 2. Pedagogical affordances and common risks of VR, virtual worlds, and the metaverse in inclusive EFL instruction

Platform	*Key affordances for ELT and Inclusion*	*Common Risks / Limitations*
Virtual Reality (VR)	- Creates highly realistic situations for speaking and listening practice (e.g. role-plays, simulations). - Allows teachers to adjust sound, light, and pace for learners with sensory differences. - Helps make abstract language concepts easier to understand through visual and interactive experiences. - Allows learners to practice safely without fear of making mistakes in public.	- Often needs expensive headsets and equipment. - Can cause cybersickness or sensory overload for some learners. - May be hard to use for learners with mobility difficulties unless designed with alternative controls. - Teachers need ongoing training to use it effectively.
Virtual Worlds	- Offer ongoing spaces for group projects and collaborative stories. - Learners can explore different identities through avatars. - Can lower anxiety by allowing text-based or slower-paced communication. - Usually run on regular computers or tablets.	- Accessibility features vary between platforms. - Open-ended spaces can be distracting. - Some platforms need active moderation to keep learners safe. - Require good internet access.
Metaverse	- Allows learners to move between different virtual spaces while keeping their avatar and progress. - Supports projects with schools or partners in other locations. - Allows communication in many forms (voice, text, objects) and joint creation of content.	- No single standard for accessibility. - Privacy and data safety may be an issue. - More complex for teachers to manage. - Risk of focusing on novelty instead of clear learning goals.

While these considerations are important, they should not discourage experimentation; with creativity, collaboration, and support from colleagues or institutions, many of these tools can be implemented at different scales, allowing educators to explore their potential while adapting to local contexts.

In fact, evidence from different immersive and game-based contexts shows that when these tools are implemented thoughtfully, they can yield tangible language-learning gains. For example, in *Second Life* weekly exchanges with native speakers, improved fluency, and communicative confidence (Kruk, 2022; Melchor-Couto, 2016). Beyond social platforms, digital games can also enhance language skills by creating interactive and motivating contexts (Peterson & Jabbari, 2022; Wu et al., 2024). As Reinders & White (2011) suggest, these digital environments hold promise for fostering learner autonomy, especially when used strategically to support active and self-directed participation.

Immersive 3D environments, especially those powered by advanced VR, extend these benefits by offering personalised and multisensory learning experiences. Studies have shown that such spaces significantly enhance motivation and engagement while adapting to individual learner profiles (Cheng & Tsai, 2019; Hu-Au & Lee, 2017;

Mystakidis, 2022; Radianti et al., 2020; Wehrmann & Zender, 2023). For neurodivergent learners, customisable setting, such as adjustable lighting, background noise, or pacing of visual transitions, can reduce sensory overload and support sustained engagement (Dahlstrom-Hakki et al., 2024; Harrison et al., 2024; Savickaite, 2023). Communication can also take multiple forms, from speech and gesture to symbolic interaction (Silva et al., 2025), broadening participation options.

Such adaptability fosters learner autonomy: learners can explore at their own pace, revisit materials, and participate without immediate peer pressure (Cowie & Alizadeh, 2022; Harrison et al., 2024; Hu-Au & Lee, 2017). This directly aligns with UDL's call for proactively designed experiences that remove barriers from the outset (CAST, 2018; Dalton, 2020). VR can also help manage environmental stimuli, a key factor in sustaining attention and reducing anxiety for learners with ASD, ADHD, or dyslexia (K. Armstrong et al., 2019; Ashburner et al., 2008; Silva et al., 2025).

These affordances - engagement, cognitive and affective skill development, and social interaction – are strengthened when immersive tools are aligned with UDL principles (Menke et al., 2020; Meyer et al., 2014)

However, inclusion requires active involvement of neurodivergent and physically diverse learners in tool design from the beginning. As Aragon et al. (2024) stress, anticipatory design must address challenges such as cybersickness, hardware access, and ethical concerns around privacy and user well-being. Without such participation, advanced technologies risk reinforcing exclusion.

Integrating VR, AR, and virtual worlds with UDL offers a powerful pathway toward equity and accessibility in EFL, creating environments that are flexible, responsive, and designed to accommodate diverse learner profiles from the start.

4.2 Applying UDL Principles to Virtual Environments

As discussed in Section 3.4, UDL offers a robust pedagogical framework for addressing learner diversity. While UDL has been successfully applied in both in-person and hybrid settings (Creed et al., 2024; Edge-Savage & Marotta, 2019; Harrison et al., 2024), its integration into immersive environments - such as virtual worlds and the metaverse - remains comparatively underexplored and seldom subjected to critical scrutiny (Menke et al., 2020; Radianti et al., 2020; Wehrmann & Zender, 2023; Yong et al., 2024). Creating truly inclusive virtual experiences demands deliberate, equity-driven design choices - from technological infrastructure to user interface and learning interactions (Aragon et al., 2024; Dahlstrom-Hakki et al., 2024; Silva et al., 2025). Without intentional planning, immersive environments may recreate, and even worsen, the same barriers that exist in traditional classrooms.

Building on this need for intentional design, Saca (2023) points out that "immersive learning experiences underscore the necessity of following accessible design guidelines, as they risk excluding many learners with disabilities" (p. 4). The author's accessibility guide offers a systematic approach grounded in reflective practice and self-evaluation, encouraging designers to identify and remove sensory, cognitive, and communicative barriers from the earliest stages of development. As Saca (2023) further explains, this process begins with guided reflection on evolving design choices, followed by structured self-assessment to highlight areas for improvement and ensure that accessibility remains a central design principle throughout. While frameworks like those proposed by Saca (2023) and (Yong et al., 2024) represent important starting points, comprehensive discussions of accessibility and inclusion in immersive environments remain limited within the field of language education.

These concerns further highlight why persistent 3D environments are not merely technologically innovative but also pedagogically promising, especially when intentionally designed to reflect inclusive frameworks. Persistent virtual spaces present unique opportunities to implement UDL principles more deeply and flexibly than traditional formats such as e-learning platforms or video-conference sessions. Building on the UDL principles outlined in Section 3.4, immersive virtual environments expand the possibilities for representation, expression, and engagement. For example, virtual worlds incorporate interactive objects, multisensory input, and customizable avatars - features that align with diverse sensory, motor, and linguistic needs in EFL contexts. For instance, VR can generate simulated environments, either mirroring the real world or constructing imaginative alternatives, to offer experiences not feasible in traditional classrooms (Almufarreh & Arshad, 2023)

This technology is particularly valuable in helping students recognise and explore abstract or hard-to-observe knowledge within risk-free settings, enabling more accurate representations of processes and systems (Almufarreh & Arshad, 2023). VR also enhances student engagement by integrating sensory inputs, including visual, auditory, olfactory, haptic, and even gustatory perception, into the learning experience. Furthermore, it enables constructivist learning through the creation of visual and manipulable objects that represent knowledge, making abstract concepts more tangible and meaningful, particularly in experiential or inquiry-based contexts (Hu-Au & Lee, 2017). Research has shown that such immersive environments not only support general learning but also benefit students with lower proficiency levels by offering individualised, concrete learning spaces tailored to their needs (Hu-Au & Lee, 2017).

These affordances are relevant in the context of EFL instruction, where abstract linguistic structures, such as tense, modality, or figurative language can be made more accessible through embodied, visual, and interactive representations. Specifically for learners with ASD, VR provides a controlled and highly customisable environment that can be adapted to their sensory and cognitive needs, allowing them to visualise and manipulate abstract concepts safely and effectively. It promotes inclusion by creating learning opportunities that may be inaccessible in traditional teaching environments and facilitates multi-channel communication through gestures, object manipulation, and symbolic interactions - modalities particularly relevant for students who struggle with verbal expression (Silva et al., 2025). An example of this would be a learner with CP, who might participate in a collaborative EFL storytelling task in a VR environment using adaptive controllers and voice-to-text input, allowing them to contribute ideas and negotiate meaning with peers without the physical strain of conventional writing tasks.

In an immersive virtual environment, a learner who finds abstract concepts difficult to grasp via text can observe those concepts in motion, interact with them contextually, and engage experientially, enhancing both understanding and retention (Bacca et al., 2014). Representation thus evolves beyond multimodality into an inherently experiential process.

Although the value of inclusive pedagogies is increasingly recognised, students with intellectual disabilities remain significantly underrepresented in general education contexts. In this regard, UDL stands out as a particularly promising framework. Rao, Smith, and Lowrey (2017) argue that it "has the potential to support meaningful inclusion of students with intellectual disability in general educational settings" (p. 37), underlining its ability to foster more active and substantive participation. This vision of inclusion becomes even more actionable when UDL principles are applied in immersive digital contexts, where the second pillar, multiple means of action and expression, can be more fully realised.

This second UDL principle gains new depth in virtual worlds, moving far beyond traditional writing or speaking modalities. Within immersive spaces, learners can act, explore, collaborate, and communicate through customised avatars situated in rich, simulated environments. Among these, VR stands out as a particularly powerful tool, offering heightened levels of presence, interactivity, and cognitive engagement that extend the affordances of virtual worlds. It addresses persistent educational challenges such as learner disengagement or the difficulty of teaching abstract concepts and 21st-century skills like empathy. VR enables immersive, hands-on learning experiences designed for active exploration and problem-solving, closely aligning with constructivist pedagogies (Wehrmann & Zender, 2023).

In Melchor-Couto's (2016) study, Spanish learners engaged in oral activities within Second Life's adapted settings, such as cafés and cinemas. These spaces facilitated realistic, curriculum-aligned communicative practice and nurtured deep emotional and social engagement. The author observed that such environments "bring learners together in realistic communicative scenarios that can contribute to a more meaningful learning experience" (p. 102), noting a marked reduction in communicative anxiety over time.

The same adaptive features that support shy or anxious learners also hold promise for neurodivergent students. For example, digital games have been shown to dismantle participation barriers by offering self-paced, feedback-rich environments that boost academic performance and motivation (Harrison et al., 2024). The use of assistive technologies - such as text-to-speech tools or writing organisers - can be normalised within inclusive classrooms, allowing all students to self-monitor performance, manage cognitive load, and prevent fatigue (Harrison et al., 2024). Peer-to-peer learning and multimodal contributions foster agency and social skill development, particularly for autistic learners, in ways that are less anxiety-inducing than traditional settings.

Importantly, in virtual worlds, these modes of expression do not compete but coexist harmoniously - an affordance of particular value in EFL contexts. One learner might choose to chat, another might record a voice message, and another might construct a virtual object to demonstrate understanding. This expressive flexibility supports authentic, personally meaningful communication that fosters fluency and confidence. Multimodal curriculum design provides neurodivergent learners with opportunities to use their preferred communication modes, including virtual whiteboards or alternative devices, thereby enhancing inclusion, and belonging (Harrison et al., 2024).

The third UDL principle - multiple means of engagement - becomes transformative within immersive environments. Here, learners can craft their own learning paths, engaging in meaningful, interactive experiences that are novel and hands-on. As Hu-Au & Lee (2017) note, VR inherently boosts engagement by enabling learners to construct their own knowledge through lived experience. In EFL settings, features like avatar customisation, storytelling, and gamification foster agency, belonging, and sustained motivation. Learners embody roles, co-construct narratives, and receive immediate feedback - creating authentic communicative contexts where language becomes purposeful and adaptive.

As Mystakidis (2022) explains, "online learning in social VR allows the wider deployment of game-based learning methods." These include playful design, gamification, and serious games (p. 491). Avatar-based identity building and shared presence in virtual spaces further contribute to inclusion and active engagement (H. J. Chen, 2024; Hupont Torres et al., 2023; Mystakidis, 2022). The sense of presence within these environments has been consistently linked to increased motivation and deeper learning immersion (Wehrmann & Zender, 2023).

While many platforms are not specifically designed for neurodivergent learners, their flexibility makes them powerful tools for fostering self-regulation and emotional and cognitive development, provided they are designed with clear pedagogical intent. As Wehrmann & Zender (2023) note, effective immersive design requires well-defined roles and goals, particularly in multi-user environments, to help learners develop strategies and sustain self-regulated learning.

The table below outlines how each of the three UDL principles can be enacted within immersive environments, providing concrete examples of their practical implementation in educational settings.

Table 3. Implementing UDL Principles in Immersive Virtual Environments

UDL Principle	*Implementation in Immersive Environments*	*Examples*
Multiple representation	Deliver content via multiple modalities - text, audio, video, 3D objects, and sensory interactions - while providing user-controlled navigation and integrated accessibility features.	Learners can listen to explanations delivered by avatars, engage with interactive simulations, or review transcripts supplemented by visual aids.
Multiple expression	Diverse modes of response and participation - such as creating virtual objects, role-playing with avatars, collaborative writing, or recording one's voice.	Learners can collaboratively enact a professional scenario within a virtual environment or create a thematic installation that showcases content they have researched.
Engagement	Learner autonomy in selecting their own pathways, customizing avatars, controlling the pace, and having safe environments for emotional self-regulation.	Learners can select level-appropriate challenges, opt for chat-based communication instead of voice, and retreat to designated sensory break areas.

Almufarreh & Arshad (2023) emphasise that the promise of emerging educational technologies, such as VR, AR, AI, and IoT (Internet of Things), hinges on embedding them within a learner-centred pedagogical framework that cultivates autonomy, digital literacy, and authentic engagement. Without this foundation, aspects such as poorly accessible menus, invisible feedback, or invasive tasks can counteract the benefits of immersion (Almufarreh & Arshad, 2023). This emphasis on design integrity aligns with UDL principles, reinforcing the notion that genuine inclusion requires thoughtful and universal design from the outset, not after the fact.

Yong et al. (2024) argue that the implementation of immersive technologies without a purposefully inclusive pedagogical framework can undermine their effectiveness and exacerbate existing inequities. As the authors observe, "the diversity of user profiles and their specific needs have frequently been an afterthought of technology design, if considered at all" (Yong et al., 2024). Consequently, many products and experiences fall short of adequately supporting the most vulnerable users.

Such design oversights are especially detrimental to marginalised groups, including Indigenous communities, ethnic minorities, women, LGBTQ+ individuals, and users with physical, sensory, or cognitive disabilities, who are already at heightened risk of exclusion (Yong et al., 2024). Hence, the development of Virtual Reality

Learning Applications (VRLAs) must be explicitly grounded in inclusive educational theory in order to avoid inadvertently excluding those learners.

In this context, true inclusion transcends basic technical accessibility. As previously discussed, it entails actively engaging with the needs, perspectives, interests, traditions, and protocols of all learners, and involving them in the design process, so that they can genuinely benefit from the resulting tools and environments (Yong et al., 2024). Without this participatory approach, immersive technologies risk undermining not only accessibility but also their cultural legitimacy, experiential authenticity, and educational effectiveness.

Moreover, Yong et al. (2024) caution that user-centred and participatory design approaches often fall short when they focus narrowly on individuals, overlooking the communal identities and shared practices that shape how learners interact. In virtual worlds and metaverse platforms, failure to acknowledge collective cultural dimensions can result in technically sophisticated environments that nonetheless feel socially alienating. By contrast, a community-centred design ethos ensures that immersive educational spaces honour group norms and promote collaboration, enhancing both cultural relevance and equitable engagement.

This shift in perspective - viewing communities as co-creators of immersive experiences - challenges conventional paradigms of designing *for* or *about* users and instead supports processes co-developed *with* and *by* users themselves (Yong et al., 2024). It also affirms the fundamental human right to equal representation of users from different ages, cultures, abilities, genders, languages, and religions in the development of next-generation virtual worlds and metaverses (Hupont Torres et al., 2023). As Yong and colleagues (2024) observe, research on inclusive, participatory VR design remains in its early stages, suggesting the need for continued critical inquiry.

While stepping into a virtual world may resemble entering a video game, the purpose within education fundamentally shifts - from completing pre-programmed tasks to fostering authentic interaction, communication, and shared educational experiences. Although the consumer market for VR is largely geared toward entertainment, its educational potential lies in creating dynamic learning activities, such as survival scenarios, storytelling games, and simulations, that prioritise connection, imagination, and reflection (W. Chen et al., 2023; Dahlstrom-Hakki et al., 2024; Peterson & Jabbari, 2022). These platforms enable "a learning community where learners can communicate, learn, and share despite different venues and geographical barriers" (W. Chen et al., 2023), and establish new forms of social learning, where "teacher-to-student or peer-to-peer learning can take place in virtual spaces without the limitations of physical space" (Hupont Torres et al., 2023).

Silva et al. (2025) highlights that VR offers "free navigation and autonomy in learning," (p. 3) enabling students to "move freely and explore three-dimensional environments" and "control their own pace of exploration and repetition of tasks" (p. 3). These affordances echo the core premise of UDL - that "each student can benefit from a flexible curriculum" (Suwannawut, 2019, p. 21) - and guide educators to "design learning based on the varied needs and interests of students, "fostering" flexible conditions that ensure access and participation by all students (Lock et al., 2020).

As Lyner-Cleophas (2020) observes, when "instructional materials are designed from the start with the variability of people in mind," individual differences are supported proactively, eliminating the need for retrofitting or accommodation. Menke et al., (2020) provide "guidelines and checklists for three UDL principles - 1) representation, 2) action and expression, and 3) engagement - to guide the design, selection, and application of learning tools, methods, and environments" (p.295).

Inclusion, in its broadest sense, is a "continuous process that ensures equal participation by removing barriers and promoting accessibility" for "all students, regardless of their backgrounds and abilities" (Wehrmann & Zender, 2023, p.74). This imperative extends to the virtual realm, where ethical considerations and societal inequities must be addressed with the same commitment as in the physical world (Hupont Torres et al., 2023). In the next section, we further this commitment by focusing specifically on neurodiversity - examining how virtual worlds can support learners with atypical cognitive profiles, unique sensory needs, and how these considerations intersect with EFL learning objectives.

4.3 Supporting Neurocognitive Diversity through Flexible Virtual Learning Environments

As established throughout this chapter, drawing on numerous authors, diverse learning profiles - including neurodivergent learners and those with neuromotor conditions such as cerebral palsy - require pedagogical strategies rooted in flexibility, personalised support, and the validation of multiple forms of participation. Neurodivergent individuals, whose neurological differences affect how they perceive and interact with the world, may process, store, and retrieve information differently, including those diagnosed with ASD and ADHD (Koreeda & Tsuge, 2020; Savickaite, 2023).

Pedagogical responses must therefore be attuned to varied needs, offering differentiated methods of engagement, representation, and expression (Lock et al., 2020). Personalised planning, aligned with learners' interests and preferences, further enables inclusive participation and supports knowledge, skill development, and motivation (K. Novak & Rose, 2016; Suwannawut, 2019).

T. Armstrong's (2010) concept of neurocognitive diversity encompasses a broad range of neurological variations that influence attention, communication, sensory processing, and self-regulation. These include sensory processing differences, distractibility, challenges in verbal and non-verbal communication (T. Armstrong, 2010; Savickaite, 2023), and difficulties with self-regulation (Lantolf, 2006). A key executive function underpinning these processes is cognitive flexibility - "thinking outside the box" and adapting to shifting demands or priorities (Diamond, 2013, p.135). It is crucial for problem-solving in "ill-structured domains" (Kapur, 2008, p.161) and, as Diamond (2013) emphasises, "more important for school readiness than IQ or entry-level reading or math skills" (p. 138). These capacities - working memory, inhibitory control, and cognitive flexibility - are central to learning and development (CAST, 2018; Diamond, 2013; Harrison et al., 2024; K. Novak & Rose, 2016).

This aligns with T. Armstrong (2010) advocacy for "niche construction," whereby learners "alter the environment to match the needs of their own unique brains" (p. 16). Inclusive pedagogical design must therefore allow for diverse modes of processing and expression (T. Armstrong, 2010; Harrison et al., 2024; K. Novak & Rose, 2016).

Immersive platforms such as the metaverse have been shown to boost engagement and support active participation, especially in blended or online learning contexts (W. Chen et al., 2023). Research has shown that VR can increase motivation, foster empathy, and creativity, and enable learners to visualise abstract concepts (Hu-Au & Lee, 2017). Such environments are often "customisable, actively engaging, and self-paced" (Hu-Au & Lee, 2017, p.219) and feature gamified and skills-based learning structures (Hupont Torres et al., 2023).

In their research, different authors identified different affordances of immersive environments:

- Personalised language practice: AI-powered VR supports adaptive, customised learning experiences and storylines (Godwin-Jones, 2024). In an EFL context, this could translate into adaptive role-play dialogues that adjust vocabulary complexity and grammar structures according to learner performance.
- Exploration of diverse identities: Learners adopt avatars and discourse styles that support identity construction and influence behaviour through the Proteus effect[8] as reported by Godwin-Jones (n.d.) and Mystakidis (2022).
- Safe, low-pressure experimentation: Research by Hu-Au & Lee, 2017; Mystakidis, 2022; Silva et al., 2025) among others has shown learners can take risks and learn from mistakes without real-world repercussions, lowering anxiety and boosting confidence.
- Learner autonomy: Students can move freely, repeat tasks, and set their own pace - crucial for engagement and retention (Silva et al., 2025).

To ensure inclusive access, these environments can incorporate features such as:

- Real-time captions for auditory content (Aragon et al., 2024; Wehrmann & Zender, 2023).
- Adjustable text-to-speech voice-overs and dynamic digital texts to improve literacy (Harrison et al., 2024; Suwannawut, 2019).
- Eye-gaze selection systems for learners with physical impairments (Borgestig et al., 2016; Hupont Torres et al., 2023; Yong et al., 2024).
- Visual cues and spatial design to support reading comprehension, organisation, and sensory regulation (Harrison et al., 2024; Menke et al., 2020; Wehrmann & Zender, 2023).

These adaptations align with UDL's emphasis on multiple means of representation and are particularly valuable for learners with sensory and motor differences. VR enables multisensory control (visual, audio, olfactory, haptic, gustatory) (Almufarreh & Arshad, 2023), allowing for finely tuned sensory input (Dahlstrom-Hakki et al., 2024; Silva et al., 2025).

For learners with cerebral palsy, avatar personalisation can extend self-expression into the virtual realm (H. J. Chen, 2024; Mystakidis, 2022). Participation is enhanced through multiple expressive modes, including speech, gesture, and symbolic interaction (Brusca-Vega & Trekles, 2020; Silva et al., 2025; Wehrmann & Zender, 2023).

In the context of ADHD, structured virtual environments help regulate stimuli and reduce overload (Dahlstrom-Hakki et al., 2024; Harrison et al., 2024; Koreeda & Tsuge, 2020; Silva et al., 2025). Virtual learning worlds thus offer a compelling model for inclusive education (Menke et al., 2020; Rose & Meyer, 2002; Wehrmann & Zender, 2023), contributing to autonomy, emotional security, and intellectual stimulation.

In sum, flexible virtual environments grounded in UDL can foster inclusive, engaging, and creative learning. By embracing diversity from the outset - not as a problem to fix, but as a strength to build upon - education can become more inclusive, engaging and equitable (Banes & Behnke, 2020; Cope & Kalantzis, 2009).

4.4 Considerations, Challenges, and Best Practices for Implementing Immersive Activities

The integration of immersive virtual environments into language teaching requires more than technological enthusiasm. It demands a sustained pedagogical commitment to equitable access, meaningful participation, and learner well-being, particularly for those whose neurocognitive or motor profiles differ from conventional norms (Cowie & Alizadeh, 2022; Silva et al., 2025). This imperative is rooted in inclusive education frameworks and supported by growing research on accessibility in virtual worlds (Creed et al., 2024; Hupont Torres et al., 2023; Saca, 2023; Savickaite, 2023).

As Bland (2023) asserts, inclusion cannot rest on rhetorical acknowledgment alone; it must inform pedagogical decisions at every level, from material selection to the creation of linguistically rich, emotionally safe learning environments.

This includes leveraging the affordances of immersive platforms, such as avatar customisation, sensory adaptation, and asynchronous participation, to reduce barriers and support diverse learners. Yet these affordances, while promising, are not neutral. Their benefits are shaped by the intentions behind their design and the frameworks guiding their use. As explored in previous sections, immersive environments aligned with UDL can provide flexible pathways for engagement, expression, and representation. However, without purposeful mediation and ethical consideration, the same technologies may reproduce or deepen the very inequities they are meant to address.

This tension between technological potential and ethical responsibility has been the focus of recent studies. Creed et al. (2024), for example, conducted two multidisciplinary "sandpits" that brought together academic researchers, AR/VR industry specialists, assistive technologists, disability advocates, and people with lived experience of physical, sensory, and cognitive impairments. Their findings confirmed both the promise and the pitfalls of immersive learning. Despite increased attention to accessibility, many commercial AR/VR tools continue to present substantial barriers. The study identified 49 challenges, grouped across four core domains: software usability, hardware usability, ethics, and collaboration and interaction (p.66, Table 3).

Their findings point to a critical reality: the growing adoption of immersive technologies, especially with the rise of the metaverse, could deepen educational exclusion if equity considerations are not embedded from the start (Aragon et al., 2024; Creed et al., 2024; Mystakidis, 2022; Silva et al., 2025). Yong et al. (2024) further note that many design frameworks adopt abstract, decontextualised notions of users, overlooking collective cultural practices and the structural factors shaping access. As they observe, "the research on inclusive participatory design in VR is in its infancy" (p. 2816), and the specific characteristics of learners must be "directly considered in the design of VR experiences to ensure proper inclusion" (p. 2817)[9].

Bridging the gap between pedagogical affordances and equitable implementation requires translating inclusive frameworks into concrete instructional practices. As established in earlier sections, immersive platforms should be grounded in UDL from the start - not retrofitted after deployment. Flexibly designed environments allow learners - particularly those with neurodivergent profiles - to modulate social and sensory input, supporting focus, autonomy, and emotional regulation (K. Novak & Rose, 2016; Rose & Meyer, 2002; Saca, 2023; Wehrmann & Zender, 2023). Dahlstrom-Hakki et al. (2024) similarly emphasise that control over ambient stimuli is crucial for maintaining engagement and reducing overload. To operationalise these principles, environments must incorporate adjustable input modalities, varied interaction formats, and options for pacing and feedback. Visual scaffolds, intuitive interfaces, and multimodal communication tools are essential design elements - not optional features (Bland, 2023; Cowie & Alizadeh, 2022; Savickaite, 2023; Silva et al., 2025). Yet inclusive design alone is not sufficient. Implementation also hinges on educator readiness.

Teacher training is key to this process. Many educators lack formal preparation in immersive tools and accessible design, often relying on peer support or self-directed online resources (Cowie & Alizadeh, 2022). Reinders and White (2011) stress the importance of fostering both learner autonomy and teacher agency in evolving digital contexts. Godwin-Jones (2024) similarly calls for sustained teacher development focused on immersive pedagogies. As such, professional development must address both technological fluency and inclusive pedagogy - including accessibility standards, UDL, and assistive technologies.

A gradual, collaborative approach is recommended. Pilot trials, co-design with learners, and iterative feedback cycles can support contextual adaptation (Radianti et al., 2020; Silva et al., 2025). Cross-sector engagement, involving educators, technology developers, policymakers, and learners, can foster sustainable adoption and ensure that solutions are aligned with both pedagogical and accessibility needs. (Creed et al., 2024; Harrison et al., 2024; Yong et al., 2024).

Despite these efforts, unequal access to immersive tools remains a major challenge. Disparities in digital infrastructure, funding, and technical support across socio-economic, geographic, and institutional lines significantly hinder implementation (Almufarreh & Arshad, 2023; Bland, 2023; Godwin-Jones, 2024; Wang et al., 2024). As Warschauer (2004) observed, "the key element is not necessarily the number of computers in the classroom but rather how they are best used" (p.12). Quoting Pimienta (2002), Warschauer (2004) calls for students to be viewed not as "from behind a screen but rather in front of a keyboard" (p.12), which remains relevant in today's immersive learning environments. Ensuring equity requires more than devices - it requires culturally responsive use, digital literacy, and technical scaffolding for both learners and families (Comas-Quinn & Borthwick, 2015; Molnar, 2019).

Ethical safeguards are also essential, particularly when working with young learners or vulnerable populations. Unregulated virtual spaces, biometric data and metadata collection, and prolonged sensory exposure carry risks that must be addressed. Bailenson (2018), Silva et al., (2025), and Aragon et al. (2024) warn that excitement about emerging tools often overshadows fundamental questions of consent, safety, and long-term cognitive impact.

To mitigate these risks, several priorities emerge. First, environments should include core accessibility features, such as adjustable voice-overs, eye-gaze navigation, and automated captions (CAST, 2018; Karlsson et al., 2019; Saca, 2023). Second, learners should participate in the evaluation and refinement of their immersive experiences (Saca, 2023; Silva et al., 2025). Third, activities must align with curriculum goals and learner interests to ensure relevance and authenticity (Bland, 2023; Hu-Au & Lee, 2017). Fourth, robust ethical protocols - particularly around informed consent and data protection - must be in place.

As Silva et al. (2025) and Savickaite (2023) make clear, inclusive education in virtual settings cannot rely on technology alone. It must be guided by a learner-centred framework that affirms agency, protects dignity, and ensures genuine access - across both physical and virtual domains.

While these considerations highlight the technical, pedagogical, and ethical dimensions of implementing immersive environments, their successful translation into classroom practice ultimately depends on the people designing and facilitating them. In inclusive EFL contexts, this places a central responsibility on educators, whose competencies, working conditions, and access to professional development directly shape the feasibility and impact of immersive learning.

4.5 Teacher Competencies for Inclusive Immersive Learning

The successful implementation of immersive technologies in inclusive EFL education depends not only on the availability of platforms and resources but also on the readiness and capacity of educators to integrate them in ways that are pedagogically sound, equitable, and responsive to learner diversity. This asks for a convergence of technological proficiency, pedagogical expertise, and awareness of accessibility and privacy concerns, underpinned by continuous professional development. Frameworks such a UNESCO's ICT Competency Framework for Teachers (2018) and the European Framework for Digital Competence of Educators (Redecker & Punie, 2017) (DigCompEdu) provide structured guidance for developing these competencies, emphasising inclusive design, accessibility, and the ethical use of digital resources. The UNESCO framework, for instance, explicitly positions UDL as a cross-cutting principle, requiring teachers to create flexible goals, methods, and assessments that meet diverse student needs. As it states "[c]urriculum designers and teachers need to be aware that students with disabilities must have access to all components of the learning process" (UNESCO, 2018, p.17), highlighting a direct link between professional competence and educational equity.

A comprehensive skill set for immersive learning includes the ability to select and adapt virtual environments to match curricular objectives, integrate assistive technologies to accommodate different cognitive and sensory profiles, and implement strategies that mitigate known risks such as sensory overload, cybersickness, or data privacy breaches (Dick, 2021; Miller et al., 2020). For example, an EFL teacher working with the autistic student with ADHD described earlier might design a VR-based conversational role-play in which visual prompts are displayed sequentially rather than all at once, reducing cognitive load, and audio cues are adjusted to minimise background noise, addressing both attention and sensory sensitivities. Such design choices require not only familiarity with VR settings but also the pedagogical insight to align them with UDL principles and individual learning goals.

However, these expectations place a considerable burden on educators who, in many contexts such as Portugal, already work under significant strain. Large class sizes, high teaching loads across multiple groups and levels, and the presence of learners with additional support needs are often not accompanied by proportional institutional support, whether in the form of (truly) smaller classes, (considerable) reduced timetables, or access to specialist assistance. Teacher education programmes, including master's degrees in EFL teaching, frequently devote limited attention to inclusive pedagogies for learners requiring additional support measures, and rarely address cutting-edge technological innovations in a sustained, practical way. Schools may also face material and infrastructural accessibility barriers, limited funding, and at times a lack of institutional will to experiment with new approaches. As a result, the gap between policy aspirations and classroom realities can be substantial. Expecting burnt-out, or inexperienced teachers to independently design and implement sophisticated immersive learning scenarios is unrealistic without robust systemic scaffolding. Instead, effective practice requires a proper structure in which educators can draw on existing, approved, and tested immersive scenarios and tasks, with the option to adapt or develop new ones as their time, skills, and interest allow, thus shifting the focus from individual burden to collective capacity.

Professional development in this area benefits from embedding technology-related competencies into ongoing training rather than treating them as one-off workshops. Tondeur et al. (2015) stress the need to cultivate "more generic competences" that can be applied across technologies and subject domains, avoiding over-specialisation in tools that may quickly become obsolete. Embedding such competencies in both pre-service and in-service training aligns with UNESCO's (2018) ICT Competency Framework for Teachers and the European Commission's DigCompEdu model (Redecker & Punie, 2017), both of which emphasise accessibility, inclusion, and the capacity to critically assess and adapt digital tools. When combined with institutional policies that ensure equitable access to resources and sustained peer collaboration, such approaches can make immersive learning a realistic and sustainable option rather than an added strain on already overstretched teachers. To make this balance between teacher skill, classroom realities, and systemic support clearer, Table 4 summarises the core immersive learning skills discussed, the most common barriers to their implementation, and the types of systemic support that can help bridge the gap between policy and practice.

Table 4. Skills, Barriers, and Systemic supports for Inclusive immersive learning

Core Skills for Immersive Learning	*Common Barriers*	*Systemic Support Needed*
Selecting and adapting VR/AR environments to align with curricular objectives and UDL principles	Limited teacher time; lack of tested, ready-to-use scenarios	Access to curated, pre-approved immersive scenarios with adaptation guidelines
Integrating assistive technologies for diverse cognitive and sensory profiles	Insufficient training; unfamiliarity with tools	Targeted training on assistive tech integration, co-design with specialists
Mitigating risks such as sensory overload, cybersickness, and data privacy breaches	Lack of awareness; limited technical control over school-owned devices	Clear institutional policies; built-in safety settings; privacy-compliant platforms
Designing tasks that balance immersion with cognitive load	Overcrowded curricula, high teacher workload	Shared resource banks with differentiated task templates
Providing personalised feedback in immersive contexts	Limited technical proficiency; time constraints	Automated feedback tools integrated into VR/AR platforms
Aligning immersive activities with inclusive pedagogies and learner agency	Lack of inclusion-focused training in pre-service programmes	Embedding inclusive digital pedagogy modules in teacher education

Part of this professional readiness includes understanding the legal and ethical frameworks that govern immersive learning environments. An important dimension of educator competence is the ability to navigate the privacy and security implications of immersive learning environments. VR and AR systems collect vast amounts of biometric and behavioural data. Often in ways that challenge existing consent frameworks (Dick, 2021; Roesner et al., 2014). Teachers therefore need to develop awareness of what data is collected, how it is processed, and how to apply relevant standards such as the Web Content Accessibility Guidelines (WCAG 2.2) (World Wide Web Consortium (W3C), 2023) and institutional privacy policies. This is particularly pertinent in inclusive settings, where vulnerable learners may be at greater risk of harm from misuse of personal or behavioural data. Embedding privacy literacy into teacher training ensures that educators can make informed choices about platform selection and classroom protocols. These considerations align with international regulatory frameworks such as the EU General Data Protection Regulation (GDPR)(European Parliament and Council of the European Union, 2016) and the U.S. Children's Oline Privacy Protection Act (COPPA)(U.S. Federal Trade Commission, 2013), which provide essential safeguards for inclusive digital learning.

The pedagogical dimension is equally critical. Research emphasises that effective integration of immersive technologies requires aligning them with learning theories such as experiential learning, constructivism, and cognitive load theory (Marougkas et al., 2023; Won et al., 2023). Teachers should be able to design tasks that leverage the strengths of immersive environments, such as embodied interaction and contextualised language use, while avoiding pitfalls such as cognitive overload or inequitable access. For instance, pairing high-end VR headsets for interactive simulations with lower-cost, phone-based VR options can expand participation in resource-limited contexts without diluting learning outcomes, a strategy identified in accessibility-focused immersive learning studies (Won et al., 2023).

Ultimately, developing educator competencies for inclusive immersive learning is not simply a matter of mastering technical tools; it is about cultivating the ability to design, implement, and evaluate experiences that are inclusive from the outset, grounded in UDL, and responsive to the social, emotional, and cognitive realities of diverse learners. By combining structured frameworks like the ICT Competency Framework for Teachers and the DigCompEdu with reflective, practice-based professional learning, educators can position immersive technologies not as novelty add-ons, but as integrated, ethical, and empowering spaces for language learning.

5. CONCLUSION AND FUTURE DIRECTIONS

Integrating immersive environments into language education stands as one of the most promising, and simultaneously demanding, frontiers of pedagogical innovation. As explored throughout this chapter, when immersive technologies such as virtual worlds and the metaverse are implemented thoughtfully and responsibly, and underpinned by UDL principles, they hold significant potential to enhance inclusivity in language learning. Far from being merely technological tools, these environments offer new ways to personalise instruction, support learner agency, and accommodate diverse cognitive and sensory needs.

Examining the opportunities, challenges, and best practices surrounding immersive environments makes it clear that adopting new platforms alone is insufficient. This chapter has explored four interrelated strands: it clarified the nature and educational affordances of virtual worlds and the metaverse; critically examined their pedagogical potential and limitations; discussed inclusive design principles for neurodivergent and physically disabled students; and proposed actionable strategies for equitable integration in EFL instruction. These explorations were unified by UDL as a guiding framework, reaffirming the central argument that true inclusion requires more than access - it demands learner-centred, ethically grounded design. What is needed is the careful crafting of pedagogical experiences that honour the full spectrum of learners' cognitive, sensory, social, and emotional diversity. These experiences must move beyond surface-level inclusion to offer meaningful, personalised, and empowering learning pathways. When designed with this intent, immersive environments can cultivate agency, personalise learning, and promote communicative competence through authentic, context-rich settings.

Nonetheless, immersive environments also carry significant risks. Without intentional design, they may exacerbate existing inequities and exclude already marginalised learners - particularly those with limited technological access or digital literacy. Inadequate moderation, cognitive overload, or culturally insensitive content may heighten stress, especially for neurodivergent users. These spaces are not inherently neutral; their impact is shaped by the pedagogical choices that inform them.

To ensure inclusion moves beyond rhetorical commitment, sustained investment is required across three critical areas: comprehensive teacher development, accessible infrastructure, and ethically grounded instructional design. Educators must be equipped not only with technological fluency but also with training in accessibility, inclusive pedagogies, and UDL principles.

Equally crucial is the creation of infrastructure that accommodates diverse needs and mitigates access barriers - physical, cognitive, and socioeconomic. Meanwhile, instructional design must align pedagogical purpose with ethical awareness, embedding flexibility, representation, and learner agency at its core.

Practical priorities for inclusive immersive EFL learning include:

- Plan for inclusion from the beginning – integrate UDL principles and accessibility features into the earliest design stages.
- Offer multiple ways to participate and respond – combine voice, text, visual, and interactive options to suit different learner profiles.
- Design with diversity in mind – anticipate cognitive, sensory, and motor differences when creating tasks, from navigation to feedback.
- Support and train educators – provide regular, hands-on training and a bank of ready-to-use (and adapt) immersive activities.
- Back it with infrastructure – ensure schools have the hardware, connectivity, and policies needed to make immersive learning sustainable.

Looking ahead, several promising avenues for research and development emerge, of which I would like to highlight:

- Conducting longitudinal studies to examine how virtual learning environments influence motivation and language development in neurodivergent learners;
- Establishing quality standards for designing inclusive immersive language-learning activities;
- Investigating teachers' and learners' perceptions of metaverse integration in educational settings;
- Developing phased, context-sensitive guidelines for implementing immersive learning across heterogeneous classrooms.

The implications of these findings extend beyond classroom practice to policy and leadership decisions. Beyond the implementation of preset frameworks, what is needed is a critically informed, context-responsive approach - one aligned with the global ethical mandate for inclusive education as articulated in the Salamanca Statement (UNESCO, 1994). This view is echoed by scholars who advocate pedagogical models grounded in sociocultural theory, digital equity, and universal design. Truly inclusive pedagogy demands purposeful curricular innovation - one that not only accommodates but actively celebrates neurocognitive diversity as an educational strength. At the same time, inclusive policy design must address persistent digital divides and ensure equitable access to meaningful learning opportunities.

For policymakers and educators, the practical implications are clear: invest in accessible infrastructure, embed immersive technology competencies into teacher training, and adopt participatory design processes that actively involve neurodivergent and physically diverse learners. In practice, this means ensuring that platforms meet accessibility standards, providing adaptable lesson templates aligned with UDL, and fostering professional communities where teachers can share and refine immersive activities. Such measures transform immersive technologies from novelty tools into sustainable, inclusive learning environments.

In the end, genuine inclusion in immersive education cannot be an afterthought - it must be the foundation from which we build, the compass by which we navigate, and the promise we uphold for every learner in the digital age.

REFERENCES

Almufarreh, A., & Arshad, M. (2023). Promising Emerging Technologies for Teaching and Learning: Recent Developments and Future Challenges. *Sustainability (Basel), 15*(6917), 6917. Advance online publication. DOI: 10.3390/su15086917

Altum, H. K., & Lee, J. (2020). Immersive Learning Technologies in English Language Teaching : A Systematic Review *. *Educational Technology International, 21*(2), 155–191.

Alvarez, B., Vergara, P. A., & Iglesias, I. (2020). Decaffeinated UDL: Chile in quest of inclusive education. In Gronseth, S. L., & Dalton, E. M. (Eds.), *International perspectives on UDL* (pp. 59–66). Routledge.

American Psychiatric Association. (2013). DSM-5. In *Atlas of Psychiatry* (5th ed.). American Psychiatric Publishing. DOI: 10.1007/978-3-031-15401-0_16

Aragon, C., Vosen Callens, M., Branham, S. M., Anicha, C., Blaser, B., & Bilen-Green, C. (2024). Expanding accessibility in immersive virtual spaces: A comprehensive approach for all disabilities. *ArXiv Preprint.* https://doi.org//arXiv.2405.05910DOI: 10.48550

Armstrong, K., Boreham, B., & Mack, T. (2019). Snapshot—Creating UDL learning and teaching strategies to address the underrepresentation of present-day Indigenous perspectives. In Gronseth, S. L., & Dalton, E. M. (Eds.), *Universal access through inclusive instructional design: International perspectives on UDL* (pp. 218–220). Routledge. DOI: 10.4324/9780429435515-27

Armstrong, T. (2010). *The power of neurodiversity: Unleashing the advantages of your differently wired brain*. DaCapo Lifelong Books.

Ashburner, J., Ziviani, J., & Rodger, S. (2008). Sensory processing and classroom emotional, behavioral, and educational outcomes in children with autism spectrum disorder. *The American Journal of Occupational Therapy, 62*(5), 564–573. DOI: 10.5014/ajot.62.5.564

Bacca, J., Baldiris, S., Fabregat, R., Graf, S., & Kinshuk. (2014). Augmented reality trends in education: A systematic review of research and applications. *Educational Technology \& Society, 17*(4), 133–149.

Bailenson, J. (2018). *Experience on demand: What virtual reality is, how it works, and what it can do*. W. W. Norton {\&} Company.

Bakhtin, M. M. (1981). *The dialogic imagination: Four essays (M. Holquist* (Emerson, C., & Holquist, M. Eds. & Trans.). University of Texas Press.

Banes, D., & Behnke, K. (2020). Future directions in universal access and assistive technology: The critical role of artificial intelligence and the internet of accessible things. In Gronseth, S. L., & Dalton, E. M. (Eds.), *International perspectives on UDL* (pp. 321–331). Routledge.

Baumer, N., & Frueh, J. (2021). What is neurodiversity? *Harvard Health Blog*. https://www.health.harvard.edu/blog/what-is-neurodiversity-202111232645

Bekteshi, S., Konings, M., Vanmechelen, I., Deklerck, J., Ortibus, E., Aerts, J. M., & Monbaliu, E. (2020). Eye Gaze Gaming Intervention in Children with Dyskinetic Cerebral Palsy: A Pilot Study of Task Performance and Its Relation with Dystonia and Choreoathetosis. *Developmental Neurorehabilitation, 23*(8), 548–556. DOI: 10.1080/17518423.2020.1770890

Bland, J. (2023). *Compelling stories for English language learners: Creativity, interculturality and critical literacy*. Bloomsbury Academic.

Blume, H. (1998). Neurodiversity: On the neurological underpinnings of geekdom. *The Atlantic*. https://www.theatlantic.com/magazine/archive/1998/09/neurodiversity/305909

Borgestig, M., Sandqvist, J., Parsons, R., Falkmer, T., & Hemmingsson, H. (2016). Eye gaze performance for children with severe physical impairments using gaze-based assistive technology — A longitudinal study. *Assistive Technology, 28*(2), 93–102. https://pubmed.ncbi.nlm.nih.gov/26496529/. DOI: 10.1080/10400435.2015.1092182

Brusca-Vega, R., & Trekles, A. (2020). Access to the curriculum for students with disabilities: Moving closer to the promise of UDL in inclusive US classrooms. In Gronseth, S. L., & Dalton, E. M. (Eds.), *International perspectives on UDL* (pp. 85–94). Routledge.

Buckle, K. L. (2020). Autscape. In Kapp, S. K. (Ed.), *Autistic community and the neurodiversity movement: Stories from the frontline* (pp. 109–122). Palgrave Macmillan., DOI: 10.1007/978-981-13-8437-0_8

Casarez, L., Hooks, D., Shipley, G., & Swafford, D. (2023). Proactive design to ensure accessibility. In Dalton, E. M., & Gronseth, S. (Eds.), *Universal access through inclusive instructional design* (pp. 30–32). Routledge.

CAST. (2018). *Universal Design for Learning guidelines version 2.2* (p. 2018). http://udlguidelines.cast.org

Chen, H. J. (2024). Gather in the metaverse : Learning outcomes, virtual presence, and perceptions of high - and low - achieving pre - service teachers of English as a Foreign Language. *Education and Information Technologies, 29*(7), 8549–8577. DOI: 10.1007/s10639-023-12135-3

Chen, W., Zhang, J., & Yu, Z. (2023). A Bibliometric Analysis of the Use of the Metaverse in Education over Three Decades. *International Journal of Information and Communication Technology Education, 19*(1), 1–16. DOI: 10.4018/IJICTE.322101

Cheng, K. H., & Tsai, C. C. (2019). A case study of immersive virtual field trips in an elementary classroom: Students' learning experience and teacher-student interaction behaviors. *Computers and Education, 140*(December 2018), 103600. DOI: 10.1016/j.compedu.2019.103600

Comas-Quinn, A., & Borthwick, K. (2015). Sharing: Open Educational Resources for Language Teachers. In Hampel, R., & Stickler, U. (Eds.), *Developing online language teaching: Research-based pedagogies and reflective practices* (pp. 96–111). Palgrave Macmillan. DOI: 10.1057/9781137412263_7

Cope, B., & Kalantzis, M. (2009). Multiliteracies: New literacies, new learning. *Pedagogies, 4*(3), 164–195. DOI: 10.1080/15544800903076044

Cosme, A. (2018). *Projeto de Autonomia e Flexibilidade Curricular: Estudo avaliativo da experiência pedagógica desenvolvida em 2017/2018 ao abrigo do Despacho n.º 5908/2017 (5 de julho).* https://www.dge.mec.pt/sites/default/files/Curriculo/Projeto_Autonomia_e_Flexibilidade/estudo_pafc.pdf

Cowie, N., & Alizadeh, M. (2022). The affordances and challenges of virtual reality for language teaching. *International Journal of TESOL Studies, 4*(3), 50–65. DOI: 10.46451/ijts.2022.03.05

Craine, M. (2020). Changing paradigms: The emergence of the autism/neurodiversity manifesto. In Kapp, S. K. (Ed.), *Autistic community and the neurodiversity movement: Stories from the frontline* (pp. 261–276). Palgrave Macmillan. DOI: 10.1007/978-981-13-8437-0_19

Creed, C., Al-Kalbani, M., Theil, A., Sarcar, S., & Williams, I. (2024). Inclusive AR/VR: Accessibility barriers for immersive technologies. *Universal Access in the Information Society, 23*(1), 59–73. DOI: 10.1007/s10209-023-00969-0

Dahlstrom-Hakki, I., Alstad, Z., Asbell-Clarke, J., & Edwards, T. (2024). The impact of visual and auditory distractions on the performance of neurodiverse students in virtual reality (VR) environments. *Virtual Reality (Waltham Cross), 28*(1), 29. DOI: 10.1007/s10055-023-00933-6

Dalton, E. M. (2020). UDL and connected laws, theories, and frameworks. In Gronseth, S. L., & Dalton, E. M. (Eds.), *International perspectives on UDL* (pp. 3–16). Routledge.

Daniels, H. (2001). *Vygotsky and pedagogy*. RoutledgeFalmer.

Diamond, A. (2013). Executive functions. *Annual Review of Psychology, 64*(1), 135–168. DOI: 10.1146/annurev-psych-113011-143750

Dick, E. (2021). *Balancing user privacy and innovation in augmented and virtual reality*. Information Technology and Innovation Foundation.

Edge-Savage, J., & Marotta, M. (2019). Spreading the word about assistive technology and universal design for learning: A model for professional teacher learning. In Gronseth, S. L., & Dalton, E. M. (Eds.), *Universal access through inclusive instructional design: International perspectives on UDL* (pp. 284–293). Routledge. DOI: 10.4324/9780429435515-38

European Parliament and Council of the European Union. (2016). *Regulation (EU) 2016/679 of the European Parliament and of the Council of 27 April 2016 on the protection of natural persons with regard to the processing of personal data and on the free movement of such data (General Data Protection Regulation)*. https://eur-lex.europa.eu/eli/reg/2016/679/oj

Fajari, L. E. W., Dayurni, P., & Rahayu, A. (2023). Meta-Analysis Study: The Effect of Augmented Reality on Student Learning Outcomes. *International Journal of Asian Education, 4*(1), 49–57. DOI: 10.46966/ijae.v4i1.301

Garzón, J., & Acevedo, J. (2019). Meta-analysis of the impact of Augmented Reality on students' learning gains. *Educational Research Review, 27*(April 2018), 244–260. DOI: 10.1016/j.edurev.2019.04.001

Germain-Rutherford, A., & Ernest, P. (2015). European language teachers and ICT: Experiences, expectations and training needs. In Hampel, R., & Stickler, U. (Eds.), *Developing online language teaching: Research-based pedagogy and practice* (pp. 8–30). Palgrave Macmillan., DOI: 10.1057/9781137412263_2

Godwin-Jones, R. (2020). Building the porous classroom: An expanded model for blended language learning. *Language Learning \& Technology, 24*(3), 1–18. http://hdl.handle.net/10125/44731

Godwin-Jones, R. (2023). Emerging spaces for language learning: AI bots, ambient intelligence, and the metaverse. *Language Learning \& Technology, 27*(2), 6–27. https://hdl.handle.net/10125/73501

Godwin-Jones, R. (2024). Distributed agency in second language learning and teaching through generative AI. *Language Learning & Technology*, *28*(2), 5–31. https://arxiv.org/abs/2403.20216. DOI: 10.64152/10125/73570

Godwin-Jones, R. (n.d.). AI and VR converge: The future of language learning in an emerging metaverse. In Chun, D., Lan, Y.-J., & Qi, G. (Eds.), *AI-mediated language education in the Metaverse era*. Springer. DOI: 10.1007/978-981-95-0245-5_11

Gomez, L. I. (2020). Immersive Virtual Reality for Learning Experiences. In D. Burgos (Ed.), *Radical Solutions and eLearning*. Springer. DOI: 10.1007/978-981-15-4952-6_12

Gronseth, S. L. (2020). Epilogue: Learning from diverse perspectives on inclusive instructional design and next steps. In Gronseth, S. L., & Dalton, E. M. (Eds.), *International perspectives on UDL* (pp. 350–357). Routledge.

Gronseth, S. L., & Dalton, E. M. (2020). Universal Access Through Inclusive Instructional Design: International Perspectives on UDL. In *Universal Access Through Inclusive Instructional Design: International Perspectives on UDL*. Routledge., DOI: 10.4324/9780429435515

Hansen, G. H. (2017). Lozanov and the teaching text. In Tomlinson, B. (Ed.), *Materials development for language learning and teaching* (2nd ed., pp. 337–342). Cambridge University Press.

Harrison, M., Rowlings, J., White, E. H., Vallence, A.-M., & Potemkin, N. (2024). *Neurodiversity and digital inclusion: Creating the conditions for inclusive education through universal design for learning*. DOI: 10.17613/xk4jx-pse60

Hehir, T., Grindal, T., Freeman, B., Lamoreau, R., Borquaye, Y., & Burke, S. (2016). A Summary of the Evidence on Inclusive Education. *Instituto Alana*, 1–34. https://alana.org.br/wp-content/uploads/2016/12/A_Summary_of_the_evidence_on_inclusive_education.pdf

Hu-Au, E., & Lee, J. J. (2017). Virtual reality in education: A tool for learning in the experience age. *International Journal of Innovation in Education*, *4*(4), 215–226. DOI: 10.1504/IJIIE.2017.091481

Hupont Torres, I., Charisi, V., De Prato, G., Pogorzelska, K., & Schade, S.. (2023). *Next generation virtual worlds – Societal, technological, economic and policy challenges for the EU*. Publications Office of the European Union., DOI: 10.2760/51579

Ikuta, S., & Hisatsune, Y. (2020). Handcrafted customized content and school activities with newly developed technologies. In Gronseth, S. L., & Dalton, E. M. (Eds.), *International perspectives on UDL* (pp. 164–171). Routledge.

Jones, E. K., & Orchard, V. (2024). Neurodiversity and disability: What is at stake? *Medical Humanities, 50*(3), 456–465. DOI: 10.1136/medhum-2023-012808

Kapp, S. K. (2020). Conclusion. In Kapp, S. K. (Ed.), *Autistic community and the neurodiversity movement: Stories from the frontline* (pp. 305–318). Palgrave Macmillan., DOI: 10.1007/978-981-13-8437-0_22

Kapp, S. K., & Ne'eman, A. (2020). Lobbying autism's diagnostic revision in the DSM-5. In Kapp, S. K. (Ed.), *Autistic community and the neurodiversity movement: Stories from the frontline* (pp. 167–194). Palgrave Macmillan., DOI: 10.1007/978-981-13-8437-0_13

Kapur, M. (2008). Productive failure. *Cognition and Instruction, 26*(3), 379–424. DOI: 10.1080/07370000802212669

Karlsson, P., Bech, A., Stone, H., Vale, C., Griffin, S., Monbaliu, E., & Wallen, M. (2019). Eyes on communication: Trialling eye-gaze control technology in young children with dyskinetic cerebral palsy. *Developmental Neurorehabilitation, 22*(2), 134–140. DOI: 10.1080/17518423.2018.1519609

Kessler, G. (2018). Technology and the future of language teaching. *Foreign Language Annals, 51*(1), 205–218. DOI: 10.1111/flan.12318

Koreeda, K., & Tsuge, M. (2020). UDL-inspired pedagogical practices in Japan. In Gronseth, S. L., & Dalton, E. M. (Eds.), *International perspectives on UDL* (pp. 111–118). Routledge.

Kruk, M. (2022). Motivational dynamics in learning English in Second Life. *ELT Journal, 76*(4), 465–475. DOI: 10.1093/elt/ccab067

Lantolf, J. P. (2000). Introducing sociocultural theory. In Lantolf, J. P. (Ed.), *Sociocultural theory and second language learning* (pp. 1–26). Oxford University Press.

Lantolf, J. P. (2006). Sociocultural theory and L2: State of the art. *Studies in Second Language Acquisition, 28*(1), 67–109. DOI: 10.1017/S0272263106060037

Lantolf, J. P., & Poehner, M. E. (2024). *Sociocultural theory and the teaching of second languages*. University of Toronto Press.

Lantolf, J. P., & Thorne, S. L. (2006). *Sociocultural theory and the genesis of second language development*. Oxford University Press.

Lock, J., Johnson, C., Hanson, J., Liu, Y., & Adlington, A. (2020). Designing an online graduate orientation program informed by UDL and studied by design-based research. In Gronseth, S. L., & Dalton, E. M. (Eds.), *Universal access through inclusive instructional design: International perspectives on UDL* (pp. 250–257). Routledge.

Long, M. H. (1996). The role of the linguistic environment in second language acquisition. In Ritchie, W. C., & Bhatia, T. K. (Eds.), *Handbook of second language acquisition* (pp. 413–468). Academic Press.

Lui, M., Maharaj, A., Shimaly, R., Atcha, A., Ali, H., Carroll, S., & McEwen, R. (2021). User experiences of eye-gaze classroom technology for children with complex communication needs. *Journal of Special Education Technology*, *37*(3), 426–436. Advance online publication. DOI: 10.1177/01626434211019399

Lyner-Cleophas, M. (2020). The prospects of universal design for learning in South Africa to facilitate the inclusion of all learners. In Gronseth, S. L., & Dalton, E. M. (Eds.), *International perspectives on UDL* (pp. 35–45). Routledge.

Marougkas, A., Troussas, C., Krouska, A., & Sgouropoulou, C. (2023). Virtual Reality in Education: A Review of Learning Theories, Approaches and Methodologies for the Last Decade. *Electronics (Basel)*, *12*(13), 2832. DOI: 10.3390/electronics12132832

Mayer, R. E. (2009). *Multimedia learning* (2nd ed.). Multimedia Learning., DOI: 10.1017/CBO9780511811678

Melchor-Couto, S. (2016). Foreign language anxiety levels in Second Life oral interaction. *ReCALL*, *29*(1), 99–119. DOI: 10.1017/S0958344016000185

Menke, K., Beckmann, J., & Weber, P. (2020). Universal design for learning in augmented and virtual reality trainings. In Gronseth, S. L., & Dalton, E. M. (Eds.), *International perspectives on UDL* (pp. 294–304). Routledge.

Meyer, A., Rose, D. H., & Gordon, D. (2014). Universal design for learning : theory and practice. In *CAST Professional Publishing*. Cast professional Pub. https://cir.nii.ac.jp/crid/1130000797493904000

Miller, M. R., Herrera, F., Jun, H., Landay, J. A., & Bailenson, J. N. (2020). Personal identifiability of user tracking data during observation of 360-degree VR video. *Scientific Reports*, *10*(1), 17404. DOI: 10.1038/s41598-020-74486-y

Molnar, S. (2019). The precarious promise of emergent tech and universal design for learning: A pivotal point. In Gronseth, S. L., & Dalton, E. M. (Eds.), *Universal access through inclusive instructional design: International perspectives on UDL* (pp. 343–345). Routledge. DOI: 10.4324/9780429435515-45

Mystakidis, S. (2022). Metaverse. *Encyclopedia*, *2*(1), 486–497. DOI: 10.3390/encyclopedia2010031

Novak, I., McIntyre, S., Morgan, C., Campbell, L., Dark, L., Morton, N., Stumbles, E., Wilson, S.-A., & Goldsmith, S. (2013). A systematic review of interventions for children with cerebral palsy: State of the evidence. *Developmental Medicine \& Child Neurology, 55*(10), 885–910. DOI: 10.1111/dmcn.12246

Novak, K., & Rose, D. H. (2016). *UDL Now! A teacher's guide to applying Universal Design for Learning in today's classrooms* (2nd ed.). CAST Professional Publishing., https://www.castpublishing.org

Pennington, L., Goldbart, J., & Marshall, J. (2004). Interaction training for conversational partners of children with cerebral palsy: A systematic review. *International Journal of Language \& Communication Disorders, 39*(2), 151–170. DOI: 10.1080/13682820310001625598

Peterson, M., & Jabbari, N. (2022). Digital games in language learning: Case studies and applications. *Digital Games in Language Learning: Case Studies and Applications*, (December), 1–184. DOI: 10.4324/9781003240075

Portugal. Ministério da Educação. (2018a). *Decreto-Lei n.º 54/2018, de 6 de julho: Estabelece o regime jurídico da educação inclusiva.* https://dre.pt/dre/detalhe/decreto-lei/54-2018-115652962

Portugal. Ministério da Educação. (2018b). *Decreto-Lei n.º 55/2018 de 6 de julho: Estabelece o currículo dos ensinos básico e secundário e os princípios orientadores da avaliação das aprendizagens.* https://dre.pt/dre/detalhe/decreto-lei/55-2018-115652962

Radianti, J., Majchrzak, T. A., Fromm, J., & Wohlgenannt, I. (2020). A systematic review of immersive virtual reality applications for higher education: Design elements, lessons learned, and research agenda. *Computers \& Education, 147*, 103778. DOI: 10.1016/j.compedu.2019.103778

Rao, K., Ok, M. W., & Bryant, B. R. (2014). A Review of Research on Universal Design Educational Models. *Remedial and Special Education, 35*(3), 153–166. DOI: 10.1177/0741932513518980

Rao, K., Smith, S. J., & Lowrey, K. A. (2017). UDL and intellectual disability: What do we know and where do we go? *Intellectual and Developmental Disabilities, 55*(1), 37–44. DOI: 10.1352/1934-9556-55.1.37

Raymaker, D. M. (2020). Shifting the system: AASPIRE and the loom of science and activism. In Kapp, S. K. (Ed.), *Autistic community and the neurodiversity movement: Stories from the frontline* (pp. 133–145). Palgrave Macmillan., DOI: 10.1007/978-981-13-8437-0_10

Redecker, C., & Punie, Y. (2017). *European Framework for the Digital Competence of Educators (DigCompEdu)*. Publications Office of the European Union., DOI: 10.2760/178382

Reinders, H., & White, C. (2011). Learner autonomy and new learning environments. *Language Learning & Technology*, *15*(3), 1–3. DOI: 10.64152/10125/44254

Roesner, F., Kohno, T., & Molnar, D. (2014). Security and privacy for augmented reality systems. *Communications of the ACM*, *57*(4), 88–96. DOI: 10.1145/2580723.2580730

Rose, D. H., & Meyer, A. (2002). *Teaching Every Student in the Digital Age: Universal Design for Learning*. Association for Supervision and Curriculum Development.

Saca, P. (2023). Designing Accessible Immersive Learning Experiences. *Journal of Technology-Integrated Lessons and Teaching*, *2*(1), 78–87. DOI: 10.13001/jtilt.v2i1.7669

Savickaite, S. (2023). *Using virtual reality to explore individual differences in perception due to neurodiversity* [University of Glasgow]. https://theses.gla.ac.uk/84098/

Silva, R. M., Martins, P., & Rocha, T. (2025). Virtual reality educational scenarios for students with ASD: Instruments validation and design of STEM programmatic contents. *Research in Autism Spectrum Disorders*, *119*, 102521. DOI: 10.1016/j.rasd.2024.102521

Singer, J. (1999). Why can't you be normal for once in your life? From a "Problem with No Name" to the emergence of a new category of difference. In Corker, M., & French, S. (Eds.), *Disability Discourse* (pp. 59–67). Open University Press.

Stickler, U., & Emke, M. (2015). Part-time and Freelance Language Teachers and their ICT Training Needs. In Hampel, R., & Stickler, U. (Eds.), *Developing online language teaching: Research-based pedagogies and reflective practices* (pp. 28–44). Palgrave Macmillan. DOI: 10.1057/9781137412263_3

Suwannawut, N. (2019). Conceptual frameworks. In Gronseth, S. L., & Dalton, E. M. (Eds.), *Universal access through inclusive instructional design: International perspectives on UDL* (pp. 18–24). Routledge. DOI: 10.4324/9780429435515-2

Swain, M. (2000). The output hypothesis and beyond: Mediating acquisition through collaborative dialogue. In Lantolf, J. P. (Ed.), *Sociocultural theory and second language learning* (pp. 97–114). Oxford University Press.

Swain, M. (2005). The output hypothesis: Theory and research. In Hinkel, E. (Ed.), *Handbook of research in second language teaching and learning* (pp. 471–483). Routledge.

Tomlinson, B. (2017). *Materials development for language learning and teaching* (2nd ed.). Cambridge University Press.

Tomlinson, C. A. (2014). *The differentiated classroom: Responding to the needs of all learners* (2nd ed.). ASCD.

Tondeur, J., Aesaert, K., Pynoo, B., van Braak, J., Fraeyman, N., & Erstad, O. (2015). Developing a validated instrument to measure pre-service teachers' ICT competencies: Meeting the demands of the 21st century. *British Journal of Educational Technology*, *52*(2), 619–636. DOI: 10.1111/bjet.12380

UNESCO. (1994). Declaração de Salamanca sobre princípios, políticas e práticas na área das necessidades educativas especiais. *Conferência Mundial de Educação Especial.* https://unesdoc.unesco.org/ark:/48223/pf0000139394

UNESCO. (2018). *ICT Competency Framework for Teachers* (3rd ed.). UNESCO. https://unesdoc.unesco.org/ark:/48223/pf0000265721

U.S. Federal Trade Commission. (2013). *Children's Online Privacy Protection Rule ("COPPA").* https://www.ftc.gov/legal-library/browse/rules/childrens-online-privacy-protection-rule-coppa

Vygotsky, L. S. (1978). *Mind in Society, The development of Higher Psychological Processes* (M. Cole, V. John-Steiner, S. Scribner, & E. Souberman, Eds.; Issue March). Harvard University Press.

Wang, F., Ni, X., Zhang, M., & Zhang, J. (2024). Educational digital inequality: A meta-analysis of the relationship between digital device use and academic performance in adolescents. *Computers & Education*, *213*(January), 105003. DOI: 10.1016/j.compedu.2024.105003

Warschauer, M. (2004). Of digital divides and social multipliers: Combining language and technology for human development. In Fitzpatrick, A. (Ed.), *Information and communication technologies in the teaching and learning of foreign languages: State of the art, needs and perspectives* (pp. 46–52). UNESCO Institute for Information Technologies in Education., https://unesdoc.unesco.org/ark:/48223/pf0000139195

Wehrmann, F., & Zender, R. (2023). Inclusive Virtual Reality Learning: Review and "Best-Fit" Framework for Universal Learning. *Electronic Journal of e-Learning*, *21*(6), 1–15. DOI: 10.34190/ejel.21.6.3265

Wertsch, J. V. (1991). *Voices of the mind: A sociocultural approach to mediated action*. Harvard University Press.

Won, M., Ungu, D. A. K., Matovu, H., Treagust, D. F., Tsai, C.-C., Park, J., Mocerino, M., & Tasker, R. (2023). Diverse approaches to learning with immersive Virtual Reality identified from a systematic review. *Computers \& Education, 195*, 104701. DOI: 10.1016/j.compedu.2022.104701

Wood, D., Bruner, J. S., & Ross, G. (1976). The role of tutoring in problem solving. *Journal of Child Psychology and Psychiatry, and Allied Disciplines, 17*(2), 89–100. DOI: 10.1111/j.1469-7610.1976.tb00381.x

World Wide Web Consortium. (W3C). (2023). *Web Content Accessibility Guidelines (WCAG) 2.2.* https://www.w3.org/TR/WCAG22/

Wu, J., Jiang, H., & Chen, S. (2024). Augmented reality technology in language learning: A meta-analysis. *Language Learning {\&} Technology, 28*(1), 1–23. https://hdl.handle.net/10125/73596

Yong, X., Chan, G., & Arya, A. (2024). Inclusion in Virtual Reality Technology: A Scoping Review. *International Journal of Human-Computer Interaction, 41*(5), 2808–2828. DOI: 10.1080/10447318.2024.2392967

Zhang, H., & Zhao, G. (2019). Universal design for learning in China. In Gronseth, S. L., & Dalton, E. M. (Eds.), *Universal access through inclusive instructional design: International perspectives on UDL* (pp. 68–75). Routledge. DOI: 10.4324/9780429435515-8

ENDNOTES

1 ***Decree-Law 54/2018*** *regulates the framework for inclusive education in Portugal, establishing the legal basis for accommodating the diverse needs of all students through flexible curricular and pedagogical practices, with an emphasis on equity, personalization, and the removal of barriers to learning and participation.*

2 ***Decree-Law 55/2018*** *defines the structure of the curriculum and its implementation across basic and secondary education, promoting curricular autonomy and flexibility, allowing schools to adapt teaching and assessment strategies to local contexts and student profiles.*

3 AAC refers to methods, systems, or devices that support or replace spoken or written communication. These can range from low-tech tools such as communication boards with pictures or symbols to high-tech speech-generating devices, text-to-speech software, and eye-gaze systems.

4 Haptic feedback refers to tactile sensations, such as vibration, pressure or resistance, produced by a device to simulate touch and physical interaction within a digital or virtual environment.

5 The notion of language as a social and situated practice, constructed through interaction with others, is particularly developed by Bakhtin in his essay *Discourse in the Novel*, included in *The Dialogic Imagination* (Bakhtin, 1981), where he introduces foundational concepts such as dialogism, social voices, and heteroglossia.

6 As of June 2024, Mozilla has terminated support for Mozilla Hubs.

7 Closed March 2023.

8 The Proteus effect refers to the phenomenon whereby users' behaviours and self-perceptions in virtual environments shift according to the characteristics of their avatars. Named after the shape-shifting Greek god Proteus, this effect was first identified by Yee and Click or tap here to enter text.Click or tap here to enter text., who found that participants assigned taller or more attractive avatars exhibited greater confidence or sociability in virtual interactions, often unconsciously. In educational contexts, the Proteus effect has implications for learner agency, participation, and identity formation in immersive environments.

9 For a comprehensive examination of this paradigm shift and its proposed participatory methodologies, refer to Yong et al. (2023).

Chapter 10
The Power of Games From Traditional to Digital for the 21st Century Survival Skills: A Case Study

Emine Şendurur
https://orcid.org/0000-0002-0340-6378
Ondokuz Mayıs University, Turkey

Neşet Mutlu
https://orcid.org/0000-0002-3378-4986
Erciyes University, Turkey

ABSTRACT

Students and teachers lacking fundamental digital literacy skills constitute a dimension of the digital divide. This study aims to enable teachers to experience the power of game-based pedagogy in a technologically restricted context and to show ways to integrate 21st-century survival skills into teachers' field of expertise. This study has a single-case research design. 26 voluntary teachers of various subject areas participated in a 5-day workshop. The pre-interview form, post-semi-structured interviews, daily field notes, and the daily activities products were the main data sources. The results indicated that participants' self-ratings on ICT usage and integration skills increased after the workshop. However, they still stated they needed time to become proficient in 21st-century skills. The participants learned how to

DOI: 10.4018/979-8-3373-7729-2.ch010

integrate game-based pedagogy into technologically restricted learning environments. They generated specific ideas within the range of board games through digital ones. Their perspectives on interdisciplinary collaboration varied across subject areas.

INTRODUCTION

The current education paradigm defines new roles for teachers, students, and technology. The teacher facilitates the student's learning experience through the affordances of technology (Reigeluth et al.., 2008). Game-based pedagogical approaches have dynamics that can support those new roles because their structure keeps players active. The teacher can sometimes act as a recordkeeper or a game master. The game environment does not always have to be digital; traditional games can be an alternative, especially in technologically restricted environments.

During the 90s, the Internet introduced a new experience of accessing information, and then the spread of uncontrolled information brought about new literacies (Chapman et al., 2019). Skills essential for the 21st century can be classified into four primary categories: "Key Subjects," encompassing language proficiency, mathematics, science, and economics; "Learning and Innovation," which includes critical thinking, communication, collaboration, and creativity; "Information, Media, and Technology"; and "Life and Career" (P21, 2019). This study presents a five-week course designed to enhance teachers' digital literacy and, as a secondary outcome, to cultivate students' 21st-century skills.

BACKGROUND

21st-century skills are sometimes referred to as survival skills; however, the digital divide, which refers to limited access and the overuse of technology, still causes inequalities in society (Robinson et al., 2020). These inequalities, primarily arising from socio-economic disparities, increase social injustice in domains such as education, employment access, healthcare, and social interaction (Cheshmehzangi et al., 2023). For example, physical conditions might hinder teachers from conducting activities supporting the development of those skills. In order to contribute to the learning of their pupils, educators employ a wide variety of instructional approaches, methods, and strategies. There are, nevertheless, several technological limitations that teachers must contend with. These limitations include difficulty in gaining access to technological devices, issues with internet connections, reluctance to change on the part of school management, instructors' low level of technological literacy, and students' unequal access to technology (Metin, 2018; Güntepe & Keles, 2022; Van

De Werfhorst et al., 2022; Yeşilyurt & Vezne, 2023). Teacher training designed to reduce the digital gap plays a vital role in achieving the United Nations' educational goals (Goal 4: Quality Education) (Grobler & Dittrich, 2024).

The Turkish Ministry of National Education (MoNE) initiated a project called FATIH in Turkey, which stands for Movement for Increasing Opportunities and Improving Technology (MoNE, 2022), which stands for Movement for Increasing Opportunities and Improving Technology (MoNE, 2022). By the conclusion of 2022, this project has resulted in the installation of interactive whiteboards in 90% of classrooms, the distribution of tablet computers to students and teachers, the establishment of information technology classrooms in schools, and the digitization of course content, which is now accessible via the Education Information Network (EBA). On the other hand, these infrastructure solutions did not adequately address the issues in actual classroom settings, particularly those concerned with sustainability and integration in addition to attitudes (Garlinska et al., 2023; Singun, 2025. There are many instructional strategies and methods to overcome these obstacles such as screenless outdoor activities for technology education (Hammes, 2007; Nikbay-Arslantaş & Bavlı, 2024), but in Turkey, the number of that kind of activities is quite limited (Özgem & Akçıl, 2022).

Game-based learning (GBL) is an important approach to help teachers and students create an effective environment for 21st-century skills acquisition (Noonoo, 2019; Xu et al., 2023; El Mawas et al., 2018; Qian & Clark, 2016). GBL can enable students to actively participate, develop higher-order skills (Dahalan et al., 2024), increase motivation (Jääskä et al., 2022).. The non-digital GBL approaches usually utilize collaborative board/card games (Kuo et al., 2023) or CS-Unplugged activities (Parlak & Şendurur, 2022). Integration of traditional street games is very rare (Durmuşkaya, 2021). The digital GBL approaches include gamification (Samala et al., 2023) or games for 21st-century skills (Partridge, 2022). The workshop, which was developed as part of this study, included activities related to using street games, such as skipping rope, hopscotch, and blindfolded tag, as well as digital games, in education. This is because teachers in rural areas do not have access to the same technological resources as teachers in big cities. Low-tech games are effective tools for reducing the negative effects of the digital divide among students. These games have similar pedagogical effects to digital games, while balancing inequalities in technology access. Teachers should have the knowledge and skills to integrate digital and traditional games into education in order to use game-based teaching models in educational settings with different technological infrastructures.

The sole integration of games into educational environments might not always be practical regarding time, location, curriculum, and other factors. Interdisciplinary approaches can make the skills turn out to be tangible experiences (Battelle for Kids, 2019; Klaassen, 2018; MoNE, 2023; OECD, 2019). Experiencing such a learning environment can improve communication skills in addition to managing real life problems (Galli, 2021; Hero & Lindfors, 2019).

MAIN FOCUS OF THE CHAPTER

The purpose of this study is to conduct a case study to examine whether there is an improvement in the potential of teachers who experience a five-day workshop with both technology-rich and technology-poor activities. The mission of the International Society for Technology in Education (ISTE) is to establish worldwide standards for the application of technology in educational settings. The International Society for Technology in Education (ISTE) standards encourage incorporating technology for educators, students, and administrators. They present a road map for educators to follow in order to make effective, ethical, and creative use of technology in their classrooms to teach students. In this study, the content of the workshop was built upon ISTE (2017) standards for students, which include the following: (i) empowered learner, (ii) digital citizen, (iii) knowledge constructor, (iv) innovative designer, (v) computational thinker, (vi) creative communicator, and (vii) global communicator. All activities served at least one of the standards. The study had two main research questions as follows:

- What are the current practices of teachers working in a technologically restricted environment regarding:
    - GBL (GBL),
    - 21st century skills,
    - interdisciplinary practice,
    - and strategies to eliminate technological restrictions?
- How does the potential of teachers working in a technologically restricted environment change:
    - perceived knowledge and skills,
    - GBL integration,
    - 21st century skills integration,
    - interdisciplinary practice,
    - and strategies to eliminate technological restrictions?

when they received a five-day workshop consisting of integration practices within various settings?

METHOD

This study aimed to examine the changes in teachers' potential to deal with technology-restricted environments through an exploratory single-case study approach(Yin, 2018). The participants are teachers working in technologically restricted environments. Their current practices and the potential changes in practices were explored during the workshop modeling how to integrate low and high technology with GBL and interdisciplinary approaches.

Data Source and Collection

Three different data sources were used in this study: The pre-interview form, daily field notes, and semi-structured interview (post-interview). The pre-interview form consists of three parts: demographics, skill ratings, and open-ended questions. They were asked to rate their 21st century, ICT usage and integration, modern instructional methods, interdisciplinary work, and instructional material creation skills in a 1-10 Likert type scale. The open-ended questions include their current practices of GBL, 21st century skills, and their link to the teaching subject, interdisciplinary practice, and strategies to deal with technologically restricted environments. The form was delivered online before the workshop. During the workshop, field notes were taken by researchers to record the observations about activities, interactions among participants, and the problems related to the logistics or any other issues. The post-interviews have the same structure as the pre-interview form, but the delivery method was face-to-face, so that the experiences about the workshop could be understood better with additional questions or comments. Data was collected under the auspices of the University Review Board. All interviews were audio recorded and transcribed verbatim. All data sources were used to understand the perspective change of participants. The pre and post skill ratings of participants served as checklists to compare the perceived skill changes. Figure 1 demonstrates how data sources are triangulated.

Figure 1. Data Sources

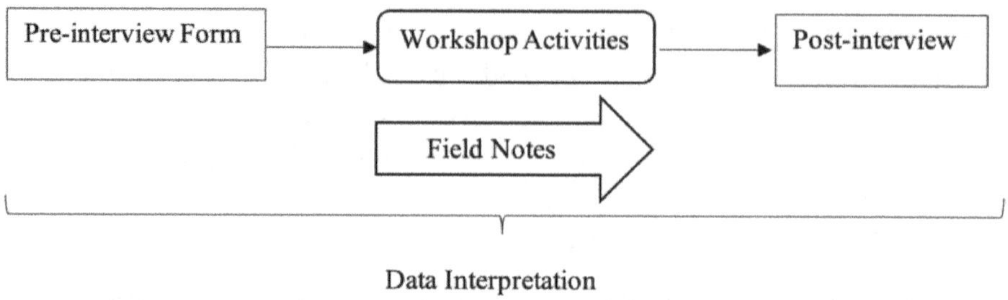

The five-day workshop provided both theoretical and practice sessions. The examples of how to use gamification/games in both technology-rich and technology-constrained environments through an interdisciplinary perspective were provided during the workshop. The activities model either digital or non-digital integration practices because the teachers might have biased approach such as no devices no 21st century skills. To change the perspectives of such malpractice, low, medium, and high technological integration activities were introduced to the paticipants. Firstly, the theoretical background of the concepts of game and gamification was explained. Next, information was provided on what kind of gamification activities can be done in technology-rich environments: "digital story", "gamification in the information search processes", "gamification with Artificial Intelligence (AI) and Web 2.0 tools", and "technology supported visualization". The workshop sessions on what kind of gamification activities can be done in technology-restricted environments included "algorithm building with traditional games", "problem solving with traditional games", "designing a computational thinking activity without a screen" and "creating concept map" topics. It was aimed to develop the 21st-century skills of teachers who experienced these activities. The remaining activities introduced technology-poor activities that teachers can implement in technology-restricted environments. In this way, teachers had a chance to provide better teaching opportunities to their students even in technology-restricted teaching environments. In addition, teachers from different disciplines were brought together and allowed to work in groups to experience different perspectives. Table 1 summarizes the details of workshop content and the relations among basic constructs (21st century skills, GBL, interdisciplinary approach, and technology integration).

Table 1. Matrix of Workshop Content

Workshop Day-Activity Number	Related 21st Century Skill(s)	GBL approach	Interdisciplinary approach	Technology Integration*	Tools
Day1-Activity1	Innovative designer	Big Risk Game (Digital)	ICT+Various disciplines	Medium	MS Power Point
Day1-Activity2	Digital citizen	Concept mapping and collaborative story telling (Non-digital)	ICT+Social science+Various disciplines	Low	Story board Colored cards Post-it
Day2-Activity1	Computational thinker	Street games (Marble and drop the handkerchief) (Non-digital)	ICT+Physical education+Various disciplines	Low	Colored cards Marbles
Day2-Activity2	Knowledge constructor	Street game (stop or istop) (Non-digital)	Physical education+Social sciences+Various disciplines	Low	Ball Hula-hoop Barcodes
Day3-Activity1	Empowered learner+Knowledge constructor	Detecting AI hallucinations Webquest (Digital+Non-digital)	ICT+Various disciplines	Low-to-high	Google search engine ChatGPT Printed text
Day3-Activity2	Knowledge constructor	Human vs. AI game (Non-digital) AI-human interaction (Digital)	ICT+Various disciplines	Low-to-high	ChatGPT Printed text
Day3-Activity3	Global collaborator	Translation using AI-assisted apps Online collaboration via platforms (Digital)	Linguistics+Various disciplinles	High	Deppl ChatGPT E-twinning platform
Day4-Activity1	Computational thinker	Concert escape game Quiz (Digital)	Linguistics+Maths ICT+Maths ICT+Science Social sciences+Visual arts	Medium	Web 2.0 tools (Educaplay & Thinglink)

continued on following page

Table 1. Continued

Workshop Day-Activity Number	Related 21st Century Skill(s)	GBL approach	Interdisciplinary approach	Technology Integration*	Tools
Day4-Activity2	Creative communicator	Data visualization 3D+AI assisted data visualization Text-to-visual (Digital)	Science+Maths ICT+Social sciences	High	3D Models AR glass Various AI platforms
Day5-Activity1	Knowledge contructor+Creative communicator	Exchange of practive Self-evaluation (Non-digital)	ICT-Various disciplines	Low	-

*Low: No screen or device; Medium: Offline device; High: Online device and tools

Participants

Purposeful sampling was used to include participants in the study. A call was published via social media, message groups, and official announcements. The following criteria were used to select the suitability of the participants for the study:

- Working in a school with technological restrictions (40 points)
- Open to integrate game-based approaches into courses (20 points)
- No previous participation in a similar project (10 points)
- Open to interdisciplinary work (10 points)
- Open to develop his/her own instructional material (10 points)
- Working in a rural area (10 points).

101 candidates applied to the call, and they were listed according to total points, but in order to include the variety among subject areas, the sorting was categorized based on the subject areas. The participants in the study were a group of twenty-six in-service teachers from various subject areas who had been selected for a workshop that lasted for five days based on the criteria presented before. Demographics were presented in Table 2. In the pre-interview form, the expectations of participants were collected. Two main themes were extracted: professional development and technology integration. Learning about new methodological approaches was the most mentioned sub-theme of professional development (n=12). The integration of game pedagogy was the most frequent sub-theme of technology integration (n=12). For both themes, teachers expect to engage in interdisciplinary activities.

Table 2. Demographics & Expectations

	n
Subject Area	9
Mathematics Education	9
Language Education	3
Social Sciences Education	1
Science education	1
Physical Education	1
Visual Arts Education	1
Guidance and Psychological Counseling	1
Religious Culture and Ethics Education	
Teaching Grade Level	26
Middle School (5-8 grades)	
Age	9
25-35 years old	14
36-45 years old	3
46+ years old	
Teaching Experience	4
4-10 years	7
11-15 years	11
16-20 years	4
21+ years	
Gender	19
Female	7
Male	
Prior Exposure to GBL	17
Yes	9
No	
Regional Background	10
Urban	16
Rural	
Expectations	
Professional development	12
New methods/techniques/strategies	6
Efficient learning environment	4
21st century skills	2
Collaboration with other disciplines	
Technology integration	12
Game pedagogy	9
Digital tools	6
Motivate students	1
Interdisciplinary activities	

Data Analysis

In-depth individual interviews and daily field notes were collected in order to improve the validity of the findings, which were based on the experiences that both the researchers and the individual participants shared. This study used an inductive thematic analysis approach. Considering the theoretical background as a starting point, the data were grouped into themes or sub-themes, and then the codes were extracted. An in-depth analysis was performed on both the transcripts of the interviews and the daily field notes. The participants' discourses were tagged with codes within this investigation's scope. Codes close to one another were grouped under the same category. In order to minimize the researcher bias, two coders worked separately, then compared the codes and themes until at least 80% consensus was provided.

FINDINGS

The Current Practices of Teachers Working in a Technologically Restricted Environment

The participants completed a pre-interview form. The form consists of questions to understand the current practices of teachers based on four dimensions: game-based pedagogy, 21st-century skills, interdisciplinary practice, and technological restrictions. The purpose of the form is to gain an understanding of the present practices of teachers. Additionally, observations of the researchers were also reported.

Teachers' Current Practices on GBL

Before participating in the workshop, most teachers were aware of the nature of GBL (n=17). Some participants described it as an integration practice (n=12), whereas a few participants saw it as an instructional method (n=5). The participants generally had an idea about GBL and pointed out its affective (n=19), cognitive (n=4), and social (n=3) advantages. The entertaining nature of the GBL was the most frequently mentioned affective feature of GBL (n=10). One participant explained this feature of GBL as follows:

"Students called Gen-Z are addicted to smartphones. Digital games are very crucial to keep students engaged during learning." (P7)

One challenge was stated by one participant, and it was related to the physical setup of the game environment (n=1). Table 3 summarizes the overall current GBL practices of participants.

Table 3. GBL approach

Theme	Sub-Theme	Code	*n*
Description	Integration of games	into the subject into learning objectives	6 6
	Method	Problem-based Student-centered	4 1
Advantages	Affective	Entertaining High motivation High engagement	10 5 4
	Cognitive	Rich/long lasting learning experience	4
	Social	Collaboration	3
Challenges	Hard to set up		1

Teachers' Current Practices on 21st Century Skills

Participants were requested to explain how they relate 21st-century skills to their field of study. Most participants had a particular point of view about these skills (n=19), whereas a few had no idea about them (n=7). One participant revealed this situation as follows:

"Honestly, I know very little about these skills, and that is the reason why I am willing to attend the project." (P1)

The participants' descriptions were divided into two sub-themes: literacy (n=21) and thinking skills (n=44). The ones defining 21st-century skills as literacy frequently equated it with technological literacy (n=7). On the other hand, the majority of participants assumed that creativity/innovativeness (n=17) and critical thinking (n=14) were closely related to those skills. The following excerpts provide the participants' points of view:

"Following the technological developments, digital literacy, critical thinking, interpreting, creativity, media literacy, and etc., I think all of them are somehow related to my subject area. (P2)"

"...I think of that problem solving as a 21st-century skill can improve collaboration skills of students." (P11)

Improved interaction (n=37) and facilitation of learning (n=13) were reported as the advantages of having 21st-century skills. The mastery of communication (n=17) and collaboration (n=13) skills were the most frequently mentioned dimensions of improved interactivity. Since the participants' subject areas varied, their perceived advantages of these skills also varied. Among them, maths was the most mentioned subject area (n=4). According to participants, it was closely related to 21st-century skills, which was perceived as an advantage. Table 4 summarizes the current practices of teachers in 21st-century skills.

Table 4. 21st Century Skills

Theme	Sub-Theme	Code	*n*
No idea	-	-	7
Description	Literacy	Technology Digital Media Information	7 6 6 2
	Thinking Skills	Creativity/ Innovativeness Critical thinking Problem solving Rationalization Analysis Interpretation	17 14 7 3 2 1
Advantages	Improve interactivity	Communication Collaboration Entrepreneurship Leadership	17 13 5 2
	Facilitate learning	Maths Language ICT Social Science	4 3 3 2 1

Teachers' Current Interdisciplinary Practices

The participants' interdisciplinary practices showed three patterns: frequent integration (n=15), rare integration (n=2), and no integration (n=9). The following subject areas were reported to apply for interdisciplinary work frequently: maths (n=11), language (n=13), social (n=7), science(n=4), ICT (n=6), and visual arts (n=3). The participants reported more than one subject area to be collaborated. The following excerpts demonstrate the way teachers explain their interdisciplinary integration:

> *"I generally collaborate with the ICT teacher. Depending on the topic, I can employ different techniques. For example, I use this site (www....) to make students practice the multiplying table. I let them play the game on that site. (P5)* "
> *"...For instance, I try to integrate the distance between planets and the sun into exponential expressions. (P2)"*

Based on the frequencies, language (Turkish and English) was the field most exposed to other subject areas. Two participants explained that they rarely apply interdisciplinary practices. On the other hand, nine participants had no integration practices at all because of having neither education (n=5) nor practice (n=4) on interdisciplinary integration. Table 5 summarizes the interdisciplinary integration practices of participants.

Table 5. Interdisciplinary Practice

Theme	Sub-Theme	Sub-Subject	*n*
Frequent Integration	Maths	Social Others	3 8
	Language	Social Others	3 10
	Social	Geography Others	2 5
	Science	Language Others	2 2
	ICT	Maths & science Others	4 2
	Visual Arts	Maths & science ICT	2 1
Rare Integration			2
No Integration	Not educated		5
	Not practiced		4

Strategies for Eliminating Technological Restrictions

Considering that the participants are employed in work environments that are technologically constrained, it was asked them to explain the strategies that they employ in order to deal with the technology integration problem. Some of them stated that they continued with traditional methods (n=10), while others employed different methods or techniques (n=22). One participant created alternative solutions, such as delivering homework via Web 2.0 tools. Games (n=7) and tangible materials (n=5) were the most frequently employed strategies to overcome the technological restrictions. One of the participants explained the strategy change due to the electric cut as follows:

> *"This is what exactly has happened to me. The new curriculum requires the utilization of Geogebra for the circle topic, but there was an electric cut. At that time, I had to think really quickly, so I decided to use the mouse cable. One*

student helped to measure and mark on the board. We did it 20 times....Then, I led them to predict the shape." (P2)

The practices of participants before the workshop were summarized in Table 6.

Table 6. Practices on Eliminating Technological Restrictions

Theme	Code	*n*
Continue with the traditional methods	-	10
Employing different methods/techniques	Game	7
	Tangible materials	5
	Demonstration	4
	CS-Unplugged	2
	Collaboration	2
	Problem-based	2
Alternative technology integration	Homework via WhatsApp	1

Changes in the Potential of Teachers on Integration Practices

Perceived Knowledge and Skills

The participants were asked to rate their skills in certain integration practices both before and after the workshop. The average ratings tended to increase in all skills. The minimum average pre-rating belonged to instructional material development skills (M=6.66) but became the highest average post-rating (M=8.6). Moreover, the maximum change in ratings from pre to post was observed in these skills with a 1.94 point increase. The minimum change in ratings occurred in ICT usage skills with a .87 point increase. The highest pre-rating was about employing interdisciplinary approaches, but the change was similar to ICT integration and adopting new integration approaches. All post-ratings were equal to or above 8 points. The summary of rating changes is presented in Table 7.

Table 7. Self-Ratings: Pre & Post

Skills	Mpre	Mpost	Change (Mpost-Mpre)
Developing instructional materials	6.66	8.6	1.94
Adopting new integration approaches	6.94	8.4	1.46
ICT integration	6.88	8.3	1.42
Employing interdisciplinary approaches	7.22	8.4	1.18
ICT usage	7.13	8	.87

The researchers conducted post-interviews with participants to understand how they perceived their potential change after such an intense workshop. The first dimension is about the perceived benefits of the workshop experience. Two main themes were extracted for this dimension: technological and methodological benefits. The workshop's most mentioned perceived benefit was improved in technology-related knowledge and skills (n=36), especially those with new and trendy tools. Material development (n=33), especially the ones including digital games (n=14), was also among the highly mentioned benefits. One participant explained how his/her perspective changed about material development as follows:

> *"I generally tend to use ready-to-use materials, which publishers provide, but this project made me aware of the tools to create instructional materials. For example, I can easily create a game using Web 2.0 tools. (P24)"*

Moreover, the participants also noted that their integration skills (n=26) and perspective changes on ICT (n=8) were also changed. Two participants explained their potential change as follows:

> *"Integration of modern approaches into my subject area was 4 before, but now, after the project, it became like 8... I usually follow recent trends in education, but such projects make it easier to update myself. I learned the tools I have never heard of in addition to those I already knew but never thought about using in such an innovative way. (P3)"*

> *"Of course, integration is a long process. It does not mean that I will use all the skills that I have earned here, which will turn out to be the exact practice. Assuming such a thing would not be realistic....On the other hand, this workshop serves as a prescription to decide where to start, what to do, how to do it, how to combine learning outcomes and technology, exactly when the technology should be used, etc. The workshop provided us with a map to achieve this. As I stated, it will, of course, take time to master the skills. I think my skills will keep improving as I insist on using them frequently. (P17)"*

In terms of methodological changes, GBL (n=17), interdisciplinary strategies (n=17), and gamification (n=10) were the most mentioned ones. One participant gave an example of an interdisciplinary strategy to embed games into the curriculum as follows:

> *"Van Cat or Çanakkale Strait....I can both let students discover the misspelling and the location on the map. Anyways, it can also be an interdisciplinary game. It just came to my mind quickly. (P1)"*

Two participants explained how they had realized the potential game/gamification integration with the tools that they already use in another way as follows:

> *"For example, yesterday there was a tool making the visuals interactive...The instructor showed us how to turn it into a game, which can be integrated into my topics....I was actually using some of the tools, but as I said before, I realized that*

I lacked certain knowledge and skills....For instance, this project improved my skills by 2 points, I can say that. Of course, this will be obvious when I practice myself. (P6)"

"I know several Web2.0 tools, but I had never thought that they could be used like that...I mean, the way they were used for games and gamification was very creative, I had never imagined like that. (P8)" Table 8 summarizes the perceived benefits according to participants.

Table 8. Perceived Benefits of the Workshop

Theme	Sub-Theme	Code	n
Technology (ICT)	Knowledge/Skills	AI/AR/VR	21
		New tools	17
	Material development	Digital games	14
		Traditional games	8
		The power of games (digital/traditional)	7
		Board games	4
	Integration skills	Technology	16
		Game integration	10
	Perspective change	Entertaining way of ICT	8
Methods (Pedagogy)	GBL	-	17
	Interdisciplinary strategies		17
	Gamification		10

GBL Integration

The second dimension of potential change is about the integration of GBL. Integration approaches fall into two categories: gamification (n=12) and technology integration into games (n=5). Street games (rope jumping, hopscotch, stop game, blind man's game, etc.) (n=14), AI or VR-based games (n=7), puzzles (n=8), mind games (n=3), and knowledge contests (n=2) were the examples of games that teachers provided examples of integration. Teaching concepts/rules (n=9), thinking skills (n=2), and famous scientists/artists (n=1) were the main content of games mentioned by teachers.

The participants explained the benefits of GBL within three sub-themes: affective (n=26), cognitive (n=24), and social (n=4). Gaining attention (n=21) was the most mentioned affective benefit perceived by participants, and then improving learning (n=16) came as a popular cognitive benefit of GBL. Although the frequency of social benefits was lower than the others, peer learning (n=2) and engagement (n=2) were emphasized by participants. The following excerpts indicate how this workshop led teachers to discover the potential of games:

"I see here that street games, I think is one of best ways to create an interdisciplinary learning environment. (P13)"

"Well, a GBL approach is very crucial for motivating students, especially for complex and intense courses, I mean the ones we call 'exam courses'. For example, I would plan 5-minute, 10-minute short games at the beginning of a lesson or add 1-minute, 2-minute long games in the middle of the lesson that can increase motivation... games are in demand in this century. I mean, the students do not enjoy it when we assign homework, but they can approach it in a positive way if I assign them to play games in the evenings. That is why this workshop made me aware that the games should definitely be integrated into our lessons." (P14)

"We think of games as a big deal, but here I realized that small steps can be taken to integrate games into lessons...I mean, you do not have to be a tech nerd or a game expert; you can just be inspired by games. (P16)"

"...I found it difficult to use games for national history because they are quite abstract for students, especially in terms of the chronological dimension and locations. Now, I can see how to design digital games to make them visible and concrete." (P19)

On the other hand, curriculum (n=10), individual (n=6), physical (n=4), and administration (n=3) were listed as the main factors hindering GBL practice. Exam-oriented politics (n=5) and tight schedule of curriculum (n=5) serve as curriculum-related barriers. The lack of time (n=2), skills (n=2), and resources (n=2) were mentioned as individual barriers. Class population (n=2) and limited outdoor space (n=2) were the codes of physical barriers. For a few teachers, having administrative pressure (n=2) and not being appreciated by administrators (n=1) were the fundamental barriers to GBL environments. One teacher explains the barriers as follows:

"I would love to use modern approaches, but my subject area is the most sophisticated. We have a time pressure... Well, our curriculum is very intense compared to other countries." (P14)

Table 9 summarizes the perceived benefits and barriers of GBL.

Table 9. GBL Benefits and Barriers

Theme	Sub-Theme	Code	*n*
Benefits	Affective	Gain attention	21
		Motivation	5
	Cognitive	Improve learning	16
		Speeding up	4
		Skill improvement	4
	Social	Peer learning	2
		Engagement	2
Barriers	Curriculum	Schedule	5
		Exam-orientedness	5
	Individual	Lack of time	2
		Lack of skills	2
		Lack of resources	2
	Physical	Class population	2
		Limited outdoor space	2
	Administration	Pressure	2
		Not appreciated	1

Twenty-First Century Skills Integration

The third dimension of potential change is about 21st-century skills and relatedness to the subject areas. All participants declared that these skills are required for their subject areas due to their basic skills. Problem-solving (n=12) and collaboration (n=11) were among the highly preferred skills. Having such 21st-century skills was associated with certain benefits, such as improvement in the learning process (n=17). Nevertheless, according to the participants, lack of motivation (n=8), integration skills (n=3), and resources (n=1) serve as the main barriers to mastering these skills in lessons. Teachers explained the reason why these were the barriers as follows:

"I realized how much I left behind the new trends because such in-service training is not designed...Honestly, I think I do not have the motivation to explore the trends by myself. (P1)"

"Sometimes, I have seen students who have had their homework done by artificial intelligence, like writing a poem, but I did not know how. However, now I have discovered how it is possible; there are endless opportunities. I was not aware that the information generated might be wrong. For example, one workshop

was about making myself famous, and I was like an artist....I mean, we can be successful as long as we have these skills to model students." (P2)

"For instance, on the first day of the workshop, I used PowerPoint in the big risk game, but I had never thought of using it that way. I mean, it was just very easy to create the game; I can do it; it is not a big deal, I see now...I used the tools shown here, but I suppose I created the materials without purpose. This workshop showed the ways to use and develop them on purpose." (P9)

"I think the undergraduate programs do not equip teachers with 21st-century skills. I really struggle with this issue. I feel like my digital skills are very limited. I perceive that I do not know how to use them in my class....We need qualified training such as this project. Knowing what to do caused relief for me. I think I will at least try to create my own material. Of course, I might need to watch YouTube videos, but I know where to start now." (P22)

Table 10 summarizes the findings about the subject areas and 21st-century skills relation.

Table 10. 21st Century Skills and the Subject Areas

Theme	Sub-Theme	*n*
Basic skills for my subject area	Problem solving	12
	Collaboration	11
	Critical thinking	7
	Digital literacy	7
	Creativity	6
	Communication	5
Benefits	Improved learning	17
	Mastering digital skills	6
	Motivation increase	2
Barriers	Lack of motivation (for older teachers)	8
	Lack of integration skills	3
	Lack of resources	1

Interdisciplinary Practice

The fourth dimension of potential change is about the potential change in interdisciplinary practice. The most mentioned benefit was improved collaboration among teachers (n=23). According to the participants, ICT (n=11) and science education (n=7) were among the most popular subject areas suitable for interdisciplinary approaches. On the other hand, failing to connect bonds between subject areas (n=10), lack of colleagues' interest (n=3), and time (n=1) were nominated as the main barriers to handling interdisciplinary work. One teacher noted the disinterest of colleagues as follows: "I think teachers are not willing to collaborate. I mean, they do not want to leave their comfort zone. (P23)". Table 11 summarizes the potential changes in interdisciplinary practice.

Table 11. Changes in Interdisciplinary Practice Potential

Theme	Sub-Theme	*n*
Benefits	Improved collaboration	23
	Enhanced learning experience	5
	Tangible learning experience	1
Fits best to	ICT	11
	Science education	7
	Maths	5
	Physical education	5
	Social sciences	5
Barriers	Fail to connect bonds	10
	Lack of others'interest	3
	Lack of time	1

Strategies to Eliminate Technology Restrictions

The fifth dimension of potential change is about the strategies to deal with technological restrictions. Unplugged (screenless) activities (n=12) and traditional street games (n=15) were two main strategies to eliminate the technological restrictions. The unplugged activities were perceived as sustainable (n=5), modeling the computational thinking (n=4), and easy to prepare (n=3). Puzzle, wheel of fortune, and role-playing were the unplugged activities listed by teachers. Traditional games were noted as appropriate to the new curriculum (n=13) with its ready-to-use structure (n=2). One teacher explains his/her interest in street game integration as follows:

> *"I have learned many modern approaches here, especially the ones without digital tools...I think these will all help me adopt to the new curriculum's needs because it advices such game-based activities...Indeed, all of the street games can be integrated, but the class hours are limited. In addition, we had a tight curriculum schedule. Alternatively, I can use interactive boards for gamification activities if I do not have time. Students can work collaboratively on the projected*

activity. Otherwise, I prefer traditional street games; they are perfect, but time matters." (P2)

Although these strategies were frequently reported, teachers' perspectives on the barriers to implementation remain. Teachers reported that administration (n=2) and restricted outside space (n=2) were the primary obstacles that needed to be overcome in order to eliminate the technological limits. Table 12 provides a summary of the various strategies and barriers.

Table 12. Strategies and Barriers to Deal with Technological Restrictions

Theme	Sub-Theme	*n*
Unplugged activities	Sustainable	5
	Modeling the computational thinking	4
	Easy to prepare	3
Traditional street games	Appropriate to the new curriculum	13
	Ready-to-use structure	2
Barriers	Administration	2
	Limited outdoor space	2

Researchers' Observations

During the session, the researchers took an active role in the activities and observed the participants and their interaction with each other. On the first day, it was obvious that the participants lacked the abilities necessary for the 21st century. Individuals with lower skill levels were left behind in the gamification activities. On the second day, during screenless activities, all teachers were both physically and cognitively active due to the engaging nature of the games. As they lasted all day, the teachers got exhausted. They were taken aback when they saw the connection between the curriculum and the games played on the street. Throughout all of the activities, they had a good time. On the third day, the actions using artificial intelligence were carried out. Every participant exhibited a high level of motivation. The participants were surprised by AI's screenless activities. On the other hand, the online collaboration and communication tools did not appeal to them. Web 2.0 activities, particularly the concert escape game, captured participants' attention on the fourth day of the event. The virtual reality and augmented reality activities were also exciting. The last day was full of opportunities for participants to share their experiences. Every participant was willing to discuss their experiences and how their viewpoints shifted throughout the workshop. All of the participants agreed that the workshop was beyond their expectations. On the other hand, most of them demanded longer content durations to complete mastery of skills (n=11). Some of them asked for AI-focused workshops (n=7), more practice-oriented content (n=10), and new follow-up modules (n=5).

SOLUTIONS AND RECOMMENDATIONS

Examples of Successful Integration

During the workshop, teachers of various subjects collaborated to engage in activities. One of the low-tech and non-digital integration was a street game called "wheels on the bus" (also known as box box nippers). Physical education teacher collaborated with maths teachers. In the original version, children make a circle and move around singing wheels on the bus and a name, who is required to turn backwards and continue moving. In the integrated version, each child had an even or odd number, and they needed to turn backwards when the number was announced by others based on whether it was even or odd. An interdisciplinary integration belonged to a Turkish language teacher, who combined misspelling detection and geography. The students are assigned to locate the place on the map and correct the mistake in the meantime. Boom game was another example. In its original form, it goes like one, two, three boom. In the integrated version, students are required to pronounce boom at each 3 multiplies and decide on the abstractness or concreteness of the word presented. Therefore, Turkish and maths teachers worked together to develop the game. Another integration example was the "drop the handkerchief" game. This example was created by a participant after a while in the workshop. The English teacher used grammar rules as the content and the rules of the game.

FUTURE RESEARCH DIRECTIONS

There are various approaches to mastering technological and pedagogical knowledge and skills, and such short but focused workshops, as offered in this study, might help teachers equip themselves with the necessary skills in a short time. The practicing part may not always be possible in short periods of workshop activities, but it can lead to understanding where and how to start. This study investigated how a focused workshop changes the potential of teachers. The first research question puts forth teachers' current practices before participation in the workshop, and the second research question compares the potential change among participants. The main dimensions to focus on were the GBL, 21st-century skills, interdisciplinary approaches, and strategies to deal with technology restrictions.

Changes in perceived skills and knowledge

The participants were asked to rate themselves both before and after the workshop regarding specific skills. The maximum change was recorded in instructional material development skills, and the minimum change was in ICT usage skills. However, the most beneficial part of the workshop was ICT-related knowledge and skills, according to the participants. Material development and integration skills were the followers. Having a low or high confidence level in ICT usage might influence the learning experience during the workshop. In Pongsakdi et al.'s (2021) study, the teachers with low confidence levels showed a significant improvement in confidence levels, but they also needed high ICT support to benefit from the workshop content. In the current study, various ICT knowledge and skills resulted in various task completion. Moreover, highly competent teachers were impatient with them. The pre-training sessions might be designed for teachers with lower confidence levels to eliminate this risk.

Regarding methodological change, GBL and interdisciplinary strategies were the most frequently mentioned ones. This study's results align with the findings of other investigations that have been published in the academic literature. One of these studies involved a group of 27 physiotherapists who participated in an educational intervention considered essential for developing the ability to adapt to new technologies and methods (Bonet-Collantes, 2024). This study was conducted to evaluate the extent to which a telerehabilitation educational intervention affects the knowledge and perspectives of physiotherapists. Through participation in the training program, participants were able to significantly improve their ICT-related skills and conceptual knowledge in their respective professions. Oktaviani and Utami (2024) conducted a different study in which they developed a training program based on TPACK and utilized the ADDIE paradigm in order to enhance the digital abilities of instructors. Through the course of the research, it was revealed that the participants successfully gained essential TPACK competencies, which significantly aided in their professional development in employing educational technology and generating pertinent educational materials. Pedagogical content knowledge is a crucial part of the teaching profession as it might directly affect learning outcomes, and such professional workshops can contribute to the improvement of content knowledge (Chang et al., 2020; Stammen et al., 2018). The current study is another example showing the effectiveness of focused professional workshops designed for teachers.

GBL

Before the implementation of the workshop, the majority of participants were aware of games to be used for educational purposes, but a few of them had no idea about the game's potential for learning. The entertaining and motivational nature of games was mentioned frequently, which comes into prominence of the affective dimension of games. A few participants listed cognitive and social dimensions as advantages. For some teachers, digital games can be important tools for communicating GenZ. After the implementation, research results revealed that gamification and technology integration into games were highly referred to as the ways of GBL integration. Participants provided many examples of street game integrations to teach concepts and rules. The affective features were the most mentioned benefit of GBL, and then cognitive and social benefits came (Csikszentmihalyi et. al., 2014). The vast majority of participants reported that they now understand how to blend digital and traditional GBL methodologies into their lesson plans. They emphasized that games that require less technology are effective and accessible educational tools for classroom activities. These findings demonstrate that the study yielded relevant results on both theoretical and practical levels. The curriculum intensity resulting in exam-orientedness and tight schedule was frequently called a strict barrier. Another aspect that is shared by other studies working in this field is the significance of providing sufficient training to in-service teachers in GBL. This is due to the considerable knowledge gap before and after the intervention, which underlines the need for this training. Researchers carried out a study investigating the development of an efficient GBL course for teachers already in the classroom (Palha et al., 2024). The results of the study showed that there was an increase in the use of GBL in practice as well as an improvement in competencies. As an additional benefit, the research provides a design solution as well as a framework for GBL training. Ragni et al. (2023) conducted a different study that investigated the use of GBL for teacher training as well as the viewpoints of educators regarding its application in their professional activity. The GBL instruction developed by the researchers was effective for both in-service and pre-service teachers. The findings of the study suggested that the effectiveness of training in GBL for teachers includes the inclusion of digital technologies, the enhancement of digital competencies, an increase in motivation, opportunities for collaborative learning, and the identification of facilitators and obstacles that affect teachers' perceptions of GBL.

21st Century Skills

Before the implementation of the five-day workshop, the majority of participants were aware of the skills, but there were still teachers who had no idea about those skills. They generally associated the skills with thinking skills. They generally believe that those skills can facilitate interaction with students rather than improvement in learning. However, after the implementation, all participants believe in the crucial role of those skills in their subject areas. Problem-solving and collaboration were the featured skills for all fields. The most important benefit of integrating those skills was improvement in learning. On the other hand, the lack of motivation and skills constitute an important barrier to integration. According to some participants, their undergrad education did not prepare them for mastering the skills. These feedbacks show that the participants have demonstrated an increased awareness of how to include skills relevant to the 21st century into their classes. They also stated that students' key abilities for the 21st century, such as problem-solving and collaboration, can be effectively taught through the use of GBL.

It is essential for educators to receive training in 21st-century competencies in order to effectively apply pedagogical methods and respond to the requirements of an ever-changing educational environment. Sophie Barat Achieng (2024) conducted a study that revealed that good professional development is essential for increasing teachers' knowledge, abilities, and attitudes regarding relevant skills in the 21st century. These training programs should have an emphasis on digital literacy, the transformation of information into practice, and the creation of educational innovations that offer educators the ability to improve the learning outcomes of their students (Mopara & Sanrattana, 2023). In accordance with our results, Martinez (2022) discovered that there was a significant change in knowledge both before and after the intervention. This finding highlights the need to provide adequate training in skills relevant to the 21st century. She also stressed that the utilization of project-based learning (PBL) as a unified teaching and learning technique in teacher training has the potential to raise the level of self-efficacy required to satisfy the curriculum needs in order to address 21st-century skills learning opportunities.

Interdisciplinary Approach

Before the training, the participants reported frequent integration of interdisciplinary approaches, especially the language and math teachers. According to the participants, inadequate training in undergraduate education and a lack of practice were the reasons for this situation. A notable point from our results is that the participants generally believed in the importance of an interdisciplinary approach after the training, which is supported by Lazou et al. (2023). They also believe that information and communication technology (ICT) and science education are two of the most preferred subject areas for collaboration. An interdisciplinary approach was utilized in this study as part of a professional development training program. The objective of the program was to expand the knowledge and capabilities of educators in order to meet the changing needs of contemporary educational practices. Training led to improved digital and media literacy skills among teachers. In this training, collaboration, peer tutoring, and peer assessment were encouraged among teachers. Anyolo et al. (2024) also found that teachers' knowledge and skills are enhanced when trained in an interdisciplinary approach, fostering a more integrated understanding of diverse educational contexts. An interdisciplinary approach equips teachers with essential skills to tackle complex challenges. This method encourages the development of innovative pedagogical approaches. However, failure to connect bonds between areas, lack of interest, and time were reported as the main barriers to the integration practice of an interdisciplinary approach. In parallel, Singh (2023) found significant obstacles to implementing a multidisciplinary approach in education, including restrictive departmental structures, insufficient resources, and bureaucratic processes. Leon and Lipuma (2024) also identified significant obstacles to interdisciplinary research, such as varied disciplinary terminology, methodological disparities, and a dominant culture of disciplinary isolation. These constraints impede efficient collaboration and communication among participants from diverse professions.

Strategies Changes Against Technological Restrictions

Participants generally find solutions by proceeding with traditional methods, but the majority put forth various strategies, such as games and tangible materials, according to interview results conducted before the implementation of the workshop. However, after implementation, unplugged or screenless activities and street games were mentioned as the favorite strategies to eliminate the technological restrictions because they were easy to integrate and sustainable. The reason for the interest in street game integration was because the new curriculum's structure is quite appropriate for that. On the other hand, administrative approaches and limited outdoor space were still seen as barriers. A prior study carried out in China sought to assist educators in applying teaching strategies designed to enhance student motivation and engagement in the learning process (Li & Jones, 2019). Educators observed a shift in their attitudes and beliefs concerning the influence of group activities on student motivation and achievement, acknowledging the necessity for proficient implementation of active learning strategies to involve students in the classroom.

CONCLUSION

This study attempts to disseminate the GBL both in technologically rich and technologically restricted environments by utilizing interdisciplinary approaches. The findings of this study are limited to the participants of this study and the boundaries of the case, and therefore, one should be cautious when generalizing the findings. Further studies can be designed to specifically observe the interaction between disciplines during the planning of GBL activities. In this study, although teachers believed and were convinced of the importance of GBL, some of them stated that they needed more practice. That is why practicing sessions should be extended and modeling how to collaborate with other disciplines. The overall duration of the workshop should also be extended because teachers with lower prior knowledge and skills demand much more support for both understanding the approaches and practicing them. Researchers found that GBL methodologies can effectively lessen the digital divide among students. However, testing the findings with a larger number of participants would improve the study's generalizability in future research. There is a need for empirical studies that thoroughly investigate the impact of GBL on student outcomes, especially in settings with limited technology resources. It would also be useful to evaluate other pedagogical strategies aimed at closing the digital gap, such as collaborative learning, project-based learning, or the utilization of open educational materials. This would assist in creating a more comprehensive body of literature on effective teaching strategies for different contexts.

ACKNOWLEDGMENTS

Grammarly and QuillBot were used to correct spelling and grammar for this book chapter. This project was funded by TUBITAK (Project ID: 123B947).

REFERENCES

Anyolo, E., Iipinge, S., & Hako, A. (2024) *Achieving Sustainability Through Interdisciplinary Approach: An Analysis of Teacher Education Transformed Curriculum*. The Asian Conference on Education & International Development 2024 Official Conference Proceedings, 411-420. https://doi.org/DOI: 10.22492/issn.2189-101X.2024.33

Battelle for Kids. (2019). *Framework for 21st Century Learning*. P21 Partnership for 21st Century Learning. https://static.battelleforkids.org/documents/p21/P21_Framework_Brief.pdf

Bonet-Collantes, M., Niño-Pinzón, D. M., Chaustre-Porras, A. D., Salas-Poloche, Y. A., & Angarita-Fonseca, A. (2024). Enhancing physiotherapists' knowledge and perceptions of telerehabilitation: A before-after educational intervention study. *Physiotherapy Research International*, *29*(4), e2120. Advance online publication. DOI: 10.1002/pri.2120 PMID: 39192801

Chang, S. H., Ward, P., & Goodway, J. D. (2020). The effect of a content knowledge teacher professional workshop on enacted pedagogical content knowledge and student learning in a throwing unit. *Physical Education and Sport Pedagogy*, *25*(5), 493–508. DOI: 10.1080/17408989.2020.1743252

Chapman, R., Likhanov, M., Selita, F., Zakharov, I., Smith-Woolley, E., & Kovas, Y. (2019). New literacy challenge for the twenty-first century: Genetic knowledge is poor even among well educated. *Journal of Community Genetics*, *10*(1), 73–84. DOI: 10.1007/s12687-018-0363-7 PMID: 29589204

Cheshmehzangi, A., Zou, T., Su, Z., & Tang, T. (2023). The growing digital divide in education among primary and secondary children during the COVID-19 pandemic: An overview of social exclusion and education equality issues. *Journal of Human Behavior in the Social Environment*, *33*(3), 434–449. DOI: 10.1080/10911359.2022.2062515

Csikszentmihalyi, M., Csikszentmihalyi, M., Abuhamdeh, S., & Nakamura, J. (2014). Flow. *Flow and the foundations of positive psychology: The collected works of Mihaly Csikszentmihalyi*, 227-238 https://doi.org/DOI: 10.1007/978-94-017-9088-8

Dahalan, F., Alias, N., & Shaharom, M. S. N. (2024). Gamification and game based learning for vocational education and training: A systematic literature review. *Education and Information Technologies, 29*(2), 1279–1317. DOI: 10.1007/s10639-022-11548-w PMID: 36688221

Durmuşkaya, S. (2021). *Blok tabanlı kodlamaya geçiş sürecinde sokak oyunlarına entegre edilmiş kodlama etkinliklerinin etkisi [The effect of coding activities integrated into street games in the transition to block-based coding]* (Publication No. 688549) [Doctoral dissertation, Ondokuz Mayıs University]. Higher Education Institution Database.

El Mawas, N., Bradford, M., Andrews, J., Pathak, P., & Muntean, C. H. (2018, June). A Case study on 21st century skills development through a computer based maths game. In *EdMedia+ Innovate Learning,* 1160-1169. Association for the Advancement of Computing in Education (AACE).

Galli, B. J. (2021). Effective Strategies for Communicating and Managing Communication in a Project Team: My Perspective. *International Journal of Applied Industrial Engineering*, *8*(1), 0. Advance online publication. DOI: 10.4018/IJAIE.20210101oa01

Garlinska, M., Osial, M., Proniewska, K., & Pregowska, A. (2023). The influence of emerging technologies on distance education. *Electronics (Basel)*, *12*(7), 1550. DOI: 10.3390/electronics12071550

Grobler, S., & Dittrich, A. K. (2024). Envisioning quality education for sustainability transformation in teacher education: Perspectives from an international dialogue on Sustainable Development Goal 4. *International Journal of Comparative Education and Development*, *26*(3), 270–285. DOI: 10.1108/IJCED-06-2023-0048

Güntepe, E. T., & Keles, E. (2022). Eğitim Fakültesindeki Öğretim Elemanlarının Teknoloji Entegrasyon Süresinin Eş Merkezli Halka Modeline Göre Değerlendirilmesi. *Ahi Evran Üniversitesi Kırşehir Eğitim Fakültesi Dergisi*, *23*(2), 1639–1690.

Hammes, R. (2007). Orienteering with Adventure Education: New Games for the 21st Century. *Strategies (Reston, VA)*, *20*(5), 7–13. DOI: 10.1080/08924562.2007.10590733

Hero, L. M., & Lindfors, E. (2019). Students' learning experience in a multidisciplinary innovation project. *Education + Training*, *61*(4), 500–522. DOI: 10.1108/ET-06-2018-0138

ISTE. (2017). ISTE 21st Century Standards for Students. https://iste.org/standards/students

Jääskä, E., Lehtinen, J., Kujala, J., & Kauppila, O. (2022). GBL and students' motivation in project management education. *Project Leadership and Society*, *3*, 100055. DOI: 10.1016/j.plas.2022.100055

Klaassen, R. G. (2018). Interdisciplinary education: A case study. *European Journal of Engineering Education*, *43*(6), 842–859. DOI: 10.1080/03043797.2018.1442417

Kuo, H. C., Weng, T. L., Chang, C. C., & Chang, C. Y. (2023). Designing Our Own Board Games in the Playful Space: Improving High School Student's Citizenship Competencies and Creativity through GBL. *Sustainability (Basel)*, *15*(4), 2968. DOI: 10.3390/su15042968

Lazou, C., Panagiotou, N., & Tsinakos, A. (2023). Training Teachers in an Interdisciplinary Approach through EMI: A Case Study in Greece. In *English Language Teacher Education in Changing Times* (pp. 50–65). Routledge., DOI: 10.4324/9781003295723-7

Leon, C., & Lipuma, J. (2024). Overcoming Obstacles to Interdisciplinary Research: Empirical Insights and Strategies. *Journal of Systemics, Cybernetics and Informatics*, *22*(6), 18–34. DOI: 10.54808/JSCI.22.06.18

Li, M., & Jones, B. D. (2019). Transforming traditional teaching: A professional development program for the college EFL teachers. *Theory and Practice in Language Studies*, *9*(12), 1494–1500. DOI: 10.17507/tpls.0912.05

Martinez, C. (2022). Developing 21st century teaching skills: A case study of teaching and learning through project-based curriculum. *Cogent Education*, *9*(1), 2024936. Advance online publication. DOI: 10.1080/2331186X.2021.2024936

Metin, E. (2018). Eğitimde teknoloji kullanımında öğretmen eğitimi: Bir durum çalışması [Teacher training in the use of technology in education: a case study]. *Journal of STEAM Education*, *1*(1), 79–103.

MoNE. (2023). 21. Yüzyıl Becerileri ve Değerlere Yönelik Araştırma Raporu [Research Report on 21st Century Skills and Values]. https://ttkb.meb.gov.tr/meb_iys_dosyalar/2023_05/11153521_21.yy_becerileri_ve_degerlere_yonelik_arastirma_raporu.pdf

MoNE (Ministry of National Education). (2022). *FATİH Projesi Hakkında* [About the FATIH project]. https://olur.meb.gov.tr/www/fatih-projesi-hakkinda/icerik/370

Mopara, R., & Sanrattana, W. (2023). Developing Teachers to Develop Students' 21st Century Skills. *World Journal of Education*, *13*(3), 94–104. DOI: 10.5430/wje.v13n3p94

Nikbay Arslantaş, Ç., & Bavlı, B. (2024). School-based outdoor education: A neglected practice at secondary level. *Journal of Adventure Education and Outdoor Learning, 24*(2), 270–286. DOI: 10.1080/14729679.2022.2143385

Noonoo, S. (2019). *Playing games can build 21st-century skills. Research explains how.* https://www.edsurge.com/news/2019-02-12-playing-games-can-build-21st-century-skills-research-explains-how

OECD. (2019). OECD future of education and skills 2030: OECD learning compass 2030. *A Series of Concept Notes,* https://www.oecd.org/content/dam/oecd/en/about/projects/edu/education-2040/1-1-learning-compass/OECD_Learning_Compass_2030_Concept_Note_Series.pdf

Oktaviani, H. I., & Utami, D. D. (2024). Development Of Training Programs to Enhance Teachers' Digital Skills with Technological Pedagogical Content Knowledge (TPACK). *Journal of Educational Technology Studies and Applied Research, 1*(2). Advance online publication. DOI: 10.70125/jetsar.v1i2y2024a23

Özgem, K., & Akçıl, U. (2022). An Investigation of Preschool Level Out-of-Class Education Activities in Finland, Estonia, Ireland, and Turkey within the Framework of 21st Century Skills. *Sustainability (Basel), 14*(14), 8736. DOI: 10.3390/su14148736

Palha, S., Bouwer, A., Webb, K., van Smaalen, D., & Agterberg, D. (2024, October). Game-based Pedagogy in Teacher Training: Results of a Pilot Course. In *European Conference on Games Based Learning*, 677-684. Academic Conferences International Limited. https://doi.org/DOI: 10.34190/ecgbl.18.1.2698

Parlak, B., & Sendurur, E. (2022). The Integration of GBS into a Technologically Restricted Context to Improve Digital Literacy. *Journal of Educational Multimedia and Hypermedia, 31*(2), 149–178.

Partridge, J. (2022). *Digital games-based learning: Minecraft in the 21st century classroom* (Doctoral dissertation, University of British Columbia). ProQuest Dissertations & Theses Global.

Pongsakdi, N., Kortelainen, A., & Veermans, M. (2021). The impact of digital pedagogy training on in-service teachers' attitudes towards digital technologies. *Education and Information Technologies, 26*(5), 5041–5054. DOI: 10.1007/s10639-021-10439-w

Qian, M., & Clark, K. R. (2016). GBL and 21st century skills: A review of recent research. *Computers in Human Behavior, 63*, 50–58. DOI: 10.1016/j.chb.2016.05.023

Ragni, B., Toto, G. A., di Furia, M., Lavanga, A., & Limone, P. (2023). The use of Digital GBL (DGBL) in teachers' training: a scoping review. In *Frontiers in Education, 8*. Frontiers Media SA. https://doi.org/DOI: 10.3389/feduc.2023.1092022

Reigeluth, C. M., Watson, W. R., Watson, S. S. L., Dutta, P., Chen, Z., & Powell, N. D. (2008). Roles for technology in the information-age paradigm of education: Learning management systems. *Educational Technology*, *48*(6), 32–39. DOI: 10.4018/978-1-61350-347-8.ch003

Robinson, L., Schulz, J., Blank, G., Ragnedda, M., Ono, H., Hogan, B., Mesch, G. S., Cotten, S. R., Kretchmer, S. B., Hale, T. M., Drabowicz, T., Yan, P., Wellman, B., Harper, M.-G., Quan-Haase, A., Dunn, H. S., Casilli, A. A., Tubaro, P., Carvath, R., & Khilnani, A. (2020). Digital inequalities 2.0: Legacy inequalities in the information age. *First Monday*, *25*(7). Advance online publication. DOI: 10.5210/fm.v25i7.10842

Samala, A. D., Bojic, L., Vergara-Rodríguez, D., Klimova, B., & Ranuharja, F. (2023). Exploring the impact of gamification on 21st-century skills: Insights from DOTA 2. *International Journal of Interactive Mobile Technologies*, *17*(18), 33–54. Advance online publication. DOI: 10.3991/ijim.v17i18.42161

Singh, A. (2023). Challenges of a multidisciplinary approach in higher education. *International Journal of Advanced Academic Studies*, *5*(9), 30–32. DOI: 10.33545/27068919.2023.v5.i9a.1049

Sophie Barat Achieng, D. M. (2024). Teacher professional development and learning outcomes in the 21st century. *IJRDO-. The Journal of Educational Research*, *10*(3), 46–54. DOI: 10.53555/er.v10i3.6190

Stammen, A. N., Malone, K. L., & Irving, K. E. (2018). Effects of modeling instruction professional development on biology teachers' scientific reasoning skills. *Education Sciences*, *8*(3), 119. DOI: 10.3390/educsci8030119

Van De Werfhorst, H. G., Kessenich, E., & Geven, S. (2022). The digital divide in online education: Inequality in digital readiness of students and schools. *Computers and Education Open*, *3*, 100100. DOI: 10.1016/j.caeo.2022.100100 PMID: 40478103

Xu, M., Luo, Y., Zhang, Y., Xia, R., Qian, H., & Zou, X. (2023). GBL in medical education. *Frontiers in Public Health*, *11*, 1113682. DOI: 10.3389/fpubh.2023.1113682 PMID: 36935696

Yeşilyurt, E., & Vezne, R. (2023). Digital literacy, technological literacy, and internet literacy as predictors of attitude toward applying computer-supported education. *Education and Information Technologies, 28*(8), 9885–9911. DOI: 10.1007/s10639-022-11311-1 PMID: 36688220

Yin, R. K. (2018). *Case Study Research and Applications: Design and Methods* (6th ed.). Sage.

ADDITIONAL READING

Børte, K., Nesje, K., & Lillejord, S. (2023). Barriers to student active learning in higher education. *Teaching in Higher Education, 28*(3), 597–615. DOI: 10.1080/13562517.2020.1839746

Chu, S. K. W., Reynolds, R. B., Tavares, N. J., Notari, M., & Lee, C. W. Y. (2021). *21st century skills development through inquiry-based learning from theory to practice*. Springer International Publishing.

Mahlangu, B. G., & Goosen, L. (2023). The Impact of a Lack of Information and Communication Technologies at Rural Schools: Digitalization in a Changing Education Environment. In *Contemporary Challenges in Education: Digitalization, Methodology, and Management* (pp. 254-275). IGI Global.

Morel, G. M., & Spector, J. M. (2022). *Foundations of educational technology: Integrative approaches and interdisciplinary perspectives*. Routledge.

Nasir, N. I. S., Lee, C. D., Pea, R., & McKinney de Royston, M. (2021). Rethinking learning: What the interdisciplinary science tells us. *Educational Researcher, 50*(8), 557–565. DOI: 10.3102/0013189X211047251

Ong, Q. K. L., & Annamalai, N. (2024). Technological pedagogical content knowledge for twenty-first century learning skills: The game changer for teachers of industrial revolution 5.0. *Education and Information Technologies, 29*(2), 1939–1980. DOI: 10.1007/s10639-023-11852-z

Tay, J., Goh, Y. M., Safiena, S., & Bound, H. (2022). Designing digital GBL for professional upskilling: A systematic literature review. *Computers & Education, 184*, 104518. DOI: 10.1016/j.compedu.2022.104518

Tobias, S., Fletcher, J. D., & Wind, A. P. (2014). GBL. *Handbook of research on educational communications and technology*, 485-503.

Vienni-Baptista, B., Lindvig, K. E., van Goch, M., & van Lambalgen, R. (2024). *Interdisciplinary practices in higher education*. Routledge. DOI: 10.4324/9781003286004

KEY TERMS AND DEFINITIONS

21st Century Surviving Skills: A dynamic set of skills including various literacies (information, computer, artificial intelligence, etc.). Their boundaries can change as technology evolves.

CS-Unplugged: It refers to screenless teaching-learning activities focusing on computer science concepts.

Digital Games: Digital games have the potential to be adapted as a GBL activity.

GBL: The learning environment is enhanced with game dynamics to facilitate learning.

Interdisciplinary Approach: An instructional design approach to create instructional materials, utilize, and evaluate them to enrich learners' learning experience and connect the bonds between different courses.

Technologically Restricted Environments: Teaching and learning environments that have a limited number or amount of technological devices, tools, and infrastructure.

Traditional Games: The street games have the potential to be adapted as a GBL activity.

Chapter 11
Piece by Piece:
Awakening Computational and Geometric Thinking in the 1st Cycle of Basic Education – The Manipulation of Pattern Blocks

Joana Martins
https://orcid.org/0009-0004-4819-5377
School of Education, Polytechnic Institute of Porto, Portugal

Daniela Mascarenhas
https://orcid.org/0000-0001-5854-536X
Centre for Research and Innovation in Education, School of Education, Polytechnic Institute of Porto, Portugal

Sara Paredes
https://orcid.org/0000-0003-4801-5386
Colégio Oceanus, Portugal

ABSTRACT

The materials manipulation plays a key role in mathematics education by transforming abstract concepts into concrete experiences. This paper presents an exploratory qualitative study focused on how Pattern Blocks promote computational and geometric thinking in 25 first grade students from a Portuguese private school. Over five formative sessions, children participated in practical activities which echoed the national curriculum such as identifying, composing and decomposing shapes. Observations of classes, video recordings and document analysis were used to collect data. Both physical and digital Pattern Blocks facilitate mathematical learning by promoting spatial awareness, logical reasoning, pattern recognition,

DOI: 10.4018/979-8-3373-7729-2.ch011

and problem-solving skills. The students developed their out-of-the-box and critical thinking, abstraction and collaboration. The study concludes that the integration of structured material promotes meaningful, student centered, active, and collaborative learning, while effectively developing computational and geometric thinking in early mathematics education.

INTRODUCTION

The integration of tangible learning tools in mathematics education has long been recognized for its effectiveness in making abstract concepts accessible to young learners. This idea is cemented by Mascarenhas (2012) who argues that "manipulable materials play an important role in learning geometry and measurements and should be used to facilitate the understanding and articulation of mathematical concepts and ideas" (p.147).

The Portuguese curriculum states that "learning to use multiple representations in mathematics is essential, verbal expression of ideas is valued, as well as representations involving manipulable materials" (ME, 2021, p. 9). Furthermore, the use of Pattern Blocks as manipulative tools serves not only to enhance engagement but also to promote deeper learning of both geometric and computational thinking skills.

This chapter presents findings from a qualitative exploratory study conducted in a private Portuguese primary school involving 25 first grade students. These students generally have a positive attitude towards exploring new mathematical concepts and, because their school fosters a hybrid learning environment – integrating technologies along all learning areas –, they are indeed comfortable with using digital tools.

That being the case, the study focus is on the use of Pattern Blocks by the students, which features a unique role in gathering computational and geometric thinking together. Pattern Blocks allow students to manipulate each piece of the set, arrange and rearrange the pieces, creating geometric figures and consequently developing a tangible understanding of shapes and their composition and decomposition. By physically building shapes and understanding their properties, students gain an entrance point into concepts that might otherwise seem abstract at this age and at the corresponding stage of mathematical thinking (concrete, pictorial and abstract).

The experience is rooted in hands-on learning which allows students to see and touch the shapes, make their own discoveries, and connect geometric forms with computational thinking processes. According to Bessa, Mascarenhas, Silva, Fernandes and Quadros-Flores (2023), this combination of abstract thinking with concrete material leads to a deeper grasp of these fundamental concepts.

In the context of the Basic Education in Portugal, it is advocated that "no one should be excluded from mathematics and that everyone should have the opportunity to be the subject of mathematically rich and challenging learning experiences" (ME, 2021). Unequivocally believing this, it is important to notice that this study is grounded in the belief that multiple representations, multiple means of engagement and expression are keys points to the holistic understanding of mathematical concepts, and pedagogical differentiation, aligning with the Universal Design for Learning allowing students to access learning in diverse ways, catering to different learning preferences and abilities (CAST, 2018).

This being the scenario, it is essential to contextualize computational thinking in basic education, geometric thinking in basic education and geometry and its relationship with manipulative materials within a theoretical framework.

Theoretical Framework

Computational Thinking in Basic Education

As digital technologies increasingly shape modern society, computational thinking has emerged as a vital competency for preparing learners to navigate complex, information-rich environments. Therefore, computational thinking is increasingly recognized as a fundamental competency for 21st-century learners. Papert (1980) emphasized the potential of children to engage in computational thinking through concrete experiences. Computational thinking includes skills like problem decomposition, abstraction, and pattern recognition which are essential not only for computing but for mathematics as well (Grover & Pea, 2013; Wing, 2006).

Far from being limited to digital competences, programming or technological applications, it incorporates several cognitive processes and problem-solving strategies that extend across disciplines, including mathematics, supporting interdisciplinary applications.

According to the Mathematic Teachers Association (APM), developing computational thinking requires more than simply introducing programming tasks; it demands meaningful, intentional learning experiences that promote reflection, abstraction, and structured reasoning (Carvalho, Espadeiro & Branco, 2023). Unlike information technology or the simple use of machines like plugged-in computers, computational thinking can be approached in an unplugged format, without reliance on digital devices (Vicari, 2018).

Building on these foundational concepts, Wing (2006) identifies five interconnected stages that form the backbone of computational thinking: decomposition, pattern recognition, abstraction, algorithms, and debugging, which are represented in Figure 1 and briefly outlined below.

Figure 1. Computational Thinking Stages (Wing, 2006)

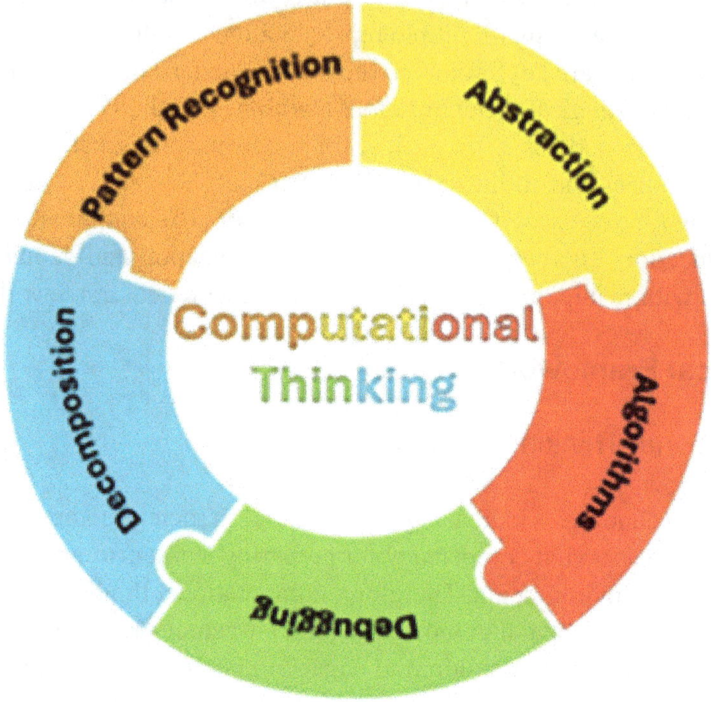

Decomposition is a crucial element of computational thinking, because it implies breaking down complex problems into smaller parts, facilitating students understanding and leading to solving strategies (Liukas, 2015 cited by Vicari, 2018). As Csizmadia (2015, cited by Vicari, 2018) notes, this strategy simplifies problem-solving, enabling learners to better grasp new or unfamiliar situations.

Pattern Recognition focuses on identifying recurring features or structures within problems. According to Wing (2006, p.31), these are "characteristics that problems share and that can be exploited so that they are solved more efficiently". Once a problem has been decomposed, recognizing similar patterns within each part can facilitate more efficient solutions. Wing (2006, p.32) also highlights that this stage often leads to automation, where one can create and navigate relationships across different levels of abstraction.

Abstraction compels the understanding the problem statement through the action of selecting and organizing relevant information, discarding irrelevant elements, and concentrating on the elements most critical to solving the problem. This step produces an abstract representation of the situation (Wing, 2006, p.34), although its conceptual complexity often makes it the most challenging to apply in practice.

Algorithms represent the procedural side of computational thinking. They are often associated with programming and consist of repeatable sequences of actions or instructions. Algorithms are structured processes that take an input, follow a finite series of steps, and deliver an output that meets a defined goal (Wing, 2006, p.35). This process-oriented approach links directly to abstraction, as it requires constructing a logical framework for action.

Debugging, the last step, entails finding and fixing mistakes in every solution. This phase is vital for enhancing the problem-solving process since entails testing, refining, and optimizing answers (APM, 2020, p.1).

These five equally relevant steps are part of a transversal mathematical competency identified as *Computational Thinking*, which integrates the mathematics Portuguese curriculum for all basic education and subsequently the Essential Learning of Mathematics for the first year of schooling (ME, 2021).

Computational thinking gives students "the methods, techniques, and courage to examine, evaluate, and create possible solutions to a complex problem," which are understandable by both humans and machines, claims Figueiredo (2017, p. 101). Engaging in this type of thinking strengthens its educational value by helping students make connections between their academic and real-world experiences and by clarifying their understanding of a variety of subjects (Figueiredo, 2017).

The dynamics and interactions between the teacher and the students in the classroom are an important part of encouraging computational thinking (Carvalho, Espadeiro & Branco, 2023). As the APM (2020) points out, a major element in making sure that computational thinking practices are actively developed is the teacher's intentionality, particularly their use of strategic questioning when students are having trouble and the way they guide the understanding and clarifying of the doubts. By encouraging students to think outside of the box and consider how they solve problems, this interaction goes beyond traditional teaching.

Furthermore, rather than focusing only on programming, computational thinking highlights the ideas that underpin it. It entails having the capacity to deal with situations through reflective analysis and various levels of abstraction. For this reason, computational thinking assignments should be faced as chances to encourage students to think deeply and creatively, organize their ideas in logical ways, and investigate problems in a meaningful way, broadening horizons from the typical technical exercises.

Teachers can develop cross-cutting skills like creativity, perseverance, and teamwork in addition to content knowledge by incorporating Computational Thinking into the mathematics curriculum. This method is in line with contemporary pedagogical frameworks that support dynamic, student-focused classrooms where thought processes are valued equally to results (Wing, 2006; Grover & Pea, 2013; Sullivan & Bers, 2019).

Ultimately, computational thinking should be considered as a potent teaching tool rather than because it teaches students to code; rather, it will equip them to think, reason, and solve problems in an ordered and creative manner. Its inclusion into mathematical education improves students' capacity to evaluate complexity, create answers, and adjust to a digital environment always changing.

Geometric Thinking in Basic Education

A basic element of mathematics education, geometry is also very important for strengthening students' logical thinking, spatial reasoning, and visualization ability. Early years of education allow geometric thinking to help children make sense of the space around them, understand shapes and their properties, and start to describe, model, and interpret physical and abstract environments, recognizing, naming, describing, constructing, comparing, and sorting two-dimensional and three-dimensional shapes. It also requires developing spatial awareness and grasping positional language—that is, "above," "next to," "between".

Geometry in the curriculum progressively includes study of angles, symmetry, transformations and the properties of shapes increasing their presence throughout the school years.

Though geometric learning starts in early years, educational policies, cultural elements, and curriculum priorities shape the approaches to encourage geometric thinking across nations. Globally, people agree increasingly on the need for early childhood geometric thinking promotion since it develops major competencies needed to life.

The Trends in International Mathematics and Science Study (TIMSS) and other major tests have exposed ongoing difficulties in students' grasp of geometric ideas across many educational systems (Mullis *et al.*, 2020). Specifically in the early years of schooling, geometry is often underrepresented even if many nations have made great improvements in other areas related to numbers.

In the United States, the National Research Council (2001) emphasized the need for a balanced mathematics curriculum that includes geometry from the early years. The Common Core State Standards for Mathematics (CCSSM) identify geometry as one of the five critical strands beginning in kindergarten, encouraging students to explore shapes, their attributes, and spatial relationships through drawing, building, and manipulation (National Governors Association Center for Best Practices & Council of Chief State School Officers, 2010).

In Singapore – a system consistently recognized for high mathematics achievement – geometry is introduced as early as kindergarten, using concrete-pictorial-abstract approaches. Students manipulate objects, draw diagrams, and engage in visual reasoning tasks, which are later formalized into more abstract geometric reasoning (Toh *et al.*, 2017).

Van Hiele's levels of geometric thinking have also gained international recognition. Van Hiele's (1986) theory states that learners advance through different stages, starting with visual shape recognition and moving on to property analysis, informal and formal deduction, and finally rigor, as illustrated in the scheme below (Table 1).

Table 1. Van Hiele Levels of Geometric Thinking (Van Hiele, 1986)

Level	Name	Description
0	Visualization	Recognizes shapes by their overall appearance, without analyzing properties.
1	Analysis	Identifies specific properties of shapes.
2	Informal Deduction	Understands relationships between properties and figures but does not use formal logic.
3	Formal Deduction	Uses formal logic and can construct proofs within an axiomatic system.
4	Rigor	Understands and compares different axiomatic systems and their logical foundations.

The idea that geometric thinking is not innate and therefore requires time, investment and practice is supported by Vygotsky's scaffolding strategy, as it implies the inclusion of appropriate tasks to evolve supported by these levels, which offer a developmental framework based on curriculum development and teacher training in many countries.

Although changes in national education policies and reforms have affected its emphasis over time, geometry has historically played a significant role in Portugal's mathematics curriculum. Geometry and measurement are reaffirmed as one of the fundamental areas of mathematics in basic education in the current curriculum (Essential Learnings of Mathematics, ME, 2021). Figure 2 demonstrates through a graphic the evolution of mathematic themes preponderance throughout the years considering the curriculum changes in the years 2001, 2007, 2013, 2018 and 2021.

Figure 2. Evolution of the mathematic themes in Portuguese curriculum through the years (ME, 2001, 2007, 2013, 2018, 2021).

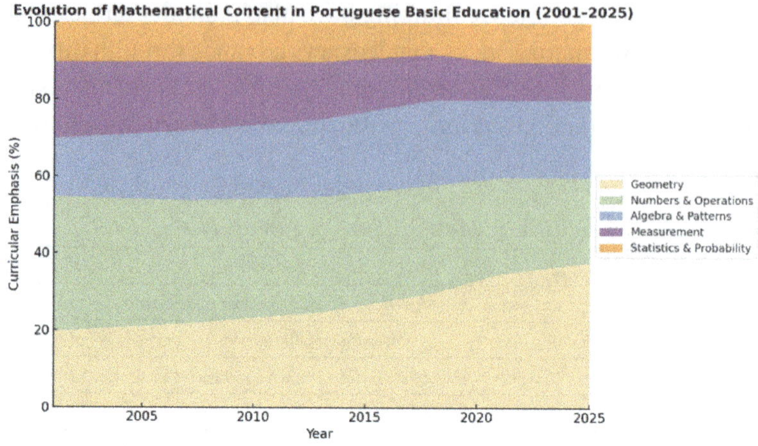

The graphic shows the evolution over the years of the weight that each of the mathematical themes has in Portuguese Basic Education, which corresponds to the period between the 1st year and the 9th year of schooling. Over time, educational reforms have prioritized different areas, taking into account the educational objectives defined by the curriculum itself.

Interpreting the graphic, it is possible to say that *Geometry* is the theme that has increased its presence in the curriculum, possibly due to the gradually greater appreciation of geometric reasoning as a crucial component in the development of mathematical literacy (NCTM, 2000; Clements & Sarama, 2007), a fact that has been confirmed internationally. As a result, the theme of *Numbers and Operations* has become less dominant in the curriculum. In order to contextualize the evolution of the Portuguese curriculum over the years, follows a brief explanation of the milestones of change in 2001, 2007, 2013, 2018 and 2021.

In 2001, clear structuring into content domains was introduced in the curriculum (ME, 2001), organizing it in the five themes of the graphic – *Geometry, Number and Operations, Algebra and Patterns, Measurement, Statistics and Probability*. Although *Geometry* had a considerable presence in this curriculum, the subject of *Numbers and Operations* was clearly dominant.

Throughout the grades, geometry was visibly more incorporated in the program (ME, 2007), and educators were urged to employ visual aids and manipulatives. Despite this, its impact was slowed by resistance and implementation issues.

The *Curriculum Goals* (Metas Curriculares, ME, 2013) of 2013 placed more of an emphasis on quantifiable results and introduced grade-level-specific learning objectives. While arithmetic continued to dominate, *Geometry* gained more structure, especially in terms of *Measurement*, shape classification, and spatial visualization.

In 2018, Essential Leanings of Mathematics (ME, 2018) was implemented with an emphasis on reasoning, problem-solving, and mathematical communication, this reform indicated a return to curriculum flexibility and depth. *Geometry* was rethought as a context for fostering transversal competencies as well as content. It was suggested that there be more open tasks, visual aids, and links to computational thinking.

The latest actualization of the Portuguese curriculum of mathematics was in 2021, which was fully implemented in 2022, where six themes were structured - *Mathematical Skills, Numbers, Algebra, Data and Probability, Geometry and Measurement* (ME, 2021). Nowadays, *Geometry and Measurement* is consolidated as one of the core areas of mathematics. Beginning in 1st grade, it promoted the use of digital tools like GeoGebra and manipulatives like Pattern Blocks to foster conceptual exploration, pattern construction, and spatial reasoning. Specifically in the first year of schooling the topics approached in *Geometry and Measurement* are spatial orientation, solids, plane figures, operations with figures, length and time.

Portuguese curricular guidelines promote a vision of geometry as a mean to foster mathematical reasoning, problem-solving, and modelling. Children are expected to use both digital and tangible manipulatives to investigate, create, and explain geometric figures since the Portuguese mathematics curriculum argues that "technological tools should be considered as unavoidable and powerful resources for the teaching and learning of mathematics" (ME, 2021).

In order to facilitate the transition from intuitive to analytical geometric reasoning, educators are urged to incorporate tangible resources. Some difficulties in the development of geometric thinking have been brought to light by recent Portuguese research, specifically the overemphasis on memorization shape identification at the expense of more complex spatial reasoning and understanding (Oliveira & Ribeiro, 2019).

The realization that geometric thinking involves more than just shapes and definitions is increasing not only in Portugal but also around the world, acknowledging that it also contains learning to reason spatially, communicate mathematically, and solve challenging problems. Active exploration, the use of precise language, the incorporation of technology, and progressive tasks that advance students through understanding levels are all essential components of an effective geometry education in the early years of schooling.

With the intention of accomplishing this, curriculum designers and educators must aim a balance between conceptual depth and content coverage, making sure that students are not just naming shapes but also developing deeper knowledge by using comparison, decomposition, transformation, and justification to support their arguments.

It is imperative for educators to establish learning environments that inspire students to explore, investigate, inquire, and deliberate their thoughts and mathematical reasoning. This requests the teacher continual professional development so that it is possible to increase confidence and pedagogical knowledge in geometry and the addition of access to high-quality resources and materials.

Despite all the given arguments that sustain geometry importance, it can be difficult for young students to develop geometric thinking, especially because it involves abstract thinking and a level of spatial visualization that may not be fully explored in formal education environments. The use of manipulative materials has become a potent tactic to close this gap by promoting conceptual understanding and encouraging interest in geometry education, making its leaning more attractive and significant to students.

Research highlights that young learners benefit most when abstract mathematical concepts are connected to tangible experiences (Clements & Sarama, 2007). In this sense, geometry is particularly suited to be taught through concrete representations. Manipulatives enable students to see, touch, and physically explore the properties and relationships of geometric shapes, turning passive learning into active discovery.

Geometry and Manipulative Materials

Manipulative Materials: Definition and Pedagogical Role

Manipulative materials are physical or digital objects that students can handle and use to model mathematical ideas. These may include, but are not limited to, pattern blocks, tangrams, geoboards, linking cubes, 3D solids, attribute blocks, mirrors (for exploring symmetry), and software tools like dynamic geometry environments.

Their effectiveness in learning geometry depends on how the students bridge the gap between concrete and abstract thinking. According to Piaget's theory of cognitive development, children move from the concrete operational stage to the formal operational stage between the ages of 7 and 12. Manipulatives serve as essential tools during this transition, enabling learners to explore, manipulate, and internalize geometric ideas through physical action and visualization before they can reason abstractly (Piaget, 1952).

Moreover, manipulative-based learning aligns with the constructivist approach to education. In this view, learning is most effective when students actively construct their own understanding through hands-on experiences and social interaction (Vygotsky, 1978). Teachers act as facilitators who pose questions, encourage exploration, and guide students in connecting their manipulative work to formal geometric concepts.

It is believed that students are more likely to deeply understand geometric concepts when they learn them through manipulatives. With the manipulatives integrated in classrooms, children can visualize how smaller shapes can be combined to form larger ones, or vice versa, by using Pattern Blocks, for example, to compose and decompose shapes. The fundamental idea of part-whole relationships, which is crucial to both geometry and number sense, is developed through this type of practical exercise.

Additionally, through working with geometric shapes, students learn visual-spatial reasoning, which lays the groundwork for later geometry and algebra by recognizing how shapes can rotate, reflect, or translate.

Over and above that, manipulatives accommodate different learning styles, like kinesthetic and visual learners. Physical materials provide alternative paths to introduce a concept and learning about it, particularly for students who have trouble with abstract representations, even though traditional instruction may favor verbal or auditory learning. This is in line with Universal Desing for Learning (UDL) principles, which support a variety of representational and expressive mediums to guarantee accessibility for every student (CAST, 2018).

UDL, as defined by the Center for Applied Special Technology, is a research-based framework that guides the design of learning experiences to meet the needs of all learners by offering multiple means of engagement, representation, action and expression (CAST, 2018). The framework draws on neuroscience and cognitive psychology to promote inclusive practices that reduce barriers to learning (Meyer et al., 2014).

More recent developments emphasize the role of flexible learning environments and the use of digital tools to foster agency and autonomy in learners (Ok et al., 2022). Meanwhile, Lambert et al. (2023) further articulate that UDL is most effective when embraced as a "way of thinking" - a responsive, empathetic mindset that enables educators to adapt in real time to the diverse and evolving needs of students.

By incorporating UDL principles, educators can ensure that manipulatives are not only engaging tools, but also intentional supports that align with inclusive pedagogy and equitable access to content.

The frequent use of manipulatives generally leads to group projects where students' mathematical communication is encouraged since they have to debate tactics, defend their positions, and pick up tips from their peers. One of the most important skills in contemporary curricula is, exactly, *Mathematical Communication*, which is fostered by these activities. Students' reasoning improves and their use of mathematical language becomes more accurate and refined as they describe how they applied materials in the process of problem solving.

Taking all these factors into account, it is possible to affirm that Geometry can become more engaging when students are allowed to construct knowledge actively. This aligns with Vale (2002), who argues that "in a learning situation with materials

(...) learning becomes an active process of constructing knowledge that is meaningful to the child" (p. 21). The tactile and creative nature of manipulatives can transform geometry lessons into enjoyable, game-like experiences that spark curiosity and a willingness to persevere through challenges. This sense of play can be especially impactful in early education, laying the foundation for a positive mathematical identity.

In order to make the most diverse abstract mathematical concepts a reality, many other manipulable materials have emerged. Some of them and their characteristics are described below.

Tangrams support learning about spatial reasoning, transformations, and problem-solving. Students practice rotation, reflection, and congruence while honing skills related to transformation geometry by rearranging seven geometric pieces to create different figures.

Rubber bands are used to create shapes on geoboards, which are square boards with pegs. This material helps students in exploring and investigating concepts like area, perimeter, and polygons characteristics. Geoboards also may facilitate the use of coordinate geometry and the study of congruent and similar figures.

On the other hand, physical models of 3D solids – such as cubes, spheres, and pyramids – provide students with the concrete representations to better understand volume, surface area, and the relationship between 2D and 3D representations.

Regarding digital manipulatives, they provide new ways for geometry exploration in contemporary classrooms. Students can manipulate geometric figures with accuracy and speed in dynamic, interactive environments with tools like GeoGebra, virtual Pattern Blocks, and interactive whiteboards. By altering a triangle's angle and immediately seeing how it affects side lengths or area, for example, these tools enhance exploration that with physical objects is commonly not rigorous enough. Despite the mentioned advantages, digital manipulatives shouldn't completely replace physical ones given that including both representations of concepts accommodate a greater variety of learning needs and preferences.

Pattern Blocks

It is commonly acknowledged that Pattern Blocks are adaptable and useful manipulatives in mathematics education, especially in the early and primary grades. These geometric shapes were first created by the Educational Development Center (EDC) in the 1960s with the goal of assisting students in investigating mathematical ideas through experiential, hands-on learning.

The materials consist of a standard set of six geometric shapes – equilateral triangle (green), square (orange), trapezoid (red), hexagon (yellow), rhombus (blue), and a thinner rhombus (beige or tan) – all color-coded and proportionally sized to encourage composition and decomposition of figures, supporting the development of these skills by allowing students to explore shape properties, equivalencies, and spatial relationships (Figure 3).

Figure 3. Pattern Blocks set

Moreover, they are used to explore symmetry, tiling, congruency, and fraction relationships and allow children to investigate shape composition and create intricate designs, promoting both artistic and geometric thinking. In general, practical shape experiences foster geometry learning, logical reasoning, and spatial reasoning (Clements & Sarama, 2007).

Examining the features in more detail, each shape in a standard Pattern Blocks set has uniform proportions, enabling students to mix and match them to create new patterns and shapes. For example, two green triangles fit into one blue rhombus and for its turn three blue rhombuses form one yellow hexagon, as shown in Figure 4.

Figure 4. Examples of overlaying pieces

Students can investigate equivalency, symmetry, and spatial reasoning thanks to the inherent relationships of this manipulative. Usually, it is made of wood or plastic but nowadays they are widely accessible in digital form through educational apps and virtual manipulatives. Pattern Blocks are a good example of modularity and scalability from a geometric perspective. Their design promotes early comprehension of geometric transformations like rotation, reflection, and translation by helping students to understand the part-whole relationship between shapes (Clements & Sarama, 2007).

They also support early work in fractions and proportional reasoning by allowing learners to compare the size and area of different shapes through visual and tactile exploration.

Regarding pedagogical applications, Pattern Blocks are employed across various domains of mathematical learning. They support students' exploration of geometric reasoning, understanding of attributes (sides, angles, and symmetry), and identification and analysis of shapes.

As students construct sequences and forecast subsequent elements, they aid in the recognition of patterns and the development of generalization skills in algebraic thinking. With Pattern Blocks, students can make informal comparisons and estimates of area and perimeter in measurement. For instance, students can start to grasp units of measurement in a tangible way by figuring out how many triangles fit into a hexagon implying the rotation of the geometric shapes to fit them into a specific pattern or structure, fostering spatial reasoning skills within simple tasks.

These pieces also provide a starting point for the development of computational thinking by allowing students to practice the fundamentals of computational logic when working on tasks that request decomposition (breaking shapes into parts), pattern recognition, and iterative construction (Grover & Pea, 2013; Wing, 2006). Mathematical communication and collaboration are supported by tasks that require problem-solving with pattern blocks, which frequently result in meaningful discourse (NCTM, 2014).

Pattern Blocks can work as a strategy to foster an inclusive classroom since it provides learning by differentiated instruction enabling students to tackle ideas at different levels of difficulty. For example, when the students are not all in the same level of comprehension, some might need time to concentrate on naming and recognizing shapes, while others might focus on studying fractional relationships, symmetry, or tiling patterns. Pattern Blocks reveal themselves as useful tools in a variety of educational contexts thanks to their adaptability advantages.

Manipulating Pattern Blocks helps students develop their critical thinking abilities – such as analysis, synthesis, and evaluation – as well as their creativity, particularly when they use them to create mosaics, images or work through open-ended design challenges. In this way it is possible to promote interdisciplinary teaching and learning by incorporating Pattern Blocks into other areas of knowledge, for instance, in science by modeling biological forms or crystalline structures, or in art by looking at pavements and cultural patterns like the Portuguese sidewalk (example in Figure 5).

Figure 5. Example of pavements with Pattern Blocks

In early education, these manipulatives provide a developmentally appropriate method to transition from concrete to abstract reasoning. According to Piaget theory, this transition is critical for learners between the concrete operational and formal operational stages (Piaget, 1952). Pattern Blocks serve as a bridge in this cognitive development by offering meaningful context and tactile engagement.

The Role of Formative Assessment in Learning

In the context of early mathematics education, assessment is not only a mean to measure academic achievement but also a crucial element of the teaching and learning processes. When teaching involves manipulative materials such as Pattern Blocks, formative assessment becomes a particularly valuable approach, since it provides real-time insights of the students' reasoning.

Formative assessment is commonly defined as a process through which teachers gather evidence of student understanding in order to inform and improve teaching and learning, concomitantly with Black and Wiliam (2009) who argue that "Formative assessment refers to all those activities undertaken by teachers and by their students in assessing themselves which provide information to be used as feedback to modify teaching and learning activities." (p. 7).

Unlike summative assessments, which are designed to evaluate what students have learned at the end of a unit or term, formative assessment is extended in time, integrated into everyday classroom practice. It involves continuous observation, feedback, and dialogue between the actors in the educational process, helping both teachers and students make adjustments.

This process is especially aligned with exploratory, hands-on learning environments developed in the present study. In activities involving Pattern Blocks, children are often observed manipulating geometric figures, testing ideas, collaborating with peers, and articulating their reasoning. These moments offer rich opportunities to assess not just the outcome of a task, but the processes and strategies students use to reach their conclusions.

Recent literature emphasizes the importance of structured observation tools in formative assessment. According to Heritage (2013), the use of observational checklists and multimodal narrative records can help teachers identify specific indicators of mathematical thinking of their students. In the *Geometry* theme, for example with the manipulation of the Pattern Blocks, observing how a student composes a hexagon using triangles and trapezoids can reveal their spatial structuring.

One of the defining characteristics of formative assessment is its dialogic nature since everyone involved in the educational process must have an active voice and the space to share reflections on their experiences. Feedback is not a unidirectional transmission of information from teacher to student; on the contrary, it is a reciprocal process that encourages students to reflect on their own thinking. As Sadler (1989) argued, for feedback to be effective, learners must understand the learning goal, recognize the gap between their current performance and that goal, and know how to close that gap.

In the specific case of this study, feedback may occur in spontaneous moments such as the teacher asking *"What would happen if you flipped that shape?"* or in more structured reflections, where students are encouraged to explain their reasoning to peers or record their design process with Pattern Blocks. These interactions support metacognition, helping children become aware of their strategies and adjust them accordingly.

Furthermore, formative assessment fosters the positioning of learners as active participants in their own learning because they are invited to evaluate their work, justify their decisions, or improve their designs, developing a mindset that values growth, experimentation, acceptance of failures and revision core components of both mathematical and computational thinking.

Digital tools also facilitate multimodal assessment, allowing students to express understanding through visual, verbal, and kinesthetic means. This is another aspect of this study that aligns with Universal Design for Learning principles (CAST, 2018), promoting equitable assessment for diverse learners.

It is not always easy for the teacher in a class full of students to observe every learner closely or provide individualized feedback in real time, which turns out to be a challenge in formative assessment. Effective implementation of formative assessment depends on the teacher's intentional planning. Teachers must design tasks that are rich enough to elicit meaningful responses, anticipate potential misconceptions, and be prepared to give constructive feedback. Wiliam (2011) even believes that the development in assessment literacy, especially in mathematics, is essential to support teachers in this endeavor.

To sum up, Formative assessment should be integrated when manipulative-based learning is fostered. Through the listed strategies, teachers can gain insight into student thinking while simultaneously guiding them forward.

Building on these theoretical insights, the following section describes the research design and methods used to examine how young learners engage with Pattern Blocks in both physical and digital environments. An action-research approach was selected to capture the dynamic, process-oriented nature of student learning in context.

RESEARCH METHODOLOGY

In order to investigate and interpret a phenomenon in its natural setting, based on the meanings that the participants themselves ascribe to it, this study used a qualitative methodology (Gómez, 1996). Action-research, which is distinguished by its formative, reflective, and transformative influence on pedagogical practices, was also incorporated into the research design (Ribeiro, 2020). The study focus on cooperation, participant involvement, and dialogical interaction—both between participants and between researchers and participants—further supports this methodological decision (Leuverink, 2018).

There were 25 first-grade participants that had unequivocal enthusiasm for both mathematics and digital learning providing a great foundation for the introduction of Pattern Blocks, as a concrete material that allows for initial sensory exploration to introduce mathematical content. The focus was to harness their natural curiosity and comfort with technology to introduce computational and geometric thinking in a playful, engaging way. The researchers were also able to see how Pattern Blocks affected a group of young students who were already interested in mathematics in this setting.

Thus, the main goal was to determine in what extent working with Physical and Digital Pattern Blocks could improve children's mathematical comprehension and encourage fundamental computational thinking abilities like pattern recognition, abstraction, and decomposition.

Despite being in their first year in Primary School, this group demonstrates an impressive level of autonomy. They are confident in navigating tasks independently, making decisions about their learning process, and showing initiative in exploring new ideas.

A particularly striking feature of this group is their natural inclination towards collaborative learning. They enjoy working in pairs or small groups and thrive in social learning environments. This preference encourages rich dialogue, cooperative problem-solving and the sharing of strategies, which deepens their understanding and strengthens peer relationships. Their interactions are respectful and supportive, and they frequently seek out each other's input when completing tasks.

The use of Pattern Blocks fits seamlessly into this dynamic. As a hands-on, manipulative resource, it allows students to physically explore abstract mathematical concepts through play and experimentation. The tactile nature of the shapes engages their senses and supports the development of spatial reasoning, pattern recognition and geometry skills. Additionally, integrating digital tools alongside physical manipulatives provides an added layer of interactivity. Students can engage with app-based versions of Pattern Blocks that offer guided challenges, immediate feedback, and opportunities for self-paced exploration.

In addition to their collaborative nature, this group is highly expressive. They enjoy explaining their reasoning, using both verbal and visual means, often supporting their ideas with drawings, gestures, or digital tools. They are also reflective learners, frequently revisiting their work to make improvements or consider alternative strategies. Their openness to feedback and ability to self-correct contributes significantly to their growth mindset, particularly in mathematics.

The children also show a strong inclination toward creativity. They approach mathematical tasks not only with logic but with imagination, often devising original ways to use Pattern Blocks beyond the initial instructions. Their ability to explore and create novel patterns, symmetrical designs, and playful constructions demonstrates a deep engagement with the material.

Moreover, they are comfortable with digital tools and transition seamlessly between physical and digital learning contexts. Their intuitive understanding of touch-based applications makes the digital version of Pattern Blocks especially engaging and effective. They respond well to challenges presented in digital format, often treating them as puzzles to solve rather than assignments to complete.

Overall, this group's combination of enthusiasm, independence, and collaboration makes them exceptionally well-suited to benefit from a blended approach to early math education. Their readiness to explore, coupled with a supportive peer culture, creates an ideal environment for meaningful and joyful learning experiences. Thus, the main goal was to determine in what extent working with Physical and Digital Pattern Blocks could improve children's mathematical comprehension and encourage fundamental computational thinking abilities like pattern recognition, abstraction, and decomposition.

Document analysis, video recordings, and in-class observations were the primary techniques used to collect information. This qualitative approach allowed the researchers to observe and document the learning process in real time, capturing not only the students' final answers but also their reasoning and problem-solving strategies along the way.

Regarding implementation, the study was organized into five structured work sessions, each lasting approximately one hour. These sessions were carefully sequenced to promote continuity in learning, with each building on the previous one to deepen understanding. The primary focus was on exploring mathematical concepts in geometry through both guided tasks and open-ended exploration.

The sessions were designed to encourage hands-on engagement with Pattern Blocks, allowing students to manipulate and investigate the materials while developing key spatial skills. The blend of physical and digital tools supported varied learning styles and maintained a high level of interest and participation throughout.

Having outlined the methodological approach, the next section presents key findings from the five-session intervention. These results illustrate how students interacted with the Pattern Blocks, the strategies they employed, and the development of their geometric and computational thinking.

PRESENTATION AND ANALYSIS OF RESULTS

In the first session, the Pattern Blocks material was introduced and provided to the students with a learning guide, which guided the students through the first three sessions. This guide, through problems and challenges, covered fundamental operations with shapes, such as composition and decomposition – essentially how shapes can be combined or broken down into smaller pieces and the other way round (Figure 6 and Figure 7).

Figure 6. Learning guide – Part I

Figure 7. Learning Guide - Part II

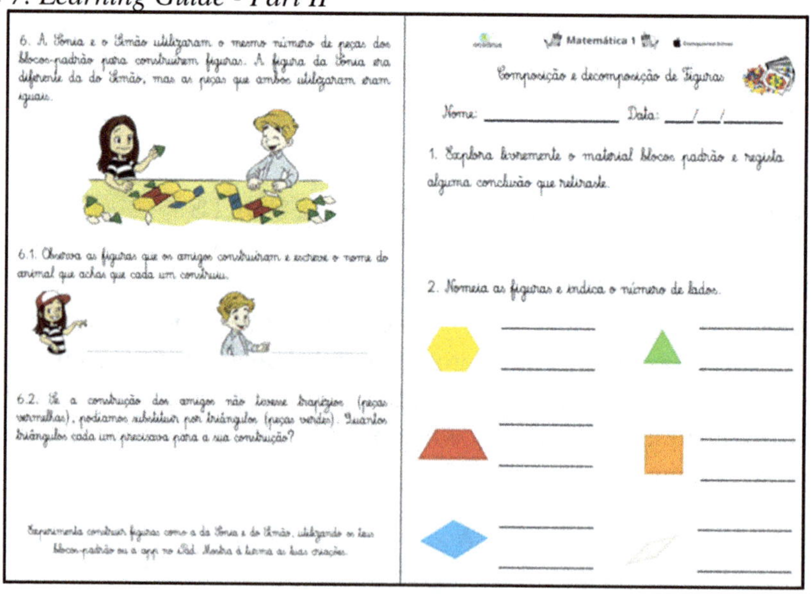

6. A Sónia e o Simão utilizaram o mesmo número de peças dos blocos-padrão para construírem figuras. A figura da Sónia era diferente da do Simão, mas as peças que ambos utilizaram eram iguais.

6.1. Observa as figuras que os amigos construíram e escreve o nome do animal que achas que cada um construiu.

6.2. Se a construção dos amigos não tivesse trapézios (peças vermelhas), podíamos substituir por triângulos (peças verdes). Quantos triângulos cada um precisava para a sua construção?

Experimenta construir figuras como a da Sónia e do Simão, utilizando os teus blocos-padrão ou a app no iPad. Mostra à turma as tuas criações.

Matemática 1

Composição e decomposição de Figuras

Nome: ______________ Data: ___/___/______

1. Explora livremente o material blocos padrão e regista alguma conclusão que retiraste.

2. Nomeia as figuras e indica o número de lados.

In the second session, students were asked to identify different geometric shapes within the Pattern Blocks set, count their sides, and discuss these features with each other. It's important to point out that each pair worked at their own pace according to the learning guide. They were then given time for free exploration in pairs, allowing them to become comfortable with the shapes and start making initial discoveries (Figure 8). This phase stimulated a range of key competences, including spatial awareness, pattern recognition (computational thinking stage), collaborative problem-solving, and mathematical reasoning. As they manipulated the shapes, students developed their visualization skills and deepened their understanding of geometric relationships, while the paired setting encouraged communication, negotiation, and shared decision-making.

Figure 8. Different ways of manipulating Pattern Blocks

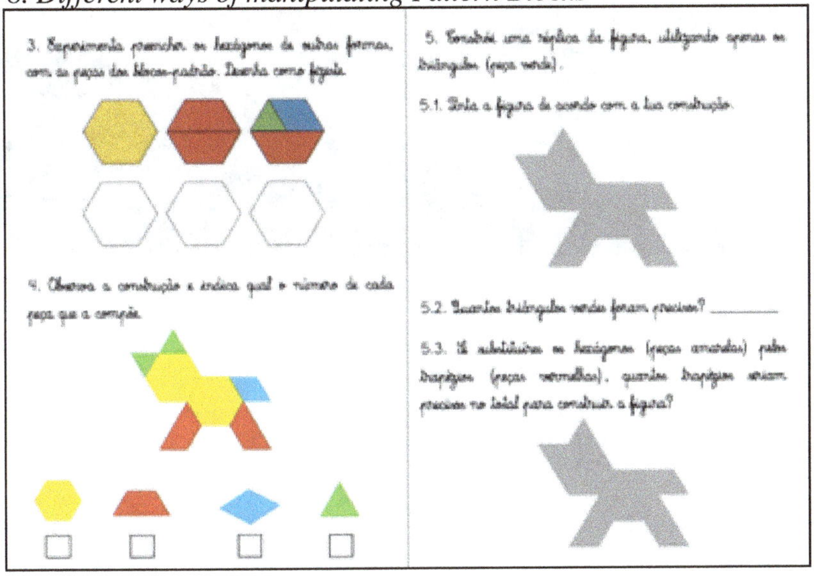

The group of students appreciate feeling autonomous and are motivated to learn when they have the freedom to explore and talk about their learning. For this reason, this exploratory period encouraged them to experiment and record what they found without specific instructions, which allowed them to take ownership of their learning, making it meaningful. In this second session, the students had the opportunity to manipulate the concrete material, but also to manipulate the application related to this material in their iPads. This allowed us to work according to the Universal Design for Learning (UDL) strategy providing different means of representation and different means of expression (Figure 9 and Figure 10), promoting pedagogical differentiation in an equitable way.

Figure 9. Physical exploration of Pattern Blocks

Figure 10. Digital exploration of Pattern Blocks

In the third session, as the pairs solved the tasks in the learning guide, made records and discovered part-whole relationships between the Pattern Shape pieces, the students had to share their work with each other, using Keynote presentations (Figure 11). This encouraged them to explain their reasoning and reinforced their ability to communicate mathematical ideas, an essential skill in both computational and geometric thinking. In these moments, they also were questioned and led to reflect on their resolutions, debugging and correcting their mistakes. Through this iterative process, students not only strengthened their conceptual understanding but also developed persistence and resilience – key traits in problem-solving.

Figure 11. Keynote presentation by the pairs of mathematical discoveries through the manipulation of the Pattern Blocks

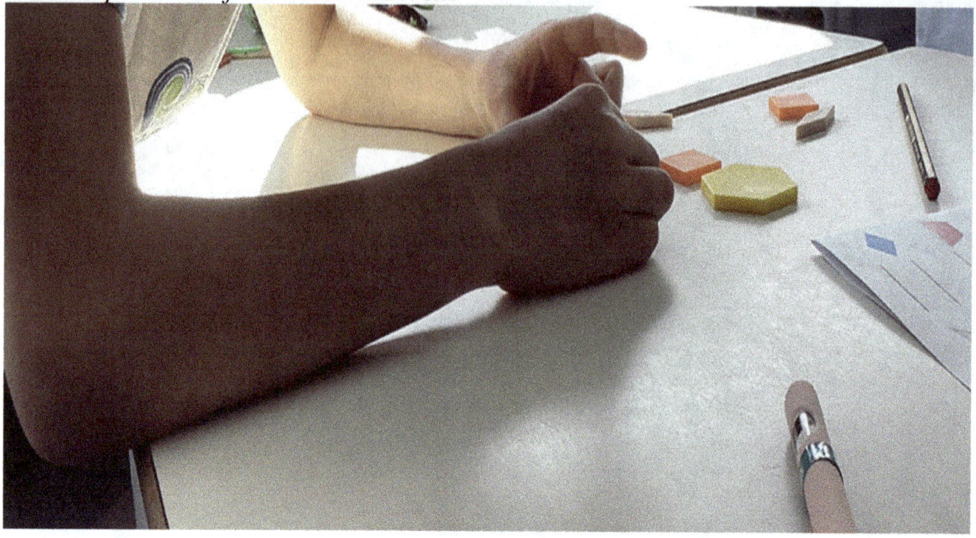

The back-and-forth dialogue, whether with peers or teacher, cultivated a classroom culture of inquiry, where mistakes were seen as learning opportunities rather than setbacks. This environment empowered students to take intellectual risks, articulate their thought processes more clearly, and build connections between abstract concepts and practical applications. It should be added that this is a class that was in its first year of learning to read and write, and in these records, they added everyday language as a form of expression, which allowed them to develop their spelling skills.

In this third session, the students finished the learning guide and systematized their mathematical learning through this moment of sharing. This final phase served not only as a consolidation of their geometric and computational understanding but also as an opportunity to reflect on their individual and collective learning journeys. As students explained their strategies, justified their reasoning, and listened to alternative approaches, they deepened their conceptual grasp and gained new perspectives.

By the end of the session, the students had not only met the learning objectives but also strengthened transversal competences such as critical thinking, communication, collaboration, and perseverance. The classroom environment – characterized by exploration, dialogue, and mutual respect – supported the development of a growth mindset, laying the foundation for continued success in both mathematics and interdisciplinary contexts.

Through these three sessions, students were making significant discoveries about geometry. For example, one student noted that two trapezoids could be combined to form a hexagon, while another realized that a hexagon could be created using six triangles (Figure 12).

Figure 12. A student's problem solving

These observations demonstrated a grasp of shape equivalency and decomposition, in this way, they improved geometric learning. By engaging with these shapes and sharing their discoveries, students developed not only mathematical reasoning but also the ability to communicate these ideas. This aligns with foundational aspects of computational thinking, such as abstraction and pattern recognition, as students noticed patterns and made generalizations about shape relationships. As they identified recurring configurations and explored how shapes could be transformed or substituted, they began to internalize key mathematical concepts such as congruence, symmetry, and transformation. Furthermore, articulating their insights encouraged metacognition – thinking about their own thinking – which supports deeper, more reflective learning. The collaborative environment allowed for peer-to-peer dialogue, fostering active listening and constructive feedback, and reinforcing the social aspect of learning. Through this process, students also honed transversal competences such as critical thinking, creativity, and logical reasoning, all of which are essential not only in mathematics but across another curriculum areas and in real-world problem-solving contexts.

Another important skill that emerged from these sessions was pattern recognition, a key component of computational thinking. As students organized and manipulated shapes, they began to see that complex figures could be broken down into simpler parts. For example, when a student realized that a trapezoid could fit three triangles and, therefore, two trapezoids would equal six triangles, they were actively practicing decomposition, a computational process of breaking down complex problems into manageable steps. This hands-on exploration allowed them to connect abstract thinking with a concrete activity, reinforcing both their computational and geometric skills.

Moreover, through these discoveries, students developed number sense and an initial and foundational understanding of equivalency, proportions, and fractional relationships – crucial mathematical concepts that often serve as a bridge to more advanced topics to explore in the future. Their ability to justify their reasoning, compare outcomes, and test their hypotheses also supported the development of logical reasoning and analytical thinking.

The students were challenged to experiment with replacing shapes to explore equivalencies. One student discovered that a trapezoid could fit three triangles, and therefore, two trapezoids would fit six triangles. This observation reflects not only an understanding of shape equivalency but also the ability to apply logic and recognize patterns (Figure 13). In making this connection, the student demonstrated, once again, key aspects of both geometric reasoning and computational thinking, particularly decomposition and pattern recognition.

Figure 13. A student's problem solving

The activity also stimulated mathematical reasoning, as the student used proportional thinking and relational understanding to connect different shapes. By justifying the relationship between the trapezoids and triangles, the student engaged in abstract thinking and began to generalize rules based on their hands-on experiences. This process supported the development of number sense, spatial awareness, and logical sequencing.

Additionally, the task encouraged perseverance and active problem-solving. As the students tested and confirmed their ideas through manipulation of the materials, they practiced self-correction and strategic thinking. Communicating their discovery to peers further developed their ability to express mathematical ideas clearly, reinforcing both oral communication and metacognitive skills – thinking about how they reached the conclusion. These are essential competences that foster deeper learning and contribute to the student's confidence as an independent and reflective learner.

By engaging in this type of activity, students were learning geometry at the same time as practicing key aspects of computational thinking, such as abstraction, decomposition, and pattern recognition. This foundational understanding supports later skills in math and computing, showing how activities, such as those presented, with Pattern Blocks go beyond traditional learning to encourage flexible, critical thinking in young learners.

Through the manipulation of Patter Blocks, students are given the opportunity to explore mathematical ideas in a tangible and meaningful way. Handling and arranging shapes allowed them to make sense of abstract concepts through direct experience, supporting a deeper and more intuitive understanding. This kind of hands-on engagement promotes curiosity and encourages learners to test out ideas, make discoveries, and reflect on the relationships they observe.

It's important to add that such activities create space for open-ended inquiry, where multiple strategies and solutions are not only possible but welcomed. Rather than being guided to a single "correct" answer, students are empowered to follow their own reasoning, revise their thinking, and explain their processes. This nurtures independence, creativity, and a strong sense of ownership over learning.

Additionally, working with others during these explorations promotes collaborative learning and the development of communication skills. As students articulate their thoughts, listen to others, and build on shared ideas, they strengthen both their conceptual understanding and their ability to express it clearly. These learning experiences illustrate how mathematical development is enriched through play, exploration, and meaningful interaction with materials - fostering learners who are not only proficient in content but also confident, reflective, and actively engaged in making sense of the world around them.

In the following sessions, particularly the fourth one, new tasks and challenges were introduced to deepen students' engagement with Pattern Blocks, as the manipulation of this material with a different intentionality. For instance, in the activity called 'Which Animal?' students worked in pairs and used Pattern Blocks to build animal figures (Figure 14).

Figure 14. "Which animal" activity

This task combined creativity with problem-solving as they chose and arranged shapes to resemble animals. The activity required them to consider shape composition and spatial orientation, which in turn strengthened their geometric understanding, but also, had to mobilize their computational thinking.

As students experimented with different configurations, they engaged in decomposition—breaking down a complex figure into smaller, manageable parts—and pattern recognition, both core aspects of computational thinking. They also practiced sequencing and algorithmic thinking as they determined the order in which shapes should be placed to achieve the desired figure.

In addition to enhancing spatial reasoning and visualization, the task stimulated creativity, perseverance, and decision-making. Collaboration further encouraged communication, adaptability, and peer learning, while the open-ended nature of the task fostered autonomy and initiative, key competences for lifelong learning. Through the dialogue between them as they carried out this activity, it was possible to see the development of these skills and competences.

The main aim of the fifth and final session was to systematize the students' knowledge by carrying out some challenges in the in the App on the iPads and sharing ideas.

Therefore, through the data collection process it was possible to observe the development of computational thinking through decomposition. It was observed how students learn to break down complex shapes into simpler components, mirroring the problem-solving process of dividing a larger task into manageable steps. This aligns with concepts introduced by Papert (1980) and Grover & Pea (2013) about how computational thinking skills can be developed even at an early age (Figure 15 and Figure 16).

Figure 15. Manipulating Pattern Blocks in the app

Figure 16. Exploration of equivalencies with Pattern Blocks in the app

The ability to decompose shapes not only revealed the students' growing spatial awareness and understanding of part-whole relationships but also highlighted how young learners can approach problems with increasingly strategic and analytical mindsets. As they manipulated Pattern Blocks to construct or reconstruct figures, they instinctively engaged in iterative thinking—testing, adjusting, and refining their arrangements. This process mirrors the computational approach to problem-solving where solutions are built through cycles of trial, evaluation, and improvement.

Moreover, the use of physical manipulatives allowed learners to externalize their thinking, making abstract processes visible and easier to communicate. Students could physically isolate components, observe recurring structures, and transfer strategies from one task to another—demonstrating an emergent ability to recognize and apply patterns, a further hallmark of computational thinking.

What's particularly significant is that these developments emerged not through explicit instruction in algorithms or coding, but through rich, embodied experiences with mathematical content. This supports the idea that computational thinking is not limited to computer science contexts but can be meaningfully cultivated across subject areas, especially when learners are given the freedom to explore, test ideas, and construct understanding collaboratively.

In this way, the observed progress in decomposition was not merely a mathematical achievement – it was an indicator of broader cognitive growth. It showed how young children, when provided with the right tools and learning environment, are capable of complex reasoning and problem-solving. These observations reinforce the value of early exposure to computational thinking through playful, hands-on, and conceptually rich activities that reflect real-world processes of learning and discovery.

It is important to emphasize that the assessment approach is formative. Students were observed and the conclusions and discoveries they made were recorded. The moment of sharing was also rich because it allowed the teacher to realize the children's understanding of this content. Rather than relying on traditional tests or fixed outcomes, assessment was embedded within the learning process itself emerging naturally through observation, dialogue, and reflection.

This formative approach created a dynamic feedback loop between teaching and learning, enabling the teacher to adapt instruction in real time based on the students' needs, misunderstandings, and emerging insights. Through attentive observation and purposeful listening, the teacher could identify not only what students knew, but how they were thinking – what strategies they used, what connections they made, and where they might need support or challenge.

As students articulated their discoveries and explained their reasoning to peers, the teacher could assess the depth of their understanding and their ability to transfer knowledge to new situations. These moments also supported metacognition, as students reflected on their own processes and clarified their thinking through communication.

Additionally, the formative assessment approach fostered a supportive and low-stakes environment in which students felt encouraged to take risks, experiment with ideas, and learn from mistakes. This atmosphere promoted confidence and resilience, helping students see learning as a continuous journey rather than a fixed performance.

Ultimately, formative assessment in this context was not a separate activity but an integral part of the learning experience – used to inform instruction, celebrate progress, and empower students to take ownership of their learning. It honored the complexity of students' thinking and provided a holistic picture of their development in both computational and geometric understanding.

To synthesize the core outcomes of the study, Table 2 presents a summary of the key findings derived from the five-session intervention. Each finding is accompanied by a brief description and the specific cognitive and transversal competencies it supports.

Table 2. Key findings and corresponding description and competencies

Key Findings	Description	Competencies	
Shape Composition and Decomposition	Students learned to make and break down shapes (e.g., forming hexagons with triangles), supporting spatial reasoning and proportional understanding.	Abstraction, Decomposition	Geometric Reasoning & Computational Thinking
Pattern Recognition	Students identified recurring configurations (e.g. 2 trapezoids = 6 triangles), demonstrating early pattern recognition and generalization.	Pattern Recognition	
Collaborative Problem Solving and Communication	Working in pairs, students articulated strategies and reasoning, fostering mathematical language and peer learning.	Communication, Collaboration, Metacognition	
Integration of Physical and Digital Manipulatives	Dual modality enhanced engagement and understanding, particularly for diverse learners with different learning styles.	Multimodal Learning	
Development of Algorithmic Thinking and Debugging	Through iteration, trial, and reflection, students adjusted their strategies and refined solutions, mirroring algorithmic and debugging processes.	Algorithmic Thinking, Logical Reasoning, Debugging	

This structured overview not only illustrates the pedagogical impact of Pattern Block manipulation but also reinforces the multidimensional nature of students' learning, about geometric reasoning, computational thinking, and social-emotional development. By mapping these outcomes, the table provided a concise reference to understand the diverse educational benefits associated with manipulative-based learning in early mathematics education. These findings are now discussed considering the study's aims and theoretical foundations, drawing implications for future educational practices.

CONCLUSIONS

This study shows how using Pattern Blocks to encourage the development of geometric and computational thinking in early childhood education has significant educational benefits. Through real-world, exploratory activities that fostered the growth of critical transversal skills like creativity, teamwork, perseverance, and communication, referenced by the *Profile of Students Leaving Compulsory Education* (Martins, 2017) as well as cognitive development in areas like abstraction, decomposition, and debugging, students actively engaged with mathematical content (ME, 2021).

In pairs and small groups, students shared their thoughts and worked through issues as a team. This social aspect of learning (Vygotsky, 1978) allowed them to develop the emotional and interpersonal skills required for a well-accomplished education, as well as to think more critically and listen to other people's viewpoints. The collaborative nature of the activities fostered the growth of shared understanding and critical thinking, both of which improved the learning process.

The open-ended nature of the task encouraged curiosity and experimentation, providing space for students to ask "what if" questions and explore multiple pathways to a solution. These are hallmarks of an inquiry-based learning environment and closely tied to scientific reasoning. They improved their ability to explain procedures, support conclusions, and modify their ideas in response to criticism as they practiced accuracy in language and representation while sharing their findings with peers. All things considered, the tasks fostered a combination of social, cognitive, and metacognitive abilities that are critical for comprehensive and continuous learning.

By combining Pattern Blocks in both digital and physical formats, students were able to make significant connections between abstract mathematical ideas and practical manipulation. The dual modality increased accessibility and engagement by promoting inclusive educational practices and taking into account a variety of learning preferences. The tasks were approached with curiosity and persistence, demonstrating how playful yet structured exploration can lead to increased understanding and internal motivation.

Importantly, the lessons naturally guided students through the basic stages of computational thinking, which Wing (2006) defines as decomposition, pattern recognition, abstraction, algorithmic thinking, and debugging. These activities were expertly integrated into mathematical problem-solving activities, showing how carefully thought-out, hands-on learning experiences can support the growth of computational thinking in a natural, age-appropriate way.

Students actively create knowledge in the classroom rather than passively absorbing it when geometry is taught with manipulatives. These resources support a diverse student body while encouraging creativity, spatial reasoning, teamwork, and conceptual understanding. As education continues to evolve, embracing a balanced integration of digital and physical manipulatives is a promising strategy for helping students develop deep, lasting mathematical thinking.

However, the effectiveness of manipulatives in the classroom is greatly influenced by the role of the teacher. It is essential to use open-ended questioning, deliberate task design, and continuous scaffolding to ensure that manipulatives are beneficial learning tools rather than distractions. Teachers must also help students connect their manipulative experiences to formal geometric and computational concepts. For example, when constructing a hexagon from triangles and trapezoids, students should be encouraged to discuss the geometric properties – such as symmetry, angles, and side relationships – involved.

Despite all their benefits, manipulatives have disadvantages. Because they become overly reliant on concrete, some students may find it difficult to transition to more abstract reasoning. These issues highlight how important it is for educators to receive continual professional development and training, both in the technical use of materials and in their pedagogical integration into worthwhile educational frameworks.

In dynamic, exploratory learning environments, formative assessment is crucial because it enables teachers to learn about students' thought processes rather than just their knowledge. Teachers can learn a great deal about students' thinking, tactics, and misconceptions through observation, discussion, and group reflection. This ongoing feedback supports customized guidance and informs instructional decisions.

Formative assessment promotes deeper engagement and assists in identifying emerging understandings in practical exercises like those involving Pattern Blocks. Through low-stakes exploration, it helps students express their ideas, gain knowledge from their peers, and develop their confidence. In the end, it fosters an adaptable, student-centered methodology that values development.

Despite the rich insights gathered, some limitations must be acknowledged. First of all, the study was conducted within a small context, involving a relatively small and demographically homogenous group. This restricts the generalization of the findings to other educational contexts.

Moreover, the duration of the intervention may not have been sufficient to capture the long-term impacts of Pattern Block manipulation on the development of computational and geometric thinking.

This study lays the groundwork for future research in early mathematics education by highlighting the potential of combining physical and digital manipulatives to foster computational and geometric thinking. Longitudinal studies could examine how early exposure to structured manipulatives like Pattern Blocks impacts mathematical performance and reasoning in later school years. Further research could examine the role of teacher professional development in enhancing the efficacy of manipulative-based instruction, particularly in the implementation of formative assessment strategies.

Overall, this study demonstrates that Pattern Blocks are useful tools for developing young students' geometric and computational thinking skills. They offer a developmentally appropriate way to explore challenging mathematical concepts, foster inclusive, student-centered learning environments, and inspire motivation. It is recommended that future research examine the long-term impacts of manipulative-based learning and its applicability in diverse educational settings.

Recent studies indicate that early mathematics education should include structured, exploratory learning experiences – experiences that cultivate not only knowledge but also the joy of learning and discovery.

As suggested by the title, *Piece by Piece: Awakening Computational and Geometric Thinking in the 1st Cycle of Basic Education – The Manipulation of Pattern Blocks*, this study shows how learning develops gradually through intentional, practical interaction with each geometric piece. By exploring, combining, breaking down, and reflecting on their constructions, students were able to literally build their understanding piece by piece, connection by connection through Pattern Blocks. Every shape manipulation turned into a chance to explore important aspects of geometric and computational thinking, encouraging logic, imagination, and teamwork. This metaphor of constructing knowledge incrementally, through interaction with tangible elements, captures the essence of early mathematics learning – concrete, exploratory, and deeply connected to the learner's developmental stage.

REFERENCES

APM. (2020). *Práticas do pensamento computacional.* Mathematic.

Bessa, L., Mascarenhas, D., Silva, N., Fernandes, D., & Quadros-Flores, P. (2023). UMA ABORDAGEM DA GRANDEZA ÁREA NO 2.º ANO DE ESCOLARIDADE PÓS-PANDEMIA. *PRATICA - Revista Multimédia De Investigação Em Inovação Pedagógica E Práticas De E-Learning*, 6(1), 104–130. https://doi.org/ DOI: 10.34630/pel.v6i1.5126

Black, P., & Wiliam, D. (2009). Developing the theory of formative assessment. *Educational Assessment, Evaluation and Accountability, 21*(1), 5–31. DOI: 10.1007/s11092-008-9068-5

Carvalho, R., Espadeiro, R. G., & Branco, N. C. V. (2023). Contributos para o desenvolvimento do pensamento computacional em Matemática: *Materiais de apoio para os professores do 1. º ciclo do ensino básico.*

CAST. (2018). Universal Design for Learning Guidelines version 2.2. http://udlguidelines.cast.org

Clements, D. H., & Sarama, J. (2007). Early childhood mathematics learning. In Lester, F. K.Jr., (Ed.), *Second handbook of research on mathematics teaching and learning* (pp. 461–555). Information Age.

Figueiredo, J., & García-Peñalvo, F. (2017). *Desenvolver o Pensamento Computacional Usando Seguir e Dar Instruções.* IEEE.

Grover, S., & Pea, R. (2013). Computational thinking in K-12. *Educational Researcher, 42*(1), 38–43. DOI: 10.3102/0013189X12463051

Heritage, M. (2013). *Formative assessment in practice: A process of inquiry and action.* Harvard Education Press.

Lambert, R., McNiff, A., Schuck, R., Imm, K., & Zimmerman, S. (2023). "UDL is a way of thinking": Theorizing UDL teacher knowledge, beliefs, and practices. *Frontiers in Education, 8*, 1145293. DOI: 10.3389/feduc.2023.1145293

Martins, G. (2017). Perfil dos Alunos à Saída da Escolaridade Obrigatória. Lisboa, Portugal: Ministério da Educação/Direção Geral de Educação. Obtido de https://dge.mec.pt/sites/default/files/Curriculo/Projeto_Autonomia_e_Flexibilidade/perfil_dos_alunos.pdf

Mascarenhas, D. (2012). *Dificuldades e estratégias de ensino e aprendizagem da geometria e grandezas no 5º. Ano de Escolaridade do Ensino Básico nas Escolas EB 2/3 da Madalena e EB 2/3 de Pedrouços do Distrito do Porto*. Universidad de Granada.

Meyer, A., Rose, D. H., & Gordon, D. (2014). *Universal Design for Learning: Theory and Practice*. CAST Professional Publishing.

Ministério da Educação. (2001). *Programa de Matemática do Ensino Básico*. Departamento de Educação Básica.

Ministério da Educação. (2007). *Programa de Matemática do Ensino Básico*. DGIDC.

Ministério da Educação. (2013). *Metas curriculares de matemática – Ensino básico*. Direção-Geral da Educação.

Ministério da Educação, (2018). Aprendizagens Essenciais de Matemática no Ensino Básico.

Ministério da Educação. (2021). Aprendizagens Essenciais de Matemática no Ensino Básico. Available from: https://www.dge.mec.pt/noticias/aprendizagens-essenciais-de-matematica

National Council of Teachers of Mathematics (NCTM). (2014). *Principles to actions: Ensuring mathematical success for all*. NCTM.

Ok, M. W., Rao, K., Bryant, B. R., & McDougall, D. (2022). Universal Design for Learning in inclusive classrooms: Recent trends and directions for future research. *Learning Disabilities Research & Practice*, *37*(2), 75–84. DOI: 10.1111/ldrp.12238

Papert, S. (1980). *Mindstorms: Children, Computers, and Powerful Ideas*. Basic Books.

Piaget, J. (1952). *The origins of intelligence in children* (Cook, M., Trans.). International Universities Press. (Original work published 1936) DOI: 10.1037/11494-000

Sadler, D. R. (1989). Formative assessment and the design of instructional systems. *Instructional Science*, *18*(2), 119–144. DOI: 10.1007/BF00117714

Sullivan, A., & Bers, M. U. (2019). Computer science education in early childhood: The case of ScratchJr. *Journal of Information Technology Education: Innovations in Practice*, *18*, 113–138. DOI: 10.28945/4437

Vale, I. (2002). *Materiais manipuláveis*. ESEVC-LEM.

Van Hiele, P. M. (1986). *Structure and Insight: A Theory of Mathematics Education*. Academic Press.

Vicari, R. M., Moreira, A. F., Menezes, P. F. B., (2018). Pensamento computacional: *revisão bibliográfica.*

Vygotsky, L. S. (1978). *Mind in Society: The Development of Higher Psychological Processes*. Harvard University Press.

Wiliam, D. (2011). *Embedded formative assessment*. Solution Tree Press.

Wing, J. M. (2006). Computational thinking. *Communications of the ACM*, *49*(3), 33–35. DOI: 10.1145/1118178.1118215

Chapter 12
Distance Learning Tools in Health Sciences: A Training Course for Higher Education Faculty

Raquel Simões de Almeida
https://orcid.org/0000-0003-4703-1712
E2S, Polytechnic Institute of Porto, Portugal

Maria João Trigueiro
https://orcid.org/0000-0003-4439-7196
E2S, Polytechnic Institute of Porto, Portugal

ABSTRACT

Higher education is rapidly shifting towards distance learning, particularly in health sciences. However, many educators feel unprepared for effective digital tool integration, leading to challenges in teaching quality. The COVID-19 pandemic highlighted this gap, emphasizing the need to equip teachers with both technical and pedagogical digital skills to create engaging learning environments. To address this, the "Technological Modernization in Health: Digital Tools for Distance Learning in Health Education" course was developed. This month-long program covered 5 essential modules and included both formative and summative assessments. Of the 32 participants, 25 successfully completed the course, demonstrating strong interest in utilizing digital resources. This initiative not only helps educators adapt but also drives pedagogical evolution. By enhancing educators' digital fluency, the program aims to democratize access to education, encourage new teaching approaches, and ultimately improve outcomes in health sciences.

DOI: 10.4018/979-8-3373-7729-2.ch012

INTRODUCTION

In recent years, higher education has seen a significant transformation in how teaching and learning are provided. The need for change in training provision and educational practices on the part of Higher Education Institutions (HIEs) stems from current challenges on a global scale, such as the climate crisis and the sustainability of the planet, tensions between political blocs and divergent social interests, migratory movements and problems of social inclusion and cohesion, inequalities in access to education as a support for social and economic development, digitalization and the impact of technologies on production and the labour market, globalization of markets or transdisciplinarity (Almeida et al, 2022). In all these areas, higher education can take on a leading role in the research and innovation it ensures, as well as in the human and technical training of young people and people throughout their lives. However, we live in an age in which information is vast and easily accessible, questioning the traditional role of the educator as the depository of knowledge. The pedagogy of transformation challenges the traditional model of education, proposing teaching that not only diffuses knowledge, but also empowers students to transform the reality around them (Libâneo, 2001). Implementing this pedagogy requires methods that value students' experience and socio-cultural context, recognizing them as co-creators of knowledge. Indeed, the urgency of an educational transformation is unavoidable. Learning must go beyond the mere acquisition of fact-based knowledge, i.e. it must involve students in enriching experiences that foster skills such as collaboration, effective communication and the capacity for autonomous and continuous learning.

The integration of digital technologies into education represents one of the most significant transformations in the teaching and learning process in the 21st century. This evolution is not only a response to the widespread digitalisation of society, but also an opportunity to rethink pedagogical practices and promote a more interactive, collaborative, and learner-centred education. Marc Prensky, in *Digital Natives, Digital Immigrants* (2001), introduced an important distinction between students, who are born into and immersed in the digital age, and educators, who are often less familiar with digital technologies. This gap highlights the need to adapt teaching methods that capitalise on students' innate digital competencies. At the same time, James Paul Gee, in his work *What Video Games Have to Teach Us About Learning and Literacy* (2003), explores how video games can be used to foster complex cognitive skills, such as problem-solving and strategic thinking.

Indeed, digital technologies, from online learning platforms to augmented reality tools and educational video games, can be integrated into pedagogy to create rich, engaging, and personalised learning environments (Selwyn, 2016). However, it is imperative to reflect on the challenges associated with the digitalisation of education, such as disparities in access to technology, the need for teacher training in digital tools, and the importance of developing students' digital literacy (Redecker, 2017; Ferrari, 2013).

One of the most pressing challenges is the inequality in access to quality education. This issue is not limited to geographic or socioeconomic differences but also extends to disparities in access to technological resources and adaptive teaching methodologies that address a diversity of learning styles and special educational needs (OECD, 2021). Inclusion, therefore, emerges as a fundamental principle, requiring policies and practices that ensure all students have the right to an education that respects and values their individualities (UNESCO, 2020). Inclusive education seeks to meet the needs of all students, valuing diversity and promoting equal opportunities by using differentiated strategies, curricular adaptations, and a supportive environment that encourages the participation of every learner (UNESCO, 2017). The adoption of Universal Design for Learning (UDL), an educational framework aimed at making learning environments accessible to all students regardless of their abilities, needs, or individual characteristics, enables educators to recognise student diversity and design teaching strategies that address this diversity and empower all learners to succeed academically (CAST, 2018; Meyer, Rose, & Gordon, 2014). Thus, digital technologies have emerged as powerful tools to promote inclusive education in higher education settings. By offering flexible, personalized, and accessible learning environments, they help meet the diverse needs of students, including those with disabilities, neurodiverse profiles, and other learning differences. Moreover, digital technologies support UDL, providing multiple means of engagement, representation, and expression, all of which can be facilitated through digital tools (CAST, 2018).

It is also necessary to reflect on the future of technology in education, considering emerging trends such as artificial intelligence and adaptive learning. These technologies have the potential to personalise education at scale and provide real-time feedback tailored to each learner's profile (Holmes et al., 2019; Luckin et al., 2016). The goal is to implement an educational approach that fully harnesses the potential of digital technologies to personalise teaching, respond to the individual needs of each student, and prepare them for an increasingly digital world (Redecker, 2017). When aligned with sound pedagogical principles and a clear vision of inclusion and accessibility, the use of digital technologies in education can be a powerful force for educational transformation, equipping students with the skills they need to navigate and thrive in 21st-century society (Voogt et al., 2015; Fullan & Langworthy, 2014).

In addition to technical skills, contemporary education must emphasise the development of values such as empathy, critical thinking and social responsibility. This holistic approach is essential to prepare students to face not only professional challenges, but also to contribute as active citizens in solving global problems (UNESCO, 2015). Educational innovation often faces resistance, both at institutional level and within the teaching community. Overcoming this resistance means creating school cultures that value experimentation, critical reflection, and adaptability to change. Collaboration between educators, students, families, and communities can facilitate the transition to more flexible, inclusive, and student-centred educational approaches (Fullan, 2007; OECD, 2018).

Ongoing teacher training is a critical element in this scenario, emphasising the need for preparation that enables teachers to integrate educational technologies, apply active learning methodologies, and develop inclusive pedagogical practices. Investment in teacher training is essential to transform challenges into opportunities for pedagogical innovation, promoting education that is relevant, interactive, and adapted to the challenges of the 21st century (Darling-Hammond et al., 2017; Redecker, 2017). Moreover, teaching approaches in the context of higher education are based on educational theories that guide curriculum development, classroom interaction and learning assessment. Pedagogical philosophy must therefore be aligned with teaching practices. In the digital age, connectivism emerges as a relevant approach, recognising learning in distributed networks and the role of technology (Siemens, 2004). This approach emphasises the importance of teaching students to navigate complex and ever-changing information environments. Teaching approaches shape the way educators conceive learning and interact with students, directly influencing pedagogical effectiveness. Choosing an approach that considers educational objectives and students' needs is key to fostering an enriching and inclusive learning environment (Biggs & Tang, 2011). Unlike traditional theories such as behaviourism, cognitivism, or constructivism, connectivism views knowledge as distributed across a network of connections and learning as the ability to construct and traverse those networks. This makes it particularly relevant to the context of education in higher education. Higher education institutions increasingly rely on distance education to expand access, promote lifelong learning, and support diverse learner populations. This reliance on distance learning (delivered either entirely online or through blended models that incorporate face-to-face and virtual elements) has been a growing trend. In this context, connectivism provides a theoretical foundation that legitimizes collaborative, technology-mediated, and self-directed learning (Siemens, 2004). It encourages students to engage in networks, curate content, and develop digital literacies essential for contemporary knowledge economies (Bell, 2011). Moreover, connectivist principles align with the flexibility and learner autonomy that characterize effective distance education. The ability to access up-to-date information, connect with global learning communities, and personalize learning pathways fosters deeper engagement and relevance in higher education curricula.

This shift is especially evident in health sciences, where flexible and accessible formats can better serve the diverse students and teaching/learning staff (Regmi & Jones, 2020; Pei & Wu, 2019). But not every educator feels ready for this change.

Many are still not trained or experienced enough when it comes to the use of digital tools to use social networks or blogs effectively when designing and delivering online courses (Rapanta et al., 2020). This skills gap can lead to substantial real-world consequences, because it slices through education into “muddy waters”, as when teachers are unsure whether it be the digital platform or replicating the pedagogical context of their funnel with it, they are risking learning, resulting in poor engagement and disorganized course layouts for students that ultimately result in poorer learning outcomes (Bond et al., 2020). The COVID-19 pandemic just made this clearer, since for many lecturers, the abrupt shift to (emergency) remote learning required an overnight adjustment without adequate training or different types of support from the institution. That moment also emphasized the need to give educators the digital know-how, not just to deal with an emergency but to thrive in a perpetually changing educational environment (Carrillo & Flores, 2020; Czerniewicz et al., 2020). However digital training should not stop at technical know-how; it is just as important that educators learn how to use technology in ways that enhance learning - by creating interactive, accessible, and engaging learning environments. Research shows that when lecturers receive proper support, students benefit from better-designed courses and are more likely to stay motivated and involved throughout their studies (Sequí-Domínguez et al., 2024). Thus, investing in continuous professional development focused on digital pedagogy is no longer optional, it is essential. Higher education organizations must recognise that technology in education is not just about access, it is about how technology is been used. Institutions can only guarantee that innovation results in genuine advancements in teaching and learning by providing educators with the resources and information they require.

This chapter presents information on the development and implementation of a micro-course - “Technological Modernization in Health: Digital Tools for Distance Learning in Health Education”- designed to train teachers to effectively integrate digital technologies in health teaching. The course curriculum was structured into five key modules, delivered both synchronously and asynchronously over one month, covering: (1) Digital Education and Virtual Pedagogical Models, exploring foundational concepts and the transition from traditional to digital learning environments; (2) Communication, Collaboration, and Digital Resources, focusing on tools and methodologies for fostering interactive and engaging educational experiences; (3) Development of Digital Learning Activities and Experiences, providing hands-on practice in creating and managing digital learning activities; (4) Assessment in Digital Contexts; (5) Trends and Innovations in Digital Education, addressing best practices for evaluating student progress and delivering effective feedback using digital tools. A number of formative (compulsory) and summative (optional) assessment tasks were also drawn up in order to monitor the progress of the trainees' acquisitions: as formative assessments, a total of 5, we have included multiple-choice tests that covered the theoretical concepts about the topics given and a logbook on the creation of a course in a digital context, reflecting on assessment practice and identifying 2 assessment tasks and 2 tools for this purpose. The summative assessments took a variety of formats, such as using a whiteboard collaboratively among all the trainees, reading and critically appraising articles on the topics given, reflecting on the potential and challenges of planning and implementing a course in a specific technical-scientific area, with concrete examples, creating a collaborative mural, reflecting on the use of social networks/platforms by students, professionals and teachers in the health area, both in clinical practice and in higher education, various quizzes, and writing tests. Out of 32 enrolled participants, 25 successfully completed the course, achieving scores above 95% in the assigned (compulsory) tasks. The rest of those enrolled said they were unable to complete the tasks given and view the lessons in the time given to complete the course due to a mix of tasks linked to their professional teaching activity. For those who completed the training, participation in the optional activities was quite high, with an average of 21 people submitting the required tasks. The silver lining is the positive results that indicate a welcome change in teachers' readiness to incorporate digital resources into their classroom practice. Not only indicators of an ability to conform to changing educational environments this increasing openness shows emerging commitment to pedagogical evolution more in concert with the requirements of contemporary learners. As the skills are integrated into practices, we do expect to see more student-focused and inclusive methods of teaching across the board and those methods are likely to include, as they have in health education, adaptability and real-world relevance (Pei & Wu, 2019; Regmi & Jones, 2020). This format is especially relevant for health science educators, many of whom balance clinical responsibilities with academic work and therefore benefit from the flexibility that online learning provides. In addition, such initiatives advance important wide-ranging goals in higher education, including equity, quality and student engagement, through the promotion of digital literacy and pedagogical capability among faculty. As digital tools proliferate, the capacity to implement them thoughtfully becomes not only a technical capability but an essential component of professional teaching identity (Bond et al., 2021). In this regard, improving educators' digital fluency is critical for democratizing access to education, especially in disciplines where hands-on experience and theoretical knowledge must coexist. Moreover, literature has shown that, when teachers are confident in their use of technology, they are likely to try out various approaches, like flipped classrooms, simulation-oriented courses, or interactive studies, which have been associated with increased performance in health-related subjects (Nichat et al., 2023; Elendu et al., 2024). This shift towards active and participatory learning environments is also correlated with demands for greater personalization in higher education which can lead to more meaningful experiences for diverse student populations. Therefore, the use of digital learning through faculty development systems is a crucial development that can completely change education not only in the case of skill acquisition but also a pedagogical factor for education. As health education continues to change with the world and advancements in technology, initiatives that give educators the tools they need to teach with confidence and creativity are paramount to maintaining momentum for the future and ensuring higher education remains relevant. These findings indicate a growing willingness among educators to integrate technology into their teaching practices. The expectation is that the skills acquired in this process will lead to more innovative, inclusive, and effective methodologies in health education. Additionally, the results suggest that the online course format can be a valuable approach to pedagogical training for higher education faculty. By promoting digital literacy among educators, this initiative not only expands access to quality education but also helps improve learning outcomes in the health sciences.

MAIN FOCUS OF THE CHAPTER

This chapter will focus on a detailed exploration of the "Technological Modernization in Health: Digital Tools for Distance Learning in Health Education" course. We will begin by describing the development and implementation of the course, with a particular emphasis on its theoretical framework and the five key modules that structured its curriculum: Digital Education and Virtual Pedagogical Models; Communication, Collaboration, and Digital Resources; Development of Digital Learning Activities and Experiences; Assessment in Digital Contexts; Trends and Innovations in Digital Education. Following the module breakdown, we will examine the formative and summative assessment strategies used to monitor trainee progress and acquisition of skills. We will then present recommendations for the effective integration of technology in health education, drawing from the course's outcomes. The chapter will conclude by summarizing the key findings and broader implications of this initiative, emphasizing the vital role of continuous professional development in empowering educators and enhancing learning outcomes in the digital age.

THEORETICAL FRAMEWORK FOR THE COURSE PROPOSAL

Developing a robust theoretical framework is important for any successful course proposal, ensuring the course is not merely a technical training program but a comprehensive development initiative aimed at fostering deeper learning and effective teaching practices in health education. The European University Association ([EUA]

2021) has defined a general orientation for a student-centred education, globally characterized as follows:

> *The higher education learning experience will nurture and enable the development of learners as creative and critical thinkers, problem solvers and active and responsible citizens equipped for lifelong learning. It will kindle curiosity and creativity and support personal development through familiarity with the scientific method and the traditions of human knowledge and commitment to evidence-based discourse (pp. 7-8).*

The rise of technological and digital media in the information society has profoundly reshaped how individuals access and engage with learning. Technologies and digital environments have enabled the transfer of significant portions of learning, both knowledge and know-how, from formal education, often structured and hierarchical, to new forms of flexible, informal, and self-directed instruction (Anderson, 2008; Selwyn, 2015). One of the most striking examples of this shift is the growing popularity of DIY (Do It Yourself) practices. These illustrate how individuals without formal qualifications can become experts in various fields through engagement with digital platforms and communities (Gauntlett, 2011). Such practices are not merely hobbies; they represent a redefinition of what it means to learn and to be knowledgeable in a digital society.

Higher Education Institutions must pay close attention to these emerging movements and learning cultures. They serve as indicators of how people are learning, often in ways that are socially connected, interest-driven, and fluid (Livingstone, 2009). The increasing preference for informal and networked learning environments demonstrates the power of the internet and digital media to foster participation, collaboration, and lifelong learning (Selwyn, 2012; Illeris, 2009). Rather than resisting these shifts, HEIs can harness them to reimagine curricula and pedagogical models, aligning more closely with the values of autonomy, flexibility, and engagement that define learning in the 21st century (Anderson, 2008; Redecker & Punie, 2017).

Our approach is primarily informed by Constructivism, which suggests that learners actively build their own understanding and knowledge (Pelech, 2010). In the context of this course, participants are not perceived as passive recipients of information; instead, they engage in hands-on activities, such as designing digital learning experiences and developing online assessment tasks appropriate to their subjects and classes. This active engagement, coupled with reflection and iterative improvement, facilitates a more profound and personalized acquisition of digital pedagogical skills.

Complementing this, Andragogy, or adult learning theory, is central to our course's structure and delivery. Recognizing that adult learners are typically self-directed, bring diverse prior experiences, and are goal-oriented, the course offers flexible learning paths through its synchronous and asynchronous components (Knowles,

Holton, & Swanson, 2012). This flexibility also accommodates the professional demands of health educators, allowing them to integrate learning effortlessly into their busy schedules. Moreover, the emphasis on practical application ensures that the skills acquired are immediately relevant and applicable to their teaching contexts, fostering intrinsic motivation.

Furthermore, the course acknowledges the principles of Connectivism, particularly relevant in the digital age. This theory suggests that learning involves making connections between specialized information sources and that the ability to navigate and create these connections is crucial (Dunaway, 2011). Our modules, especially those on communication, collaboration, and digital resources, equip educators with the tools to build and participate in online communities of practice, share knowledge, and leverage digital networks for continuous professional development. This aligns with the understanding that knowledge often resides within diverse networks and that effective digital literacy involves the ability to connect with and contribute to these networks.

In the constructivist model of Ubiquitous Learning (ulearning), learning has no time or place limits. Students learn whatever, wherever and whenever with the help of (mobile) technologies and digital connectivity (computer-mediated learning), considering the learning context. The ubiquitous learning environment promotes study and research in digital sources and is characterized by permanence, accessibility, immediacy, interactivity, context awareness and adaptability (Cárdenas--Robledo & Peña-Ayala, 2018; Phumeechanya & Wannapiroon, 2014). Ubiquitous learning is active in MOOCs, which are increasingly valued as they allow access to international students and a wider audience, are cost-effective, easy to update and disseminate, and make use of LMS (Learning Management Systems) platforms that are already widespread in ES and easy to manage and use. Even in the classroom, the intensive use of apps and other digital software is becoming increasingly visible, allowing students to access information, search for different content and make their voice heard in pedagogical interactions with classmates and teachers. In these scenarios, teachers reinforce their tutoring, content curation and teaching resource production roles, discovering new creative and daring ways to carry out educational activity (Pantoja & Gonçalves, 2020).

Finally, Experiential Learning is constructed throughout the curriculum (Wijnen-Meijer, et al., 2022). The modules are designed to move participants through a cycle of concrete experience (e.g., using a new digital tool), reflective observation (e.g., analysing its pedagogical utility), abstract conceptualization (e.g., understanding its underlying principles), and active experimentation (e.g., applying it in a course design).

Professors are already competent and expert in their respective technical-scientific domains. Through this course, we leverage their existing knowledge (in line with

Ausubel's dictum: 'The most important single factor influencing learning is what the learner already knows.') to provide them with an expanded toolkit for their daily practice, thereby fostering a more personalized, dynamic, and significant teaching-learning process, ultimately enhancing student outcomes (Bryce & Blown, 2024).

The course was implemented on the institutional Moodle platform (Figure 1) over one month. Defined deadlines for tasks allowed participants the flexibility to learn at their own pace, fostering a personalized and adaptable experience.

Figure 1. Homepage of the course on Moodle platform

MODULE 1: DIGITAL EDUCATION AND VIRTUAL PEDAGOGICAL MODELS

This foundational module, "Digital Education and Virtual Pedagogical Models," serves as the initial step in the training program, welcoming participants to the evolving landscape of higher education and it is designed to immerse learners in the core concepts and paradigm shifts associated with digital learning environments.

The module begins with Lecture 1, providing an introductory overview of e-learning and blendend learning in higher education. To supplement this, participants are directed to a diverse array of resources. These include a "Whiteboard" task, encouraging interactive engagement based on a KWL strategy (Know/Want to Know/Learned), and essential readings such as the "Handbook of e-Learning Strategy" and "Digital Pedagogies in Higher Education" which offer comprehensive insights into strategic and pedagogical approaches to digital education. Further expanding on the current trends, "The Future of Digital and Online Learning in Higher Education" is provided, alongside "Decreto-Lei n.º 133/2019 - Ensino a Distância," a crucial legal framework for distance learning in Portugal.

Lecture 2 builds upon the initial concepts, guiding participants through further exploration. Supporting resources for this segment include an introduction to "Plataforma NAU," a key national e-learning platform, and resources from prominent international organizations like "WHO - Open Learning" and "UNESCO - Open Learning," emphasizing global perspectives and initiatives in open education. Additionally, Open Educational Resources are highlighted, promoting accessibility and sharing. An asynchronous classes guide provided practical guidance on designing flexible learning experiences.

The module culminates with Lecture 3, which is complemented by practical and reflective tasks. Participants can access "Tutorials - Moodle," "Differences between LMS (Moodle, Classroom e Teams)," offering practical tips into learning management systems and their tailored applications.

Within each module, participants found multiple video lectures, supplementary support materials, optional tasks designed to offer further insights into the subject (these do not contribute to course completion status), and a compulsory evaluation activity or quiz. In this module, the optional task was reading the paper "Online Learning in Health Professions Education – Teaching and Learning in Online Environments" (MacNeill et al., 2024) and reflect on some topics proposed; the compulsory task was a quiz to assess participants understanding of the module's core concepts.

MODULE 2: COMMUNICATION, COLLABORATION, AND DIGITAL RESOURCES

Module 2 focused on the importance of "Communication, Collaboration, and Digital Resources" in distance education. This module aimed to equip participants with both the theoretical understanding and practical competencies necessary to engage effectively in digitally mediated learning and professional environments. Grounded in contemporary theories of online education and networked learning (Anderson, 2008; Siemens, 2005), this module encouraged learners to explore how digital technologies shape interpersonal interaction, knowledge sharing, and community building.

A core objective of the module was to foster a deep understanding of how communication operates in online environments, distinguishing between synchronous and asynchronous modes, and analysing their impact on learner engagement and outcomes (Garrison, Anderson, & Archer, 2000). Participants also critically examined the role of collaboration in digital learning, drawing on research that highlighted how shared problem-solving, dialogue, and co-construction of meaning supported deeper learning and critical thinking (Laurillard, 2012; Hrastinski, 2009).

Beyond theoretical insight, the module placed strong emphasis on the development of practical skills. Learners engaged with a range of digital tools and platforms, including learning management systems, collaborative editing software, video-conferencing tools, and discussion forums, with the aim of enhancing their digital fluency and communication strategies (Bates, 2015).

The first lecture focused on effective digital communication, highlighting the need to adapt traditional face-to-face teaching methods to virtual learning environments. While the core principles of education remain unchanged, the strategies employed must consider the specific characteristics of distance learning (Anderson, 2008; Moore, Dickson-Deane, & Galyen, 2011). It was emphasised that online and in-person education differs in several key aspects. For instance, in terms of interaction and engagement, face-to-face classes allow spontaneous exchanges through direct discussions, immediate feedback, and non-verbal cues, whereas online learning demands intentional strategies to actively engage students (Hrastinski, 2009). Flexibility and accessibility also differ significantly. In-person classes are generally structured around fixed schedules and physical locations, which can be limiting for some learners. Online education, however, offers increased flexibility, allowing students to access content at their own pace and from different contexts, which can be particularly advantageous for diverse learner profiles (Garrison, Anderson, & Archer, 2000). Communication in traditional classrooms enables immediate clarification of doubts and dynamic discussions, while virtual environments require the establishment of clear and consistent communication channels to ensure students' understanding (Boettcher & Conrad, 2021). Assessment and feedback are another point of contrast. While face-to-face teaching typically enables supervised assessments and direct, verbal feedback, online learning relies more on digital tools such as automated quizzes and peer review systems to ensure timely and meaningful feedback (Gikandi, Morrow, & Davis, 2011). Moreover, the social dimension of learning is more naturally fostered in physical classrooms, where a sense of community can develop organically. In online settings, building a collaborative and supportive learning environment requires deliberate and structured efforts (Rovai, 2002). To address these challenges and support effective digital communication, the session discussed several pedagogical strategies. These included establishing transparent and consistent channels of communication, fostering interactive learning environments, providing timely and constructive feedback, incorporating multimedia resources to enrich content delivery, encouraging social learning through group interaction and collaboration, and maintaining awareness of appropriate digital communication etiquette (Salmon, 2000). Several digital tools were suggested to facilitate the implementation of these strategies - Google Classroom, Zoom, Slack, Nearpod, Mentimeter Socrative, and others.

The second and third sessions consisted of practical examples of the use of digital tools in the context of synchronous and asynchronous classes, with the addition of collaborative tasks. These included platforms such as Miro and Mural, interactive digital whiteboards that enable teamwork in real time or asynchronously. Both platforms allow users to brainstorm, visualise workflows, and co-create content using templates, sticky notes, diagrams, and embedded media. These tools are particularly effective for supporting design thinking, project planning, and collaborative learning in online education (Mehta et al., 2021). Examples were also given of Padlet and Wakelet, two content curation and collaborative wall platforms.

In this module, the optional task consisted of creating a collaborative mural using Padlet or Wakelet on a topic related to the content normally taught by the teacher; the compulsory task was a quiz to assess the participants' understanding of the fundamental concepts of the module.

MODULE 3: DEVELOPMENT OF DIGITAL LEARNING ACTIVITIES AND EXPERIENCES

Module 3, named "Development of Digital Learning Activities and Experiences", focused particularly in how to design digital learning experiences for higher education instructors. This entailed selecting pedagogically sound activities that effectively integrate technology. The aim was, therefore, to provide a variety of tools, applicable to health teaching, that would respond to different areas of knowledge and serve a variety of purposes. Edpuzzle, for instance, lets teachers transform videos into interactive lessons by embedding questions and gathering analytics. Research has shown that Edpuzzle improves engagement, reduces cognitive load, and fosters self-regulated learning, especially in flipped classroom settings and among students needing additional support (Álvarez & Mischel, 2024; Dwyer, 2018). Also, interactive "icebreaker" and gamified quiz tools such as Quizizz and Quizalize stimulate motivation, creativity, and engagement in university contexts. Assemblr Edu offers educators augmented-reality experiences to create 3D interactive learning, promoting spatial learning and immersion (Danesh et al., 2020). Anatomix, BodyInteract, and Osso VR permit simulation-based experiential learning: Anatomix provides virtual anatomy exploration; BodyInteract facilitates clinical-scenario practice; Osso VR supports surgical training, studies show these tools enhance skill acquisition and critical decision-making (Roueche et al., 2021; Mütterlein & Hess, 2020). Labster's virtual science labs have compelling empirical support: use of Labster simulations significantly boosts STEM pass rates, lowers dropout rates, and increases retention, simulations embedded as pre-labs strongly predict continued STEM engagement and career intentions, which makes it an impossible tool for higher education teachers to ignore.

In addition to these tools, we focused on the contribution that the use of branching can make to distance learning. Incorporating gamification across these tools aligns with educational design principles that leverage game-elements (such as points, badges, narrative, and immediate feedback) to increase motivation, engagement, and metacognitive awareness (Deterding et al., 2011; Kapp, 2012). Empirical work shows gamified environments can boost performance and engagement in both general university settings and domain-specific disciplines like software testing (Shelby et al., 2021).

Furthermore, this module also focused on how, in the context of higher education, particularly in distance learning environments, social media platforms have emerged as valuable tools to enhance communication, engagement, and collaborative learning. Social media facilitates the creation of informal and participatory learning spaces, bridging the gap between institutional content delivery and student-centred, networked learning experiences (Manca & Ranieri, 2016).

Platforms such as Facebook, Twitter, LinkedIn, and Instagram can be adopted by educators for a variety of academic purposes: discussion, peer feedback, networking, knowledge sharing, and community building (Tess, 2013). The negative aspects of using social networks were also highlighted, such as the possibility of them serving as a distraction, inequity in participation, or privacy concerns (Greenhow & Lewin, 2016). To address this, educators were encouraged to set clear boundaries and ethical guidelines, while also promoting digital literacy and responsible online behaviour among students (Redecker & Punie, 2017).

In this module, the optional task consisted of a reflection on the use of social networks as a tool for dissemination and teaching in health; the compulsory task was a quiz to assess the participants' understanding of the fundamental concepts of the module.

MODULE 4: ASSESSMENT IN DIGITAL CONTEXTS

Module 4, titled "Assessment in Digital Contexts," represents the final module, inviting participants to thoroughly explore the critical domain of evaluation within contemporary digital learning environments. The module begins by instructing learners to review a provided file that visually outlines all module content and associated tasks, establishing a clear roadmap for the learning journey. The initial segment of the module explores into the ongoing discourse surrounding online assessment, acknowledging its complexities and the diverse perspectives from experts.

To facilitate a comprehensive understanding, participants are presented with two distinct viewpoints: "Webinar Practices of Assessment in Online Learning" and "Alternative Methods of Assessment the Experience of UCDublin". Both resources offer pertinent and adaptable approaches relevant to higher education, allowing learners to critically compare different methodologies.

Building on this introductory understanding, the module then provides a set of highly valuable resources pertaining to assessment strategies in digital contexts. These include online assessment recommendations, offering practical guidelines, and an Assessment and Bloom's Taxonomy Infographic, which visually connects assessment practices with cognitive learning levels. Furthermore, a synthesis document showcases various assessment strategies, complete with illustrative examples and practical tools, enriching the participants' toolkit.

The module prepares participants for a synchronous session by providing a video tutorial on "Learning to create a Test in Moodle". This hands-on preparation culminates in a task designed to reinforce the practical application of Moodle for assessment. This module included additionally a synchronous session where participants can engage in real-time discussion, clarify doubts, and practice their newly acquired assessment skills in a guided environment.

At the end, a mandatory task was defined - this task requires participants to reflect on their assessment practices and propose improvements. Specifically, they are instructed to consider their course/discipline that intends to create digital content, identify two assessment tasks and two tools suitable for this purpose.

COURSE EVALUATION AND TRAINEE FEEDBACK

Out of the 32 enrolled participants, 25 successfully finished the course, with scores above 95% on the compulsory activities. The remaining enrolled students stated that they were unable to accomplish the tasks assigned to them and see the lessons within the time frame specified for completing the course owing to a combination of obligations related to their professional teaching activities. For those who finished the program, participation in the optional activities was quite high, with an average of 21 persons completing each of the required tasks. As an example of this high level of adherence, we can mention, for example, in the activity of creating a collaborative mural, 21 participants created a Padlet with various themes, such as "Imaging Methods", "Cocaine Addiction", "Obesity and Inflammation", "Non-Invasive Brain Stimulation" or "Food Sustainability", which they injected with numerous learning-promoting contents and activities. In the Reflection on the Course/Distance UC activities and on the use of social networks/platforms by students, professionals and teachers in the health field, both in clinical practice and in higher education, 19 participants submitted texts that reflected their interpretation of the content learned in the modules taught and how they could adapt this knowledge in their teaching practice.

Later, a feedback questionnaire was designed to gather participant perspectives on the "Digital Tools for Distance Learning in Health Education" course to inform future improvements and ensure an optimal learning experience for all participants. Participants are asked to indicate their level of agreement with various statements using a 5-point Likert scale (1 = Strongly Disagree 2 = Disagree 3 = Neutral 4 = Agree 5 = Strongly Agree). The questionnaire is structured into four main sections (Figure 2), each containing a statement to be rated on the Likert scale:

- Overall satisfaction with the course: "I am satisfied with the overall content and structure of the course."
- Learning experience: "I feel I have gained valuable knowledge regarding digital education, virtual pedagogical models, and digital tools to use."
- Usefulness of resources and tools: "The recommended resources (e.g., EBooks, articles, guides, links) were useful for my learning and are relevant to my teaching practice."
- Course structure and workload: "The pace and workload of the course were appropriate."

Figure 2. Participants feedback

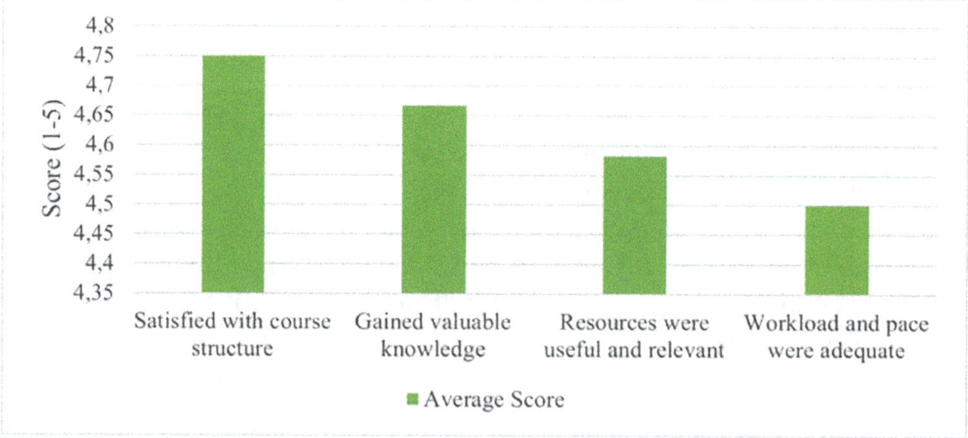

Following the Likert scale questions, the questionnaire includes a single open-ended question designed to elicit more detailed and qualitative feedback: "What was the most valuable aspect of the course and, if anything, what could be improved? (Please be specific)".

Twelve participants completed the feedback questionnaire, including nine women and three men. On average, participants had 10 years of teaching experience. The results show a generally positive response to the course content and delivery. Most participants "agreed" or "strongly agreed" with the clarity of the instructions and the relevance of the digital tools presented. Some qualitative comments emphasized the usefulness of the content, said that most of the tools demonstrated had great applicability in their professional practice, whether in distance or face-to-face classes, to make teaching a more interactive and enriching experience, and suggested the desire for more practical demonstrations of the use of these and other tools in future editions of the course.

While many existing training models in health sciences distance education focus primarily on either technical proficiency or isolated pedagogical strategies, they often lack an integrated, interdisciplinary approach that addresses the complex realities of academic and clinical teaching in digital environments. For instance, most faculty development programs prioritize basic LMS navigation or generic instructional design without tailoring content to the specific demands of health professions education, such as virtual clinical supervision, ethical considerations, or simulation-based learning (Philipsen et al., 2019; Cutri et al., 2020). This course distinguishes itself by offering a holistic, modular, and context-sensitive framework that combines pedagogical innovation and technological fluency, designed specifically for higher education faculty navigating hybrid or fully online health education settings. By embedding peer collaboration, continuous assessment, and flexible delivery formats, it responds more effectively to the dynamic needs of health sciences educators than traditional one-size-fits-all models (Bond et al., 2021).

In addition, this course is closely aligned with the World Health Organization's *Global Strategy on Digital Health 2020–2025*, which emphasizes the need to strengthen the digital competencies of health professionals and promote equitable, ethical, and sustainable use of digital technologies in health systems. By equipping faculty in health sciences with the pedagogical, technical, and ethical skills required for high-quality distance education, the initiative supports key strategic objectives such as workforce capacity-building, inclusive digital transformation, and governance for digital health education. In particular, the course contributes to the WHO's call for member states and institutions to "develop digitally competent health workforce[s] through accessible and context-relevant education and training programmes" (WHO, 2021, p. 22). It reinforces the strategy's vision of leveraging digital tools to improve access, quality, and equity in health education, particularly in higher education contexts where clinical and academic responsibilities intersect.

Despite the strengths of the course, several limitations must be acknowledged. First, the lack of detailed data on faculty digital readiness prior to participation limited the ability to tailor content to varying levels of technological competence. Without a formal baseline, it was difficult to assess progress or target differentiated support. Second, while participation and completion rates were tracked, there was limited discussion of robust evaluation metrics to assess the effectiveness of training in terms of actual pedagogical impact or behavioral change. Third, critical discussions on the inherent limitations of e-learning in health education, such as the fidelity of virtual simulations, learner fatigue, or privacy concerns, were largely absent. Moreover, the course engaged educators from a diverse range of health disciplines, including pharmacy, occupational therapy, biomedical sciences, functional sciences, orthotics, and radiotherapy. Nonetheless, the under-exploration of how disciplinary background influences digital training uptake and engagement remains a notable gap that warrants further investigation.

RECOMMENDATIONS

Realizing the potential of integrating technology into higher education, particularly regarding its role in teaching and learning processes, does not just depend on investment in acquiring and making available technological resources. It is also essential to invest in adequate infrastructure, such as broadband internet access, good quality Wi-Fi connectivity and adequate technical support, but above all, it is necessary to invest in the professional development of teaching staff for the pedagogical and critical use of digital technologies in teaching and learning processes, which will enable teachers to design and implement innovative and transformative pedagogical approaches (Almeida et al., 2022; Rabello & Tavares, 2016). To effectively foster the widespread adoption and proficient use of distance learning tools among higher education faculty in Health Sciences, a strategic, multi-faceted approach is essential. This can be achieved through the establishment of a dedicated central hub in each organisation, orchestrating initiatives across four key pillars:

1. Tailored Training & Capacity Building
    - Curriculum Development: Design and deliver a continuous professional development curriculum that directly addresses the specific pedagogical and technical challenges faced by health sciences faculty in distance learning. This includes advanced modules on instructional design for online environments, effective use of virtual simulation tools, strategies for online clinical supervision, and ethical considerations in digital health education. According to George et al. (2014), targeted training in

instructional design significantly enhances educators' ability to adapt content for virtual modalities. Moreover, the integration of virtual simulations has been shown to improve clinical reasoning and decision-making skills in students (Cook et al., 2010), making their inclusion in faculty training essential.

- Modular and Flexible Offerings: Provide training in diverse, flexible formats (e.g., micro-courses, workshops, bootcamps, synchronous webinars, asynchronous modules) to accommodate the demanding schedules of faculty often balancing academic and clinical responsibilities. Luo & Li, (2025) highlight that integrating structured, discipline-specific microlearning into university curricula can effectively bridge academic-industry skill gaps. Offering certifications or micro-credentials upon completion not only serves as an incentive but also contributes to formal recognition of newly acquired competencies (Kirkwood & Price, 2014). Flexibility in scheduling and modality (e.g., asynchronous delivery) is particularly effective in fostering access and equity in faculty development programs (Philipsen et al., 2019).
- Peer-to-Peer Learning Initiatives: Facilitate communities of practice, supervision, or mentorship programs where experienced faculty can share best practices, troubleshooting tips, and innovative approaches to distance learning in health sciences. This fosters a supportive environment and leverages internal expertise. Wenger et al. (2002) argue that communities of practice are critical in sustaining professional growth, particularly in dynamic fields like digital education. Moreover, mentoring relationships and peer feedback have been associated with improved teaching efficacy and resilience among educators during transitions to online teaching (Bond et al., 2021).

2. Comprehensive Resources & Technical Support
    - Centralized Digital Resource Repository: Develop and maintain an easily accessible, curated repository of high-quality digital learning resources, templates for online course design, assessment rubrics for virtual activities, and examples of successful distance learning implementations in health sciences. Repositories like these can improve consistency in course quality, reduce preparation time, and promote the reuse of proven strategies. In the context of health education, curated resources have been shown to support faculty in aligning digital content with learning outcomes, especially when paired with instructional design templates (Philipsen et al., 2019). Furthermore, sharing exemplars of successful online teaching practices encourages innovation and adaptation among faculty (Bond et al., 2021).

- Dedicated Technical Support Team: Establish a responsive and specialized technical support team specifically for distance learning tools. This team should offer tiered support, from basic troubleshooting to advanced platform customization and integration assistance, ensuring faculty feel confident and supported when encountering technical challenges. Faculty members often report technical difficulties as a major barrier to adopting online teaching tools; therefore, providing structured and timely support has been identified as a key factor in successful distance education implementation (Cutri et al., 2020). Also, dedicated support tailored to the pedagogical tools used in health sciences (e.g., simulations, remote assessment platforms) greatly enhances faculty satisfaction and course quality (Czerniewicz et al., 2020).
- Software and Hardware Provision: Advocate for and facilitate access to necessary software licenses, specialized health education tools (e.g., virtual dissection apps, escape rooms, patient simulators), and essential hardware (e.g., quality microphones, webcams) to ensure faculty have the right equipment for effective online delivery. Provision of necessary hardware and software not only improves teaching effectiveness but also reduces cognitive load, allowing educators to focus on pedagogy rather than logistics. Access to discipline-specific tools, such as virtual reality in anatomy or simulation software in nursing, is particularly crucial in maintaining clinical relevance in online environments (Kononowicz et al., 2019).

3. Innovation & Dissemination
   - Pilot Programs and Grant Opportunities: Actively encourage and support faculty in piloting innovative distance learning technologies and pedagogical approaches. This could involve offering seed grants or dedicated time for faculty to experiment and develop new solutions. According to Laurillard (2012), supporting innovation through small-scale pilot initiatives enables the exploration of emerging technologies in low-risk environments. Pilot funding can also empower faculty to adapt pedagogy to the unique needs of health sciences education, where simulation and experiential learning play central roles (Garrison & Vaughan, 2008).
   - Research and Evaluation: Promote and conduct research on the effectiveness of distance learning tools and methodologies within health sciences education. This evidence-based approach allows for continuous refinement of strategies and validates the impact of digital pedagogical innovations. Means et al. (2013) emphasize that systematic evaluation is essential to determine not just if digital interventions "work," but how

and under what conditions they are most effective. In health professions education, contextualized research using big data and analytics helps ensure that digital strategies align with clinical competence frameworks (Ellaway et al., 2014).

- Dissemination of Best Practices: Organize regular internal and external dissemination events (e.g., symposia, conferences, online showcases) to share successful case studies, research findings, and lessons learned. This promotes knowledge exchange, celebrates achievements, and inspires further adoption. Communities that openly share innovations tend to accelerate institutional learning and increase the uptake of effective strategies (Wenger et al., 2002). Furthermore, visibility of successful implementations encourages replication and scaling (Philipsen et al., 2019).
- Recognition and Incentives: Establish formal recognition programs and incentives for faculty who excel in integrating distance learning tools and demonstrate innovative digital pedagogical practices. This could include awards, promotion criteria considerations, or funding for further professional development. Recognition is a powerful motivator in academic environments, and when innovation is tied to tangible incentives, faculty engagement with digital transformation efforts increases significantly (Kirkwood & Price, 2013).

4. Inclusitvity and Continuous Improvement
    - Digital Inclusion and Skills Development: Promote digital inclusion by ensuring that all members of the academic community, regardless of background or ability, have access to the necessary tools and training to fully engage in distance education. This includes initiatives to strengthen digital skills, reduce technological barriers, and provide equitable access to resources. Digital inequality encompasses not only access to devices and internet, but also disparities in digital literacy and confidence, which must be addressed through targeted training programs (Van Dijk, 2020; Beaunoyer et al., 2020). In health sciences education, ensuring digital inclusion is critical to preventing the amplification of existing educational inequities.
    - Universal Accessibility Compliance: Ensure that all educational materials, platforms, and tools meet established accessibility standards such as the Web Content Accessibility Guidelines (WCAG) and conform to national and institutional policies. Accessible design is a legal and ethical imperative, particularly in health education where diverse learner needs are common. Universal design principles, such as providing captions, screen-reader compatibility, and keyboard navigation, enhance learn-

ing for all students, including those with disabilities (Burgstahler, 2015; Seale, 2014).
- Assessment and Impact Evaluation: Apply structured and systematic evaluation tools to assess the quality, impact, and sustainability of digital learning strategies and training initiatives. These evaluations should be based on clear indicators of pedagogical effectiveness and informed by educational research. Using validated frameworks and data-driven analytics can help institutions refine their approaches and ensure alignment with learning outcomes and professional competencies in health sciences (Laurillard, 2012).
- Continuous Feedback and Iterative Improvement: Maintain institutional responsiveness and relevance by embedding continuous feedback loops into all digital education initiatives. This involves regular monitoring, stakeholder input, and agile adaptation mechanisms to respond to emerging needs and evolving educational contexts. A dynamic, iterative approach to digital innovation fosters resilience and promotes a culture of continuous pedagogical improvement (Viczko, 2016).

5. Ethical Considerations
    - Ethical Use of Educational Technology: The integration of digital tools in education must be guided by clear ethical principles. Faculty should be prepared to address issues such as data privacy, academic integrity, and equitable access. Ethical awareness is essential to prevent unintended harms, including surveillance and algorithmic bias (Selwyn, 2016).
    - Responsible Innovation and AI: As artificial intelligence becomes more common in education, educators must understand its ethical implications, such as bias in learning analytics or lack of transparency in automated feedback systems. Clear guidelines are needed to ensure responsible use and protect students' rights (Luckin et al., 2016; Floridi et al., 2018).
    - Fostering an Ethical Culture: Institutions should promote a culture of digital ethics by offering training, establishing codes of conduct, and encouraging critical reflection on technology's societal impact. This ensures innovation in education is both effective and aligned with academic values.

To sum up, the dynamic landscape of healthcare demands an equally agile and forward-thinking approach to education. To cultivate highly competent and adaptable professionals, higher education health schools must proactively embrace pedagogical innovation and digital transformation. This necessitates the establishment of dedicated centers designed to champion these critical advancements. Thus, these centers' core mission should align seamlessly with institutional strategic objectives, providing tailored support to the entire academic community: faculty, students, and non-teaching staff. This involves designing and delivering professional development programs specifically adapted to the unique demands of health sciences. Such central hub would actively promote and disseminate innovative teaching and learning practices, advocating for student-centered, active methodologies suitable for "Education 4.0."

CONCLUSIONS

The "Technological Modernization in Health: Digital Tools for Distance Learning in Health Education" course demonstrated that structured pedagogical training in digital competencies can effectively enhance educators' readiness for remote teaching in health sciences. By combining theoretical foundations with hands-on application, the program addressed a critical gap in faculty development, fostering both digital fluency and pedagogical innovation.

The high completion rate and strong engagement with both formative and summative assessments indicate that health educators are not only capable of adopting digital tools but are also motivated to integrate them meaningfully into their practice. This initiative shows the importance of sustained, targeted professional development to support the ongoing evolution of teaching strategies in increasingly digital academic environments.

Ultimately, the findings suggest that investing in digital pedagogical training contributes to more adaptive, inclusive, and student-centered teaching approaches in health education. Such initiatives are essential to ensuring that higher education remains responsive to technological change and aligned with the needs of contemporary learners.

REFERENCES

Almeida, L. da S., & Gonçalves, S. Ramos do Ó, J., Rebola, F., Soares, S., & Vieira, F. (2022). *Inovação Pedagógica no Ensino Superior: Cenários e Caminhos de Transformação* (A3ES Readings nº 16). Lisboa: Agência de Avaliação e Acreditação do Ensino Superior.

Álvarez, C., & Mischel, L. (2024). Edpuzzle for e-learning: A study of perceived advantages and limitations. *International Journal of Education and Development Using Information and Communication Technology*, *20*(1), 134–145.

Anderson, T. (Ed.). (2008). *The theory and practice of online learning* (2nd ed.). AU Press. DOI: 10.15215/aupress/9781897425084.01

Bates, T. (2015). *Teaching in a digital age: Guidelines for designing teaching and learning*. Tony Bates Associates Ltd.

Beaunoyer, E., Dupéré, S., & Guitton, M. J. (2020). COVID-19 and digital inequalities: Reciprocal impacts and mitigation strategies. *Computers in Human Behavior*, *111*, 106424. DOI: 10.1016/j.chb.2020.106424 PMID: 32398890

Bell, F. (2011). Connectivism: Its place in theory-informed research and innovation in technology-enabled learning. *International Review of Research in Open and Distance Learning*, *12*(3), 98–118. DOI: 10.19173/irrodl.v12i3.902

Biggs, J., & Tang, C. (2011). *Teaching for quality learning at university: What the student does* (4th ed.). McGraw-Hill Education.

Boettcher, J. V., & Conrad, R. M. (2021). *The online teaching survival guide: Simple and practical pedagogical tips* (2nd ed.). Jossey-Bass.

Bond, M., Bedenlier, S., Marín, V. I., & Händel, M. (2021). Emergency remote teaching in higher education: Mapping the first global online semester. *International Journal of Educational Technology in Higher Education*, *18*(1), 50. DOI: 10.1186/s41239-021-00282-x PMID: 34778537

Bond, M., Bedenlier, S., Marín, V. I., & Händel, M. (2021). Emergency remote teaching in higher education: Mapping the first global online semester. *International Journal of Educational Technology in Higher Education*, *18*(1), 50. DOI: 10.1186/s41239-021-00282-x PMID: 34778537

Bond, M., Buntins, K., Bedenlier, S., Zawacki-Richter, O., & Kerres, M. (2020). Mapping research in student engagement and educational technology in higher education: A systematic evidence map. *International Journal of Educational Technology in Higher Education, 17*(1), 2. DOI: 10.1186/s41239-019-0176-8

Bryce, T. G. K., & Blown, E. J. (2024). Ausubel's meaningful learning re-visited. *Current Psychology (New Brunswick, N.J.), 43*(5), 4579–4598. DOI: 10.1007/s12144-023-04440-4 PMID: 37359615

Burgstahler, S. (2015). *Universal design in higher education: From principles to practice* (2nd ed.). Harvard Education Press.

Cárdenas-Robledo, L. A., & Peña-Ayala, A. (2018). Ubiquitous learning: A systematic review. *Telematics and Informatics, 35*(5), 1097–1132. DOI: 10.1016/j.tele.2018.01.009

Carrillo, C., & Flores, M. A. (2020). COVID-19 and teacher education: A literature review of online teaching and learning practices. *European Journal of Teacher Education, 43*(4), 466–487. DOI: 10.1080/02619768.2020.1821184

CAST. (2018). *Universal Design for Learning guidelines version 2.2.* http://udlguidelines.cast.org

Cook, D. A., Levinson, A. J., Garside, S., Dupras, D. M., Erwin, P. J., & Montori, V. M. (2010). Instructional design variations in internet-based learning for health professions education: A systematic review and meta-analysis. *Academic Medicine, 85*(5), 909–922. DOI: 10.1097/ACM.0b013e3181d6c319 PMID: 20520049

Cutri, R. M., Mena, J., & Whiting, E. F. (2020). Faculty readiness for online crisis teaching: Transitioning to online teaching during the COVID-19 pandemic. *European Journal of Teacher Education, 43*(4), 523–541. DOI: 10.1080/02619768.2020.1815702

Cutri, R. M., Mena, J., & Whiting, E. F. (2020). Faculty readiness for online crisis teaching: Transitioning to online teaching during the COVID-19 pandemic. *European Journal of Teacher Education, 43*(4), 523–541. DOI: 10.1080/02619768.2020.1815702

Czerniewicz, L., Agherdien, N., Badenhorst, J., Belluigi, D., Chambers, T., Chili, M., & Prinsloo, P. (2020). A wake-up call: Equity, inequality and COVID-19 emergency remote teaching and learning. *Postdigital Science and Education, 2*(3), 946–967. DOI: 10.1007/s42438-020-00187-4 PMID: 40477091

Danesh, A., et al. (2020). Effectiveness of augmented reality in education. Journal of Educational Technology.

Darling-Hammond, L., Hyler, M. E., & Gardner, M. (2017). *Effective Teacher Professional Development*. Learning Policy Institute. https://learningpolicyinstitute.org/product/effective-teacher-professional-development-report

Deterding, S., Dixon, D., Khaled, R., & Nacke, L. (2011). From game design elements to gamefulness: defining "gamification". *Proceedings of the 15th International Academic MindTrek Conference*. DOI: 10.1145/2181037.2181040

Dunaway, M. K. (2011). Connectivism: Learning theory and pedagogical practice for networked information landscapes. *RSR. Reference Services Review*, *39*(4), 675–685. DOI: 10.1108/00907321111186686

Dwyer, S. (2018). Gameful engagement: Gamification, critical thinking, and first-year composition. Double Helix: A Journal of Critical Thinking and Writing, 6(1), 1–13. https://doi.org/DOI: 10.37514/DB-H-J.2018.6.1.07

Elendu, C., Amaechi, D. C., Okatta, A. U., Amaechi, E. C., Elendu, T. C., Ezeh, C. P., & Elendu, I. D. (2024). The impact of simulation-based training in medical education. *Revista de Medicina (São Paulo)*, *103*(27), e38813. DOI: 10.1097/MD.0000000000038813 PMID: 38968472

Ellaway, R. H., Pusic, M. V., Galbraith, R. M., & Cameron, T. (2014). Developing the role of big data and analytics in health professional education. *Medical Teacher*, *36*(3), 216–222. DOI: 10.3109/0142159X.2014.874553 PMID: 24491226

European University Association. (2021). Universities Without Walls: A Vision For 2030. https://eua.eu/resources/publications/983:pathways-to-the-future.html

Ferrari, A. (2013). *DIGCOMP: A Framework for Developing and Understanding Digital Competence in Europe*. Joint Research Centre, European Commission., DOI: 10.2788/52966

Floridi, L., Cowls, J., Beltrametti, M., Chatila, R., Chazerand, P., Dignum, V., Luetge, C., Madelin, R., Pagallo, U., Rossi, F., Schafer, B., Valcke, P., & Vayena, E. (2018). AI4People—An ethical framework for a good AI society. *Minds and Machines*, *28*(4), 689–707. DOI: 10.1007/s11023-018-9482-5 PMID: 30930541

Fullan, M. (2007). *The new meaning of educational change* (4th ed.). Teachers College Press.

Fullan, M., & Langworthy, M. (2014). *A rich seam: How new pedagogies find deep learning*. Pearson.

Garrison, D. R., Anderson, T., & Archer, W. (2000). Critical inquiry in a text-based environment*: Computer conferencing in higher education. The Internet and Higher Education*, *2*(2–3), 87–105. DOI: 10.1016/S1096-7516(00)00016-6

Garrison, D. R., & Vaughan, N. D. (2008). *Blended learning in higher education: Framework, principles, and guidelines*. Jossey-Bass.

Gauntlett, D. (2011). *Making is connecting: The social meaning of creativity from DIY and knitting to YouTube and Web 2.0*. Polity Press.

Gee, J. P. (2003). *What video games have to teach us about learning and literacy*. Palgrave Macmillan. DOI: 10.1145/950566.950595

George, P. P., Papachristou, N., Belisario, J. M., Wang, W., Wark, P. A., Cotic, Z., & Car, J. (2014). Online eLearning for undergraduates in health professions: A systematic review of the impact on knowledge, skills, attitudes, and satisfaction. *Journal of Global Health*, *4*(1), 010406. DOI: 10.7189/jogh.04.010406 PMID: 24976965

Gikandi, J. W., Morrow, D., & Davis, N. E. (2011). Online formative assessment in higher education: A review of the literature. *Computers & Education*, *57*(4), 2333–2351. DOI: 10.1016/j.compedu.2011.06.004

Greenhow, C., & Lewin, C. (2016). Social media and education: Reconceptualizing the boundaries of formal and informal learning. *Learning, Media and Technology*, *41*(1), 6–30. DOI: 10.1080/17439884.2015.1064954

Holmes, W., Bialik, M., & Fadel, C. (2019). *Artificial Intelligence in Education: Promises and Implications for Teaching and Learning*. Center for Curriculum Redesign.

Hrastinski, S. (2009). *A theory of online learning as online participation*. Computers & Education, 52(1), 78–82. https://doi.org/DOI: 10.1016/j.compedu.2008.06.009

Illeris, K. (2009). *Contemporary theories of learning: Learning theorists... In their own words*. Routledge. DOI: 10.4324/9780203870426

Kapp, K. M. (2012). *The gamification of learning and instruction: Game-based methods and strategies for training and education*. Pfeiffer.

Kirkwood, A., & Price, L. (2013). Technology-enhanced learning and teaching in higher education: What is 'enhanced' and how do we know? A critical literature review. *Learning, Media and Technology*, *39*(1), 6–36. DOI: 10.1080/17439884.2013.770404

Kirkwood, A., & Price, L. (2014). Technology-enhanced learning and teaching in higher education: What is 'enhanced' and how do we know? A critical literature review. *Learning, Media and Technology*, *39*(1), 6–36. DOI: 10.1080/17439884.2013.770404

Knowles, M. S., Holton, E. F.III, & Swanson, R. A. (2012). *The adult learner: The definitive classic in adult education and human resource development* (7th ed.). Routledge. DOI: 10.4324/9780080964249

Kononowicz, A. A., Woodham, L. A., Edelbring, S., Stathakarou, N., Davies, D., Saxena, N., & Zary, N. (2019). Virtual patient simulations in health professions education: Systematic review and meta-analysis by the digital health education collaboration. *Journal of Medical Internet Research, 21*(7), e14676. DOI: 10.2196/14676 PMID: 31267981

Laurillard, D. (2012). *Teaching as a design science: Building pedagogical patterns for learning and technology*. Routledge.

Libâneo, J. C. (2001). Educação no século XXI: pedagogia da reprodução ou pedagogia da transformação? In *J. C. Libâneo, M. L. Oliveira & N. T. Toschi (Orgs.), Educação escolar: políticas, estrutura e organização* (pp. 31–50). Alternativa.

Livingstone, S. (2009). *Children and the internet: Great expectations, challenging realities*. Polity Press.

Luckin, R.. (2016). *Intelligence Unleashed: An Argument for AI in Education*. Pearson.

Luckin, R., Holmes, W., Griffiths, M., & Forcier, L. B. (2016). *Intelligence Unleashed: An Argument for AI in Education*. Pearson Education.

Luo, H., & Li, W. (2025). Impact of microlearning on developing soft skills of university students across disciplines. *Frontiers in Psychology, 16*, 1491265. DOI: 10.3389/fpsyg.2025.1491265 PMID: 40351600

MacNeill, H., Masters, K., Nemethy, K., & Correia, R. (2024). Online learning in health professions education. Part 1: Teaching and learning in online environments: AMEE Guide No. 161. *Medical Teacher, 46*(1), 4–17. DOI: 10.1080/0142159X.2023.2197135 PMID: 37094079

Manca, S., & Ranieri, M. (2016). Is Facebook still a suitable technology-enhanced learning environment? An updated critical review of the literature from 2012 to 2015. *Journal of Computer Assisted Learning, 32*(6), 503–528. DOI: 10.1111/jcal.12154

Means, B., Toyama, Y., Murphy, R., & Baki, M. (2013). The effectiveness of online and blended learning: A meta-analysis of the empirical literature. *Teachers College Record, 115*(3), 1–47. DOI: 10.1177/016146811311500307

Mehta, K. J., Agrawal, A., & Sanghi, S. (2021). Digital whiteboards as collaborative learning spaces: Case studies using Miro and Mural in remote education. *International Journal of Educational Technology in Higher Education, 18*, 26. Advance online publication. DOI: 10.1186/s41239-021-00262-4

Meyer, A., Rose, D. H., & Gordon, D. (2014). *Universal Design for Learning: Theory and practice*. CAST Professional Publishing. https://www.cast.org/products-books/udl-theory-practice

Moore, M. G., Dickson-Deane, C., & Galyen, K. (2011). E-learning, online learning, and distance learning environments: Are they the same? *The Internet and Higher Education, 14*(2), 129–135. DOI: 10.1016/j.iheduc.2010.10.001

Mütterlein, J., & Hess, T. (2020). The role of immersive technologies in skill acquisition. Journal of VR in Learning.

Nichat, A., Gajbe, U., Bankar, N. J., Singh, B. R., & Badge, A. K. (2023). Flipped Classrooms in Medical Education: Improving Learning Outcomes and Engaging Students in Critical Thinking Skills. *Cureus, 15*(11), e48199. DOI: 10.7759/cureus.48199 PMID: 38054140

OECD. (2018). *Teaching for the Future: Effective Classroom Practices To Transform Education*. OECD Publishing., DOI: 10.1787/9789264293243-

OECD. (2021). *21st-Century Readers: Developing Literacy Skills in a Digital World*. OECD Publishing., DOI: 10.1787/a83d84cb-

Pantoja, A., & Gonçalves, S. (2020). El tutor como agente de cambio y las buenas prácticas. In Pantoja, A. (Ed.), *Buenas prácticas en la tutoría universitária* (pp. 17–38). Editorial Síntesis.

Pei, L., & Wu, H. (2019). Does online learning work better than offline learning in undergraduate medical education? A systematic review and meta-analysis. *Medical Education Online, 24*(1), 1666538. DOI: 10.1080/10872981.2019.1666538 PMID: 31526248

Pelech, J. (2010). *The comprehensive handbook of constructivist teaching: From theory to practice* (Pieper, G., Ed.). IAP Information Age Publishing.

Philipsen, B., Tondeur, J., Roblin, N. P., Vanslambrouck, S., & Zhu, C. (2019). Improving teacher professional development for online and blended learning: A systematic meta-aggregative review. *Educational Technology Research and Development, 67*(5), 1145–1174. DOI: 10.1007/s11423-019-09645-8

Philipsen, B., Tondeur, J., Roblin, N. P., Vanslambrouck, S., & Zhu, C. (2019). Improving teacher professional development for online and blended learning: A systematic meta-aggregative review. *Educational Technology Research and Development, 67*(5), 1145–1174. DOI: 10.1007/s11423-019-09645-8

Phumeechanya, N., & Wannapiroon, P. (2014). Ubiquitous scaffold learning environment using problem-based learning to enhance problem-solving skills and context awareness. https://arxiv.org/pdf/1401.2234.pdf

Prensky, M. (2001). Digital natives, digital immigrants. *On the Horizon, 9*(5), 1–6. DOI: 10.1108/10748120110424816

Rabello, C., & Tavares, K. (2016). Tecnologias digitais no ensino superior: Das possibilidades e tendências à superação de barreiras e desafios. In J. Farbiarz, A. Farbiarz & B. Hemais (Orgs.), Design para uma educação inclusiva (pp. 25-36). Blucher. DOI: 10.5151/9788580392012-02

Rapanta, C., Botturi, L., Goodyear, P., Guàrdia, L., & Koole, M. (2020). Online University Teaching During and After the Covid-19 Crisis: Refocusing Teacher Presence and Learning Activity. *Postdigit Sci Educ, 2*(3), 923–945. DOI: 10.1007/s42438-020-00155-y PMID: 40477148

Redecker, C. (2017). *European Framework for the Digital Competence of Educators: DigCompEdu*. Joint Research Centre, European Commission., DOI: 10.2760/159770

Regmi, K., & Jones, L. (2020). A systematic review of the factors – enablers and barriers – affecting e-learning in health sciences education. *BMC Medical Education, 20*(1), 91. DOI: 10.1186/s12909-020-02007-6 PMID: 32228560

Roueche, B.. (2021). Virtual simulation in medical training: A review. *Medical Education.*

Rovai, A. P. (2002). Building sense of community at a distance. *International Review of Research in Open and Distance Learning, 3*(1), 1–16. DOI: 10.19173/irrodl.v3i1.79

Seale, J. (2014). *E-learning and disability in higher education: Accessibility research and practice* (2nd ed.). Routledge.

Selwyn, N. (2016). *Education and Technology: Key Issues and Debates* (2nd ed.). Bloomsbury Academic.

Sequí-Domínguez, I., Cavero-Redondo, I., Álvarez-Bueno, C., López-Gil, J. F., Martínez-Vizcaíno, V., & Pascual-Morena, C. (2024). Effectiveness of eHealth Interventions Promoting Physical Activity in Children and Adolescents: Systematic Review and Meta-Analysis. *Journal of Medical Internet Research*, *26*, e41649. DOI: 10.2196/41649 PMID: 38381490

Shelby, S. J., & Fralish, Z. D. (2021). Using Edpuzzle to improve student experience and performance in the biochemistry laboratory. *Biochemistry and Molecular Biology Education*, *49*(5), 529–534. DOI: 10.1002/bmb.21494 PMID: 33666326

Siemens, G. (2004). Connectivism: A learning theory for the digital age. *International Journal of Instructional Technology and Distance Learning*, *1*(2), 1–8. http://www.itdl.org/Journal/Jan_05/article01.htm

Tess, P. A. (2013). The role of social media in higher education classes (real and virtual) – A literature review. *Computers in Human Behavior*, *29*(5), A60–A68. DOI: 10.1016/j.chb.2012.12.032

Tess, P. A. (2013). The role of social media in higher education classes (real and virtual) – A literature review. *Computers in Human Behavior*, *29*(5), A60–A68. DOI: 10.1016/j.chb.2012.12.032

UNESCO. (2015). *Rethinking education: Towards a global common good?* UNESCO Publishing. https://unesdoc.unesco.org/ark:/48223/pf0000232555

UNESCO. (2017). *A guide for ensuring inclusion and equity in education*. UNESCO Publishing. https://unesdoc.unesco.org/ark:/48223/pf0000248254

UNESCO. (2020). *Global Education Monitoring Report 2020: Inclusion and education – All means all*. UNESCO Publishing. https://unesdoc.unesco.org/ark:/48223/pf0000373718

Van Dijk, J. A. G. M. (2020). *The digital divide*. Polity Press.

Viczko, M. (2016). *A Rich Seam: How New Pedagogies Find Deep Learning*, by Michael Fullan and Maria Langworthy: (2014). London: Pearson. *Leadership and Policy in Schools*, *15*(2), 231–233. DOI: 10.1080/15700763.2015.1073331

Voogt, J., Erstad, O., Dede, C., & Mishra, P. (2015). Challenges to learning and schooling in the digital networked world of the 21st century. *Journal of Computer Assisted Learning*, *31*(5), 403–413. DOI: 10.1111/jcal.12029

Wang, A. I. (2015). The wear out effect of a game-based student response system. *Computers & Education*, *82*, 217–227. DOI: 10.1016/j.compedu.2014.11.004

Wenger, E., McDermott, R., & Snyder, W. M. (2002). *Cultivating communities of practice: A guide to managing knowledge*. Harvard Business School Press.

Wijnen-Meijer, M., Brandhuber, T., Schneider, A., & Berberat, P. O. (2022). Implementing Kolb's Experiential Learning Cycle by Linking Real Experience, Case-Based Discussion and Simulation. *Journal of Medical Education and Curricular Development*, *9*, 23821205221091511. DOI: 10.1177/23821205221091511 PMID: 35592131

World Health Organization. (2021). *Global strategy on digital health 2020–2025*. World Health Organization. https://www.who.int/publications/i/item/9789240020924

KEY TERMS AND DEFINITIONS

Asynchronous Learning: A flexible approach to distance education where learners access and complete course materials at different times and locations, often at their own pace. This is a contrast to synchronous learning, where all participants are online simultaneously.

Digital Literacy: The ability to find, evaluate, create, and communicate information using digital technologies. It includes both technical skills and critical thinking to use these tools effectively.

Distance Learning: A mode of education where students and instructors are separated by location, and instruction is delivered through various technologies. This can include fully online or blended formats.

Micro-course: A short, focused training program designed to teach a specific skill or set of skills. In the context of the chapter, it is a targeted training initiative for health educators to learn how to integrate digital tools into their teaching practices effectively.

Pedagogical Innovation: Involves introducing new or significantly improved teaching methods, learning strategies, and educational materials, often by integrating new technologies and active learning approaches, to improve student engagement and outcomes.

Pedagogical Innovation: The introduction of new or significantly improved teaching methods, learning strategies, and educational materials. This often involves integrating new technologies and active learning approaches to enhance student engagement and outcomes.

Professional Development: The process of a professional acquiring new skills or knowledge after their initial training. In this context, it refers to ongoing training for health educators, particularly in digital and pedagogical skills.

Compilation of References

Aayog, N. I. T. I. (2022). Atal Innovation Mission: Atal Tinkering Labs and STEM Education in India. https://niti.gov.in

Abuodha, L., & Kipkebut, A. (2024). Disruptive AI in Education: Transforming Learning in the Digital Age. *International Journal for Research in Applied Science and Engineering Technology*, *12*(2), 195–199. DOI: 10.22214/ijraset.2024.58283

Acemoğlu, D., & Restrepo, P. (2019). *The wrong kind of AI? Artificial intelligence and the future of labor demand.* DOI: 10.3386/w25682

Adamopoulou, E., & Moussiades, L. (2020). Chatbots: History, technology, and applications. *Machine Learning with Applications*, *2*, 100006. DOI: 10.1016/j.mlwa.2020.100006

Adewale, M. D., Azeta, A. A., Abayomi-Alli, A., & Sambo-Magaji, A. (2024). Impact of artificial intelligence adoption on students' academic performance in open and distance learning: A systematic literature review. *Heliyon*, *10*(22), e40025. Advance online publication. DOI: 10.1016/j.heliyon.2024.e40025 PMID: 39605813

Admiraal, W. (2014). Meaningful learning from practice: Web-based video in professional preparation programs in university. *Technology, Pedagogy and Education*, *23*(4), 491–506. DOI: 10.1080/1475939X.2013.813403

Admiraal, W., & Berry, A. (2016). Video narratives to assess student-teachers' competence as new teachers. *Teachers and Teaching*, *22*(1), 21–34. DOI: 10.1080/13540602.2015.1023026

Admiraal, W., Hoeksma, M., van de Kamp, M.-T., & van Duin, G. (2011). Assessment of teacher competence using video portfolios: Reliability, construct validity and consequential validity. *Teaching and Teacher Education*, *27*(6), 1019–1028. DOI: 10.1016/j.tate.2011.04.002

Admiraal, W., Huizenga, J., Akkerman, S., & ten Dam, G. (2011). The concept of flow in game-based learning. *Computers in Human Behavior, 27*(3), 1185–1194. DOI: 10.1016/j.chb.2010.12.013

Admiraal, W., Vermeulen, J., & Bulterman-Bos, J. (2020). Teaching with learning analytics: How to connect computer-based assessment data with classroom instruction? *Technology, Pedagogy and Education, 29*(5), 577–591. DOI: 10.1080/1475939X.2020.1825992

Ajani, O. A., Gamede, B. T., & Matiyenga, T. C. (2024*). Leveraging artificial intelligence to enhance teaching and learning in higher education: Promoting quality education and critical engagement.* Journal of Pedagogical Sociology and Psychology. DOI: 10.33902/JPSP.202528400

Akavova, A., Temirkhanova, Z., & Lorsanova, Z. M. (2023). *Adaptive learning and artificial intelligence in the educational space.* E3S Web of Conferences, 451, 6011. DOI: 10.1051/e3sconf/202345106011

Akgun, S., & Greenhow, C. (2022). Artificial intelligence in education: Addressing ethical challenges in K-12 settings. *AI and Ethics, 2*(3), 431–440. DOI: 10.1007/s43681-021-00096-7 PMID: 34790956

Akhmadieva, R. Sh., Kalmazova, N., Belova, T. V., Prokopyev, A. I., Molodozhnikova, N. M., & Spichak, V. Y. (2024). Research trends in the use of artificial intelligence in higher education. *Frontiers in Education, 9*, 1438715. Advance online publication. DOI: 10.3389/feduc.2024.1438715

Akinwalere, S. N., & Ivanov, V. (2022). Artificial Intelligence in higher education: Challenges and opportunities. *BORDER CROSSING, 12*(1), 1–15. DOI: 10.33182/bc.v12i1.2015

Akram, N. A., Kiren, N. A., Sabir, N. S., & Aslam, N. S. (2025). The effect of AI based scaffolding on problem solving and metacognitive awareness in learners. ˜the œCritical Review of Social Sciences Studies, 3(3), 1074–1089. DOI: 10.59075/ja7dvy78

Akram, H., Abdelrahman, L., & Al Halbusi, H. (2022). Teachers' perceptions of technology integration in teaching-learning practices: A systematic review. *Frontiers in Psychology, 13*, 920317. DOI: 10.3389/fpsyg.2022.920317 PMID: 35734463

Alam, M.Dr. Md. Mahmood Alam. (2018). Digital technologies in teaching and learning. *International Journal of Indian Psychology, 6*(2), 34–39. DOI: 10.25215/0602.045

Albuquerque, J. G. M., de Abreu, M. T. C., & de Lima, I. N. (2024). O impacto da Inteligência Artificial na personalização do ensino. *Rebena-Revista Brasileira de Ensino e Aprendizagem, 9*, 182-192. https://rebena.emnuvens.com.br/revista/article/view/242

AlGerafi, M. A. M., Zhou, Y., Oubibi, M., & Wijaya, T. T. (2023). Unlocking the potential: A comprehensive evaluation of augmented reality and virtual reality in education. *Electronics (Basel), 12*(18), 3953. DOI: 10.3390/electronics12183953

Alharbi, W. (2023). AI in the Foreign Language Classroom: A Pedagogical Overview of Automated Writing Assistance Tools. *Education Research International, 2023*, 1–15. DOI: 10.1155/2023/4253331

Allen, L. K., & Kendeou, P. (2024). ED-AI Lit: An Interdisciplinary Framework for AI Literacy in Education. *Policy Insights from the Behavioral and Brain Sciences, 11*(1), 3–10. DOI: 10.1177/23727322231220339

Almatrafi, O., & Johri, A. (2018). Systematic review of discussion forums in massive open online courses (MOOCs). *IEEE Transactions on Learning Technologies, 12*(3), 413–428. DOI: 10.1109/TLT.2018.2859304

Almazrou, S., Alanezi, F., Almutairi, S. A., AboAlsamh, H. M., Alsedrah, I. T., Arif, W. M., & Attar, R. W. (2024). Enhancing medical students' critical thinking skills through ChatGPT: An empirical study with medical students. *Nutrition and Health (Berkhamsted, Hertfordshire), 02601060241273627*. Advance online publication. DOI: 10.1177/02601060241273627 PMID: 39150341

Almeida, L. da S., & Gonçalves, S. Ramos do Ó, J., Rebola, F., Soares, S., & Vieira, F. (2022). *Inovação Pedagógica no Ensino Superior: Cenários e Caminhos de Transformação* (A3ES Readings nº 16). Lisboa: Agência de Avaliação e Acreditação do Ensino Superior.

Almufarreh, A., & Arshad, M. (2023). Promising Emerging Technologies for Teaching and Learning: Recent Developments and Future Challenges. *Sustainability (Basel), 15*(6917), 6917. Advance online publication. DOI: 10.3390/su15086917

Al-Rahmi, W., Aldraiweesh, A., Yahaya, N., & Kamin, Y. (2018). Massive open online courses (MOOCS): Systematic literature review in Malaysian higher education. *Int. J. Eng. Technol., 7*(4), 2197–2202. DOI: 10.14419/ijet.v7i4.15156

Alsaqqa, A., Alkahlout, M., & Abu-Naser, S. (2022). Using Deep Learning to Classify Different Types of Vitamin. *International Journal of Academic Engineering Research, 6*(1), 1–6.

Alsowat, H. H. (2022). Hybrid learning or virtual learning? Effects on students' essay writing and digital literacy. *Journal of Language Teaching and Research, 13*(4), 872–883. DOI: 10.17507/jltr.1304.20

Altum, H. K., & Lee, J. (2020). Immersive Learning Technologies in English Language Teaching : A Systematic Review *. *Educational Technology International, 21*(2), 155–191.

AlTwijri, L., & Alghizzi, T. M. (2024). *Investigating the integration of artificial intelligence in English as a foreign language classes for enhancing learners' affective factors: A systematic review [Review of Investigating the integration of artificial intelligence in English as a foreign language classes for enhancing learners' affective factors: A systematic review].* Heliyon, 10(10). Elsevier BV. DOI: 10.1016/j.heliyon.2024.e31053

Alvarez, B., Vergara, P. A., & Iglesias, I. (2020). Decaffeinated UDL: Chile in quest of inclusive education. In Gronseth, S. L., & Dalton, E. M. (Eds.), *International perspectives on UDL* (pp. 59–66). Routledge.

Álvarez, C., & Mischel, L. (2024). Edpuzzle for e-learning: A study of perceived advantages and limitations. *International Journal of Education and Development Using Information and Communication Technology, 20*(1), 134–145.

Al-Zahrani, A. M. (2024). Unveiling the shadows: Beyond the hype of AI in education. *Heliyon, 10*(9), e30696. Advance online publication. DOI: 10.1016/j.heliyon.2024.e30696 PMID: 38737255

Al-Zahrani, A. M., & Alasmari, T. M. (2025). A comprehensive analysis of AI adoption, implementation strategies, and challenges in higher education across the Middle East and North Africa (MENA) region. *Education and Information Technologies, 30*(8), 1–51. DOI: 10.1007/s10639-024-13300-y

American Psychiatric Association. (2013). DSM-5. In *Atlas of Psychiatry* (5th ed.). American Psychiatric Publishing. DOI: 10.1007/978-3-031-15401-0_16

Amiel, T. (2013). Identifying barriers to the remix of translated open educational resources. *International Review of Research in Open and Distance Learning, 14*(1), 126–144. DOI: 10.19173/irrodl.v14i1.1351

Anderson, T. (Ed.). (2008). *The theory and practice of online learning* (2nd ed.). AU Press. DOI: 10.15215/aupress/9781897425084.01

Anghel, G. A., Zanfir, C. M., Matei, F. L., Voicu, C. D., & Neac a, R. A. (2025). The Integration of artificial intelligence in academic learning practices: A Comprehensive approach. *Education Sciences, 15*(5), 616. DOI: 10.3390/educsci15050616

Annetta, L. A. (2010). The “I’s” have it: A framework for serious educational game design. *Review of General Psychology*, *14*(2), 105–113. DOI: 10.1037/a0018985

Anyolo, E., Iipinge, S., & Hako, A. (2024) *Achieving Sustainability Through Interdisciplinary Approach: An Analysis of Teacher Education Transformed Curriculum*. The Asian Conference on Education & International Development 2024 Official Conference Proceedings, 411-420. https://doi.org/DOI: 10.22492/issn.2189-101X.2024.33

APM. (2020). *Práticas do pensamento computacional*. Mathematic.

Aqazade, M., Mauntel, M., & Atabas, S. (2025, January 29). Empowering mathematics teacher educators: Exploring Artificial Intelligence-driven mathematical tasks. *School Science and Mathematics*, ssm.18339. Advance online publication. DOI: 10.1111/ssm.18339

Araiza-Alba, P., Keane, T., & Kaufman, J. (2022). Are we ready for virtual reality in K–12 classrooms? *Technology, Pedagogy and Education*, *31*(4), 471–491. DOI: 10.1080/1475939X.2022.2033307

Armstrong, K., Boreham, B., & Mack, T. (2019). Snapshot—Creating UDL learning and teaching strategies to address the underrepresentation of present-day Indigenous perspectives. In Gronseth, S. L., & Dalton, E. M. (Eds.), *Universal access through inclusive instructional design: International perspectives on UDL* (pp. 218–220). Routledge. DOI: 10.4324/9780429435515-27

Armstrong, T. (2010). *The power of neurodiversity: Unleashing the advantages of your differently wired brain*. DaCapo Lifelong Books.

Asha, V., Reddy, G. P., Nithya, B., Tungal, K., Durgaprasad, V., & Kruthik, T. N. (2023). Implication and advantages of machine learning-based chatbots in diverse disciplines. In *2023 International Conference on Sustainable Computing and Data Communication Systems (ICSCDS)* (pp. 22–28). IEEE. DOI: 10.1109/ICSCDS56580.2023.10104649

Ashburner, J., Ziviani, J., & Rodger, S. (2008). Sensory processing and classroom emotional, behavioral, and educational outcomes in children with autism spectrum disorder. *The American Journal of Occupational Therapy*, *62*(5), 564–573. DOI: 10.5014/ajot.62.5.564

Atal, D., Admiraal, W., & Saab, N. (2024). Effects of 360 video virtual reality-supported reflection on student teachers’ classroom management self-efficacy and their stress levels. *Teaching and Teacher Education*, *144*(July), 104573. DOI: 10.1016/j.tate.2024.104573

Bacca, J., Baldiris, S., Fabregat, R., Graf, S., & Kinshuk. (2014). Augmented reality trends in education: A systematic review of research and applications. *Educational Technology \& Society, 17*(4), 133–149.

Baig, A., Cressler, J. D., & Minsky, M. (2024). The future of ai in education: Personalized learning and intelligent tutoring systems. AlgoVista. *Journal of AI and Computer Science*, *1*(1), 592648.

Baig, M. I., & Yadegaridehkordi, E. (2023). Flipped classroom in higher education: A systematic literature review and research challenges. *International Journal of Educational Technology in Higher Education*, *20*(1), 61. DOI: 10.1186/s41239-023-00430-5

Bailenson, J. (2018). *Experience on demand: What virtual reality is, how it works, and what it can do*. W. W. Norton {\&} Company.

Baker, R. S., & Inventado, P. S. (2014). Educational data mining and learning analytics. In *Springer eBooks* (p. 61). Springer Nature., DOI: 10.1007/978-1-4614-3305-7_4

Bakhadirov, M., Alasgarova, R., & Rzayev, J. (2024). Factors influencing teachers' use of artificial intelligence for instructional purposes. *IAFOR Journal of Education*, *12*(2), 10–32. DOI: 10.22492/ije.12.2.01

Bakhtin, M. M. (1981). *The dialogic imagination: Four essays (M. Holquist* (Emerson, C., & Holquist, M. Eds. & Trans.). University of Texas Press.

Ballantine, J., Boyce, G., & Stoner, G. (2024). A critical review of AI in accounting education: Threat and opportunity. *Critical Perspectives on Accounting*, *99*, 102711. Advance online publication. DOI: 10.1016/j.cpa.2024.102711

Bancoro, J. C.Jaysone Christopher M. Bancoro. (2024). The Relationship between artificial intelligence (AI) usage and academic performance of business administration students. *International Journal of Asian Business and Management*, *3*(1), 27–48. DOI: 10.55927/ijabm.v3i1.7876

Barak, M. (2006). Instructional principles for fostering learning with ICT: Teachers' perspectives as learners and instructors. *Education and Information Technologies*, *11*(2), 121–138. DOI: 10.1007/s11134-006-7362-9

Bardin, L. (1997). *Content analysis* (70th ed.).

Barz, N., Benick, M., Dörrenbächer-Ulrich, L., & Perels, F. (2024). The effect of digital game-based learning interventions on cognitive, metacognitive, and affective-motivational learning outcomes in school: A meta-analysis. *Review of Educational Research*, *94*(2), 193–227. DOI: 10.3102/00346543231167795

Baskoro, G., Mariza, I., & Sutapa, I. N. (2023). Innovation to Improve Critical Thinking Skills in the Generation Z using Peeragogy as a Learning Approach and Artificial Intelligence (AI) as a Tool. *Deleted Journal*, *25*(2), 121–130. DOI: 10.9744/jti.25.2.121-130

Bates, T. (2015). *Teaching in a digital age: Guidelines for designing teaching and learning*. Tony Bates Associates Ltd.

Battelle for Kids. (2019). Framework for 21st Century Learning Definitions. https://www.battelleforkids.org/wp-content/uploads/2023/11/P21_Framework_DefinitionsBFK.pdf

Battelle for Kids. (2019). *Framework for 21st Century Learning*. P21 Partnership for 21st Century Learning. https://static.battelleforkids.org/documents/p21/P21_Framework_Brief.pdf

Baumer, N., & Frueh, J. (2021). What is neurodiversity? *Harvard Health Blog*. https://www.health.harvard.edu/blog/what-is-neurodiversity-202111232645

Beatty, B. J. (2019). *Hybrid flexible course design: Implementing student-directed hybrid classes*. EdTech Books. DOI: 10.59668/33

Beaunoyer, E., Dupéré, S., & Guitton, M. J. (2020). COVID-19 and digital inequalities: Reciprocal impacts and mitigation strategies. *Computers in Human Behavior*, *111*, 106424. DOI: 10.1016/j.chb.2020.106424 PMID: 32398890

Bekteshi, S., Konings, M., Vanmechelen, I., Deklerck, J., Ortibus, E., Aerts, J. M., & Monbaliu, E. (2020). Eye Gaze Gaming Intervention in Children with Dyskinetic Cerebral Palsy: A Pilot Study of Task Performance and Its Relation with Dystonia and Choreoathetosis. *Developmental Neurorehabilitation*, *23*(8), 548–556. DOI: 10.1080/17518423.2020.1770890

Belikov, O. M., & Bodily, R. (2016). Incentives and barriers to OER adoption: A qualitative analysis of faculty perceptions. *Open Praxis*, *8*(3), 235–246. DOI: 10.5944/openpraxis.8.3.308

Belkina, M., Daniel, S., Nikolic, S., Haque, R., Lyden, S., Neal, P., Grundy, S., & Hassan, G. M. (2025, April). Implementing Generative AI (GenAI) in higher education: A systematic review of case studies. *Computers and Education: Artificial Intelligence*, *8*, 100407. DOI: 10.1016/j.caeai.2025.100407

Belland, B. R., Walker, A. E., Kim, N. J., & Lefler, M. (2017). Synthesizing results from empirical research on computer-based scaffolding in STEM education: A meta-analysis. *Review of Educational Research*, *87*(2), 309–344. DOI: 10.3102/0034654316670999 PMID: 28344365

Bell, F. (2011). Connectivism: Its place in theory-informed research and innovation in technology-enabled learning. *International Review of Research in Open and Distance Learning*, *12*(3), 98–118. DOI: 10.19173/irrodl.v12i3.902

Bell, J., Sawaya, S., & Cain, W. (2014). Synchromodal classes: Designing for shared learning experiences between face-to-face and online students. *International Journal of Designs for Learning*, *5*(1). Advance online publication. DOI: 10.14434/ijdl.v5i1.12657

Bender, E. M., Gebru, T., McMillan-Major, A., & Shmitchell, S. (2021). On the dangers of stochastic parrots: Can language models be too big? In *Proceedings of the 2021 ACM Conference on Fairness, Accountability, and Transparency* (pp. 610–623). DOI: 10.1145/3442188.3445922

Bessa, L., Mascarenhas, D., Silva, N., Fernandes, D., & Quadros-Flores, P. (2023). UMA ABORDAGEM DA GRANDEZA ÁREA NO 2.º ANO DE ESCOLARIDADE PÓS-PANDEMIA. *PRATICA - Revista Multimédia De Investigação Em Inovação Pedagógica E Práticas De E-Learning*, 6(1), 104–130. https://doi.org/ DOI: 10.34630/pel.v6i1.5126

Biggs, J., & Tang, C. (2011). *Teaching for quality learning at university: What the student does* (4th ed.). McGraw-Hill Education.

Binns, R. (2018). Fairness in machine learning: Lessons from political philosophy. Journal of Machine Learning Research. https://ora.ox.ac.uk/objects/uuid:2ff2785b-b0d4-447a-8326-a1fcc4c80840

Black, P., & Wiliam, D. (2009). Developing the theory of formative assessment. *Educational Assessment, Evaluation and Accountability*, *21*(1), 5–31. DOI: 10.1007/s11092-008-9068-5

Bland, J. (2023). *Compelling stories for English language learners: Creativity, interculturality and critical literacy*. Bloomsbury Academic.

Blessing, S. B., Gilbert, S. B., Ourada, S., & Ritter, S. (2009). Authoring model-tracing cognitive tutors. *International Journal of Artificial Intelligence in Education*, *19*(2), 189–210. DOI: 10.3233/IRG-2009-19(2)04

Blume, H. (1998). Neurodiversity: On the neurological underpinnings of geekdom. *The Atlantic*. https://www.theatlantic.com/magazine/archive/1998/09/neurodiversity/305909

Boateng, S. L., & Boateng, R. (Eds.). (2025). *AI and Society: Navigating Policy, Ethics, and Innovation in a Transforming World*. CRC Press. DOI: 10.4324/9781003595670

Bobrytska, V. I., Krasylnykova, H. V., Beseda, N., Krasylnykov, S. R., & Skyrda, T. S. (2024). Artificial intelligence (AI) in Ukrainian Higher Education: A Comprehensive Study of Stakeholder Attitudes, Expectations and Concerns. *International Journal of Learning. Teaching and Educational Research, 23*(1), 400–426. DOI: 10.26803/ijlter.23.1.20

Boettcher, J. V., & Conrad, R. M. (2021). *The online teaching survival guide: Simple and practical pedagogical tips* (2nd ed.). Jossey-Bass.

Bogdan, R. C., & Biklen, S. K. (1994). *Qualitative research in education: An introduction to theory and methods*. Porto Editora.

Bond, M., Bedenlier, S., Marín, V. I., & Händel, M. (2021). Emergency remote teaching in higher education: Mapping the first global online semester. *International Journal of Educational Technology in Higher Education, 18*(1), 50. DOI: 10.1186/s41239-021-00282-x PMID: 34778537

Bond, M., Buntins, K., Bedenlier, S., Zawacki-Richter, O., & Kerres, M. (2020). Mapping research in student engagement and educational technology in higher education: A systematic evidence map. *International Journal of Educational Technology in Higher Education, 17*(1), 2. DOI: 10.1186/s41239-019-0176-8

Bonet-Collantes, M., Niño-Pinzón, D. M., Chaustre-Porras, A. D., Salas-Poloche, Y. A., & Angarita-Fonseca, A. (2024). Enhancing physiotherapists' knowledge and perceptions of telerehabilitation: A before-after educational intervention study. *Physiotherapy Research International, 29*(4), e2120. Advance online publication. DOI: 10.1002/pri.2120 PMID: 39192801

Bontchev, B. P., Terzieva, V., & Paunova-Hubenova, E. (2021). Personalization of serious games for learning. *Interactive Technology and Smart Education, 18*(1), 50–68. DOI: 10.1108/ITSE-05-2020-0069

Borgestig, M., Sandqvist, J., Parsons, R., Falkmer, T., & Hemmingsson, H. (2016). Eye gaze performance for children with severe physical impairments using gaze-based assistive technology — A longitudinal study. *Assistive Technology, 28*(2), 93–102. https://pubmed.ncbi.nlm.nih.gov/26496529/. DOI: 10.1080/10400435.2015.1092182

Bower, M., Dalgarno, B., Kennedy, G. E., Lee, M. J. W., & Kenney, J. (2015). Design and implementation factors in blended synchronous learning environments: Outcomes from a cross-case analysis. *Computers & Education, 86*, 1–17. DOI: 10.1016/j.compedu.2015.03.006

Brown, J. L., Collins, A., & Duguid, P. (1989). Situated cognition and the culture of learning. *Educational Researcher, 18*(1), 32–42. DOI: 10.3102/0013189X018001032

Bryce, T. G. K., & Blown, E. J. (2024). Ausubel's meaningful learning re-visited. *Current Psychology (New Brunswick, N.J.), 43*(5), 4579–4598. DOI: 10.1007/s12144-023-04440-4 PMID: 37359615

Bryman, A. (2016). *Social research methods* (5th ed.). Oxford University Press.

Buckle, K. L. (2020). Autscape. In Kapp, S. K. (Ed.), *Autistic community and the neurodiversity movement: Stories from the frontline* (pp. 109–122). Palgrave Macmillan., DOI: 10.1007/978-981-13-8437-0_8

Burgstahler, S. (2015). *Universal design in higher education: From principles to practice* (2nd ed.). Harvard Education Press.

Burrell, J. (2016). How the machine 'thinks': Understanding opacity in machine learning algorithms. *Big Data & Society, 3*(1), 2053951715622512. DOI: 10.1177/2053951715622512

Buskist, W., & Irons, J. G. (2008). Buskist, W., & Irons, J. G. (2008). Simple Strategies for Teaching Your Students to Think Critically. American Psychological Association, 49–57. DOI: 10.1002/9781444305173.ch5

Busuttil, L., & Calleja, J. (2025). Teachers' beliefs and practices about the potential of ChatGPT in teaching mathematics in secondary schools. *Digital Experiences in Mathematics Education, 11*(1), 140–166. DOI: 10.1007/s40751-024-00168-3

Butcher, N. (2015). *A basic guide to Open Educational Resources (OER)*. Commonwealth of Learning and UNESCO. https://unesdoc.unesco.org/ark:/48223/pf0000215804

Cabero-Almenara, J., Palacios-Rodríguez, A., Loaiza-Aguirre, M. I., & Rivas-Manzano, M. R. (2024). Acceptance of educational artificial intelligence by teachers and its relationship with some variables and pedagogical beliefs. *Education Sciences, 14*(7), 740. DOI: 10.3390/educsci14070740

Cárdenas-Robledo, L. A., & Peña-Ayala, A. (2018). Ubiquitous learning: A systematic review. *Telematics and Informatics, 35*(5), 1097–1132. DOI: 10.1016/j.tele.2018.01.009

Carreon, A., Smith, S. J., Mosher, M., Rao, K., & Rowland, A. (2022). A review of virtual reality intervention research for students with disabilities in K–12 settings. *Journal of Special Education Technology, 37*(1), 82–99. DOI: 10.1177/0162643420962011

Carrillo, C., & Flores, M. A. (2020). COVID-19 and teacher education: A literature review of online teaching and learning practices. *European Journal of Teacher Education, 43*(4), 466–487. DOI: 10.1080/02619768.2020.1821184

Carson, S. (2010). The unwalled garden: Growth of the OpenCourseWare Consortium, 2001–2008. *Open Learning*, *25*(1), 5–10.

Caruajulca, C. B. (2021). CRITICAL THINKING IN THE EDUCATIONAL IN THE FIELD OF EDUCATION. *ASEAN Journal of Psychiatry*, *22*(10). Advance online publication. DOI: 10.54615/2231-7805.47233

Carvalho, R., Espadeiro, R. G., & Branco, N. C. V. (2023). Contributos para o desenvolvimento do pensamento computacional em Matemática: *Materiais de apoio para os professores do 1. º ciclo do ensino básico.*

Casarez, L., Hooks, D., Shipley, G., & Swafford, D. (2023). Proactive design to ensure accessibility. In Dalton, E. M., & Gronseth, S. (Eds.), *Universal access through inclusive instructional design* (pp. 30–32). Routledge.

CAST. (2018). *Universal Design for Learning guidelines version 2.2* (p. 2018). http://udlguidelines.cast.org

CAST. (2018). *Universal Design for Learning guidelines version 2.2.* http://udlguidelines.cast.org

CAST. (2018). Universal Design for Learning Guidelines version 2.2. http://udlguidelines.cast.org

Castañeda, R., Martínez-Gómez-Aldaraví, A., Mercadé, L., Gómez, V. J., Mengual, T., Díaz-Fernández, F. J., Sinusia Lozano, M., Navarro Arenas, J., Barreda, Á., Gómez, M., Pinilla-Cienfuegos, E., & Ortiz de Zárate, D. (2024). Use of ChatGPT as a virtual mentor on K-12 students learning science in the fourth industrial revolution. *Knowledge (Beverly Hills, Calif.)*, *4*(4), 582–614. DOI: 10.3390/knowledge4040031

Cavanagh, M. (2021). Pre-service teacher reflection and feedback using an online video platform during professional experience. *The Australian Journal of Teacher Education*, *46*(2), 72–85. DOI: 10.14221/ajte.2021v46n2.5

Ceci, S. J., & Papiero, P. B. (2005). The rhetoric and reality of gap closing: When the "have-nots" gain but the "haves" gain even more. *The American Psychologist*, *60*(2), 149–160. DOI: 10.1037/0003-066X.60.2.149 PMID: 15740447

Celik, I., Gedrimiene, E., Siklander, S., & Muukkonen, H. (2024). The affordances of artificial intelligence-based tools for supporting 21st-century skills. *Australasian Journal of Educational Technology*. Advance online publication. DOI: 10.14742/ajet.9069

Cen, H., Koedinger, K. R., & Junker, B. (2007). Is Over Practice Necessary?-Improving Learning Efficiency with the Cognitive Tutor through Educational Data Mining. Frontiers in artificial intelligence and applications, 158, 511.

Chan, C. (2024). Holistic competencies and AI in education: A synergistic pathway. *Australasian Journal of Educational Technology, 40*(5), 1–12. DOI: 10.14742/ajet.10191

Chan, C. K. Y., & Hu, W. (2023). Students' voices on generative AI: Perceptions, benefits, and challenges in higher education. *International Journal of Educational Technology in Higher Education, 20*(1), 43. DOI: 10.1186/s41239-023-00411-8

Chang, S. H., Ward, P., & Goodway, J. D. (2020). The effect of a content knowledge teacher professional workshop on enacted pedagogical content knowledge and student learning in a throwing unit. *Physical Education and Sport Pedagogy, 25*(5), 493–508. DOI: 10.1080/17408989.2020.1743252

Chapman, R., Likhanov, M., Selita, F., Zakharov, I., Smith-Woolley, E., & Kovas, Y. (2019). New literacy challenge for the twenty-first century: Genetic knowledge is poor even among well educated. *Journal of Community Genetics, 10*(1), 73–84. DOI: 10.1007/s12687-018-0363-7 PMID: 29589204

Chaudhry, M. A., & Kazim, E. (2021). Artificial intelligence in education (AIEd): A high-level academic and industry note 2021. *AI and Ethics, 2*(1), 157–165. DOI: 10.1007/s43681-021-00074-z PMID: 34790953

Chen, L., Chen, P., & Lin, Z. (2024). Artificial intelligence in teaching and teacher professional development: A systematic review. Computers and Education: X Reality, 3, 100089. DOI: 10.1016/j.cexr.2024.100089

Chen, C., Jamiat, N., Rabu, S. N. A., & Du, S. (2025). Effects of augmented reality with pedagogical agent on EFL primary students' vocabulary acquisition, motivation, and technology perceptions. *International Journal of Human-Computer Interaction, 41*(18), 1–19. DOI: 10.1080/10447318.2024.2443534

Cheng, K. H., & Tsai, C. C. (2019). A case study of immersive virtual field trips in an elementary classroom: Students' learning experience and teacher-student interaction behaviors. *Computers and Education, 140*(December 2018), 103600. DOI: 10.1016/j.compedu.2019.103600

Chen, H. J. (2024). Gather in the metaverse : Learning outcomes, virtual presence, and perceptions of high - and low - achieving pre - service teachers of English as a Foreign Language. *Education and Information Technologies, 29*(7), 8549–8577. DOI: 10.1007/s10639-023-12135-3

Chen, L., Chen, P., & Lin, Z. (2020). Artificial intelligence in education: A review. *IEEE Access : Practical Innovations, Open Solutions*, *8*, 75264–75278. DOI: 10.1109/ACCESS.2020.2988510

Chen, W., Zhang, J., & Yu, Z. (2023). A Bibliometric Analysis of the Use of the Metaverse in Education over Three Decades. *International Journal of Information and Communication Technology Education*, *19*(1), 1–16. DOI: 10.4018/IJICTE.322101

Cheshmehzangi, A., Zou, T., Su, Z., & Tang, T. (2023). The growing digital divide in education among primary and secondary children during the COVID-19 pandemic: An overview of social exclusion and education equality issues. *Journal of Human Behavior in the Social Environment*, *33*(3), 434–449. DOI: 10.1080/10911359.2022.2062515

Chetry, K. K. (2024). Transforming education: How AI is revolutionizing the learning experience. *International Journal of Research Publication and Reviews*, *5*(5), 6352–6356. DOI: 10.55248/gengpi.5.0524.1277

Chinta, S. V., Wang, Z., Yin, Z., Hoang, N., Gonzalez, M., Quy, T. L., & Zhang, W. (2024). FairAIED: Navigating fairness, bias, and ethics in educational AI applications. *arXiv preprint arXiv:2407.18745*. https://doi.org//arXiv.2407.18745DOI: 10.48550

Chiu, T. K. F., & Chai, C. (2020). Sustainable curriculum planning for artificial intelligence education: A self-determination theory perspective. *Sustainability (Basel)*, *12*(14), 5568. DOI: 10.3390/su12145568

Choi, J., Thompson, C. E., Choi, J., Waddill, C. B., & Choi, S. (2022). Effectiveness of immersive virtual reality in nursing education: Systematic review. *Nurse Educator*, *47*(3), 57–61. DOI: 10.1097/NNE.0000000000001117 PMID: 34657101

Chounta, I. A., Bardone, E., Raudsep, A., & Pedaste, M. (2022). Exploring teachers' perceptions of artificial intelligence as a tool to support their practice in Estonian K-12 education. *International Journal of Artificial Intelligence in Education*, *32*(3), 725–755. DOI: 10.1007/s40593-021-00243-5

Clements, D. H., & Sarama, J. (2007). Early childhood mathematics learning. In Lester, F. K.Jr., (Ed.), *Second handbook of research on mathematics teaching and learning* (pp. 461–555). Information Age.

CNE. (2024). *Estado da Nação 2023*. Conselho Nacional de Educação (CNE). www.cnedu.pt

Cohen, L., Manion, L., & Morrison, K. (2018). *Research methods in education* (8th ed.). Routledge.

Coleman, J. P. H. (2021). AI and our understanding of intelligence. In Arai, K., Kapoor, S., & Bhatia, R. (Eds.), *Intelligent systems and applications* (pp. 209–223). Springer., DOI: 10.1007/978-3-030-55180-3_15

Comas-Quinn, A., & Borthwick, K. (2015). Sharing: Open Educational Resources for Language Teachers. In Hampel, R., & Stickler, U. (Eds.), *Developing online language teaching: Research-based pedagogies and reflective practices* (pp. 96–111). Palgrave Macmillan. DOI: 10.1057/9781137412263_7

Commonwealth of Learning (COL). (2020). *Skills for Work Program.* https://www.col.org/programmes/skills-work

Cook, D. A., Levinson, A. J., Garside, S., Dupras, D. M., Erwin, P. J., & Montori, V. M. (2010). Instructional design variations in internet-based learning for health professions education: A systematic review and meta-analysis. *Academic Medicine*, *85*(5), 909–922. DOI: 10.1097/ACM.0b013e3181d6c319 PMID: 20520049

Cooper, G. (2023). Examining science education in ChatGPT: An exploratory study of generative artificial intelligence. *Journal of Science Education and Technology*, *32*(3), 444–452. DOI: 10.1007/s10956-023-10039-y

Cope, B., & Kalantzis, M. (2009). Multiliteracies: New literacies, new learning. *Pedagogies*, *4*(3), 164–195. DOI: 10.1080/15544800903076044

Cordero, J., Torres-Zambrano, J., & Cordero-Castillo, A. (2024). Integration of generative artificial intelligence in higher education: Best practices. *Education Sciences*, *15*(1), 32. DOI: 10.3390/educsci15010032

Cosme, A. (2018). *Projeto de Autonomia e Flexibilidade Curricular: Estudo avaliativo da experiência pedagógica desenvolvida em 2017/2018 ao abrigo do Despacho n.º 5908/2017 (5 de julho).* https://www.dge.mec.pt/sites/default/files/Curriculo/Projeto_Autonomia_e_Flexibilidade/estudo_pafc.pdf

Cossio, S., Chiappinotto, S., Dentice, S., Moreal, C., Magro, G., Dussi, G., Palese, A., & Galazzi, A. (2025). Cybersickness and discomfort from head-mounted displays delivering fully immersive virtual reality: A systematic review. *Nurse Education in Practice*, *85*, 104376. DOI: 10.1016/j.nepr.2025.104376 PMID: 40267853

Cotton, D. R., Cotton, P. A., & Shipway, J. R. (2024). Chatting and cheating: Ensuring academic integrity in the era of ChatGPT. *Innovations in Education and Teaching International*, *61*(2), 228–239. DOI: 10.1080/14703297.2023.2190148

Cowie, N., & Alizadeh, M. (2022). The affordances and challenges of virtual reality for language teaching. *International Journal of TESOL Studies*, *4*(3), 50–65. DOI: 10.46451/ijts.2022.03.05

Craft, A. (2005). *Creativity in schools: Tensions and dilemmas*. Routledge., DOI: 10.4324/9780203357965

Creed, C., Al-Kalbani, M., Theil, A., Sarcar, S., & Williams, I. (2024). Inclusive AR/VR: Accessibility barriers for immersive technologies. *Universal Access in the Information Society, 23*(1), 59–73. DOI: 10.1007/s10209-023-00969-0

Creswell, J. W. (2021). *Qualitative research methods* (Bütün, M., & Demir, S. B., Trans.). Siyasal Kitabevi. (Original work published 2013)

Creswell, J. W., & Plano Clark, V. L. (2011). *Designing and conducting mixed methods research* (2nd ed.). SAGE Publications.

Crompton, H., & Song, D. (2020). El potencial de la inteligencia artificial en la educación superior. *Revista Virtual Universidad Católica Del Norte*, (62), 1–4. DOI: 10.35575/rvucn.n62a1

Cross, J. I., & Boag-Hodgson, C. C. (2025). A collaborative virtual reality flight simulator: Efficacy, challenges, and potential. *IEEE Transactions on Learning Technologies, 18*, 119–129. DOI: 10.1109/TLT.2025.3526863

Csikszentmihalyi, M., Csikszentmihalyi, M., Abuhamdeh, S., & Nakamura, J. (2014). Flow. *Flow and the foundations of positive psychology: The collected works of Mihaly Csikszentmihalyi*, 227-238 https://doi.org/DOI: 10.1007/978-94-017-9088-8

Csikszentmihalyi, M. (1990). *Flow: The psychology of optimal experience*. Harper-Perennial.

Cuban, L., Kirkpatrick, H., & Peck, C. (2001). High access and low use of technologies in high school classrooms: Explaining an apparent paradox. *American Educational Research Journal, 38*(4), 813–834. DOI: 10.3102/00028312038004813

Cutri, R. M., Mena, J., & Whiting, E. F. (2020). Faculty readiness for online crisis teaching: Transitioning to online teaching during the COVID-19 pandemic. *European Journal of Teacher Education, 43*(4), 523–541. DOI: 10.1080/02619768.2020.1815702

Czerniewicz, L., Agherdien, N., Badenhorst, J., Belluigi, D., Chambers, T., Chili, M., & Prinsloo, P. (2020). A wake-up call: Equity, inequality and COVID-19 emergency remote teaching and learning. *Postdigital Science and Education, 2*(3), 946–967. DOI: 10.1007/s42438-020-00187-4 PMID: 40477091

Dahalan, F., Alias, N., & Shaharom, M. S. N. (2024). Gamification and game based learning for vocational education and training: A systematic literature review. *Education and Information Technologies, 29*(2), 1279–1317. DOI: 10.1007/s10639-022-11548-w PMID: 36688221

Dahlstrom-Hakki, I., Alstad, Z., Asbell-Clarke, J., & Edwards, T. (2024). The impact of visual and auditory distractions on the performance of neurodiverse students in virtual reality (VR) environments. *Virtual Reality (Waltham Cross), 28*(1), 29. DOI: 10.1007/s10055-023-00933-6

Dai, W., Lin, J., Jin, H., Li, T., Tsai, Y. S., & Gašević, D.. (2023). Can large language models provide feedback to students? A case study on ChatGPT. In *2023 IEEE International Conference on Advanced Learning Technologies (ICALT)*, (pp. 323–325). DOI: 10.1109/ICALT58122.2023.00100

Danesh, A., et al. (2020). Effectiveness of augmented reality in education. Journal of Educational Technology.

Daniel, B. (2015). Big Data and analytics in higher education: Opportunities and challenges. *British Journal of Educational Technology*, *46*(5), 904–920. DOI: 10.1111/bjet.12230

Daniels, H. (2001). *Vygotsky and pedagogy*. RoutledgeFalmer.

Darabi, A., Arrastia, M. C., Nelson, D. W., Cornille, T., & Liang, X. (2011). Cognitive presence in asynchronous online learning: A comparison of four discussion strategies. *Journal of Computer Assisted Learning*, *27*(3), 216–227. DOI: 10.1111/j.1365-2729.2010.00392.x

Darling-Hammond, L., Hyler, M. E., & Gardner, M. (2017). *Effective Teacher Professional Development*. Learning Policy Institute. https://learningpolicyinstitute.org/product/effective-teacher-professional-development-report

Darwin, N., Rusdin, D., Mukminatien, N., Suryati, N., Laksmi, E. D., & Marzuki, N. (2023). Critical thinking in the AI era: An exploration of EFL students' perceptions, benefits, and limitations. *Cogent Education*, *11*(1), 2290342. Advance online publication. DOI: 10.1080/2331186X.2023.2290342

Davar, N. F., Dewan, M. A., & Zhang, X. (2025). AI chatbots in education: Challenges and opportunities. *Information (Basel)*, *16*(3), 235. DOI: 10.3390/info16030235

Davenport, T., Guha, A., Grewal, D., & Breßgott, T. (2019). How artificial intelligence will change the future of marketing. *Journal of the Academy of Marketing Science*, *48*(1), 24–42. DOI: 10.1007/s11747-019-00696-0

de Frutos, N. D., Carrasco, L. C., de la Maza, M. S., & Etxabe-Urbieta, J. M. (2024). Application of Artificial Intelligence (AI) in Education: Benefits and Limitations of AI as Perceived by Primary, Secondary, and Higher Education Teachers. *Revista Electronica Interuniversitaria de Formacion Del Profesorado*, *27*(1). Advance online publication. DOI: 10.6018/reifop.577211

Delahunty, J., Verenikina, I., & Jones, P. (2014). Socio-emotional connections: Identity, belonging and learning in online interactions. A literature review. *Technology, Pedagogy and Education, 23*(2), 243–265. DOI: 10.1080/1475939X.2013.813405

Delcker, J., Heil, J., & Ifenthaler, D. (2025). Evidence-based development of an instrument for the assessment of teachers' self-perceptions of their artificial intelligence competence. *Educational Technology Research and Development, 73*(1), 115–133. DOI: 10.1007/s11423-024-10418-1

Delello, J. A., Sung, W., Mokhtari, K., Hebert, J., Bronson, A., & Giuseppe, T. D. (2025). AI in the Classroom: Insights from educators on usage, challenges, and mental health. *Education Sciences, 15*(2), 113. DOI: 10.3390/educsci15020113

Deng, F., Chai, C. S., Tsai, C. C., & Lee, M. H. (2014). The relationships among Chinese practicing teachers' epistemic beliefs, pedagogical beliefs and their beliefs about the use of ICT. *Journal of Educational Technology & Society, 17*(2), 245–256.

DeRosa, R., & Jhangiani, R. S. (2017). Open pedagogy. In Jhangiani, R. S., & Biswas-Diener, R. (Eds.), *Open: The philosophy and practices that are revolutionizing education and science* (pp. 115–124). Ubiquity Press. DOI: 10.5334/bbc.i

Deterding, S., Dixon, D., Khaled, R., & Nacke, L. (2011). From game design elements to gamefulness: defining "gamification". *Proceedings of the 15th International Academic MindTrek Conference*. DOI: 10.1145/2181037.2181040

Devasani, S., Gilbert, S. B., & Blessing, S. B. (2012). Evaluation of two intelligent tutoring system authoring tool paradigms: Graphical user interface-based and text-based. In *Proceedings of the 21st Conference on Behavior Representation in Modeling and Simulation* (pp. 54-61).

DeVellis, R. F. (2017). *Scale development: Theory and applications* (4th ed.). SAGE Publications.

Dey, D. (2025). Enhancing educational tools through artificial intelligence in perspective of need of AI. DOI: 10.2139/ssrn.5031275

Diamond, A. (2013). Executive functions. *Annual Review of Psychology, 64*(1), 135–168. DOI: 10.1146/annurev-psych-113011-143750

Dick, E. (2021). *Balancing user privacy and innovation in augmented and virtual reality*. Information Technology and Innovation Foundation.

Dilling, F. (2025, July). ChatGPT's Perspectives on Real Numbers, Straight Lines and Probability-A Quantitative Study on the Influence of Prompting. In *Frontiers in Education* (Vol. 10, p. 1577322). Frontiers., DOI: 10.3389/feduc.2025.1577322

Dipaola, D., Moore, K. S., Ali, S., Perret, B., Zhou, X., Zhang, H., & Lee, I. (2023). Make-a-Thon for Middle School AI Educators. *SIGCSE 2023 - Proceedings of the 54th ACM Technical Symposium on Computer Science Education, 1*, 305–311. DOI: 10.1145/3545945.3569743

Doherty, I., Sharma, N., & Harbutt, D. (2023). Technology use for teacher professional development in low- and middle-income countries: A systematic review. *Computers and Education Open, 4*, 100088. DOI: 10.1016/j.caeo.2022.100088

du Boulay, B. (2023). Artificial intelligence in education and ethics. In *Handbook of Open* (p. 93). Distance and Digital Education., DOI: 10.1007/978-981-19-2080-6_6

Duan, Y., Edwards, J. S., & Dwivedi, Y. K. (2019). Artificial intelligence for decision making in the era of Big Data – Evolution, challenges and research agenda. *International Journal of Information Management, 48*, 63–71. DOI: 10.1016/j.ijinfomgt.2019.01.021

Dunaway, M. K. (2011). Connectivism: Learning theory and pedagogical practice for networked information landscapes. *RSR. Reference Services Review, 39*(4), 675–685. DOI: 10.1108/00907321111186686

Durán, M., Gutiérrez, I., & Prendes, M. P. (2019). Analysis of variables that influence the digital competence of teachers. *Revista Electrónica Interuniversitaria de Formación del Profesorado, 22*(3), 115–132. DOI: 10.6018/reifop.373611

Durmuşkaya, S. (2021). *Blok tabanlı kodlamaya geçiş sürecinde sokak oyunlarına entegre edilmiş kodlama etkinliklerinin etkisi [The effect of coding activities integrated into street games in the transition to block-based coding]* (Publication No. 688549) [Doctoral dissertation, Ondokuz Mayıs University]. Higher Education Institution Database.

Dwi, M., Akmal, A. N. A., & Alifatul Kamila, A. N. (2024). Navigating ethical dilemmas in AI-enhanced language education: addressing bias and ensuring inclusivity. *Available at SSRN* 4936530. http://dx.doi.org/DOI: 10.2139/ssrn.4936530

Dwivedi, Y. K., Kshetri, N., Hughes, L., Slade, E. L., Jeyaraj, A., Kar, A. K., Baabdullah, A. M., Koohang, A., Raghavan, V., Ahuja, M., Albanna, H., Albashrawi, M. A., Al-Busaidi, A. S., Balakrishnan, J., Barlette, Y., Basu, S., Bose, I., Brooks, L., Buhalis, D., & Wright, R. (2023). "So what if ChatGPT wrote it?" Multidisciplinary perspectives on opportunities, challenges and implications of generative conversational AI for research, practice and policy. *International Journal of Information Management, 71*, 102642. DOI: 10.1016/j.ijinfomgt.2023.102642

Dwyer, S. (2018). Gameful engagement: Gamification, critical thinking, and first-year composition. Double Helix: A Journal of Critical Thinking and Writing, 6(1), 1–13. https://doi.org/DOI: 10.37514/DB-H-J.2018.6.1.07

Eager, B., & Brunton, R. (2023). Prompting higher education towards AI-augmented teaching and learning practice. *Journal of University Teaching & Learning Practice, 20*(5). Advance online publication. DOI: 10.53761/1.20.5.02

Eaton, S. E. (2025). Global trends in education: Artificial intelligence, postplagiarism, and future-focused learning for 2025 and beyond–2024–2025 Werklund Distinguished Research Lecture. *International Journal for Educational Integrity, 21*(1), 12. DOI: 10.1007/s40979-025-00187-6

Echeverria, V., Yang, K., Lawrence, L., Rummel, N., & Aleven, V. (2023). Designing hybrid human–AI orchestration tools for individual and collaborative activities: A technology probe study. *IEEE Transactions on Learning Technologies, 16*(2), 191–205. DOI: 10.1109/TLT.2023.3248155

EDSAFE Alliance. (2025). *AI and Education: Toward a Global Framework for Ethical and Safe Use.* https://www.edsafe.org/framework

Educational Initiatives. (2020). MindSpark Adaptive Learning Platform: Enhancing Student Understanding and Critical Thinking in Mathematics. https://uplink.weforum.org/uplink/s/uplink-contribution/a012o00001pTbgMAAS/personalised-adaptive-learning-with-mindspark

Egunjobi, D., & Adeyeye, O. (2024). *Revolutionizing learning: The impact of augmented reality (AR) and artificial intelligence.* (AI on Education. *International Journal of Research Publication and Reviews, 5*(10), 1157–1170. DOI: 10.55248/gengpi.5.1024.2734

Ehlers, U.-D. (2011). From open educational resources to open educational practices. *eLearning Papers, 23*, 1–8.

Ehlers, U.-D. (2011). Extending the territory: From open educational resources to open educational practices. *Journal of Open. Flexible and Distance Learning, 15*(2), 1–10.

EkStep Foundation. (2021). Digital Learning for All: Case Studies and Impact of EkStep's Personalised Learning Platform. EkStep Foundation (https://ekstep.org). Home - EKStep. (2023, August 12). EkStep. https://ekstep.org/

El Mawas, N., Bradford, M., Andrews, J., Pathak, P., & Muntean, C. H. (2018, June). A Case study on 21st century skills development through a computer based maths game. In *EdMedia+ Innovate Learning,* 1160-1169. Association for the Advancement of Computing in Education (AACE).

Elder, L., & Paul, R. (2020). *Critical thinking: Tools for taking charge of your learning and your life*. Rowman & Littlefield.

Elendu, C., Amaechi, D. C., Okatta, A. U., Amaechi, E. C., Elendu, T. C., Ezeh, C. P., & Elendu, I. D. (2024). The impact of simulation-based training in medical education. *Revista de Medicina (São Paulo), 103*(27), e38813. DOI: 10.1097/MD.0000000000038813 PMID: 38968472

Ellaway, R. H., Pusic, M. V., Galbraith, R. M., & Cameron, T. (2014). Developing the role of big data and analytics in health professional education. *Medical Teacher, 36*(3), 216–222. DOI: 10.3109/0142159X.2014.874553 PMID: 24491226

Ennis, R. H. (1996). *Critical thinking*. Prentice Hall.

Etcuban, J. O. (2025). The use of ChatGPT in addressing Algebra anxiety and promoting confidence. *International Electronic Journal of Mathematics Education, 20*(2), em0825. Advance online publication. DOI: 10.29333/iejme/16008

European Parliament and Council of the European Union. (2016). *Regulation (EU) 2016/679 of the European Parliament and of the Council of 27 April 2016 on the protection of natural persons with regard to the processing of personal data and on the free movement of such data (General Data Protection Regulation).* https://eur-lex.europa.eu/eli/reg/2016/679/oj

European University Association. (2021). Universities Without Walls: A Vision For 2030. https://eua.eu/resources/publications/983:pathways-to-the-future.html

Facione, P. A. (2011). Critical thinking: What it is and why it counts. *Insight assessment, 1*(1), 1-23. https://insightassessment.com/wp-content/uploads/2023/12/Critical-Thinking-What-It-Is-and-Why-It-Counts.pdf

Fahim, M., & Ghamari, M. R. (2011). Critical thinking in Education: Globally developed and locally applied. *Theory and Practice in Language Studies, 1*(11). Advance online publication. DOI: 10.4304/tpls.1.11.1632-1638

Fajari, L. E. W., Dayurni, P., & Rahayu, A. (2023). Meta-Analysis Study: The Effect of Augmented Reality on Student Learning Outcomes. *International Journal of Asian Education, 4*(1), 49–57. DOI: 10.46966/ijae.v4i1.301

Farrokhnia, M., Banihashem, S. K., Noroozi, O., & Wals, A. (2023). A SWOT analysis of ChatGPT: Implications for educational practice and research. *Innovations in Education and Teaching International*, •••, 1–15.

Fawns, T. (2022). An entangled pedagogy: Looking beyond the pedagogy—technology dichotomy. *Postdigital Science and Education*, *4*(3), 711–728. DOI: 10.1007/s42438-022-00302-7 PMID: 40477872

Fehrman, S., & Watson, S. L. (2021). A systematic review of asynchronous online discussions in online higher education. *American Journal of Distance Education*, *35*(3), 200–213. DOI: 10.1080/08923647.2020.1858705

Feng, M., Heffernan, N., & Koedinger, K. (2011). Student modeling in an intelligent tutoring system. In *Intelligent tutoring systems in e-learning environments: Design, implementation and evaluation* (pp. 208–236). IGI Global. DOI: 10.4018/978-1-61692-008-1.ch011

Fernández-Sánchez, M. R., Garrido-Arroyo, M. C., & Porras-Masero, I. (2022). Curricular integration of digital technologies in teaching processes. *Frontiers in Education*, *7*, 1005499. DOI: 10.3389/feduc.2022.1005499

Ferrari, A. (2013). *DIGCOMP: A Framework for Developing and Understanding Digital Competence in Europe*. Joint Research Centre, European Commission., DOI: 10.2788/52966

Figueiredo, J., & García-Peñalvo, F. (2017). *Desenvolver o Pensamento Computacional Usando Seguir e Dar Instruções*. IEEE.

Filak, V. F., & Sheldon, K. M. (2008). Teacher support, student motivation, student need satisfaction, and college teacher course evaluations: Testing a sequential path model. *Educational Psychology*, *28*(6), 711–724. DOI: 10.1080/01443410802337794

Fischer, L., Hilton, J.III, Robinson, T. J., & Wiley, D. (2015). A multi-institutional study of the impact of open textbook adoption on the learning outcomes of post-secondary students. *Journal of Computing in Higher Education*, *27*(3), 159–172. DOI: 10.1007/s12528-015-9101-x PMID: 32269452

Floridi, L. (2023). AI as agency without intelligence: On ChatGPT, large language models, and other generative models. *Philosophy & Technology*, *36*(1), 15. DOI: 10.1007/s13347-023-00621-y

Floridi, L., Cowls, J., Beltrametti, M., Chatila, R., Chazerand, P., Dignum, V., Luetge, C., Madelin, R., Pagallo, U., Rossi, F., Schafer, B., Valcke, P., & Vayena, E. (2018). AI4People—An Ethical Framework for a Good AI Society: Opportunities, Risks, Principles, and Recommendations. *Minds and Machines*, *28*(4), 689–707. DOI: 10.1007/s11023-018-9482-5 PMID: 30930541

Foo, S. Y., & Quek, C. L. (2019). Developing students' critical thinking through asynchronous online discussions: A literature review. *Malaysian Online Journal of Educational Technology*, *7*(2), 37–58. DOI: 10.17220/mojet.2019.02.003

Fredricks, J. A., Blumenfeld, P. C., & Paris, A. H. (2004). School engagement: Potential of the concept, state of the evidence. *Review of Educational Research*, *74*(1), 59–109. DOI: 10.3102/00346543074001059

Fredricks, J. A., Blumenfeld, P., Friedel, J., & Paris, A. (2005). School engagement. In Moore, K. A., & Lippmann, L. (Eds.), *Conceptualizing and measuring indicators of positive development. What do children need to flourish?* (pp. 419–446). Kluwer. DOI: 10.1007/0-387-23823-9_19

Freeman, S., Eddy, S. L., McDonough, M., Smith, M. K., Okoroafor, N., Jordt, H., & Wenderoth, M. P. (2014). Active learning increases student performance in science, engineering, and mathematics. *Proceedings of the National Academy of Sciences of the United States of America*, *111*(23), 8410–8415. DOI: 10.1073/pnas.1319030111 PMID: 24821756

Fullan, M. (2021). *The right drivers for whole system success*. Center for Strategic Education. https://michaelfullan.ca/wp-content/uploads/2021/03/Fullan-CSE-Leading-Education-Series-01-2021R2-compressed.pdf

Fullan, M. (2007). *The new meaning of educational change* (4th ed.). Teachers College Press.

Fullan, M., & Langworthy, M. (2014). *A rich seam: How new pedagogies find deep learning*. Pearson.

Galikyan, I., Admiraal, W., & Kester, L. (2021). MOOC discussion forums: The interplay of the cognitive and the social. *Computers & Education*, *165*, 104133. DOI: 10.1016/j.compedu.2021.104133

Galli, B. J. (2021). Effective Strategies for Communicating and Managing Communication in a Project Team: My Perspective. *International Journal of Applied Industrial Engineering*, *8*(1), 0. Advance online publication. DOI: 10.4018/IJAIE.20210101oa01

Garlinska, M., Osial, M., Proniewska, K., & Pregowska, A. (2023). The influence of emerging technologies on distance education. *Electronics (Basel), 12*(7), 1550. DOI: 10.3390/electronics12071550

Garrison, D. R., Anderson, T., & Archer, W. (2000). Critical inquiry in a text-based environment*: Computer conferencing in higher education. The Internet and Higher Education*, *2*(2–3), 87–105. DOI: 10.1016/S1096-7516(00)00016-6

Garrison, D. R., Anderson, T., & Archer, W. (2001). Critical thinking, cognitive presence, and computer conferencing in distance education. *American Journal of Distance Education, 15*(1), 7–23. DOI: 10.1080/08923640109527071

Garrison, D. R., & Vaughan, N. D. (2008). *Blended learning in higher education: Framework, principles, and guidelines*. Jossey-Bass.

Garzón, J., & Acevedo, J. (2019). Meta-analysis of the impact of Augmented Reality on students' learning gains. *Educational Research Review, 27*(April 2018), 244–260. DOI: 10.1016/j.edurev.2019.04.001

Gašević, D., Dawson, S., & Siemens, G. (2015). Let's not forget: Learning analytics are about learning. *TechTrends*, *59*(1), 64–71. DOI: 10.1007/s11528-014-0822-x

Gauntlett, D. (2011). *Making is connecting: The social meaning of creativity from DIY and knitting to YouTube and Web 2.0*. Polity Press.

Gee, J. P. (2003). What video games have to teach us about learning and literacy. *ACM Computers in Entertainment*, *1*(1), 1–4. DOI: 10.1145/950566.950595

Gehring, D. R., Titus, S. K., Bleistein, T. M., & Li, H. (2025). Guidelines of discussion board prompts in higher education: A scoping review protocol. *International Journal of Educational Research Open*, *9*, 100470. DOI: 10.1016/j.ijedro.2025.100470

George, B., & Wooden, O. S. (2023). Managing the strategic transformation of higher education through artificial intelligence. *Administrative Sciences*, *13*(9), 196. DOI: 10.3390/admsci13090196

George, P. P., Papachristou, N., Belisario, J. M., Wang, W., Wark, P. A., Cotic, Z., & Car, J. (2014). Online eLearning for undergraduates in health professions: A systematic review of the impact on knowledge, skills, attitudes, and satisfaction. *Journal of Global Health*, *4*(1), 010406. DOI: 10.7189/jogh.04.010406 PMID: 24976965

Germain-Rutherford, A., & Ernest, P. (2015). European language teachers and ICT: Experiences, expectations and training needs. In Hampel, R., & Stickler, U. (Eds.), *Developing online language teaching: Research-based pedagogy and practice* (pp. 8–30). Palgrave Macmillan., DOI: 10.1057/9781137412263_2

Ghomi, M., & Redecker, C. (2019, May). Digital Competence of Educators (DigCompEdu): Development and Evaluation of a Self-assessment Instrument for Teachers' Digital Competence. In CSEDU (1) (pp. 541-548).

Giannakos, M., Azevedo, R., Brusilovsky, P., Cukurova, M., Dimitriadis, Y., Hernandez-Leo, D., & Rienties, B. (2024). The promise and challenges of generative AI in education. *Behaviour & Information Technology*, •••, 1–27. DOI: 10.1080/0144929X.2024.2394886

Gikandi, J. W., Morrow, D., & Davis, N. E. (2011). Online formative assessment in higher education: A review of the literature. *Computers & Education*, *57*(4), 2333–2351. DOI: 10.1016/j.compedu.2011.06.004

Gillani, N., Eynon, R., Chiabaut, C., & Finkel, K. (2023). Unpacking the "Black Box" of AI in Education. *Journal of Educational Technology & Society*, *26*(1), 99–111. DOI: 10.30191/ETS.202301_26(1).0008

Gillies, R. M. (2016). Cooperative Learning: Review of Research and Practice. *The Australian Journal of Teacher Education*, *41*(3), 39–54. Advance online publication. DOI: 10.14221/ajte.2016v41n3.3

Gkintoni, E., Antonopoulou, H., Sortwell, A., & Halkiopoulos, C. (2025). *Challenging cognitive load theory: The role of educational neuroscience and artificial intelligence in redefining learning efficacy [Review of challenging cognitive load theory: The role of educational neuroscience and artificial intelligence in redefining learning efficacy]*. Brain Sciences, 15(2), 203. Multidisciplinary Digital Publishing Institute. DOI: 10.3390/brainsci15020203

Gligorea, I., Cioca, M., Oancea, R., Gorski, A.-T., Gorski, H., & Tudorache, P. (2023). *Adaptive learning using artificial intelligence in e-learning: A literature review [Review of adaptive learning using artificial intelligence in e-learning: A Literature review]*. Education Sciences, 13(12), 1216. Multidisciplinary Digital Publishing Institute. DOI: 10.3390/educsci13121216

Global Educational Studies Review. (2020). *In global educational studies review*. https://doi.org/DOI: 10.31703/gesr

Godwin-Jones, R. (2020). Building the porous classroom: An expanded model for blended language learning. *Language Learning \& Technology, 24*(3), 1–18. http://hdl.handle.net/10125/44731

Godwin-Jones, R. (2023). Emerging spaces for language learning: AI bots, ambient intelligence, and the metaverse. *Language Learning \& Technology, 27*(2), 6–27. https://hdl.handle.net/10125/73501

Godwin-Jones, R. (2024). Distributed agency in second language learning and teaching through generative AI. *Language Learning & Technology*, *28*(2), 5–31. https://arxiv.org/abs/2403.20216. DOI: 10.64152/10125/73570

Godwin-Jones, R. (n.d.). AI and VR converge: The future of language learning in an emerging metaverse. In Chun, D., Lan, Y.-J., & Qi, G. (Eds.), *AI-mediated language education in the Metaverse era*. Springer. DOI: 10.1007/978-981-95-0245-5_11

Gomez, L. I. (2020). Immersive Virtual Reality for Learning Experiences. In D. Burgos (Ed.), *Radical Solutions and eLearning*. Springer. DOI: 10.1007/978-981-15-4952-6_12

Gonzaga, K. V. P., Graça, V. G. D., & Quadros-Flores, P. (2024). A cultura e metodologia maker na formação de professores: Uma proposta criativa, interdisciplinar, inovadora, sustentável e inclusiva. *Dialogia*, (50), e27733–e27733. DOI: 10.5585/50.2024.27733

Gouseti, A., James, F., Fallin, L., & Burden, K. (2025). The ethics of using AI in K-12 education: A systematic literature review. *Technology, Pedagogy and Education*, *34*(2), 161–182. DOI: 10.1080/1475939X.2024.2428601

Government of Portugal. (2020). *Action Plan for Digital Transition*. Council of Ministers Resolution no. 30/2020. https://portugaldigital.gov.pt/wp-content/uploads/2022/01/Plano_Acao_Transicao_Digital.pdf

Grabb, D. (2023). The impact of prompt engineering in large language model performance: A psychiatric example. *Journal of Medical Artificial Intelligence*, *6*, 6. DOI: 10.21037/jmai-23-71

Grace, E., & Vidhyavathi, P. L., & P. Malathi, L. (2023). A STUDY ON "AI IN EDUCATION: OPPORTUNITIES AND CHALLENGES FOR PERSONALISED LEARNING. Industrial Engineering Journal (Vol. 52, Issue 5, pp. 750–759). http://www.journal-iiie-india.com/1_may_23/82_online.pdf

Grech, A., & Camilleri, A. F. (2017). *Blockchain in education*. Joint Research Centre, European Commission.

Greenhow, C., & Lewin, C. (2016). Social media and education: Reconceptualizing the boundaries of formal and informal learning. *Learning, Media and Technology*, *41*(1), 6–30. DOI: 10.1080/17439884.2015.1064954

Greller, W., & Drachsler, H. (2012). Translating learning into numbers: A generic framework for learning analytics. *Journal of Educational Technology & Society*, *15*(3), 42–57.

Griffiths, D., Frías-Martínez, E., Tlili, A., & Burgos, D. (2024). A Cybernetic Perspective on Generative AI in Education: From Transmission to Coordination. *International Journal of Interactive Multimedia and Artificial Intelligence*, *8*(5), 15–24. DOI: 10.9781/ijimai.2024.02.008

Grobler, S., & Dittrich, A. K. (2024). Envisioning quality education for sustainability transformation in teacher education: Perspectives from an international dialogue on Sustainable Development Goal 4. *International Journal of Comparative Education and Development*, *26*(3), 270–285. DOI: 10.1108/IJCED-06-2023-0048

Gronseth, S. L., & Dalton, E. M. (2020). Universal Access Through Inclusive Instructional Design: International Perspectives on UDL. In *Universal Access Through Inclusive Instructional Design: International Perspectives on UDL*. Routledge., DOI: 10.4324/9780429435515

Grover, S., & Pea, R. (2013). Computational thinking in K-12. *Educational Researcher*, *42*(1), 38–43. DOI: 10.3102/0013189X12463051

Guan, L., Zhang, Y., & Gu, M. M. (2024). Pre-service Teachers Preparedness for AI-integrated Education: An Investigation from Perceptions, Capabilities, and Teachers' Identity Changes. *Computers and Education Artificial Intelligence*, *100341*. Advance online publication. DOI: 10.1016/j.caeai.2024.100341

Gudoniene, D., Staneviciene, E., Huet, I., Dickel, J., Dieng, D., Degroote, J., Rocio, V., Butkiene, R., & Casanova, D. (2025). Hybrid teaching and learning in higher education: A systematic literature review. *Sustainability (Basel)*, *17*(2), 756. DOI: 10.3390/su17020756

Guha, A., Grewal, D., & Atlas, S. (2024). Generative AI and Marketing Education: What the Future Holds. *Journal of Marketing Education*, *46*(1), 6–17. DOI: 10.1177/02734753231215436

Güntepe, E. T., & Keles, E. (2022). Eğitim Fakültesindeki Öğretim Elemanlarının Teknoloji Entegrasyon Süresinin Eş Merkezli Halka Modeline Göre Değerlendirilmesi. *Ahi Evran Üniversitesi Kırşehir Eğitim Fakültesi Dergisi*, *23*(2), 1639–1690.

Guo, P. J., Kim, J., & Rubin, R. (2014, March). How video production affects student engagement: An empirical study of MOOC videos. In *Proceedings of the first ACM conference on Learning@ scale conference*, (pp. 41-50). DOI: 10.1145/2556325.2566239

Guo, P., Saab, N., Post, L. S., & Admiraal, W. (2020). A review of project-based learning in higher education: Student outcomes and measures. *International Journal of Educational Research*, *102*, 101586. DOI: 10.1016/j.ijer.2020.101586

Guo, S., Halim, H. B. A., & Saad, M. R. B. M. (2025). Leveraging AI-enabled mobile learning platforms to enhance the effectiveness of English teaching in universities. *Scientific Reports*, *15*(1), 15873. Advance online publication. DOI: 10.1038/s41598-025-00801-0 PMID: 40335582

Habgood, M. J., & Ainsworth, S. E. (2011). Motivating children to learn effectively: Exploring the value of intrinsic integration in educational games. *Journal of the Learning Sciences*, *20*(2), 169–206. DOI: 10.1080/10508406.2010.508029

Habib, S., Vogel, T., Anli, X., & Thorne, E. (2024). How does generative artificial intelligence impact student creativity? *Journal of Creativity*, *34*(1), 1–7. DOI: 10.1016/j.yjoc.2023.100072

Hamari, J., Koivisto, J., & Sarsa, H. (2014). Does gamification work?-A literature review of empirical studies on gamification. In *2014 47th Hawaii International Conference on System Sciences* (pp. 3025-3034). Ieee.

Hamilton, L., Halverson, R., Jackson, S., Mandinach, E., Supovitz, J., & Wayman, J. (2009). *Using student achievement data to support instructional decision making* (NCEE 2009-4067). Washington, DC: National Center for Education Evaluation and Regional Assistance, Institute of Education Sciences, U.S. Department of Education. Retrieved from https://ies.ed.gov/ncee/wwc/publications/practiceguides/

Hammes, R. (2007). Orienteering with Adventure Education: New Games for the 21st Century. *Strategies (Reston, VA)*, *20*(5), 7–13. DOI: 10.1080/08924562.2007.10590733

Hansen, G. H. (2017). Lozanov and the teaching text. In Tomlinson, B. (Ed.), *Materials development for language learning and teaching* (2nd ed., pp. 337–342). Cambridge University Press.

Harrison, M., Rowlings, J., White, E. H., Vallence, A.-M., & Potemkin, N. (2024). *Neurodiversity and digital inclusion: Creating the conditions for inclusive education through universal design for learning*. DOI: 10.17613/xk4jx-pse60

Harry, A., & Sayudin, S. (2023). Role of AI in education. [INJURITY]. *Interdisciplinary Journal and Humanity*, *2*(3), 260–268. DOI: 10.58631/injurity.v2i3.52

Harvey, T., Carlson, J., Struck, M., & Moroz, K. (2018). Feeling real: Social presence within online discussions. *Distance Learning : for Educators, Trainers, and Leaders*, *15*(4), 13–27.

Hasan, S., Nasreen, N. S., & Rasul, N. S. S. U. (2025). Leveraging artificial intelligence (AI) in higher education: fostering soft skills communication, collaboration, creativity and critical thinking among university students. *Insights-Journal of Life and Social Sciences*, *3*(2), 1–7. DOI: 10.71000/c42srm97

Hazzan-Bishara, A., Kol, O., & Levy, S. (2025). The factors affecting instructors' adoption of AI technologies: A unified model of external and internal determinants. *Education and Information Technologies, 30*(11), 15043–15069. Advance online publication. DOI: 10.1007/s10639-025-13393-z

Hehir, T., Grindal, T., Freeman, B., Lamoreau, R., Borquaye, Y., & Burke, S. (2016). A Summary of the Evidence on Inclusive Education. *Instituto Alana*, 1–34. https://alana.org.br/wp-content/uploads/2016/12/A_Summary_of_the_evidence_on_inclusive_education.pdf

Hemminki-Reijonen, U., Hassan, N. M., Huotilainen, M., Koivisto, J. M., & Cowley, B. U. (2025). Design of generative AI-powered pedagogy for virtual reality environments in higher education. *npj Science of Learning, 10*(1), 1-15. https://doi.org/DOI: 10.1038/s41539-025-00326-1

Henderson, M., & Phillips, M. (2015). Video-based feedback on student assessment: Scarily personal. *Australasian Journal of Educational Technology, 31*(1). Advance online publication. DOI: 10.14742/ajet.1878

Heritage, M. (2013). *Formative assessment in practice: A process of inquiry and action*. Harvard Education Press.

Herodotou, C., Naydenova, G., Boroowa, A., Gilmour, A., & Rienties, B. (2020). How can predictive learning analytics and motivational interventions increase student retention and enhance administrative support in distance education? *Journal of Learning Analytics, 7*(2), 72–83. DOI: 10.18608/jla.2020.72.4

Hero, L. M., & Lindfors, E. (2019). Students' learning experience in a multidisciplinary innovation project. *Education + Training, 61*(4), 500–522. DOI: 10.1108/ET-06-2018-0138

Hershkovitz, A. (2015). Towards data-driven instruction. *Technology, Instruction. Cognition and Learning, 10*, 1–4.

Hew, K. F., & Cheung, W. S. (2012). *Student participation in online discussions: Challenges, solutions, and future research*. Springer Science & Business Media. DOI: 10.1007/978-1-4614-2370-6

Hew, K. F., Cheung, W. S., & Ng, C. S. L. (2010). Student contribution in asynchronous online discussion: A review of the research and empirical exploration. *Instructional Science, 38*(6), 571–606. DOI: 10.1007/s11251-008-9087-0

Hilton, J.III. (2016). Open educational resources and college textbook choices: A review of research on efficacy and perceptions. *Educational Technology Research and Development, 64*(4), 573–590. DOI: 10.1007/s11423-016-9434-9

Hitchcock, J. H., & Onwuegbuzie, A. J. (2020). Developing mixed methods crossover analysis approaches. *Journal of Mixed Methods Research, 14*(1), 63–83. DOI: 10.1177/1558689819841782

Holmes, W., Bialik, M., & Fadel, C. (2019). *Artificial intelligence in education promises and implications for teaching and learning*. Center for Curriculum Redesign. https://discovery.ucl.ac.uk/id/eprint/10139722

Holmes, W., Bialik, M., & Fadel, C. (2019). Artificial intelligence in Education: Promises and implications for teaching and learning. https://oro.open.ac.uk/60255/

Holmes, W., Bialik, M., & Fadel, C. (2019). *Artificial intelligence in education promises and implications for teaching and learning*. Center for Curriculum Redesign.

Holmes, W., Bialik, M., & Fadel, C. (2019). *Artificial Intelligence in Education: Promises and Implications for Teaching and Learning*. Center for Curriculum Redesign.

Holmes, W., & Miao, F. (2023). *Guidance for generative AI in education and research*. Unesco Publishing.

Holmes, W., Porayska-Pomsta, K., Holstein, K., Sutherland, E., Baker, T. T., Shum, S. B., Santos, O. C., Rodrigo, M., Cukurova, M., Bittencourt, I. I., & Koedinger, K. R. (2021). Ethics of AI in education: Towards a community-wide framework. *International Journal of Artificial Intelligence in Education, 32*(3), 504–526. DOI: 10.1007/s40593-021-00239-1

Home - Casel schoolguide. (2025, August 12). Casel Schoolguide. https://schoolguide.casel.org/

Hong, Y., Saab, N., & Admiraal, W. (2024). Approaches and game elements used to tailor digital gamification for learning: A systematic literature review. *Computers & Education, 212*(April), 105000. DOI: 10.1016/j.compedu.2024.105000

Hong, Y., Saab, N., & Admiraal, W. (2025). EFL university students' game element preferences and learning needs: Implications for the instructional design of digital gamified classes. *System, 131*(July), 103670. DOI: 10.1016/j.system.2025.103670

Hrastinski, S. (2009). *A theory of online learning as online participation*. Computers & Education, 52(1), 78–82. https://doi.org/DOI: 10.1016/j.compedu.2008.06.009

Hrastinski, S. (2008). Asynchronous and synchronous e-learning. *EDUCAUSE Quarterly, 31*(4), 51–55.

Huang, A. Y. Q., Lu, O. H. T., & Yang, S. J. H. (2022). Effects of artificial intelligence-enabled personalized recommendations on learners' learning engagement, motivation, and outcomes in a flipped classroom. *Computers & Education, 194*, 104684. DOI: 10.1016/j.compedu.2022.104684

Hu-Au, E., & Lee, J. J. (2017). Virtual reality in education: A tool for learning in the experience age. *International Journal of Innovation in Education*, *4*(4), 215–226. DOI: 10.1504/IJIIE.2017.091481

Hughes, J. N., Luo, W., Kwok, O.-M., & Loyd, L. K. (2008). Teacher-student support, effortful engagement, and achievement: A 3-year longitudinal study. *Journal of Educational Psychology*, *100*(1), 1–14. DOI: 10.1037/0022-0663.100.1.1 PMID: 19578558

Huizenga, J. C., & Dam, G. T. M. (2017). Teachers' practice-based perceptions of the value of game-based learning in secondary education. *Computers & Education, 110*, 105–115. DOI: 10.1016/j.compedu.2017.03.008

Huizenga, J., Admiraal, W., Akkerman, S., & ten Dam, G. (2009). Mobile game-based learning in secondary education: Engagement, motivation and learning in a mobile city game. *Journal of Computer Assisted Learning*, *25*(4), 332–344. DOI: 10.1111/j.1365-2729.2009.00316.x

Hupont Torres, I., Charisi, V., De Prato, G., Pogorzelska, K., & Schade, S.. (2023). *Next generation virtual worlds – Societal, technological, economic and policy challenges for the EU*. Publications Office of the European Union., DOI: 10.2760/51579

Hu, S. (2024). The effect of artificial intelligence-assisted personalized learning on student learning outcomes: A meta-analysis based on 31 empirical research papers. *Science Insights Education Frontiers*, *24*(1), 3873–3894. DOI: 10.15354/sief.24.re395

Hu, X., Sui, H., Geng, X., & Zhao, L. (2024). Constructing a teacher portrait for the artificial intelligence age based on the micro ecological system theory: A systematic review. *Education and Information Technologies*, *29*(13), 16679–16715. DOI: 10.1007/s10639-024-12513-5

Hwang, S. (2022). Examining the effects of artificial intelligence on elementary students' mathematics achievement: A meta-analysis. *Sustainability (Basel)*, *14*(20), 13185. DOI: 10.3390/su142013185

Ifenthaler, D., Mah, D. K., & Yau, J. Y. K. (2019). Utilising Learning Analytics for Study Success: Reflections on Current Empirical Findings. In Ifenthaler, D., Mah, D. K., & Yau, J. Y. K. (Eds.), *Utilizing learning analytics to support study success*. Springer. DOI: 10.1007/978-3-319-64792-0_2

Illeris, K. (2009). *Contemporary theories of learning: Learning theorists... In their own words*. Routledge. DOI: 10.4324/9780203870426

Imran, M., & Almusharraf, N. (2023). Analyzing the role of ChatGPT as a writing assistant at higher education level: A systematic review of the literature. In *Contemporary Educational Technology* (Vol. 15, Issue 4, pp. 1–14). DOI: 10.30935/cedtech/13605

Imran, M., Almusharraf, N., Ahmed, S., & Mansoor, M. I. (2024). Personalization of E-Learning: Future Trends, Opportunities, and Challenges. *International Journal of Interactive Mobile Technologies*, *18*(10), 4–18. DOI: 10.3991/ijim.v18i10.47053

Indian Institute of Technology Gandhinagar. (2020). Innovative Approaches in Education: Design Thinking at IIT Gandhinagar. https://dic.iitgn.ac.in/wp/

Ironside, P. M. (2000). Thinking in nursing education. Part II. A teacher's experience. PubMed, 20(5), 243–247. https://pubmed.ncbi.nlm.nih.gov/10754846

ISTE. (2017). ISTE 21st Century Standards for Students. https://iste.org/standards/students

Jääskä, E., Lehtinen, J., Kujala, J., & Kauppila, O. (2022). GBL and students' motivation in project management education. *Project Leadership and Society*, *3*, 100055. DOI: 10.1016/j.plas.2022.100055

Jatileni, C. N., Sanusi, I. T., Olaleye, S. A., Ayanwale, M. A., Agbo, F. J., & Oyelere, P. B. (2024). Artificial intelligence in compulsory level of education: Perspectives from Namibian in-service teachers. *Education and Information Technologies*, *29*(10), 12569–12596. DOI: 10.1007/s10639-023-12341-z

Jiang, J., & Fryer, L. K. (2024). The effect of virtual reality learning on students' motivation: A scoping review. *Journal of Computer Assisted Learning*, *40*(1), 360–373. DOI: 10.1111/jcal.12885

Jian, M. J. K. O. (2023). Personalized learning through AI. *Advances in Engineering Innovation*, *5*(1), 16–19. DOI: 10.54254/2977-3903/5/2023039

Jobin, A., Ienca, M., & Vayena, E. (2019). The global landscape of AI ethics guidelines. *Nature Machine Intelligence*, *1*(9), 389–399. DOI: 10.1038/s42256-019-0088-2

Johnson, D. W., & Johnson, R. T. (2018). Cooperative learning: The foundation for active learning. *Active learning-Beyond the future*, 59-71. https://doi.org/DOI: 10.5772/intechopen.81086

Johnson, D. W., & Johnson, R. T. (2009). Energizing learning: The instructional power of conflict. *Educational Researcher*, *38*(1), 37–51. DOI: 10.3102/0013189X08330540

Johnson, S. D., & Aragon, S. A. (2003). An instructional strategy framework for online learning environments. In Aragon, S. A. (Ed.), *Facilitating learning in online environments. New Directions for Adult and Continuing Education* (Vol. 10, pp. 31–44). Jossey-Bass. DOI: 10.1002/ace.117

Jonassen, D., Peck, K., & Wilson, B. (1999). *Learning with technology: A constructivist approach*. Prentice Hall.

Jones, E. K., & Orchard, V. (2024). Neurodiversity and disability: What is at stake? *Medical Humanities*, *50*(3), 456–465. DOI: 10.1136/medhum-2023-012808

Joshi, M. (2023). *Adaptive learning through artificial intelligence*. SSRN Electronic Journal. DOI: 10.2139/ssrn.4514887

Kabudi, T., Pappas, I. O., & Olsen, D. H. (2021). AI-enabled adaptive learning systems: A systematic mapping of the literature. *Computers and Education Artificial Intelligence*, *2*, 100017. DOI: 10.1016/j.caeai.2021.100017

Kaledio, P., Robert, A., & Frank, L. A. (2024). *The impact of artificial intelligence on students' learning experience*. SSRN Electronic Journal. DOI: 10.2139/ssrn.4716747

Kalniņa, D., Nīmante, D., & Baranova, S. (2024). Artificial intelligence for higher education: Benefits and challenges for pre-service Instructors. *Frontiers in Education*, *9*, 1501819. Advance online publication. DOI: 10.3389/feduc.2024.1501819

Kamali, J., Alpat, M. F., & Bozkurt, A. (2024). AI ethics as a complex and multifaceted challenge: Decoding educators' AI ethics alignment through the lens of activity theory. *International Journal of Educational Technology in Higher Education*, *21*(1), 62. DOI: 10.1186/s41239-024-00496-9

Kandel, R. K. (2015). Resolving ELT Challenges Through Critical Thinking Strategies. https://www.researchgate.net/publication/281692231_Resolving_ELT_Challenges_Through_Critical_Thinking_Strategies

Kapoor, H., & Kaufman, J. C. (2021). Basic concepts of creativity. *The Cambridge handbook of lifespan development of creativity*, 5-19.

Kapp, K. M. (2012). *The gamification of learning and instruction: Game-based methods and strategies for training and education*. Pfeiffer.

Kaptanoğlu, M. Y., & Kavanoz, S. (2024). Self-regulation and self-efficacy of EFL learners in hybrid educational settings in Türkiye. *Psychology in the Schools*, *61*(12), 4517–4537. DOI: 10.1002/pits.23293

Kapur, M. (2008). Productive failure. *Cognition and Instruction*, *26*(3), 379–424. DOI: 10.1080/07370000802212669

Karadag, I., Güzelci, O. Z., & Alaçam, S. (2023). EDU-AI: A twofold machine learning model to support classroom layout generation. *Construction Innovation*, *23*(4), 898–914. DOI: 10.1108/CI-02-2022-0034

Karakuş, N., Gedik, K., & Kazazoğlu, S.KARAKUŞ. (2025). Ethical decision-making in education: A comparative study of instructors and artificial intelligence in ethical dilemmas. *Behavioral Sciences (Basel, Switzerland)*, *15*(4), 469. DOI: 10.3390/bs15040469 PMID: 40282090

Karlsson, P., Bech, A., Stone, H., Vale, C., Griffin, S., Monbaliu, E., & Wallen, M. (2019). Eyes on communication: Trialling eye-gaze control technology in young children with dyskinetic cerebral palsy. *Developmental Neurorehabilitation*, *22*(2), 134–140. DOI: 10.1080/17518423.2018.1519609

Kasneci, E., Sessler, K., & Küchenhoff, H.. (2023). ChatGPT for good? On opportunities and challenges of large language models for education. *Learning and Individual Differences*, *103*, 102274. DOI: 10.1016/j.lindif.2023.102274

Kearsley, G., & Shneiderman, B. (1998). Engagement theory. *Educational Technology*, *38*(5), 20–23.

Ke, F. (2008). A case study of computer gaming for math: Engaged learning from gameplay? *Computers & Education*, *51*(4), 1609–1620. DOI: 10.1016/j.compedu.2008.03.003

Kennedy, H., & Wanless, L. (2022). Artificial intelligence. In *The Routledge Handbook of Digital Sport Management* (1st ed.). Routledge. DOI: 10.4324/9781003088899-29

Kerlinger, F. N., & Kaya, E. (1959). The construction and factor analytic validation of scales to measure attitudes toward education1. *Educational and Psychological Measurement*, *19*(1), 13–29. DOI: 10.1177/001316445901900102

Kessler, G. (2018). Technology and the future of language teaching. *Foreign Language Annals*, *51*(1), 205–218. DOI: 10.1111/flan.12318

Khalil, M., Wong, J., de Koning, B., Ebner, M., & Paas, F. (2018). Gamification in MOOCs: A review of the state of the art. In *2018 IEEE Global Engineering Education Conference (EDUCON)*, (pp. 1629-1638). IEEE. DOI: 10.1109/EDUCON.2018.8363430

Khatri, B. B., & Karki, P. D. (2023). Artificial intelligence (AI) in higher education: Growing academic integrity and ethical concerns. *Nepalese Journal of Development and Rural Studies*, *20*(01), 1–7. DOI: 10.3126/njdrs.v20i01.64134

Khazanchi, R., Di Mitri, D., & Drachsler, H. (2025). The effect of AI-based systems on mathematics achievement in rural context: A quantitative study. *Journal of Computer Assisted Learning*, *41*(1), e13098. DOI: 10.1111/jcal.13098

Khlaif, Z. N., Ayyoub, A., Hamamra, B., Bensalem, E., Mitwally, M. A. A., Ayyoub, A., Hattab, M. K., & Shadid, F. (2024). University teachers' views on the adoption and integration of generative AI tools for student assessment in higher education. *Education Sciences*, *14*(10), 1090. DOI: 10.3390/educsci14101090

Kim, J. (2024). Types of teacher-AI collaboration in K-12 classroom instruction: Chinese teachers' perspective. *Education and Information Technologies*, *29*(13), 17433–17465. DOI: 10.1007/s10639-024-12523-3

Kimmons, R. (2016). OER adoption and perceptions in American higher education. *Open Praxis*, *8*(2), 111–123.

Kimmons, R., Rosenberg, J., & Allman, B. (2021). Trends in educational technology: What Facebook, Twitter, and Scopus can tell us about current research and practice. *TechTrends*, *65*(2), 125–136. DOI: 10.1007/s11528-021-00589-6 PMID: 33644781

Kim, N. J., & Kim, M. K. (2022). Teacher's perceptions of using an artificial intelligence-based educational tool for scientific writing. *Frontiers in Education*, *7*, 755914. Advance online publication. DOI: 10.3389/feduc.2022.755914

Kim, Y. R., Park, M. S., & Joung, E. (2025). Exploring the integration of artificial intelligence in math education: Preservice Teachers' experiences and reflections on problem-posing activities with ChatGPT. *School Science and Mathematics*, ssm.18336. Advance online publication. DOI: 10.1111/ssm.18336

Kirkwood, A., & Price, L. (2013). Technology-enhanced learning and teaching in higher education: What is 'enhanced' and how do we know? A critical literature review. *Learning, Media and Technology*, *39*(1), 6–36. DOI: 10.1080/17439884.2013.770404

Kitcharoen, P., Howimanporn, S., & Chookaew, S. (2024). Enhancing Teachers' AI Competencies through Artificial Intelligence of Things Professional Development Training. *International Journal of Interactive Mobile Technologies*, *18*(2), 4–15. Advance online publication. DOI: 10.3991/ijim.v18i02.46613

Kizilcec, R. F. (2024). To Advance AI Use in Education, Focus on Understanding Educators. In *International Journal of Artificial Intelligence in Education* (Vol. 34, Issue 1). DOI: 10.1007/s40593-023-00351-4

Klaassen, R. G. (2018). Interdisciplinary education: A case study. *European Journal of Engineering Education*, *43*(6), 842–859. DOI: 10.1080/03043797.2018.1442417

Klimova, B., Pikhart, M., & Kacetl, J. (2023). Ethical issues of the use of AI-driven mobile apps for education. *Frontiers in Public Health, 10*, 1–8. DOI: 10.3389/fpubh.2022.1118116 PMID: 36711343

Klunder, S., Smit, B., Slegers, K., Saab, N., Nahon, A., Mainhard, T., & Admiraal, W. (2023). Meedoen op afstand in een hybride klas. Interactie met leerlingen met een chronische aandoening. NWO-NRO 40.5.20500.139. ICLON Universiteit Leiden, the Netherlands.

Klunder, S., Saab, N., & Admiraal, W. (2022). A teacher perspective on using a hybrid virtual classroom for students with a chronic illness in mainstream primary and secondary schools. *Technology, Pedagogy and Education, 31*(4), 493–508. DOI: 10.1080/1475939X.2022.2033824

Knowles, M. S., Holton, E. F.III, & Swanson, R. A. (2012). *The adult learner: The definitive classic in adult education and human resource development* (7th ed.). Routledge. DOI: 10.4324/9780080964249

Kodaganallur, V., Weitz, R. R., & Rosenthal, D. (2005). A comparison of model-tracing and constraint-based intelligent tutoring paradigms. *International Journal of Artificial Intelligence in Education, 15*(2), 117–144. DOI: 10.3233/IRG-2005-15(2)03

Kodavali, S. K., Gilbert, S., & Blessing, S. B. (2010, June). Expansion of the xPST framework to enable non-programmers to create intelligent tutoring systems in 3D game environments. In *International Conference on Intelligent Tutoring Systems* (pp. 365-367). Springer, Berlin, Heidelberg. DOI: 10.1007/978-3-642-13437-1_72

Koedinger, K. R., Aleven, V., Heffernan, N., McLaren, B., & Hockenberry, M. (2004, August). Opening the door to non-programmers: Authoring intelligent tutor behavior by demonstration. In *International Conference on Intelligent Tutoring Systems* (pp. 162-174). Springer, Berlin, Heidelberg. DOI: 10.1007/978-3-540-30139-4_16

Koedinger, K. R., Anderson, J., Hadley, W., & Mark, M. (1997). Intelligent tutoring goes to school in the big city. *International Journal of Artificial Intelligence in Education, 8*, 30–43.

Kok, C. L., Ho, C. K., Koh, Y. Y., & Heng, W., J. B., & Teo, T. H. (2024). Psychological aspects of AI enhanced learning experiences. In *Proceedings of TENCON 2024 – 2024 IEEE Region 10 Conference* (pp. 1302–1305). IEEE. DOI: 10.1109/TENCON61640.2024.10902839

Kononowicz, A. A., Woodham, L. A., Edelbring, S., Stathakarou, N., Davies, D., Saxena, N., & Zary, N. (2019). Virtual patient simulations in health professions education: Systematic review and meta-analysis by the digital health education collaboration. *Journal of Medical Internet Research*, *21*(7), e14676. DOI: 10.2196/14676 PMID: 31267981

Korkmaz Guler, N., Dertli, Z. G., Boran, E., & Yildiz, B. (2024). An artificial intelligence application in mathematics education: Evaluating ChatGPT's academic achievement in a mathematics exam. *Pedagogical Research*, *9*(2), em0188. Advance online publication. DOI: 10.29333/pr/14145

Kouzov, O. (2019). The New Paradigms In Education and Support of Critical Thinking with Artificial Intelligence (AI) Tools. *Serdica Journal of Computing*, *13*(1–2), 27–40. DOI: 10.55630/sjc.2019.13.27-40

Kruk, M. (2022). Motivational dynamics in learning English in Second Life. *ELT Journal*, *76*(4), 465–475. DOI: 10.1093/elt/ccab067

Küçük, S., Turan, Z., Özkan, Ç. N., Taş, Y. F., & Gürsoy, T. (2024). An innovative approach in middle school science courses: Effects of collaborative augmented reality activities on motivation, cognitive load, and satisfaction. *Interactive Learning Environments*, *33*(3), 2355–2373. DOI: 10.1080/10494820.2024.2408582

Kuhail, M. A., Alturki, N., Alramlawi, S., & Alhejori, K. (2023). Interacting with educational chatbots: A systematic review. *Education and Information Technologies*, *28*(1), 973–1018. DOI: 10.1007/s10639-022-11177-3

Kumar, S. (2023). Developing human skills in the era of Artificial intelligence: challenges and opportunities for education and training. Scholedge International Journal of Multidisciplinary & Allied Studies ISSN 2394-336X, 10(2), 11. DOI: 10.19085/sijmas100201

Kuo, H. C., Weng, T. L., Chang, C. C., & Chang, C. Y. (2023). Designing Our Own Board Games in the Playful Space: Improving High School Student's Citizenship Competencies and Creativity through GBL. *Sustainability (Basel)*, *15*(4), 2968. DOI: 10.3390/su15042968

Labadze, L., Grigolia, M., & Machaidze, L. (2023). Role of AI chatbots in education: systematic literature review. In *International Journal of Educational Technology in Higher Education* (Vol. 20, Issue 1). DOI: 10.1186/s41239-023-00426-1

Lai, E. R. (2011). Critical Thinking: a literature review. http://paluchja-zajecia.home .amu.edu.pl/seminarium_fakult/sem_f_krytyczne/Critical%20Thinking%20A%20 Literature%20Review.pdf

Lambert, R., McNiff, A., Schuck, R., Imm, K., & Zimmerman, S. (2023). "UDL is a way of thinking": Theorizing UDL teacher knowledge, beliefs, and practices. *Frontiers in Education*, *8*, 1145293. DOI: 10.3389/feduc.2023.1145293

Lampou, R. (2023). The Integration of Artificial Intelligence in Education: Opportunities and Challenges. *Review of Artificial Intelligence in Education*, *4*(00), e015. Advance online publication. DOI: 10.37497/rev.artif.intell.educ.v4i00.15

Lantolf, J. P. (2000). Introducing sociocultural theory. In Lantolf, J. P. (Ed.), *Sociocultural theory and second language learning* (pp. 1–26). Oxford University Press.

Lantolf, J. P. (2006). Sociocultural theory and L2: State of the art. *Studies in Second Language Acquisition*, *28*(1), 67–109. DOI: 10.1017/S0272263106060037

Lantolf, J. P., & Poehner, M. E. (2024). *Sociocultural theory and the teaching of second languages*. University of Toronto Press.

Lantolf, J. P., & Thorne, S. L. (2006). *Sociocultural theory and the genesis of second language development*. Oxford University Press.

Laurillard, D. (2012). *Teaching as a design science: Building pedagogical patterns for learning and technology*. Routledge.

Lazarus, M. D., Truong, M., Douglas, P., & Selwyn, N. (2024). Artificial intelligence and clinical anatomical education: Promises and perils. *Anatomical Sciences Education*, *17*(2), 249–262. DOI: 10.1002/ase.2221 PMID: 36030525

Lazou, C., Panagiotou, N., & Tsinakos, A. (2023). Training Teachers in an Interdisciplinary Approach through EMI: A Case Study in Greece. In *English Language Teacher Education in Changing Times* (pp. 50–65). Routledge., DOI: 10.4324/9781003295723-7

LeCun, Y., Bengio, Y., & Hinton, G. (2015). Deep learning. *Nature*, *521*(7553), 436–444. DOI: 10.1038/nature14539 PMID: 26017442

Lee, D., Son, T., & Yeo, S. (2025). Impacts of interacting with an AI chatbot on preservice teachers' responsive teaching skills in math education. *Journal of Computer Assisted Learning*, *41*(1), e13091. DOI: 10.1111/jcal.13091

Lee, D., & Yeo, S. (2022). Developing an AI-based chatbot for practicing responsive teaching in mathematics. *Computers & Education*, *191*, 104646. DOI: 10.1016/j.compedu.2022.104646

Lee, J., Alonzo, D., Beswick, K., Abril, J. M. V., Chew, A. W., & Oo, C. Z. (2024). Dimensions of teachers' data literacy: A systematic review of literature from 1990 to 2021. *Educational Assessment, Evaluation and Accountability*, *36*(2), 145–200. DOI: 10.1007/s11092-024-09435-8

Lee, J., Hong, M., & Cho, J. (2024). Development of a Content Framework of Artificial Intelligence Integrated Education Considering Ethical Factors. *International Journal on Advanced Science, Engineering and Information Technology*, *14*(1), 205–213. DOI: 10.18517/ijaseit.14.1.19558

Leikin, R. (2013). Evaluating mathematical creativity: The interplay between multiplicity and insight1. *Psychological Test and Assessment Modeling*, *55*(4), 385–400.

Leon, C., & Lipuma, J. (2024). Overcoming Obstacles to Interdisciplinary Research: Empirical Insights and Strategies. *Journal of Systemics, Cybernetics and Informatics*, *22*(6), 18–34. DOI: 10.54808/JSCI.22.06.18

Liang, J., Stephens, J. M., & Brown, G. (2025*). A systematic review of the early impact of artificial intelligence on higher education curriculum, instruction, and assessment [Review of A systematic review of the early impact of artificial intelligence on higher education curriculum, instruction, and assessment].* Frontiers in Education, 10. Frontiers Media. DOI: 10.3389/feduc.2025.1522841

Libâneo, J. C. (2001). Educação no século XXI: pedagogia da reprodução ou pedagogia da transformação? In *J. C. Libâneo, M. L. Oliveira & N. T. Toschi (Orgs.), Educação escolar: políticas, estrutura e organização* (pp. 31–50). Alternativa.

Li, F., & Mohammad, M. (2025). Artificial Intelligence and Education in China: Exploring the Future of Personalized Learning and Its Social Implications. *Uniglobal Journal of Social Sciences and Humanities*, *4*(1), 216–222.

Li, L., Hew, K. F., & Du, J. (2024). Gamification enhances student intrinsic motivation, perceptions of autonomy and relatedness, but minimal impact on competency: A meta-analysis and systematic review. *Educational Technology Research and Development*, *72*(2), 765–796. DOI: 10.1007/s11423-023-10337-7

Li, M., & Jones, B. D. (2019). Transforming traditional teaching: A professional development program for the college EFL teachers. *Theory and Practice in Language Studies*, *9*(12), 1494–1500. DOI: 10.17507/tpls.0912.05

Lin, C.-C., Huang, A. Y. Q., & Lu, O. H. T. (2023). *Artificial intelligence in intelligent tutoring systems toward sustainable education: a systematic review [Review of Artificial intelligence in intelligent tutoring systems toward sustainable education: a systematic review].* Smart Learning Environments, 10(1). Springer Nature. DOI: 10.1186/s40561-023-00260-y

Lin, H., & Qiu, C. (2024). Artificial intelligence (AI) -integrated educational applications and college students' creativity and academic emotions: Students' and instructors' perceptions and attitudes. *BMC Psychology, 12*(1), 487. Advance online publication. DOI: 10.1186/s40359-024-01979-0 PMID: 39285268

Lin, L., Zhou, D., Wang, J., & Wang, Y. (2024). A systematic review of big data driven education evaluation. *SAGE Open, 14*(2), 21582440241242180. DOI: 10.1177/21582440241242180

Li, P. H., Lee, H. Y., Cheng, Y. P., Starčič, A. I., & Huang, Y. M. (2023). Solving the self-regulated learning problem: Exploring the performance of ChatGPT in mathematics. In *International Conference on Innovative Technologies and Learning* (pp. 77–86). Springer. DOI: 10.1007/978-3-031-40113-8_8

Liu, H. H. B. (2024). Learning evaluation method based on artificial intelligence technology and its application in education. *Journal of Electrical Systems, 20*(1833), 1842. DOI: 10.52783/jes.1722

Livingstone, S. (2009). *Children and the internet: Great expectations, challenging realities*. Polity Press.

Li, Y., Sha, L., Yan, L., Lin, J., Rakovič, M., & Galbraith, K.. (2023). Can large language models write reflectively. *Computers and Education: Artificial Intelligence, 4*, 100140.

Lo, C. K., & Hew, K. F. (2017). A critical review of flipped classroom challenges in K-12 education: Possible solutions and recommendations for future research. *Research and Practice in Technology Enhanced Learning, 12*(1), 4. DOI: 10.1186/s41039-016-0044-2 PMID: 30613253

Lockhorst, D., Admiraal, W., & Pilot, A. (2010). CSCL in teacher training: What tasks lead to teacher collaboration? *Technology, Pedagogy and Education, 19*(1), 63–78. DOI: 10.1080/14759390903579190

Lokman, A. S., & Ameedeen, M. A. (2019). Modern chatbot systems: A technical review. In *Proceedings of the Future Technologies Conference (FTC) 2018: Volume 2* (pp. 1012–1023). Springer. DOI: 10.1007/978-3-030-02683-7_75

Lo, L. S. (2023). The CLEAR path: A framework for enhancing information literacy through prompt engineering. *Journal of Academic Librarianship*, *49*(4), 102720. DOI: 10.1016/j.acalib.2023.102720

Long, D., & Magerko, B. (2020). *What is ai literacy? Competencies and design considerations.* 1. DOI: 10.1145/3313831.3376727

Long, P., & Siemens, G. (2011). Penetrating the fog: Analytics in learning and education. *EDUCAUSE Review (Online).*

Long, M. H. (1996). The role of the linguistic environment in second language acquisition. In Ritchie, W. C., & Bhatia, T. K. (Eds.), *Handbook of second language acquisition* (pp. 413–468). Academic Press.

López Costa, M. (2025). Artificial Intelligence and Data Literacy in Rural Schools' Teaching Practices: Knowledge, Use, and Challenges. *Education Sciences*, *15*(3), 352. DOI: 10.3390/educsci15030352

Lucas, B., & Spencer, E. (2017). *Teaching Creative Thinking: Developing learners who generate ideas and can think critically (Pedagogy for a Changing World series).* Crown House Publishing Ltd.

Luckin, R. (2017). Towards artificial intelligence-based assessment systems. *Nature Human Behaviour, 1*(3), 0028. https://doi.org/DOI: 10.1038/s41562-016-0028

Luckin, R., Holmes, W., Griffiths, M., & Forcier, L. B. (2016). *Intelligence Unleashed: An Argument for AI in Education*. Pearson Education. https://www.pearson.com/content/dam/corporate/global/pearson-dot-com/files/innovation/Intelligence-Unleashed-Publication.pdf

Luckin, R., Holmes, W., Griffiths, M., & Forcier, L. B. (2016). Intelligence unleashed: An argument for AI in education. Pearson Education. https://www.pearson.com/content/dam/one-dot-com/one-dot-com/global/Files/about-pearson/innovation/open-ideas/Intelligence-Unleashed-Publication.pdf

Luckin, R., Holmes, W., Griffiths, M., & Forcier, L. B. (2016). *Intelligence unleashed: An argument for AI in education*. Pearson. https://www.pearson.com/content/dam/one-dot-com/one-dot-com/global/Files/about-pearson/innovation/open-ideas/Intelligence-Unleashed-Publication.pdf

Luckin, R.. (2016). *Intelligence Unleashed: An Argument for AI in Education*. Pearson.

Lui, M., Maharaj, A., Shimaly, R., Atcha, A., Ali, H., Carroll, S., & McEwen, R. (2021). User experiences of eye-gaze classroom technology for children with complex communication needs. *Journal of Special Education Technology*, *37*(3), 426–436. Advance online publication. DOI: 10.1177/01626434211019399

Luo, B., Lau, R. Y., Li, C., & Si, Y. W. (2022). A critical review of state-of-the-art chatbot designs and applications. *Wiley Interdisciplinary Reviews. Data Mining and Knowledge Discovery*, *12*(1), e1434. DOI: 10.1002/widm.1434

Luo, H., & Li, W. (2025). Impact of microlearning on developing soft skills of university students across disciplines. *Frontiers in Psychology*, *16*, 1491265. DOI: 10.3389/fpsyg.2025.1491265 PMID: 40351600

Lu, Q., Yao, Y., Xiao, L., Yuan, M., Wang, J., & Zhu, X. (2024). Can ChatGPT effectively complement teacher assessment of undergraduate students' academic writing? *Assessment & Evaluation in Higher Education*, *49*(5), 616–633. DOI: 10.1080/02602938.2024.2301722

Lydia, E. G., Vidhyavathi, P., & Malathi, P. (2023). A Study On "Ai In Education: Opportunities And Challenges For Personalized Learning. *Industrial Engineering Journal*, *52*(05), 750–759. DOI: 10.36893/IEJ.2023.V52I05.750-759

MacLellan, C. J., Koedinger, K. R., & Matsuda, N. (2014, June). Authoring tutors with SimStudent: An evaluation of efficiency and model quality. In International conference on intelligent tutoring systems (pp. 551-560). Springer, Cham.

MacNeill, H., Masters, K., Nemethy, K., & Correia, R. (2024). Online learning in health professions education. Part 1: Teaching and learning in online environments: AMEE Guide No. 161. *Medical Teacher*, *46*(1), 4–17. DOI: 10.1080/0142159X.2023.2197135 PMID: 37094079

Maghsudi, S., Lan, A., Xu, J., & van der Schaar, M. (2021). Personalized Education in the AI Era: What to Expect Next? arXiv. DOI: 10.48550/ARXIV.2101.10074

Maghsudi, S., Lan, A., Xu, J., & van der Schaar, M. (2021). Personalized Education in the Artificial Intelligence Era: What to Expect Next. *IEEE Signal Processing Magazine*, *38*(3), 37–50. DOI: 10.1109/MSP.2021.3055032

Mahmoud, C., & Sørensen, J. T. (2024). Artificial Intelligence in Personalized Learning with a Focus on Current Developments and Future Prospects. *Research and Advances in Education*, *3*(8), 25–31. DOI: 10.56397/RAE.2024.08.04

Maity, S., & Deroy, A. (2024). Human-Centric eXplainable AI in Education. *arXiv preprint arXiv:2410.19822*.https://doi.org//arXiv.2410.19822DOI: 10.35542/osf .io/k5u9b

Ma, K., Zhang, Y., & Hui, B.-H. (2024). How Does AI Affect College? The Impact of AI Usage in College Teaching on Students' Innovative Behavior and Well-Being. *Behavioral Sciences (Basel, Switzerland), 14*(12), 1223. DOI: 10.3390/bs14121223 PMID: 39767364

Makransky, G., & Mayer, R. E. (2022). Benefits of taking a virtual field trip in immersive virtual reality: Evidence for the immersion principle in multimedia learning. *Educational Psychology Review, 34*(3), 1771–1798. DOI: 10.1007/s10648-022-09675-4 PMID: 35475019

Malik, G., Tayal, D. K., & Vij, S. (2018). An analysis of the role of artificial intelligence in education and teaching. In Advances in intelligent systems and computing (pp. 407–417). DOI: 10.1007/978-981-10-8639-7_42

Mallillin, L. L. D. (2024). Artificial Intelligence (AI) Towards Students' Academic Performance. *Innovare Journal of Education, 16*, 16–21. Advance online publication. DOI: 10.22159/ijoe.2024v12i4.51665

Manca, S., & Ranieri, M. (2016). Is Facebook still a suitable technology-enhanced learning environment? An updated critical review of the literature from 2012 to 2015. *Journal of Computer Assisted Learning, 32*(6), 503–528. DOI: 10.1111/jcal.12154

Mandernach, B. J. (2006). Thinking Critically about Critical Thinking: Integrating Online Tools to Promote Critical Thinking. *InSight a Journal of Scholarly Teaching, 1*, 41–50. DOI: 10.46504/01200603ma

Mandinach, E. B., & Gummer, E. S. (2016). What does it mean for teachers to be data literate: Laying out the skills, knowledge, and dispositions. *Teaching and Teacher Education, 60*, 366–376. DOI: 10.1016/j.tate.2016.07.011

Mandinach, E. B., & Schildkamp, K. (2021). Misconceptions about data-based decision making in education: An exploration of the literature. *Studies in Educational Evaluation, 69*, 100842. DOI: 10.1016/j.stueduc.2020.100842

Mao, J., Chen, B., & Liu, J. C. (2023). Generative artificial intelligence in education and its implications for assessment. *TechTrends*, •••, 1–9.

Maphalala, M. C., & Ajani, O. A. (2025). Leveraging artificial intelligence as a learning tool in higher education. *Interdisciplinary Journal of Education Research, 7*(1), a01. Advance online publication. DOI: 10.38140/ijer-2025.vol7.1.01

Marougkas, A., Troussas, C., Krouska, A., & Sgouropoulou, C. (2023). Virtual reality in education: A review of learning theories, approaches and methodologies for the last decade. *Electronics (Basel), 12*(13), 2832. DOI: 10.3390/electronics12132832

Marshall, S., Blaj-Ward, L., Dreamson, N., Nyanjom, J., & Bertuol, M. T. (2024). The reshaping of higher education: Technological impacts, pedagogical change, and future projections. *Higher Education Research & Development*, *43*(3), 521–541. DOI: 10.1080/07294360.2024.2329393

Martinez, C. (2022). Developing 21st century teaching skills: A case study of teaching and learning through project-based curriculum. *Cogent Education*, *9*(1), 2024936. Advance online publication. DOI: 10.1080/2331186X.2021.2024936

Martin, F., & Bolliger, D. U. (2018). Engagement matters: Student perceptions on the importance of engagement strategies in the online learning environment. *Online Learning : the Official Journal of the Online Learning Consortium*, *22*(1), 205–222. DOI: 10.24059/olj.v22i1.1092

Martins, G. (2017). Perfil dos Alunos à Saída da Escolaridade Obrigatória. Lisboa, Portugal: Ministério da Educação/Direção Geral de Educação. Obtido de https://dge.mec.pt/sites/default/files/Curriculo/Projeto_Autonomia_e_Flexibilidade/perfil_dos_alunos.pdf

Mascarenhas, D. (2012). *Dificuldades e estratégias de ensino e aprendizagem da geometria e grandezas no 5º. Ano de Escolaridade do Ensino Básico nas Escolas EB 2/3 da Madalena e EB 2/3 de Pedrouços do Distrito do Porto*. Universidad de Granada.

Maurino, P. S. M. (2007). Looking for critical thinking in online threaded discussions. *Journal of Educational Technology Systems*, *35*(3), 241–260. DOI: 10.2190/P4W3-8117-K32G-R34M

Ma, W., Adesope, O. O., Nesbit, J. C., & Liu, Q. (2014). Intelligent tutoring systems and learning outcomes: A meta-analysis. *Journal of Educational Psychology*, *106*(4), 901–918. DOI: 10.1037/a0037123

Mayer, R. E. (2009). *Multimedia learning* (2nd ed.). Multimedia Learning., DOI: 10.1017/CBO9780511811678

Mayer, R. E. (2024). The past, present, and future of the cognitive theory of multimedia learning. *Educational Psychology Review*, *36*(1), 8. DOI: 10.1007/s10648-023-09842-1

Mazhar, A., & Al Rifaee, M. M. (2023). A systematic review of the use of virtual reality in education. In *2023 International Conference on Information Technology (ICIT), (422-427)*, Amman, Jordan. DOI: 10.1109/ICIT58056.2023.10225794

McDonald, N., Johri, A., Ali, A., & Collier, A. H. (2025). Generative artificial intelligence in higher education: Evidence from an analysis of institutional policies and guidelines. *Computers in Human Behavior: Artificial Humans, 3*, 100121. DOI: 10.1016/j.chbah.2025.100121

Means, B., Toyama, Y., Murphy, R., & Baki, M. (2013). The effectiveness of online and blended learning: A meta-analysis of the empirical literature. *Teachers College Record, 115*(3), 1–47. DOI: 10.1177/016146811311500307

Mehta, K. J., Agrawal, A., & Sanghi, S. (2021). Digital whiteboards as collaborative learning spaces: Case studies using Miro and Mural in remote education. *International Journal of Educational Technology in Higher Education, 18*, 26. Advance online publication. DOI: 10.1186/s41239-021-00262-4

Melchor-Couto, S. (2016). Foreign language anxiety levels in Second Life oral interaction. *ReCALL, 29*(1), 99–119. DOI: 10.1017/S0958344016000185

Méndez Alarcón, C. M., Lasekan, O. A., & Godoy Pena, M. T. (2025). AI concerns among educators: A thematic analysis. [IRJMS]. *International Research Journal of Multidisciplinary Scope, 6*(1), 1031–1045. DOI: 10.47857/irjms.2025.v06i01.01929

Mergen, M., Graf, N., & Meyerheim, M. (2024). Reviewing the current state of virtual reality integration in medical education-a scoping review. *BMC Medical Education, 24*(1), 788. DOI: 10.1186/s12909-024-05777-5 PMID: 39044186

Merino-Campos, C. (2025). *The Impact of Artificial Intelligence on Personalized Learning in Higher Education: A Systematic Review [Review of The Impact of Artificial Intelligence on Personalized Learning in Higher Education: A Systematic Review].* Trends in Higher Education, 4(2), 17. Multidisciplinary Digital Publishing Institute. DOI: 10.3390/higheredu4020017

Metin, E. (2018). Eğitimde teknoloji kullanımında öğretmen eğitimi: Bir durum çalışması [Teacher training in the use of technology in education: a case study]. *Journal of STEAM Education, 1*(1), 79–103.

Meyer, A., Rose, D. H., & Gordon, D. (2014). Universal design for learning : theory and practice. In *CAST Professional Publishing*. Cast professional Pub. https://cir.nii.ac.jp/crid/1130000797493904000

Meyer, A., Rose, D. H., & Gordon, D. (2014). *Universal Design for Learning: Theory and practice*. CAST Professional Publishing. https://www.cast.org/products-books/udl-theory-practice

Meyer, A., Rose, D. H., & Gordon, D. (2014). *Universal Design for Learning: Theory and Practice*. CAST Professional Publishing.

Miller, M. R., Herrera, F., Jun, H., Landay, J. A., & Bailenson, J. N. (2020). Personal identifiability of user tracking data during observation of 360-degree VR video. *Scientific Reports, 10*(1), 17404. DOI: 10.1038/s41598-020-74486-y

Ministério da Educação, (2018). Aprendizagens Essenciais de Matemática no Ensino Básico.

Ministério da Educação. (2001). *Programa de Matemática do Ensino Básico*. Departamento de Educação Básica.

Ministério da Educação. (2013). *Metas curriculares de matemática – Ensino básico*. Direção-Geral da Educação.

Ministério da Educação. (2021). Aprendizagens Essenciais de Matemática no Ensino Básico. Available from: https://www.dge.mec.pt/noticias/aprendizagens-essenciais-de-matematica

Mir, R., Mir, G. M., Raina, N. T., Mir, S., Mir, S. M., Miskeen, E., Alharthi, M. H., & Alamri, M. M. S. (2023). *Application of Artificial Intelligence in Medical Education: Current Scenario and Future Perspectives. [Review of Application of Artificial Intelligence in Medical Education: Current Scenario and Future Perspectives.]*. PubMed, 11(3), 133. National Institutes of Health. DOI: 10.30476/jamp.2023.98655.1803

Mishra, P., & Koehler, M. J. (2006). Technological pedagogical content knowledge: A framework for teacher knowledge. *Teachers College Record, 108*(6), 1017–1054. DOI: 10.1111/j.1467-9620.2006.00684.x

Mohd Amin, M. R., Ismail, I., & Sivakumaran, V. M. (2025). Revolutionizing education with artificial intelligence (AI)? Challenges, and implications for open and distance learning (ODL). *Social Sciences & Humanities Open, 11*, 101308. Advance online publication. DOI: 10.1016/j.ssaho.2025.101308

Molenaar, I., & Knoop-van Campen, C. A. N. (2019). How teachers make dashboard information actionable. *British Journal of Educational Technology, 50*(5), 2341–2356. DOI: 10.1111/bjet.12810

MoNE (Ministry of National Education). (2022). *FATİH Projesi Hakkında* [About the FATIH project]. https://olur.meb.gov.tr/www/fatih-projesi-hakkinda/icerik/370

MoNE. (2023). 21. Yüzyıl Becerileri ve Değerlere Yönelik Araştırma Raporu [Research Report on 21st Century Skills and Values]. https://ttkb.meb.gov.tr/meb_iys_dosyalar/2023_05/11153521_21.yy_becerileri_ve_degerlere_yonelik_arastirma_raporu.pdf

Moore, M. G., Dickson-Deane, C., & Galyen, K. (2011). E-learning, online learning, and distance learning environments: Are they the same? *The Internet and Higher Education, 14*(2), 129–135. DOI: 10.1016/j.iheduc.2010.10.001

Moore, R. L., & Miller, C. N. (2022). Fostering cognitive presence in online courses: A systematic review (2008-2020). *Online Learning : the Official Journal of the Online Learning Consortium, 26*(1), 130–149. DOI: 10.24059/olj.v26i1.3071

Mopara, R., & Sanrattana, W. (2023). Developing Teachers to Develop Students' 21st Century Skills. *World Journal of Education, 13*(3), 94–104. DOI: 10.5430/wje.v13n3p94

Moustaghfir, S., & Brigui, H. (2024). Navigating Critical Thinking in the Digital Era: An informative exploration. *International Journal of Linguistics Literature & Translation, 7*(1), 137–143. DOI: 10.32996/ijllt.2024.7.1.11x

Muhie, Y. A., & Woldie, A. B. (2020). *Integration of Artificial Intelligence Technologies in Teaching and Learning in Higher Education.* Science and Technology, 10(1), 1. http://www.sapub.org/global/showpaperpdf.aspx?doi=10.5923/j.scit.20201001.01

Mütterlein, J., & Hess, T. (2020). The role of immersive technologies in skill acquisition. Journal of VR in Learning.

Mystakidis, S. (2022). Metaverse. *Encyclopedia, 2*(1), 486–497. DOI: 10.3390/encyclopedia2010031

National Council of Teachers of Mathematics (NCTM). (2014). *Principles to actions: Ensuring mathematical success for all.* NCTM.

National Council of Teachers of Mathematics (NCTM). (2023). Artificial Intelligence in mathematics teaching: A position of the National Council of Teachers of Mathematics. https://www.nctm.org/standards-and-positions/Position Statements/Artificial-Intelligence-and-Mathematics-Teaching/

Neji, W., Boughattas, N., & Ziadi, F. (2023). Exploring New AI-Based Technologies to Enhance Students' Motivation. *Issues in Informing Science and Information Technology, 20*, 95. DOI: 10.28945/5149

Ng, D. T. K., Leung, J. K. L., Su, J., Ng, R. C. W., & Chu, S. K. W. (2023). Teachers' AI digital competencies and twenty-first century skills in the post-pandemic world. *Educational Technology Research and Development, 71*(1), 137–161. DOI: 10.1007/s11423-023-10203-6 PMID: 36844361

Nguyen, V. (2025). The Use of Generative AI Tools in Higher Education: Ethical and Pedagogical Principles. *Journal of Academic Ethics, 23*(3), 1435–1455. Advance online publication. DOI: 10.1007/s10805-025-09607-1

Nichat, A., Gajbe, U., Bankar, N. J., Singh, B. R., & Badge, A. K. (2023). Flipped Classrooms in Medical Education: Improving Learning Outcomes and Engaging Students in Critical Thinking Skills. *Cureus, 15*(11), e48199. DOI: 10.7759/cureus.48199 PMID: 38054140

Nikbay Arslantaş, Ç., & Bavlı, B. (2024). School-based outdoor education: A neglected practice at secondary level. *Journal of Adventure Education and Outdoor Learning, 24*(2), 270–286. DOI: 10.1080/14729679.2022.2143385

Ning, J., Ma, Z., Yao, J., Wang, Q., & Zhang, B. (2025). Personalized learning supported by learning analytics: A systematic review of functions, pathways, and educational outcomes. *Interactive Learning Environments, 33*(8), 1–23. DOI: 10.1080/10494820.2025.2478437

Noetel, M., Griffith, S., Delaney, O., Sanders, T., Parker, P., del Pozo Cruz, B., & Lonsdale, C. (2021). Video improves learning in higher education: A systematic review. *Review of Educational Research, 91*(2), 204–236. DOI: 10.3102/0034654321990713

Noonoo, S. (2019). *Playing games can build 21st-century skills. Research explains how.* https://www.edsurge.com/news/2019-02-12-playing-games-can-build-21st-century-skills-research-explains-how

Norman, G. (2010). Likert scales, levels of measurement, and the "laws" of statistics. *Advances in Health Sciences Education : Theory and Practice, 15*(5), 625–632. DOI: 10.1007/s10459-010-9222-y PMID: 20146096

Novak, I., McIntyre, S., Morgan, C., Campbell, L., Dark, L., Morton, N., Stumbles, E., Wilson, S.-A., & Goldsmith, S. (2013). A systematic review of interventions for children with cerebral palsy: State of the evidence. *Developmental Medicine \& Child Neurology, 55*(10), 885–910. DOI: 10.1111/dmcn.12246

Novak, K., & Rose, D. H. (2016). *UDL Now! A teacher's guide to applying Universal Design for Learning in today's classrooms* (2nd ed.). CAST Professional Publishing., https://www.castpublishing.org

Nwana, H. S. (1990). Intelligent tutoring systems: An overview. *Artificial Intelligence Review, 4*(4), 251–277. DOI: 10.1007/BF00168958

O'Dea, X., & O'Dea, M. (2023). Is Artificial Intelligence Really the Next Big Thing in Learning and Teaching in Higher Education? A Conceptual Paper. *Journal of University Teaching & Learning Practice, 20*(5). Advance online publication. DOI: 10.53761/1.20.5.06

Oates, G. (2011). Sustaining integrated technology in undergraduate mathematics. *International Journal of Mathematical Education in Science and Technology, 42*(6), 709–721. DOI: 10.1080/0020739X.2011.575238

OECD. (2018). *Teaching for the Future: Effective Classroom Practices To Transform Education*. OECD Publishing., DOI: 10.1787/9789264293243-

OECD. (2019). OECD future of education and skills 2030: OECD learning compass 2030. *A Series of Concept Notes,* https://www.oecd.org/content/dam/oecd/en/about/projects/edu/education-2040/1-1-learning-compass/OECD_Learning_Compass_2030_Concept_Note_Series.pdf

OECD. (2019). OECD Learning Compass 2030: A series of concept notes. oecd/en/about/projects/edu/education-2040/1-1-learning-compass/OECD_Learning_Compass_2030_Concept_Note_Series.pdf

OECD. (2019). PISA 2018 results (Volume I): What students know and can do. OECD Publishing. https://www.oecd.org/en/publications/2019/12/pisa-2018-results-volume-i_947e3529.html

OECD. (2021). *21st-Century Readers: Developing Literacy Skills in a Digital World*. OECD Publishing., DOI: 10.1787/a83d84cb-

OECD. (2023). *Artificial Intelligence and the Future of Skills: Capabilities and Assessments*. OECD Publishing., DOI: 10.1787/5ee71f34-

Ofosu-Asare, Y. (2024). Cognitive imperialism in artificial intelligence: Counteracting bias with indigenous epistemologies. *AI & Society*. Advance online publication. DOI: 10.1007/s00146-024-02065-0

Ok, M. W., Rao, K., Bryant, B. R., & McDougall, D. (2022). Universal Design for Learning in inclusive classrooms: Recent trends and directions for future research. *Learning Disabilities Research & Practice, 37*(2), 75–84. DOI: 10.1111/ldrp.12238

Oktaviani, H. I., & Utami, D. D. (2024). Development Of Training Programs to Enhance Teachers' Digital Skills with Technological Pedagogical Content Knowledge (TPACK). *Journal of Educational Technology Studies and Applied Research, 1*(2). Advance online publication. DOI: 10.70125/jetsar.v1i2y2024a23

Omughelli, D., Gordon, N., & Al Jaber, T. (2024). Fairness, bias, and ethics in AI: Exploring the factors affecting student performance. *Journal of International Communication*, *3*(2), 100–110.

Onesi-Ozigagun, O., Ololade, Y. J., Eyo-Udo, N. L., & Ogundipe, D. O. (2024). *Revolutionizing education through AI: A comprehensive review of enhancing learning experiences [review of revolutionizing education through AI: A comprehensive review of enhancing learning experiences]*. International Journal of Applied Research in Social Sciences, 6(4), 589. Fair East Publishers. DOI: 10.51594/ijarss.v6i4.1011

Onions, P. (2009). Thinking Critically An introduction. https://www.semanticscholar.org/paper/Thinking-Critically-An-introduction-Onions/0409cf62b55da25a6ebbe64a3114c921edb43f5a

OpenStax. (2023). *About us*. https://openstax.org/about

Opesemowo, O. A. G., & Adewuyi, H. O. (2024). *A systematic review of artificial intelligence in mathematics education: The emergence of 4IR [Review of A systematic review of artificial intelligence in mathematics education: The emergence of 4IR]*. Eurasia Journal of Mathematics, Science and Technology Education, 20(7). Modestum Limited. DOI: 10.29333/ejmste/14762

Oruganti, N. R. (2024). The Transformative Impact of AI in Education: A Technical Analysis. *International Journal of Scientific Research in Computer Science Engineering and Information Technology*, *10*(6), 1457–1464. DOI: 10.32628/CSEIT241061181

Ouyang, F., Wu, M., Zheng, L., Zhang, L., & Jiao, P. (2023). Integration of artificial intelligence performance prediction and learning analytics to improve student learning in online engineering course. *International Journal of Educational Technology in Higher Education*, *20*(1), 4. Advance online publication. DOI: 10.1186/s41239-022-00372-4 PMID: 36683653

Özgem, K., & Akçıl, U. (2022). An Investigation of Preschool Level Out-of-Class Education Activities in Finland, Estonia, Ireland, and Turkey within the Framework of 21st Century Skills. *Sustainability (Basel)*, *14*(14), 8736. DOI: 10.3390/su14148736

Palacios-Hidalgo, F. J., & Huertas-Abril, C. A. (2021). Effects of hybrid education in pre-service EFL and bilingual primary teachers' digital literacy. In *2021 1st Conference on Online Teaching for Mobile Education (OT4ME)*, (pp. 73-77). IEEE.

Palha, S., Bouwer, A., Webb, K., van Smaalen, D., & Agterberg, D. (2024, October). Game-based Pedagogy in Teacher Training: Results of a Pilot Course. In *European Conference on Games Based Learning*, 677-684. Academic Conferences International Limited. https://doi.org/DOI: 10.34190/ecgbl.18.1.2698

Pantoja, A., & Gonçalves, S. (2020). El tutor como agente de cambio y las buenas prácticas. In Pantoja, A. (Ed.), *Buenas prácticas en la tutoría universitária* (pp. 17–38). Editorial Síntesis.

Papamitsiou, Z., & Economides, A. A. (2014). Learning analytics and educational data mining in practice: A systematic literature review of empirical evidence. *Journal of Educational Technology & Society*, *17*(4), 49–64.

Papert, S. (1980). *Mindstorms: Children, Computers, and Powerful Ideas*. Basic Books.

Park, D. M., & Lee, H. J. (2024). Literature review of AI hallucination research since the advent of ChatGPT: Focusing on papers from arXiv. *Informatization Policy*, *31*(2), 3–38.

Park, J., Teo, T. W., Teo, A., Chang, J., Huang, J. S., & Koo, S. (2023). Integrating artificial intelligence into science lessons: Teachers' experiences and views. *International Journal of STEM Education*, *10*(1), 61. Advance online publication. DOI: 10.1186/s40594-023-00454-3

Park, S. (2023). Discovering unproductive learning patterns of wheel-spinning students in intelligent tutors using cluster analysis. *TechTrends*, *67*(3), 489–497. DOI: 10.1007/s11528-023-00847-9

Parlak, B., & Sendurur, E. (2022). The Integration of GBS into a Technologically Restricted Context to Improve Digital Literacy. *Journal of Educational Multimedia and Hypermedia*, *31*(2), 149–178.

Partridge, J. (2022). *Digital games-based learning: Minecraft in the 21st century classroom* (Doctoral dissertation, University of British Columbia). ProQuest Dissertations & Theses Global.

Paskevicius, M., & Irvine, V. (2019). Open education and learning design: Open pedagogy in practice. *Journal of Interactive Media in Education*, *2019*(1), 1–13. DOI: 10.5334/jime.512

Pasquale, F. (2015). *The black box society: The secret algorithms that control money and information*. Harvard University Press. DOI: 10.4159/harvard.9780674736061

Patton, M. Q. (2002). *Qualitative research and evaluation methods* (3rd ed.). SAGE Publications.

Pavlova, N. H. (2024). Flipped dialogic learning method with ChatGPT: A case study. *International Electronic Journal of Mathematics Education, 19*(1), em0764. Advance online publication. DOI: 10.29333/iejme/14025

Pei, L., & Wu, H. (2019). Does online learning work better than offline learning in undergraduate medical education? A systematic review and meta-analysis. *Medical Education Online, 24*(1), 1666538. DOI: 10.1080/10872981.2019.1666538 PMID: 31526248

Pelech, J. (2010). *The comprehensive handbook of constructivist teaching: From theory to practice* (Pieper, G., Ed.). IAP Information Age Publishing.

Pennington, L., Goldbart, J., & Marshall, J. (2004). Interaction training for conversational partners of children with cerebral palsy: A systematic review. *International Journal of Language \& Communication Disorders, 39*(2), 151–170. DOI: 10.1080/13682820310001625598

Perla, L., Agrati, L. S., & Beri, A. (2025). Post-teaching and professional learning: An investigation on teachers attitudes towards AI. *Professional Development in Education, 51*(3), 1–12. DOI: 10.1080/19415257.2025.2465970

Perry, A. M. (2022). Student engagement, nol earning without it. *Creative Education, 13*(04), 1312–1326. DOI: 10.4236/ce.2022.134079

Perryman, L. A., & de los Arcos, B. (2016). Women's empowerment through openness: OER, OEP and the Sustainable Development Goals. *Open Praxis, 8*(2), 163–180. DOI: 10.5944/openpraxis.8.2.289

Pesovski, I., Santos, R., Henriques, R., & Trajkovik, V. (2024). Generative AI for customizable learning experiences. *Sustainability (Basel), 16*(7), 3034. DOI: 10.3390/su16073034

Peters, M., Elasri Ejjaberi, A., Martínez, M. J., & Fàbregues, S. (2022). Teacher digital competence development in higher education: Overview of systematic reviews. *Australasian Journal of Educational Technology, 38*(3), 122–139. DOI: 10.14742/ajet.7543

Peterson, M., & Jabbari, N. (2022). Digital games in language learning: Case studies and applications. *Digital Games in Language Learning: Case Studies and Applications*, (December), 1–184. DOI: 10.4324/9781003240075

Philipsen, B., Tondeur, J., Roblin, N. P., Vanslambrouck, S., & Zhu, C. (2019). Improving teacher professional development for online and blended learning: A systematic meta-aggregative review. *Educational Technology Research and Development, 67*(5), 1145–1174. DOI: 10.1007/s11423-019-09645-8

Phillips, A., Pane, J. F., Reumann-Moore, R., & Shenbanjo, O. (2020). Implementing an adaptive intelligent tutoring system as an instructional supplement. *Educational Technology Research and Development, 68*(3), 1409–1437. DOI: 10.1007/s11423-020-09745-w

Phua, J. T. K., Neo, H. F., & Teo, C.-C. (2025). Evaluating the Impact of Artificial Intelligence Tools on Enhancing Student Academic Performance: Efficacy Amidst Security and Privacy Concerns. *Big Data and Cognitive Computing, 9*(5), 131. DOI: 10.3390/bdcc9050131

Phumeechanya, N., & Wannapiroon, P. (2014). Ubiquitous scaffold learning environment using problem-based learning to enhance problem-solving skills and context awareness. https://arxiv.org/pdf/1401.2234.pdf

Piaget, J. (1952). *The origins of intelligence in children* (Cook, M., Trans.). International Universities Press. (Original work published 1936) DOI: 10.1037/11494-000

Pierres, O., Christen, M., Schmitt-Koopmann, F. M., & Darvishy, A. (2024). Could the Use of AI in Higher Education Hinder Students With Disabilities? A Scoping Review. *IEEE Access, 12*(December 2023), 27810–27828. DOI: 10.1109/ACCESS.2024.3365368

Pirker, J., & Dengel, A. (2021). The potential of 360° virtual reality videos and real VR for education—A literature review. *IEEE Computer Graphics and Applications, 41*(4), 76–89. DOI: 10.1109/MCG.2021.3067999 PMID: 33755559

Pithers, R., & Soden, R. (2000). Critical thinking in education: A review. *Educational Research, 42*(3), 237–249. DOI: 10.1080/001318800440579

Ploetzner, R. (2024). The effectiveness of enhanced interaction features in educational videos: A meta-analysis. *Interactive Learning Environments, 32*(5), 1597–1612.

Pohn, B., Mehnen, L., Fitzek, S., Choi, K., Braun, R. J., & Hatamikia, S. (2025). Integrating artificial intelligence into pre-clinical medical education: Challenges, opportunities, and recommendations. *Frontiers in Education, 10*, 1570389. Advance online publication. DOI: 10.3389/feduc.2025.1570389

Pongsakdi, N., Kortelainen, A., & Veermans, M. (2021). The impact of digital pedagogy training on in-service teachers' attitudes towards digital technologies. *Education and Information Technologies*, *26*(5), 5041–5054. DOI: 10.1007/s10639-021-10439-w

Popenici, S. A., & Kerr, S. (2017). Exploring the impact of artificial intelligence on teaching and learning in higher education. *Research and Practice in Technology Enhanced Learning*, *12*(1), 22. DOI: 10.1186/s41039-017-0062-8 PMID: 30595727

Portugal. Ministério da Educação. (2018a). *Decreto-Lei n.º 54/2018, de 6 de julho: Estabelece o regime jurídico da educação inclusiva*. https://dre.pt/dre/detalhe/decreto-lei/54-2018-115652962

Portugal. Ministério da Educação. (2018b). *Decreto-Lei n.º 55/2018 de 6 de julho: Estabelece o currículo dos ensinos básico e secundário e os princípios orientadores da avaliação das aprendizagens*. https://dre.pt/dre/detalhe/decreto-lei/55-2018-115652962

Prensky, M. (2001). Digital natives, digital immigrants. *On the Horizon*, *9*(5), 1–6. DOI: 10.1108/10748120110424816

Przybylski, A. K., Murayama, K., DeHaan, C. R., & Gladwell, V. (2013). Motivational, emotional, and behavioral correlates of fear of missing out. *Computers in Human Behavior*, *29*(4), 1841–1848. DOI: 10.1016/j.chb.2013.02.014

Qian, M., & Clark, K. R. (2016). GBL and 21st century skills: A review of recent research. *Computers in Human Behavior*, *63*, 50–58. DOI: 10.1016/j.chb.2016.05.023

Qiao, J., Xu, J., Li, L., & Ouyang, Y. Q. (2021). The integration of immersive virtual reality simulation in interprofessional education: A scoping review. *Nurse Education Today*, *98*, 104773. DOI: 10.1016/j.nedt.2021.104773 PMID: 33497990

Qiu, Y., Pan, J., & Ishak, N. A. (2022). Effectiveness of Artificial Intelligence (AI) in Improving Pupils' Deep Learning in Primary School Mathematics Teaching in Fujian Province. *Computational Intelligence and Neuroscience*, *1*, 1–10. Advance online publication. DOI: 10.1155/2022/1362996 PMID: 36193186

Rabello, C., & Tavares, K. (2016). Tecnologias digitais no ensino superior: Das possibilidades e tendências à superação de barreiras e desafios. In J. Farbiarz, A. Farbiarz & B. Hemais (Orgs.), Design para uma educação inclusiva (pp. 25-36). Blucher. DOI: 10.5151/9788580392012-02

Rad, H. S. (2025). Reinforcing L2 reading comprehension through artificial intelligence intervention: Refining engagement to foster self-regulated learning. *Smart Learning Environments*, *12*(1), 23. Advance online publication. DOI: 10.1186/s40561-025-00377-2

Radianti, J., Majchrzak, T. A., Fromm, J., & Wohlgenannt, I. (2020). A systematic review of immersive virtual reality applications for higher education: Design elements, lessons learned, and research agenda. *Computers & Education*, *147*, 103778. DOI: 10.1016/j.compedu.2019.103778

Raes, A., Detienne, L., Windey, I., & Depaepe, F. (2020). A systematic literature review on synchronous hybrid learning: Gaps identified. *Learning Environments Research*, *23*(3), 269–290. DOI: 10.1007/s10984-019-09303-z

Ragni, B., Toto, G. A., di Furia, M., Lavanga, A., & Limone, P. (2023). The use of Digital GBL (DGBL) in teachers' training: a scoping review. In *Frontiers in Education, 8*. Frontiers Media SA. https://doi.org/DOI: 10.3389/feduc.2023.1092022

Rahman, M. M., & Watanobe, Y. (2023). ChatGPT for education and research: Opportunities, threats, and strategies. *Applied Sciences (Basel, Switzerland)*, *13*(9), 5783. DOI: 10.3390/app13095783

Rao, K., Ok, M. W., & Bryant, B. R. (2014). A Review of Research on Universal Design Educational Models. *Remedial and Special Education*, *35*(3), 153–166. DOI: 10.1177/0741932513518980

Rao, K., Smith, S. J., & Lowrey, K. A. (2017). UDL and intellectual disability: What do we know and where do we go? *Intellectual and Developmental Disabilities*, *55*(1), 37–44. DOI: 10.1352/1934-9556-55.1.37

Rapanta, C., Botturi, L., Goodyear, P., Guàrdia, L., & Koole, M. (2020). Online University Teaching During and After the Covid-19 Crisis: Refocusing Teacher Presence and Learning Activity. *Postdigit Sci Educ*, *2*(3), 923–945. DOI: 10.1007/s42438-020-00155-y PMID: 40477148

RASHMI. (2023). Unlocking the Potential of AI in Education: Challenges and Opportunities. *International Journal For Multidisciplinary Research*, *5*(4), 1–11. DOI: 10.36948/ijfmr.2023.v05i04.5955

Ravitz, J. L., Becker, H. J., & Wong, Y. (2000). Constructivist-Compatible Beliefs and Practices among US Teachers. Teaching, Learning, and Computing: 1998 National Survey Report# 4.

Ray, S., & Ray, D. P. (2024). Artificial Intelligence in Education: Navigating the Nexus of Innovation and Ethics for Future Learning Landscapes. *International Journal of Research -GRANTHAALAYAH, 11*(12), 163–174. DOI: 10.29121/granthaalayah.v11.i12.2023.5464

Redecker, C., & Punie, Y. (2017). *European framework for the digital competence of educators - DigCompEdu*. Publications Office of the European Union. https://data.europa.eu/doi/10.2760/159770

Redecker, C. (2017). *European Framework for the Digital Competence of Educators: DigCompEdu*. Joint Research Centre, European Commission., DOI: 10.2760/159770

Redecker, C., & Punie, Y. (2017). *European Framework for the Digital Competence of Educators (DigCompEdu)*. Publications Office of the European Union., DOI: 10.2760/178382

Regmi, K., & Jones, L. (2020). A systematic review of the factors - enablers and barriers - affecting e-learning in health sciences education. *BMC Medical Education, 20*(1), 91. DOI: 10.1186/s12909-020-02007-6 PMID: 32228560

Reigeluth, C. M. (2014). The learner-centered paradigm of education: Roles for technology. *Educational Technology*, •••, 18–21.

Reigeluth, C. M., Watson, W. R., Watson, S. S. L., Dutta, P., Chen, Z., & Powell, N. D. (2008). Roles for technology in the information-age paradigm of education: Learning management systems. *Educational Technology, 48*(6), 32–39. DOI: 10.4018/978-1-61350-347-8.ch003

Reinders, H., & White, C. (2011). Learner autonomy and new learning environments. *Language Learning & Technology, 15*(3), 1–3. DOI: 10.64152/10125/44254

Ribeiro, N., & Subrahmanyam, S. (2021). Emotional challenges of teaching online during pandemic. In Sony, K. K., Verma, N., & Uddin, M. (Eds.), *Psychosocial issues in Covid-19 pandemic* (pp. 244–255). SHINE Publication. RED.

Ritchhart, R. (2015). *Creating cultures of thinking: The 8 forces we must master to truly transform our schools*. John Wiley & Sons.

Rizvi, M. (2023). Exploring the landscape of artificial intelligence in education: Challenges and opportunities. (2023, June 8). IEEE Conference Publication | IEEE Xplore. https://ieeexplore.ieee.org/document/10156773

Robinson, L., Schulz, J., Blank, G., Ragnedda, M., Ono, H., Hogan, B., Mesch, G. S., Cotten, S. R., Kretchmer, S. B., Hale, T. M., Drabowicz, T., Yan, P., Wellman, B., Harper, M.-G., Quan-Haase, A., Dunn, H. S., Casilli, A. A., Tubaro, P., Carvath, R., & Khilnani, A. (2020). Digital inequalities 2.0: Legacy inequalities in the information age. *First Monday, 25*(7). Advance online publication. DOI: 10.5210/fm.v25i7.10842

Roesner, F., Kohno, T., & Molnar, D. (2014). Security and privacy for augmented reality systems. *Communications of the ACM, 57*(4), 88–96. DOI: 10.1145/2580723.2580730

Romero Rodríguez, L., Sánchez-Alzola, A., & Salazar, A. (2025). Serious games in engineering education: Assessing novelty effects and the influence of prior gaming experience. *Computer Applications in Engineering Education, 33*(3), e70021. DOI: 10.1002/cae.70021

Rönnlund, M., Ledman, K., Nylund, M., & Rosvall, P. (2019). Life skills for 'real life': How critical thinking is contextualised across vocational programmes. *Educational Research, 61*(3), 302–318. DOI: 10.1080/00131881.2019.1633942

Rose, D. H., & Meyer, A. (2002). *Teaching Every Student in the Digital Age: Universal Design for Learning*. Association for Supervision and Curriculum Development.

Roshanaei, M., Olivares, H., & Lopez, R. R. (2023). Harnessing AI to Foster Equity in Education: Opportunities, Challenges, and Emerging Strategies. *Journal of Intelligent Learning Systems and Applications, 15*(4), 123–143. DOI: 10.4236/jilsa.2023.154009

Roueche, B.. (2021). Virtual simulation in medical training: A review. *Medical Education.*

Rovai, A. P. (2002). Building sense of community at a distance. *International Review of Research in Open and Distance Learning, 3*(1), 1–16. DOI: 10.19173/irrodl.v3i1.79

Rumberger, R. W., & Rotermund, S. (2012). The relationship between engagement and high school dropout. In Christenson, S. L., Reschly, A. L., & Wylie, C. (Eds.), *Handbook of research on student engagement* (pp. 491–513). Springer. DOI: 10.1007/978-1-4614-2018-7_24

Runco, M. A., & Jaeger, G. J. (2012). The standard definition of creativity. *Creativity Research Journal, 24*(1), 92–96. DOI: 10.1080/10400419.2012.650092

Saavedra, A. R., & Opfer, V. D. (2012). Learning 21st-century skills requires 21st-century teaching. *Phi Delta Kappan, 94*(2), 8–13. DOI: 10.1177/003172171209400203

Saca, P. (2023). Designing Accessible Immersive Learning Experiences. *Journal of Technology-Integrated Lessons and Teaching*, *2*(1), 78–87. DOI: 10.13001/jtilt.v2i1.7669

Sadler, D. R. (1989). Formative assessment and the design of instructional systems. *Instructional Science*, *18*(2), 119–144. DOI: 10.1007/BF00117714

Sailer, M., & Homner, L. (2020). The gamification of learning: A meta-analysis. *Educational Psychology Review*, *32*(1), 77–112. DOI: 10.1007/s10648-019-09498-w

Sailer, M., Maier, R., Berger, S., Kastorff, T., & Stegmann, K. (2024). Learning activities in technology-enhanced learning: A systematic review of meta-analyses and second-order meta-analysis in higher education. *Learning and Individual Differences*, *112*, 102446. DOI: 10.1016/j.lindif.2024.102446

Sajja, R., Sermet, Y., Cwiertny, D., & Demir, I. (2023). Platform-independent and curriculum-oriented intelligent assistant for higher education. *International Journal of Educational Technology in Higher Education*, *20*(1), 42. DOI: 10.1186/s41239-023-00412-7

Saleh, S. E. (2019). *CRITICAL THINKING AS a 21st CENTURY SKILL: CONCEPTIONS, IMPLEMENTATION AND CHALLENGES IN THE EFL CLASSROOM*. European Journal of Foreign Language Teaching., DOI: 10.46827/ejfl.v0i0.2209

Salomon, G. (1998). Novel constructivist learning environments and novel technologies: Some issues to be considered. *Learning and Instruction*, *1*(1), 3–12. DOI: 10.1016/S0959-4752(98)00007-3

Samala, A. D., Bojic, L., Vergara-Rodríguez, D., Klimova, B., & Ranuharja, F. (2023). Exploring the impact of gamification on 21st-century skills: Insights from DOTA 2. *International Journal of Interactive Mobile Technologies*, *17*(18), 33–54. Advance online publication. DOI: 10.3991/ijim.v17i18.42161

Samuel, Y., Brennan-Tonetta, M., Samuel, J., Kashyap, R., Kumar, V., Krishna Kaashyap, S., Chidipothu, N., Anand, I., & Jain, P. (2023). Cultivation of human centered artificial intelligence: Culturally adaptive thinking in education (CATE) for AI. *Frontiers in Artificial Intelligence*, *6*, 1–13. DOI: 10.3389/frai.2023.1198180 PMID: 38106981

Sanabria-Z, J., Alfaro-Ponce, B., Argüelles-Cruz, A., & Ramírez-Montoya, M. S. (2023). AI-Based Platform Design for Complex Thinking Assessment: A case study of an Ideathon using the Transition Design approach. *Computers in the Schools*, *40*(4), 391–411. DOI: 10.1080/07380569.2023.2256711

Sanusi, I. T., Ayanwale, M. A., & Tolorunleke, A. E. (2024). Investigating pre-service teachers' artificial intelligence perception from the perspective of planned behavior theory. *Computers and Education: Artificial Intelligence*, *6*(100202), 1–15. DOI: 10.1016/j.caeai.2024.100202

Saputra, I., Astuti, M., Sayuti, M., & Kusumastuti, D. (2023). Integration of Artificial Intelligence in Education: Opportunities, Challenges, Threats and Obstacles. A Literature Review. *Indonesian Journal of Computer Science*, *12*(4). Advance online publication. DOI: 10.33022/ijcs.v12i4.3266

Savickaite, S. (2023). *Using virtual reality to explore individual differences in perception due to neurodiversity* [University of Glasgow]. https://theses.gla.ac.uk/84098/

Schellens, T., & Valcke, M. (2006). Fostering knowledge construction in university students through asynchronous discussion groups. *Computers & Education*, *46*(4), 349–370. DOI: 10.1016/j.compedu.2004.07.010

Schildkamp, K., Lai, M. K., & Earl, L. (2019). *Data-based decision making in education: Challenges and opportunities*. Springer.

Schildkamp, K., & Poortman, C. (2015). Factors influencing the functioning of data teams. *Teachers College Record*, *117*(4), 1–42. DOI: 10.1177/016146811511700403

Schleicher, A. (2020). *The Impact of COVID-19 on Education: Insights from" Education at a Glance 2020*. OECD Publishing.

Seale, J. (2014). *E-learning and disability in higher education: Accessibility research and practice* (2nd ed.). Routledge.

Seebut, S., Wongsason, P., & Kim, D. (2024). Combining GPT and Colab as learning tools for students to explore the numerical solutions of difference equations. *Eurasia Journal of Mathematics, Science and Technology Education*, *20*(1), em2377. DOI: 10.29333/ejmste/13905

Self, J. (1990). Theoretical foundations for intelligent tutoring systems. *Journal of Artificial Intelligence in Education*, *1*(4), 3–14.

Selwyn, N. (2016). *Education and Technology: Key Issues and Debates* (2nd ed.). Bloomsbury Academic.

Selwyn, N. (2019). *Should robots replace teachers? AI and the future of education*. John Wiley & Sons.

Sequí-Domínguez, I., Cavero-Redondo, I., Álvarez-Bueno, C., López-Gil, J. F., Martínez-Vizcaíno, V., & Pascual-Morena, C. (2024). Effectiveness of eHealth Interventions Promoting Physical Activity in Children and Adolescents: Systematic Review and Meta-Analysis. *Journal of Medical Internet Research*, *26*, e41649. DOI: 10.2196/41649 PMID: 38381490

Sha, L., Rakovic, M., Whitelock-Wainwright, A., Carroll, D., Yew, V. M., Gasevic, D., . . . (2021). *Assessing algorithmic fairness in automatic classifiers of educational forum posts. In Artificial Intelligence in Education: 22nd International Conference, AIED 2021*, (pp. 381-394), Utrecht, The Netherlands. DOI: 10.1007/978-3-030-78292-4_31

Shal, T., Ghamrawi, N., & Naccache, H. (2024). Leadership styles and AI acceptance in academic libraries in higher education. *Journal of Academic Librarianship*, *50*(2), 102849. Advance online publication. DOI: 10.1016/j.acalib.2024.102849

Shapiro, S. S., & Wilk, M. B. (1965). An analysis of variance test for normality (complete samples). *Biometrika*, *52*(3-4), 591–611. DOI: 10.1093/biomet/52.3-4.591

Sharma, S., Mittal, P., Kumar, M., & Bhardwaj, V. (2025). *The role of large language models in personalized learning: a systematic review of educational impact [Review of the role of large language models in personalized learning: a systematic review of educational impact]*. Discover Sustainability, 6(1). Springer Nature. DOI: 10.1007/s43621-025-01094-z

Sharples, M. (2023). Towards social generative AI for education: Theory, practices and ethics. *Learning: Research and Practice*, *9*(2), 159–167. Advance online publication. DOI: 10.1080/23735082.2023.2261131

Sharrab, Y., Almutiri, N. T., Tarawneh, M., Alzyoud, F., Al-Ghuwairi, A. R. F., & Al-Fraihat, D. (2023). Toward Smart and Immersive Classroom based on AI, VR, and 6G. *International Journal of Emerging Technologies in Learning*, *18*(2), 4–16. DOI: 10.3991/ijet.v18i02.35997

Shelby, S. J., & Fralish, Z. D. (2021). Using Edpuzzle to improve student experience and performance in the biochemistry laboratory. *Biochemistry and Molecular Biology Education*, *49*(5), 529–534. DOI: 10.1002/bmb.21494 PMID: 33666326

Sherin, M. G., & Van Es, E. A. (2009). Effects of video club participation on teachers' professional vision. *Journal of Teacher Education*, *60*(1), 20–37. DOI: 10.1177/0022487108328155

Siemens, G. (2005). Connectivism: A learning theory for the digital age. *International Journal of Instructional Technology and Distance Learning*, *2*(1), 3–10.

Siemens, G., & Gasevic, D. (2012). Guest editorial- learning and knowledge analytics. *Journal of Educational Technology & Society*, *15*(3), 1–2.

Silva, R. M., Martins, P., & Rocha, T. (2025). Virtual reality educational scenarios for students with ASD: Instruments validation and design of STEM programmatic contents. *Research in Autism Spectrum Disorders*, *119*, 102521. DOI: 10.1016/j.rasd.2024.102521

Singer, J. (1999). Why can't you be normal for once in your life? From a "Problem with No Name" to the emergence of a new category of difference. In Corker, M., & French, S. (Eds.), *Disability Discourse* (pp. 59–67). Open University Press.

Singh, A. (2023). Challenges of a multidisciplinary approach in higher education. *International Journal of Advanced Academic Studies*, *5*(9), 30–32. DOI: 10.33545/27068919.2023.v5.i9a.1049

Slade, S., & Prinsloo, P. (2013). Learning analytics: Ethical issues and dilemmas. *The American Behavioral Scientist*, *57*(10), 1510–1529. DOI: 10.1177/0002764213479366

Slimi, Z. (2023). The impact of artificial intelligence on higher education: An empirical study. *European Journal of Educational Sciences*. DOI: 10.19044/ejes.v10no1a17

Smutny, P., & Schreiberova, P. (2020). Chatbots for learning: A review of educational chatbots for the Facebook Messenger. *Computers & Education*, *151*, 103862. DOI: 10.1016/j.compedu.2020.103862

Snyder, L. G., & Snyder, M. (2008). Teaching critical thinking and problem solving skills. In The Delta Pi Epsilon Journal (Vols. 2–2). https://dme.childrenshospital.org/wp-content/uploads/2019/02/Optional-_Teaching-Critical-Thinking-and-Problem-Solving-Skills.pdf

Sophie Barat Achieng, D. M. (2024). Teacher professional development and learning outcomes in the 21st century. *IJRDO-. The Journal of Educational Research*, *10*(3), 46–54. DOI: 10.53555/er.v10i3.6190

Soylu, M. Y., & Lee, J. (2024, October). Analyzing interplay of metacognition, cognitive presence, and course performance in MOOCs and Master course forums. In *2024 IEEE Digital Education and MOOCS Conference (DEMOcon)*, (pp. 1-6). IEEE. DOI: 10.1109/DEMOcon63027.2024.10748167

Spasić, A. J., & Janković, D. S. (2023, June). Using ChatGPT standard prompt engineering techniques in lesson preparation: Role, instructions and seed-word prompts. In *2023 58th International Scientific Conference on Information, Communication and Energy Systems and Technologies (ICEST)* (pp. 47–50). IEEE.

Sperling, K., Stenberg, C. J., McGrath, C., Åkerfeldt, A., Heintz, F., & Stenliden, L. (2024). In search of artificial intelligence (AI) literacy in teacher education: A scoping review. *Computers and Education Open*, *6*, 100169. DOI: 10.1016/j.caeo.2024.100169

Squire, K. (2013). Video games and learning: Teaching and participatory culture in the digital age. *The Alberta Journal of Educational Research*, *59*(1), 129–132. DOI: 10.55016/ojs/ajer.v59i1.55771

Stacey, P. (2013). Government support for open educational resources: Policy, funding, and strategies. *International Review of Research in Open and Distance Learning*, *14*(2), 67–80. DOI: 10.19173/irrodl.v14i2.1537

Stammen, A. N., Malone, K. L., & Irving, K. E. (2018). Effects of modeling instruction professional development on biology teachers' scientific reasoning skills. *Education Sciences*, *8*(3), 119. DOI: 10.3390/educsci8030119

Steenbergen-Hu, S., & Cooper, H. (2013). A meta-analysis of the effectiveness of intelligent tutoring systems on K–12 students' mathematical learning. *Journal of Educational Psychology*, *105*(4), 970–987. DOI: 10.1037/a0032447

Subrahmanyam, S. (2024). Implementing agile talent management practices to adapt to changing higher education landscapes. In Kayyali, M. (Ed.), *Cultivating creativity and navigating talent management in academia* (pp. 187–210). IGI Global Scientific Publishing. DOI: 10.4018/979-8-3693-6880-0.ch009

Subrahmanyam, S. (2025). Qualitative Research Designs in Higher Education. In Mdikana, A. (Ed.), *Social Implications of Research in Higher Education* (pp. 263–296). IGI Global Scientific Publishing. DOI: 10.4018/979-8-3373-0654-4.ch010

Sullivan, A., & Bers, M. U. (2019). Computer science education in early childhood: The case of ScratchJr. *Journal of Information Technology Education: Innovations in Practice*, *18*, 113–138. DOI: 10.28945/4437

Sumakul, D. T. Y. G., & Hamied, F. A. (2023). Amotivation in AI injected EFL classrooms: Implications for teachers. *Indonesian Journal of Applied Linguistics*, *13*(1), 26–34. DOI: 10.17509/ijal.v13i1.58254

Sung, H., & Nathan, M. J. (2024). Your body tells how you engage in collaboration: Machine-detected body movements as indicators of engagement in collaborative math knowledge building. *British Journal of Educational Technology*, *55*(5), 1950–1973. DOI: 10.1111/bjet.13473

Su, Y., Lin, Y., & Lai, C. (2023). Collaborating with ChatGPT in argumentative writing classrooms. *Assessing Writing*, *57*, 100752. DOI: 10.1016/j.asw.2023.100752

Swain, M. (2005). The output hypothesis: Theory and research. In Hinkel, E. (Ed.), *Handbook of research in second language teaching and learning* (pp. 471–483). Routledge.

Swidan, A., Lee, S. Y., & Romdhane, S. B. (2025). College Students' Use and Perceptions of AI Tools in the UAE: Motivations, Ethical Concerns and Institutional Guidelines. *Education Sciences*, *15*(4), 461. DOI: 10.3390/educsci15040461

Tahir, M., Hassan, F. D., & Shagoo, M. R. (2024). *Role of artificial intelligence in education: A conceptual review [Review of Role of artificial intelligence in education: A conceptual review].* World Journal of Advanced Research and Reviews, 22(1), 1469. GSC Online Press. DOI: 10.30574/wjarr.2024.22.1.1217

Tan, C. (2017). Teaching critical thinking: Cultural challenges and strategies in Singapore. *British Educational Research Journal*, *43*(5), 988–1002. DOI: 10.1002/berj.3295

Tan, M. J. T., & Maravilla, N. M. A. T. (2024). Shaping integrity: Why generative artificial intelligence does not have to undermine education. *Frontiers in Artificial Intelligence*, *7*, 1471224. Advance online publication. DOI: 10.3389/frai.2024.1471224 PMID: 39512399

Tess, P. A. (2013). The role of social media in higher education classes (real and virtual) – A literature review. *Computers in Human Behavior*, *29*(5), A60–A68. DOI: 10.1016/j.chb.2012.12.032

The Impact of AI on Teaching and Learning in Higher Education Technology. (2022). The Impact of AI on Teaching and Learning in Higher Education Technology. *Journal of Higher Education Theory and Practice*, *22*(13). Advance online publication. DOI: 10.33423/jhetp.v22i13.5514

The MIT Press, Massachusetts Institute of Technology. (2025, June 23). Book details - MIT Press. MIT Press. https://mitpress.mit.edu/9780262538282/critical-thinking/

Theeuwes, B., Saab, N., Denessen, E., & Admiraal, W. (2025). Unraveling expert teachers' intercultural competence when facing a simulated multicultural classroom context. *Teaching and Teacher Education*, *162*(August), 105053. DOI: 10.1016/j.tate.2025.105053

Thelma, C. C., Sain, Z. H., Shogbesan, Y. O., Phiri, E. V., & Akpan, W. M. (2024). *Ethical* Implications of AI and Machine Learning in Education: A Systematic Analysis. 3(1), 1. DOI: 10.33650/ijit.v3i1.9364

Tlili, A., Shehata, B., Adarkwah, M. A., Bozkurt, A., Hickey, D. T., Huang, R., & Agyemang, B. (2023). What if the devil is my guardian angel: ChatGPT as a case study of using chatbots in education. *Smart Learning Environments, 10*(1), 15. DOI: 10.1186/s40561-023-00237-x

Tomlinson, C. A. (2014). *The differentiated classroom: Responding to the needs of all learners* (2nd ed.). ASCD.

Tondeur, J., Aesaert, K., Pynoo, B., van Braak, J., Fraeyman, N., & Erstad, O. (2015). Developing a validated instrument to measure pre-service teachers' ICT competencies: Meeting the demands of the 21st century. *British Journal of Educational Technology, 52*(2), 619–636. DOI: 10.1111/bjet.12380

Tondeur, J., Van Braak, J., Ertmer, P. A., & Ottenbreit-Leftwich, A. (2017). Understanding the relationship between teachers' pedagogical beliefs and technology use in education: A systematic review of qualitative evidence. *Educational Technology Research and Development, 65*(3), 555–575. DOI: 10.1007/s11423-016-9481-2

Trucano, M. & Information for Development Program. (2005). Knowledge Maps: ICT in Education. infoDev / World Bank. https://documents1.worldbank.org/curated/en/457411468341334749/pdf/319530WP0REVIS0800PUBLIC0Box379827B.pdf

U.S. Federal Trade Commission. (2013). *Children's Online Privacy Protection Rule ("COPPA").* https://www.ftc.gov/legal-library/browse/rules/childrens-online-privacy-protection-rule-coppa

UNESCO & Teacher Task Force. (2023). *Global report on teachers: Addressing teacher shortages*. UNESCO Publishing. https://www.unesco.org/en/articles/global-report-teachers-addressing-teacher-shortages-and-transforming-profession

UNESCO. (1994). Declaração de Salamanca sobre princípios, políticas e práticas na área das necessidades educativas especiais. *Conferência Mundial de Educação Especial.* https://unesdoc.unesco.org/ark:/48223/pf0000139394

UNESCO. (2012). *2012 Paris OER Declaration.* https://unesdoc.unesco.org/ark:/48223/pf0000217019

UNESCO. (2015). *Rethinking education: Towards a global common good?* UNESCO Publishing. https://unesdoc.unesco.org/ark:/48223/pf0000232555

UNESCO. (2017). *A guide for ensuring inclusion and equity in education.* UNESCO Publishing. https://unesdoc.unesco.org/ark:/48223/pf0000248254

UNESCO. (2017). *Ljubljana OER Action Plan 2017.* https://unesdoc.unesco.org/ark:/48223/pf0000259349

UNESCO. (2018). *ICT Competency Framework for Teachers* (3rd ed.). UNESCO. https://unesdoc.unesco.org/ark:/48223/pf0000265721

UNESCO. (2019). *Recommendation on Open Educational Resources (OER)*. https://unesdoc.unesco.org/ark:/48223/pf0000370936

UNESCO. (2020). *Global Education Monitoring Report 2020: Inclusion and education – All means all*. UNESCO Publishing. https://unesdoc.unesco.org/ark:/48223/pf0000373718

UNESCO. (2021). *Recommendation on the Ethics of Artificial Intelligence*. https://unesdoc.unesco.org/ark:/48223/pf0000380455

UNESCO. (2024). AI competency framework for teachers. UNESCO Publishing. Retrieved from https://unesdoc.unesco.org/ark:/48223/pf0000391104

Uribe-Enciso, O. L., Uribe-Enciso, D. S., & Vargas-Daza, M. D. (2017). Critical thinking and its importance in education: Some reflections. *Rastros Rostros*, *19*, 78–88. DOI: 10.16925/ra.v19i34.2144

Urrutia, F., & Araya, R. (2024). Who's the best detective? Large language models vs. traditional machine learning in detecting incoherent fourth grade math answers. *Journal of Educational Computing Research*, *61*(8), 187–218. DOI: 10.1177/07356331231191174

Uygun, D. (2024). Teachers' perspectives on artificial intelligence in education. *Advances in Mobile Learning Educational Research*, *4*(1), 931–939. Advance online publication. DOI: 10.25082/AMLER.2024.01.005

Vale, I. (2002). *Materiais manipuláveis*. ESEVC-LEM.

Van De Werfhorst, H. G., Kessenich, E., & Geven, S. (2022). The digital divide in online education: Inequality in digital readiness of students and schools. *Computers and Education Open*, *3*, 100100. DOI: 10.1016/j.caeo.2022.100100 PMID: 40478103

van der Rijst, R., Guo, P., & Admiraal, W. (2023). Student engagement in hybrid approaches to teaching in higher education. *Revista de Investigación Educacional*, *41*(2), 315–336. DOI: 10.6018/rie.562521

Van Dijk, J. A. G. M. (2020). *The digital divide*. Polity Press.

Van Hiele, P. M. (1986). *Structure and Insight: A Theory of Mathematics Education*. Academic Press.

VanLehn, K. (2011). The relative effectiveness of human tutoring, intelligent tutoring systems, and other tutoring systems. *Educational Psychologist*, *46*(4), 197–221. DOI: 10.1080/00461520.2011.611369

Vasconcelos, M. A. R., & Santos, R. P. D. (2023). Enhancing STEM learning with ChatGPT and Bing Chat as objects to think with: A case study. *arXiv preprint arXiv:2305.02202*.

Velander, J., Ahmed Taiye, M., Otero, N., Milrad, M., & Zijlema, A. (2023). Reflections on methods for eliciting teachers' understanding, attitudes and emotions about AI. In M. Milrad et al. (Eds.), *Methodologies and intelligent systems for technology enhanced learning. 13th International Conference, MIS4TEL 2023* (Lecture Notes in Networks and Systems, Vol. 764, pp. 124–135). Springer. https://doi.org/DOI: 10.1007/978-3-031-41226-4_13

Velli, K., & Zafiropoulos, K. (2024). Factors that affect the acceptance of educational AI tools by greek teachers—A structural equation modelling study. *European Journal of Investigation in Health, Psychology and Education*, *14*(9), 2560–2579. DOI: 10.3390/ejihpe14090169 PMID: 39329837

Viberg, O., Grönlund, Å., & Andersson, A. (2020). Integrating digital technology in mathematics education: A Swedish case study. *Interactive Learning Environments*, *31*(1), 232–243. DOI: 10.1080/10494820.2020.1770801

Vicari, R. M., Moreira, A. F., Menezes, P. F. B., (2018). Pensamento computacional: *revisão bibliográfica*.

Viczko, M. (2016). *A Rich Seam: How New Pedagogies Find Deep Learning*, by Michael Fullan and Maria Langworthy: (2014). London: Pearson. *Leadership and Policy in Schools*, *15*(2), 231–233. DOI: 10.1080/15700763.2015.1073331

Vieriu, A. M., & Petrea, G. (2025). The Impact of Artificial Intelligence (AI) on Students' Academic Development. *Education Sciences*, *15*(3), 343. DOI: 10.3390/educsci15030343

Vistorte, A. O. R., Deroncele-Acosta, Á., Ayala, J. L. M., Barrasa, Á., López-Granero, C., & Martí-González, M. (2024). Integrating artificial intelligence to assess emotions in learning environments: A systematic literature review. *Frontiers in Psychology*, *15*, 1387089. Advance online publication. DOI: 10.3389/fpsyg.2024.1387089 PMID: 38966729

Voogt, J., Erstad, O., Dede, C., & Mishra, P. (2015). Challenges to learning and schooling in the digital networked world of the 21st century. *Journal of Computer Assisted Learning*, *31*(5), 403–413. DOI: 10.1111/jcal.12029

Voulgari, I., Komis, V., & Sampson, D. G. (2014). Learning outcomes and processes in massively multiplayer online games: Exploring the perceptions of players. *Educational Technology Research and Development*, *62*(2), 245–270. DOI: 10.1007/s11423-013-9312-7

Vygotsky, L. S. (1978). *Mind in Society, The development of Higher Psychological Processes* (M. Cole, V. John-Steiner, S. Scribner, & E. Souberman, Eds.; Issue March). Harvard University Press.

Vygotsky, L. S. (1978). *Mind in society: The development of higher psychological processes* (Cole, M., Vera John-Steiner, S. S., & Souberman, E., Eds. & Trans.). Harvard University Press.

Vygotsky, L. S. (1978). *Mind in Society: The Development of Higher Psychological Processes*. Harvard University Press.

Wachira, P., & Keengwe, J. (2011). Technology integration barriers: Urban school mathematics teachers perspectives. *Journal of Science Education and Technology*, *20*(1), 17–25. DOI: 10.1007/s10956-010-9230-y

Walter, Y. (2024). Embracing the future of Artificial Intelligence in the classroom: The relevance of AI literacy, prompt engineering, and critical thinking in modern education. *International Journal of Educational Technology in Higher Education*, *21*(1), 15. Advance online publication. DOI: 10.1186/s41239-024-00448-3

Wang, X. (2025). Research and Practice on the Digital Transformation Path of Local Higher Education in the Era of Digital Intelligence. In *Proceedings of the 2nd International Conference on Educational Development and Social Sciences (EDSS 2025)* (Vol. 924, p. 360). Springer Nature. DOI: 10.2991/978-2-38476-400-6_44

Wang, A. I. (2015). The wear out effect of a game-based student response system. *Computers & Education*, *82*, 217–227. DOI: 10.1016/j.compedu.2014.11.004

Wang, F., Ni, X., Zhang, M., & Zhang, J. (2024). Educational digital inequality: A meta-analysis of the relationship between digital device use and academic performance in adolescents. *Computers & Education*, *213*(January), 105003. DOI: 10.1016/j.compedu.2024.105003

Wang, M. T., & Degol, J. (2014). Staying engaged: Knowledge and research needs in student engagement. *Child Development Perspectives*, *8*(3), 137–143. DOI: 10.1111/cdep.12073 PMID: 27087833

Wang, M., Wang, M., Xu, X., Yang, L., Cai, D., & Yin, M. (2023). Unleashing ChatGPT's power: A case study on optimizing information retrieval in flipped classrooms via prompt engineering. *IEEE Transactions on Learning Technologies*, *17*, 629–644. DOI: 10.1109/TLT.2023.3324714

Wang, N., Wang, X., & Su, Y. S. (2024). Critical analysis of the technological affordances, challenges and future directions of Generative AI in education: A systematic review. *Asia Pacific Journal of Education*, *44*(1), 139–155. DOI: 10.1080/02188791.2024.2305156

Wang, Q., & Li, Y. (2024). How virtual reality, augmented reality and mixed reality facilitate teacher education: A systematic review. *Journal of Computer Assisted Learning*, *40*(3), 1276–1294. DOI: 10.1111/jcal.12949

Ward, B., Bhati, D., Neha, F., & Guercio, A. (2025). *Analyzing the Impact of AI Tools on Student Study Habits and Academic Performance*. 2022 IEEE 12th Annual Computing and Communication Workshop and Conference (CCWC), 434. DOI: 10.1109/CCWC62904.2025.10903692

Wardat, Y., Tashtoush, M. A., AlAli, R., & Jarrah, A. M. (2023). ChatGPT: A revolutionary tool for teaching and learning mathematics. *Eurasia Journal of Mathematics, Science and Technology Education*, *19*(7), em2286. Advance online publication. DOI: 10.29333/ejmste/13272

Warschauer, M. (2004). Of digital divides and social multipliers: Combining language and technology for human development. In Fitzpatrick, A. (Ed.), *Information and communication technologies in the teaching and learning of foreign languages: State of the art, needs and perspectives* (pp. 46–52). UNESCO Institute for Information Technologies in Education., https://unesdoc.unesco.org/ark:/48223/pf0000139195

Wehrmann, F., & Zender, R. (2023). Inclusive Virtual Reality Learning: Review and "Best-Fit" Framework for Universal Learning. *Electronic Journal of e-Learning*, *21*(6), 1–15. DOI: 10.34190/ejel.21.6.3265

Wei, X. (2024, September). Evaluating chatGPT-4 and chatGPT-4o: performance insights from NAEP mathematics problem solving. In *Frontiers in education* (Vol. 9, p. 1452570). Frontiers Media SA. DOI: 10.3389/feduc.2024.1452570

Wei, X., Saab, N., & Admiraal, W. (2021). Assessment of cognitive, behavioral, and affective learning outcomes in massive open online courses: A systematic literature review. *Computers & Education*, *163*, 104097. DOI: 10.1016/j.compedu.2020.104097

Wenger, E., McDermott, R., & Snyder, W. M. (2002). *Cultivating communities of practice: A guide to managing knowledge*. Harvard Business School Press.

Wertsch, J. V. (1991). *Voices of the mind: A sociocultural approach to mediated action*. Harvard University Press.

What Works Clearinghouse. (2010, March). WWC intervention report middle school math: Plato Achieve Now. Retrieved from Department of Education, Institute of Education Sciences, website: http://ies.ed.gov/ncee/wwc/interventionreport.aspx?sid378

Wijnen-Meijer, M., Brandhuber, T., Schneider, A., & Berberat, P. O. (2022). Implementing Kolb's Experiential Learning Cycle by Linking Real Experience, Case-Based Discussion and Simulation. *Journal of Medical Education and Curricular Development*, *9*, 23821205221091511. DOI: 10.1177/23821205221091511 PMID: 35592131

Wiley, D. (2014). The access compromise and the 5th R. *Iterating Toward Openness*. https://opencontent.org/blog/archives/3221

Wiley, D., Bliss, T. J., & McEwen, M. (2014). Open educational resources: A review of the literature. In Spector, J. M. (Eds.), *Handbook of research on educational communications and technology* (pp. 781–789). Springer. DOI: 10.1007/978-1-4614-3185-5_63

Wiley, D., & Hilton, J.III. (2018). Defining OER-enabled pedagogy. *International Review of Research in Open and Distance Learning*, *19*(4), 133–147. DOI: 10.19173/irrodl.v19i4.3601

Wiley, D., Hilton, J.III, Ellington, S., & Hall, T. (2012). A preliminary examination of the cost savings and learning impacts of using open textbooks in middle and high school science classes. *International Review of Research in Open and Distance Learning*, *13*(3), 262–276. DOI: 10.19173/irrodl.v13i3.1153

Wiliam, D. (2011). *Embedded formative assessment*. Solution Tree Press.

Williamson, B. (2024). The Social life of AI in Education. In *International Journal of Artificial Intelligence in Education* (Vol. 34, Issue 1, pp. 97–104). DOI: 10.1007/s40593-023-00342-5

Williamson, B., & Eynon, R. (2020). Historical threads, missing links, and future directions. *AI in education. Learning, Media and Technology*, *45*(3), 223–235. DOI: 10.1080/17439884.2020.1798995

Wing, J. M. (2006). Computational thinking. *Communications of the ACM*, *49*(3), 33–35. DOI: 10.1145/1118178.1118215

Winn, W. (2002). Research into practice: Current trends in educational technology research: The study of learning environments. *Educational Psychology Review, 14*(3), 331–351. DOI: 10.1023/A:1016068530070

Wolfenden, F., Buckler, A., & Keraro, F. (2012). OER adaptation and reuse across cultural contexts in Sub-Saharan Africa: Lessons from TESSA (Teacher Education in Sub-Saharan Africa). *Journal of Interactive Media in Education, 2012*(1), 5. DOI: 10.5334/2012-03

Won, M., Ungu, D. A. K., Matovu, H., Treagust, D. F., Tsai, C.-C., Park, J., Mocerino, M., & Tasker, R. (2023). Diverse approaches to learning with immersive Virtual Reality identified from a systematic review. *Computers \& Education, 195*, 104701. DOI: 10.1016/j.compedu.2022.104701

Wood, D., Bruner, J. S., & Ross, G. (1976). The role of tutoring in problem solving. *Journal of Child Psychology and Psychiatry, and Allied Disciplines, 17*(2), 89–100. DOI: 10.1111/j.1469-7610.1976.tb00381.x

World Health Organization. (2021). *Global strategy on digital health 2020–2025.* World Health Organization. https://www.who.int/publications/i/item/9789240020924

World Wide Web Consortium. (W3C). (2023). *Web Content Accessibility Guidelines (WCAG) 2.2.* https://www.w3.org/TR/WCAG22/

Wu, J., Jiang, H., & Chen, S. (2024). Augmented reality technology in language learning: A meta-analysis. *Language Learning {\&} Technology, 28*(1), 1–23. https://hdl.handle.net/10125/73596

Wu, Y. T., & Wang, L. J. (2016). Research trends in technology-enhanced knowledge building pedagogies: A review of selected empirical research from 2006 to 2015. *Journal of Computers in Education, 3*(3), 353–375. DOI: 10.1007/s40692-016-0065-2

Xing, W., Song, Y., Li, C., Liu, Z., Zhu, W., & Oh, H. (2025). Development of a generative AI-powered teachable agent for middle school mathematics learning: A design-based research study. *British Journal of Educational Technology, 56*(5), 2043–2077. Advance online publication. DOI: 10.1111/bjet.13586

Xu, X. (2025). *AI optimization algorithms enhance higher education management and personalized teaching through empirical analysis [Review of AI optimization algorithms enhance higher education management and personalized teaching through empirical analysis].* Scientific Reports, 15(1). Nature Portfolio. DOI: 10.1038/s41598-025-94481-5

Xu, M., Luo, Y., Zhang, Y., Xia, R., Qian, H., & Zou, X. (2023). GBL in medical education. *Frontiers in Public Health, 11*, 1113682. DOI: 10.3389/fpubh.2023.1113682 PMID: 36935696

Xu, W., & Ouyang, F. (2022). A systematic review of AI role in the educational system based on a proposed conceptual framework. *Education and Information Technologies*, *27*(3), 4195–4223. DOI: 10.1007/s10639-021-10774-y

Yanar, A. N., & Ergene, Ö. (2025). Integrating artificial intelligence in education: How pre-service mathematics teachers use ChatGPT for 5E lesson plan design. *Journal of Pedagogical Research*, *9*(2), 158–176. DOI: 10.33902/JPR.202533163

Yang, X., Cheng, P. Y., Liu, X., & Shih, S. P. (2024). The impact of immersive virtual reality on art education: A study of flow state, cognitive load, brain state, and motivation. *Education and Information Technologies*, *29*(5), 6087–6106. DOI: 10.1007/s10639-023-12041-8

Yan, L., Greiff, S., Teuber, Z., & Gašević, D. (2024). Promises and challenges of generative artificial intelligence for human learning. *Nature Human Behaviour*, *8*(10), 1839–1850. DOI: 10.1038/s41562-024-02004-5 PMID: 39438686

Yan, L., Sha, L., Zhao, L., Li, Y., Martinez-Maldonado, R., & Chen, G.. (2023). Practical and ethical challenges of large language models in education: A systematic scoping review. *British Journal of Educational Technology*, •••, 1–23.

Yaseen, H., Mohammad, A. S., Ashal, N., Abusaimeh, H., Ali, A. A. A., & Sharabati, A. A. (2025). The Impact of Adaptive Learning Technologies, Personalized Feedback, and Interactive AI Tools on Student Engagement: The Moderating Role of Digital Literacy. *Sustainability (Basel)*, *17*(3), 1133. DOI: 10.3390/su17031133

Yeadon, W., & Hardy, T. (2024). The impact of AI in physics education: A comprehensive review from GCSE to university levels. *Physics Education*, *59*(2), 1–19. DOI: 10.1088/1361-6552/ad1fa2

Yeşilyurt, E., & Vezne, R. (2023). Digital literacy, technological literacy, and internet literacy as predictors of attitude toward applying computer-supported education. *Education and Information Technologies*, *28*(8), 9885–9911. DOI: 10.1007/s10639-022-11311-1 PMID: 36688220

Yıldırım, A., & Şimşek, H. (2021). *Qualitative research methods in social sciences* (12th ed.). Seçkin Publishing. [in Turkish]

Yildirim-Erbasli, S. N., & Bulut, O. (2023). Conversation-based assessment: A novel approach to boosting test-taking effort in digital formative assessment. *Computers and Education: Artificial Intelligence*, *4*, 100135. DOI: 10.1016/j.caeai.2023.100135

Yin, R. K. (2018). *Case Study Research and Applications: Design and Methods* (6th ed.). Sage.

Yong, X., Chan, G., & Arya, A. (2024). Inclusion in Virtual Reality Technology: A Scoping Review. *International Journal of Human-Computer Interaction*, *41*(5), 2808–2828. DOI: 10.1080/10447318.2024.2392967

Yue, M., Jong, M. S.-Y., & Ng, D. T. K. (2024). Understanding K–12 teachers' technological pedagogical content knowledge readiness and attitudes toward artificial intelligence education. *Education and Information Technologies*, *29*(15), 19505–19536. DOI: 10.1007/s10639-024-12621-2

Zaharuddin, C. Y., Chen Yu, , & Yao, G. (2024). Enhancing student engagement with AI-driven personalized learning systems. [ITEE]. *International Transactions on Education Technology*, *3*(1), 1–8. DOI: 10.33050/itee.v3i1.662

Zaman, B. U. (2023). Transforming Education Through AI, Benefits, Risks, and Ethical Considerations. DOI: 10.36227/techrxiv.24231583

Zawacki-Richter, O., Marín, V. I., Bond, M., & Gouverneur, F. (2019). Systematic review of research on artificial intelligence applications in higher education–where are the educators? *International Journal of Educational Technology in Higher Education*, *16*(1), 1–27. DOI: 10.1186/s41239-019-0171-0

Zhai, X., Chu, X., Chai, C. S., Jong, M. S., Starčič, A. I., Spector, M., Liu, J., Jing, Y., & Li, Y. (2021). *A Review of Artificial Intelligence (AI) in Education from 2010 to 2020 [Review of A Review of Artificial Intelligence (AI) in Education from 2010 to 2020]*. Complexity, 2021(1). Hindawi Publishing Corporation. DOI: 10.1155/2021/8812542

Zhai, X. (2022, December 27). *ChatGPT user experience: Implications for education. SSRN*. https://doi.org/DOI: 10.2139/ssrn.4312418

Zhang, D., Zhou, L., Briggs, R. O., & Nunamaker, J. F.Jr. (2006). Instructional video in e-learning: Assessing the impact of interactive video on learning effectiveness. *Information & Management*, *43*(1), 15–27. DOI: 10.1016/j.im.2005.01.004

Zhang, H. (2023). Similarities, differences, and limitations of humans and AI behavior. *Computer Sciences & Mathematics Forum*, *8*(1), 43. DOI: 10.3390/cmsf2023008043

Zhou, C., & Zhang, W. (2024). Computational Thinking (CT) towards Creative Action: Developing a Project-Based Instructional Taxonomy (PBIT) in AI Education. *Education Sciences*, *14*(2), 1–14. DOI: 10.3390/educsci14020134

Zhuang, Y. (2025). Lessons from Using ChatGPT in Calculus: Insights from Two Contrasting Cases. *Journal of Formative Design in Learning*, *9*(1), 25–35. DOI: 10.1007/s41686-025-00098-2

Zou, X., Su, P., Li, L., & Fu, P. (2023). AI-generated content tools and students' critical thinking: Insights from a Chinese university. *IFLA Journal*, *50*(2), 228–241. DOI: 10.1177/03400352231214963

Zou, Y. L., Kuek, F., Feng, W. Z., & Cheng, X. (2025). Digital learning in the 21st century: Trends, challenges, and innovations in technology integration. *Frontiers in Education*, *10*, 1562391. Advance online publication. DOI: 10.3389/feduc.2025.1562391

Zydney, J. M., McKimmy, P., Lindberg, R., & Schmidt, M. (2019). Here or there instruction: Lessons learned in implementing innovative approaches to blended synchronous learning. *TechTrends*, *63*(2), 123–132. DOI: 10.1007/s11528-018-0344-z

About the Contributors

Mário Cruz is a Professor at the School of Education of the Polytechnic Institute of Porto (P.PORTO), where he coordinates the Master's in Teaching English in the 1st Cycle of Basic Education and is a member of the Technical-Scientific and Pedagogical Councils. He is also the Director of the Center for Pedagogical Innovation at P.PORTO, leading initiatives in digital learning, teacher training, and pedagogical transformation. He holds a PhD in Didactics and Training from the University of Aveiro (2011) and a PhD in Linguistic Studies from the University of Vigo (2019). His academic background also includes a Master's in Didactics of Languages (2005, University of Aveiro), a Master's in Teaching English and Spanish in Basic Education (2012, Polytechnic of Porto), a Master's in Teaching English and Spanish in the 3rd Cycle of Basic Education and Secondary Education (2015, University of Aveiro), a Postgraduate Specialization in Special Education (2008, Polytechnic of Porto), and a Licentiate Degree in Teaching English and German (2002, University of Aveiro). His research focuses on language didactics, bilingual education (CLIL), digital gamification, intercultural communication, with a strong emphasis on technology-enhanced learning, experiential approaches, virtual learning communities, and generative artificial intelligence applied to education. He has played a key role in several Erasmus+ and national research projects.. He has an extensive publication record, including 57 journal articles, 15 authored books/chapters, and 14 book chapters, as well as participation in 18 international conferences as an organizer and over 20 academic events as a speaker. Additionally, he has supervised three PhD theses, 25 Master's dissertations. His collaborative research network includes over 123 co-authors worldwide, and he actively contributes as an editorial board member and peer reviewer for international journals. His research is particularly focused on the integration of AI, gamification, and digital tools in teacher training, promoting adaptive and inclusive education methodologies. Recently, he has also acted as an external expert at the Agency for Assessment and Accreditation of Higher Education in Portugal (A3ES).

Ricardo Queirós holds a PhD in Computer Science and is an Associate Professor at the Media Arts and Design School of the Polytechnic Institute of Porto (P.PORTO), where he teaches Web and Mobile programming. He is a researcher at the Center for Research in Advanced Computing Systems (CRACS) at INESC TEC Porto, with expertise in Generative Artificial Intelligence, programming education, e-learning interoperability, and gamification. As a specialist in Generative AI in education, Ricardo has taught courses on its applications in teaching and learning and has published extensively on the subject. He is also the Conference Chair of the International Computer Programming Education Conference (ICPEC), the first international event dedicated to programming education. Additionally, he is an editorial board member of high-impact journals and a Guest Editor of several special issues in Computer Science. Ricardo is the author of more than 12 books on Web/Mobile development and has published over 150 scientific works, particularly in AI-driven education, gamification, and e-learning interoperability. His contributions include European research projects aimed at developing AI-powered and gamified learning environments to enhance digital education.

Daniela Mascarenhas is a Professor at the School of Education at Polytechnic of Porto (P.PORTO), where she coordinates the Master's in Teaching for the 1st Cycle of Basic Education and in Mathematics and Natural Sciences for the 2nd Cycle of Basic Education and is a member of both the Pedagogical Council and Technical-Scientific Council. She is also the Coordinator of the Training and Pedagogical Development Office at the Pedagogical Innovation Center. She She holds a Post-Doctorate in Education Sciences (Pedagogical Supervision) and a PhD in Mathematics Didactics, with extensive experience in teacher training, inclusive education, and digital learning strategies. Her research interests include AI-driven education, inclusive learning methodologies, gamified learning experiences, and pedagogical innovation. She has coordinated and participated in several Erasmus+ projects focusing on STEAM education, competency-based learning, and the integration of technology in teacher training. Daniela has published numerous research papers and book chapters on mathematics didactics, digital education, and professional development for teachers, contributing to high-impact academic forums. She also collaborates on curriculum design for digital education, AI-driven assessment tools, and innovative teaching methodologies aimed at enhancing engagement and accessibility in learning.

***

Wilfried Admiraal is full professor Educational Sciences with a focus on Teaching, Teachers and Technology. His research interest combines the areas of teaching, technology and social psychology in secondary and higher education. Current projects relate to simulations and virtual reality in higher education, learner engagement and interaction in online learning, and students' and teachers' scientific literacy.

I Wayan Heka Arcana Putra is a doctoral student at the Centre for the Study of Professions at OsloMet and a research fellow at the Norwegian Research School on Digitalization, Culture, and Society. His research focuses on teaching and teachers' professional practices, media and information literacies, and the role of technology in education and schooling. His current project explores teachers' professional practices and development, and the pedagogical approaches needed to support students in developing the competences to evaluate online information.

Zeynep Gül Dertli is a research assistant in the Department of Mathematics Education at the Faculty of Education, Istanbul Aydin University, Turkey, and a doctoral student in Mathematics Education at Hacettepe University. Her research interests include mathematics education, mathematical modeling, technology-enhanced learning, and the integration of artificial intelligence into teaching and learning processes.

Azadeh Eskandarzadeh is a faculty member specializing in business and communication, currently pursuing her Doctor of Business Administration (DBA) with a focus on marketing. She holds multiple academic degrees, including a Bachelor's in Creative Multimedia, and an MBA in Project Management from Malaysia. Master of Administrative Studies - Global Technology Administration and Master of Philosophy from UCAM.Azadeh has extensive experience teaching undergraduate courses in marketing, organizational behavior, and business communication across diverse institutions in Canada.

Yunona Gogia is an experienced higher education professional with 20 years of teaching various career colleges, business schools, and university courses. She holds a Master of Arts Degree in Journalism from Tbilisi State University (TSU), a Master of Arts Degree in Tourism and Hospitality from Global Barcelona School of Business (GBSB), and a University Diploma in Japanese Linguistics from Moscow State University. Yunona is a Bachelor of Hospitality Management Instructor at Acsenda School of Management and a Business Management Instructor at the University Canada West in Vancouver, BC. Yunona's professional experience includes 15 years of ownership and management of food and beverage and light industrial businesses, hence her interest in practical knowledge transfer.

Sandra Luna is currently an Invited Lecturer at P.Porto, where she teaches a wide range of Curricular Units in EFL, Communication and Skills Competences. She also collaborates with a Portuguese Publisher on inclusive materials for EFL textbooks and other. She holds a degree in Languages, Literatures, and Cultures and a Master's in Anglo-American Studies and is currently pursuing a PhD in Language Sciences, specializing in Didactics. Her research interests include pedagogy, foreign language acquisition, and the development of inclusive educational materials,with a particular focus on neurodivergent students. She is also dedicated to teacher training, exploring how multimodal approaches and Universal Design for Learning (UDL) can enhance the teaching and learning process.

Graça Magalhães has a degree in Mathematics - Educational Branch (five years) from the Faculty of Sciences of the University of Porto, completed in 1994. In 2011, she completed a Master's Degree in Educational Sciences - Pedagogical Supervision in Mathematics Education, at the University of Minho. In addition, she has a Postgraduate Degree - Specialized Training Course in School Administration and Organization in the Area of School and Educational Administration, certified by the Scientific-Pedagogical Council for Continuing Education (Accreditation Register CCPFC/CFE-3184/17, completed on July 18, 2018). She is currently in the 2nd year of her PhD in Educational Sciences at the University of Trás-os-Montes and Alto Douro, with research focused on "Cooperative Learning as a promoter of Critical and Creative Thinking in Mathematics A students". She is a collaborating researcher at the Center for Educational Research and Intervention (CIIE) of the I&D of Educational Sciences at the University of Porto. She has also been a member of the 500 group as a secondary school Mathematics A teacher for 30 years. Since 2003, she has been coordinator of the Mathematics Section at the Henrique Medina Secondary School in Esposende. She currently coordinates the Mathematics and Experimental Sciences Department and is a member of the school's Pedagogical Council.

Joana Martins is an invited assistant professor at the School of Education of the Polytechnic Institute of Porto (ESE-IPP) and is part of the Technical-Scientific Unit of Mathematics, Sciences and Technologies. She holds a Master's Degree in Teaching 1st Cycle of Basic Education and Mathematics and Natural Sciences in the 2nd Cycle of Basic Education (2023) and a Degree in Basic Education (2021) from ESE-IPP. She has actively participated in national and international teacher training initiatives, including participation in the Erasmus+ KA-131 project focused on the articulation of knowledge, mathematics education and robotics (Bilbao, 2023) and also in the Erasmus+ KA-220 project focused on sustainability, technology and teacher training (Florence, 2023). Her research activity has focused on the area of mathematics education, with a special interest in the intersections between mathematics, technology and pedagogical innovation, with several notable national and international publications.

Neşet Mutlu is an assistant professor in the faculty of education at the Erciyes University, Turkey. His areas of interest are online education, blended learning, and the use of smart mobile devices in education. Preparing in-service courses for teachers with online learning environments and developing digital literacy applications for students are some of the latest projects he has completed. He has served as an expert and trainer in large-scale projects of organizations such as the European Union, Deutsche Gesellschaft für Internationale Zusammenarbeit, Scientific and Technological Research Council of Turkey.

Sara Paredes is a dedicated primary and second cycle of basic education school teacher, currently based at Colégio Oceanus in Valadares. She holds a Master's degree in Education from the School of Education of Porto (2023), where she deepened her understanding of teaching methodologies, reflective practices and child development. With a strong passion for education and research, she embraces her dual role as both educator and investigator. Her pedagogical approach is grounded in reflection and inquiry, guided by the belief that thoughtful and critical analysis of teaching practices leads to more meaningful and effective learning. She sees the classroom not only as a place for learning, but as a space for cultivating curiosity, encouraging critical thinking and inspiring a lifelong love of learning in her students. She continues to collaborate closely with researchers and teachers from the School of Education of Porto, engaging in dialogue and shared practices that contribute to the ongoing improvement of her teaching. This collaboration allows her to remain up to date with current educational research, refine her approaches, and deepen her understanding of how to support pupils' learning in more impactful ways. Her work is driven by a constant desire to improve—both personally and professionally—and to contribute to the development of more inclusive, engaging, and thoughtful educational environments. She is particularly interested in how reflective teaching can support both teacher growth and student success, and how a questioning attitude can open new paths in the educational journey.

Purushothaman R, is a dedicated researcher and academician, currently serving as a Research Assistant at the Srinivasa Ramanujan Center, SASTRA University, Kumbakonam. His research interests span across multiple disciplines, including circular economy, supply chain management, operations management, general management, and human resource management. With a passion for advancing knowledge in these fields, he actively contributes to academia through research and scholarly pursuits.

Emine Sendurur received her PhD in Computer Education and Instructional Technology from Middle East Technical University, Turkey, in 2012. In 2005, she was hired as a research assistant in the same department. After completing her PhD, she worked as an instructor in Computer Programming department. She recently works as an instructor in Computer Education and Instructional Technologies department at Ondokuz Mayıs University, Turkey. She teaches courses including instructional design, computer science, learning theories, Internet based programming and human-computer interaction. Her main research interests consist of user experience, informal learning, social networking sites, cognitive load theory, instructional message design, and eye-tracking methodology.

Raquel Simões de Almeida is a lecturer at E2S, Polytechnic of Porto. She has a BSc in Occupational Therapy, an MSc in Mental Health and Psychosocial Rehabilitation, and a Ph.D. in Psychology. She is a researcher in the field of Health and Technologies at the Center for Rehabilitation Research, and she has a postgraduate degree in Digital Health and in Pedagogical Innovation and Educational Change.

Satya Subrahmanyam is a distinguished academic leader, researcher, and institutional strategist with over 27 years of experience in higher education, leadership, and research management. He holds two PhDs and a Postdoctoral qualification from the Polytechnic Institute of Leiria, Portugal. Currently serving as Professor and Dean (Research) at Holy Spirit University of Kaslik (USEK), Lebanon, he spearheads research initiatives that enhance academic excellence and institutional reputation. He played a pivotal role in the development of the Catholic University in Erbil, Kurdistan, where he established new departments, led research programs, and collaborated on international educational projects. As a founding member and Managing Partner of Vignan Institute of Technology and Management, India, he contributed to its transformation into a premier institution. With expertise in AI-driven business strategies, HR analytics, and leadership in technology adoption, he has published extensively, guided PhD research, and led training programs in corporate and academic settings.

Maria João Trigueiro is an occupational therapist and lecturer with interest in the field of pediatrics, neurology and lifestyle redesign. Full Professor at the Health School (ESS-P.Porto). She has contributed in several national and international research projects regarding disability and social exclusion. As Professor she teaches at the degree and master levels both at ESS-P.Porto and at the Faculty of Psychology and Educational Sciences – University of Porto (FPCEUP). She participates as a staff member in the Psychosocial Rehabilitation Lab, and on the Porto Interactive Neuroscience Group, Her research interests are related with the wellbeing of people who suffer from neuro, musculoskeletal and motor control dysfunction (children and adults) throughout helping with their Lifestyle Redesign, and the Use of Interactive and Virtual Reality Technologies in the treatment of different pathologies, in both children and adults.

Seema Yadav has academic qualifications of M. Sc. (Chemistry), M Ed (RIE), UGC-NET, and PhD in Education. Presently she is working as an Assistant Professor, in the Department of Education at The Bhopal School of Education, Bhopal. She has almost 18 years of teaching experience. Her areas of specialization are educational psychology, environmental education, digital learning, and curriculum development.

Index

Symbols

A

C

P

R

S

T

U

V

www.ingramcontent.com/pod-product-compliance
Lightning Source LLC
LaVergne TN
LVHW081316300926
849161LV00008B/1778